BOOKS TO BUILD ON

A Grade-by-Grade
Resource Guide for
Parents and Teachers

THE · CORE · KNOWLEDGE
SERIES

BOOKS TO BUILD ON

A Grade-by-Grade Resource Guide for Parents and Teachers

edited by
John Holdren and

E. D. HIRSCH, JR.
Author of *Cultural Literacy*

Delta
Trade Paperbacks

A Delta Book
Published by
Dell Publishing
a division of
Bantam Doubleday Dell Publishing Group, Inc.
1540 Broadway
New York, New York 10036

Library of Congress Cataloging in Publication Data
Hirsch, E. D. (Eric Donald), 1928–
   Books to build on : a grade-by-grade resource guide for parents and teachers / edited by
E.D. Hirsch and John Holdren.
      p.   cm.
   ISBN 0-385-31640-2
   1. Children—United States—Books and reading.   I. Holdren, John.   II. Core Knowledge
Foundation.   III. Title.
Z1037.H646   1996
011.62—dc20   96-17200
                                                                          CIP

Manufactured in the United States of America
Published simultaneously in Canada

November 1996

10   9   8   7   6   5   4   3

BRG

To the parents and teachers
who pioneered the Core Knowledge movement
and to those who will join them.
E.D.H.

With love to my wife, Tricia, and my daughters, Sara and Hannah.
J.H.

Editor-in-Chief, Core Knowledge Series: E. D. Hirsch, Jr.
Editor: John Holdren

Project Manager: Tricia Emlet

Writers: Tricia Emlet, Susan Tyler Hitchcock, John Holdren, Mary Beth Klee

Researchers, Consultants, and Assistants:
Julie D. Bauer, Carolyn Bradley, Cheryl Cannard, Tricia Emlet, Maria Goldstein, Pamela Griffith, Susan Tyler Hitchcock, John Holdren, Deborah Hyland, Blair Logwood Jones, Mary Beth Klee, Michael Marshall, Kathleen Lingle Pond, Chris N. Regan, Jeanne Nicholson Siler, Janet Smith, Nancy Strother, Martha Clay Sullivan, Linda Williams, Lois Williams

ACKNOWLEDGMENTS

Benefactors: The Brown Foundation, The Challenge Foundation, The Walton Family Foundation

Thanks to: Georgette Fraser and the staff of
        The Book Rack
        12 Scott Adam Road
        Cockeysville, MD 21030
        410-667-6897

Special thanks to the teachers and parents who, over the years, have shared with us and their children their love of books and their enthusiasm for Core Knowledge.

CONTENTS

Acknowledgments   vii
Introduction   1
A Note to Teachers   5
How to Use This Book   7
Core Knowledge: Building Knowledge Year by Year or
    "Why Should I Teach Ancient Egypt to a First Grader?"   9

LANGUAGE ARTS

Introduction   25
General Resources   32
    Guides to Good Reading   32
    Poetry Collections   33
        General collections   33
        "Mother Goose" poems   35
        For younger children   36
        For older children   38
    Stories: Collections and Series   38
    Shakespeare for Children   43
    Biography Collections   44
    About Language   44
        Sayings, Phrases, and Wordplay   45
Reading and Writing: Kindergarten—Grade 2   46
    Alphabet Books   47
    Phonics and Phonetically Controlled Readers   47
Beginning Reading Materials (not phonetically controlled)   48
Kindergarten   50
    Poems   50
    Stories   51
    Aesop's Fables   54
Grade 1   56
    Poems   56
    Stories   57
    Aesop's Fables   62
    Different Lands, Similar Stories   62
Grade 2   64
    Poems   64
    Stories   65
    Mythology of Ancient Greece   68

American Tall Tales 70
Grade 3 72
  Poems 72
  Stories 73
  Mythology 75
    More Myths of Ancient Greece and Rome 75
    Norse Mythology 76
Grade 4 77
  Poems 77
  Stories 78
  Legends of King Arthur and the Knights of the Round Table 80
Grade 5 83
  Poems 83
  Stories 84
  Myths and Legends 86
  Speeches 87
Grade 6 88
  Poems 88
  Stories 89
  Myths of Ancient Greece and Rome 90

HISTORY AND GEOGRAPHY

Introduction 93

WORLD HISTORY AND GEOGRAPHY

General Resources 103
  History Resources and References 103
  Series 105
  Geography Resources and References 107
  Atlases 108
  Periodicals 110
Kindergarten 111
Grade 1 112
  Ancient Civilizations 112
    Ancient Egypt 113
  History of World Religions 114
    General Reference: Teacher/Parent Resources 114
    Stories from Sacred Texts 115
    Stories Inspired by World Religions 117
  Mexico 118
Grade 2 119
  India 119
  Hinduism and Buddhism 119
  Ancient China 120

Japan   121
Ancient Greece   122
Geography of the Americas   123
Grade 3   125
Ancient Rome   125
The Vikings   126
Topics in Geography   127
Canada   127
Important Rivers of the World   127
Grade 4   129
Europe in the Middle Ages   129
Activity Books   131
Historical Fiction   132
The Rise of Islam and the "Holy Wars"   132
Early and Medieval Africa   133
Geography of Africa   133
Medieval China   134
Grade 5   135
Mesoamerican Civilizations   135
European History from the Age of Exploration to the English Bill of Rights   136
The Age of Exploration   136
The Renaissance   137
The Reformation   138
England from Elizabeth to William and Mary   138
Feudal Japan   139
Russia: Early Growth and Expansion   139
Grade 6   141
Lasting Ideas from Ancient Civilizations   141
Judaism and Christianity   141
Ancient Greece and Rome   142
Toward the Modern World: From the Enlightenment to the
    Industrial Revolution   143
The Enlightenment   143
The French Revolution   144
The Industrial Revolution   145
Latin American Independence Movements   145

AMERICAN HISTORY AND GEOGRAPHY

General Resources   147
Kindergarten   152
Native American Peoples, Past and Present   152
Early Exploration and Settlement   152
Columbus   152
Pilgrims   153

Presidents Past and Present   153
Grade 1   155
    The Earliest People: Hunters and Nomads   155
    Introduction to Maya, Inca, and Aztec Civilizations   155
    Early Exploration and Settlement   157
        Columbus   157
        The English Colonies: An Introduction   157
    From Colonies to Independence: The American Revolution   158
    Early Exploration of the American West   160
Grade 2   161
    American Government: The Constitution   161
    The War of 1812   161
    Westward Expansion   162
        Pioneers   162
        Native Americans   163
    The Civil War: An Introduction   164
    Immigration and Citizenship   166
        Historical Fiction on Immigration   166
    Civil Rights   168
Grade 3   170
    The Earliest Americans   170
    Early Exploration of North America   171
    The Thirteen Colonies: Life and Times Before the Revolution   172
Grade 4   175
    General Resources   175
    The American Revolution   175
        Books on the American Revolution—General Studies   175
        Biographies   176
        Historical Fiction   177
    Making a Constitutional Government   178
    Early Presidents and Politics   179
    Reformers   180
Grade 5   182
    The Civil War: Causes, Conflicts, Consequences   182
        Historical Fiction   183
    Reconstruction   184
    Westward Expansion   184
    Native Americans: Culture and Life   186
Grade 6   188
    General Resources   188
    Immigration   188
    Industrial and Urban America   189
    Reformers and Reform Movements   190
    The Spanish-American War   191

VISUAL ARTS

Introduction   193
General Resources   197
    Art Prints and Reproductions   197
    How-To and Activity Books   198
    Elements of Art   200
    Series About Art and Artists   200
    Art Histories   202
    Biography Collections   202
    Architecture   202
    Books About Art Museums   203
    Art and Literature   204
Kindergarten   205
    How-To and Activity Books   205
    Elements of Art   205
    Artists and Works   206
Grade 1   208
    How-To and Activity Books   208
    Elements of Art   208
    Ancient Art   208
    Artists and Works   209
Grade 2   211
    How-To and Activity Books   211
    Elements of Art   211
    Artists and Works   211
Grade 3   213
    How-To and Activity Books   213
    American Indian Art   213
    Artists and Works   213
Grade 4   215
    How-To and Activity Books   215
    Art and Architecture of the Middle Ages in Europe   215
    Islamic Art and Architecture   215
    The Art of Africa   216
    The Art of a New Nation: The United States   216
Grade 5   218
    How-To and Activity Books   218
    Elements of Art   218
    Renaissance Art and Artists   218
        General Books on Renaissance Art   218
        Books on Specific Artists   219
    American Art of the Nineteenth Century   220

Grade 6   221
   Art Histories (including books about periods and schools)   221
   Elements of Art   222
   Artists and Works   222

MUSIC

Introduction   225
General Resources   228
Mail-Order Music Sources   228
General Resources   229
   Songbooks   229
   Songs—Recordings   230
   Musical Activities   232
   Musical Instruments and the Orchestra   233
   Multicultural Music   235
   Composers (books and recordings)   236
   Dance   240
   Opera   241
   Jazz   242
   Storybooks About Music and Songs   243

SCIENCE

Introduction   247
General Resources   252
   Science Curriculum Modules for Schools   252
   Series (on various topics)   253
   General Science and Reference   254
   Experiments and Activities   255
   The Human Body   256
   Biography Collections   257
   Magazines   258
Kindergarten   259
   Plants and Plant Growth   259
   Animals and Their Needs   260
   Pets and Their Care   260
   The Human Body: Health and the Five Senses   261
   Magnetism   262
   Seasons and Weather   262
   Taking Care of the Earth   263
   Biographies   263
Grade 1   265
   Living Things and Their Environments   265
   Oceans and Undersea Life   266
   Habitat Destruction and Endangered Species   267

Extinct Animals (mostly dinosaurs)   268
The Human Body: Basic Body Systems and Health   268
    Basic Body Systems   268
    Health and Disease: Taking Care of Your Body   269
Matter   269
Electricity   270
The Solar System   270
The Earth (outside and inside)   271
Biographies   272
Grade 2   274
    Seasonal Cycles   274
    Life Cycles   274
    Weather   275
    Insects   276
    The Human Body   278
        Cells   278
        Digestive and Excretory Systems   278
    Magnetism   279
    Tools and Simple Machines   279
    Biographies   280
Grade 3   281
    Fish   281
    Amphibians and Reptiles   281
    Birds   281
    Mammals   282
    The Human Body   282
    Sound and Hearing   283
    Light and Optics: An Introduction   284
    Ecology   284
    Astronomy   285
    Biographies   287
Grade 4   288
    The Human Body   288
    Chemistry: Basic Terms and Concepts   288
    Electricity   289
    Geology: The Earth and Its Changes   289
    History of the Earth   291
    Meteorology   291
    Biographies   292
Grade 5   294
    Life Sciences: Life Cycles and Cell Processes   294
    The Human Body   295
        Adolescence   295
        Human Reproduction   295

Chemistry: Matter and Change   296
Introduction to Physics: Speed, Work, Power   297
Biographies   297
Grade 6   299
History of Science   299
Energy   299
Light and the Electromagnetic Spectrum   300
Astronomy: Stars and Galaxies   301
Genetics, Adaptation, and Evolution   302
The Human Body: Immune System and Disease   303
Biographies   303

MATHEMATICS: SUPPLEMENTARY RESOURCES

Introduction   305
General Resources   317
Computer Software   319
Numbers and Counting   320
Computation   322
Fractions   322
Time (including telling time, days of the week, months of the year)   323
Money   323

Index   325

BOOKS TO BUILD ON

A Grade-by-Grade
Resource Guide for
Parents and Teachers

INTRODUCTION

"Can you recommend some good books on . . . ?"

This book is intended to lead you to many other books—books about history, geography, literature, language, science, math, and the fine arts. It was written to meet a need expressed to us by many parents and teachers. Since 1991, when we wrote *What Your First Grader Needs to Know*—the first book in what are now seven volumes in the Core Knowledge Series (*What Your Kindergartner–Sixth Grader Needs to Know*)—many parents and teachers have called or written the Core Knowledge Foundation. They have told us that their children and students are excited by the topics in the Core Knowledge books, and are eager to know more. And they have asked, "What *other* good books would you recommend for our children on astronomy? Ancient Greece and Rome? Magnetism and electricity? Frederick Douglass? Susan B. Anthony? Impressionist painters? American tall tales? Africa? Japan?"

To answer the requests for help, we have developed this annotated bibliography that briefly describes many good books for children. We hope *Books to Build On* will help parents select some of the best books for their children. We also hope this guide will help the growing number of teachers who are using the books in the Core Knowledge Series. These teachers have often said to us, "It's been a while since I studied Ancient Egypt or plant photosynthesis. Can you recommend some books that will help me brush up on these and other topics?" For teachers (and interested parents), this guide includes some books to help you continue to be a "lifelong learner" as you work with young learners.

Since there are thousands and thousands of children's books to choose from, we have tried to be selective in this guide. Our purpose in recommending specific titles, however, is not to exclude others but to help you get started. Our researchers—who include the staff of the Core Knowledge Foundation and teachers and librarians in many Core Knowledge schools—have tried to take a broad look at the wide range of available books, and from those to recommend ones that are informative, appealing, well written, and, in many cases, well illustrated. But no doubt we have missed some good titles, perhaps one of your favorites. If so, please let us know.

Also, in the sometimes fickle world of children's publishing, many books, even good ones, go out of print with little notice. In advance we express our regrets for any frustration you may experience in seeking out a recommended title that has gone out of print since *Books to Build On* went to press.

A Focus on Nonfiction

The great nineteenth-century American poet Emily Dickinson wrote

> *There is no frigate like a book*
> *To take us lands away.*

Sometimes those lands are real: China, Africa, Australia, Mars, the bottom of the ocean. Sometimes those lands are imaginary: Narnia, Middle Earth, the Hundred Acre Wood.

The books in *Books to Build On* will take you to both real and imaginary lands, but to one more than the other. In the extensive Language Arts section of *Books to Build On*, we do recommend many of works of poetry and fiction: Aesop's fables, fairy tales, Native American legends, Greek myths, tall tales, historical novels, and more. But the main focus of this guide is on nonfiction: history, geography, biography, science, math, and the fine arts.

This focus on nonfiction is in no way intended to suggest that exploring the solar system is more valuable than visiting Narnia or the Hundred Acre Wood. Children need a literary diet rich in both imaginative literature and nonfiction. There are a number of good guides that recommend even more fiction and poetry for children than we do here, and we encourage you to consult them. (Some of these guides are described on pages 32–33 under "Guides to Good Reading.")

In this guide we focus on nonfiction in order to support parents and teachers who want to help their children build strong foundations of important, interesting knowledge about a great many things, such as:

why the pyramids were built
what happens when you turn on a light switch
what instruments make up an orchestra
why Americans fought each other in the Civil War
what's beneath the surface of the Earth
who built the Great Wall
how the Plains Indians lived and the stories they told
what some brave American women did to get the right to vote
why most people in "Latin America" speak Spanish
why Americans celebrate the Fourth of July
what Mozart was like as a child
what the samurai did in ancient Japan
what happens when a volcano erupts.

This guide directs you to good books on those topics and dozens more. Taken collectively, these topics can form the core of a strong, well-rounded early education.

Building Knowledge Year by Year

Through reading (or listening to) some of the books recommended in this guide, your child can start building strong foundations of knowledge when she is young, and then continue to build on those foundations year by year. We have organized the recommended books in a year-by-year or, more precisely, grade-by-grade scheme, from kindergarten to sixth grade.

Why do we recommend books about the Great Wall of China for second graders, or about pyramids and mummies for first graders? Shouldn't you just help your child find good books on whatever interests him whenever it interests him? That's always a good idea, especially for parents helping their children at home. Parents who are using this guide to enrich or supplement their children's learning may want to think of the grade-level designations as flexible recommendations, depending on their children's interests.

Nevertheless, there are very good reasons for organizing this guide in a grade-by-grade *sequence* of topics that builds, logically and coherently, year by year through the elementary grades. These reasons are explained in detail in "Core Knowledge: Building Knowledge Year by Year" (see pages 9–23).

Books, Books, and (Mostly) More Books

This resource guide recommends a few cassettes, videos, and CD-ROMs, but it mainly suggests books. Our focus on books is not meant, in this day of high-tech interactive media, to be old fashioned. Nor is it meant to suggest that children should engage only in "book-learning" as opposed to hands-on projects and explorations. Children thrive when they can do experiments, art projects, dramatic performances, and other forms of "active" learning.

But it's a mistake to think that reading or listening to a good book is not active. Good books inform, engage, and challenge the mind. They can "take us lands away." They help build and expand a child's vocabulary (having a big vocabulary is one sign of having a broad foundation of knowledge on which to build later learning). Books, said William Ellery Channing, "give to all who will faithfully use them."

E. D. Hirsch, Jr., and John Holdren
Charlottesville, Virginia

A NOTE TO TEACHERS

We hope you will find this book useful, especially those of you who are teaching in the growing national network of Core Knowledge schools. If you are interested in the ideas of teachers in Core Knowledge schools, please write or call the Core Knowledge Foundation (2012-B Morton Drive, Charlottesville, VA 22903 [804] 977-7550) for information on ordering collections of lessons created and shared by teachers in Core Knowledge schools. Also, you can get access to more lessons and ideas shared by teachers through the Core Knowledge Home Page on the Internet at the following address:

http://www.coreknowledge.org

HOW TO USE THIS BOOK

Books to Build On is a companion volume to the Core Knowledge Series (currently seven volumes, *What Your Kindergartner–Sixth Grader Needs to Know*). This resource guide for parents and teachers identifies and briefly describes many good books for children. To locate books on a specific topic, you can scan the topics in the Table of Contents or look up a subject, author, or title in the alphabetized Index at the back of this book. Or, you can browse through the entries in a specific subject area and grade level.

How This Book Is Organized

The following diagram shows how this guide is organized and provides a sample entry:

[subject area and grade level]	**American History and Geography: Grade 2**
[topic]	**THE CIVIL WAR: AN INTRODUCTION**
	[annotated listing]
[title]	*Just a Few Words, Mr. Lincoln: The Story of the Gettysburg Address*
[author]	by Jean Fritz
[illustrator]	illustrated by Charles Robinson
[publisher, date]	Grosset & Dunlap, 1993
[description]	An All Aboard Reading book, Level 3 (for grades 2–3), this illustrated book does a fine job of giving a glimpse at the private life of Lincoln and dramatizing the events surrounding his brief and immortal speech. "It took longer to boil an egg" than to give this speech, the author notes. Includes the text of the Gettysburg Address.

Entries in this resource guide are organized according to the following **subject areas:**
• Language Arts
• World History and Geography
• American History and Geography
• Visual Arts
• Music
• Science
• Math

Within each subject area, entries are organized according to **grade level (kindergarten through sixth).** And, within each grade level, entries are further organized according to **topics** (and occasionally subtopics) as specified in the *Core Knowledge Sequence* (for information on the

Sequence, see in this book "Core Knowledge: Building Knowledge Year by Year," especially pages 15–17). Each entry provides bibliographic information and a brief description of the book, book series, or other resource.

Grade-by-Grade Summaries for Each Subject Area: In *Books to Build On*, each section devoted to a major subject-area—Language Arts; World History and Geography; American History and Geography; Visual Arts; Music; Science; and Math—begins with a brief grade-by-grade summary of topics. For example, at the beginning of the section on World History and Geography, you will find a grade-by-grade outline that progresses from an introduction to the continents in kindergarten to the study of the French Revolution in sixth grade. You may find it helpful to begin by skimming these outlines, which will give you an overview of the specific topics in each grade level and how they build year by year.

"General Resources": Some books are pertinent to topics in more than one grade level. These books are listed at the beginning of each subject-area section under the heading of "General Resources."

Series: Some children's books are part of a series. We provide information on a book series in the General Resources listings. We then organize specific titles within the series under the appropriate grade level and topic (as specified in the *Core Knowledge Sequence).* For example, under Visual Arts "General Resources" you will find a listing for the Getting to Know the World's Greatest Artists series by Mike Venezia. You will find a specific title in this series, *Picasso,* listed under grade 2 (with a cross-reference to the listing for the complete series).

CC—The "Core Collection": The researchers who compiled this guide—including the staff of the Core Knowledge Foundation and teachers and librarians in many Core Knowledge schools—have tried to take a broad look at the wide range of available books, and from those to recommend ones that are informative, appealing, well written, and, in many cases, well illustrated. On some topics—such as the American Revolution or Ancient Egypt—there is a potentially confusing abundance of titles to choose from. To help you choose among these, we have selected a few that we admire most, and designated them with the symbol **CC,** which stands for **"Core Collection."**

Books designated as "Core Collection" titles are the ones we would look for first in the library, or the ones we would first consider purchasing for schools (especially if we had a limited budget—and who doesn't?). Our choices for the "Core Collection" are not the result of polling thousands of teachers or writers, but they do reflect the considered opinions of many experienced writers and educators. If you don't agree with our choices, or if you think we should add a title to the "Core Collection," let us hear from you. If you can't find a "Core Collection" book on a particular topic, don't be concerned. Look for other recommended titles, and look through the books in your library or bookstore to see if they meet *your* "core collection" standards.

> For more information on Core Knowledge, please write to the Core Knowledge Foundation, 2012-B Morton Drive, Charlottesville, VA 22903, or call (804) 977-7550.

CORE KNOWLEDGE:
BUILDING KNOWLEDGE YEAR BY YEAR

or

"Why Should I Teach Ancient Egypt to a First Grader?"

by E. D. Hirsch, Jr., and John Holdren

If you thumb through the pages of *Books to Build On*, you'll see that this resource guide is organized not just by topics but also by grade levels. You'll find, for example, books on the Renaissance for fifth graders; on Africa for fourth graders; on astronomy for third graders; on Greek myths for second graders; on ancient Egypt for first graders.

Now, you might ask, "Why should I teach ancient Egypt to a first grader rather than a third grader? Or Greek myths to a second grader but not a fourth grader? Why are *any* of these topics assigned to a specific grade level? Who selected these topics and put them in specific grades? What's the point?"

To answer these sensible questions, we need to explain the ideas behind this book, which are the ideas behind the education reform initiative known as "Core Knowledge." First, however, we should note that the way you use this guide may depend on whether you are a parent or a teacher. Parents who use this guide to enrich their children's learning may want to think of the grade-level designations as flexible recommendations. After all, when your child expresses curiosity about a topic, it's a good idea to strike while the iron is hot. Teachers, too, will always want to help a child find good resources whenever he or she expresses eagerness to know more about a certain topic, whether it's baseball statistics, black holes, or ballet.

But teachers also know—at least, teachers in the growing national network of Core Knowledge schools know—that for a school to be successful, teachers need to have a shared vision of what they want their students to know and be able to do. They need to have clear and specific agreements about what children should learn in each grade. That is why many teachers have found it helpful to follow the specific topics, grade by grade, that are spelled out in the model curriculum guidelines called the *Core Knowledge Sequence*, upon which this resource guide is based. These teachers know that by "sticking to the *Sequence*" they are helping their students make steady progress as they gain knowledge that builds coherently year by year, without a lot of repetition or gaps.

But we're getting ahead of ourselves. Let's step back and begin at the beginning with the commonsense idea that schools need to follow a sequential curriculum that helps children build knowledge year by year.

The Myth of the Existing Curriculum

A curriculum is a course of study. A curriculum should say what is to be taught and learned. Parents assume that the schools to which they send their children have a clearly defined curriculum. Parents *trust* schools to know what the children should be learning, and to teach it to them. But too many American schools fail this trust.

This failure is often the result of good intentions and a sincere desire to "put children first." But such attitudes, however honorable, are based on flawed ideas that lead to faulty practices, such as those dramatized in the following excerpt from an article published in October 1993, called "Back in the Classroom." The article was written by a district superintendent who decided that, to remind himself of "what education is *really* about," he would, incognito, become a classroom teacher once again. After he filled out job applications and went through interviews, he secured a teaching position, and the first day of school approached.

Now this "new" teacher faced a question: what should he teach? This, he wrote, is what happened:

> *I began walking the dangerous line of pretending that I knew what I was doing while frantically trying to find out how to do it. I talked with my team leader, who gave me some ideas on how she planned her year. When I asked* what *we were supposed to teach she said, "Oh, there are district guidelines in your cupboard, but we don't really use them." I talked with the school's curriculum specialist, who told me: "Teach what comes from the kids. Concentrate on the richness and texture of the curriculum. Scope and sequence will follow." I talked with the principal, who encouraged me to experiment. Although she supported the different things I tried, she was nondirective.*

Here, then, is a new teacher—and every year there are thousands of them—who has no idea of what to teach. What about the district curriculum guidelines? "[They're] in your cupboard but we don't really use them." Instead, he is told to "concentrate on . . . richness and texture"—advice more appropriate to making a pudding than preparing units and lessons. And his principal encourages him "to experiment." *To experiment!* But these are not laboratory animals; these are children—perhaps *your* children.

When this article came out in *Educational Leadership*—a mainstream educational journal with a circulation of over 200,000 among teachers and administrators—not an eyebrow was raised. There was no outcry, no protest, no righteous indignation. For the superintendent-turned-teacher was only saying what many educators now take for granted: "There are district guidelines in your cupboard, but we don't really use them." In the world of American public education, that is not the stuff of scandal. It's just commonly accepted practice: it's what "everybody" knows and many do. It is no more shocking than a newspaper headline announcing, "Americans Often Overestimate Deductions on Income Tax Returns!"

Evading Specific Content

While many educators take for granted that curriculum content is something to be quietly ignored, the general public still assumes that a curriculum is something to be followed. Parents trust schools to have a curriculum that guides teachers and provides a measure of accountability, sets reasonable standards that all children should be encouraged to achieve, and marks out a clear path along which children can make steady progress in learning.

But in many schools and districts, the curriculum marks out no clear path. Few curricula answer, in plain English, the central question: *What is your child learning in school?* Few spell out, in clear and concrete terms, a core of specific content and skills all children at a particular grade level are expected to learn by the end of the school year. Teachers, then, cannot be entirely blamed for leaving the district curriculum in the cupboard, because too often the curriculum offers very little specific guidance about what to teach.

Most curricula speak in general terms of vaguely defined skills, processes, and attitudes, often in an abstract, pseudotechnical jargon calling for children to "analyze patterns and data," or "investigate the structure and dynamics of living systems," or "work cooperatively in a group." Rarely do our school curricula say anything like the following:

Geography, Grade 1: Working with maps, globes, and other geographic tools

Students will:

- Locate themselves on maps and globes, and name their continent, country, state, and community.
- Understand that maps have keys or legends with symbols and their uses.
- Find directions: east, west, north, south.
- Locate: the equator; North and South Poles
- Identify major oceans: Pacific, Atlantic, Indian
- Review the seven continents: Asia, Europe, Africa, North America, South America, Australia, Antarctica
- Locate: United States, Canada, Mexico, Central America.

Those specific content guidelines (taken from the *Core Knowledge Sequence*) stand in contrast to the vaguely described skills, processes, and attitudes that make up the typical American public school curriculum. In March of 1994, a reporter for *The Boston Globe* noted that a proposed new curriculum for the Massachusetts public schools went "out of its way to avoid" any specific content. The reporter wrote: "Biology is left out. . . . So is physics, Shakespeare, and the Bill of Rights. But it *does* specify that upon graduation, all students must be able to 'identify stereotyping,' 'generate original ideas,' and 'use appropriate gestures.' "

Who would not want students to be able to "identify stereotyping" or "generate original ideas"? Yet, while some of these vague guidelines may express worthwhile goals, it is difficult to imagine how *any* such guidelines could form the basis of a coherent, effective education.

In vagueness there is a kind of safety. Who will object to a curriculum that requires children to "learn how to learn" or "become lifelong learners and critical thinkers" or "develop geographic awareness" or "cultivate an appreciation for the environment"? On the other hand, people can argue with specific content recommendations. If you say that first graders should learn the seven continents, someone is sure to object that such knowledge is "developmentally inappropriate" or consists of "mere rote-learning of facts" or is "culturally biased."

As long as educators shy away from any really specific curricular content, they can both avoid disagreements and commit themselves to vague and lofty goals. At the same time, they are making it very difficult to reach those goals, because a vague curriculum leads to the kind of incoherence identified by a mother of identical twins, who (in a letter to the Core Knowledge

Foundation) wrote that her children, in the same school but in different classrooms, were learning completely different content. As a district assistant superintendent for curriculum acknowledged to a Florida newspaper reporter, when it comes to *what* to teach, "the final decision is still up to that classroom teacher who closes the door and teaches those students."[1]

In America, there is a long tradition of "local control" of education, including local control of curriculum. But the idea of "local control" is being taken to a curious extreme when the "locality" becomes the individual classroom. Localism has gone too far when a school official charged with responsibility for the curriculum can concede, without fear of recrimination, that the real decisions are made by individual teachers behind closed doors.

Repetitions and Gaps

When curricular guidelines are vague and consequently ignored; when teachers have no clearly defined body of shared content; when decisions about what to teach are made by individual teachers in isolated classrooms; then too often a child's education is marred by glaring repetition and gaps.

Consider a familiar scenario. A second-grade teacher, Ms. Jones, loves teaching about the rain forest. In the same school, a fourth-grade teacher, Ms. Smith, loves teaching about the rain forest. For both, it's a favorite unit, on which they spend about five to six weeks of class time. Neither wants to give up her favorite unit. After all, both teachers developed it to meet the district's vague elementary science requirement of "promoting environmental awareness," and both teachers put a great deal of time, energy, and even out-of-pocket money into planning activities and acquiring resources (though neither knows that they do many of the same activities and use many of the same books). And so, your child has Ms. Jones for second grade, and two years later has Ms. Smith for fourth grade: it's the rain forest all over again. For *rain forest* in that scenario, you can substitute lots of other favorites: dinosaurs, pioneers, *Charlotte's Web*, or *Charlie and the Chocolate Factory*.

When something is repeated, something else is not being taught. Thus, repetitions mean not just boredom but also lost opportunities that leave *gaps* in knowledge. We hear all too often about the high school graduates who don't know the basic freedoms guaranteed by the Bill of Rights, or in what century World War One occurred, or how to add fractions with unlike denominators, or how to compute simple interest on a loan. A 1993 poll of more than 3,100 Ivy League students— supposedly some of the brightest and best prepared—revealed that 75 percent of them could not identify the author of the Gettysburg Address.

These gaps are not only discouraging in themselves, but also threatening because they present obstacles to new learning. This is because a child's ability to learn something new depends greatly upon what he or she has already learned. It is a fundamental psychological principle that *knowledge builds on knowledge*—that we learn something new by building on what we already know. We accommodate new knowledge by connecting it to familiar knowledge. Thus, for example, many years ago, when the automobile first came along, people called it a "horseless carriage"—they connected the new mode of transportation with the old mode they already knew.

Anyone who has ever taught a class has noticed that introducing a new lesson brings smiles

---

[1] Lakeland, Fl. *Ledger*, "Special Report on Polk Schools," August 13–September 1, 1995, p. 17.

of recognition to the faces of some students but frowns of puzzlement to others. This happens not simply because students differ in ability, but because some students have the expected background knowledge, while others suffer from gaps in knowledge.

Consider another scenario. In third grade, Ms. Franklin is about to begin a unit on early explorers: Columbus, Magellan, and others. In her class, she has some students who were in Mr. Washington's second-grade class last year, and some students who were in Ms. Johnson's second-grade class. She also has a few students who have moved in from other towns. As Ms. Franklin begins the unit on explorers, she asks the children to look at a globe and use their fingers to trace a route across the Atlantic Ocean from Europe to North America. The students who had Mr. Washington look blankly at her: they didn't learn that last year. The students who had Ms. Johnson, however, eagerly point to the proper places on the globe. While two of the students who came from other towns pipe up and say, "Columbus and Magellan again? We did that last year."

The Core Knowledge Idea

Because of the basic principle that knowledge builds on knowledge, the idea of avoiding repetitions and gaps gets at the heart of a fundamental need in public education. If all children are to be given a fair chance to make steady academic progress, then we need to ensure that each student who enters a class at the beginning of the year is ready to gain the new knowledge and skills to be taught in the coming year.

When teachers in a school do not know what children in other classrooms are learning on the same grade level, much less in earlier and later grades, they cannot reliably predict that children will come prepared with a shared core of knowledge and skills. For a school to be successful, teachers need a common vision of what they want their students to know and be able to do. They need to have *clear, specific learning goals,* as well as the sense of mutual accountability that comes from shared commitment to helping all children achieve those goals.

That is the idea behind the Core Knowledge initiative. Since it was founded in 1986, the nonprofit Core Knowledge Foundation has worked to give parents, teachers—and through them, children—a guide to clearly defined learning goals in the form of a carefully sequenced body of knowledge.

American education is teeming with reforms: year-round schooling, site-based management, authentic assessment, literature-based instruction, "multiple intelligences," cooperative learning, whole language, restructuring, block scheduling, interactive technology, total quality management, and much more. But even the most thoughtful among these many proposals remain remarkably vague about curricular content. Reforms that focus on restructuring, critical thinking, or self-esteem neglect the essential fact that our students will be prepared to be responsible citizens, productive workers, and successful lifelong learners only if we begin very early in their schooling to help them acquire essential skills and strong foundations of knowledge.

The most effective elementary school systems in the world (such as those in France, Germany, and Japan) focus on teaching a coherent, specific, and shared sequence of knowledge. It is time American schools did so as well, for the following reasons:

(1) Commonly shared knowledge makes schooling more effective.

When our children enter school, we want them to be respected and recognized as unique individuals. We want their particular gifts to be nurtured; we want their weaknesses to be treated with gentleness and encouragement in hopes of turning them, with time and effort, into strengths. But classrooms do not, or should not, exist in isolation. In our public school system, classrooms are part of, and should prepare our children for life in, larger communities.

In public schools, the little community of the classroom is part of the larger community of the school, and the school itself is part of a larger system of schools. All communities require some common ground. If the community of the classroom is to be effective, its members need to share some common ground of knowledge. If the community of the school is to be effective, then the classrooms that make up the school must also share a clearly defined sense of what children in the school should know.

In any school, each teacher needs to understand that she is building on the work of her colleagues in earlier grades, and laying new foundations for teachers in later grades to build on. If students are to avoid a lot of repetition and gaps, and to make steady progress in learning, their teachers must have this shared sense of mission and mutual accountability. But this can only happen if a school has a very clear and specific sense of the knowledge and skills that children are expected to acquire at each grade level.

This is *not* to argue for a lockstep "factory model" of education. A shared core of knowledge and skill does not need to take up 100 percent of classroom time. In Core Knowledge schools, the model core provided by the Core Knowledge Foundation (see below, on the *Core Knowledge Sequence)* is intended to constitute about 50 percent of the school's curriculum, thus leaving many opportunities for local choice and individualized instruction. A school does not need to prescribe "everything every child needs to know," but a school does need a common core of content, articulated in concrete and specific terms, so that students can build on their shared knowledge as active, successful learners, always prepared for the next steps.

(2) Commonly shared knowledge makes schooling more fair and democratic.

When all the children who enter a grade can be assumed to share some of the same building blocks of knowledge, and when the teacher knows exactly what those building blocks are, then all the students are empowered to learn.

In our current system, children from disadvantaged backgrounds too often suffer from unmerited low expectations that translate into watered-down curricula. But if we specify the core of knowledge that all children should share, then we can guarantee equal access to that knowledge, and compensate for the academic advantages some students are offered at home. In a Core Knowledge school, *all* children enjoy the benefits of important, challenging knowledge that will provide the foundation for successful later learning.

(3) Commonly shared knowledge helps create cooperation and solidarity in our schools and nation.

Diversity is a hallmark and strength of our nation. American classrooms are usually made up of students from a variety of cultural backgrounds, and those different cultures should be honored by all students. At the same time, education should create a *school-based* culture that is common and welcoming to all because it includes knowledge of many cultures, and gives all students, no matter what their background, a common foundation for understanding our cultural diversity.

The Core Knowledge Sequence: *A Model of Specific, Sequenced Content*
If the curriculum in your child's school is typical, it says things like:

In first grade children shall:

• be able to identify beliefs and value systems of specific groups.
• be able to identify and explain the significance of national symbols, major holidays, historical figures and events.

Notice that such guidelines do not state *which* "beliefs" of *which* "specific groups," or *which* "national symbols, major holidays, historical figures and events."

Compare those vague district guidelines to the following guidelines from the *Core Knowledge Sequence,* which outlines a core of specific content to be taught in grades K–6. Here is only *part* of the content specified for first grade history and geography:

World History and Geography: Grade 1 *(excerpt)*
I. Early Civilizations
    A. What is "civilization"?
    B. Early Africa: geography
        1. Some scientists think humans began there.
        2. Sahara desert
        3. Nile River
    C. Ancient Egypt
        1. importance of the Nile River: floods and farming
        2. pharaohs
            a. Tutankhamen
            b. Hatshepsut (female pharaoh)
        3. pyramids
        4. mummies
        5. Sphinx
        6. animal gods
        7. hieroglyphics
American History and Geography: Grade 1 *(excerpt)*
III. From Colonies to Independence
    A. What is a colony? Locate the original thirteen colonies.
    B. American colonists wanted to be independent of English rule.
    C. Reinforce [from Kindergarten] the idea of democracy ("rule of the people").
    D. The story of the American Revolution
        1. Boston Tea Party
        2. Minutemen and Redcoats; "Yankee Doodle"
        3. Paul Revere's ride: "One if by land, two if by sea"
        4. The "shot heard round the world"
        5. The Declaration of Independence

      a. Thomas Jefferson
      b. "We hold these truths to be self-evident, that all men are created equal. . . ."
      c. Fourth of July
      d. the Liberty Bell
  6. Benjamin Franklin: patriot, inventor, writer
  7. Stories of women and the Revolution
      a. Deborah Sampson
      b. Phillis Wheatley
  8. George Washington: from military commander to our first president
      a. Martha Washington
      b. Our national capital city named Washington

Because this resource guide is organized according to the outline of specific content in the *Core Knowledge Sequence*, you will find in the first-grade section of this guide many listings for books on Ancient Egypt and on the American Revolution. The *Core Knowledge Sequence* offers a grade-by-grade model of specific content guidelines in history, geography, language arts, science, mathematics, and the fine arts, meant to constitute about 50 percent of a school's curriculum. It is important to note the grade-by-grade organization of the *Sequence*, which stands in contrast to many state curricula (as well as many proposed voluntary national standards[2]) organized in broad multiyear categories: for example, grades K–4, grades 5–8, and grades 9–12. Such broad categories leave too many chances for repetition and gaps in instruction. To encourage steady year-by-year progress, it makes more sense to define learning goals year by year, grade by grade.

In schools following the *Core Knowledge Sequence*, first graders are introduced to Ancient Egypt. In second grade, the children learn about Greek myths and civilization, which then becomes the basis for an introduction to ancient Rome in third grade, which leads to the study of medieval Europe, Africa, and China in fourth grade, which will all be built on in fifth grade when students study the "rebirth" of classical learning during the Renaissance, as well as feudal Japan.

But, you may say, that sounds a little intimidating. Ancient civilizations, the Renaissance, feudal Japan—shouldn't children study those in *later* grades, in middle and high school? In elementary school, shouldn't they be concentrating on basic skills and the "three *R*'s" (reading, 'riting, and 'rithmetic)? Yes, absolutely—elementary schools should provide plenty of practice to ensure that children master basic skills in reading, writing, and math. But schools can do more.

---

[2] As a result of the "education summit" convened by President Bush in Charlottesville, Virginia, in 1989, Congress established a bipartisan council to oversee the development of voluntary national education standards in different subjects (the arts, civics and government, economics, English, foreign languages, geography, history, science). Prominent professional and scholarly organizations were enlisted to develop the standards. These standards are *voluntary*, and those published to date vary in their degree of specificity: the arts standards, for example, are phrased in terms of broad guidelines, while the History standards are more specific. All of the voluntary national standards published to date make recommendations in broad multiyear categories rather than in a grade-by-grade sequence. In general, the proposed national standards constitute a useful starting point for further planning and discussion. Schools that base their curriculum on the *Core Knowledge Sequence* can be confident that their programs will meet or exceed the voluntary national standards.

By beginning in the early grades to introduce children to a broad range of topics in history, geography, literature, science, and the arts, schools can plant the seeds of knowledge that will grow later when, in middle and high school, students tackle topics in greater depth, detail, and sophistication. In elementary school, the goal of introducing such topics is not for the child to achieve deep, expert-level knowledge, but to become broadly familiar with people, terms, and ideas in such a way that, later, when the child hears them mentioned or reads about them, she enjoys the satisfying sense that "I *know* something about that!"

How Did We Create the Sequence?

The *Core Knowledge Sequence* is the result of a long process of research and consensus-building undertaken by the Core Knowledge Foundation. Here is how we achieved the consensus behind the *Core Knowledge Sequence*.

First we analyzed the many reports issued by state departments of education and by professional organizations—such as the National Council of Teachers of Mathematics and the American Association for the Advancement of Science—which recommend general outcomes for elementary and secondary education. We also tabulated the knowledge and skills through grade six specified in the successful educational systems of several other countries, including France, Japan, Sweden, and West Germany.

In addition, we formed an advisory board on multiculturalism that proposed a specific knowledge of diverse cultural traditions that American children should share as part of their school-based common culture. We sent the resulting materials to three independent groups of teachers, scholars, and scientists around the country, asking them to create a master list of the knowledge children should have by the end of grade six. About 150 teachers (including college professors, scientists, and administrators) were involved in this initial step.

These items were amalgamated into a master plan, and further groups of teachers and specialists were asked to agree on a grade-by-grade sequence of the items. That sequence was then sent to some one hundred educators and specialists who participated in a national conference to hammer out a working agreement on an appropriate core of knowledge for the first six grades.

This important meeting took place in March 1990. The conferees were elementary school teachers, curriculum specialists, scientists, science writers, officers of national organizations, representatives of ethnic groups, district superintendents, and school principals from across the country. A total of twenty-four working groups decided on revisions in the *Core Knowledge Sequence*. The resulting provisional *Sequence* was further fine-tuned during a year of implementation at a pioneering school, Three Oaks Elementary in Lee County, Florida.

In only a few years, many more schools—urban and rural, rich and poor, public and private—joined in the effort to teach Core Knowledge. Based largely on suggestions from these schools, the *Core Knowledge Sequence* was revised in 1995: separate guidelines were added for Kindergarten, and a few topics in other grades were added, omitted, or moved from one grade to another, in order to create an even more coherent sequence for learning. Based on the principle of learning from experience, the Core Knowledge Foundation continues to work with schools and advisors to "fine-tune" the *Sequence*, and is also conducting research that will lead to the publication of guidelines for grades 7 and 8, as well as for preschool. (The *Core Knowledge Sequence* may be ordered from the Core Knowledge Foundation; see the end of this Introduction for the address.)

Resistance and Responses

A growing national network of schools—some two hundred as of this writing—has embraced the *Core Knowledge Sequence* as a common ground of content. But there are still thousands of schools that suffer from the problems we described earlier: curricular incoherence, isolated teachers in isolated classrooms, repetition and gaps.

Old habits are hard to break. Because the ideas behind Core Knowledge require educators to break old habits, there is bound to be some resistance. This resistance takes the form of various objections and charges. Let us consider some of those here.

• *A common core of knowledge will make schools into cookie cutters that turn out the same product everywhere.*

Other countries teach a common core of knowledge: are all French, Japanese, and German children alike? A common core of knowledge that makes up only about half of American schooling will be no threat to children's individuality. A body of shared knowledge will be taught in a variety of ways by different teachers, and responded to in a variety of ways by different students. And, influential as schools are, children are shaped by a great deal outside of school as well.

• *Students are unique individuals and can't be expected all to learn the same material. Schooling should respond to the unique learning styles of each individual child.*

There is no incompatibility between teaching a core curriculum and adapting instruction to the needs of individual students. Moreover, even as we look to teachers to bring out the best in each child as a learner, we also ask them to recognize the needs of each child as part of a larger community. All communities require some common ground. The community of the classroom requires, in particular, that its members share some common knowledge, because this knowledge makes communication and progress possible.

• *Specific academic content is not developmentally appropriate for young children.*

What exactly does "developmentally appropriate" mean? Who is to decide what is "developmentally appropriate" for particular children? Are the topics recommended in existing curricula "developmentally appropriate"?

For example, to cite one state's Social Studies curriculum framework, is it "developmentally appropriate" for second graders to "learn about the community and its components—stores, recreational facilities, protective and educational services," or to "explore components of the community such as shopping centers or community services"?

Must children in the second grade have their horizons bounded by the local mall, as opposed to the much greater reach of the *Core Knowledge Sequence* for second grade, which has children learning about China and India, ancient Greece, and the Civil War?

The question of "developmental appropriateness" applies less to content than to methods of instruction. That is, within reason, specific content is itself neither developmentally appropriate nor inappropriate. Given specific content guidelines, teachers are generally aware of how to deliver the content in developmentally appropriate ways: for example, not lecturing to kindergartners about the seven continents, but singing songs, making papier-mâché globes, cutting out and coloring continent-shaped patterns, and making charts with animals characteristic of different continents.

• *A curriculum that specifies what is to be taught at each grade level takes away the creative freedom of teachers.*

Some educators argue that curricular decisions should be left up to the individual classroom teacher. They say that it is part of a teacher's "professional autonomy" to decide what should be taught. Yes, the individual teacher should have significant freedom to decide *how* to teach, and some say in *what* to teach as well. But to leave *all* decisions about what to teach up to the individual teacher is to place too great a burden on the teacher, to remove the opportunity for professional cooperation among teachers, and to lose sight of what schools need to be fair and effective.

Teaching a common core of knowledge, such as that articulated in the *Core Knowledge Sequence*, is compatible with a variety of instructional methods and additional subject matters. Teachers in Core Knowledge schools report that making the commitment to teach a shared body of specific knowledge is not confining but liberating. Given specific content guidelines, teachers can fashion a variety of creative lessons and teaching approaches, and collaborate by sharing ideas and resources. In general, teachers in Core Knowledge schools report a sense of empowerment, both personal and professional.

• *Knowledge is changing so fast that the best approach is not to teach specific knowledge but to teach children to "learn how to learn."*

"Learning how to learn" is an admirable aim but a misleading slogan. If learning is to proceed on any principle besides random chance, then schools need to follow a carefully sequenced body of knowledge. Why? Because children learn new knowledge by building upon what they already know. It's important to begin building foundations of knowledge in the early grades because that's when children are most receptive, and because academic deficiencies in the first six grades can permanently impair the quality of later schooling. The most powerful tool for later learning is not an abstract set of procedures (such as "problem solving") but a broad base of knowledge in many fields.

The idea that "knowledge is changing" is only partly true, and, as it pertains to schools, mostly misleading. It is true that some ideas and terms—such as "SCUD" missile, software, or the Commonwealth of Independent States—did not exist or were not widely known even as recently as a generation ago. But the obvious fact that the modern world is changing—sometimes, as in the case of the breakup of the Soviet Union, in dramatic and dizzying ways—in no sense leads to the conclusion that "knowledge is changing so fast that we can't keep up with it" or that "what we learn today will be obsolete by the year 2000." The basic principles of science and constitutional government, the important events of world history, the essential elements of mathematics and of oral and written expression—all of these are part of a solid core that does not change rapidly, but instead forms the basis for true lifelong learning.

• *In curriculum, "less is more"; schools should not try to cover a lot of content but instead should help students master a few areas in depth and detail.*

Many among us perhaps share grim memories of, for example, the high school history course as a superficial blitz through a heavy textbook crammed with facts, names, and dates. Courses like this are what make many people respond warmly to the idea that "less is more." Surely, we think, we would have learned more if we had been confronted with less, if we had been allowed to investigate specific issues and questions in depth and detail.

Does it follow, then, that when it comes to knowledge, less is more? Like most slogans in education, there is some truth to "less is more," but also some danger when the slogan is wrongly construed or thoughtlessly applied.

It is hard to disagree with the view that deep knowledge is better than shallow. But—particularly in the elementary years—it does not follow that deep knowledge of a few things is better than broad knowledge of many things. In fact, one needs *both*—both deep knowledge and broad knowledge.

To help children gain breadth of knowledge is to help them lay the foundation on which they can build new knowledge, including more in-depth, specialized knowledge. The best time to acquire broad general knowledge is in the early years, when children are most curious and receptive. In these early years, the idea of "less is more" does not apply, and is especially irrelevant, even potentially damaging, to students from disadvantaged backgrounds, who may be left behind while some advantaged students learn a desirable breadth of knowledge at home.

The idea of "less is more" is misleading because it flatters a strain in some educational theory that disparages challenging content and focuses instead on feelings, attitudes, and "self-esteem." But there is one sense in which "less is more" applies even to the early years. This sense is not in opposition to broad and rich knowledge, but in encouraging selectivity about the way in which broad and rich knowledge is chosen. Educational planners need to take on the responsibility of selecting a rich core of important knowledge, defined in an explicit sequence. It is this particular sense of "less is more" that informs the process of selection and consensus-building that went into the *Core Knowledge Sequence*.

• *It is elitist to specify a body of content.*

A central motivation behind the Core Knowledge initiative is *anti*-elitist. The goal is to guarantee *equal access for all* to knowledge necessary for higher literacy and learning. Such knowledge is currently possessed only by the educated elite—and that's the problem. Our aim is to make that knowledge available to all through the institution available to all: universal public schooling.

Core Knowledge is critically important for children from disadvantaged backgrounds. As Albert Shanker, president of the American Federation of Teachers, has written, as long as the curriculum remains completely a matter of local choice, "schools and school districts are free to hold students up to high standards or, as often happens in the case of disadvantaged children, to decide the kids can't do the work and give them a watered-down curriculum. The trouble with this is that it virtually guarantees these children will fall behind their more advantaged peers—and never catch up" (*New York Times*, December 16, 1991). In a Core Knowledge school, however, *all* children are taught a core of challenging, interesting knowledge that provides a foundation to build on year by year.

• *Our population is changing, and schooling needs to change to meet the needs of an increasingly diverse population. What we need is a curriculum that is more multicultural.*

Schools should foster respect for diversity, and a curriculum should include the study of many cultures. Typically, however, state and district curriculum guidelines do not define specific

multicultural content. Rather, they prescribe a set of nice-sounding but vague goals and attitudes, such as the following from one state's "Curricular Framework for Social Studies":
- Understand the characteristics and development of cultures throughout the world.
- Understand that societies reflect contributions from many cultures.
- Understand and appreciate various dimensions of world interdependence.
- Understand historic and current events from the perspective of diverse cultural and national groups.

These are admirable goals that nod in the direction of multiculturalism—but where is the specific multicultural content? Without some specificity, the door is open to repetition and gaps. How many times will children study the Woodland Indians, and yet perhaps never examine the different ways of life of the Anasazi or the Cheyenne? Will children study Mexico but not Japan, Kenya but not China? Or Kenya in second grade, then again in fourth?

If we truly want our children to know about and appreciate many cultures, then we need to specify which cultures, and teach them in a way that broadens their perspective on the world and its diversity, rather than bores them with repetition or leaves them unaware of people and places that most educated people know about.

- *The job of the teacher is to teach children, not subject matter.*

There's something warm and appealing in that slogan. After all, it gives top priority to children—and don't we all want the highest priority of teachers to be the best interests of our children?

But there's something disconcerting in the way the imperative to "teach children, not subject matter" is phrased. It suggests an either/or situation: *either* you teach children, *or* you teach subject matter. The implication is that teachers who teach "subject matter" are somehow *not* teaching children!

But what exactly does it mean to "teach children"? Are we in fact teaching children if we do not teach subject matter?

What a strange pass American education has come to when many educators assume that between children and subject matter there is some fundamental incompatibility, as though they were, as the old saying goes, like east and west, and never the twain shall meet.

One would have thought, rather, that the challenge for the teacher is to link east and west—that is, to bring children and subject matter together, through practice, hard work, and imaginative and creative endeavors that kindle in children the love of subject matter that the teacher herself or himself feels (or should feel).

- *Students don't learn from rote memorization of isolated facts. What children need is not a bunch of facts but critical thinking skills.*

Those who think that the only way to teach specific content is through rote memorization need to observe the many imaginative, resourceful, and creative ways that teachers in Core Knowledge schools have found to engage their students in active learning of important knowledge: through dramatizations, art projects, writing workshops, collaborative learning groups, research projects, and more. Yes, children may occasionally memorize a poem or the Preamble to the Constitution—but these are valid learning experiences, which, in fact, children enjoy, and from which they get a sense of pride and achievement.

Behind the outcry against "rote memorization" lies a deep prejudice—a prejudice against fact. Many educators object to any curriculum that says, for example, that children should learn the seven continents, because that is "mere fact." To teach facts, they say, is to reduce education to "Trivial Pursuit." Granted, some facts are trivial. Who starred in *Car 54, Where Are You?* That's trivial. But who was Dred Scott and what was the significance of the Supreme Court's Dred Scott decision? That's worth knowing: it gives you insight into the causes of the Civil War as well as historical perspective on race relations in the United States.

The problem is, too many educators have unreasonably dismissed *all* facts as trivia, or as irrelevant, or culturally biased. Such claims are all too easy to make; they are also intellectually irresponsible. Recently, a Colorado newspaper reported that a principal "refused to agree that every graduate should know something about the Depression, the Holocaust, and World War II." According to the principal, such knowledge is "arbitrary and, therefore, presumptuous." The logical if absurd conclusion of such thinking is that there is nothing we all need to know because everything is arbitrary.

No one wants schools to think of curriculum solely in terms of facts. We also want—and students need—opportunities to use the facts, to apply them, question them, discuss them, doubt them, connect them, analyze them, verify or deny them, solve problems with them. All these activities, however, rely upon having some facts to work with. Without factual knowledge about an issue or problem, you can't think critically about it—you can only have an uninformed opinion.

• *Many teachers may not have learned much about Ancient Egypt or the Industrial Revolution or photosynthesis. So how can you put such content in a curriculum? You can't expect teachers to teach what they don't know.*

Educators are fond of talking about preparing children to be "lifelong learners." Why don't we have equal confidence in our *teachers* as lifelong learners?

In schools that build a program on the *Core Knowledge Sequence,* many teachers express initial anxiety about having to prepare to teach topics they're unfamiliar with. But once they make the effort (and it does take hard work), they often express tremendous enthusiasm and a rekindled love of learning, which carries over to their students.

A second-grade teacher at a Core Knowledge school in the South Bronx wrote to tell us that

> *Core Knowledge has made a major difference to my students and myself. I am very excited about teaching interesting subjects. The content is thrilling and fascinating for me as a person and a teacher. I feel that my interest and energy rub off on my students. They are "turned on" because I am "turned on." In addition, I have also developed a close working relationship with other teachers. There is congruence and unity among us. My students are learning high-level concepts. They are being challenged and they love it!*

The Growing Grassroots Effort

As more and more parents and teachers consider the ideas behind Core Knowledge, many of them have come to the conclusion that elementary education must strike a better balance between the development of the "whole child" and the more limited but fundamental duty of the school to ensure that all children master a core of knowledge and skills essential to their competence as learners in later grades. But these parents and teachers cannot act on their convictions without access to an agreed-upon, concrete sequence of knowledge. Our main motivation in developing the *Core Knowledge Sequence* and this resource guide has been to give parents and teachers something concrete to work with.

It has been encouraging to see a growing number of schools respond to the Core Knowledge reform effort. The Core Knowledge Foundation is working to evaluate the effect of implementing a school program based on the *Core Knowledge Sequence*. Preliminary reports from the most experienced and fully committed Core Knowledge schools reveal increased collaboration among teachers, tremendous parent enthusiasm, active thinking and questioning by students on important topics, increased use of library resources, and gradual improvements in many standardized test scores. If you would like more information about the growing network of Core Knowledge schools, please call or write the Director of School Programs at the Core Knowledge Foundation.

Parents and teachers are urged to join in a grass-roots effort to strengthen our elementary schools. The place to start is in your own school and district. Insist that your school clearly state the core of *specific* knowledge and skills that each child in a grade must learn. Whether your school's core corresponds exactly to the Core Knowledge model is less important than the existence of *some* core—which, we hope, will be as solid, coherent, and challenging as the *Core Knowledge Sequence* has proven to be. Inform members of your community about the need for such a specific curriculum, and help make sure that the people who are elected or appointed to your local school board are independent-minded people who will insist that our children have the benefit of a solid, specific, world-class curriculum in each grade.

You are invited to become a member of the Core Knowledge Network by writing the Core Knowledge Foundation, 2012-B Morton Drive, Charlottesville, VA 22903.

LANGUAGE ARTS

Introduction

Language Arts is a term used by schools to refer to reading and writing, spelling, grammar, vocabulary, creative writing, expository writing, library and research skills, literature, drama, public speaking, and more. While all of these should be taught at some point, the emphasis varies according to grade level.

In the primary grades—kindergarten through third grade—the emphasis of schools must be, first and foremost, on *the* crucial mission of early education: teaching children to read. As Elizabeth McPike of the American Federation of Teachers has put it, in no uncertain terms,

> *If a child in a modern society like ours does not learn to read, he doesn't make it in life. If he doesn't learn to read well enough to comprehend what he is reading, if he doesn't learn to read effortlessly enough to render reading pleasurable, if he doesn't learn to read fluently enough to read broadly and reflectively across all content areas, his chances for a fulfilling life, by whatever measure—academic success, financial success, the ability to find interesting work, personal autonomy, self-esteem—are practically nil.[1]*

While it is almost universally agreed that children should learn to read in the primary grades, there is disagreement about how to achieve that goal, as suggested by the subtitle of a classic study of the teaching of reading, Jeanne Chall's *Learning to Read: The Great Debate*. But as that study and others have demonstrated,[2] while fashions come and go in education, pulling schools toward one pedagogical extreme or another, there is a reasonable middle ground that is best for children.

This middle ground *balances* two approaches to the teaching of reading and writing that some educators (wrongly) see as mutually exclusive. The first approach emphasizes the systematic teaching of the "nuts and bolts" of written language: letter-sound combinations (phonics), handwriting, punctuation, grammar, spelling, vocabulary, sentence structure, paragraph form, and other rules and conventions. The second approach emphasizes the need for children to be nourished on a rich diet of meaningful poetry, fiction, and nonfiction, and to be given frequent opportunities to use language in creative and expressive ways.

In schools, *both* of these approaches need to be embraced, for the good of the children. In

---

[1] "Learning to Read: Schooling's First Mission," *American Educator*, Volume 19 Number 2 (Summer 1995), page 3.

[2] See, for example, Marilyn Jager Adams, *Beginning to Read: Thinking and Learning about Print* (Cambridge: MIT Press, 1990). A convenient summary of this authoritative analysis of research on early reading is available from the Center for the Study of Reading, University of Illinois, 51 Gerty Drive, Champaign, IL 61820. Call (217) 244-4083 for current pricing.

particular, at the time of this writing, many elementary schools need to pay much more attention to the "nuts and bolts": they need to take steps to balance a worthwhile emphasis on literature and creative expression with an equally necessary emphasis on the basic, how-to skills of reading and writing.

Parents can support a child's growth as a reader and a writer, but the schools, not parents, are responsible for teaching the nuts and bolts of language. Parents can reinforce what is (or should be) taught in school by playing language games with their children, by helping them read books for beginning readers, by engaging them in fun and useful writing activities (letters to relatives, party invitations, grocery lists), and more. To help in these endeavors, we have included below a selection of books and other resources on "Reading and Writing: Kindergarten–Grade 2." These are meant to complement, not replace, the reading series and associated materials that schools use to teach reading and writing.

Without question, the single most important and helpful thing parents can do is to set aside fifteen or twenty minutes regularly, daily if possible, to read aloud to their children. Reading aloud is, of course, also a regular part of any good classroom. Reading aloud should continue long after children have learned to read independently.

Whether we are reading aloud to children or recommending books to them as they become independent readers, the question remains, what should they read? Some children will answer this for themselves: set loose in a library, they will walk out with a stack of books. But many children can benefit from some considered guidance and suggestions.

The world of children's literature has something for every taste and diet. It includes such sustaining fare as Newbery Award–winning titles, or the works of acclaimed writers like Frances Hodgson Burnett or Scott O'Dell or Lloyd Alexander, or such cheering series as the "Ramona" books of Beverly Cleary and the *Pippi Longstocking* stories of Astrid Lindgren, to name just a few. It includes popular "lite" fare, such as Nancy Drew or Hardy Boys mysteries, or the Baby Sitters' Club books. It includes novelizations of hit television shows and movies, such as the *Star Trek* and *Star Wars* books. It includes the literary equivalent of junk food in the Goosebumps series of horror stories.

An occasional sweet treat, of course, does no harm if you maintain a balanced diet. What's unhealthy is to make a diet of nothing but sweet treats. That is why we need to give children the opportunity to hear and read nourishing and sustaining literature. Schools in particular need to make thoughtful and responsible choices about the books they read to children and ask children to read. Especially in light of the dramatic disparity in children's home circumstances, schools should, for the sake of fairness, expose children to a common core of literature that has stood the test of time, to poems and stories with wonderful characters, adventure, humor, and language that have gripped the imaginations of readers for generation upon generation.

Even such classic literature, however, presents us with a vast field of choices. Inevitably, in choosing some titles and not others, a degree of arbitrariness enters into the selection—an arbitrariness we have endeavored to minimize by involving a wide range of people in the process of selecting the works suggested here.

Still, one might say, why read *Charlotte's Web* but not *Stuart Little*? Or why read *Charlotte's Web* instead of *Black Beauty*? Or why read *Charlotte's Web* at all? Such questions could go on forever, but they miss the point. The point of defining a core of selected works is *not* to exclude, but to ensure that children will be exposed to a broad range of enriching literature, without glaring repetitions and gaps; that the children's knowledge of good literature will build year by year; and that their experience of literature will sometimes be enriched by its connection to studies in other disciplines (such as, for example, the Greek myths recommended for second grade, which may be connected to the study of ancient Greek civilization in World History).

The works of poetry, fiction, and drama suggested here are meant to constitute a *core* of enriching literature. Teachers and parents are strongly encouraged to expose children to many more stories and poems than those listed below, including classic picture books, read-aloud books, perennial favorites by beloved children's writers, popular favorites by contemporary writers, biographies, books about art and music, lots of nonfiction, and of course books that the children themselves choose. For suggestions on more good reading, see General Resources, Guides to Good Reading (pages 32–33).

Language Arts in the *Core Knowledge Sequence:* A Summary

For information on the specific content guidelines known as the *Core Knowledge Sequence* and on the ideas behind the Core Knowledge initiative, please see in this book "Core Knowledge: Building Knowledge Year by Year" (pages 9–23, especially pages 15–17 on the *Sequence*).

The Language Arts section of the *Core Knowledge Sequence* includes guidelines for the teaching of reading and writing, and specific recommendations for works of poetry, fiction, nonfiction, drama, and great speeches. Some works are recommended because they are connected with topics in the History section of the *Sequence*. The recommended works are far from comprehensive, and are intended as a starting point for further explorations in literature and language.

Here is **a brief summary** of the main topics in the Language Arts section of the *Core Knowledge Sequence:*

• **Kindergarten:** Children are taught to recognize, name, and write the letters of the alphabet (uppercase and lowercase letters), and receive systematic instruction and practice in decoding letter-sound correspondences. They read simple, phonetically controlled stories written in words that use the letter-sound patterns they have learned. They engage in many oral language activities, and are offered many opportunities to express themselves in print. They are offered some familiar sayings and proverbs.

Children are introduced, through reading aloud, to a varied selection of poetry with strong rhyme and rhythm, including "Mother Goose" and other traditional rhymes. They are also introduced (through reading aloud complemented by discussion, role playing, art projects, and more) to a core of literature, including: Aesop's fables, tales from the Brothers Grimm and other favorite stories (for example, "Cinderella," "Snow White," "The Ugly Duckling," "Chicken Little," "Little Red Riding Hood," and more), favorite tales from diverse lands and cultures (for example, "How Many Spots Does a Leopard Have?" "Tug of War," "The Legend of Jumping Mouse," "Momotaro: Peach Boy"), some more recent children's classics ("The Velveteen Rabbit," selections from *Winnie-the-Pooh*), and selected tall tales (Johnny Appleseed, Casey Jones). Teachers and parents are encouraged to supplement this core of literature with many other works, including books the children themselves choose.

• **Grade 1:** Children continue systematic instruction and practice in decoding letter-sound correspondences, working toward the goal of more independent reading and writing. They master common "sight words" (*of, are, is,* and so on). They read phonetically controlled stories written in words that use the letter-sound patterns they have learned, and, with assistance as needed, they read "beginning reader" books that are not phonetically controlled (see pages 47–49 for suggested titles). They are offered many opportunities to express themselves in print, and they get regular practice, about thirty minutes per school day, in handwriting and in writing words and sentences dictated by the teacher. They learn some conventions of written language, including capitalization (first word of sentence, names, *I*), end punctuation (period, question mark, exclamation point), making words plural by adding *s*, and writing common contractions with an apostrophe (for example, *isn't, I'm, don't*). As they learn these conventions, they sometimes go back over what they have written and correct their mistakes. They are offered some familiar sayings and proverbs.

Children are introduced, through reading aloud, to a varied selection of poetry, both familiar (more "Mother Goose" and other traditional rhymes, selections from Robert Louis Stevenson's *A Child's Garden of Verses*, "The Owl and the Pussycat," "Thanksgiving Day: Over the river and through the wood") and more recent (poems by Robert Frost, Langston Hughes, Eloise Greenfield, and others). They are introduced (through reading aloud complemented by discussion, role playing, art projects, and more) to a core of literature, including: more Aesop's fables, folktales from around the world ("The Boy at the Dike," "Brer Rabbit" stories, "The Frog Prince," "Hansel and Gretel," "How Anansi Got Stories from the Sky God," "Issun-Boshi: One-Inch Boy," "It Could Always Be Worse," "The Knee-High Man," "Medio Pollito," "Pinocchio," "Rapunzel," "Tom Thumb," "Why the Owl Has Big Eyes," and more), and some more recent children's classics, such as "The Tale of Peter Rabbit" and selections from *The House at Pooh Corner*. They take part in a drama and learn about some terms and conventions of drama, such as actors and actresses, costumes, and scenery. Teachers and parents are encouraged to supplement this core of literature with many other works, including books the children themselves choose to read or be read.

• **Grade 2:** Children continue systematic instruction and practice in decoding letter-sound correspondences. They are given regular practice in spelling and vocabulary enrichment. They get regular practice in handwriting, and in writing words and sentences dictated by the teacher. They are offered many opportunities for writing, at least thirty minutes per school day, both imaginative and expository, with teacher guidance that strikes a balance between encouraging creativity and requiring correct use of conventions: spelling, capitalization, end punctuation, complete sentences. They learn more conventions of written language, including capitalization (months, days of the week, holidays, countries, cities, states, titles) and end punctuation. As they learn these conventions, they sometimes go back over what they have written and correct their mistakes. They learn about nouns and verbs; common prefixes and suffixes; antonyms and synonyms; and familiar abbreviations. They are offered some familiar sayings and proverbs.

Through a combination of reading aloud and independent reading, children are introduced to a varied selection of literature. They enjoy poetry by such writers as Gwendolyn Brooks, Emily Dickinson, Shel Silverstein, and Robert Louis Stevenson. They read or are read stories from around the world, including "Beauty and the Beast," "The Blind Men and the Elephant" (from India), *A Christmas Carol, Charlotte's Web*, "The Emperor's New Clothes," "From Tiger to Anansi,"

"How the Camel Got His Hump," stories of Iktomi (the Plains Indian trickster figure), "El Pajaro Cu" (an Hispanic folktale), *Peter Pan*, "The Crane Wife" (from Japan), and "The Magic Paintbrush" (from China). In connection with their study of ancient Greece (see World History Grade 2), they are introduced to a generous selection of favorite Greek myths, and learn what a "myth" is. They enjoy American tall tales, including tales about Paul Bunyan, John Henry, and Pecos Bill. And they learn more terms and conventions of drama, including comedy and tragedy, playwright, theater, stage, act, and scene. Teachers and parents are encouraged to supplement this core of literature with many other works, including books the children themselves choose to read.

• **Grade 3:** Independent reading and writing are encouraged. Reading instruction continues, with systematic attention to decoding skills as needed. Children practice giving speeches. They are given regular practice with spelling and vocabulary enrichment. They refine their handwriting skills, and continue writing from dictation by the teacher. They learn how to use the library. They are offered many opportunities for writing, at least thirty minutes per school day on average, both imaginative and expository, and in some cases work through a process that involves organizing, drafting, revising, and proofreading to correct mistakes. They are given teacher guidance that strikes a balance between encouraging creativity and requiring correct use of conventions: spelling, capitalization, end punctuation, complete sentences, subject-verb agreement, proper verb tense. They learn more grammar and conventions of written language, including parts of speech (nouns, pronouns, verbs, adjectives, articles, conjunctions), subject and predicate, sentence types (declarative, exclamatory, interrogative, imperative), helping verbs, homonyms, punctuation (of dates, and of city and state), and features of a friendly letter (date, salutation, body, closing, signature). They are offered some familiar sayings and proverbs.

Through a combination of reading aloud and independent reading, children are introduced to a varied selection of literature. They enjoy poetry by such writers as Lewis Carroll, Nikki Giovanni, Langston Hughes, Eve Merriam, and Ogden Nash. They read or are read stories from around the world, including *Alice in Wonderland,* tales from *The Arabian Nights* ("Aladdin" and "Ali Baba"), "Gone Is Gone" (a Norse and English folktale), "The Hunting of the Great Bear" (an Iroquois legend), Hans Christian Andersen's "The Little Match Girl," "The People Who Could Fly" (an African-American folktale), "Three Words of Wisdom" (a folktale from Mexico), "William Tell," and selections from *The Wind in the Willows.* They build on their second-grade introduction to mythology by reading more myths of ancient Greece and Rome (in connection with their study of ancient Rome; see World History Grade 3). They also learn about Norse mythology (in connection with their study of the Vikings; see World History Grade 3). Teachers and parents are encouraged to supplement this core of literature with many other works, including books the children themselves choose to read.

• **Grade 4:** Independent reading and writing are encouraged. Children practice giving speeches. They are given regular practice with spelling and vocabulary enrichment. They continue to use the library, and learn what a bibliography is. They are offered many opportunities for writing, both creative and expository, forty minutes per school day on average, in various contexts and subject areas, but with a stronger emphasis than in previous grades on expository writing, including summaries, book reports, and essays. They learn how to organize and develop a brief essay and the paragraphs in it. In some cases they work through a process that involves organizing, drafting, revising, and proofreading, and they are given more responsibility for (and guidance in) editing for organization and development of ideas, and proofreading to ensure correct use of conventions: spelling, capitalization, punctuation, complete sentences, subject-verb agreement, proper verb tense. They learn more grammar and conventions of written language, including parts of speech (review all learned in third grade, and add adverbs, interjections, and prepositions); regular and irregular verbs; punctuation (commas; apostrophe in possessives and contractions); and, avoiding the double negative. They are offered some familiar sayings and proverbs.

Through a combination of reading aloud and independent reading, children are introduced to a varied selection of literature. They enjoy poetry by such writers as Maya Angelou, Langston Hughes, Henry Wadsworth Longfellow, and Edna St. Vincent Millay. They learn basic terms for discussing poetry (*stanza* and *line*). They read or are read stories from around the world (in original or sometimes adapted versions) including ''The Fire on the Mountain'' (an Ethiopian folktale); selections from *Gulliver's Travels*; ''The Magic Brocade'' (a Chinese folktale); *Pollyanna; Robinson Crusoe;* and *Treasure Island*. In connection with their study of American colonial and Revolutionary history (see American History Grade 4), they read Washington Irving's ''The Legend of Sleepy Hollow'' and ''Rip Van Winkle''; and, they become familiar with Patrick Henry's speech, ''Give me liberty or give me death.'' In connection with their study of women's rights, they learn about another speech, Sojourner Truth's ''Ain't I a woman.'' In connection with their study of the Middle Ages (see World History Grade 4), they read tales of Robin Hood, St. George and the Dragon, and a selection of legends of King Arthur and the Knights of the Round Table. Teachers and parents are encouraged to supplement this core of literature with many other works, including books the children themselves choose to read.

• **Grade 5:** Independent reading and writing are encouraged, including some reading of longer works (plays, novels, biographies). Students practice giving speeches and short talks, and reciting poems and passages of drama. They are given regular practice with spelling and vocabulary enrichment. They continue to use the library, and learn more research skills. They are offered many opportunities for writing, both creative and expository, forty minutes per school day on average, in various contexts and subject areas, with an emphasis on expository writing, including summaries, book reports, and essays. They continue to work on organizing and developing essays and the paragraphs in them. They are given more responsibility for (and guidance in) revision, with the expectation that in some cases students will rewrite and edit to produce a finished essay that is thoughtful, well organized, and correct in grammar, mechanics, and spelling that have been taught so far. They learn more grammar and conventions of written language, including a review of topics studied in earlier grades; direct and indirect objects; linking verbs; pronoun case and agreement; and punctuation (colon before list; commas with appositive; quotation marks). They are offered some familiar sayings and proverbs.

Students learn and apply some literary terms and concepts. They learn what a pen name (pseudonym) is. They learn about figurative language (imagery, metaphor and simile, symbol, personification). They learn how some poetry uses alliteration and onomatopoeia.

Through a combination of reading aloud and independent reading, students are introduced to a varied selection of literature. They read poetry by such writers as William Blake, Gwendolyn Brooks, Countee Cullen, Emily Dickinson, Robert Frost, and Walt Whitman. They read or are read stories from around the world (in original or sometimes adapted versions) including *The Adventures of Tom Sawyer; Little House on the Prairie;* selections from *Little Women;* selections from the *Narrative of the Life of Frederick Douglass;* and tales of Sherlock Holmes. In connection with their study of Plains Indians (see American History Grade 5), they read legends of the Sun Dance and "trickster" stories. Also related to American History are two speeches: Lincoln's "Gettysburg Address" and Chief Joseph's "I will fight no more forever." In connection with their study of feudal Japan (see World History Grade 5), they read the Japanese folktale "A Tale of the Oki Islands." In connection with their study of the Renaissance (see World History Grade 5), they read selections from *Don Quixote* and Shakespeare's *A Midsummer Night's Dream*. Teachers and parents are encouraged to supplement this core of literature with many other works, including books the students themselves choose to read.

• **Grade 6:** Independent reading and writing are encouraged, including reading of longer works (essays, plays, novels, biographies). Students practice giving speeches and short talks, and reciting poems and passages of drama. They are given regular practice with spelling and vocabulary enrichment. They continue to use the library, and learn more research skills. They are offered many opportunities for writing, both creative and expository, on average forty-five minutes per school day, in various contexts and subject areas, with an emphasis on expository writing, including summaries, book reports, and essays. Special emphasis is placed on writing persuasive essays (with a clear thesis, logical development, and use of supporting evidence, as distinguished from mere opinion), and on writing a research essay (both the process of research and the final product). Students are given more responsibility for (and guidance in) revision, with the expectation that in some cases they will rewrite and edit to produce a finished essay that is thoughtful, well organized, and correct in grammar, mechanics, and spelling that have been taught so far. They learn more grammar and conventions of written language, including a review of topics studied in earlier grades; sentence mechanics; and sentence variety. They are offered some familiar sayings and proverbs.

Students learn and apply some literary terms and concepts. They learn what an epic is, and they are introduced to structure in poetry (meter, couplet, rhyme scheme, free verse).

Through a combination of reading aloud and independent reading, students are introduced to a varied selection of literature. They read poetry by such writers as Maya Angelou, Lord Byron, Emily Dickinson, Paul Laurence Dunbar, Robert Frost, Rudyard Kipling, Edgar Allan Poe, and William Wordsworth. They read (in original or adapted versions) *Dr. Jekyll and Mr. Hyde*; Homer's *Iliad* and *Odyssey* (see also World History Grade 6: Ancient Greece); Shakespeare's *Julius Caesar* (see also World History Grade 6: Ancient Rome); and *The Secret Garden*. They read more works from classical mythology, including the myths of Apollo and Daphne; Orpheus and Eurydice; Narcissus and Echo; and Pygmalion and Galatea. Teachers and parents are encouraged to supplement this core of literature with many other works, including books the students themselves choose to read.

LANGUAGE ARTS

General Resources

The Core Knowledge Series: *What Your Kindergartner–Sixth Grader Needs to Know*, E. D. Hirsch, Jr., editor. Published by Doubleday in hardcover and Dell in paperback.

The seven current books in the Core Knowledge Series, one each for kindergarten through sixth grade, are the companion books to this resource guide. These illustrated books provide a convenient introduction to topics in the *Core Knowledge Sequence,* including the Language Arts topics summarized on pages 27–31. Full of stories, poems, history, and discussions of topics in geography, science, math, the visual arts and music, the books can be read to children or, in the upper grades, read by children. All author's proceeds from the sale of *What Your Kindergartner–Sixth Grader Needs to Know* go to the nonprofit Core Knowledge Foundation to support its mission of helping parents and teachers help children develop strong early foundations of knowledge.

CC = a "Core Collection" book (see p. 8).

See also pages 46–49, Reading and Writing: Kindergarten–Grade 2.

Note: The entries under Language Arts General Resources are organized in the following categories:

- Guides to Good Reading
- Poetry Collections
- Stories: Collections and Series
- Shakespeare for Children
- Biography Collections
- About Language

GUIDES TO GOOD READING

Note: The stories and poems recommended in the Language Arts section of this book are meant to constitute a *core* of enriching literature. Teachers and parents are strongly en-couraged to expose children to many more stories and poems than those listed below, including classic picture books, read-aloud books, perennial favorites by beloved children's writers, popular favorites by contemporary writers, biographies, books about art and music, lots of nonfiction, and of course books that the children themselves choose. If you would like suggestions on more good reading for children, ask your child's teacher or librarian, or consult the following guides:

Books That Build Character
by William Kilpatrick, Gregory Wolfe, and
   Suzanne M. Wolfe
Simon & Schuster/Touchstone, 1994
In an earlier book, *Why Johnny Can't Tell Right*

from Wrong, Kilpatrick argued that one way to encourage moral conduct is through literature that dramatizes the virtues we want our children to have. What literature in particular? This book provides some answers, with many recommendations for good books for young children to young adults.

Children's Classics: A Book List for Parents
The Horn Book, Inc.
This brief and helpful pamphlet, prepared by the staff of *The Horn Book*, a respected journal devoted to the study of children's literature, recommends favorite fiction and poetry for children from toddlers to young adults, and includes sections on "Picture Books," "Books for Beginning Readers," "Poetry," "Folk and Fairy Tales/Myths and Legends," and "Chapter Books." For cost and ordering information, write or call The Horn Book, Inc., 11 Beacon Street, Suite 1000, Boston, MA 02108; (800) 325-1170.

Chinaberry Book Service
Not a book but a friendly, reliable mail-order source of selected books and other resources (including some story tapes), Chinaberry offers an eclectic, personal, and generously annotated catalog, conveniently organized by age levels. Each book is described in detail, and you'll sometimes learn as much about the Chinaberry founder's philosophy and family as about the books! Chinaberry offers an excellent selection for children in preschool through the primary grades; for older children, the selections are fewer and lean toward fantasy. Write or call for a catalog: 2780 Via Orange Way, Suite B, Spring Valley, CA 91978; (800) 776-2242.

The New Read-Aloud Handbook
by Jim Trelease
Penguin, 1995 (revised)
The author recommends and describes many books to read aloud to children of different ages, and provides some genial tips about how to read aloud.

CC The New York Times Parent's Guide to the Best Books for Children
by Eden Ross Lipson
Times Books, 1991 (revised and updated)
A very helpful book, well organized and with useful indexes, with more than 1,700 titles in six categories: Wordless Books, Picture Books, Story Books, Early Reading, Middle Reading, and Young Adult.

POETRY COLLECTIONS

Note: This section is divided into four categories:
- General collections
- "Mother Goose" poems
- For younger children
- For older children

General collections (with poems appropriate for younger and older children)

A Book of Nonsense
written and illustrated by Edward Lear
Alfred A. Knopf, 1992

> "How pleasant to know Mr. Lear!
> Who has written such volumes of stuff!
> Some think him ill-tempered and queer,
> But a few think him pleasant enough."

So the author introduces himself in this handsome hardback edition of a book originally published in 1846. Here are limericks galore, "The Owl and the Pussy Cat," Nonsense Alphabets, and more, many with Lear's own humorous line drawings. This volume in the Everyman's Library Children's Classics series lacks only an index of titles and first lines. About a hundred of Lear's limericks are collected in *There Was an Old Man: A Gallery of Nonsense Rhymes*, illustrated by Michele Lemieux with funny, brightly colored drawings (Morrow Junior Books, 1994). You might also look for *The Owl and the Pussy-Cat and Other Nonsense Poems*, selected and illustrated by Michael Hague (North-South Books, 1995), with extravagant, fantastical, sometimes bizarre paintings in keeping with Lear's sense of the absurd. An inexpensive paperback edition of *The Complete Nonsense Book of Edward Lear* is available from Dover Books (see address, page 39). Dover also sells a coloring book called *Edward Lear's Nonsense,* with ready-to-color versions of more than eighty of Lear's own illustrations of his verse.

Dancing Teepees: Poems of American Indian Youth
selected by Virginia Driving Hawk Sneve
illustrated by Stephen Gammell
Holiday House, 1989
This is a beautifully illustrated collection of short poems, many transcribed by the editor from oral tradition, and others written by contemporary Native American poets, including the editor herself.

The Dream Keeper and Other Poems
by Langston Hughes
illustrated by Brian Pinkney
Alfred A. Knopf, 1994
Sweet, soft, short, powerful—Hughes's collection of poems for young people, originally published in 1932, still teems with meaning and music. This edition is illustrated effectively with ink-scratch black-and-whites.

CC *Favorite Poems Old and New*
selected by Helen Ferris
illustrated by Leonard Weisgard
Doubleday, 1957
This anthology of perennial favorites has been around for a while, and if there's any justice, it will stay around. It's a great one-volume collection with over seven hundred poems, grouped into eighteen sections, such as "My Family and I," "It's Fun to Play," "Animal Pets and Otherwise," and "Almost Any Time Is Laughing Time." Just turn to any page and start reading aloud! Illustrated with only a few line drawings, but that doesn't matter: it's the words that count here.

CC *Hand in Hand: An American History Through Poetry*
collected by Lee Bennett Hopkins
illustrated by Peter M. Fiore
Simon & Schuster, 1994
Teachers and parents will find in this book a wealth of wonderful poetry, folk songs, and oratory, much of it familiar, to accompany the study of American history. The book opens with Frost's "The Gift Outright," and then proceeds thematically and chronologically from the 1600s to the present. It includes the ballads of Casey Jones and John Henry, and poems by Longfellow ("Paul Revere's Ride"), Walt Whitman, Whittier ("Barbara Frietchie"), Langston Hughes, Carl Sandburg, Gwendolyn Brooks, Lucille Clifton, and many others. Lovely color paintings enhance every page.

Make a Joyful Sound: Poems for Children by African-American Poets
edited by Deborah Slier
illustrated by Cornelius Van Wright and Ying-Hwa Hu
Checkerboard Press, 1991
This happily illustrated collection brings together familiar and not-so-familiar poems by writers such as Nikki Giovanni, Langston Hughes, Useni Eugene Perkins, Gwendolyn Brooks, Eloise Greenfield, and many others. A delightful collection with something for everyone to enjoy.

The Oxford Book of Children's Verse in America
edited by Donald Hall
Oxford University Press, 1985
A valuable collection of American poems, mostly traditional and familiar, some fresh and recent, including Rachel Field's lovely "Something Told the Wild Geese," Ogden Nash's "Adventures of Isabel," Eve Merriam's "Catch a Little Rhyme," Laura Richards's "Eletelephony," and many more. Not illustrated, but that is not a shortcoming.

***

CC = "**Core Collection**" book (see page 8).

CC *The Random House Book of Poetry for Children*
selected by Jack Prelutsky
illustrated by Arnold Lobel
Random House, 1983
Almost six hundred poems, from classic to contemporary, are collected in this rich volume and illustrated in Lobel's witty, whimsical style. Selections include poems by Lewis Carroll, Christina Rossetti, Vachel Lindsay, Robert Louis Stevenson, as well as many favorite contemporary writers. The book is a generous treasury, brimming over with verse.

Sing a Song of Popcorn
introduced by Beatrice Schenk de Regniers
Scholastic, 1988
A very attractive collection of something old and something new, this book includes familiar favorites such as Robert Frost's "Stopping by Woods," Ogden Nash's "Adventures of Isabel," and Christina Rossetti's "Who Has Seen the Wind?" It also offers a generous selection of works by modern and contemporary writers such as Theodore Roethke, David McCord, Nikki Giovanni, Eve Merriam, Jack Prelutsky, and many others. A delight to read aloud, and a delight to look at because of the illustrations by nine Caldecott Medal artists. A Teaching Guide is available from the publisher.

CC *Wishes, Lies, and Dreams: Teaching Children to Write Poetry*
HarperCollins, 1970, 1980
Rose, Where Did You Get That Red? Teaching Great Poetry to Children
Random House/Vintage, 1973, 1990
both by Kenneth Koch
After working with students in New York's P.S. 161, Koch wrote of his experiences in *Wishes, Lies, and Dreams*, a book that offers teachers and parents some wonderful suggestions on how to encourage children to write poetry. And its "sequel," *Rose, Where Did You Get That Red?* suggests ways to help children enjoy great poems as well as write their own poems.

"Mother Goose" poems

Note: There are *many* Mother Goose collections available, and just about any will do fine. Here are some favorites:

Random House Book of Mother Goose
selected and illustrated by Arthur Lobel
Random House, 1986
Some might find the illustrations slightly quaint, but this is a very generous selection, including some less well-known rhymes.

The Real Mother Goose
illustrated by Blanche Fisher Wright
Checkerboard Press, 1991 reprint
A perennial favorite and widely available edition of Mother Goose with charming old-fashioned illustrations.

Hey Diddle Diddle and Other Mother Goose Rhymes
illustrated by Tomie de Paola
Sandcastle, 1988
Classic versions of about fifty rhymes are presented in a book enhanced by the happy pastel illustrations of Tomie de Paola.

Mother Goose: A Collection of Classic Nursery Rhymes
selected and illustrated by Michael Hague
Henry Holt, 1984
Michael Hague's beautiful illustrations, full of detail and feeling, in the tradition of N. C. Wyeth, embellish this collection of fifty favorites, with text in large, readable type.

Sing a Song of Mother Goose
illustrated by Barbara Reid
Scholastic, 1987
This convenient, colorful collection of forty Mother Goose rhymes is designed with large, readable type.

Tail Feathers from Mother Goose
by Iona and Peter Opie
Little, Brown, 1988
Not the standard Mother Goose rhymes, but a
charming and interesting book with a diverse
collection of folk rhymes, including some previ-
ously unpublished and unusual variations of familiar rhymes. Illustrated by a number of distinguished children's artists, this book makes a
great resource for poems to read aloud.

For Younger Children

Note: This is an approximate category,
roughly including books of poetry appropriate for children in preschool to about third
grade. There is no hard and fast dividing line
between the books recommended here and
the books recommended below "for older
children." We have organized the books in
these categories to help you make your own
selections.

CC *A Child's Garden of Verses*
by Robert Louis Stevenson

>   illustrated by Jessie Willcox Smith
>   Charles Scribner's Sons/Atheneum, 1985

>   illustrated by Joanna Isles
>   Harry N. Abrams, 1994

>   illustrated by Eve Garnett
>   Puffin Books, 1948; reissued 1994

>   Dover, 1992
>   edited by Philip Smith
>   illustrated by Thea Kliros

Many volumes of these favorite poems are
available, and any will do. The Jessie Willcox
Smith edition reprints the original 1895 edition
of Stevenson's book of poems for children, with
line drawings throughout, occasional color
plates, and antique-looking typestyle. Joanna
Isles contributes brightly colored illustrations
and decorations to a hardbound keepsake volume. Eva Garnett's edition is a handy, inexpen-

sive paperback with attractive black-and-white
line drawings. The Dover Books edition is a
"Children's Thrift Classic" book priced at only
a dollar. Dover (see address, page 39) also sells
A Child's Garden of Verses Coloring Book, with
ready-to-color illustrations of twenty-five poems.

Favorite Poems of Childhood
edited by Philip Smith
Dover, 1992
A "Children's Thrift Classic" for only a dollar
(for Dover's address see page 39). Includes "The
Walrus and the Carpenter," "The Owl and the
Pussycat," "Wynken, Blynken, and Nod," and
many more.

*For Laughing Out Loud: Poems to Tickle Your
Funnybone*
selected by Jack Prelutsky
illustrated by Marjorie Priceman
Alfred A. Knopf, 1991
"If you have got a funnybone,/and I've no
doubt you do,/then this completely silly book/
is sure to tickle you," writes Jack Prelutsky as
an introduction to the book. Primarily contemporary, these poems run from amusing to irreverent to ridiculous, and will make everyone,
children and adults alike, laugh out loud.

Ride a Purple Pelican
by Jack Prelutsky
illustrated by Garth Williams
Greenwillow Books, 1986
These bouncy, playful rhymes are great for
reading aloud to young children. They have the
kind of rhythm that makes you want to clap or
sing. Many of the poems include place names
from the United States and Canada, so while
your child is enjoying the rhymes, he or she is
getting a little geographic vocabulary as a bonus! Colorful, funny illustrations. This is just
one of many fine books of poems for children
by Jack Prelutsky. Check your library for other
titles by him. Some of our favorites are: *The
New Kid on the Block; Something BIG Has Been
Here; Beneath a Blue Umbrella; It's Thanksgiving;*

It's Snowing! It's Snowing!; and *My Parents Think I'm Sleeping.*

CC *The Rooster Crows: A Book of American Rhymes and Jingles*
by Maud and Miska Petersham
Macmillan/Aladdin Books, 1987
This Caldecott Medal winner includes a wealth of traditional American poems, songs, finger games, rope-skipping rhymes, and jingles, with many colorful, old-fashioned illustrations.

Shake It to the One that You Love the Best: Play Songs and Lullabies from Black Musical Traditions
collected and adapted by Cheryl Warren Mattox
Warren-Mattox Productions, 1990
"Shake it to the east, shake it to the west": this brightly illustrated collection of rhymes and songs includes many that are very familiar. A cassette of the songs is available too.

Side by Side: Poems to Read Together
collected by Lee Bennett Hopkins
illustrated by Hilary Knight
Simon & Schuster, 1988
This pretty volume, with adorable illustrations by Hilary Knight framing every poem, offers a wide selection, from classic to new and unfamiliar. It includes a number of poems suggested in the *Core Knowledge Sequence,* including Stevenson's "The Swing" and "Rain," "The Three Little Kittens," "The Walrus and the Carpenter," and "The Night Before Christmas."

CC *Surprises* (1984)
    More Surprises (1987)
selected by Lee Bennett Hopkins
illustrated by Megan Lloyd
HarperCollins
For these two "I Can Read" books, with big print and illustrations on every page, Lee Bennett Hopkins has chosen a wonderful selection of short poems, some traditional and many by acclaimed writers past and present, such as Elizabeth Coatsworth, Aileen Fisher, Nikki Giovanni, Jack Prelutsky, Maxine Kumin, and Hop-

kins himself. The poems are organized in thematic chapters, such as "Who to Pet," "At the Top of My Voice," and "Body Parts." Great for reading aloud to children and, as children begin to read themselves, for children to read aloud to you! (While you're at it, check your library for books of poems by Lee Bennett Hopkins.)

Talking Like the Rain: A First Book of Poems
selected by X. J. Kennedy and Dorothy M. Kennedy
illustrated by Jane Dyer
Little, Brown, 1992
Some old favorites, some fresh and new, this beautiful volume collects over a hundred poems for children, including several suggested in the *Core Knowledge Sequence,* such as "The Owl and the Pussycat," "The Pasture," "The Purple Cow," and "The Swing." Delicate watercolor paintings illustrate every poem.

When We Were Very Young (1924, 1952)
Now We Are Six (1927, 1955)
by A. A. Milne
illustrated by Ernest H. Shepard
E. P. Dutton
With Christopher Robin and Pooh as frequent characters, these perennial poetic favorites are still available in the original editions. Wonderful for reading aloud.

You Read to Me, I'll Read to You
by John Ciardi
illustrated by Edward Gorey
HarperCollins, 1962
This clever and lighthearted volume presents poems in two different colors of type. As the table of contents instructs, in the child's point of view, "All the poems printed in black, you read to me. All the poems printed in blue, I'll read to you."

CC = "Core Collection" book (see page 8).

For Older Children

Note: This is an approximate category, roughly including books of poetry appropriate for children in about third grade and up. There is no hard-and-fast dividing line between the books recommended here and the books recommended above "for younger children." We have organized the books in these categories to help you make your own selections.

The Everyman Anthology of Poetry for Children
compiled by Gillian Avery
with illustrations by Thomas Bewick
Alfred A. Knopf/Everyman's Library, 1994
"My aim has been to assemble a collection of poems that the owner will not outgrow," says the editor of this keepsake volume, who has reached back and chosen poems by Shakespeare, Donne, Milton, Shelley, Byron, Tennyson, and Yeats, as well as more recent favorites by Hilaire Belloc, Robert Frost, Langston Hughes, Gwendolyn Brooks, and Ogden Nash. These are not easy poems, but a collection to help children stretch and grow.

Talking to the Sun: An Illustrated Anthology of Poems for Young People
by Kenneth Koch and Kate Farrell
Henry Holt, 1985
This wonderful book pairs great works of art with great poems, offering a gratifying opportunity to appreciate words, pictures, and how they can complement each other.

You Come Too: Favorite Poems for Young Readers
by Robert Frost
illustrated by Thomas W. Nason
Henry Holt, 1959
Nason's soft, wood-toned engravings capture the quiet rural spirit of some of Frost's work. Poems in this volume include "Stopping by Woods on a Snowy Evening," "Birches," "Mending Wall," "The Death of the Hired Man," and "The Road Not Taken."

Where the Sidewalk Ends
by Shel Silverstein
HarperCollins, 1974
Younger children love many of these poems, too, but some parents insist that Shel Silverstein is for older children—you decide. We know that children love to hear, read, and even memorize these sometimes irreverent, sometimes touching, often very funny, occasionally indecorous (that's a nice word for "gross") poems, illustrated with the poet's humorous drawings. A separately available cassette tape on the Columbia Records label features the poet himself reading (chanting, singing, yelling, howling) a selection of the poems in this book. If you like *Where the Sidewalk Ends*, try the poet's other collections of poems and drawings, *A Light in the Attic* (HarperCollins, 1981), a selection from which is also available on a cassette tape on the Columbia Records label; and, *Falling Up* (HarperCollins, 1996).

STORIES: COLLECTIONS AND SERIES

See also Language Arts Grade 2: Mythology of Ancient Greece; American Tall Tales.
See also Language Arts Grade 3: More Myths of Ancient Greece and Rome; Norse Mythology.
See also Language Arts Grade 4: Legends of King Arthur and the Knights of the Round Table.

Best-Loved Folktales of the World
selected by Joanna Cole
Doubleday/Anchor Books, 1982
A read-aloud treasury, more than seven hundred pages thick, with tales from around the world, some familiar, many new to our eyes and welcome indeed. This book contains many tales specified in the Language Arts section of the *Core Knowledge Sequence*. To name just a few: "Momotaro (Peach Boy)" (Japan); "The Tiger, the Brahman, and the Jackal" (India); "A Tug of War" (Africa); "A Tale of the Oki Islands" (Ja-

pan); "People Who Could Fly" (African American); "Talk" (Africa—Ashanti); "How Spider Obtained Sky God's Stories" (Africa—Ashanti); "It Could Always Be Worse" (Yiddish); "Aladdin" and "Ali Baba" (from *Arabian Nights);* Brothers Grimm tales; and many more. A valuable and convenient teacher/parent resource.

The Candlewick Book of Fairy Tales
retold by Sarah Hayes
illustrated by P. J. Lynch
Candlewick Press, 1993
A big, beautifully illustrated, well-written collection, wonderful for reading aloud, with the favorites "Snow White and the Seven Dwarfs," "The Frog Prince," "Hansel and Gretel," "The Six Swans," "The Twelve Dancing Princesses," "Sleeping Beauty," "Rapunzel," "Beauty and the Beast," and "Cinderella."

CC *Classics to Read Aloud to Your Children* (1984)
More Classics to Read Aloud to Your Children (1986)
Classic Myths to Read Aloud (1989)
compiled and edited by William F. Russell
Crown Publishers
There's a wealth of great stories and poems in these three books, designed to meet the needs and interests of children of many ages. Selections are organized into "Listening Levels": I (ages 5 and up), II (ages 8 and up), and III (ages 11 and up). A preface offers advice on reading aloud, and each selection is preceded by a short helpful introduction and a pronunciation key. There are far too many titles to list, but some familiar titles are: in *Classics,* "The Ugly Duckling"; "Androcles and the Lion"; selections from *Don Quixote, Tom Sawyer, Romeo and Juliet, The Call of the Wild;* "Casey at the Bat"; "Paul Revere's Ride"; "The Highwayman"; and O. Henry's "The Gift of the Magi." In *More Classics,* "The Emperor's New Clothes"; "The Pied Piper of Hamelin"; "The Owl and the Pussycat"; "Wynken, Blynken, and Nod"; "Pandora's

Box"; "The Village Blacksmith"; Mark Twain's "Celebrated Jumping Frog"; selections from *Treasure Island* and *Little Women;* the Gettysburg Address; and the "I have a dream" speech of Martin Luther King, Jr. *(Classic Myths* is described in more detail in Language Arts Grade 2: Mythology of Ancient Greece.)

Dover Children's Books
Dover is an unusual company that publishes some good old-fashioned books (often reprints of older but still quite good versions) at bargain prices. They also produce lots of coloring books and little activity books that children enjoy. Write for their free Children's Book Catalog. In it you'll find a listing of the Thrift Editions and Children's Thrift Classics series, which include novels, poems, and classic fairy and folktales (some of which may strike modern ears as quaint or old fashioned) in readable-type editions at the remarkably low price of $1.00 each. Occasional line drawings illustrate the children's stories. Titles include *Black Beauty, Japanese Fairy Tales, Robin Hood,* and collections of stories by Hans Christian Andersen and the Brothers Grimm. Dover Books are easily ordered by mail: Dover Publications, 31 East Second Street, Mineola, NY 11501. (No telephone or credit card orders are accepted. See—we said they're old fashioned!)

Favorite Fairy Tales Told Around the World
by Virginia Haviland
Little, Brown, 1985
Haviland has taken a few stories from each of her highly acclaimed volumes of tales from different countries and compiled them for a worldwide fairytale tour. The book includes tales from Czechoslovakia, Denmark, England, France, Greece, India, Ireland, Italy, Japan, Norway, Russia, Scotland, Spain, and Sweden. Beech Tree Books (an imprint of William Morrow) also publishes sixteen paperback volumes, each devoted to a different country, all titled *Favorite Fairy Tales Told in . . .*

CC *From Sea to Shining Sea: A Treasury of American Folklore and Folk Songs*
compiled by Amy L. Cohn
Scholastic, 1993
Illustrated by fifteen Caldecott Award–winning artists, this is a four-hundred-page collection of stories and songs from the United States, representing the work of many of today's best children's authors and illustrators. The book organizes some stories historically—Native American creation myths, then stories of coming to America, then revolutionary, then pioneer, then slavery stories. It organizes some thematically—tricksters, animals, nonsense, giants, athletes. Each section is illustrated by a different artist, including Barbara Cooney, Donald Crews, Trina Schart Hyman, Jerry Pinkney, and Chris Van Allsburg. Many of the American poems, myths, and stories recommended in the *Core Knowledge Sequence* are included, like "Paul Revere's Ride," "I Hear America Singing," stories of Daniel Boone and Davy Crockett, John Henry and Casey Jones, Johnny Appleseed and Paul Bunyan. The editor has also provided helpful comments on the stories and songs, along with a bibliography and an index, organized by ethnic tradition, geography, and story type.

Grimms' Tales for Young and Old
translated by Ralph Mannheim
Doubleday/Anchor Books, 1977; 1983
This hefty collection bills itself as "the complete stories" of the Brothers Grimm. You'll find all the familiar favorites—"The Wolf and the Seven Kids," "Rapunzel," "Hansel and Gretel," "The Fisherman and His Wife," "Ashputtle (Cinderella)," "The Musicians of Bremen"—plus many less well-known tales, including the funny tales of "Clever Else" and the hapless Hans. In all, there are 210 stories, in new translations. The language stays close to the originals and does not sound quaint or old fashioned like, for example, the Victorian-era translations by Lucy Crane (see below, *Sleeping Beauty and Other Fairy Tales*). Good for reading aloud, but note that these tales, unlike many modern retellings, do not tone down the occasional gore or vio-

lence—none of which is gratuitous, but which does make some parents a little anxious. No illustrations.

In a Circle Long Ago: A Treasury of Native Lore from North America
retold by Nancy Van Laan
illustrated by Lisa Desimini
Alfred A. Knopf/Apple Soup Books, 1995
A generous and beautifully illustrated collection of twenty-five stories, songs, and poems from over twenty different traditions, organized by region, and retold especially for younger readers, with an emphasis on stories about animals and nature. With helpful introductory notes and pronunciation guides. A delightful read-aloud, with a variety of illustrations to enjoy as well (acrylics, collage, watercolors, and more).

Jump! The Adventures of Brer Rabbit (1986)
    adapted by Van Dyke Parks and
    Malcolm Jones
Jump Again! More Adventures of Brer Rabbit (1987)
    adapted by Van Dyke Parks
    both books illustrated by Barry Moser
    Harcourt Brace
Jump! presents five Brer Rabbit stories written to be read aloud, in a style that gives the lilt and cadence of a storyteller without falling into linguistic stereotypes. Both "Brer Fox's Dinner" and "Tricking Brer Bear" are included here. The striking illustrations are scattered through the book, both color and black and white, giving Brer Rabbit a gleam in his eyes in every one. An audiotape of this book is available, with stories read by Whoopi Goldberg. *Jump Again!* offers five more Brer Rabbit stories, with illustrations on every other page, many of them amusing portraits of the main characters, including Miss Wolf, Brer Fox, Brer Coon, Brer Weasel, and of course, Brer Rabbit with that gleam in his eye. This second volume, which includes "The Wonderful Tar-Baby Story," received Redbook's Children's Picture Book Award in 1987. (See also below, *Tales of Uncle Remus*.) A third volume, *Jump on Over*, is also available.

Keepers of the Animals: Native American Stories and Wildlife Activities for Children (1991)
Keepers of the Earth: Native American Stories and Environmental Activities for Children (1988)
Keepers of Life: Discovering Plants Through Native American Stories and Earth Activities for Children (1994)
Keepers of the Night: Native American Stories and Nocturnal Activities for Children (1994)
by Michael Caduto and Joseph Bruchac
Fulcrum Publishing
The authors of these books promote ecological awareness through an interdisciplinary approach, weaving together American Indian stories and hands-on science activities. Each illustrated book follows a pattern: it offers many stories from various Native American traditions, followed by discussions of cultural and ecological issues, background information on related scientific topics, suggested questions to ask children, and instructions for nature-oriented activities.

The Maid of the North: Feminist Folktales from Around the World
by Ethel Johnston Phelps
Henry Holt, 1981
In these twenty one folk and fairy tales from many cultures, Phelps turns the spotlight on lesser-known female characters, such as Lady Ragnau from the Arthurian legends, making them the heroes of the tales she tells. Few illustrations and small print make this a read-aloud choice for younger children.

Mythology
by Edith Hamilton
illustrated by Steele Savage
Little, Brown, 1942
The classic resource on Greek myths, Hamilton's retellings sketch out the central myths of heroes and gods. A teacher/parent resource, this is not the book to use for telling the myths to younger children. The book includes a brief chapter on Norse mythology, genealogical tables, and a lengthy index.

CC *The People Could Fly: American Black Folktales*
by Virginia Hamilton
illustrated by Leo and Diane Dillon
Alfred A. Knopf/Borzoi, 1985
Written with a careful ear for dialect and word choice, this book collects stories from four different traditions, representing African-American folktales that have come out of slavery and beyond. Hamilton offers a thought-provoking introduction to the book, explaining the circumstances in which these stories were first told, and then concludes each story with a brief note about its history and significance. The Dillons illustrate each story with magical black-and-white drawings.

The Random House Book of Fairy Tales
by Amy Ehrlich
illustrated by Diane Goode
Random House, 1985
This is a wonderful book, with illustrations on every spread, alternating color and soft charcoal, with large-size type, and with eloquent retellings of nineteen favorite fairy tales, including "The Emperor's New Clothes," "Rapunzel," "Snow White," "Jack and the Beanstalk," "Red Riding Hood," "Cinderella," and more. It also includes a short introduction by Bruno Bettelheim about the psychological significance of classic fairy tales for the child's imagination.

Read Me a Story: A Child's Book of Favorite Tales
illustrated by Sophie Windham
Scholastic, 1991
This handsome, colorful, friendly-looking collection contains many read-aloud favorites, including "The Gingerbread Boy," "The Three Little Pigs," "Goldilocks," "The Little Red Hen," "The Musicians of Bremen," "The Three Billy Goats Gruff," "Little Red Riding Hood," and "The Ugly Duckling."

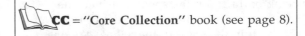
CC = "Core Collection" book (see page 8).

Seven Tales
by Hans Christian Andersen
translated by Eva Le Gallienne
illustrated by Maurice Sendak
HarperCollins, 1991
These sensitive translations, originally published in the 1950s, are still fresh today. The volume includes "The Ugly Duckling," "The Fir Tree," "Happy Family," "The Darning Needle," "The Steadfast Tin Soldier," "The Princess and the Pea," and "It's Absolutely True."

Sleeping Beauty and Other Fairy Tales
by Jacob and Wilhelm Grimm
translated by Lucy Crane
Dover, 1992
This inexpensive little paperback reprints selections from *Household Stories,* Lucy Crane's 1886 translation. The language is a bit old fashioned, yet it has a grace lacking in some modern retellings, and should be comprehensible to the modern child's ear. Ten favorites are included in the volume: "Sleeping Beauty," "The Golden Goose," "Hansel and Gretel," "The Bremen Town Musicians," "Snow White," "The Frog Prince," "Rumpelstiltskin," "Little Red Riding Hood," "Tom Thumb," and "Rapunzel." One line drawing illustrates each story. Part of the Dover Children's Thrift Classics series, the book is quite a bargain for a dollar. A reprinting of the complete *Household Stories* is also available from Dover (see address, page 39).

The Tales of Uncle Remus: The Adventures of Brer Rabbit
retold by Julius Lester
illustrated by Jerry Pinkney
Dial Books, 1987
Julius Lester has a great gift for putting a *voice* on the page. As soon as you start reading aloud, you can't help but sound good. These stories are full of wit, mischief, and mayhem. Lester tells the stories fresh, and even though some are very familiar, they have the feel of being narrated on the spot (sometimes he throws in a modern-day reference or two, but that's all in the spirit of the telling). As one

family reported to us, when they sat down one night to read aloud from *Tales of Uncle Remus,* "We were rolling on the floor!" In a foreword to one of the books, Julius Lester writes that one function of the storyteller is to "animate us with laughter and love." He succeeds admirably. Julius Lester has written three other collections of Uncle Remus tales: *More Tales of Uncle Remus* (1988); *Further Tales of Uncle Remus* (1990); and *The Last Tales of Uncle Remus* (1994). (See also above, *Jump!*)

Tatterhood and Other Tales
edited by Ethel Johnston Phelps
illustrated by Pamela Baldwin Ford
The Feminist Press, 1978
The editor begins her introduction to this interesting book by saying, "The stories in this book were chosen for a special characteristic that singles them out from other folk and fairy tales. They portray active and courageous girls and women in the leading roles." The tales come from around the world, and are good for reading aloud. A few black-and-white drawings illustrate the text.

A Treasury of Children's Literature
edited by Armand Eisen
Houghton Mifflin, 1992
This book is a generous source for fairy tales, fables, classics, American folklore, and favorite poems, many of which are suggested in the *Core Knowledge Sequence.* It collects fairy tales by the Brothers Grimm and Hans Christian Andersen, Aesop's fables, excerpts from *Alice in Wonderland* and *Peter Pan,* Br'er Rabbit stories, tales of John Henry, Paul Bunyan, Johnny Appleseed, and *The Night Before Christmas.* Some stories are retold in strong, read-aloud prose. Color paintings illustrate almost every two-page spread.

A Wonder Book for Boys and Girls
by Nathaniel Hawthorne
illustrated by Arthur Rackham
Alfred A. Knopf, 1906, 1994
Nathaniel Hawthorne may be most remembered for *The Scarlet Letter,* but he also wrote stories

for children. His *Wonder Book,* first published in 1851, is a classic collection of retold myths. You can probably find an edition of it in many libraries (the one listed here, with illustrations by Arthur Rackham, is a handsome new edition in the Everyman Library Children's Classics series). Hawthorne creates a frame story for the telling of the myths: a group of children listens to a young man named Eustace Bright who "had won great fame among the children, as a narrator of wonderful stories." Before and after each myth, Eustace and the children talk, mostly about the stories. In retelling the myths of Perseus, King Midas, Pandora, and others, Hawthorne has, he readily admits, allowed himself "great freedom of treatment." He embellishes the tales with invented episodes and commentary and fanciful language, all of which give these versions great charm, but which may make them sound quaint and flowery to some modern ears.

SHAKESPEARE FOR CHILDREN

Shakespeare
The bard merits a resource catalog all to himself. Call The Writing Company, Culver City, California, at (800) 421-4246 and ask for this catalog filled with materials to help you teach Shakespeare. While you're at it, ask for their other Language Arts catalogs as well.

Shakespeare for Children
as told by Jim Weiss
Greathall Productions
On this cassette tape, recommended by the producers for ages eight and up, storyteller Jim Weiss tells lively and accessible versions of two plays, *A Midsummer Night's Dream* and *The Taming of the Shrew.* These are stories, not drama, so if you know the plays it may take you a few minutes to get used to hearing description of what you are accustomed to as dialogue or action. Also, to turn the plays into short stories, Weiss has had to interpret them in his own way, which may not be the way you see the

plays. But most children will not have to overcome these minor obstacles. They will enjoy the spirited telling and the lively stories. This is one of many fine story tapes available from Greathall Productions: (800) 477-6234.

CC *Shakespeare for Young People* **series**
edited by Diane Davidson
Swan Books
These slender paperback volumes of some of the most popular plays—*A Midsummer Night's Dream, Romeo and Juliet, Julius Caesar,* and others—are a great way to introduce children to Shakespeare's plays—not just reading the plays, but performing them. The editor has carefully condensed the plays while retaining the original language. She has cleverly added announcers who help introduce scenes and explain difficult passages. Available from The Writing Company: (800) 421-4246.

Shakespeare Stories
by Leon Garfield
illustrated by Michael Foreman
Houghton Mifflin, 1985
The author retains some of Shakespeare's language as he recasts the plays as stories. While no substitute for the originals, these well-told stories can help introduce children to the plot and characters, and so prepare them for the wonderful but challenging language they will encounter when they read the plays themselves. "The play's the thing," but these stories are a good way to get to them. Titles include: *Twelfth Night, King Lear, The Tempest, Hamlet, Romeo and Juliet, Othello, A Midsummer Night's Dream, Macbeth,* and more. Also available from the same author, a second volume, *Shakespeare Stories II.*

CC *Shakespeare: The Animated Tales*
abridged by Leon Garfield
Alfred A. Knopf
A book-and-video series, joining artists from Wales, Russia, England, the U.S., and Japan. Each half-hour-long animated video has a companion illustrated book that matches the video script. The plays are, of course, drastically short-

ened, but in a way that is respectful of the originals, with dialogue straight from Shakespeare.
Some productions use "Claymation" animated
figures, while others are cartoon animation. In
general, the comedies come off better than the
tragedies, but all are effective ways to get
younger children interested in Shakespeare. The
tragedies include *Macbeth, Hamlet,* and *Romeo
and Juliet.* The comedies—we suggest you start
with them—include *A Midsummer Night's
Dream, The Tempest,* and *Twelfth Night.*

BIOGRAPHY COLLECTIONS

Great Lives: American Literature
by Doris Faber and Harold Faber
Simon & Schuster/Atheneum, 1995
This reference book contains thirty eight- to ten-
page biographical sketches of great American
authors from James Fenimore Cooper to Tennes-
see Williams. Each entry portrays the author's
life, major works, and the reception he or she
received. It includes contemporary photos or
portraits of the authors. Useful as a teacher/
parent resource for background information on
authors in the *Core Knowledge Sequence,* including Irving, Longfellow, Poe, Thoreau, Alcott,
Dickinson, Twain, Whitman, Frost, Hughes, and
White.

*Lives of the Writers: Comedies, Tragedies (and
What the Neighbors Thought)*
by Kathleen Krull
illustrated by Kathryn Hewitt
Harcourt Brace, 1994
This engaging, gossipy volume tells the *other*
side of the story about nineteen favorite authors. Each brief biography gives the basics of
the writer's life and works, filled in with personal details and quirky quotations that give a
more private glimpse than most standard biographies. We learn, for example, that Edgar Allan
Poe, aged twenty-seven, married his thirteen-
year-old cousin; that Emily Dickinson only al-

lowed her physician to examine her from the
room next door; and that E. B. White compli-
mented his wife-to-be once by telling her she
smelled like pencil shavings. Full-page color
caricatures of each author accompany their sections.

ABOUT LANGUAGE

Note: These are not grammar textbooks, but
books that take an imaginative approach to
grammatical topics. They can provide a pleasant supplement, especially for reading aloud
at home, but they cannot replace the explicit
instruction and regular practice in grammatical rules and conventions that children
should receive in school.

A Cache of Jewels and Other Collective Nouns
(1987)
Kites Sail High: A Book About Verbs **(1988)**
*Many Luscious Lollipops: A Book About
Adjectives* **(1989)**
Merry-Go-Round: A Book About Nouns **(1990)**
Up Up and Away: A Book About Adverbs
(1991)
by Ruth Heller
Grosset & Dunlap
Written in verse and brightly illustrated, these
books are a fun way to learn about some gram-
matical terms and concepts.

I Think I Thought and Other Tricky Verbs
by Marvin Terban
illustrated by Giulio Maestro
Houghton Mifflin/Clarion Books, 1984
In humorous, alliterative rhyming couplets,
Terban presents the present and past tenses of
thirty irregular verbs of English. If you like this,
look for other books by the same author, including *It Figures! Fun Figures of Speech* and *Your
Foot's on My Feet.*

Sayings, Phrases, and Wordplay

I Saw Esau: The Schoolchild's Pocket Book
edited by Iona and Peter Opie
illustrated by Maurice Sendak
Candlewick Press, 1992
This captivating little book is full of jingles, rhymes, and sayings from childhoods present and past. The authors, renowned collectors of children's literature, call it a "feast of laughter," and illustrator Maurice Sendak adds more fun with his whimsical interpretations of nonsense rhymes. Many of the jingles are footnoted, so you can learn something about their history and meaning.

In a Pickle and Other Funny Idioms
by Marvin Terban
illustrated by Giulio Maestro
Houghton Mifflin/Clarion Books, 1983
Thirty common English phrases, such a *chip off the old block* and *don't cry over spilled milk*, are humorously illustrated and explained. Marvin Terban has pretty much cornered the market in wordplay books. If you like this book, look for his other books, including: *Mad as a Wet Hen! and Other Funny Idioms; Punching the Clock: Funny Action Idioms; Superdupers! Really Funny Real Words; Funny You Should Ask: How to Make Up Jokes and Riddles with Wordplay; Too Hot to Hoot: Funny Palindrome Riddles*, and more.

LANGUAGE ARTS

Reading and Writing: Kindergarten–Grade 2

Note: Please see the Introduction to Language Arts (pages 25–27) for a discussion of the need for an approach to the teaching of reading and writing that balances an emphasis on meaningful literature and creative expression with an equally necessary emphasis on the "nuts and bolts"— the systematic early teaching of decoding skills and conventions of written language.

This section on Reading and Writing suggests some resources to help children in the primary grades learn the "nuts and bolts" of language, so that they can gain access, on their own, to the world of meaning in the good books recommended throughout this guide and elsewhere. It is especially important that children receive *early* instruction, and that, in kindergarten through second grade, this instruction be explicit, systematic, and well organized, with regular practice and review of such basic skills and concepts as letter names and sounds, specific letter-sound patterns that make up the English language, and how letters can be written to represent spoken words.

Schools, not parents, are responsible for teaching the nuts and bolts of language. Parents can reinforce what is (or should be) taught in school. We hope the resources recommended here will be of help to both parents and teachers. These resources are meant to complement, not substitute for, the readers and associated materials that schools use to teach reading and writing, though some teachers may find these additional resources helpful as well, especially if their school has adopted a philosophy or set of materials that neglects the systematic early teaching of decoding skills and of the conventions of written language.

The following list is intended to help you get started in locating a few of the many good resources available. Besides the books suggested below, other useful supplies are generally available from teacher supply stores and some toy stores:

- magnetic letters, letter tiles, and letter flash cards
- letter-picture cards (cards with simple pictures and a corresponding letter, for example, the letter *a* with a picture of an apple) and word-picture cards
- simple bingo or lotto games to practice recognizing letters and words
- workbooks to practice handwriting
- alphabet and "first words" activity books
- computer software for teaching the alphabet, letter sounds, and words, such as *Bailey's Book House* (Edmark), *Beginning Reading* (Sierra On-Line), *Kid Phonics* (Davidson), and the *Reader Rabbit* series (The Learning Company).

ALPHABET BOOKS

Note: The books recommended here are appropriate for *preschool*-age children. We list them here because kindergartners still enjoy and benefit from them. There are dozens of good alphabet books; here are just a few favorites.

A Was Once an Apple Pie
by Edward Lear
illustrated by Julie Lacome
Candlewick Press, 1992
This favorite alphabet jingle, a delight to read aloud, is accompanied here by colorful illustrations that evoke paper cutouts and patchwork quilts.

Alison's Zinnia
by Anita Lobel
Greenwillow Books, 1990
This is a charming alphabet book that uses alliteration, repetition, and beautiful illustrations of flowers to teach the alphabet.

Alphabears: An ABC Book
by Kathleen Hague
illustrated by Michael Hague
Henry Holt, 1984
Cute, old-fashioned bears—can any child resist?

Chicka Chicka Boom Boom
by Bill Martin, Jr., and John Archambault
illustrated by Lois Ehlert
Scholastic, 1989
This is a bouncy rhyming book about the alphabet, fun to read aloud, fun to look at, fun to chime in all together with the refrain (identified in the title).

I Spy: An Alphabet in Art
by Lucy Micklethwait
Greenwillow Books, 1992
An unusual alphabet book that asks children to search two-page illustrations for objects that begin with each letter.

On Market Street
by Arnold Lobel
illustrated by Anita Lobel
Greenwillow/Mulberry, 1981
A boy goes on a shopping spree through the letters of the alphabet in this elaborate and dazzling alphabet book.

Plant and Animal Alphabet Coloring Book
written and illustrated by Leslie Tillett
Dover, 1980
Each page contains an picture of a capital letter of the alphabet filled with images of plants and animals representing that letter. Dover has many other alphabet activity books as well. Write for a catalog of children's books (see address, page 39).

PHONICS AND PHONETICALLY CONTROLLED READERS

Note: There are *many* phonics materials available from many sources. In recommending a few here, we emphatically do not mean to exclude others. The recommendations here are for materials that are time tested and/or readily available, generally at a reasonable cost, and usable by those without special training in the teaching of reading and writing.

"Phonetically controlled readers" are simple stories written in a controlled vocabulary that corresponds to the letter-sound patterns that a child has been taught in preparation for reading the story. For example, after being taught some consonants and the short *a* sound (as in *apple*), a child might read a simple story about "Mac and Tab and the Hat." While such stories are, of course, not literature, they are very helpful in teaching children to read, especially in providing the early (and tremendously satisfying) experience of being able "to read it all by myself."

Bob Books; More Bob Books; Even More Bob Books
by Bobby Lynn Maslen
illustrated by John R. Maslen
Scholastic/Bob Books, 1976
Easy for parents to use at home, these three sets of little books—occasionally whimsical, quirky, and fun—offer cute stories and line drawings that verge on silly but which most children will probably like for that very reason. The books begin with short words and simple consonant sounds, and go on through the three sets to introduce new sounds in a nicely sequenced fashion.

Educators Publishing Service (EPS)
31 Smith Place, Cambridge, MA 02138-1000
This mail-order company has many good teacher-created resources, including such favorites as the "Primary Phonics" series of workbooks and storybooks (described below). Call (800) 225-5750 for a catalog.

Primary Phonics Workbooks and Storybooks
by Barbara Makar
Educators Publishing Service
These five sets of workbooks and coordinated readers have simple line drawings for many short stories using words with short vowels, long vowels, r-controlled vowels, and other vowel combinations in a carefully controlled sequence. Taken as a whole, they form a fairly comprehensive phonics program, more than most parents are likely to undertake at home (unless, of course, you are home-schooling). It's possible, however, to use of some of the storybooks at home to complement reading instruction in school. The storybooks have a more old-fashioned look and feel to them than the Bob Books (see above). Primary Phonics is only one of many sets of phonics materials available from Educators Publishing Service (address above); call (800) 225-5750 for a catalog.

Recipe for Reading, **third edition**
by Nina Traub and Frances Bloom
Educators Publishing Service, 1990
This practical text offers a time-tested sequence of instruction for basic letter sounds and moves into more complex sounds. The book and optional associated materials (workbooks, storybooks, writing paper) are available from Educator's Publishing Service (see address above).

BEGINNING READING MATERIALS (NOT PHONETICALLY CONTROLLED)

Note: These books are the next step after phonetically controlled reading materials. They use a wider variety of words and more complex sentences, but still have large print, a limited amount of text per page, and short chapters or a manageable number of pages per book.

CC *Ready . . . Set . . . Read: The Beginning Reader's Treasury* (1990)
Ready . . . Set . . . Read—and Laugh! A Funny Treasury for Beginning Readers (1995)
compiled by Joanna Cole and Stephanie Calmenson
Doubleday
These two colorfully illustrated collections contain stories, poems, riddles, and word games by well-known writers like Arnold Lobel and Eve Merriam. The second book puts the emphasis on humor, and offers such classics as *Come Back, Amelia Bedelia.* Both books are a good next step for the child who is growing more confident as a reader and ready for challenges beyond beginning phonic texts.

Ladybug and *Spider*
The Cricket Magazine Group
These are monthly magazines with high quality literature, stories and nonfiction articles, as well as puzzles, games and other projects. Colorful, attractive artwork illustrates each issue. *Ladybug* is for children about four to six years old: it has good read-aloud stories, simple poems, and some simple texts for beginning readers. The stories in *Spider* are written for children about

six to eight years old who have already mastered phonic readers and are ready for more challenging material. Many libraries carry these magazines. For subscription information, write to The Cricket Magazine Group (315 Fifth Street, Peru, IL 61354) or call (800) 827-0227.

Check your library for the area designated as "Beginning or Easy Readers," and for books that are part of series with names like I Can Read, Step into Reading, Let's Read and Find Out, and the like. Most are designated in some way, such as "Level 1," "Level 2," and so on, for the new reader or the reader ready for something a little more challenging. Popular favorites among such books include the following:

P. D. Eastman
Are You My Mother?
Go, Dog, Go
Sam and the Firefly

Lillian Hoban
Arthur's Prize Reader
Arthur's Honey Bear
Arthur's Loose Tooth

Syd Hoff
Chester
Danny and the Dinosaur
Sammy the Seal

Arnold Lobel
Frog and Toad Are Friends
Frog and Toad Together
Owl at Home

Edward Marshall
Fox at School
Fox in Love
Three by the Sea

James Marshall
Fox on Stage
Fox on the Job
Three Up a Tree

Else Homelund Minarik
Little Bear
Little Bear's Friend
Little Bear's Visit

Peggy Parish
Amelia Bedelia
Thank You, Amelia Bedelia
Amelia Bedelia and the Surprise Shower

Dr. Seuss
The Cat in the Hat
Green Eggs and Ham
One Fish Two Fish Red Fish Blue Fish

Jean Van Leeuwen
Tales of Oliver Pig
Amanda Pig and Her Big Brother Oliver
More Tales of Amanda Pig

LANGUAGE ARTS

Kindergarten

Note: The stories and poems recommended here are meant to constitute a *core* of enriching literature. Teachers and parents are strongly encouraged to expose children to many more stories and poems than those listed below, including classic picture books, read-aloud books, perennial favorites by beloved children's writers, popular favorites by contemporary writers, biographies, books about art and music, lots of nonfiction, and of course books that the children themselves choose. For suggestions on more good reading, see Language Arts General Resources, Guides to Good Reading (pages 32–33). **See also** pages 46–49, Reading and Writing: Kindergarten—Grade 2.

CC = a **"Core Collection"** book (see p. 8).

POEMS

See also Language Arts General Resources: Poetry Collections: General Collections; "Mother Goose"; and For Younger Children.

A Child's Garden of Verses
by Robert Louis Stevenson
See description under Language Arts General Resources: Poetry Collections for Younger Children.

Dancing Teepees: Poems of American Indian Youth
selected by Virginia Driving Hawk Sneve
Holiday House, 1989
Some of the short poems in this beautifully illustrated collection would be nice to share with children as they learn about Native American peoples (see American History: Kindergarten).

CC = **"Core Collection"** book (see page 8).

CC *The Rooster Crows: A Book of American Rhymes and Jingles*
by Maud and Miska Petersham
Macmillan/Aladdin Books, 1987
This Caldecott Medal winner includes a wealth of traditional American poems, songs, finger games, rope-skipping rhymes, and jingles.

Shake It to the One that You Love the Best: Play Songs and Lullabies from Black Musical Traditions
collected and adapted by Cheryl Warren Mattox
Warren-Mattox Productions, 1990
See description under Language Arts General Resources: Poetry Collections.

When We Were Very Young **(1924, 1952)**
Now We Are Six **(1927, 1955)**
by A. A. Milne
illustrated by Ernest H. Shepard
E. P. Dutton
See description under Language Arts General Resources: Poetry Collections for Younger Children.

STORIES

Note: Many of the stories below are available in convenient collections. **See also** Language Arts General Resources: Stories, for recommended collections of stories and fairy tales.

Animal Tales
as told by Jim Weiss
Greathall Productions
On this cassette tape, storyteller Jim Weiss tells nine tales, including ''The Three Billy Goats Gruff,'' ''The Lion and the Mouse,'' and ''The Tortoise and the Hare.'' Weiss calls attention to the stories, not himself as teller. One of many fine story tapes available from Greathall Productions: (800) 477-6234.

The Bremen-Town Musicians
    retold by Ruth Belov Gross
    illustrated by Jack Kent
    Scholastic, 1974

    retold and illustrated by Ilse Plume
    Doubleday, 1980

    retold and illustrated by Janet Stevens
    Holiday House, 1992

    retold and illustrated by Bernadette Watts
    North-South Books, 1992
It's hard to go wrong with any of the many versions of this favorite tale. Ruth Belov's simple retelling, illustrated with Jack Kent's funny cartoons, has great action scenes, like the page on which the four animals come crashing through the window, interrupting the robbers as they feast and count their stolen money. Ilse Plume's Caldecott Honor book features gentle, quiet, and colorful illustrations. Quite the opposite is Janet Stevens, who makes her characters look wild, bedraggled, and a little crazy. Bernadette Watts provides large, colorful pictures to go with her good retelling.

Cinderella
    retold by Marcia Brown
    Charles Scribner's Sons, 1954; Aladdin
      Books, 1988 (paperback)

    retold by Amy Ehrlich
    illustrated by Susan Jeffers
    Dial Books/Puffin Pied Piper, 1985
Marcia Brown's retelling won the Caldecott Medal for its illustrations, evocative line drawings in pastel colors. Its language is pleasantly old fashioned, and does not shy away from words like *alas* and *wretched*. Amy Ehrlich's version is told in more simple language, but still sounds pleasant and not watered down; and this large-format book has big, stunning, detailed illustrations by Susan Jeffers, who depicts Cinderella with a fresh, young-looking, almost childlike face.

Goldilocks and the Three Bears
    retold and illustrated by Jan Brett
    G. P. Putnam's Sons, 1987; Sandcastle, 1990

    retold and illustrated by James Marshall
    Dial Books, 1988
Two excellent versions: one plays it straight, one funny. Jan Brett's traditional version stands out because of her marvelously detailed illustrations, which are a delight to look at again and again. James Marshall's wacky interpretation of the traditional story won a Caldecott Honor medal.

Henny Penny
retold and illustrated by Paul Galdone
Clarion Books, 1968
Galdone's characteristically energetic illustrations, here in a four-color format, make this a lively retelling of the tale otherwise known as ''Chicken Little'' (''The sky is falling!''). For another version try *Chicken Little and the Little Half Chick* by Berte and Elmer Hader (Gallery Books, 1990), which includes a retelling of the Spanish folktale ''*Medio Pollito.''*

CC *How Many Spots Does a Leopard Have? and Other Tales*
by Julius Lester
illustrated by David Shannon
Scholastic, 1989
Written in a style that makes any reader turn storyteller, this book offers one big picture per story—but what wonderful pictures they are! The volume includes not only the title story but also eleven other African or Jewish folktales, including "Tug of War."

CC *In a Circle Long Ago: A Treasury of Native Lore from North America*
retold by Nancy Van Laan
illustrated by Lisa Desimini
Alfred A. Knopf/Apple Soup Books, 1995
See description under Language Arts General Resources: Stories. This is an especially good collection of tales to connect to the introduction to Native American peoples (see American History: Kindergarten). Besides this collection, there are many good picture books based on American Indian myths and legends, too many to list here. To name just a few, try Gerald McDermott's Caldecott Award winner, *Arrow to the Sun: A Pueblo Indian Tale* (Puffin, 1977), and his boisterous *Coyote: A Trickster Tale from the American Southwest* (Harcourt Brace, 1994); also, Tomie de Paola's *The Legend of the Bluebonnet* (Putnam, 1983; also available from Scholastic) and *The Legend of the Indian Paintbrush* (Macmillan/Aladdin, 1988; also available from Scholastic).

Johnny Appleseed
   poem by Reeve Lindbergh
   illustrated by Kathy Jakobsen
   Little, Brown, 1990

   retold and illustrated by Steven Kellogg
   William Morrow, 1988
The Story of Johnny Appleseed
   retold and illustrated by Aliki
   Simon & Schuster, 1971
Lindbergh has taken the legend of Johnny Appleseed and turned it into a lovely poem. Jakobsen's fascinating illustrations, inspired by American folk art, tell the story not only of Johnny Appleseed himself but also of the evolution of the United States from wilderness to settled land. Steven Kellogg's big book makes a good read-aloud, with its simple prose and vigorous, action-packed pictures. In contrast to Kellogg's high-energy tall tale, Aliki tells a gentle story, with happy and colorful drawings, and emphasizes Johnny Appleseed as a man of peace.

"King Midas and the Golden Touch"
in *A Wonder Book for Boys and Girls*
by Nathaniel Hawthorne
Alfred A. Knopf, 1906, 1994
In his 1851 *Wonder Book*, Nathaniel Hawthorne called his version of the Greek myth of King Midas "The Golden Touch." See Language Arts General Resources: Stories for a description of *A Wonder Book*. If Hawthorne's retelling is too long or old-fashioned sounding for your taste, then you can find other versions of "The Golden Touch" that condense and slightly adapt Hawthorne for present-day listeners: see *What Your Kindergartner Needs to Know* or William Russell's *Classics to Read Aloud* (described under Language Arts General Resources: Stories). There's also a fine story-on-tape version of King Midas on *Greek Myths* by Jim Weiss (see Language Arts Grade 2: Mythology of Ancient Greece). After children have heard a version of the story of King Midas and the Golden Touch, they may get a kick out of a modernized version, *Max and Ruby's Midas* by Rosemary Wells (Dial Books/Penguin, 1995), in which Max gains the power to turn anything (including his parents) into hot fudge sundaes.

The Little Red Hen
   retold and illustrated by Paul Galdone
   Clarion Books, 1973

   retold and illustrated by Margot Zemach
   Farrar, Straus & Giroux, 1983
Take your pick of these two fine retellings. Galdone's illustrations are bold, energetic, even boisterous. Zemach's are witty, lovely, and softer-toned.

Little Red Riding Hood
> retold and illustrated by Trina Schart
> Hyman
> Holiday House, 1983

Red Riding Hood
> retold and illustrated by James Marshall
> Puffin Books, 1991

Here are two very different Red Riding Hoods—both are delightful. Trina Schart Hyman's Caldecott Honor Book stays close to the original Brothers Grimm tale, and offers a detailed story with lots of dialogue and description. Her illustrations are beautiful and vivid. James Marshall offers a modern, revved-up, sometimes tongue-in-cheek retelling of the old tale, with funny, cartoonlike drawings. In Marshall's version, when the hunter pulls Granny out of the wolf, she complains, "It was so dark in there I couldn't read a *word.*" Try both if you can.

Peach Boy: A Japanese Legend
> retold by Gail Sakuri
> illustrated by Makiko Nagano
> Troll Associates, 1994

Peach Boy
> retold by William H. Hooks
> illustrated by June Otani
> Bantam Little Rooster Books, 1992

Gail Sakurai adds lively dialogue and description to make a fine read-aloud version of the longtime favorite Japanese folktale about Momotaro, "Peach Boy." Her book is illustrated with soft watercolors that take their shapes and colors from Japanese textiles. At the end of the book, she provides a page of cultural background to the story. William Hooks's version is part of the Bank Street Ready to Read series, with simple language and large print. It is in the highest of three reading levels in that series, and so still a read-aloud for kindergartners. The book has pleasant color illustrations that give glimpses of Japanese traditional costume and architecture, and depict the bad guys—the *oni*—as suitably monsterlike but not too scary.

Snow White
> retold by Paul Heins
> illustrated by Trina Schart Hyman
> Little, Brown, 1974

> retold by Josephine Poole
> illustrated by Angela Barret
> Alfred A. Knopf, 1991

> translated by Randall Jarrell
> illustrated by Nancy Eckholm Burkert
> Farrar, Straus & Giroux, 1972

So many versions of *Snow White,* and so many good ones—check your library for one that suits your fancy. The ones recommended here all tell the story very well for reading aloud, and differ in the character of their illustrations. Trina Schart Hyman creates a dark, dramatic, sometimes sensuous world in her pictures. Angela Barrett's illustrations are elegant and mysterious. Nancy Burkert's version won a Caldecott Honor medal for the finely detailed, two-page illustrations.

CC *The Story of Jumping Mouse*
retold and illustrated by John Steptoe
Lothrop, Lee & Shepard/Mulberry Books, 1984
In this large-format picture book, Steptoe retells a moving folktale from Hyemeyohsts Storm's *Seven Arrows.* The language is good for reading aloud, and the pictures, in sepia ink-wash and pencil, are fascinating glimpses of animals and nature from the mouse's point of view.

The Three Billy Goats Gruff
> retold and illustrated by Janet Stevens
> Harcourt Brace/Voyager Books, 1987

> retold and illustrated by Ellen Appleby
> Scholastic, 1985

> retold and illustrated by Glen Rounds
> Holiday House, 1993

Janet Stevens's spirited retelling of the classic story won a Parent's Choice award. The words are traditional, meant to be read aloud, and the pictures lively and humorous: the little goat wears a pacifier, the big goat sports shades and a black leather jacket, and the troll is downright nasty looking. Ellen Appleby's version is cute and traditional. In Glen Rounds's book, simple drawings complement an energetic retelling of the traditional story, with lots of BIG CAPITAL LETTERS to guide your reading aloud.

CC *The Three Little Pigs and Other Favorite Nursery Stories*
retold and illustrated by Charlotte Voake
Candlewick Press, 1992
With large type, simple language, and charming tinted sketches brightening every page, this book offers lighthearted yet faithful versions of ten fairy tales, including its title story, "Three Billy Goats Gruff," "Goldilocks," "Red Riding Hood," and "The Musicians of Bremen."

The Ugly Duckling
    retold by Marianna Mayer
    illustrated by Thomas Locker
    Macmillan, 1987

    retold by Lilian Moore
    illustrated by Daniel San Souci
    Scholastic, 1988

    retold and illustrated by Lorinda Bryan
      Cauley
    Harcourt Brace/Voyager Books, 1979
Mayer's graceful version of the story and Locker's painterly illustrations make this a beautiful book. Moore's retelling is true in spirit to the Hans Christian Andersen tale, with lovely and affecting illustrations by Daniel San Souci. Cauley also stays close to Andersen's original words, and provides vigorous, naturalistic illustrations, not in full color but color tinted (her book, by the way, is a "Reading Rainbow" selection).

CC *Winnie-the-Pooh*
by A. A. Milne
illustrated by Ernest H. Shepard
E. P. Dutton/Penguin, 1926, 1954
This whimsical children's classic is available in its original edition. Accept no substitutes! Milne's wit and wordplay make these original stories wonderful for reading aloud. The Walt Disney videos, *Winnie-the-Pooh and the Blustery Day* and *Winnie-the-Pooh and Tigger, Too*, draw much of their spirit and some of their dialogue from the original books, and are a delight to watch. But don't stop at watching: read the original with your children. You'll enjoy it as much as they do. (By the way, that bouncy fellow, Tigger, doesn't show up until the sequel, *The House at Pooh Corner*—see the description under Language Arts Grade 1: Stories.)

The Wolf and the Seven Little Kids
by Jacob and Wilhelm Grimm
illustrated by Bernadette Watts
North-South Books, 1995
This is a big, pleasant, playful picture book, with familiar household items scattered throughout the illustrations of the goats' home. Your children might also enjoy a modern variation on the basic plot of this story, *Heckedy Peg*, by Audrey Wood (Harcourt Brace Jovanovich, 1987), stunningly illustrated by Don Wood. It's a powerful story, so read it yourself first to see what you think.

AESOP'S FABLES

The Aesop for Children
illustrated by Milo Winter
Rand McNally, 1919; Checkerboard Press, 1947
A classic now for generations, this book presents over a hundred of Aesop's fables in large print with color illustrations, many full-page. Some of the language and imagery may be dated, but most is timeless and all is charming. A one-sentence moral wraps up each fable.

The Best of Aesop Fables
retold by Margaret Clark
illustrated by Charlotte Voake
Little Brown/Joy Street, 1990
This edition offers simply told tales, though the author—in order, she says, not to sound "preacherly"—has chosen not to spell out the morals at the end of the stories. Children will enjoy the funny, whimsical illustrations.

Aesop's Fables
selected and illustrated by Michael Hague
Henry Holt, 1985
Rich, detailed, warm-toned illustrations accompany thirteen of the well-known fables, including "The Hare and the Tortoise" and "The Lion and the Mouse." The text is written in satisfying style and printed in large, readable type; often two illustrations accompany a single fable.

Aesop's Fables
illustrated by Heidi Holder
Viking, 1981; Puffin Books, 1991
This book retells eight fables with elegant, elaborate color illustrations. Selected fables include "The Hare and the Tortoise" and "The Fox and the Grapes."

 **CC** = "**Core Collection**" book (see page 8).

Animal Fables from Aesop
by Barbara McClintock
David R. Godine, 1991
This witty volume introduces a cast of animal characters who then "perform" in nine fables, including "The Fox and the Crow," "The Fox and the Grapes," and "The Town Mouse and the Country Mouse." McClintock has fleshed out the fables slightly so they read more like stories, with just a bit of dialogue and description. Many lively, colorful illustrations make these stories come to life.

CC *The Children's Aesop*
retold by Stephanie Calmenson
illustrated by Robert Byrd
Boyds Mills Press, 1992
This collection of twenty-eight fables, with big, bright, colorful illustrations, is distinguished by lively writing and engaging dialogue to bring the stories to life for modern-day young readers (or listeners).

LANGUAGE ARTS

Grade 1

> *Note:* The stories and poems recommended here are meant to constitute a *core* of enriching literature. Teachers and parents are strongly encouraged to expose children to many more stories and poems than those listed below, including classic picture books, read-aloud books, perennial favorites by beloved children's writers, popular favorites by contemporary writers, biographies, books about art and music, lots of nonfiction, and of course books that the children themselves choose. For suggestions on more good reading, see Language Arts General Resources, Guides to Good Reading (pages 32–33). **See also** pages 46–49, Reading and Writing: Kindergarten–Grade 2.

 **CC** = a "**Core Collection**" book (see p. 8).

POEMS

See also Language Arts General Resources: Poetry Collections: General Collections; "Mother Goose"; and For Younger Children. **See also** the books recommended in Language Arts Kindergarten: Poems.

A Child's Garden of Verses
by Robert Louis Stevenson
See description under Language Arts General Resources: Poetry Collections for Younger Children.

Over the River and Through the Wood
by Lydia Maria Child

> illustrated by Brinton Turkle
> Scholastic, 1987

> illustrated by Iris Van Rynbach
> Little, Brown, 1989

An inexpensive paperback, Brinton Turkle's edition of the 1844 poem alternates between black-and-white charcoal drawings of grandparents rolling out pie dough and carving a turkey, and softly tinted paintings of a Victorian family traveling through snowy landscapes to their house. In Iris Van Rynbach's book, a "Reading Rainbow" selection, the warm, detailed watercolors are lovely to look at. Both books provide the music for the song.

The Owl and the Pussycat
by Edward Lear

> illustrated by Jan Brett
> G. P. Putnam's Sons, 1991

> illustrated by Hilary Knight
> Macmillan/Aladdin Books, 1983

Imagine the Owl and the Pussycat traveling between Caribbean islands, and imagine that under their little pea-green boat you can see every colorful reef fish and sea turtle swimming, every coral fan swaying below—that's how the wonderful illustrator, Jan Brett, envisions this poem. Hilary Knight takes a different and unusual approach—in fact, the official title of her little book is *Hilary Knight's The Owl and the Pussycat*. She does not alter Edward Lear's poem but places it inside a story about a fat and jolly Professor Comfort, who tells the poem to two young listeners. A fun idea, and fun pictures too. See also Language Arts General Resources: Poetry Collections, for Michael Hague's book of "The Owl and the Pussycat" and other Edward Lear poems.

CC *Ready . . . Set . . . Read: The Beginning Reader's Treasury*
Ready . . . Set . . . Read—and Laugh! A Funny Treasury for Beginning Readers
compiled by Joanna Cole and Stephanie Calmenson
Doubleday, 1990; 1995
See description under Language Arts: Reading and Writing: Beginning Reading Materials.

When We Were Very Young (1924, 1952)
Now We Are Six (1927, 1955)
by A. A. Milne
illustrated by Ernest H. Shepard
E. P. Dutton
See description under Language Arts General Resources: Poetry Collections for Younger Children.

Wynken, Blynken, and Nod
by Eugene Field

> illustrated by Susan Jeffers
> E. P. Dutton, 1982

> illustrated by Johanna Westerman
> North-South Books, 1995

In Susan Jeffers's lovely version, the illustrations interpret the poem as the story of two brothers and a sister playing make-believe in the attic. The shoe is a boat they make of sofas, the moon and the wind are imaginary guides in the sky. In Joanna Westerman's rendition, the illustrations take their cues from the poem: the moon smiling, the herring fish in the sea, and the children aloft in a Dutch-style wooden shoe.

STORIES

See also Language Arts General Resources: Stories, for recommended collections of stories and fairy tales.

The Adventures of Pinocchio
adapted by Sue Kassirer
illustrated by Mary Haverfield
Random House, 1992
Bright watercolors illustrate a clear, readable version of the story in this inexpensive paperback. This is not the story told in the Walt Disney film but a very condensed and softened version of the original *Pinocchio*, a short novel by C. Collodi. We do not recommend Collodi's complete, original *Pinocchio* for first grade: it is too long and a little too dark. In *What Your First Grader Needs to Know (revised edition)*, you can find a retelling of one humorous episode from Collodi's book.

Anansi and the Moss-Covered Rock **(1988)**
Anansi and the Talking Melon **(1994)**
Anansi Goes Fishing **(1992)**
by Eric Kimmel
Holiday House
These three Anansi stories combine spirited text and funny illustrations of the trickster spider's adventures with other animals. (See also below, *A Story, A Story*.)

CC *The Boy Who Held Back the Sea*
retold by Lenny Hort
illustrated by Thomas Locker
Dial Books, 1987
Lenny Hort retells the old tale of "The Boy at the Dike" with a bit of a twist. While the young hero of most traditional versions is a good boy who does a good deed, the hero of this version is a mischievous boy who does a lot that he shouldn't do before he does the good deed of plugging the hole in the dike with only his finger until at long last help comes. The most striking thing about this book, however, are the paintings by Thomas Locker, done in the style of Rembrandt and Vermeer, with extraordinary

light and shade. A delight to read aloud and look at again and again.

Fairytale Favorites in Story and Song
as told by Jim Weiss
Greathall Productions
On this cassette tape (also available on compact disc), storyteller Jim Weiss tells "Puss in Boots," "Rapunzel," "The Shoemaker and the Elves," and "Stone Soup," all with energy and flair, but in a way that calls attention to the stories, not himself as teller. A Parent's Choice award winner. One of many fine story tapes available from Greathall Productions: (800) 477-6234.

The Frog Prince
retold by Jan Ormerod and David Lloyd
illustrated by Jan Ormerod
Lothrop, Lee & Shepard, 1990

retold by Edith Tarcov
illustrated by James Marshall
Scholastic, 1987

Jan Ormerod's version of the story is enhanced by a recurring rhyme, first heard from the frog as it lifts its head up out of the water: "What is the matter, my honey, my heart?" The color in this book is limited, but Ormerod makes up for it with fascinating marginal decorations on every page. The version published by Scholastic is part of their "Hello Reader!" series, told in simple language with big print and goofy, colorful pictures. It is suitable for first graders to try reading with a little help. For an amusing parody that starts where the original fairy tale ends, try *The Frog Prince Continued* by Jon Scieszka (Viking, 1991), who has also written another "fractured fairy tale," *The True Story of the Three Little Pigs* (Viking, 1989).

CC = "Core Collection" book (see page 8).

Hansel and Gretel
by the Brothers Grimm

retold and illustrated by Susan Jeffers
Dial Books, 1980

retold by Rika Lesser
illustrated by Paul O. Zelinsky
G. P. Putnam's Sons/Sandcastle Books, 1984

retold and illustrated by James Marshall
Dial Books for Young Readers, 1990

The pictures in Susan Jeffers's fine retelling are light, bright, and lovely. Their gentleness softens some of the darkness of the tale. The Rika Lesser edition stays close to the Brothers Grimm text and won a Caldecott Honor award for Paul Zelinsky's warm-toned, detailed oil paintings. James Marshall's version is altogether different—funny, cartoonish illustrations complement a retelling that maintains the basic story line but throws in a few wisecracks and one-liners to lighten the proceedings. Best to read a more traditional version first, we think, and later turn to Marshall's for a laugh or two. By the way, a *Hansel and Gretel Coloring Book* is available from Dover (see address, page 39), with simple text and twenty-nine illustrations.

CC The House at Pooh Corner
by A. A. Milne
illustrated by Ernest Shepard
E. P. Dutton, 1928, 1956

As we said about *Winnie the Pooh* (described under Language Arts Kindergarten: Stories), accept no substitutes! Milne's wit and wordplay make these original stories wonderful for reading aloud. The Walt Disney videos, *Winnie-the-Pooh and the Blustery Day* and *Winnie-the-Pooh and Tigger, Too*, draw much of their spirit and some of their dialogue from the original books, and are a delight to watch. But don't stop at watching: read the original with your children. You'll enjoy it as much as they do.

It Could Always Be Worse
retold and illustrated by Margot Zemach
Farrar, Straus & Giroux, 1976
This Caldecott Honor book tells the Yiddish

folktale with just the right rhythm for reading aloud and just the right chaos in the illustrations for getting a good laugh out of the story.

Jack and the Beanstalk
illustrated by Matt Faulkner
Scholastic, 1986

retold and illustrated by John Howe
Little, Brown, 1989

There are many versions of this tale to choose from, and many in story collections. Matt Faulkner offers a simple retelling with clever colored pencil illustrations that play with perspective and size in fun ways. John Howe's excellent read-aloud version stands out for its vivid, dramatic paintings and a fierce-looking (but not really scary) giant.

The Knee-High Man and Other Tales
by Julius Lester
illustrated by Ralph Pinto
Dial Books, 1972

Lester collected and retold the humorous "Knee-High Man" along with five other stories because, as he explains in his introduction, he found them all reflecting thoughts and feelings about the slave/master relationship, yet also having meaning today. Lester writes in a way that makes it easy to read aloud, as he captures rhythms and inflections of voice. Each tale in this small volume is illustrated with humorous color paintings.

"Medio Pollito"
in *Favorite Fairy Tales Told in Spain*
retold by Virginia Haviland
illustrated by Monique Passicott
William Morrow/Beech Tree Books, 1995

This collection has an excellent read-aloud version of a tale recommended for first grade in the *Core Knowledge Sequence*, "Medio Pollito" or, as it is called here, "The Half-Chick." Haviland's version is a bit longer and more detailed than the retelling in *What Your First Grader Needs to Know*. Black-and-white drawings accompany Haviland's retelling, and four other

tales from Spain round out her book. (See also Language Arts General Resources: Series, for a description of Haviland's *Favorite Fairy Tales from Around the World.*)

The Pied Piper of Hamelin
retold by Deborah Hautzig
illustrated by S. D. Schindler
Random House, 1989

This is a Step into Reading book, with simple language, big print, and colorful pictures. It can be read aloud, and as first graders gain skill in reading, they may be able to read parts to you. In libraries you can find Robert Browning's poem "The Pied Piper of Hamelin," which is a classic of narrative verse, though it may be complex even to read aloud to first graders. The retelling of "The Pied Piper" in *What Your First Grader Needs to Know (revised edition)* incorporates some of Browning's rhymes and rhythms into a prose version of the story.

The Princess and the Pea
by Hans Christian Andersen

retold and illustrated by Suçie Stevenson
Dell Picture Yearling, 1992

retold and illustrated by Janet Stevens
Scholastic, 1984

illustrated by Dorothée Duntze
North-South Books, 1984

The first two of these picture books take a light-hearted approach to Andersen's tale. Both depict amusing animal characters in bright and lively pictures. The third book, by Dorothée Duntze, is quite different in its look and feel: it tells the story as Andersen wrote it, but the pictures are highly stylized, elegant and intricate, in an art nouveau style. All are fine for reading aloud.

 **CC** = "Core Collection" book (see page 8).

Puss in Boots
by Charles Perrault

 CC translated by Malcolm Arthur
illustrated by Fred Marcellino
Farrar, Straus & Giroux, 1990

retold and illustrated by Paul Galdone
Clarion Books, 1976

retold by Susan Saunders
illustrated by Elizabeth Miles
Scholastic, 1989

The book by Arthur and Marcellino, a Caldecott Honor Book, provides a fine read-aloud version of the tale of the clever cat who wins a kingdom for his master. It's a book children will want to return to again and again because of the magnificent illustrations, from the stunning full-face portrait of Puss on the dust jacket to the clever and stylish paintings that grace every page. Paul Galdone's retelling also makes a good read-aloud, with vigorous and funny drawings that convey the sense of mischief in the tale. The Saunders and Miles book tells the story in simple language with lovely watercolor illustrations that place the story in a medieval setting.

Rapunzel
by Amy Ehrlich
illustrated by Kris Waldherr
Dial Books, 1989

retold and illustrated by Alix Berenzy
Henry Holt, 1995

retold by Barbara Rogasky
illustrated by Trina Schart Hyman
Holiday House, 1982

retold by Bernice Chardiet
illustrated by Julie Downing
Scholastic, 1990

Amy Ehrlich offers a quiet, poetic retelling of the story illustrated with soft colored-pencil drawings. Each page is bordered distinctively, with rampion garlands or rose thorns or forest trees, to suit the stage of the story. In contrast,

Alix Berenzy's version is emotionally charged, with bold, vibrant powerful paintings, strongly contrasting light and dark, that convey the power of this story. Another dramatic version comes from Barbara Rogasky, with the drama heightened by the intricate and evocative art of Trina Schart Hyman. Lovely illustrations and simple prose make Bernice Chardiet's version, a Scholastic Easy to Read Folktale, one that can be read aloud or by first graders with a little help.

Rumpelstiltskin

 CC retold and illustrated by Paul O.
Zelinsky
E. P. Dutton, 1986

retold by Alison Sage
illustrated by Gennady Spirin
Dial Books for Young Readers, 1991

Here are two beautiful picture books. Paul Zelinsky's extraordinary Caldecott Honor book is distinguished by opulent, detailed paintings for every page, setting the story in a medieval castle and envisioning Rumpelstiltskin as a skinny-legged, bug-eyed little elf. Alison Sage retells the story in a way that fleshes out the Brothers Grimm tale with added description and dialogue; in her book, Spirin's detailed paintings are admirable, but the Zelinsky book is more likely to appeal to a child's imagination.

Sleeping Beauty
retold and illustrated by Trina Schart
Hyman
Little, Brown, 1977

retold and illustrated by Mercer Mayer
Macmillan, 1984

Here are two beautiful picture books, both of which tell the traditional story with spectacular illustrations. A classic read-aloud version (unillustrated) may be found in *Sleeping Beauty and Other Fairy Tales*, translated by Lucy Crane (see description under Language Arts General Resources: Stories). For a twist, try *Sleeping Ugly* by Jane Yolen (Putnam/Coward McCann, 1981), in which Princess Miserella, Plain Jane, and a fairy fall under a sleeping spell. A prince undoes the spell in a surprising way. It's fun to compare this easy reader with one of the traditional versions of the Sleeping Beauty story.

CC *A Story a Story*
retold and illustrated by Gail E. Haley
Macmillan, 1988
Spider and the Sky God: An Akan Legend
retold by Deborah M. Newton Chocolate
illustrated by Dave Albers
Troll Associates, 1993
Both of these books tell the legend of how stories, once the exclusive property of the sky god, came to people on earth by virtue of that tricky spider, Anansi. Gail Haley's 1971 Caldecott Medal winner remains a classic. Bold woodblock illustrations and clear, rhythmic text, written with an ear for the sounds of nature and language, make this an especially wonderful book to read aloud. Deborah M. Newton Chocolate's book is also a good retelling, though her language is not as musical as Haley's. Albers's illustrations borrow shapes and colors from African textiles, and the book's last page provides information about the Akan people, the Ananse tradition, and African storytelling. (See also above, *Anansi and the Moss-Covered Rock.*)

The Tale of Peter Rabbit
written and illustrated by Beatrix Potter
Frederick Warne and Company, 1902, 1987
Some children will have heard this story read aloud since they could eat solid food. Fine, read it again! Avoid imitations and retellings. The original story and art by Beatrix Potter are *the real* Peter Rabbit. Yes, it's all veddy, veddy proper and British, but would you have it any other way? If you don't already know Beatrix Potter's other children's classics, try the following titles, all of which begin with *The Tale of . . .* : *The Flopsy Bunnies; Squirrel Nutkin; Two Bad Mice; Mr. Jeremy Fisher; Benjamin Bunny.* Have we left out one of your favorites? We apologize! By the way, *The Tale of Peter Rabbit Coloring Book* is available from Dover (see address, page 39), with twenty-seven illustrations in the style of Beatrix Potter.

The Tales of Uncle Remus: The Adventures of Brer Rabbit (1987)
More Tales of Uncle Remus: Further Adventures of Brer Rabbit, His Friends, Enemies, and Others (1988)
retold by Julius Lester
illustrated by Jerry Pinkney
Dial Books
Two of four books of Uncle Remus tales retold by Julius Lester (see Language Arts General Resources: Stories for a description of Lester's other volumes). These are to read aloud, and contain versions of stories suggested in the *Core Knowledge Sequence,* such as "Brer Rabbit Gets Brer Fox's Dinner" and "Brer Rabbit Tricks Brer Bear."

The Velveteen Rabbit
by Margery Williams
illustrated by Michael Hague
Henry Holt, 1983
There are *many* editions of this classic children's story; this just happens to be an especially handsome one, with Michael Hague's lovely illustrations, and the complete text. Another edition, illustrated in soft shades by David Jorgensen (Alfred A. Knopf/Dragonfly, 1985), very slightly condenses the original story, which does no harm, and is a companion book for a video version narrated by Meryl Streep (produced by Rabbit Ears). Any reasonably complete edition of this tale will do. We only recommend that you steer clear of versions that too greatly shorten the story, for much of the charm is in the language, quaint, delicate, and lyrical. By the way, Dover (see address, page 39) publishes a *Velveteen Rabbit Coloring Book,* with the complete story and ready-to-color illustrations.

CC = "Core Collection" book (see page 8).

Aesop's Fables

See listings under Language Arts Kindergarten: Aesop's Fables (pages 54–55).

Different Lands, Similar Stories

Note: To give children a sense that people around the world tell stories that, while they differ in details, have much in common, the *Core Knowledge Sequence* recommends that children be introduced to similar stories from different lands, such as the following:

Lon Po-Po: A Red Riding Hood Story from China
translated and illustrated by Ed Young
G. P. Putnam's Sons, 1989; Scholastic, 1990
This Caldecott Medal winner tells a story that will make Western readers think not only of "Red Riding Hood" but also "The Wolf and Seven Kids." Young's fascinating pastel illustrations are wonderful and sometimes chilling, especially those in which the wolf's eye dominates the page. A teaching guide for this book is available from Scholastic.

Thumbelina
retold by Amy Ehrlich
illustrated by Susan Jeffers
Penguin/Puffin Books, 1979
Try this beautifully illustrated edition of Hans Christian Andersen's story and compare it to "Tom Thumb" and "Issun Boshi" ("The Inch Boy").

CC *Tom Thumb*
retold and illustrated by Richard Jesse Watson
Harcourt Brace/Voyager Books, 1989
This book retells a version of "Tom Thumb" from the English folk tradition, which you may find it interesting to compare with the story of German origin retold in *What Your First Grader Needs to Know (revised edition)*. Beautiful, lifelike paintings distinguish this fine book. (Compare it

also to the Japanese tale of "Issun Boshi," or "The Inch Boy"; see below).

The Inch Boy
retold and illustrated by Junko Morimoto
Puffin Books, 1988
This is a beloved Japanese folk tale that, like the Tom Thumb story, has a tiny hero. The illustrations play with perspective and size, while echoing the lines and texture of Japanese brush paintings. For another version, try *Little Inchkin*, retold and illustrated by Fiona French (Dial Books, 1994), with magnificent paintings and exquisite decorative borders.

The Egyptian Cinderella
retold by Shirley Climo
illustrated by Ruth Heller
HarperCollins, 1992
This is the story of a young slave girl who is distraught when one of her shoes is stolen, though all works out well (of course!) when the shoe ends up with the pharaoh. Brightly colored illustrations light up the pages. (See also World History Grade 1: Ancient Egypt.) You might also enjoy, by the same author and illustrator, *The Korean Cinderella* (HarperCollins, 1993), a rags-to-riches fairy tale from Korea.

The Golden Slipper: A Vietnamese Legend
retold by Darrell Lum
illustrated by Makiko Nagano
Troll Associates, 1994
Although set to work in the rice fields by her stepmother, Tam is assured by magical creatures all around her that she is a princess. A flock of birds helps her husk the rice, then clothe her in golden brocade. The golden slipper she loses becomes the key to her royal destiny. For another version of this tale, see *The Brocaded Slipper and Other Vietnamese Tales* by Lynette Dyer Vuong (Addison-Wesley, 1982).

CC = "Core Collection" book (see page 8).

CC *Mufaro's Beautiful Daughters: An African Tale*
retold and illustrated by John Steptoe
Lothrop, Lee & Shepard, 1987
This African tale may remind you of Cinderella with its message about the foolishness of excessive pride and the dignity of quiet humility. The author says that the lush illustrations, which won a Caldecott Honor medal, were inspired by the flora and fauna of Zimbabwe and by the ruins of an ancient city found among them. A wonderful read-aloud.

The Rough-Face Girl
by Rafe Martin
illustrated by David Shannon
G. P. Putnam's Sons, 1992
This Algonquin folktale tells of three sisters, two presumptuous and haughty, the third humble yet rough faced, since her sisters made her tend the fire. Yet it is the rough-face girl who sees the Invisible Being, an embodiment of the forces of nature, and wins her place as his bride. Martin tells the tale with a storyteller's rhythms; Shannon has painted mystical illustrations for this beautiful tale.

Moss Gown
by William Hooks
illustrated by Donald Carrick
Clarion Books, 1987
Elements of the Cinderella story and the underlying plot of Shakespeare's *King Lear* are part of this story, based on tales the author heard as a child growing up in the North Carolina tidewater region. Lovely illustrations.

Yeh-Shen: A Cinderella Story from China
retold by Ai-Ling Louie
illustrated by Ed Young
Putnam & Grosset/Philomel Books, 1982
More than a thousand years older than any known European version of Cinderella, this is the story of Yeh-Shen, who has a mean stepmother, and is left alone at home while the great festival is going on, until . . . well, you have to read it to find out. (Yes, there's a slipper involved!) A good read-aloud, with many dreamlike, soft-toned illustrations.

The Talking Eggs
retold by Robert San Souci
illustrated by Jerry Pinkney
Dial Books, 1989
Although not as close a parallel to Cinderella as many of the stories listed here, this Creole story from the American South features two sisters, one greedy and one kind, whose different behavior causes them to receive different rewards in life. An engaging read aloud and a beautiful book.

CC = "Core Collection" book (see page 8).

LANGUAGE ARTS

Grade 2

Note: The stories and poems recommended here are meant to constitute a *core* of enriching literature. Teachers and parents are strongly encouraged to expose children to many more stories and poems than those listed below, including classic picture books, read-aloud books, perennial favorites by beloved children's writers, popular favorites by contemporary writers, biographies, books about art and music, lots of nonfiction, and of course books that the children themselves choose. For suggestions on more good reading, see Language Arts General Resources: Guides to Good Reading (pages 32–33). **See also** pages 46–49, Reading and Writing: Kindergarten–Grade 2.

CC = a "Core Collection" book (see p. 8).

POEMS
See also Language Arts General Resources: Poetry Collections: General Collections; and, For Younger Children.

The Night Before Christmas
by Clement Clark Moore

    illustrated by Douglas Gorsline
    Random House, 1975

    illustrated by James Marshall
    Scholastic, 1991

Gorsline's illustrations are appropriately Victorian in style. With engraving-like detail of line, he evokes the traditional trappings of a house at Christmastime. James Marshall adds humor to the traditional poem with his cartoon illustrations. The children may sleep, but the family's pets—cats, bulldogs, a chicken, and a mouse—greet Santa and his reindeer with great merriment. Whatever the source you use for this poem, it's great for reading aloud, and also nice to memorize favorite parts.

The Owl and the Pussy-Cat and Other Nonsense Poems
Edward Lear
illustrated by Michael Hague
North-South Books, 1995

Despite its title, the majority of poems in this picture book are Lear's limericks, eighteen in all. With extravagant, fantastical, sometimes bizarre paintings. See also Language Arts General Resources: Poetry Collections, for *A Book of Nonsense* and other collections of Lear's nonsense poetry.

CC *Surprises* (1984)
    More Surprises (1987)
selected by Lee Bennett Hopkins
illustrated by Megan Lloyd
HarperCollins

Two delightful "I Can Read" books. See complete description under Language Arts General Resources: Poetry Collections for Younger Children.

You Read to Me, I'll Read to You
by John Ciardi
illustrated by Edward Gorey
HarperCollins, 1962
See description under Language Arts General
Resources: Poetry Collections for Younger Children.

STORIES

See also Language Arts General Resources:
Stories.

Beauty and the Beast

CC retold and illustrated by Jan Brett
Clarion Books, 1989

retold by Deborah Hautzig
illustrated by Kathy Mitchell
Random House, 1995

retold by Marianna Mayer
illustrated by Mercer Mayer
Macmillan, 1978; Aladdin Books, 1987
Here are two gorgeous read-aloud picture book
versions, as well as an easy-reader. The Marianna Mayer retelling has elaborate illustrations
that turn the story into an intense, romantic
drama. The Jan Brett version emphasizes fun
and, in clever ways, the moral of the story.
Brett's characteristically lovely and detailed
illustrations fill every page; children will want
to return to them often to find the ''hidden''
messages and images. Deborah Hautzig's excellent retelling, a Step into Reading book with
simple language and big print, is a fine choice
for second graders to read independently. It has
many colorful pictures that are more attractive
than what one often finds in easy-reader books.

The Blind Men and the Elephant
retold by Karen Backstein
illustrated by Annie Mitra
Scholastic, 1992
Second graders can read this book on their own,
which has big print, simple language, and colorful pictures. You might also like *Seven Blind
Mice* by Ed Young (Philomel Books, 1992),
which, with minimal text and striking cut-paper
illustrations, retells the story of ''The Blind Men
and the Elephant'' but with seven blind mice
who scurry up and down different parts of the
huge beast, mistaking every one.

A Christmas Carol
by Charles Dickens
abridged by Vivian French
illustrated by Patrick Benson
Candlewick Press, 1992
This book streamlines Dickens's story into a
large-type story of thirty pages, including many
amusing illustrations. The abridgment maintains
a good sense of Dickens's language. The story is
divided into sections, so this could be read
aloud over a few days.

Charlotte's Web
by E. B. White
illustrated by Garth Williams
HarperCollins, 1952
A modern classic, a great read-aloud, and only
one of the books by E. B. White that children
love to have read to them and later reread on
their own, including *Stuart Little* and *The Trumpet of the Swan*.

The Crane Wife
retold by Sumiko Yagawa and translated by
Katherine Paterson
illustrated by Suekichi Akaba
William Morrow, 1981; Mulberry Books, 1987
This beautiful book retells the Japanese story in
elegant language and soft illustrations that look
as if they are classic ink-brush paintings on rice
paper. (See World History Grade 2: Japan.)

CC = ''Core Collection'' book (see page 8).

The Emperor's New Clothes
by Hans Christian Andersen

> retold and illustrated by Virginia Lee
>   Burton
> Houghton Mifflin, 1949, 1979

> adapted by Janet Stevens
> Holiday House, 1985

> retold by Ruth Belov Gross
> illustrated by Jack Kent
> Scholastic, 1977

> in *The Ugly Duckling and Other Fairy Tales*
> Dover, 1992

Virginia Lee Burton's edition, with quaint illustrations, makes a good read-aloud. Janet Stevens retells the story with animal characters: the emperor is a well-dressed pig. Ruth Belov Gross's small, slender paperback, with cartoonlike illustrations, while not billed as an easy-reader book, is written in clear, direct sentences with big print, and so a good choice for second graders to read, with a little help on the occasional big words. The inexpensive little volume from Dover presents a close translation of Hans Christian Andersen's story, with more detail and more demanding language than the picture-book versions, and illustrated with only one drawing. The volume contains seven other Andersen stories. By the way, after they get to know "The Emperor's New Clothes," children may enjoy *The Principal's New Clothes* by Stephanie Calmenson, illustrated by Denise Brunkus (Scholastic, 1989), a modern version in which a vain principal is snookered into parading around in his underwear by two fast-talking fashion experts.

The Fisherman and His Wife
> translated by Randall Jarrell
> illustrated by Margot Zemach
> Farrar, Straus & Giroux, 1987

The Magic Fish
> by Freya Littledale
> illustrated by Winslow Pinney Pels
> Scholastic, 1985

Jarrell's translation from the German tells the story in elegant language, with illustrations that overflow the page with colors and characters. A fine read-aloud. Freya Littledale's little picture book, *The Magic Fish,* tells the story of "The Fisherman and His Wife" in simple language, readable by many second graders, with amusing illustrations that make the wife particularly haughty and the fish particularly huge.

"How the Camel Got His Hump"
in *The Elephant's Child and Other Just So Stories*
by Rudyard Kipling
Dover, 1993

Listen now, O best beloved! Kipling's "Just So" stories, with their broad humor and wonderful rhythms and sounds, are meant to be read aloud. Unfortunately, many of the stories reflect the writer's times and culture, and show a degree of stereotyping that is generally no longer tolerated today. But that is not the case with "How the Camel Got His Hump." Read it aloud with gusto and enjoy yourselves. This book is part of Dover's inexpensive Children's Thrift Classics series, described under Language Arts General Resources: Stories. A picture book collection, *Just So Stories,* beautifully illustrated by Michael Foreman (Viking/Puffin, 1987), is available, as is an illustrated edition of "How the Camel Got His Hump" in the Rabbit Ears Storybook Classics series (1989), which you can buy with a cassette tape of Jack Nicholson reading the story.

CC *Iktomi and the Berries* **(1989)**
   Iktomi and the Boulder **(1988)**
   Iktomi and the Buffalo Skull **(1991)**
   Iktomi and the Ducks **(1990)**
retold and illustrated by Paul Goble
Orchard Books

Goble, renowned for picture books that tell American Indian tales with lyrical language and distinctive illustrations, has written four books about the trickster figure, Iktomi. The Lakota people, writes Goble, call these stories "*ohunkaka*: amusing stories which are not meant to be believed, but which often have moral lessons wrapped up inside them." Goble's Iktomi books play tricks on the reader, too, with unexpected twists of language and image that second graders will enjoy discovering. A delight in every way, not to be missed. (See American History Grade 2: Native Americans: Plains Indians.)

Peter Pan
by J. M. Barrie

> illustrated by Michael Hague
> Henry Holt, 1978

> adapted by Cathy East Dubowski
> illustrated by Jean Zallinger
> Random House, 1991

The original book by J. M. Barrie is wonderful and rich, but also dense and wandering to the modern ear. Many editions are available in libraries; the one we list here has wild, magical paintings by Michael Hague sprinkled throughout the volume. For an edition appropriate for reading aloud or for strong second-grade readers to read independently, try Cathy East Dubowski's "Bullseye Classic" adapted for early readers. Occasional pencil sketches illustrate this hundred-page chapter-book.

Talk, Talk: An Ashanti Legend
by Deborah M. Newton Chocolate
illustrated by Dave Albers
Troll Associates, 1993
Here is a humorous legend about a time when everything decides to talk, much to the surprise of the human characters. The woodblock-type illustrations strengthen the book with many visual references to West African crafts and culture. The book's last page explains something of this legend's homeland and significance in Ashanti culture. For a lively retelling of this tale good for reading aloud (small print, limited illustrations), see *The Cow-Tail Switch*, a collection of West African stories retold by Harold Courlander and George Herzog (Henry Holt, 1947, 1986). You might also try *Too Much Talk* by Angela Shelf Medearis, illustrated by Stefano Vitale (Candlewick Press, 1995), an exuberantly illustrated book that tells the legend of "too much talk" in simple language that many children

may be able to read independently or with just a bit of help.

"The Tiger, the Brahman, and the Jackal"
in *Favorite Fairy Tales Told in India*
retold by Virginia Haviland
illustrated by Vera Rosenberry
William Morrow/Beech Tree Books, 1973, 1994
The very funny Indian folktale of the hapless Brahman, the duplicitous tiger, and the clever jackal is retold with just the right wit and pace by Virginia Haviland in this book, which is one of sixteen paperback volumes, each devoted to a different country, all titled *Favorite Fairy Tales Told in . . .*

Tiger Soup: An Anansi Story from Jamaica
retold and illustrated by Frances Temple
Orchard Books, 1994
Will hungry little Anansi get to drink Tiger's soup? Come along and see; you might also find out why monkeys live in trees and why tigers eat meat. The language occasionally hints at spoken dialect (example: "Sure is hot today, not so, Brother Tiger?"). Fun, brightly colored illustrations on every page. The hardback edition of this book has a play version of the story on the inside of the book jacket. (For more Anansi stories, see Language Arts Grade 1: Stories.)

The Tongue-Cut Sparrow
retold by Momoko Ishii
translated by Katherine Paterson
E. P. Dutton, 1987
Paterson's knowledge of the culture and language of Japan make this book a delightful version of the classic tale. Intermingled with the translation are Japanese words, whose meaning can be detected from their sounds and context. (See World History Grade 2: Japan.)

Tye May and the Magic Brush
> retold and illustrated by Molly Garrett Bang
> Mulberry Books, 1981
Liang and the Magic Paintbrush
> retold and illustrated by Demi
> Henry Holt, 1980
Here are two good versions of a favorite Chi-

nese folktale. In Molly Bang's version, the main character, Tye May, is a girl. This is an enchanting easy-reader version of the traditional Chinese story, divided into six chapters that could be read independently by most second graders. With attractive drawings printed in black and red. In Demi's version, the main character, Liang, is a boy. This elegant version of the story, better suited for reading aloud, demonstrates economy of word and line, and has illustrations that look very much like ancient Chinese miniatures. (See World History Grade 2: Ancient China.)

MYTHOLOGY OF ANCIENT GREECE

See also World History Grade 2: Ancient Greece.

CC *D'Aulaire's Book of Greek Myths*
written and illustrated by Ingri and Edgar
   Parin d'Aulaire
Dell Yearling, 1962
This is a rich, welcoming book, with large pages, graceful illustrations, and interesting text (best for reading aloud at this grade). Starting with the creation and Gaea (Mother Earth), moving through the major and minor gods and the mortal descendants of Zeus, the book identifies each character by relation to others in the genealogy and by telling familiar stories associated with him or her. The book includes the myths of Midas, Heracles, and Oedipus, as well as all the gods and goddesses. It also offers an excellent index and several helpful illustrated charts of genealogy and relationships. Either this or *The Macmillan Book of Greek Myths* (see below) would make a great text to turn to for Greek myths in second grade.

Classic Myths to Read Aloud
compiled and edited by William F. Russell
Crown Publishers, 1989
An excellent and generous collection of Greek and Roman myths, retold in a language that has

a suitably old-fashioned feel. The editor provides a brief helpful introduction to each myth, a pronunciation key, and a chart that cross-references the Greek and Roman gods. Those who are seeking a source for the Greek myths recommended for second grade in the *Core Knowledge Sequence* will find many included in this book: "Icarus and Daedalus"; "The Origin of the Seasons (Demeter and Persephone)"; "Pegasus the Winged Horse"; "The Spinning Contest (Arachne)"; "The Story of Theseus"; "The Riddle of the Sphinx (Oedipus)"—though this version, meant for older children, goes on to tell of Oedipus's terrible fate, which is a story we think best left for a later grade; and "The Wooden Horse." Good read-aloud versions of other *Core Knowledge Sequence* titles may be found in Russell's companion books (described under Language Arts General Resources: Stories): "Ulysses and the Cyclops" in *Classics to Read Aloud;* and "Pandora's Box" in *More Classics to Read Aloud.*

Cyclops
retold and illustrated by Leonard Everett Fisher
Holiday House, 1991
This big picture book offers a good read-aloud retelling of the episode from Homer's *Odyssey* in which Odysseus encounters the one-eyed, man-eating giant, and must use his wits to find a way to get himself and his crew out of the giant's clutches before they are all eaten. The author's paintings vividly illustrate the scenes, including the one bound to draw cries of "Oooooo!" and "Ugh!" from children, in which Odysseus puts out Cyclops's eye.

Favorite Greek Myths
retold by Mary Pope Osborne
illustrated by Troy Howell
Scholastic, 1989
Suitable for reading aloud, this book offers graceful, respectful retellings of a dozen myths, including King Midas; Arachne; Persephone; and Atalanta. The author generally uses the Roman names rather than the Greek (for example, Ceres, Proserpine, and Pluto rather than Deme-

ter, Persephone, and Hades), each illustrated with a full-page color painting and occasional black-and-white line drawings. The tone and presentation of this book are, in a way, the opposite of Marcia Williams's *Greek Myths* (see below). Try both if you can.

The Gods and Goddesses of Olympus
written and illustrated by Aliki
HarperCollins, 1994

This is an interesting read-aloud introduction to the Greek gods and goddesses. Aliki tells the Greek myth of creation, then goes on to introduce Zeus, Hera, Hephaestus, Aphrodite, Eros, Ares, Poseidon, Athena, Hermes, Artemis, Apollo, Hades, Demeter (and Persephone), Dionysus, and Hestia. The illustrations are big, bold, and vividly colored, a departure from Aliki's usually more subtle and delicate art.

CC *Greek Myths*
as told by Jim Weiss
Greathall Productions

On this cassette tape (also available on compact disc), storyteller Jim Weiss tells favorite Greek myths, including King Midas, Hercules, Perseus and Medusa, and Arachne. You'll also want to hear another collection of myths-on-tape by Jim Weiss, called *She and He: Adventures in Mythology,* which includes the story of Atalanta and the Golden Apples (as well as myths recommended for third grade in the *Core Knowledge Sequence*). These are just two of many fine story tapes available from Greathall Productions: (800) 477-6234.

CC *Greek Myths for Young Children*
by Marcia Williams
Candlewick Press, 1991

Here's a book that many children like to pore over and return to again and again. At first glance the book appears to be filled with comic strips—and that's just the point. Williams has turned the myths into clever, colorful, and readable cartoons. Myths retold here include Pandora's Box, Prometheus, Daedalus, Arachne,

and Heracles. Inside the story frames, conversation balloons let beginning readers chime into the telling of the stories when read aloud. The illustrations are cute, lively, and engaging. A delightful book, but take note: if you like your mythology straight up and serious, this is *not* the book for you.

CC *The Macmillan Book of Greek Gods and Heroes*
by Alice Low
illustrated by Arvis Stewart
Macmillan, 1985

Like the d'Aulaires' big *Book of Greek Myths* (see above), this single volume conveniently collects many of the great stories and retells them in prose suitable for reading aloud, accompanied by illustrations, many in color, on almost every page. Included are the stories of Prometheus, Pandora, Persephone, Arachne, Atalanta, the labors of Heracles, Theseus and the Minotaur, Daedalus, the Trojan Horse, and Odysseus and the Cyclops.

Persephone
retold and illustrated by Warwick Hutton
Macmillan/Margaret K. McElderry Books, 1994

Persephone and the Pomegranate: A Myth from Greece
retold and illustrated by Kris Waldherr
Dial Books for Young Readers, 1993

Here are two beautifully illustrated, read-aloud picture books that tell the myth of why we have seasons. Lovely watercolors accompany Warwick Hutton's eloquent retelling of the myth. Kris Waldherr offers a graceful and lyrical vision in her illustrations.

Theseus and the Minotaur
retold and illustrated by Warwick Hutton
Macmillan/Margaret K. McElderry Books, 1989

With soft watercolor illustrations, this picture book tells the story of Theseus with clearly written text, appropriate for reading aloud. Also try, from the same author, an excellent read-aloud picture-book version of *The Trojan Horse* (Macmillan/Margaret K. McElderry Books, 1992).

The Trojan Horse: How the Greeks Won the War
by Emily Little
illustrated by Michael Eagle
Random House, 1988
The story of the Trojan Horse and its place in the war between Greece and Troy is told in simple language and big print in this "Step into Reading" book for grades 2 to 4. The text will probably prove very challenging for all but strong second-grade readers, so you may want to read aloud part and ask the children to read part. The color illustrations help convey the times. The final chapter brings in Homer and Schliemann, explaining how the story and the historic understanding of Troy have come to us.

CC *Wings*
by Jane Yolen
illustrated by Dennis Nolan
Harcourt Brace Jovanovich, 1991
Jane Yolen's dramatic, eloquent retelling of the myth of Icarus and Dedalus is brought to life in Dennis Nolan's extraordinary paintings, in which the Greek gods are depicted as ever-watching, and very human, faces in the clouds. A great read-aloud.

AMERICAN TALL TALES

American Tall Tales
by Mary Pope Osborne
illustrated by Michael McCurdy
Alfred A. Knopf, 1991
This beautiful book retells many traditional legends, including the stories of Paul Bunyan, Johnny Appleseed, John Henry, and Pecos Bill. The lyrical language is good for reading aloud, and "Notes on the Story" precede every chapter, providing historical background

on each tale. The artist's strong illustrations fall on almost every spread: bold woodblock renderings, tinted with colored pencil, capturing the energy of these tales.

Cut from the Same Cloth: American Women of Myth, Legend, and Tall Tale
by Robert D. San Souci
illustrated by Brian Pinkney
Philomel Books, 1993
Tall tales aren't just about men, as this collection proves, with tales about strong women from Native American, African-American, Mexican-American, Eskimo, Hawaiian, and Anglo-American traditions. The stories are fast paced and fun to read out loud. The ink-scratch illustrations are wonderful but few and far between. The author begins each of the fifteen stories with a note on sources, and includes lengthy source notes and bibliography.

CC *John Henry*
by Julius Lester
illustrated by Jerry Pinkney
Dial Books/Penguin, 1994
This is a powerful, uplifting picture-book version of the John Henry legend, based upon extensive research into the folk-song tradition that tells the tale. In the book's introduction, Julius Lester says that in the legend he finds "the courage to hammer until our hearts break and to leave our mourners smiling in their tears." The words almost speak themselves; just start reading aloud and you'll catch the spirit. Superb illustrations; the book received a Caldecott Honor medal.

John Henry: An American Legend
retold and illustrated by Ezra Jack Keats
Alfred A. Knopf/Dragonfly, 1965
Called by the *Washington Post* Keats's "finest work," this retelling of the John Henry story sings with rhythmic prose and glows with Keats's distinctive collagelike art. A fine read-aloud.

John Henry and His Mighty Hammer
    illustrated by Roseanne Litzinger
Johnny Appleseed Goes a'Planting
    illustrated by Pat Hoggan
Paul Bunyan and His Blue Ox
    illustrated by Jean Pidgeon
Pecos Bill: The Roughest, Toughest, Best
    illustrated by Ben Mahan
    all retold by Patsy Jensen
    Troll Associates, 1994
Teachers should welcome these four little books, part of Troll's "First-Start Tall Tale" series, written in big print and easy words suitable for independent reading by second graders. All are colorfully illustrated, and all humorously relate the larger-than-life stories. The John Henry story has an interesting new character, Polly Ann, John Henry's wife, who could "drive steel almost as fast as John Henry." The Pecos Bill story also introduces Slue-foot Sue. You may also enjoy a video of *Pecos Bill* from Rabbit Ears productions, energetically narrated (that's an understatement) by Robin Williams.

Johnny Appleseed: A Tall Tale
    retold and illustrated by Steven Kellogg
    William Morrow, 1988
The Story of Johnny Appleseed
    written and illustrated by Aliki
    Simon & Schuster, 1971
Kellogg's picture book begins in history and ends in fable and imagination, weaving the story of Johnny Appleseed into a tableau of tall tales of bravery and accomplishment in the wilderness. Kellogg tells the stories vigorously, with his energetic, entertaining illustrations. Good for reading aloud, and written in a way that some second graders can read with a little help. In contrast to Kellogg's high-energy tall tale, Aliki tells a gentle story, with happy and colorful drawings, and emphasizes Johnny Appleseed as a man of peace. Her version is suitable for independent reading by many second graders.

Paul Bunyan
retold and illustrated by Steven Kellogg
William Morrow, 1984
Kellogg makes Paul Bunyan into a friendly-looking giant whose adventures we follow through the lively prose and funny, frenetic drawings that convey the tall-tale spirit of exaggeration. A good read-aloud that some second graders may be able to read with a little help.

CC = "Core Collection" book (see page 8).

LANGUAGE ARTS

Grade 3

> *Note:* The stories and poems recommended here are meant to constitute a *core* of enriching literature. Teachers and parents are strongly encouraged to expose children to many more stories and poems than those listed below, including classic picture books, read-aloud books, perennial favorites by beloved children's writers, popular favorites by contemporary writers, biographies, books about art and music, lots of nonfiction, and of course books that the children themselves choose. Regular reading aloud to children should continue long after they can read independently. For suggestions on more good reading, see Language Arts General Resources: Guides to Good Reading (pages 32–33).

CC = a "**Core Collection**" book (see p. 8).

POEMS

See also Language Arts General Resources: Poetry Collections: General Collections; and For Younger Children.

CC *Favorite Poems Old and New*
selected by Helen Ferris
illustrated by Leonard Weisgard
Doubleday, 1957
See description under Language Arts General Resources: Poetry Collections.

Make a Joyful Sound: Poems for Children by African-American Poets
edited by Deborah Slier
illustrated by Cornelius Van Wright and Ying-Hwa Hu
Checkerboard Press, 1991
See description under Language Arts General Resources: Poetry Collections.

CC *The Random House Book of Poetry for Children*
selected by Jack Prelutsky
illustrated by Arnold Lobel
Random House, 1983
See description under Language Arts General Resources: Poetry Collections.

Where the Sidewalk Ends **(1974)**
A Light in the Attic **(1981)**
by Shel Silverstein
HarperCollins
See description under Language Arts General Resources: Poetry Collections for Older Children.

You Read to Me, I'll Read to You
by John Ciardi
illustrated by Edward Gorey
HarperCollins, 1962
See description under Language Arts General

Resources: Poetry Collections for Younger Children.

STORIES

See also Language Arts General Resources: Stories.

Aladdin and the Magic Lamp
    retold by Deborah Hautzig
    illustrated by Kathy Mitchell
    Random House, 1993
Aladdin and the Wonderful Lamp
    retold by Carol Carrick
    illustrated by Donald Carrick
    Scholastic, 1993
The Tale of Aladdin and the Wonderful Lamp: A Story from the Arabian Nights
    retold by Eric Kimmel
    illustrated by Ju-Hong Chen
    Holiday House, 1992
Will children want to *read* Aladdin after Disney and Robin Williams? Well, we like the movie, and we hope children will like one of these books as well. Deborah Hautzig offers an illustrated, easy-to-read version of the well-known tale, part of the "Step into Reading" series, that should be easy for third graders. Carol and Donald Carrick offer a straightforward retelling, vividly illustrated, that suffers only at the climax—the death of the evil magician—which comes across as an anticlimax. Eric Kimmel gives a spirited retelling with colorful illustrations and text set in the shape of Islamic arches.

CC *Ali Baba and the Forty Thieves*
retold by Walter McVitty
illustrated by Margaret Early
Harry N. Abrams, 1988
This gorgeous picture-book tells the story of Ali Baba in word and especially in picture, with gilt-edged full-page illustrations in the style of ancient Persian miniatures. This version of the story emphasizes the role of the servant Morgiana in saving Ali Baba's life.

CC *Alice in Wonderland*
by Lewis Carroll
illustrated by John Tenniel
Scholastic/Apple Classic, 1988
This complete and original edition of Lewis Carroll's book also has the traditional illustrations by John Tenniel. A teaching guide to this edition is available from Scholastic. Strong readers can read this independently, and the book is a joy to read aloud. An elegant hardbound keepsake edition is available as part of the Children's Classics series in the Everyman Library (Alfred A. Knopf, 1992).

The Arabian Nights
    retold by Neil Philip
    illustrated by Sheila Moxley
    Orchard Books, 1994
The Arabian Nights
    by Brian Alderson
    illustrated by Michael Foreman
    William Morrow/Books of Wonder, 1992
The Arabian Nights Entertainments
    edited by Andrew Lang
    Dover, 1969
There are many good read-aloud collections of the tales that, so goes the legend, Scheherazade told to entertain her master, and to save her life! Neil Philip retells most of the well-known and some of the lesser-known tales from *The Arabian Nights* in strong, spare prose. And the illustrations are as sumptuous as they should be—full of purple elephants, royal-blue backdrops, and golden skies. Brian Alderson's opulent edition of the full collection of stories is decorated with 120 illustrations, some moody full-color paintings, some gilt-touched ornamental borders. A reviewer of the London *Times* called this book "*the* version" of the Arabian tales. Andrew Lang's retellings date from 1898. They are elegant, detailed, and to modern ears may sound a bit old fashioned. See also in this section the individual listings for picture books of *Aladdin* and *Ali Baba*.

CC = "Core Collection" book (see page 8).

"Gone Is Gone"
in *Clever Gretchen and Other Forgotten Folktales*
retold by Alison Lurie
illustrated by Margot Tomes
HarperCollins, 1980
The hilarious Norse folktale of the husband who minds the house while the wife is away—and you can just imagine what happens!—is retold in Alison Lurie's collection. The best version we know is out of print: *Gone Is Gone* by Wanda Gag (Coward-McCann, 1935). Some enterprising publisher needs to reissue it; until then, check your library. A version of this tale, titled "The Man Who Was to Mind the House," is reprinted in *Stories for Seven-Year-Olds*, edited by Sara and Stephen Corrin (Faber and Faber, 1964). A very similar tale told in Wales, titled "The Cow on the Roof," may be found in *Best Loved Folktales of the World*, edited by Joanna Cole (Doubleday/Anchor, 1982).

Iroquois Stories: Heroes and Heroines, Monsters and Magic
retold by Joseph Bruchac
illustrated by Daniel Burgevin
The Crossing Press, 1985
Bruchac retells twenty-nine stories from the Iroquois. An excellent resource, this book includes the story recommended in Language Arts Grade 3 in the *Core Knowledge Sequence*, "The Hunting of the Great Bear." (See also American History Grade 3: Eastern "Woodland" Indians.)

The Little Match Girl
by Hans Christian Andersen

  illustrated by Rachel Isadora
  G. P. Putnam's Sons, 1987

  retold by Christine San José
  illustrated by Anastassija Archipowa
  Boyds Mills Press, 1994
Here are two beautifully illustrated versions of Andersen's sad and quietly moving story. Both place the tale in a Victorian winter setting. An unillustrated version of the tale may be found in the inexpensive collection, *The Ugly Duckling*

and Other Fairy Tales (Dover, 1992; see address, page 39).

The People Could Fly: American Black Folktales
by Virginia Hamilton
illustrated by Leo and Diane Dillon
Alfred A. Knopf/Borzoi, 1985
Written with a careful ear for dialect, this book collects many African-American folk stories, including the one that gives the book its title. See Language Arts General Resources for a full description.

"Three Words of Wisdom"
in *Cuentos: Tales from the Hispanic Southwest*
  retold by José Maestas and Juan Rael
  Museum of New Mexico Press, 1980
in *Mexican Folktales from the Borderland*
  retold by Riley Aiken
  Southern Methodist University Press, 1980
The humorous Mexican story "Three Words of Wisdom" is perhaps most conveniently available in the Core Knowledge book *What Your Third Grader Needs to Know* (Doubleday, 1992). If you are interested in other versions, you can try the volumes listed above, both of which are academic, adult resources. To share with your children a similar story as told in a different land (Greece), try *Three Gold Pieces*, retold and illustrated by Aliki (Pantheon, 1967; HarperTrophy, 1994).

William Tell
  retold and illustrated by Margaret Early
  Harry N. Abrams, 1991
The Apple and the Arrow: The Legend of William Tell
  retold and illustrated by Mary and Conrad Buff
  Scholastic, 1951
For her elegant picture-book version of the adventures of Switzerland's hero, Margaret Early created illustrations that echo the patterns, colors, and style of medieval art. *The Apple and the Arrow*, a Newbery Honor Book, tells the William

Tell story from the perspective of his young son, in the form of a short (eighty-page) novel. Strong third-grade readers could read this book independently, and it's a good read-aloud as well.

The Wind in the Willows
by Kenneth Grahame
illustrated by Ernest H. Shepard
Charles Scribner's Sons, 1908, 1933
There are many editions of *The Wind in the Willows;* any (unabridged) will do fine. The Scribner's edition has a special charm because of the inimitable ink drawings of the characters. Retellings and videos of these stories of Rat, Mole, Badger, and the irrepressible Mr. Toad are available, but try sharing at least some of the stories in the original versions, with their lyrical language and fine wit. While the language is wonderful, it is sometimes difficult, so these stories may be enjoyed most when read aloud. Try reading aloud the first two chapters, "The River Bank" and "The Open Road," and then see if your children ask for more. We think they will! If you would like a retelling for third graders to read independently, try the "Great Illustrated Classics" edition, adapted by Malvina G. Vogel (Baronet Books/Playmore Publishers, 1994), sold in some discount stores and chain bookstores, or call the publisher at (212) 924-7447.

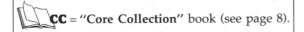 **CC** = "Core Collection" book (see page 8).

MYTHOLOGY

More Myths of Ancient Greece and Rome
See also World History Grade 3: Ancient Rome.
See also Language Arts Grade 2: Mythology of Ancient Greece. The books recommended there are also useful in this grade.

Androcles and the Lion
written and illustrated by Janet Stevens
Holiday House, 1989
This lively picture-book retelling of the story of the slave and the lion (who returns kindness with kindness) should be enjoyable and easy reading for third graders.

CC *The Arrow and the Lamp: The Story of Psyche*
by Margaret Hodges
illustrated by Donna Diamond
Little, Brown, 1989
This breathtakingly lovely picture book offers a wonderful read-aloud retelling of the Cupid and Psyche myth.

The Book of Virtues
edited by William J. Bennett
Simon & Schuster, 1993
This compendious anthology includes *many* good stories, including some Roman legends recommended in the *Core Knowledge Sequence* for third grade. Bennett was smart to turn to James Baldwin for good old versions of "Androcles and the Lion," "The Sword of Damocles," and "Horatius at the Bridge." Also included in this book is the story of "Damon and Pythias."

CC *Classic Myths to Read Aloud*
compiled and edited by William F. Russell
Crown Publishers, 1989
For a complete description of this helpful resource, see Language Arts Grade 2: Mythology of Ancient Greece. Those who are seeking a source for the myths recommended for third grade in the *Core Knowledge Sequence* will find many in this book: "Perseus and the Gorgon's Head," "Cupid and Psyche," "The Sword of Damocles," "Damon and Pythias," and a very good three-part version of "Jason and the Golden Fleece." (Another selection recommended for third grade, "Androcles and the Lion," is retold in Russell's companion book, *Classics to Read Aloud to Your Children.* See Language Arts General Resources: Stories.)

Jason and the Golden Fleece
written and illustrated by Leonard Everett
    Fisher
Holiday House, 1990
This is a vividly illustrated account of Jason and
the Argonauts in their search for the golden
fleece. The retelling proceeds at a brisk clip and
sometimes reads more like a summary than a
story.

The Macmillan Book of Greek Gods and Heroes
by Alice Low
illustrated by Arvis Stewart
Macmillan, 1985
This single volume conveniently collects many
of the great stories and retells them in prose
suitable for reading aloud or for independent
reading by strong third-grade readers. Included
are stories of Jason and the Golden Fleece, and
of Perseus and Medusa. With illustrations, many
in color, on almost every page.

CC *Perseus*
retold and illustrated by Warwick Hutton
Macmillan, 1993
This clear and direct retelling of the myth of
Perseus and Medusa is distinguished by War-
wick Hutton's watercolor illustrations.

A Wonder-Book for Girls and Boys
by Nathaniel Hawthorne
illustrated by Arthur Rackham
Alfred A. Knopf, 1994
Hawthorne's *Wonder-Book* offers an elegant read-
aloud version of the myth of Perseus and Medusa, which he entitled "The Gorgon's Head."
Two of Rackham's illustrations accompany this
story, but none of Medusa—too bad. For a complete description of this book, see Language
Arts General Resources: Stories.

Norse Mythology
See also World History Grade 3, The Vikings.

CC *D'Aulaire's Norse Gods and Giants*
retold and illustrated by Ingri and Edgar Parin
    d'Aulaire
Doubleday, 1967
This big, full, engaging book is a companion to
the d'Aulaires's excellent compendium of stories
about the Greek gods and goddesses. It is organized by character (Thor, Loki, Balder, Odin,
Freya, etc.), relates the familiar and sometimes
violent myths of Norse gods and giants, and offers helpful charts of relationships and a good
index. Great for reading aloud, readable by
strong third-grade readers. With many enjoyable
illustrations.

Favorite Norse Myths
retold by Mary Pope Osborne
illustrated by Troy Howell
Scholastic, 1996
From the myth of creation to the twilight of the
gods, this book, good for reading aloud, retells
fourteen tales from Norse mythology. Perhaps
in part because of the writer's quiet, measured
style, these myths seem more "civilized," less
fierce and gory than those told in *D'Aulaire's
Norse Gods and Giants* (see above). Full-page or
two-page paintings accompany each myth.
Compare this to the D'Aulaires' and see which
you prefer.

LANGUAGE ARTS

Grade 4

Note: The stories and poems recommended here are meant to constitute a *core* of enriching literature. Teachers and parents are strongly encouraged to expose children to many more stories and poems than those listed below, including perennial favorites by beloved children's writers, popular favorites by contemporary writers, biographies, books about art and music, lots of nonfiction, and of course books that the children themselves choose. Regular reading aloud to children should continue long after they can read independently. For suggestions on more good reading, see Language Arts General Resources: Guides to Good Reading (pages 32–33).

CC = a **"Core Collection"** book (see p. 8).

POEMS
See also Language Arts General Resources: Poetry Collections (General Collections, and Collections for Older Children).

CC *Favorite Poems Old and New*
selected by Helen Ferris
illustrated by Leonard Weisgard
Doubleday, 1957
See description under Language Arts General Resources: Poetry Collections.

Make a Joyful Sound: Poems for Children by African-American Poets
edited by Deborah Slier
illustrated by Cornelius Van Wright and Ying-Hwa Hu
Checkerboard Press, 1991
See description under Language Arts General Resources: Poetry Collections.

CC *Paul Revere's Ride*
by Henry Wadsworth Longfellow
illustrated by Ted Rand
E. P. Dutton, 1990
"Listen, my children, and you shall hear/Of the midnight ride of Paul Revere." This atmospheric picture-book adds nighttime visions of Paul Revere's ride to the full text of the Longfellow poem. Full-page watercolors help children see costume, architecture, and landscape of the time. Endpapers offer a map of the ride, and a final note tells the historical background for the poem. (See also American History Grade 4: American Revolution.)

CC *The Random House Book of Poetry for Children*
selected by Jack Prelutsky
illustrated by Arnold Lobel
Random House, 1983
See description under Language Arts General Resources: Poetry Collections.

Where the Sidewalk Ends (1974)
A Light in the Attic (1981)
by Shel Silverstein
HarperCollins
See description under Language Arts General Resources: Poetry Collections for Older Children.

STORIES

See also Language Arts General Resources: Stories.

The Fire on the Mountain and Other Ethiopian Stories
retold by Harold Courlander and Wolf Leslau
Henry Holt, 1950; 1995
This collection, one of many compiled by the prolific Harold Courlander, contains the story recommended for fourth grade in the *Core Knowledge Sequence*, "The Fire on the Mountain." This same story is also reprinted in the collection, *Best-Loved Folktales of the World*, edited by Joanna Cole (Doubleday/Anchor, 1982).

Gulliver's Travels
by Jonathan Swift

    adapted by James Riordan
    illustrated by Victor G. Ambrus
    Oxford University Press, 1992

    adapted by Malvina Vogel
    illustrated by Pablo Marcus
    Playmore, Inc./Baronet Books, 1995
Gulliver's Stories
    retold by Edward Dolch, Marguerite Dolch,
      and Beulah Jackson
    Scholastic/Little Apple Classics, 1960
Jonathan Swift's tale of little Lilliputians and giant Brobdingnagians has long been told to children in one form or another. James Riordan has condensed Swift's novel, but he maintains some of the rhythm and diction representative of the eighteenth-century, so it gives young readers a good feel for the original. Though condensed,

this version is still challenging for fourth-grade readers, and perhaps best as a read-aloud or a "shared reading"—parts read aloud, and parts independently. Those seeking a simpler retelling for the fourth-grade classroom should examine two different versions, one by Vogel, the other by Dolch. Vogel's retelling is part of the "Great Illustrated Classics" series, sold in some discount stores and chain bookstores, or available from the publisher by calling (212) 924-7447; the black-and-white drawings are nothing to cheer about, but the text is engagingly told, though it takes liberties with the original story. Dolch's competent but less lively retelling was written for ease of reading, and includes episodes from Gulliver's voyages to Lilliput and Brobdingnag. (For a story-on-tape version, see also below, *Rip Van Winkle/Gulliver's Travels*.)

CC *The Legend of Sleepy Hollow*
retold by Robert D. San Souci
illustrated by Daniel San Souci
Dell Picture Yearling Books, 1986
Highly condensed but well told, this version of the tale of Ichabod Crane and the Headless Horseman is about the most "user-friendly" book around for fourth-grade readers. Good pictures, too, on almost every page. If you'd like to read aloud some or all of Washington Irving's substantially longer original text, there are many editions available, including one illustrated by Arthur Rackham (Random House/Derrydale, 1994).

Pollyanna
by Eleanor H. Porter
Grosset, 1912; Scholastic/Apple Classics, 1987
This inexpensive paperback edition offers the full, unabridged original novel, without illustrations or commentary. As William Kilpatrick writes in his book *Why Johnny Can't Tell Right from Wrong*, "Forget the saccharine reputation; . . . the *real* Pollyanna, found only in the book, is well worth knowing." Also available as a paperback published by Dell Yearling Books.

Rip Van Winkle
  adapted by Freya Littledale
  illustrated by Michael Dooling
  Scholastic, 1991

CC *Washington Irving's Rip Van Winkle*
  adapted and illustrated by Thomas Locker
Dial Books, 1988
Littledale's illustrated version is simplified for easy reading at about a third-grade level. It tells the story well enough, but misses the flavor of Washington Irving's language. Thomas Locker also condenses and adapts Irving's story, but his telling is closer to the original and is accompanied by luminous paintings. You can find the original Irving text (unillustrated) in William Russell's *Classics to Read Aloud* (described under Language Arts General Resources: Stories). Also, Dover Books (see address, page 39) offers a *Rip Van Winkle Coloring Book*, with the complete text by Washington Irving and ready-to-color line drawings based on illustrations by Arthur Rackham.

Rip Van Winkle/Gulliver's Travels
as told by Jim Weiss
Greathall Productions
On this cassette tape, storyteller Jim Weiss tells lively, if highly condensed, versions of two classics. Weiss does not read from the originals, nor does he attempt to capture their language. Nevertheless, his "storyteller's versions" (as he calls them) are, in their own right, fun listening. Weiss also adds a song, "Rip's Rap," with an antidrug message. It's no masterpiece, but it doesn't detract from the story, and you can always push "Stop." This is one of many fine story tapes available from Greathall Productions: (800) 477-6234.

Robin Hood/The Three Musketeers
as told by Jim Weiss
Greathall Productions
On this cassette tape, storyteller Jim Weiss tells his "storyteller's versions," as he calls them, of these classic tales. Both are exciting, humorous, and told in a way that serves the stories rather than drawing attention to the teller. One of many fine story tapes available from Greathall Productions: (800) 477-6234.

CC *Robin Hood of Sherwood Forest*
by Ann McGovern
illustrated by Tracy Sugarman
Scholastic/Apple Classics, 1968
This inexpensive paperback tells the major tales about Robin Hood, including his confrontation with Little John, his meeting with Friar Tuck, his continuing battles with the Sheriff of Nottingham, and his winning of Maid Marian. The stories have been recast in language that fourth graders can read independently, but still retain some of the old-fashioned English that gives the appropriate feeling of a far-off time.

Robinson Crusoe
retold by Edward W. Dolch, Marguerite P.
  Dolch, and Beulah F. Jackson
illustrated after designs by J. J. Grandville
Scholastic/Little Apple Classics, 1990
This volume greatly simplifies the story and language of Defoe's original, making it a 120-page, large-print novel, which should not prove too challenging for a fourth-grade reader. The occasional illustrations are reminiscent of Victorian magazine engravings. You might also try the "Great Illustrated Classics" version, adapted by Malvina Vogel (Baronet Books/Playmore Publishers, 1992), sold in some discount stores and chain bookstores or available from the publisher by calling (212) 924-7447, but note that the illustrations leave something to be desired.

CC *Saint George and the Dragon*
retold by Margaret Hodges
illustrated by Trina Schart Hyman
Little, Brown, 1984
This is an exquisite picture book that draws its story line from Spenser's *Faerie Queene*, telling the story of Red Cross Knight and Una as they confront the dreadful dragon. Trina Schart Hyman's illustrations are bold and fascinating: some seem to be stained-glass windows, others illuminations from a medieval manuscript. Suit-

able for independent reading by fourth graders, and for reading aloud as well.

Treasure Island
by Robert Louis Stevenson
illustrated by Mervyn Peake
Alfred A. Knopf, 1992
In any library you can probably find a version of the complete and unabridged *Treasure Island.* Try reading it aloud, giving the pirates appropriately growly and snarly voices—it's fun, even though the nautical vocabulary may sometimes mystify. If you want to own the book, you can find many paperback editions including a handsome Puffin Classics paperback; the edition from Knopf listed here is part of their Everyman's Library Children's Classics series, a relatively inexpensive hardbound book with acclaimed illustrations. What about a version at a fourth-grade reading level? You might try the readable "Great Illustrated Classics" version, adapted by Deidre Laiken (Baronet Books/Playmore Publishers, 1992), sold in some discount stores and chain bookstores or available from the publisher by calling (212) 924-7447; or the adequate retelling in the "Simple English Classics Series," adapted by Elizabeth V. DiSomma and Mary Louise McTiernan, (Dormac, Inc., 1987; distributed by Edmark, P.O. Box 3218, Redmond, WA 98073; call [800] 426-0856), for which a Teacher's Guide and Student Workbook are also available.

CC *The Weaving of a Dream: A Chinese Folktale*
retold and illustrated by Marilee Heyer
Puffin Books, 1986
This favorite Chinese folktale (also known as "The Chuang Brocade" and "The Magic Brocade") is told here in eloquent words and utterly stunning pictures. An old widow weaves a picture of a glorious palace into a brocade, but the wind carries it away. Her three sons set out to find it and, in classic folktale fashion, only one, untainted by selfish motives, succeeds. A beautiful book, not to be missed. A very good (unillustrated) version of this tale, called "The

Magic Brocade," is collected in *Best-Loved Folktales of the World*, edited by Joanna Cole (Doubleday/Anchor, 1982).

LEGENDS OF KING ARTHUR AND THE KNIGHTS OF THE ROUND TABLE

Note: Children enjoy legends of King Arthur from an early age, and there are many good books of Arthurian legends for younger readers, including picture books and easy readers like the "Step-Up Classic" volume *Knights of the Round Table*, adapted by Gwen Gross for a second-grade reading level (Random House, 1985). We recommend the following books in this grade because in the *Core Knowledge Sequence*, the reading of Arthurian legends is connected to the introduction in fourth grade to medieval Europe and feudalism. See World History Grade 4: The Middle Ages.

Arthur, High King of Britain
by Michael Morpurgo
illustrated by Michael Foreman
Harcourt Brace, 1995
This book begins with a clever imaginative premise: a modern-day twelve-year-old boy, for reasons too complicated to explain here, comes upon King Arthur, and it is Arthur himself who tells the boy stories of Merlin, Excalibur, Lancelot and Guinevere, Sir Gawain and the Green Knight, Percival, and more. Michael Foreman's full-page watercolor illustrations accompany each story.

CC *King Arthur and His Knights*
as told by Jim Weiss
Greathall Productions
On this cassette tape, storyteller Jim Weiss brings drama, humor, and atmosphere to a selection of Arthurian legends, including "The Sword in the Stone," "King Arthur and Guine-

vere," "Sir Percival Meets a Lady," "Sir Lancelot's Journey," "Merlin's Magic," and more. One of many fine story tapes available from Greathall Productions: (800) 477-6234.

CC *The Kitchen Knight: A Tale of King Arthur*
retold by Margaret Hodges
illustrated by Trina Schart Hyman
Holiday House, 1990
This beautiful picture book tells the story of Sir Gareth of Orkney, one of the knights of the Round Table, in his battle against the Knight of the Red Plain near the Castle Perilous. The language is eloquent and challenging but still suitable for independent reading by fourth graders.

Knights of the Kitchen Table
by Jon Scieszka
illustrated by Lane Smith
Puffin Books, 1991
After they know about King Arthur and the Round Table, kids will laugh at this silly satire. When three boys find themselves called "vile knaves" by a guy in armor, they quickly call him "Sir" back, "because that's the way they talk in knight books." A bit more investigation, and they discover they have time-traveled to Camelot! A quick read with cute illustrations, this book would make a nice light dessert after a main course of Arthurian legends.

The Legend of King Arthur
retold by Robin Lister
illustrated by Alan Baker
Doubleday, 1988
Lister retells the legends in modern-day prose, clear and easy to understand, though without any of the antique "thee and thou" diction that some readers prefer in these tales. Bold color illustrations accompany many of the stories, which include "Merlin and the Dragons," "The Sword in the Stone," "Excalibur," "The Fellowship of the Round Table," "Lancelot, Guinevere and Elayne," "The Holy Grail," "The Day of Destiny," and others.

Sir Gawain and the Green Knight
retold by Selina Hastings
illustrations by Juan Wijngaard
Lothrop, Lee & Shepard, 1981
This feels like an old book, with its red-and-gold marginal decorations and its paintings in the Renaissance style. It tells the story of how the courageous knight Gawain stood up to the test put to him by the supernatural Green Knight. Challenging but readable by many fourth graders, and good for reading aloud as well.

Sir Gawain and the Loathly Lady
retold by Selina Hastings
illustrations by Juan Wijngaard
Lothrop, Lee & Shepard/Mulberry Books, 1985
As intricately detailed as an illuminated manuscript, this book portrays in picture and word the story of King Arthur's quest to answer what remains a tough question: "What is it that women most desire?" It goes on to tell the story of Sir Gawain's obligatory marriage to the ugliest woman imaginable, and how his chivalry turned her beautiful again. This story brings back memories of "Beauty and the Beast," and also brilliantly conveys the ideas of chivalry and romance among the Knights of the Round Table. (Teachers and parents should read the book themselves first to determine if they are uncomfortable with the curses spoken by the Black Knight who challenges Arthur.)

The Sword in the Stone
by T. H. White
illustrated by Dennis Nolan
Philomel Books, 1993
Here is a vividly illustrated edition of the first section of T. H. White's witty, exciting, and magical novel, *The Once and Future King*. The vocabulary is sometimes quite challenging, so this book is probably best as a read-aloud. (White's *Sword in the Stone* is also available in inexpensive paperback editions.)

CC = "Core Collection" book (see page 8).

Young Guinevere
by Robert D. San Souci
illustrated by Jamichael Henterly
Doubleday, 1993
Myth and magic echo through this vivid and beautiful picture-book, which tells the story of the adventures of Guinevere as a young, brave, athletic woman. The story is not "official" Arthurian legend; as the author notes, the story "draws on a variety of classical and contemporary sources. It also reflects the author's reading of the 'might-have-beens' between the lines of legends, folktales, ballads, poems, and works of literature that touch—all too briefly—on Guinevere's early life." So, this may not be for Arthurian purists, but for others, it's a delightful book.

LANGUAGE ARTS

Grade 5

> *Note:* The stories and poems recommended here are meant to constitute a *core* of enriching literature. Teachers and parents are strongly encouraged to expose children to many more stories and poems than those listed below, including perennial favorites by beloved children's writers, popular favorites by contemporary writers, biographies, books about art and music, lots of nonfiction, and, of course, books that the children themselves choose. Regular reading aloud to children should continue long after they can read independently. For suggestions on more good reading, see Language Arts General Resources: Guides to Good Reading (pages 32–33).

 **CC** = a "**Core Collection**" book (see p. 8).

POEMS

See also Language Arts General Resources: Poetry Collections (General Collections, and Collections for Older Children).

Casey at the Bat
by Ernest L. Thayer
illustrated by Patricia Polacco
G. P. Putnam's Sons, 1988
You can find "Casey at the Bat" in many collections of poetry. If you'd like a picture-book edition, take a look at this book. It gives the poem a brief introduction and conclusion, setting it in the context of a modern Little League game, with humorous, exaggerated illustrations.

The Dream Keeper and Other Poems
by Langston Hughes
illustrated by Brian Pinkney
Alfred A. Knopf, 1994
See description under Language Arts General Resources: Poetry Collections.

The Everyman Anthology of Poetry for Children
compiled by Gillian Avery
with illustrations by Thomas Bewick
Alfred A. Knopf/Everyman's Library, 1994
See description under Language Arts General Resources: Poetry Collections for Older Children.

CC *Favorite Poems Old and New*
selected by Helen Ferris
illustrated by Leonard Weisgard
Doubleday, 1957
See description under Language Arts General Resources: Poetry Collections.

Poetry for Young People
by Emily Dickinson
edited by Frances Schoonmaker Bolin
illustrated by Chi Chung
Sterling, 1994
This lovely book collects about fifty of the more accessible poems of Emily Dickinson and presents them with gentle, evocative paintings,

some of which soften the edges or diffuse the mystery of Dickinson's words. A brief note discusses Dickinson's life and work at the opening of the book, and a bibliography and index appear at the close. Difficult or unusual words in individual poems are defined at the bottom of the page.

You Come Too: Favorite Poems for Young Readers
by Robert Frost
illustrated by Thomas W. Nason
Henry Holt, 1959
See description under Language Arts General Resources: Poetry Collections for Older Children.

STORIES

See also Language Arts General Resources: Stories.

CC *The Adventures of Tom Sawyer*
by Mark Twain
Scholastic/Apple Classics, 1993
Any version of the original novel will do. The "Apple Classic" from Scholastic is a standard inexpensive paperback version with good-sized print. We encourage fifth graders to read the original novel, and perhaps to be read parts of it aloud. Condensed or adapted versions cannot do justice to Twain's humor and language. If you have reason for using a condensed version, then you might examine *Tom Sawyer* as adapted by June Edwards, illustrated by Joel Naprstek (Steck-Vaughn, 1991), which turns the novel into seven short chapters, simplified in plot and language, but through dialogue conveying a tiny bit of the style and rhythm of Twain's own writing.

To round out the reading of *Tom Sawyer*, you might also read *"Mark Twain"—What Kind of a Name Is That? A Story of Samuel Langhorne Clemens* by Robert Quackenbush (Prentice Hall, 1980). This entertaining biography was written by an author with an eye for interesting details—for instance, we learn the names of

Twain's favorite cats (Beelzebub, Blatherskite, Buffalo Bill, and Apollinaris). The amusing cartoon drawings and text emphasize Twain's rebellious nature.

CC *Don Quixote and Sancho Panza*
adapted by Margaret Hodges
illustrated by Stephen Marchesi
Charles Scribner's Sons, 1992
This lovely book selects six central episodes from *Don Quixote* and retells them with grace and respect for not only Cervantes's Spanish but also the long line of English translations of this classic. Marchesi's illustrations, some in pencil and some in colored chalk, enliven almost every spread. The author provides a thoughtful introduction to Cervantes, his work, and its meaning. The length, style, and design of this book makes it a perfect fifth-grade introduction to the work. Now, would the publisher *please* issue a paperback edition? (See also World History Grade 5: The Renaissance.)

CC *Little House on the Prairie*
by Laura Ingalls Wilder
illustrated by Garth Williams
HarperCollins, 1935; uniform edition, 1953
Many children will have read, or had read to them, this and other "Little House" books in their younger years. We recommend this book for independent reading by fifth graders as a way to complement their study of the settlement of the American West (see American History Grade 5: Westward Expansion). The crystalline clarity of Wilder's prose makes her books seem deceptively easy. They are rich and have depths that reveal themselves in rereading. Students who are curious about Wilder's life and times might also enjoy *On the Way Home* by Laura Ingalls Wilder and Rose Wilder Lane (HarperCollins, 1962), a book made out of Laura's diary entries by her daughter, Rose.

CC *Little Women*
by Louisa May Alcott
abridged by Muriel Fuller
Scholastic/Apple Classics [no date]
Any child who wants to read the complete,

original novel should certainly be encouraged to do so, but we can recommend this respectful abridgement by Muriel Fuller, which keeps the spirit and tone of Alcott's original, as a good choice, especially for a class text. (Note, however, that the "novelization" based on the fine recent movie of *Little Women* does *not* stay true to Alcott's spirit or tone, and thus cannot be recommended.) Students who take an interest in Louisa May Alcott and are ready for a challenging but rewarding book might try *Invincible Louisa* by Cornelia Meigs (Little, Brown, 1933; also a Scholastic paperback), an engaging biography of a woman whose life would make a good novel!

CC *A Midsummer Night's Dream for Young People*
edited and illustrated by Diane Davidson
Swan Books, 1986
Recommended by the Folger Shakespeare Library, this is part of Diane Davidson's excellent "Shakespeare for Young People" series. This slim volume condenses the play into about a forty-minute production, which encourages reading aloud and acting out scenes, which is the best way to get to know Shakespeare—through hearing and seeing, not just reading. Davidson keeps Shakespeare's original words and provides clear stage directions, as well as spoken parts by two "Announcers," who introduce scenes and help explain the action. This is the best version we know to get fifth graders interested in and liking Shakespeare, and ready for his complete plays when they get a little older. (Swan Books, P.O. Box 2498, Fair Oaks, CA 95628)

Those who prefer a condensed text more for reading than performance may want to examine *A Midsummer Night's Dream* as adapted by Diana Stewart (Steck-Vaughn, 1991). This adaptation, written as a play, considerably shortens the original but still retains Shakespeare's diction, imagery, and rhythm, and includes some stage directions and scenery descriptions.

To learn more about Shakespeare's life and times, students can read *Bard of Avon: The Story of William Shakespeare* by Diane Stanley and Peter Vennema (William Morrow, 1992), a handsome picture-book biography. Stanley's illustrations include images of Elizabethan stage productions of *A Midsummer Night's Dream, Romeo and Juliet,* and *Macbeth.* The text introduces the spirit of the theater of the time, the building of the Globe, well-known actors of the day, and the growth of Shakespeare's reputation. An author's postscript comments on Shakespeare's language, in terms comprehensible to a fifth grader.

Also, see Language Arts General Resources for more on Shakespeare (page 43), including a Shakespeare resource catalog, prose versions of the plays, and the video series *Shakespeare: The Animated Tales.*

CC *Escape from Slavery: The Boyhood of Frederick Douglass in His Own Words*
edited and illustrated by Michael McCurdy
foreword by Coretta Scott King
Alfred A. Knopf, 1994
This striking volume offers a representative set of excerpts from the *Narrative of the Life of Frederick Douglass.* Each of the book's nine chapters is introduced with a brief passage to orient the reader. The prose is eloquent and demanding, but that is because it is Douglass's own, and not a modern adaptation. Strong woodblock prints illustrate the book throughout. Michael McCurdy has done young readers a great service in creating this accessible edition of an important work.

A good biography of Douglass, readable by fifth grade students, is *Frederick Douglass: The Black Lion* by Patricia and Fredrick McKissack (Childrens Press, 1987). See also the interesting and readable articles in the February 1989 issue of *Cobblestone,* a history magazine for young people. (For information on *Cobblestone,* see American History General Resources.)

The Adventures of Sherlock Holmes (vols. 1–4)
adapted by Catherine Edwards Sadler
illustrated by Andrew Glass
Avon Camelot Books, 1981, 1981, 1981, 1988
The four volumes in this series offer engaging and accessible versions of many stories about

the extraordinary Sherlock Holmes and his trusted friend, Dr. Watson. The language is sufficiently challenging to sustain fifth graders' interest but not too difficult for independent reading. Among the favorite stories in these volumes you will find, in Book One, "The Red-Headed League"; in Book Two, "The Adventure of the Speckled Band"; in Book Three, "The Adventure of the Musgrave Ritual"; and, in Book Four, "The Adventure of the Crooked Man," among many others.

Children may also enjoy the books in the eight-volume Match Wits with Sherlock Holmes series, adapted by Murray Shaw, and illustrated by George Overlie (Carolrhoda Books/First Avenue Editions, 1990), designed to entice young readers into the mysteries that Sherlock Holmes solves by simplifying the language, occasionally illustrating the stories, and, at each story's end, outlining the logic that Holmes used to unravel the mystery. For the story suggested in the *Core Knowledge Sequence,* see the volume titled *The Adventure of the Copper Beeches and The Red-Headed League.*

After reading, treat yourself to *Sherlock Holmes for Children* (Greathall Productions). On this cassette tape, Jim Weiss offers lively renditions of four stories. He gives Holmes a properly cool voice, and gives the villains voices reminiscent of bad guys from the melodramatic Saturday-morning serials of long ago (we're showing our age here). Weiss does not read from the original stories, nor does he attempt to capture their language. Nevertheless, his "storyteller's versions" (as he calls them) are, in their own right, delightful listening. Also try another tape by Weiss, *Mystery! Mystery! for Children,* which features one Sherlock Holmes story—"The Red-Headed League"—along with a retelling of Edgar Allan Poe's "The Purloined Letter" and even a Father Brown mystery! These are two of many fine story tapes available from Greathall Productions: (800) 477-6234.

 **CC** = "Core Collection" book (see page 8).

MYTHS AND LEGENDS

The Samurai's Daughter
retold by Robert D. San Souci
illustrated by Stephen T. Johnson
Dial Books, 1992
This book is recommended for reading in connection with learning about feudal Japan (see World History Grade 5). It tells the story of a strong-willed girl, Tokoyo, the daughter of a *samurai,* and her struggle to help her exiled father. This beautifully illustrated picture book should be enjoyable and easy reading for fifth graders.

Another version of this Japanese legend is told as "A Tale of the Oki Islands," as collected in *Best-Loved Folktales of the World,* selected by Joanna Cole (Doubleday/Anchor, 1982). This book is not illustrated, but the story is well told, very suitable for a fifth-grade classroom, and the book offers a wealth of tales from around the world to boot.

The Legend of Scarface: A Blackfeet Indian Tale
by Robert San Souci
illustrated by Daniel San Souci
Doubleday, 1991
With beautiful illustrations in earth colors and a quiet, deliberate writing style, this picture-book version of the legend of Scarface and Morning Star should be enjoyable and easy reading for fifth graders. Recommended for reading in connection with learning about the Plains Indians (see American History Grade 5).

CC *Native American Stories*
told by Joseph Bruchac
illustrated by John Kahionhes Fadden
Fulcrum, 1991
This volume conveniently collects the stories from *Keepers of the Earth* by Joseph Bruchac and Michael Caduto (described under Language Arts General Resources: Series). The stories, straightforwardly told in the manner of Native American oral tradition, should be easy and enjoyable reading for fifth graders. The stories are grouped by theme: Creation, Fire, Earth, Wind

and Weather, Water, Sky, Seasons, Plants and Animals, Life Death Spirit, and Unity of Earth. Bruchac includes a number of tales featuring "trickster" figures, including "How Grandmother Spider Stole the Sun" (Muskogee), "Old Man Coyote and the Rock" (Pawnee), and "How Raven Made the Tides" (Tsimshian—Pacific Northwest). More trickster tales of Coyote, Spider, and Raven may be found in *American Indian Myths and Legends,* edited by Richard Erdoes and Alfonso Ortiz (Pantheon, 1984), but this book should be considered a teacher/parent resource, as a number of the tales are racy or scatological.

SPEECHES

See American History Grade 5 for recommended resources on Abraham Lincoln's Gettysburg Address, and Chief Joseph's "I will fight no more forever."

LANGUAGE ARTS

Grade 6

> *Note:* The stories and poems recommended here are meant to constitute a *core* of enriching literature. Teachers and parents are strongly encouraged to expose children to many more stories and poems than those listed below, including perennial favorites by beloved children's writers, popular favorites by contemporary writers, biographies, books about art and music, lots of nonfiction, and, of course, books that the children themselves choose. Regular reading aloud to children should continue long after they can read independently. For suggestions on more good reading, see Language Arts General Resources: Guides to Good Reading (pages 32–33).

CC = a **"Core Collection"** book (see p. 8).

POEMS
See also Language Arts General Resources: Poetry Collections (General Collections, and Collections for Older Children).

The Dream Keeper and Other Poems
by Langston Hughes
illustrated by Brian Pinkney
Alfred A. Knopf, 1994
See description under Language Arts General Resources: Poetry Collections.

The Everyman Anthology of Poetry for Children
compiled by Gillian Avery
with illustrations by Thomas Bewick
Alfred A. Knopf/Everyman's Library, 1994
See description under Language Arts General Resources: Poetry Collections for Older Children.

CC *Favorite Poems Old and New*
selected by Helen Ferris
illustrated by Leonard Weisgard
Doubleday, 1957
See description under Language Arts General Resources: Poetry Collections.

One Hundred and One Famous Poems
compiled by Roy J. Cook
Contemporary Books, 1958
Here's a convenient collection of very traditional poems from days past, including Tennyson's "Charge of the Light Brigade"; famous passages from Shakespeare's plays ("The quality of mercy is not strained," Polonius's advice to Hamlet, Hamlet's "To be or not to be" soliloquy); Emerson's "The Snowstorm"; Wordsworth's "The Daffodils"; selections from Byron's *Childe Harold's Pilgrimage*; Kipling's "If";

Longfellow's "Psalm of Life"; Poe's "The Raven," and many more.

Poetry for Young People
by Emily Dickinson
edited by Frances Schoonmaker Bolin
illustrated by Chi Chung
Sterling, 1994
See description under Language Arts Grade 5: Poetry.

The Raven and Other Favorite Poems
by Edgar Allan Poe
Dover, 1991
Forty-one of Poe's best known poems are reprinted in this edition. Part of Dover's Thrift Editions series (see page 39 for Dover's address).

You Come Too: Favorite Poems for Young Readers
by Robert Frost
illustrated by Thomas W. Nason
Henry Holt, 1959
See description under Language Arts General Resources: Poetry Collections for Older Children.

STORIES
See also Language Arts General Resources: Stories.

Dr. Jekyll and Mr. Hyde
by Robert Louis Stevenson
You should be able to find many editions of this classic thriller at your library. We recommend that sixth graders read the original text, not a retelling. An inexpensive "Thrift Edition" is available from Dover Books (see address, page 39).

 **CC** = "Core Collection" book (see page 8).

Julius Caesar
by William Shakespeare
adapted by Diana Stewart
illustrated by Charles Shaw
Steck-Vaughn, 1991
Julius Caesar for Young People
edited and illustrated by Diane Davidson
Swan Books, 1990
Julius Caesar in the original is a more than daunting text for the sixth grade. But the play offers such valuable opportunities for added insight and enjoyment when studying ancient Rome (see World History Grade 6), not to mention such great speeches—"Friends, Romans, countrymen . . ."—that it would be a shame to just "wait until high school." Here, then, are two admirably well-adapted versions for young readers. Diana Stewart's is a shortened and simplified version of the play, written for ease of reading and comprehension, yet respectful of Shakespeare's language, especially in the more memorable speeches. Diane Davidson's edition is designed to encourage a classroom or community performance. She has simplified the dialogue and action to create material for a practical stage production. She also offers advice to the classroom or neighborhood stage director for scenery, costumes, and organization. (Swan Books, P.O. Box 2498, Fair Oaks, CA 95628) See also Language Arts General Resources: Shakespeare (page 43).

The Secret Garden
by Frances Hodgson Burnett
illustrated by Tasha Tudor
HarperCollins, 1962
This is a good edition of the full and original 1911 novel. Some children will have heard this read aloud to them at a younger age, and some will have read abridged versions, perhaps even the original. In sixth grade, the novel can be read independently and, at this age, with attention not just to the story (which is wonderful) but to the way it is told. Like Laura Ingalls Wilder's *Little House* books, *The Secret Garden* is written in such clear prose that it may seem transparent. But there is a great deal more to

this book that students can appreciate when they read it with attention to, for example, the garden as a symbol of Mary's development. Are we saying that you should analyze the book to death? Goodness, no—just encourage children to read it with a new degree of awareness and appreciation.

A Tale of Two Cities
by Charles Dickens
This novel, available in many libraries and paperback editions, may be connected to the sixth-grade introduction to the French Revolution (see World History Grade 6). Although this is one of Dickens's most tightly structured novels, and one of his shortest, it will still be a great challenge to many sixth-grade readers, and so is perhaps best for reading aloud. One retelling, adapted by Patricia Krapesh (Steck-Vaughn, 1991), is a forty-page version that maintains the plot line but loses the language and energy of the original. Another retelling, in the "Great Illustrated Classics" series (Baronet/Playmore, 1994; [212] 924-7477), is easy and engaging but also sacrifices Dickens's language.

MYTHS OF ANCIENT GREECE AND ROME

Black Ships Before Troy: The Story of the Iliad
    retold by Rosemary Sutcliff
    illustrated by Alan Lee
    Delacorte Press, 1993

CC *The Children's Homer: The Adventures of Odysseus and the Tale of Troy*
    by Padraic Colum
    Macmillan, 1918; Aladdin Paperbacks
The Iliad and *The Odyssey*
    retold by Barbara Leonie Picard
    Oxford University Press, 1960; 1952
The Trojan War and *The Adventures of Ulysses*
    by Bernard Evslin
    Scholastic, 1988; 1989
In connection with their sixth-grade study of lasting ideas from ancient Greece and Rome (as recommended in the *Core Knowledge Sequence*;

see World History Grade 6), students can enjoy reading one of many versions of the great Homeric epics, the *Iliad* and the *Odyssey*, adapted for young readers. One of our favorite versions is *The Children's Homer*. In lovely prose that often approaches poetry, Padraic Colum retells the Homeric epics in a style comprehensible to young readers, without losing important elements of meaning and image from the stories.

Colum is our first choice, but you may wish to consider others. A recent retelling comes from Rosemary Sutcliff, whose *Black Ships Before Troy* tells the story of the *Iliad* in prose marked by both vigor and dignity. Barbara Leonie Picard's elegant prose retellings, in two volumes, are more challenging, and perhaps best for the ambitious reader. Bernard Evslin's two slim paperbacks are simple, readable retellings of the major episodes in the epics. They get across the plot but come nowhere near the literary quality of Colum's version, not to mention Sutcliff's or Picard's.

We should mention an out-of-print retelling of *The Iliad and the Odyssey of Homer* by Alfred J. Church. Available in many libraries, these old-fashioned prose retellings do soften and civilize Homer's sometimes savage world, but they have a grace and dignity missing, or available in only small quantity, from some more recent adaptations for children. (William Russell based his "read-aloud" versions on Alfred Church; see below, *Classic Myths to Read Aloud.*) Finally, we should not rule out the possibility of some enterprising sixth graders reading one of the great poetic translations, such as the especially clear and vigorous renderings of Robert Fitzgerald (Doubleday/Anchor Books).

CC *Classic Myths to Read Aloud*
compiled and edited by William F. Russell
Crown Publishers, 1989
An excellent and generous collection of Greek and Roman myths, retold in a language that has a suitably old-fashioned feel. The editor provides a brief helpful introduction to each myth, a pronunciation key, and a chart that cross-references the Greek and Roman gods. He also of-

fers an unusual and interesting feature after each tale, called "A Few Words More," in which he discusses the origins of words and phrases that appear in the tales and have made their way into our language, such as *Achilles' heel, cereal, dog days, the face that launched a thousand ships, laconic,* and dozens more. For older listeners (or readers), there are retellings of generous portions of Homer's *Iliad and Odyssey* (based on the good old Alfred Church versions for children), and even of Virgil's *Aeneid.* Those who are seeking a source for the myths recommended for sixth grade in the *Core Knowledge Sequence* will find a few included in this book: "Echo and Narcissus," "Orpheus and Eurydice," and "Pygmalion and Galatea."

Favorite Greek Myths
retold by Mary Pope Osborne
illustrated by Troy Howell
Scholastic, 1989
See description under Language Arts Grade 2, Mythology of Ancient Greece. This book is suitable for independent reading by sixth graders, and includes the myths of Apollo and Daphne, Echo and Narcissus, and Orpheus and Eurydice.

HISTORY AND GEOGRAPHY

Introduction

For many years the early grades of our schools have taught "Social Studies" rather than history, teaching lessons about the family, neighborhood, and community. This narrow teaching focus is based on an idea called "expanding horizons," which can be pictured as a series of concentric circles, at the center of which is The Child. According to the expanding horizons model, schools should start by teaching the child about himself and only gradually move into larger circles of knowledge, from the Self outward to the Family, the School, the Community, the State, and so on.

While such studies can be of some value, we need to ask whether they are sufficient, and whether they are based on an accurate model of childhood. While it is true that learning does move from the familiar to the unfamiliar, the theorists who invented the expanding horizons model failed to take account of how familiar to children are things they have never seen, like elves or fairies. The expanding-horizons model assumes that the child's greatest interest is in himself, in the immediate and the personal. But why, then, are children so interested in dinosaurs, in medieval castles, or knights in armor?

We should take advantage of children's natural curiosity and begin *early* to broaden their horizons by introducing them to a broad range of knowledge about other people, places, and times. In starting at an early age to teach our children about history and geography, we can foster the beginnings of understanding about the world beyond the child's immediate surroundings, and about varied people and ways of life. We can also begin to develop our children's sense of our nation's past and its significance.

Learning history is not a matter of being able to recall a bunch of names and dates. Children need to know some of these, to be sure, but they also need to grasp how the facts fit into a bigger picture. Nowadays, however, given the minor role of history in the curriculum, it's very hard for children to get a sense of the bigger picture. Many schools teach too little history too late, and squeeze that little into a few grades rather than teaching it over several years.

Rather than teaching history only in occasional grades, we urge that schools teach history in a sequenced and coherent fashion, beginning in Kindergarten, and building year by year. Young children (and adults too) need to be attracted by the "story" in history. This does not mean abandoning facts for legends, but it does mean putting the facts into narrative form, with people and plots, problems and resolutions. Many books do a good job of telling history in an appealing way that takes advantage of children's naturally active imaginations as they "visit" people and places in the past. In the classroom, too, we can help children learn about history through art projects, drama, music, and discussions.

History and Geography in the *Core Knowledge Sequence:* A Summary

> For information on the specific content guidelines known as the *Core Knowledge Sequence* and on the ideas behind the Core Knowledge initiative, please see in this book "Core Knowledge: Building Knowledge Year by Year" (pages 9–23, especially pages 15–17 on the *Sequence).*

From kindergarten on, the *Core Knowledge Sequence* recommends specific topics in the history and geography of America and the world, organized in a way that builds year by year.

Recommended topics in World History and Geography in the *Core Knowledge Sequence* are organized in a mostly chronological fashion, building from ancient civilizations in first grade to recent times in sixth grade. This does not mean that once a first grader has studied ancient Egypt, she never needs to study it again. Middle and high school students can tackle topics in greater depth, detail, and sophistication. But by introducing topics early, we plant the seeds of knowledge that can grow later. When children are introduced to world history in a way that builds year by year, then they can develop, by the time they enter middle school, a sense of the larger chronology of events that gives meaning and coherence to their later studies.

In American history, the *Core Knowledge Sequence* recommends topics for kindergarten through second grade that give children a broad glimpse of major events and figures in American history, from early to recent times. This constitutes a kind of overture, which touches upon main themes to be developed later. Beginning in third grade, the *Core Knowledge Sequence* organizes the study of major topics in American history in chronological fashion.

The American History guidelines intersect chronologically with the World History guidelines in sixth grade, thus preparing for the integrated study of modern world and American history in grades seven and eight.

• **Kindergarten:** *World History and Geography:* By working with maps and globes, children become familiar with basic geographic terms and concepts. They learn to identify and locate the seven continents, the Atlantic and Pacific Oceans, and the North and South Poles. Their knowledge of the continents is reinforced through connection with familiar landmarks and plant and animal life on each continent.

American History and Geography: Working with maps and globes, children learn to name and locate the town or city and state in which they live. They locate North America and the United States, including Alaska and Hawaii.

They come to understand the different ways of life of different Native American peoples by learning about specific tribes or nations, past and present: how the people lived, what they wore and ate, the homes they lived in, and the current life of the tribe or nation.

They learn about the early exploration and settlement of this country, including stories about Columbus, and about the Pilgrims and Thanksgiving. They are introduced to the Fourth of July, "Independence Day," as the birthday of our nation. They learn about the injustice that during part of our nation's history, some people—the slaves—were not free.

Children are introduced to stories about some American presidents: Washington, Jefferson, Lincoln, and Theodore Roosevelt. They learn who is the current president of the United States.

They learn about national symbols, including the American flag, the Statue of Liberty, Mount Rushmore, and the White House.

• **Grade 1:** *World History and Geography:* Children learn more about working with maps and globes. They review the seven continents and major oceans (Atlantic, Pacific, Indian), learn the major directions (east, west, north, south), and locate places relevant to the historical topics they are studying. They learn about the equator, as well as geographical terms such as *peninsula* and *island.*

Children begin their study of ancient civilizations. They are encouraged to consider what things make up a civilization. They learn about the "cradle of civilization," Mesopotamia, and about the importance of two rivers (the Tigris and Euphrates). They are introduced to ancient Egypt, including the Nile River, pharaohs (such as "King Tut"), hieroglyphics, and—always a favorite!—pyramids and mummies.

Since religion is so important in the story of civilization, children are introduced to the history of major world religions. The goal is to be respectful and descriptive, not prescriptive, to focus on major symbols, figures, and stories that will be the basis for deeper understanding in the future. In first grade, children are introduced to Judaism, Christianity, and Islam.

Also in World History, children learn about modern Mexico. (This can be connected to their historical study of the ancient Maya and Aztec civilizations; see American History Grade 1).

American History and Geography: Children learn about very early hunters and nomads who crossed what was in those ancient times a land bridge from Asia to North America. They are introduced to three great early civilizations in the Americas: Maya, Inca, and Aztec.

After a brief review of the story of Columbus, children learn about other explorers and settlers. They learn about the Spanish conquistadors, and about English settlers, including stories of the "Lost Colony," Jamestown, and the Puritans in the Massachusetts Bay Colony.

They are introduced to the story of the American Revolution, including the Boston Tea Party, Paul Revere's ride, the "shot heard round the world," the signing of the Declaration of Independence, and the progress of George Washington from military commander to our first president. (Students study the American Revolution in greater depth in fourth grade.)

They learn about Thomas Jefferson and the Louisiana Purchase, and the story of the Lewis and Clark expedition, including the role of Sacagawea. On maps they locate the Appalachian Mountains, the Rocky Mountains, and the Mississippi River.

Children learn about national symbols, including the Liberty Bell, the eagle, and the American flag.

• **Grade 2:** *World History and Geography:* In second grade, children extend their knowledge of ancient civilizations and world religions. They learn major geographical features of Asia, and as they learn about India they are introduced to Hinduism and Buddhism. They learn about China, including Confucius, the building of the Great Wall, and important inventions.

They learn about modern civilization and culture in Japan, about the geography of this island nation, and about the mix of traditional customs and modern industries and ways of life.

They are introduced to the civilization of ancient Greece (in connection with the introduction of Greek myths: see Language Arts, grade 2), and about the Mediterranean Sea, Athens, the Olympic games, the Parthenon, and Alexander the Great.

American History and Geography: Children are introduced to the beginnings of Constitutional government in America. They learn about James Madison and the idea that "we the people" govern ourselves.

They learn the story of the War of 1812, including the Battle of Lake Erie, the burning of the White House, and Francis Scott Key's writing of "The Star Spangled Banner."

They learn more about the westward expansion of the nation, studying the pioneers who headed west on such routes as the Oregon Trail. They learn how this westward movement affected American Indians, including the near extermination of the buffalo and the story of the "Trail of Tears."

They are introduced to the story of the Civil War as a great conflict that divided our nation. They learn about the controversy over slavery, and about such figures as Harriet Tubman, Ulysses S. Grant, Robert E. Lee, and President Lincoln. (Students study the Civil War in greater depth in fifth grade.)

Through narrative and biography, children are introduced to the importance of immigration in our history. They learn about various motives people have had for coming to America, about the experience of immigration, and the meaning of citizenship.

In connection with these historical studies, children learn about the geography of the Americas, including the Appalachian and Rocky Mountains, the Great Lakes, the Gulf of Mexico, the Caribbean Sea, and major countries in South America. They add to their vocabulary such geographic terms as *horizon, desert, oasis,* and *prairie.*

They learn about national symbols, including earlier versions of the American flag, the Statue of Liberty, and the Lincoln Memorial.

• **Grade 3:** *World History and Geography:* In third grade, children build on their earlier study of Greece and learn about Ancient Rome. They learn about the legend of Romulus and Remus, and how the Romans adapted the Greek religion and gods. They are introduced to Julius Caesar and familiar phrases such as *"Veni, vidi, vici"* ("I came, I saw, I conquered"). They explore life in the Roman Empire, and the story of the eruption of Mt. Vesuvius and the destruction of Pompeii. They learn about Constantine, the first Christian emperor of Rome, and about the "decline and fall" of the Western Roman Empire and the rise of the Eastern Roman—or Byzantine—Empire. They learn about the city of Constantinople, and the Byzantine emperor Justinian and his wife Theodora, and about Byzantine art. As part of their introduction to Roman and Byzantine times, they learn about the geography of the Mediterranean region.

Children learn about the Vikings, including their exploration of North America before Columbus. (See also Language Arts Grade 3: Norse Mythology; and, American History Grade 3: Early Exploration of North America.)

Their study of world geography includes important rivers of the world, and they add to their geographic vocabulary such terms as *source, tributary, delta,* and *strait.* They are also introduced to the use of an atlas, and to the use of a bar scale to measure distance on a map.

American History and Geography: Children learn about the different ways of life of some early Native Americans, including those of the Southwest and the Eastern Woodlands.

Children extend their earlier studies of exploration and settlement by learning about early Spanish explorers, such as Ponce de Leon and Hernando de Soto, about the settlement of St. Augustine and settlements in the Southwest, as well as conflicts with Southwestern American Indians.

They are introduced to the story of the long search for a "Northwest Passage," including the efforts of John Cabot, Jacques Cartier, and Henry Hudson. They learn associated geography of the United States and Canada.

Building upon what they learned in first grade, children now learn more about the settlement of the original thirteen colonies in America. They learn about the different motivations—religious, economic, and otherwise—for settling in America. They study how the Dutch settled in "New Netherland," soon to become New York, and how William Penn and the "Quakers" settled in Pennsylvania. They look in some detail at Virginia, including the early settlement of Jamestown, the interactions and conflicts with the Powhatan Indians, the story (fact or legend?) of John Smith and Pocahontas, the development of tobacco as a cash crop, and the beginnings of slavery. They also look in some detail at Massachusetts. They learn the story of the Pilgrims and the Mayflower Compact. They learn about the Puritans in the Massachusetts Bay Colony. They also consider the development of slavery in colonial America, and learn about the experience of the Middle Passage.

• **Grade 4:** *World History and Geography:* In fourth grade, children are introduced to the history of Europe leading up to and including the Middle Ages. They learn about the invasions of Germanic tribes after the fall of Rome. They are introduced to developments in the history of the Christian church, including the origin of the Roman Catholic Church and the rise of the monasteries as centers of learning. They study life in feudal times, including castles, knights in armor, and chivalry. (This can be connected to reading legends of King Arthur: see Language Arts Grade 4.) They learn about the Norman Conquest, King John and the Magna Carta, and Joan of Arc. They find out about the terrible plague that swept across Europe. Throughout these studies, they learn about associated European geography, including important rivers, mountain ranges, and more.

Building upon their introduction to Islam in first grade, children deepen their knowledge by learning about the Five Pillars of Islam. They learn about the spread and development of Islamic civilization in such thriving cities as Córdoba (in Spain). They meet figures like Saladin and Richard the Lionhearted as they are introduced to the Crusades, and they learn how these wars between Christians and Muslims led to growing trade and cultural interaction between East and West.

Children are introduced to the history of early and medieval African kingdoms. Building upon their knowledge of ancient Egypt, they learn about the early kingdom of Kush (Nubia) and the medieval kingdoms of the Sudan in Ghana, Mali, and Songhai, and about such leaders as Sundiata Keita and Mansa Musa of Mali. They also learn about the geography of Africa, including major rivers and mountains, and contrasting climates in different regions (desert, rain forest, savanna).

Building upon their introduction to China in second grade, children learn more about powerful medieval dynasties, about China's growing influence on its neighbors, about the growth of the silk trade, about Genghis Khan, and about Kublai Khan and Marco Polo.

Children expand their work with maps and globes by learning about longitude and latitude, the Prime Meridian and the International Date Line, and the representation of elevations and depressions on relief maps. They are also introduced to major mountains and mountain ranges around the world (which can be connected to their study of how mountains are formed: see Science Grade 4).

American History and Geography: Children begin with a brief look at the French and Indian

War. They then take an extended look at the American Revolution: causes, major figures, and consequences. Along the way, they meet not only Paul Revere, Thomas Jefferson, and George Washington, but also Tom Paine, Deborah Sampson, Phillis Wheatley, Lafayette, Molly Pitcher, Benedict Arnold, John Paul Jones, and Nathan Hale. (See also Visual Arts Grade 4: Gilbert Stuart's portrait of Washington, and Leutze's "Washington Crossing the Delaware.")

Children learn about the making of a constitutional government in America, and are introduced to some of the basic values and principles of American democracy as defined in the Declaration of Independence and the Constitution. They learn about some of the struggles, conflicts, and compromises that went into the making of the Constitution. They consider some basic questions about the purposes of government as they learn about the separation of powers, checks and balances, and other features of American government. They study the main precepts of the Bill of Rights. They consider some of the responsibilities and functions of government today at local, state, and national levels.

Children continue their study of American history by learning about early presidents and politics. They are introduced to the ideas behind the arguments between such figures as Jefferson and Hamilton, and the eventual growth of political parties. They learn some basic facts about the administrations of Jefferson and Madison. They are introduced to Andrew Jackson's presidency of the "common man," and to his Indian removal policies.

They explore some of the ideas and people in social reform movements before the Civil War. They meet abolitionists such as William Lloyd Garrison and Frederick Douglass. They are introduced to feminists such as Elizabeth Cady Stanton and Sojourner Truth. They learn about Horace Mann and public schooling, and about Dorothea Dix and her campaign for better treatment of the mentally ill.

• **Grade 5:** *World History and Geography:* Having been introduced in first grade to the Maya, Aztec, and Inca civilizations, children in fifth grade now learn more about their achievements, ways of life, and beliefs.

Children already know the stories of Columbus and other European explorers: now they get a sense of the historical context for those stories by studying the causes and consequences of European exploration, trade, and the clash of cultures. They learn about the European desire to take over trade routes controlled by Muslims. They learn about the explorations of the Portuguese, Spanish, Dutch, and English, and the various rivalries between these nationalities. Throughout these studies, they expand their knowledge of relevant geography.

Children are introduced to the Renaissance as a "rebirth" of learning. They learn first about the role of Islamic scholars in preserving works of classical civilization. They learn about the rise of Italian city states and powerful families such as the Medici family. They get a sense of the ideals of the Renaissance as embodied in such figures as the ideal courtier of Castiglione and the "prince" described by Machiavelli. By meeting Copernicus and Galileo, they learn about the conflicts between science and the church. They also learn about the great artists of the Renaissance (for specifics, see Visual Arts Grade 5). (Note: see Language Arts Grade 5 for related literary works: selections from Cervantes's *Don Quixote* and Shakespeare's *A Midsummer Night's Dream.*)

Children continue their chronological study of world history by being introduced to the Reformation. They learn about Martin Luther, John Calvin, and the Counter-Reformation.

They learn about some turning points in the history of England. Along the way they meet Henry VIII and Queen Elizabeth, and learn the story of the defeat of the Spanish Armada. They learn about the English Revolution, from the beheading of Charles I through the reign of Cromwell to the Restoration of Charles II. They go on to learn about the Glorious Revolution, Parliament, and the English Bill of Rights.

Children look back to the history of feudal Japan and review the geography of the region. They learn about the strict code of the samurai. They review Buddhism (to which they were introduced in second grade when learning about India), and they are introduced to Shintoism. They learn about the closing of Japan to outsiders.

Children learn about the early growth of Russia, and meet such figures as Ivan the Terrible, Peter the Great, and Catherine the Great. They also study the geography of Russia.

To their work with maps and globes, children add new knowledge of the Tropics of Cancer and Capricorn and time zones. They also examine great lakes of the world, and get an overview of the political geography of Europe.

American History and Geography: In first and second grades children had been introduced to the westward expansion of the United States; now, in fifth grade, they examine that story in more detail. They take a closer look at various pioneers and their different motivations. They learn about related American geography, including major lakes, rivers, and mountains. They explore the causes and consequences of the American Indian resistance to the westward movement of the pioneers. They learn what "Manifest Destiny" meant to nineteenth-century Americans, how such ideas led to war with Mexico, and why many Americans were opposed to that war.

Having been introduced in second grade to the Civil War, children now study it in some detail. They examine causes and events leading up to the conflict, including the growing division between an industrial North and agricultural South. They learn about the Missouri Compromise, Harriet Beecher Stowe's *Uncle Tom's Cabin,* the Dred Scott decision, John Brown, and the Lincoln-Douglas debates.

During their study of the war itself, they learn about Jefferson Davis, Robert E. Lee, Ulysses S. Grant, and Stonewall Jackson. They examine a few crucial battles, including the First Battle of Bull Run, Antietam Creek, Vicksburg, and Gettysburg. They consider the words and ideas of Lincoln's Gettysburg Address. They learn about African-American troops such as the Massachusetts 54th. They learn about Sherman's March to the Sea, the burning of Atlanta, the fall of Richmond, and the surrender at Appomattox, followed by the assassination of Lincoln.

Children move on to learn about the Reconstruction era. They learn what carpetbaggers and scalawags were. They learn about the impeachment of Andrew Johnson. They explore the significance of the thirteenth, fourteenth, and fifteenth amendments to the Constitution. They learn about the rise of the Ku Klux Klan, and about "Black Codes."

They learn more about the American West after the Civil War. They study railroads, cowboys, and the "Wild West." They learn about the culture and life of Plains Indians and Pacific Northwest Indians, and about American government policies toward Indians. They learn about forced removal, the battle at Little Big Horn, and Wounded Knee.

As part of their studies, children review the geography of the United States, including a cumulative review of all fifty states and capitals.

• **Grade 6:** *World History and Geography:* In sixth grade, students begin by taking a byway from the chronological path on which their previous studies have proceeded. They now have an opportunity to deepen their knowledge of topics to which they were introduced in earlier grades. They explore lasting ideas from ancient civilizations. They review what they have learned about

Judaism, Christianity, Greece, and Rome, but with an emphasis on the legacy of enduring ideas about right and wrong, and about democracy and government. They examine concepts of law, justice, and social responsibility in Judaism. In their consideration of Christianity, they discuss the ideas in the Sermon on the Mount. Connected to these studies they also learn about the geography of the Middle East.

Building upon their second-grade introduction to ancient Greece, students now examine the roots of democracy in the Greek *polis* and Athenian assembly. They learn about Pericles and the "Golden Age," and about the wisdom of Socrates, Plato, and Aristotle.

Building upon their third-grade introduction to ancient Rome, students learn about the Punic Wars, Roman government, Julius Caesar, Roman law, Christianity under the Roman Empire, and the ways in which historians have perceived Rome's "decline and fall" as an object lesson for later generations and societies. (In connection with these topics, see Language Arts Grade 6: Shakespeare's *Julius Caesar*.)

After this study of our legacy from ancient civilizations, students pick up the chronological thread where it left off in fifth grade by learning more about main ideas and figures of the Enlightenment. They consider the two opposed views of human nature expressed by John Locke and Thomas Hobbes. They also learn about the influence of the Enlightenment on the beginnings of the United States (as, for example, the idea of "natural rights").

Building upon their prior knowledge of the American Revolution (studied in first and fourth grade), students learn about the French Revolution. They learn about the three estates, Louis XIV and Versailles, Marie Antoinette, the fall of the Bastille, the Reign of Terror, and the rise and fall of Napoleon Bonaparte. (See also Language Arts Grade 6: Dickens's *A Tale of Two Cities*; and Visual Arts Grade 6, David and Delacroix.)

Students go on to examine the social and cultural movement known as Romanticism. They learn about the ideas of Jean-Jacques Rousseau. They are introduced to Romanticism in literature (see for example poems of Wordsworth and Byron; Language Arts Grade 6), in painting (see Visual Arts Grade 6), and in music (see Music Grade 6).

Students study the great changes brought about by the Industrial Revolution. They learn about the factory system, and the growing divide between social classes. They explore the competing ideas and values of capitalism and socialism, and are introduced to Karl Marx's theory of class struggle. (Note: these topics can be connected, historically and thematically, to the sixth-grade study of American history, which is focused on approximately concurrent topics.)

Students are introduced to major figures and events in Latin American independence movements. They learn about Toussaint L'Ouverture and the Haitian Revolution; about the Mexican revolutions, and the role of such leaders as Miguel Hidalgo and Benito Juárez; about Simón Bolívar and other Latin American "liberators"; and, about José Martí and the Cuban war for independence. They are also introduced to associated geography of Central America and South America.

American History and Geography: In sixth grade, students learn about America as it enters the modern age. They build upon their second-grade introduction to immigration. They learn about how America was shaped by great waves of immigration in the nineteenth century. They consider the meaning of the poem by Emma Lazarus inscribed on the Statue of Liberty. They examine how major cities were affected by new immigrants. They examine the "nativist" resistance to immigrants.

Students study how America was changed by industrialization and urbanization during the "Gilded Age." They examine the growth of organized labor, and learn about violent confrontations such as occurred at Haymarket Square. They consider the rise of big business, including such figures as Carnegie, Morgan, and Rockefeller. They learn about the growth of reform movements, including the "populist" movement and the appeal of William Jennings Bryan. They meet various reformers of the "Progressive" era, including the "muckrakers," Jane Addams, Jacob Riis, and President Theodore Roosevelt. They learn about those who worked for better lives for African-Americans, such as Ida Tarbell, Booker T. Washington, and W. E. B. Du Bois. They build on their fourth-grade introduction to reformers for women's rights as they learn about Susan B. Anthony and the campaign for woman's suffrage.

Students explore the troubling decisions and compromises faced by the emergence of America as a world power. They examine the main ideas, events, and debates associated with the increasingly complex role of the United States in international affairs, including the annexation of Hawaii, the Spanish-American War, war with the Philippines, and the case of the Panama Canal.

• **Grades 7 and 8:** Students in these grades will focus on selected topics in twentieth-century history and geography, for which guidelines are being developed by the Core Knowledge Foundation. Please call or write for more information.

WORLD HISTORY AND GEOGRAPHY

General Resources

> **The Core Knowledge Series:** *What Your Kindergartner–Sixth Grader Needs to Know*, E. D. Hirsch, Jr., editor. Published by Doubleday in hardcover and Dell in paperback.
>
> The seven current books in the Core Knowledge Series, one each for kindergarten through sixth grade, are the companion books to this resource guide. These illustrated books provide a convenient introduction to topics in the *Core Knowledge Sequence*, including the World History and Geography topics summarized on pages 94–101. Full of stories, poems, and discussions of topics in science, math, the visual arts, and music, the books can be read to children or, in the upper grades, read by children. All author's proceeds from the sale of *What Your Kindergartner–Sixth Grader Needs to Know* go to the nonprofit Core Knowledge Foundation to support its mission of helping parents and teachers help children develop strong early foundations of knowledge.

CC = a "Core Collection" book (see p. 8).

HISTORY RESOURCES AND REFERENCES

The Ancient World of the Bible
by Malcolm Day
Viking, 1994
This attractive book contains concise, skillful re-tellings of more than two dozen famous stories from the Bible, and places them in a larger context of history and geography. The book is organized in sections as follows: "The First People," "Abraham's Family," "The Israelites in Egypt," "The Promised Land," "David's Kingdom," "The Time of the Prophets," "The Exile." The text is supported by colorful illustrations, diagrams, maps, and photos of artifacts and landscapes that convey the environment of the Middle East and the daily life of ancient Israelites.

The Democracy Reader
edited by Diane Ravitch and Abigail Thernstrom
HarperCollins, 1993
This collection of great speeches and writings on the theme of democracy, including such works as the French Declaration of the Rights of Man and of the Citizen, is a valuable parent/teacher resource for the upper grades.

Festivals Together: A Guide to Multi-cultural Celebration
by Sue Fitzjohn, Minda Weston, and Judy Large
illustrated by John Gibbs with Sarah Fitzjohn and Abigail Large
Hawthorn Press, 1993
This book offers stories from various cultures and religious traditions (including Judaism, Is-

lam, Buddhism, and Hinduism) appropriate for reading aloud to young children, as well as suggested activities and songs designed to go along with the celebrations and festivals of various traditions. Ideas for hands-on activities make this a helpful resource for the teacher or parent who is introducing major world religions to children in the early grades. (Available from West Music: [800] 397-9378.)

Herstory: Women Who Changed the World
edited by Ruth Ashby and Deborah Gore Ohrn
Viking, 1995
This fascinating collection would make an excellent teacher/parent resource. It offers brief, well-written, upbeat biographical sketches of 120 women from Hatshepsut of ancient Egypt to contemporary Nobel laureate Rigoberta Menchú, and profiles many women specified in the *Core Knowledge Sequence,* including the Byzantine Empress Theodora, Joan of Arc, Queen Isabella I, Queen Elizabeth I, Deborah Sampson, Sacagawea, Sojourner Truth, Elizabeth Cady Stanton, Dorothea Dix, Margaret Fuller, Harriet Beecher Stowe, Elizabeth Blackwell, Jane Addams, Ida B. Wells, Marie Curie, Mary McLeod Bethune, Eleanor Roosevelt, and many more. Includes black-and-white illustrations and photographs, as well as an introduction by Gloria Steinem.

In the Beginning: The Nearly Complete History of Almost Everything
by Richard Platt
illustrated by Brian Delf
Dorling Kindersley, 1995
The scheme of this dazzlingly illustrated large-format volume is to take a subject—homes, clothing, bridges, cars, writing and printing—and trace its development through history. Concise captions with each image convey fascinating nuggets of information—how the Jeep got its name, why mailboxes at first failed (because messengers planted mice in them to eat the letters). A terrific browsing book for older children, and for teachers and parents as well. You may want to know that one section treats the

Big Bang theory of the creation of the universe, and another provides a detailed pictorial record of evolution. Of course the subtitle is a wild exaggeration, but it gets your attention, right? Includes a biographical index of inventors and engineers.

The Kingfisher Book of the Ancient World: From the Ice Age to the Fall of Rome
by Hazel Mary Martell
Kingfisher Books, 1995
Clearly written and generously illustrated, this overview of early civilizations will interest readers from about fourth grade up. The prehistory and migration routes of early peoples get strong treatment. There are brief discussions of early American, African, and Chinese civilizations, and more detailed presentations of the Mediterranean civilizations. A helpful teacher/parent resource, and a good book for older children to learn from.

The Kingfisher Illustrated History of the World
edited by Jack Zevin
Kingfisher Books, 1993
Attractively and informatively illustrated, this big general reference book is encyclopedic in scope and chronological in its presentation, beginning the story of humankind in the Ice Age and surveying it up to the collapse of the Soviet Union, all in about 750 pages. Besides the typical coverage of politics and war, it includes sections on art, buildings, communications, economics, food, religion, and science. Sidebars trace chronologies and offer thumbnail biographies. A helpful teacher/parent resource, and a good book for older children to pore over or use for research.

Knowledge Unlimited, Inc.
This is a mail-order company that offers many classroom teaching aids, especially on history (which they insist on calling "Social Studies"). You'll find big, colorful posters on ancient civilizations; hieroglyphics; great explorers; multicultural art; world religions; leaders, inventors, authors, and lots more. Also many videos, CD-

ROMs, and other curricular aids. Write or call for a catalog: Knowledge Unlimited, P.O. Box 52, Madison, WI 53701-0052; (800) 356-2303.

My First Book of Biographies: Great Men and Women Every Child Should Know
by Jean Marzollo
illustrated by Irene Trivas
Scholastic, 1994
A collection of forty-five short biographies, good for reading aloud to young children, each accompanied with a color drawing. The book offers sketches of Rachel Carson, George Washington Carver, Cesar Chavez, Walt Disney, Amelia Earhart, Albert Einstein, Duke Ellington, Mohandas Gandhi, Katsushika Hokusai, Helen Keller and Annie Sullivan, Rosa Parks, Yo-Yo Ma, Jesse Owens, Beatrix Potter, Sequoya, and many more.

Questions and Answers About Explorers
by Christopher Maynard
Kingfisher Books, 1995
With large, informative illustrations and short simple texts, readable by children in about third grade and up, this attractive book touches on high points of exploration by asking the sort of questions children ask: Why leave home in the first place? How did explorers figure out where they were headed? The stories of Marco Polo, Ibn Batuta, Columbus, Captain Cook, and Stanley and Livingstone are told, as are the exploits of Arab sailors, ancient Egyptians, and the seekers of the Northwest Passage, among others.

Social Studies School Service
This is a mail-order company that offers many books (including some recommended in this resource guide) and classroom teaching aids, including activity books, posters, software, videos, and more. The materials vary greatly in quality, but there's enough good stuff here to make it worth your while to write or call for their K–6 catalog: 10200 Jefferson Boulevard, Room P31, P.O. Box 802, Culver City, CA 90232-0802; (800) 421-4246.

Wonders of the World
by Giovanni Caselli
Dorling Kindersley, 1992
Here's an attractive collection that can help you see many of the human creations that are part of the study of history recommended in the *Core Knowledge Sequence*. The fabled monuments of the ancients (pyramids, ziggurats, Hanging Gardens, Colossus, the lighthouse of Alexandria) and the achievements of later builders (Gothic cathedrals, the Eiffel Tower, the Statue of Liberty) are appealingly drawn on a big show-and-tell scale and accompanied by short descriptions. Also included are the giant statue of Buddha in Myanmar (Burma) and the Taj Mahal, and, as a last word, the world's tallest modern skyscrapers.

SERIES

Ancient Civilizations Time Traveler series
by Jane Pofahl
T. S. Denison and Company
These activity books say they're meant for grades three and up but we think that's too high an estimate, and that they can be used or adapted for use in grades one and two. They offer black-line reproducible pages with writing activities, games, pictures, and patterns for hands-on projects. Titles in the series include *Mesopotamia, Egypt, Greece,* and *Rome.* Like most such books, they're a mix of good ideas and fluff, so use with discretion. Available in many teacher's supply stores, or call Knowledge Unlimited ([800] 356-2303) or Social Studies School Service ([800] 421-4246).

The Ancient World series
Silver Burdett
Each volume in this series, written for middle school and above, focuses on a different ancient culture, and offers brief discussions of family life, religion, governments, art and architecture, transportation and communication. Illustrated with color photos, drawings, diagrams, and maps. There are separate volumes on the an-

cient Aztecs, Chinese, Egyptians, Greeks, Incas, Israelites, Japanese, Mayas, Phoenicians, Romans, Sumerians, and Vikings. Good teacher/parent resources.

Bellerophon Activity Books
Bellerophon produces many coloring books, as well as paper doll books, on a variety of topics in both world and American history and geography. Drawings in some of the coloring books may be too intricate or detailed for very young children; in the grade-level listings that follow, we recommend some individual titles that we think are appropriate. Note that the written text accompanying the drawings is directed toward older readers, and is marked by a sometimes offbeat humor. For a catalog, send a long envelope with three first-class stamps to Bellerophon Books, 122 Helena Avenue, Santa Barbara, CA 93101.

Dover Activity Books
Dover offers a variety of fun activity books for children. Their coloring books have detailed line illustrations, sometimes a bit too detailed for very young children, with useful historical information (written for adults, not children). Coloring book titles include: *Knights and Armor, Life in a Medieval Castle and Village, Cathedrals of the World, Uniforms of the Napoleonic Wars,* and *Story of the Vikings.* Dover's "Cut and Assemble" books present the pieces for scale models of historically accurate buildings and models, including, for example, a medieval castle, an English village, and an Egyptian mummy case. They also offer paper dolls representing a variety of times and places. For a catalog, write Dover Publications, 31 East Second Street, Mineola, NY 11501.

The Inside Story series
Peter Bedrick Books
The books in this series contain detailed accounts of engineering and architectural techniques from the past, as well as information on daily life of the times. Precisely detailed color illustrations and informative text blocks are aimed at upper-level students, although younger readers can learn from looking at the pictures with you. Titles include *An Egyptian Pyramid, A Greek Temple, A Medieval Cathedral,* and *The Voice of the Middle Ages.*

New True Book series
Childrens Press
There are New True Books in many fields, not just history and geography, and they are generally reliable and informative, like mini-encyclopedia articles for children. They are some of the few nonfiction books written for the beginning reader, in short sentences and big type, suitable for reading aloud, but meant for children to read independently in about second or third grade and up (we approximate because some of the books are more challenging than others). Each volume has plenty of color illustrations on every page and concludes with a glossary and an index.

The See Through History series
Viking
These books rely primarily on their visuals to convey major periods of history. On large-format pages, they combine detailed color illustrations and brief, informative blocks of text. Each volume includes four see-through plastic overlays, so the reader can peer into the "anatomy" of historic buildings, vessels, and neighborhoods. Currently the series includes *Ancient Egypt, Ancient Greece, Ancient Rome, The Aztecs, The Middle Ages, The Renaissance, The Vikings,* and *The Industrial Revolution.*

Young Discovery Library
These pocket-sized hardcover (but not expensive) books, originally published by Éditions Gallimard in French, introduce thematic topics in history and geography with color illustrations and simple text, readable by children in about third grade and up. Each page presents a key idea, and the topic sentence is set in boldface type. Titles include *The Barbarians; Cathedrals: Stone Upon Stone; Japan: Land of Samurai and Robots; On the Banks of the Pharaoh's Nile.* For a

catalog, write to Young Discovery Library, 217 Main Street, Ossining, NY 10562, or call (800) 343-7854.

GEOGRAPHY RESOURCES AND REFERENCES

CC *Circling the Globe: A Young People's Guide to Countries and Cultures of the World*
Kingfisher Books, 1995
A big, heavy, excellent reference book, readable from about fourth grade and up. All the world's nearly two hundred independent countries are individually presented in this attractive encyclopedia of world geography. Larger countries get at least four pages of description, photographs, and illustrations, along with a good but not very large map. The USA, Russia, China, Japan, and the industrialized nations of Europe get several pages each, organized by major topics like economy, geography, history, and people. The book also includes sections on global topics such as the oceans, the earth's formation and geological history, world population and environmental issues, mapmaking and geographical terms. Includes a comprehensive index.

CC *Geography From A to Z: A Picture Glossary*
by Jack Knowlton
illustrated by Harriett Barton
HarperCollins, 1988
This glossary uses colorful illustrations to introduce sixty-three terms for geographic features such as *island, lake, gulch, sound, strait, palisade,* and *isthmus*. It is an excellent resource, especially helpful for showing younger children the meaning of some funny-sounding terms. Just dip in and read aloud—it's more fun than you might think. Children in about third grade and up can read it independently.

CC = "Core Collection" book (see page 8).

Janice VanCleave's Geography for Every Kid: Easy Activities That Make Learning Geography Fun
Janice VanCleave
John Wiley & Sons, 1993
The subtitle pretty much sums up this friendly little book, written for children ages 8 to 12. The author suggests many questions to ask and things to do to get children thinking about geography. Chapters address such topics as "The Earth in Space," "The History of Mapmaking," "Explorers," "Global Addresses," "Mapping a Sphere: The Earth," "Using a Map Scale," "Finding Places," "Compass Rose," "Mapping the Ocean Floor," "Contour Mapping," "Time Zones," and more. Many line drawings.

Maps and Globes
by Ray Broekel
Childrens Press, 1983
Beginning readers can navigate this New True Book, written in simple language and large-sized type, and illustrated throughout. It presents geographic terms and concepts, and discusses how to use maps and globes. Appropriate for strong third-grade readers and up.

CC *Maps and Globes*
by Jack Knowlton
illustrated by Harriet Barton
HarperCollins, 1985
A wonderful, easy-to-read (in about third grade and up), clear introduction to all kinds of maps, globes, and basic elements of geography, this book explains concepts such as hemisphere, latitude and longitude, elevation, and contour maps. With friendly, colorful illustrations.

The Visual Dictionary of the Earth
edited by Geoffrey Stalker
Dorling Kindersley, 1993
Part of the *Eyewitness Visual Dictionaries* series, this is an attractive, beautifully designed reference book. The illustrations are extremely clear, and many are large enough to hold up to show a group. Its cross-section diagrams vividly illustrate the "insides" of mountains, oceans, and

many other landforms. A helpful book for teachers to show geographic terms and concepts.

Where on Earth: A Geografunny Guide to the Globe
by Paul Rosenthal
illustrated by Marc Rosenthal
Alfred A. Knopf, 1992
This book offers a hip, entertaining introduction to the seven continents. Its clear, often funny analogies and examples put difficult or abstract information in perspective. For example, "imagine that the Earth is a bowl of breakfast cereal. The land would take up about as much room as four round banana slices adrift in all that milk." This might be the book that engages older children otherwise not enthusiastic about the subject of geography.

ATLASES

Children's Atlas of Civilizations
by Antony Mason
Millbrook, 1994
Best for third grade and up, this colorful oversized volume may help adults teaching the earlier grades too. It presents the ancient civilizations of the world continent by continent, from the Stone Age to the Renaissance. Asian civilizations, such as the Aryans and the Guptas of India and the Chinese dynasties, are covered well, but African civilizations are covered scantily. More than three dozen subjects each get two-page spreads, including a short description of the culture, a map, photographs of artifacts, and sidebars with particular points of interest. The illustrations are plentiful and helpful, though some maps are short on detail, small, or awkwardly cut off from surrounding regions.

Children's Atlas of Exploration
by Antony Mason
Millbrook, 1993
An interesting book for adults and children alike, this atlas reproduces ancient maps beside modern ones, and uses period art and vintage photographs beside quality modern photography to accompany its informative and lively text. Following the format of the *Children's Atlas of Civilizations*, listed above, this volume presents famous explorers—Alexander the Great, the Vikings, Marco Polo—as well as Egyptian explorations of Africa under the pharaohs, Jesuit missions into Asia, Darwin's travels, adventurers at the poles and on the threshold of space. Amply illustrated with color photographs and drawings, and with good, simple maps.

Children's Atlas of People and Places
by Jenny Wood
Millbrook, 1993
This colorfully and generously illustrated book provides maps and text on climate, the distribution of resources, political boundaries, dominant physical features, national flags, local building styles, and costume. Scanning the world's countries continent by continent, this book can serve as a teacher/parent resource for the early grades, and is readable by older children on their own. The simple maps show topographical features and locations of major cities, and are accompanied by a small graphic of a globe showing where in the world the mapped country is located.

The Doubleday Children's Atlas
edited by Jane Olliver
Doubleday, 1987
An informative and easy-on-the-eye book for children in the upper elementary grades, this atlas, organized by continent and within those sections by country or groups of countries, provides good-sized physical maps, a few paragraphs of text about a country or region, pictures of the countries' flags, photographs of often famous places or landmarks, and an appendix of fact charts. This atlas does not offer the dazzling array of pictures you can find in some others, but that may be a virtue, as its pages are uncluttered by potentially distracting little images.

The Eyewitness Atlas of the World
Dorling Kindersley, 1994
This very big, colorful, busy book combines the features of an atlas—large, detailed maps, by region or by nation, and a thorough index to everything on them—with the features of the popular Eyewitness books, that is, a wealth of stunning pictures, with bits of text that invite browsing and add geographical, economic, and cultural information to each map. Organized by continent, the book begins each section with a two-page spread on physical geography (landscapes, climate, animals, vegetation), then proceeds to look at the "human geography" of countries or groups of countries, providing information both important and trivial (did you know that "it has been calculated that in every second of the day, two hundred Americans are eating a hamburger"?).

The Great Atlas of Discovery
by Neil Grant
illustrated by Peter Morter
Alfred A. Knopf, 1992
The earliest explorers—the Phoenicians, Vikings, ancient Chinese, and Marco Polo—all receive brief treatment in this superbly illustrated, large-format volume, useful for children in the upper elementary grades. The book is a collage of words and pictures, not a straightforward narrative. Most of the book is devoted to explorations by Europeans since the late fifteenth century. The attractive, watercolor-style maps emphasize journey routes and physical features.

CC *New Puffin Children's World Atlas: An Introductory Atlas for Young People*
by Jacqueline Tivers and Michael Day
Puffin Books, 1994
An excellent first book of world maps, with twenty simplified maps showing contours and locations of countries, mountains, essential resources, predominant agriculture and industry. Genial icons (a cow, stacked logs, a fish) help draw children's attention to different features. Bold outlines clearly convey the shapes of different countries. Accompanying photographs

show representative people and places. This is a friendly little book for children in the primary grades.

Rand McNally Children's Atlas of World History
Rand McNally, 1991 (revised printing)
A useful book for children in the upper elementary grades, this atlas takes you on a whirlwind tour of history from the Stone Age to the Space Age. Two-page spreads focus on a civilization or theme, such as "Mesopotamia," "Egypt," "The Bible Lands," "Ancient Greece," "Travel and Trade," "The Spread of Christianity," "The Rise of Islam," "America Before Columbus," "Renaissance and Reformation," "The Empire Builders," "The Industrial Revolution," and more. Brief essays lightly touch upon major events, and a few color illustrations (thankfully, not too many, which can clutter the page) accompany good-sized maps that show topographical features. A very handy reference to have around.

Rand McNally Children's Atlas of World Wildlife
by Elizabeth G. Fagan
illustrated by Jan Wills
Rand McNally, 1990
Organized by continent, and within continent by regions (for example, Africa: Savanna, Rain Forest, Desert, East Africa, Madagascar), this informative atlas is a good teacher/parent resource, with good-sized topographical maps and, as the title indicates, information and many color pictures (both drawings and photographs) of animals around the world.

CC *Rand McNally Picture Atlas of the World*
by Richard Kemp
illustrated by Brian Delf
Rand McNally, 1993
An excellent atlas for older students, this book has beautiful physical and pictorial maps illuminated by illustrations showing representative highlights—plants, animals, architecture, natural

resources, and so on. Brief but informative essays accompany each map. There are also sections on such interesting topics as "Where People Live" and "The Biggest, Highest, and Longest on Earth."

The Young People's Atlas of the United States
by James Harrison and Eleanor Van Zandt
Kingfisher Books, 1992
Remember when you had to do that report on one of the fifty states? Well, this oversized, generously illustrated book would have come in handy. First it gives an overview of the U.S. by region, then devotes a two-page spread to each state, providing the state nickname, symbols (bird, tree, flower), relief map, fact boxes, pictures of famous persons, and color illustrations and photographs. That's a lot of visual information, but because the book is so big the pages don't look cluttered. The text is readable by students in the upper elementary grades.

PERIODICALS

Calliope
Calliope is a magazine about world history for young readers in about fifth to eighth grade. Each issue focuses upon a specific topic—for example, "Pharaohs of Egypt," "Islamic Spain," and "Independence Movements of Spanish South America." Clearly written articles illustrated in black and white are accompanied by features such as related literature, etymology of words, hands-on activities, and current-day features by scholars in the field. Many libraries

subscribe to *Calliope*. Subscriptions and back issues are available; call (800) 821-0115, or write to Cobblestone Publishing, 7 School Street, Peterborough, NH 03458.

CC *Kids Discover*
This is an excellent, engaging magazine designed to get kids from about ages 7 to 12 interested in geography, science, and history. Each issue is devoted to a single topic, such as Australia, Columbus, or Knights and Castles. The illustrations, photographs, and design are first rate, lively but not too busy, and most issues have a game, puzzle, or other activity. Kids in fourth grade and up should be able to read it independently. Published monthly September through June; back issues are available. Write or call Kids Discover, 170 Fifth Avenue, New York, NY 10010. (212) 242-5133; fax (212) 242-5628.

National Geographic World
This is "the official magazine for junior members of the National Geographic Society," appropriate for children in about grades 4–7. It's an odd mix of lively articles on geographic topics—for example, "Backyard Bugs," "Hot Spot: Rome," and "Saving Orangutans"—and more frenzied pieces on cool-neat-rad stuff like "Meet the Simpsons' Creator" and "Bankshot: A New Ball Game." Oh, well, maybe the *National Geographic* people think a spoonful of sugar makes the medicine go down. Very slick, with a flashy, busy layout, sometimes hard to distinguish from advertising (though the magazine accepts no ads). Subscriptions are available by becoming a "junior member"; call (800) 647-5463.

WORLD HISTORY AND GEOGRAPHY

Kindergarten

See also World History and Geography: General Resources.

See also Music General Resources: Multicultural Music for song tapes and books that suggest activities you can connect with the introduction of different continents and countries.

See also Language Arts: Kindergarten for many stories that you can connect with the introduction of different continents and countries.

A *Is for Africa*
written and photographed by Ifeoma Onyefulu
Cobblehill Books, 1993
"This alphabet is based on my own favorite images of the Africa I know," writes the Nigerian author of this book. Colorful, lively photos portray the people and customs of Africa, and a bit of text on each page helps explain how the photos and their topics typify Africa today.

New True Book series (on the continents)
Childrens Press
There's a New True Book on each of the seven continents. The titles—surprise!—are *Africa, Antarctica, Asia, Australia, Europe, North America, South America*. The books convey information in simple language, large-format type, and small color photographs on every page. The books go into more detail than you will probably want to share with kindergartners, but parts can be read aloud, and the many pictures can be very helpful.

CC *New Puffin Children's World Atlas: An Introductory Atlas for Young People*
by Jacqueline Tivers and Michael Day
Puffin Books, 1994
An excellent first book of world maps, with twenty simplified maps showing contours and locations of countries, mountains, essential resources, predominant agriculture and industry. Accompanying photographs show representative scenes. A good book to look at and talk about with kindergartners.

What Your Kindergartner Needs to Know
edited by E. D. Hirsch, Jr., and John Holdren
Doubleday, 1996
The World History and Geography section of this book presents a friendly and engaging introduction to our big world and some of the people and places in it. It offers a read-aloud world tour that takes your child to each of the seven continents, with pictures of interesting wildlife, familiar landmarks, and more. With color maps and illustrations.

WORLD HISTORY AND GEOGRAPHY

Grade 1

ANCIENT CIVILIZATIONS

Ancient Civilizations: Mesopotamia
by Jane Pofahl
T. S. Denison and Company, 1993
This activity book is part of the "Ancient Civilizations Time Traveler Series" meant for grades three and up, but which can readily be adapted for use with younger children. It offers blackline reproducible pages with writing activities, games, pictures of the ziggurat at Ur, and patterns for hands-on projects. Available in many teacher's supply stores, or call Knowledge Unlimited ([800] 356-2303) or Social Studies School Service ([800] 421-4246).

The Ancient Near East: A Bellerophon Coloring Book
Bellerophon Books, 1992
Ready-to-color line drawings of gods, heroes, animals, and scenes convey some sense of the ancient cultures of Mesopotamia, Assyria, and Persia. A little bit of text (for older readers) helps to identify the subject matter of each drawing. Includes scenes such as "Gilgamesh conquers two bulls" and "Gilgamesh grappling with a lion"; "Hammurabi receives the laws"; and, winged lions and other neat creatures. (For Bellerophon address, see page 106.)

CC *Gilgamesh the King*
retold and illustrated by Ludmila Zeman
Tundra Books, 1992
Powerful illustrations accompany this picture-book retelling of the world's oldest story of the god-man who learns what it means to be human. It was first told by the Sumerians, who wrote it on clay tablets found in Iraq and Syria in the nineteenth century. Zeman tells it in simple prose and colorful, detailed pictures. (Note: there is what you might call a "love scene" in this children's story, though you might not notice if you aren't looking for it. It's all very sweet and not at all erotic, but read it yourself first to see if you have any problem with the fact that Enkidu and Shamhat "explored the ways of love together.")

Mesopotamia
by Rosalind Bayley
Butterfly Books/Librairie du Liban, 1991
This book, which appears to be imported and translated (though no translator or illustrator is credited), is written for middle school students but useful here as a teacher/parent resource and for its many color pictures, including images of a scribe writing cuneiform, the ziggurat at Ur, the city of Babylon, and the Ishtar Gate.

"Mesopotamia"
A helpful teacher/parent resource, and a source of good ideas that could be adapted for use with younger children, this is the September/October 1993 issue of *Calliope*, a magazine about world history for children in the upper elementary grades and above. This issue provides lively and brief articles on historical topics (including Hammurabi and Babylon), stories and myths, and craft projects. (See address, page 110.)

CC = "Core Collection" book (see page 8).

Ancient Egypt

Ancient Egypt **(1990)**
    by George Hart
Mummy **(1993)**
    by James Putnam
Pyramid **(1993)**
    by James Putnam
    Alfred A. Knopf
Three Eyewitness books with words well beyond a first-grade level, but great pictures, like having a little museum in your home or classroom. *Ancient Egypt* is an excellent resource on art, culture, and daily life, with many drawings and photographs of artifacts. *Pyramid* includes a few pyramids from outside Egypt but concentrates on those around the Nile. *Mummy* has chapters on "Making a Mummy," "Mummy Masks," and "Curse of the Mummy," with fascinating photos of artifacts from Egypt and other cultures that practiced mummification.

CC *Bill and Pete Go down the Nile*
written and illustrated by Tomi dePaola
G. P. Putnam's Sons, 1987
History? No, not really. But along the way in this quirky, charming, funny story about Bill (a crocodile) and his friend Pete (his toothbrush—a bird, of course) you'll encounter the Nile, mummies, sarcophaguses, and more. A sample: " 'Today we learned about the stinks, Mama,' said Bill. 'You mean *sphinx*, Bill,' said Pete."

A Coloring Book of Ancient Egypt **(1994)**
Tut-Ankh-Amun and His Friends **(1995)**
by Cyril Aldred
Bellerophon Books
Here are two good coloring books from which you can pick pages to go along with what your children are learning about ancient Egypt. The line drawings are adapted from ancient Egyptian art, ready for coloring. Informative captions describe the pictures, but the prose is for adults. There is a good line drawing of the famous bust of Queen Nefertiti in the *Tut-Ankh-Amun and His Friends* book. (See address, page 106.)

The Egyptian Cinderella
by Shirley Climo
illustrated by Ruth Heller
HarperCollins, 1989
Vivid, colorful, and informative illustrations distinguish this story of Rhodopis, a slave girl who loses her slipper, but then it ends up in the hands of the pharaoh, and—well, you know the rest. A fun read-aloud.

Life in Ancient Egypt Coloring Book **(1989)**
    text by Stanley Appelbaum
    illustrations by John Green
Cut and Make Egyptian Masks **(1993)**
    by A. G. Smith and Josie Hazen
Egyptian Punch-Out Mummy Case **(1993)**
    by A. G. Smith
    Dover
Hands-on activities from Dover (see address, page 106). The coloring book features detailed, full-page line drawings of the arts, crafts, architecture, and daily life of ancient Egypt, with explanatory captions that will help adults interpret the images for children. The booklet of five authentic masks is printed on high-quality paper, ready to cut and assemble, and includes King Tut, the jackal god Anubis, and the falcon god Horus. First graders will need help making the masks. They will also need help making the "punch-out mummy case," but they will enjoy the product: an historically accurate mummy sarcophagus, $11 \times 4 \times 3 \frac{1}{2}$ inches assembled.

Fun with Hieroglyphics
by Catherine Roehrig
Viking, 1990
This activity kit, complete with twenty-four rubber stamps and a book explaining the meaning and practice of writing through hieroglyphics, introduces children to this Egyptian form of picture writing. The stamps allow children to express themselves the Egyptian way. The kit is prepared with historical accuracy by the curator of the Egyptian collection of the Metropolitan Museum of Art.

CC *I Wonder Why Pyramids Were Built and Other Questions About Ancient Egypt*
by Philip Steele
Kingfisher Books, 1995
This big book has lots of color drawings, some realistic and some cartoonish, that go along with text written in a lively, sometimes humorous question-and-answer format. Questions include: "Could a woman be a pharaoh? Why were mummies brainless? Why were the pyramids built? Who made mud pies? Who looked really cool? Did Egyptians like parties? Did people have pets? Why is paper called paper?" Informative and fun.

Into the Mummy's Tomb: The Real Life Discovery of Tutankhamun's Treasures
by Nicholas Reeves
Scholastic, 1993
This book uses the experience of early twentieth-century archaeologists as a path into the discovery of King Tut's tomb and the riches of his culture. Intended for older readers, the book will nonetheless captivate first graders with its many color illustrations and photographs, while adults can adapt and retell its fascinating stories about the Egyptian boy-king and those who discovered his remains.

Mummies Made in Egypt
written and illustrated by Aliki
HarperCollins, 1979
In a quiet, matter-of-fact tone, and with her characteristically detailed and friendly-looking drawings, Aliki explains everything you want to know about mummies, sure to elicit lots of ooos and ahhs and ughs when you read this aloud. A Reading Rainbow selection.

On the Banks of the Pharaoh's Nile
by Corinne Courtalon
illustrated by Christian Broutin
Young Discovery Library, 1988
This little book brings together a lot of information about ancient Egypt. Color illustrations are sometimes realistic, sometimes reminiscent of ancient Egyptian art. A good read-aloud. Part of

the Young Discovery Library, listed under World History General Resources: Series.

Temple Cat
by Andrew Clements
illustrated by Kate Kiesler
Clarion Books, 1996
This is the delightful story of a cat who grows tired of being worshiped as a god and escapes into the real world beyond the temple. Beautiful illustrations convey a lot of information about ancient Egypt.

CC *Tut's Mummy: Lost . . . and Found*
by Judy Donnelly
illustrated by James Watling
Random House, 1988
This is a "Step into Reading" book (intended for grades 2–3) that begins with a chapter about the death of Tutankhamen and then describes the twentieth-century discovery of the tomb and its treasures. It would make an engaging read-aloud, because it gets across a lot of history in a way that emphasizes the story. It is illustrated on every page with a few photographs and with color pictures.

HISTORY OF WORLD RELIGIONS

General Reference: Teacher/Parent Resources

Note: The following books are not written for young children but are valuable resources for parents and teachers. Some provide text that may be adapted for use in first grade.

The Ancient World of the Bible
by Malcolm Day
Viking, 1994
See description under World History General Resources: History Resources and References.

Beliefs and Believers
by Michael Pollard
Garrett Educational Corporation, 1992
An informative but brief reference book on many of the world's religions written for the upper elementary and middle school grades. Specific sections could be adapted for first graders, particularly the section on Islam. Good (but small) photos accompany the text.

Comparing Religions **series**
Thomson Learning, 1993
A very thoughtful series of five slender volumes comparing different aspects of world religions. Some sections could be read or adapted to first grade. The five titles in the series are *Birth Customs, Food and Fasting, Pilgrimages and Journeys, Initiation Customs,* and *Death Customs.*

How Do You Spell **God?** *Answers to the Big Questions from Around the World*
by Rabbi Marc Gellman and Monsignor Thomas Hartman
illustrated by Jos. A. Smith
Morrow Junior Books, 1995
Intended for upper elementary students, but a marvelous resource to help teach the history of world religions in the primary grades. The text is engaging, balanced, sensitive, and often humorous. There are chapters on such topics as: "How Are Religions Different?" "What Question Does Each Religion Want to Answer the Most?" "What Are the Holy Books?" "Where Are the Holy Places?" "Why Do Religions Split Up?" "How Do You Build a House for God?" This book, written by a Rabbi and a Catholic priest, was endorsed by everyone from the Dalai Lama to the National Council of Islamic Affairs.

CC = "Core Collection" book (see page 8).

Stories from Sacred Texts

Note: The books listed here are retellings or picture book versions of stories from the sacred texts of Judaism, Christianity, and Islam, suitable for reading aloud in first grade.

A Child Is Born: The Christmas Story
by Elizabeth Winthrop
illustrated by Charles Mikolaycak
Holiday House, 1983
Winthrop faithfully adapts Biblical texts for understanding by young children. The dramatic illustrations carry this very fine book.

A Child's First Bible
by Sandol Stoddard
illustrated by Tony Chen
Dial Books, 1990
This is a lovely compilation of basic Bible stories, told with simplicity and grace, each story no more than a page, and each accompanied by one of Tony Chen's superb illustrations.

A Coloring Book of the Old Testament
A Coloring Book of the New Testament
Bellerophon Books, 1992
Two fine coloring books to accompany activities at home or school with illustrations from artists of the Middle Ages. (See address, page 106.)

The Easter Story
written and illustrated by Carol Heyer
Ideals, 1990
Despite the title, this beautiful picture book follows the life of Jesus from birth to resurrection. The haunting illustrations are through the eyes of Jesus—the reader never actually sees Jesus's face.

Esther's Story
by Diane Wolkstein
illustrated by Juan Wijngaard
William Morrow, 1996
A stunningly illustrated retelling of the story in which one woman's courage and faithfulness save her people. When the king's advisor, Ha-

man, hatches a plot against the Jewish people, Queen Esther (whose husband does not know she is Jewish) intercedes for her people. She wins the king's support.

Exodus
written by Miriam Chaikin
illustrated by Charles Mikolaycak
Holiday House, 1987
This beautifully illustrated book tells the story of Moses leading the Hebrews out of Egyptian captivity.

CC *Festival of Freedom: The Story of Passover*
retold by Maida Silverman
illustrated by Carolyn S. Ewing
Simon & Schuster, 1988
Fine illustrations and age-appropriate text tell the story of the Exodus, including the captivity in Egypt, the life of Moses, the ten plagues, and deliverance of the children of Israel.

The First Christmas
illustrated with paintings from the National Gallery
Simon & Schuster, 1992
With text from the gospels of Matthew and Luke, the strength of this volume comes from the astonishing quality of the art. A visual treasure for the retelling of the Nativity story.

Hanukkah: The Festival of Lights
by Jenny Koralek
illustrated by Juan Wijngaard
Lothrop, Lee & Shepard, 1990
Haunting illustrations and dramatic text tell the story of Matathias and his sons retaking the temple from pagan invaders.

Islamic Calligraphy Coloring Book
by Ahmad Massasati
American Trust Publications, 1992
Islamic calligraphy has long been an art form as well as a means of communications. These beautiful reproducible pages allow children to

experience the intricacy and beauty of the patterns. (Publisher's address: 10900 West Washington Street, Indianapolis, IN 46231.)

Jonah and the Great Fish
    retold and illustrated by Warwick Hutton
    Atheneum, 1984
The Story of Jonah
    by Kurt Baumann
    illustrated by Allison Reed
    North-South Books, 1987
Here are two fine illustrated versions of the story of stubborn Jonah, who decides not to do the Lord's bidding and ends up in the belly of the whale. Both offer distinctive watercolor paintings and engaging text.

CC *Moses in the Bulrushes*
retold and illustrated by Warwick Hutton
Macmillan, 1986/Aladdin Books, 1992
In clear, simple, and balanced language, perfect for reading aloud, Warwick Hutton tells the story of the baby Moses, accompanied by gentle pen-and-watercolor illustrations.

CC *The Nativity*
illustrated by Ruth Sanderson
Little, Brown, 1993
With text from the gospels of Matthew and Luke, Ruth Sanderson's extraordinary artistic talents bring the Nativity story to life, from the announcement by the angel Gabriel to the birth of Jesus to flight into Egypt and return. Her book combines elaborate borders characteristic of illuminated manuscripts with Renaissance-inspired illustrations.

Noah's Ark
illustrated by Jane Ray
E. P. Dutton, 1990
The story is told in the words of the King James Bible and accompanied by the vibrant folk art illustrations of Jane Ray. Through its extraordinary art this book celebrates the wonder of creation and a world renewed.

CC *The Parables of Jesus*
retold and illustrated by Tomie de Paola
Holiday House, 1987
A bright and beautiful compilation of the stories
Jesus told to teach his followers. Tomie de
Paola's joyful art brightens each page.

CC *The Story of Hanukkah*
by Amy Ehrlich
illustrated by Ori Sherman
Dial Books, 1989
Dramatic illustrations and splendid, age-appropriate text distinguish this retelling of the Hanukkah story of the Maccabees' retaking of the
temple.

CC *Tales from the Old Testament*
as told by Jim Weiss
Greathall Productions
Not a book but a story tape. On this cassette,
storyteller Jim Weiss does an admirable job of
telling the stories of "Abraham and the Idols,"
"The Story of Ruth," "Noah and the Ark,"
"Queen Esther," "David and Goliath," "David's
Dance," and "Wise King Solomon." The tellings
are respectful, quietly dramatic, and, according
to the producers, "nondenominational." One of
many fine story tapes available from Greathall
Productions: (800) 477-6234.

When Solomon Was King
by Sheila MacGill-Callahan
illustrated by Stephen T. Johnson
Dial Books, 1995
A moving and beautifully illustrated story of
Solomon as a young boy, helping a wounded
lioness, learning the ways of mercy, and then as
a proud adult needing to relearn the lessons of
his youth.

CC = "Core Collection" book (see page 8).

Stories Inspired by World Religions

Note: These enjoyable stories are not from sacred texts but can help children understand
the religions that inspired them.

A Carol for Christmas
by Ann Tompert
illustrated by Laura Kelly
Macmillan, 1994
In a humble Austrian village the church organ
is broken and the parishioners will need a special hymn to lift their spirits on Christmas Eve.
This is a beautiful retelling of how the carol "Silent Night" came to be written.

CC *The Hundredth Name*
by Shulamith Levey Oppenheim
illustrated by Michael Hays
Boyds Mills Press, 1995
Salah, a Muslim child, wishes with all his heart
to lift the sadness of his friend and constant
companion, the camel Qadiim. This is a rich
story of a child's faith and the love that leads
him to ask Allah to reveal to Qadiim the hundredth name of God, which human beings can
never know. Set in Egypt and lavishly illustrated. (Publisher's address: 815 Church Street,
Honesdale, PA 18431; [800] 949-7777.)

In the Month of Kislev: A Story for Hanukkah
written and illustrated by Nina Jaffe
Viking, 1992
Impoverished Mendel the Peddler and his children teach their wealthy neighbors the meaning
of charity.

CC *Yussel's Prayer*
retold by Barbara Cohen
illustrated by Michael J. Deraney
Lothrop, Lee & Shepard, 1981
On the feast of Yom Kippur (Jewish Day of
Atonement) the wealthy merchants and well-ed-
ucated rabbi take time to pray, repent, and
spend the day in synagogue. Little Yussel, the
penniless and poorly educated shepherd boy, is

not allowed—there is work to be done. But in the end, it is Yussel's humble prayer that is heard by God, and his song teaches a lesson to the rabbi and merchants.

MEXICO

Note: For historical connections, see also American Civilization Grade 1: Introduction to Maya and Aztec civilizations; Conquistadors.

Count Your Way Through Mexico
by Jim Haskins
illustrations by Helen Byers
Carolrhoda Books, 1989
Using the numbers from one to ten, this book explores ten features of Mexican history and culture, including its Indian and Spanish heritage and some familiar Mexican foods. Each feature is explained in a brief paragraph and illustrated with an attractive colored-pencil drawing.

Fiesta! Mexico and Central America: A Global Awareness Program for Children in Grades 2–5
by Barbara Linse and Dick Judd
Fearon Teacher Aids, 1993
See description under Music General Resources: Multicultural Music.

CC *Mexico*
by Karen Jacobsen
Childrens Press, 1982
For a first-grade unit on Mexico, this little book could serve well as a central text for reading aloud and discussion. It's a New True Book, with big print, clear and simple language, and many colorful photographs and illustrations. It introduces the land and people of Mexico, discusses the Indian and Spanish heritage, and gives a glimpse of modern Mexico.

Mexico: The Culture
by Bobbie Kalman
Crabtree, 1993
Colorful photos and illustrations, narrated in short blocks of text, give the flavor of Mexican life, landscape, and culture. There are details in this book that will especially delight first graders, like the hand-clap rhyme, the recipes, and the instructions on how to make a piñata.

CC = "Core Collection" book (see page 8).

WORLD HISTORY AND GEOGRAPHY

Grade 2

INDIA

Count Your Way Through India
by Jim Haskins
illustrated by Liz Brenner Dodson
Carolrhoda Books, 1990
One of the *Count Your Way* series, this book uses the numbers one to ten to introduce children to, among other topics, the "Wheel of Law" symbol, Mohandas Gandhi, the Taj Mahal, *Diwali* (a Hindu festival), geography of India, wildlife, and Ravana the ten-headed demon. A fun and informative read-aloud, with color illustrations.

India: The Culture
by Bobbie Kalman
Crabtree, 1990
This book uses color photographs and straightforward explanatory text to explore present-day India, but also gives insight into ancient customs and religion relevant to the study of ancient India. Chapters include "Rooted in Religion," "Holy Water," "Everyday Crafts," and "Festivals and Celebrations." Good for reading aloud and sharing the pictures.

Living in India
by Anne Singh
illustrated by Aline Riquier
Young Discovery Library, 1988
While this book focuses on life in modern-day India, it offers useful information relevant to historical studies as well, including a discussion of climate, customs, castes, the Hindu religion, and the Ganges River. The language is clear and straightforward, good for reading aloud, and every page has color illustrations. Part of the Young Discovery Library, listed under World History General Resources: Series.

HINDUISM AND BUDDHISM

Ancient India: A Coloring Book
Bellerophon Books, 1991
A good activity book that offers line drawings of Hindu deities (Brahma, Vishnu, Shiva, and others) and of Buddha based on authentic art. (See address, page 106.)

CC Buddha
by Susan Roth
Doubleday, 1994
This beautiful picture book portrays the early years of Siddhārtha's life, from his birth to the time that he renounces his earthly existence, leaving riches, wife, and son to become a holy man. The text is sweet and simple, an excellent read-aloud, and every page is illustrated with exquisitely detailed cut-paper artwork.

CC The Cat Who Went to Heaven
by Elizabeth Coatsworth
Macmillan, 1930; 1958
This lovely chapter book chronicles the life of Siddhārtha Gautama, the Buddha, through the eyes of an impoverished Japanese artist who paints a mural for the temple, as well as through the eyes of his housekeeper and his cat, who desperately wants to be in the painting! A classic, great to read aloud.

Festivals Together: A Guide to Multi-cultural Celebration
by Sue Fitzjohn, Minda Weston, and Judy Large
illustrated by John Gibbs with Sarah Fitzjohn
    and Abigail Large
Hawthorn Press, 1993
See description under General Resources: History Resources and References.

The Golden Deer
by Margaret Hodges
illustrated by Daniel San Souci
Macmillan, 1992
Buddha, incarnated as a golden deer, protects his herd and is prepared to lay down his life to save the life of a pregnant doe. In the process he instructs a heedless king in the way of mercy to all creatures. One of Buddhism's *Jataka* tales (stories of Buddha's various incarnations). With lovely illustrations.

Hidden in Sand
by Margaret Hodges
illustrated by Paul Birling
Macmillan, 1994
Set in the Rajasthan Desert in northern India, this is the story of a small boy's tireless effort and enterprise to save his caravan from death in the desert. (One of the *Jataka* tales of Buddha's various incarnations.)

The Little Lama of Tibet
by Lois Raimondo
Scholastic, 1994
A great second-grade introduction to one of the spiritual leaders of Tibetan Buddhism, six-year-old Ling Rinpoche, the "little lama." Through photos and simple text children learn of the little lama's spiritual training, dress, and daily activity. We are also treated to the lama's words of advice to American children: "Number one: Everyone should study very hard. Number two: You should respect your teachers and take action according to the teachers' advices," and more.

Rama and Sita: A Folk Tale from India
written and illustrated by Govinder Ram
Peter Bedrick Books, 1988
Retold from Hinduism's *Ramayana*, this is the story of Princess Sita, who is captured by the King of the Demons. She is rescued by her beloved hero, Prince Rama, working with Hanuman, King of the Monkeys. Beautifully illustrated, this is one of the few picture-book presentations of basic stories of Hinduism.

CC *Sacred River*
written and illustrated by Ted Lewin
Clarion Books, 1995
A rich watercolor picture book presentation of Hinduism's most sacred river, the Ganges. More than one million pilgrims a year come to renew themselves at the Ganges. Exquisite art and simple, descriptive text give a vivid look at present-day devotionals and convey the bustling life and activities of modern Indians living near and visiting the Ganges.

Silent Lotus
written and illustrated by Jeanne M. Lee
Farrar, Straus & Giroux, 1991
A simple and elegant tale of a deaf-mute Hindu girl, who uses her talents to dance for the gods and worshipers in the temple of Angkor Wat (in Cambodia). Beautiful illustrations.

ANCIENT CHINA

Ancient China
by Robert Nicholson and Claire Watts
Chelsea House/Chelsea Juniors, 1994
This slender book is written for children in the upper elementary grades, but its text is clear enough that, with a little adaptation, you could effectively read parts of it aloud and share the many colorful pictures. It includes a variety of dynasties in its definition of "ancient" (Qin, Ming, etc.), with chapters on "The Great Wall," "The Forbidden City," "Inventions," "Paper," "Great Thinkers" (including Confucius), and more.

A Coloring Book of Ancient China
Bellerophon Books, 1991
These line drawings, ready for coloring, replicate a variety of ancient Chinese art, from a twelfth-century B.C. elephant-shaped vessel to a lion with wings to a portrait of Confucius. Brief notes identify each image. (See address, page 106.)

The Dragon's Robe
  written and illustrated by Deborah Nourse Lattimore
  HarperCollins, 1990
The Empty Pot
  written and illustrated by Demi
  Henry Holt, 1990
The Journey of Meng
  by Doreen Rappaport
  illustrated by Yang Ming-Yi
  Dial Books, 1991
The Seven Chinese Brothers
  by Margaret Mahy
  illustrated by Jean and Mou-sien Tseng
  Scholastic, 1990
These books are fiction, not history, but they can be used to supplement second-grade studies of ancient China. *The Dragon's Robe* is a magical story inspired by ancient Chinese art and reflects the history of Hui Tsung, the last emperor of the Northern Sung dynasty, in the thirteenth century. The story is engaging, and the magnificent illustrations reflect Chinese silkwork and brush-painting styles. *The Empty Pot* features Demi's characteristically delicate and lovely artwork. The story does not claim to have any roots in Chinese folklore, but this inspiring moral tale about a boy who lived "a long time ago in China" is too good to pass up. In *The Journey of Meng*, beautiful, foggy watercolor illustrations accompany an ancient (and sad) Chinese story of love, honor, and self-sacrifice. When Meng's husband is conscripted to build the Great Wall, she pursues a magical journey to bring him warm clothes, ultimately confronting the cruel emperor himself. The traditional Chinese tall tale, *The Seven Chinese Brothers*, pits seven clever brothers against Ch'in Shih

Huang, the emperor from the third century B.C. who masterminded the Great Wall of China. The story is engaging, the illustrations colorful and lively. A fine read-aloud. See also Language Arts Grade 2, Stories: *Tye May and the Magic Brush*.

CC *The Great Wall of China*
by Leonard Everett Fisher
Macmillan, 1986
Fisher's beautiful charcoal illustrations and brief, gripping text make this picture book about the building of the Great Wall powerful and interesting. Each page contains a phrase in Chinese calligraphy, translated at the end of the book.

Growing Up In Ancient China
by Ken Teague
illustrated by Richard Hook
Troll Associates, 1994
This little illustrated book explores ancient Chinese culture by focusing on various aspects of daily life through the experience of children: houses, clothing, school, travel, festivals, and more. A good read-aloud.

Lóng Is a Dragon: Chinese Writing for Children
by Peggy Goldstein
Scholastic, 1991
This book introduces several dozen Chinese characters, showing how they are written in ancient and modern Chinese, how they are pronounced, and what they mean. With guidance from adults, second graders could enjoy learning to write a little Chinese, thanks to this book.

JAPAN

A to Zen
by Ruth Wells
illustrated by Yoshi
Picture Book Studio, 1992
From the moment you open this clever book—reading pages from right to left—you enter the Japanese culture. The Roman alphabet letters

guide the tour, from *Aikido* to *Zen*, including *Hiroshima*, *Kimono*, *Origami*, and *Sushi*.

How My Parents Learned to Eat
by Ina R. Friedman
illustrated by Allen Say
Houghton Mifflin, 1984
CC *The Bicycle Man*
written and illustrated by Allen Say
Houghton Mifflin, 1982

Here are two works of fiction that would nicely supplement learning about Japan. Both have to do with interactions between Japanese and American characters. *How My Parents Learned to Eat* is told in the voice of a daughter of a Japanese mother and American father, who thinks back to the awkward moments during their courtship caused by the differences between forks and chopsticks. This is a subtle, charming story that says a lot about people and cultures, not just eating utensils. It has soft-toned, attractive illustrations by Allen Say, who is both the writer and illustrator of *The Bicycle Man*, a lyrical picture book that recalls the day when two American soldiers happen upon a schoolyard full of Japanese children. At first the children are scared and shy, but then, when one soldier begins to do tricks on the principal's bicycle, a kind of communication occurs that goes beyond words.

Japan
by Karen Jacobsen
Childrens Press, 1982

This New True Book, written in simple language and big print with many color illustrations, is good for reading aloud or for reading (with a little help) by many second graders. It discusses the geography of the island nation, the city of Tokyo, people, homes, food, education, sports, kabuki theater, and more.

CC *Japan: Land of Samurai and Robots*
by Laurence Ottenheimer
illustrated by Michelle Nikly
Young Discovery Library, 1988
Despite its silly title, this little book offers a lot of interesting information about Japan in an intelligent overview. The language is clear and straightforward, good for reading aloud, and every page has color illustrations. Topics include climate, homes, customs, schools, writing, holidays, judo and sumo, food, religion, and more. Part of the Young Discovery Library, listed under World History General Resources: Series.

ANCIENT GREECE
See also Language Arts Grade 2: Mythology of Ancient Greece.

American Classical League Catalog of Teaching Materials for Teachers of Latin, Greek, and Classical Humanities
This catalog lists a number of excellent resources relevant to ancient Greece, Rome, and classical mythology, including songbooks, coloring books, puzzle books, and activity books, as well as some textbooks. You can order it by writing to the American Classical League, Teaching Materials and Resource Center, Miami University, Oxford Ohio 45056; or, call (513) 529-7741.

Ancient Greece
by Daniel Cohen
illustrated by James Seward
Doubleday, 1990
This big and dramatically illustrated volume has brief sections on Achilles, Homer, the Minotaur, Atlantis, Greek geography, the Olympics, the Delphic Oracle, military life, rule by the people, the Persian Wars, Greek gods, drama, philosophers, the "Golden Age," the war between Athens and Sparta, Socrates, and Alexander the Great. There's a great deal in this book worth sharing, if you are willing to adapt the words for young ears.

Ancient Greece
by Robert Nicholson and Claire Watts
Chelsea House/Chelsea Juniors, 1994
This slender book is written for children in the

upper elementary grades, but its text is clear enough that, with some adaptation, you could effectively read parts of it aloud and share the many colorful pictures. Includes chapters on "City-States," "Citizens and Slaves," "Philosophers and Scientists," "Food," "Arts and Crafts," and "Growing Up." It also includes a brief discussion of "How We Know" about the ancient Greeks.

Ancient Greece
by Anne Pearson
Alfred A. Knopf, 1992
This Eyewitness book contains sharp color photos of many artifacts from ancient Greece: statues, ruins, friezes, vases. It's a beautiful book to look at, and the apparent age of many objects may help convey to children that *ancient* means really, really long ago.

A Coloring Book of Ancient Greece
     Bellerophon Books, 1994
Life in Ancient Greece Coloring Book
     by John Green
     Dover, 1993
The Bellerophon (see address, page 106) coloring book includes simple line drawings of figures and scenes from Greek mythology and ancient Greek life, all based on ancient art works: Hercules, Hermes, Cerberus, Theseus battling the Minotaur, Zeus, Hera, and even "Nike"— and it's not a shoe. Dover's *Life in Ancient Greece* coloring book features more detailed line drawings with informative captions (for adults to read), with pictures of domestic life, the naval battle at Salamis, boys at school, the marketplace in Athens, Olympian games, Plato teaching in the Academy, Aristotle tutoring the young Alexander, and more. (See address, page 106.)

CC *The Great Alexander the Great*
by Joe Lasker
Viking Penguin/Puffin Books, 1983, 1990
This little book conveys the high points in the life of Alexander. The author has dramatized key moments, so the book reads more like an adventure story, illustrated with energetic watercolors.

The Greeks
by A. Susan Williams
Thomson Learning, 1993
Though written for the upper elementary grades, this attractive book can be readily adapted for younger children as an introduction to ancient Greece. Its thirteen short chapters (each is a two-page spread) and excellent color pictures give just enough information about important topics, including language, buildings, theater, myths, sports, clothes, and culture.

Growing Up in Ancient Greece
by Chris Chelepi
illustrated by Chris Molan
Troll Associates, 1994
This little illustrated book imagines daily life in ancient Greece from the point of view of children living in that time. In simple, straightforward prose the author describes houses in the country and city, schools, festivals, the marketplace, and more. A good read-aloud.

GEOGRAPHY OF THE AMERICAS

Living in South America
by Chantal Henry-Biabaud
illustrated by Bernard Dagan
Young Discovery Library, 1991
This colorfully illustrated and informative little book begins with a brief glimpse into history, then discusses different regions and peoples of South America, wildlife in the Amazon jungles, modern Rio de Janeiro and São Paulo, and more. Clear and simple prose, good for reading aloud. Part of the Young Discovery Library, listed under World History General Resources: Series.

CC = "Core Collection" book (see page 8).

New Puffin Children's World Atlas: An
Introductory Atlas for Young People
by Jacqueline Tivers and Michael Day
Puffin Books, 1994
See description under World History General
Resources: Atlases.

North America **(1986)**
South America **(1986)**
by D. V. Georges
Childrens Press
These two New True Books, with large print

and simple language, give a brief overview
of the geography of North and South America. You can read aloud parts of these generously illustrated books to introduce children to
major mountain ranges, important seaports,
natural resources, and other interesting information.

CC = **"Core Collection"** book (see page 8).

WORLD HISTORY AND GEOGRAPHY

Grade 3

See also World History General Resources.

ANCIENT ROME

See also Language Arts Grade 3: More Myths of Ancient Greece and Rome.

American Classical League Catalog of Teaching Materials for Teachers of Latin, Greek, and Classical Humanities
See the description of this catalog under World Civilization Grade 2, Ancient Greece.

"Byzantium, Constantinople, Istanbul"
A teacher/parent resource, this November/December 1990 issue of *Calliope* (see address, page 110), the history magazine for young people, includes information on Constantine, Justinian, Theodora, Hagia Sophia, the legacy of the Byzantine Empire, and the coming of the Turks. For ordering information, see *Calliope* under World History General Resources: Periodicals.

A Coloring Book of Rome
Bellerophon Books, 1994
This book offers ready-to-color line drawings taken from ancient Roman art, especially portraits in sculpture, busts, and coins. Many drawings are accompanied by passages in Latin, translated alongside. (See address, page 106.)

The Dark Ages
by Tony Gregory
Facts on File, 1993
This is a good teacher/parent resource on the late Roman Empire and the rise of Byzantine civilization. Part of an *Illustrated History of the World* series, this book covers the fall of the Roman Empire, the Byzantine Empire, India, China and the silk road, and the rise of Islam, using a large-page format, an assortment of photos, drawings, maps, and charts. Eight informative, illustration-packed pages on the Byzantine Empire introduce Mediterranean trade; the city of Constantinople; Byzantine art and culture (including the Hagia Sophia); and Justinian and Theodora.

Everyday Life in Roman Times
by Mike Corbishley
Franklin Watts, 1994
This nicely designed book explores aspects of daily life in ancient Rome—food, housing, clothing, bathing, shopping, reading and writing, the theater—with brief informative paragraphs and a number of suggested activities: follow ancient Roman recipes for sweets, tie a toga accurately, learn to read and write the original Roman alphabet. Many color illustrations and clear writing make this a good read-aloud.

Growing Up in Ancient Rome
by Peter Corbishley
Troll Associates, 1994
This book introduces ancient Roman civilization by describing the daily life of young people, with illustrated sections on family, town and country, trade and shopping, festivals and ceremonies, and school. Strong third-grade readers may be able to read this with some help.

CC *Living in Ancient Rome*
by Odile Bombarde and Claude Moatti
illustrated by François Place
Young Discovery Library, 1988
Most third graders should be able to read this
informative, colorful, hold-in-your-hand size
book. In clear language and with plentiful illustrations, it tells what the city of ancient Rome
was like, how some Romans lived, what schools
were like, and, of course in extra detail, about
the games and gladiator fights in the Coliseum.
It briefly discusses the Roman armies and the
spread of the Roman empire. Part of the Young
Discovery Library, listed under World History
General Resources: Series.

"Pompeii"
Here's a typically lively and packed issue of the
children's magazine *Kids Discover* (see address,
page 110). The reading level may challenge
third graders, but the information is engaging,
and the many pictures fascinating. Includes a
discussion of how a volcano erupts, as well as
activities (a maze, an acrostic, a time capsule).

Pompeii . . . Buried Alive
by Edith Kunhardt
illustrated by Michael Eagle
Random House, 1987
This "Step into Reading" book (designated for
grades 2 and 3) relates the experience of living
in Pompeii during the eruption of Vesuvius. A
final chapter discusses archaeologists' finds in
the ruins. This should be easy reading for third
graders.

A Roman Villa
by Jacqueline Morley
illustrated by John James
Peter Bedrick Books, 1992
This highly detailed and primarily visual book
focuses on the design, construction, and daily
life of a villa, the typical upper-class Roman res-
idence. Many of the drawings include cutaways
to reveal interiors and emphasize examples of

Roman technical accomplishments, such as un-
der-floor heating.

The Romans
by Peter Crisp
Chelsea House/Chelsea Juniors, 1994
Very strong third grade readers could read this
on their own. The book provides brief, clear discussions of many topics, including: "The Roman
World," "The City of Rome," "Republic and
Emperors," "Slaves," "Gods and Temples,"
"Food," and "Clothes." It provides a good version of the legend of Romulus and Remus. It
offers directions for making a mosaic. Every
page has color illustrations, including a few excellent photographs of, for example, Roman
arches and the Forum as it looks today. It also
includes a brief discussion of "How We Know"
about the ancient Romans.

What Do We Know About the Romans?
by Mike Corbishley
Peter Bedrick Books, 1991
This book introduces ancient Roman history and
culture by using a question-and-answer format
that involves children in the pursuit of interesting information. It is also very attractively designed, has a glossary, word lists with Latin
roots, Roman numerals, and a time line and
maps.

THE VIKINGS

See also American History Grade 3: Early Exploration of North America. You may want to
study the Vikings after Rome and Byzantium
and before the European settlement of the
Americas, as a way of moving from the
World History to the American History topics
recommended for third grade in the *Core
Knowledge Sequence*.
See also, in connection with the Vikings, Language Arts Grade 3: Norse Mythology.

Growing Up in Viking Times
by Dominic Tweddle
illustrated by Angus McBride
Troll Associates, 1994
This slender illustrated book will answer children's questions about how the Vikings lived: their houses, clothes, food, education, beliefs, rules, ships, "trading and raiding," and more. An informative book with interesting details, suitable for reading aloud.

Story of the Vikings Coloring Book
by A. G. Smith
Dover, 1988
This Dover coloring book has line drawings of people, ships, villages, home life, raids, Erik the Red, and more. (See address, page 106.)

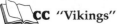 **CC** "Vikings"
This November 1995 issue of *Kids Discover* magazine (see address, page 110) is devoted to the Vikings. With excellent color illustrations, it describes the Vikings' love of ships and exploration, their governance by "Thing," Erik the Red, Leif Erikson, and much more.

The Vikings
by Robert Nicholson and Claire Watts
Scholastic, 1991
The cover says that inside you'll find "facts, stories, activities." There are facts about geography, longships, trade, runes, crafts, food, and clothing. There's a brief section on the Norse gods, and an okay story, "Thor Visits the Land of the Giants." Activities are few but feasible, such as making "Viking jewelry." Clearly written, but challenging vocabulary for many third graders. With vivid color photographs and color drawings on every page.

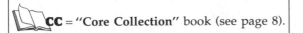
CC = "Core Collection" book (see page 8).

TOPICS IN GEOGRAPHY

Canada

Canada
by E. Schemenaur
Childrens Press, 1994
This New True Book, written in simple language and big print with many color illustrations, should be readable by third graders. It provides an introduction to the people, land, and natural resources of Canada.

Canada
by Donna Bailey
Raintree/Steck-Vaughn, 1992
Part of the "Where We Live" series, this book, told as though spoken by a child, introduces the land and people of Canada. With color photos and drawings. Most third graders should be able to read this book independently.

The Great St. Lawrence Seaway
written and illustrated by Gail Gibbons
William Morrow, 1992
This readable and colorfully illustrated book follows a ship as it carries a load of iron from an Atlantic seaport along the St. Lawrence to the Great Lakes.

Important Rivers of the World

"Rivers"
This is an issue of the excellent children's magazine, *Kids Discover*, with articles on great rivers of the world, river explorers, river ecosystems, and the water cycle. For ordering information, see address, page 110.

Minn of the Mississippi
written and illustrated by Holling Clancy
   Holling
Houghton Mifflin, 1951; 1979
"This is a book," the author writes, "about a river, and a turtle in it." The author has a gift

for understatement. This is a book about a great river and a little turtle, all right, but it's also about all sorts of fascinating topics in natural and human history. This is a book to read aloud, not quickly but, like the river, moving steadily ahead, taking your time, getting there whenever you get there. Illustrated on every page; a Newbery Honor Book. If you like this, try Holling's other wonderful books, *Paddle to the Sea* and *Seabird*.

"Up and Down Rivers"
This September 1987 issue of *Faces* ("The Magazine About People") has a number of short, in-

teresting articles on or related to important rivers, including two that might be helpful for this grade: "River Traffic," which takes you to rivers around the world; and "River Match," a game in which you match the name of a river with a fact about it. For ordering and pricing information, call (800) 821-0115, or write to Cobblestone Publishing, 7 School Street, Peterborough, NH 03458.

 **CC** = **"Core Collection"** book (see page 8).

WORLD HISTORY AND GEOGRAPHY

Grade 4

See also World History General Resources.

EUROPE IN THE MIDDLE AGES
See also Language Arts Grade 4: Legends of King Arthur and the Knights of the Round Table.

Anno's Medieval World
written and illustrated by Mitsumasa Anno
G. P. Putnam's Sons/Philomel Books, 1980
This ingenious picture book could, according to its author, bear a longer title: *How People Living in the Era of the Ptolemaic Theory Saw Their World.* With quiet, simple language and detailed, imaginative drawings of a town and its people, Anno dramatizes the changing concepts of world and self that must have gone through the minds of people as their sense of the world and their place in it slowly began to change. Of course the change is not as neat or swift as it comes across in this short book, but that is a quibble. A book for fourth graders to read independently, as well as a good read-aloud.

Canterbury Tales
by Geoffrey Chaucer
selected and retold by Barbara Cohen
illustrated by Trina Schart Hyman
Lothrop, Lee & Shepard, 1988
Not history but wonderful literature to complement your exploration of medieval times. Barbara Cohen has done a fine job of turning Chaucer's Middle English verse into readable, engaging modern English prose. She provides Chaucer's Prologue, which establishes the frame: pilgrims on their way to Canterbury

agree to pass the time by telling tales. We get four tales here, including the comic, mock-heroic tale of Chanticleer the rooster, told by the Nun's Priest; the dark moral fable told by the immoral Pardoner; and, the story that asks "What do women want most?" told by the irrepressible Wife of Bath. Wonderful for reading aloud or independently (though the text will be challenging for fourth graders), and gorgeously illustrated.

CC *Castles*
by Philip Steele
Kingfisher Books, 1995
This big, impressive, colorful picture book is readable by fourth graders. It is not a linear narrative but a collection of brief two-page spreads on a variety of topics, such as: "People and Power," "Building a Castle," "Gates and Walls," "Market Day," "Warriors and Arms," "Becoming a Knight," "Food and Drink," "The Great Hall," "The Chapel," "Hunting and Hawking," "The Joust," "Heraldry," "Under Attack," and more. Detailed color drawings on every page.

Castle (1994)
Knight (1993)
by Christopher Gravett
Alfred A. Knopf
Two Eyewitness Books that display abundant excellent photographs to help you see the Middle Ages. Text is brief; the pictures tell the story here. In *Castle,* several pages portray real people dressed in medieval costume and using medieval tools, like a crossbow and a carpenter's chisel. The twenty-nine pictorial chapters in *Knight* focus on separate topics such as armor,

tournaments, heraldry, the Crusades, arming for a fight, and the castle at peace.

Castle (1977)
Cathedral: The Story of Its Construction (1973)
written and illustrated by David Macaulay
Houghton Mifflin
Two fascinating books, both Caldecott Honor winners, from renowned author/illustrator David Macaulay. With short text and beautiful line drawings, Macaulay chronicles the construction of a medieval castle and a Gothic cathedral. The buildings are imaginary, but the processes of construction are so historically accurate and marvelously rendered from various perspectives that Macaulay was awarded a medal from the American Institute of Architects for *Cathedral*. *Castle* is also valuable for its detailed description of the process of construction, not just from an engineering perspective but as a social fact: we are reminded that the castle is not only the place where the lords and ladies feasted, but the place that quarrymen, blacksmiths, mortar makers, masons, carpenters, and diggers built (and let's not forget, as one humorous illustration notes, Master James's dog).

CC *Cathedrals: Stone Upon Stone*
by Brigitte Gandiol-Coppin
illustrated by Dominique Thibault
Young Discovery Library, 1989
This neat little book explains why, where, and how the great cathedrals of Europe were built. Only thirty-five pages long, with lovely illustrations of medieval town life and cathedrals under construction, it is written in language appropriate for fourth grade readers, with key ideas emphasized in boldface type. Part of the Young Discovery Library, listed under World History General Resources: Series.

"Defenders of France"
This March/April 1992 issue of *Calliope* (see address, page 110), the world history magazine for young people, includes articles on Charlemagne and Joan of Arc, as well as instructions for a classroom activity, "Design a Coat of Arms."

Written for middle school, so most useful as a teacher/parent resource.

Illuminations
written and illustrated by Jonathan Hunt
Macmillan, 1989/Aladdin Books, 1993
An alphabet book for fourth graders? Yes, indeed, when it's as informative and attractive as this one, illustrated in the style of a medieval illuminated manuscript. *A* is for "alchemist," *B* is for "Black Death," *C* is for "Coat of Arms," et cetera. Go ahead, try to guess *Z*. (It's "zither"!) This may not be the main text for your studies, but it's a lovely and interesting book that fourth graders can read on their own.

A Medieval Cathedral
by Fiona MacDonald and John James
Peter Bedrick Books, 1991
Using the cathedral as a point of reference, this informative book looks at many aspects of medieval life. It includes two-page spreads on craftsmen, gargoyles, pilgrims, monks, and miracle plays, for example, all illustrated with detailed color drawings and cutaway diagrams. Glossary and index included. Challenging vocabulary and sometimes small print make this a good book for teachers and parents to read and share with children.

CC *A Medieval Feast*
written and illustrated by Aliki
HarperCollins/HarperTrophy, 1983
This fascinating and easy-to-read picture book is full of details that suggest what life must have been like in a medieval castle by describing the preparations for a grand feast (for no less a visitor than the king!). Aliki gives a nice view of life in the different social classes, and provides some interesting information in a brief author's note at the end.

The Middle Ages
by Sarah Howarth
Viking, 1993
Part of the *See Through History* series, this book has a special feature children love—four illustra-

tions with see-through pages that lift to reveal cutaway views of an abbey, a medieval town, a castle, and a mill. It covers many topics in brief chapters on "The Family," "Lords and Peasants," "Becoming a Knight," "Living in a Castle," "The Crusades," "The Monastic Life," and more. The text, while informative, is dry and "textbookish."

Picture the Middle Ages: The Middle Ages Resource Book
written by Linda Honan
illustrated by Ellen Kosmer
Golden Owl Publishing, 1994
Teachers may find this resource book especially helpful. It is designed to provide "all the information needed for upper-elementary and middle-school teachers to create a five- to eight-week unit on the Middle Ages." Chapters are devoted to historical background, the town (craftsmen and guilds), the castle, heraldry, the monastery, the manor, costumes and armor, music and dance, art and literature, and the "grand finale," a medieval festival. The spiral-bound book includes black-line reproducible readings, activities, games, puzzles, patterns, and more. Available directly from Golden Owl Publishing, P.O. Box 503, Amawalk, NY 10501; or call (800) 789-0022.

CC A Tournament of Knights
written and illustrated by Joe Lasker
HarperCollins, 1986
Pleasing watercolors and an energetic text tell the fictional story of Justin, a young English knight facing an experienced jouster. As they cheer their hero on, students are also learning about the great medieval ritual of tournament in this enjoyable little book that fourth graders can read independently.

Walter Dragun's Town: Crafts and Trade in the Middle Ages
written and illustrated by Sheila Sancha
HarperCollins, 1989
Referring to actual public records of the English town Stanford, dated 1275, and cathedral sculptures from nearby Lincoln Cathedral, the au-

thor/illustrator recreates the bustling commercial and social life of a medieval town. This is a good book to convey the sense of daily life, a reminder that not everyone was a knight in armor, not every day a feast or tournament. Illustrated with black-and-white sketches.

Activity Books

Design Your Own Coat of Arms: An Introduction to Heraldry (1987)
by Rosemary Chorzempa
Knights and Armour Coloring Book (1985)
by A. G. Smith
The Middle Ages (1971)
by Edmund V. Gillon, Jr.
Stained Glass Windows Coloring Book (1992)
by Paul E. Kennedy
Dover
Inexpensive activity books from Dover (see address, page 106). Coat of Arms contains drawings and explanations of heraldry, designed to provide ideas for creating an original coat of arms. Knights and Armor prints simple line drawings based on medieval art and armor design. The Middle Ages coloring book presents over fifty woodcut images enlarged from actual medieval sources, representing daily life, historic events, and legend. Stained Glass Windows is a tiny book that makes it very easy to make your own "stained glass windows" by coloring these reproductions printed on translucent paper.

A Coloring Book of the Middle Ages (1995)
A Medieval Alphabet to Illuminate (1994)
Bellerophon Books
These two coloring books from Bellerophon (see address, page 106) present line drawings based on medieval sources. The Middle Ages presents pictures of King Arthur, Saint George and the Dragon, a monk copying a book, William the Conqueror, the Normans crossing the channel to invade England, a plowman, a miller, Chaucer, and many more. The Medieval Alphabet offers elaborately designed initials from which children can learn about illuminated manuscript,

and that they are likely to enjoy coloring even though they may not notice the occasional wry humor ("C is for 'confusion,' " "Q is for 'quantum theory' ").

Historical Fiction

Adam of the Road
by Elizabeth Janet Gray
illustrated by Robert Lawson
Viking, 1942/Puffin Books, 1987
A Newbery Award winner, this novel set in thirteenth-century England tells the story of eleven-year-old Adam. When his father disappears and his dog is stolen, Adam, alone, takes to the road, where he meets merchants, pilgrims, priests, and sinners, all as he goes in search of his father and his dog.

The Castle in the Attic
by Elizabeth Winthrop
Holiday House, 1985
This children's novel tells a magical story about a timid boy named William who travels through a toy castle back in time to the Middle Ages. Once there, he goes on a quest, meets a dragon and a wicked wizard, and proves his courage in the end.

The Door in the Wall
by Marguerite de Angeli
Dell Yearling, 1949, 1989
A Newbery Award winner, this novel tells the story of young Robin who, "ever since he could remember . . . had been told what was expected of him as son of his father. Like other sons of noble family . . . he would learn all the ways of knighthood." But everything changes when Robin falls ill and loses the use of his legs. This moving, inspiring story conveys a feel for life and times in medieval England.

A Proud Taste for Scarlet and Miniver
by E. L. Konigsburg
Dell, 1985
While waiting in heaven for divine judgment to be passed on her second husband, Eleanor of Aquitaine and three of the people who knew her well recall the events of her life. This is a wonderful, rich novel, though very challenging for fourth-grade readers.

THE RISE OF ISLAM AND THE "HOLY WARS"

See also Visual Arts Grade 4: Islamic Art and Architecture.

The Arabs in the Golden Age
by Mokhtar Moktefi
illustrated by Véronique Ageorges
Millbrook, 1992
This book introduces Islam (including the Five Pillars of Islam, and two meanings of *jihad*—one as "holy war," one as "the work of the soul," the lifelong struggle against pride, selfishness, and other vices), then goes on to discuss the growth and development of Arab civilization from about the eighth to thirteenth centuries, including culture, everyday life, and advances in science, medicine, and mathematics. Colorful illustrations, some in the style of illuminated manuscripts. Written for middle-school readers in clear, direct prose; good for selective reading aloud or as a teacher/parent resource.

AWAIR
"AWAIR" stands for Arab World and Islamic Resources and School Services, a nonprofit educational organization that offers materials (including teaching units) on Islam and the Arab world for schools and teachers at the precollegiate level. For more information, write to them at 1865 Euclid Avenue, Suite 4, Berkeley, CA 94709.

"The First Crusade"
In this January/February 1995 issue of *Calliope* (see address, page 110), the magazine of world history for young people, articles and activity ideas help children come to understand "Pope Urban's Call," "The Siege of Antioch," and

"The Fall of Jerusalem." There are also interesting excerpts from an eyewitness account written by fourteen-year-old Anna Comena, daughter of the Byzantine emperor.

"Islamic Spain"

This November/December 1995 issue of *Calliope* (see address, page 110), the magazine of world history for young people, features Córdoba, Seville, and Granada, centers of Islamic culture and learning in Spain.

A Sixteenth Century Mosque

by Fiona MacDonald and Mark Bergin
Peter Bedrick Books, 1994
This large-scale, fabulously illustrated book is about much more than mosques. There are sections on the spread of Islam (with fine maps), the Islamic faith, love of learning, and regard for charity, as well as sections on Islamic design, the first mosques, and basic elements of Islamic architecture.

The World of Islam

written and compiled by Richard Tames
Jackdaw Publications, 1976
This "Jackdaw" is a packet of posters, readings, art prints, and reproduced primary sources. It includes pictures and text on the Qur'an, the spread of Islam, mosques, the arts of Islam, Islamic cities, and more. Though intended for older students, the materials in this package can also be useful for the teacher who is willing to select from them and adapt them for younger students. Teachers may also want to examine the optional Study Guide, which provides reproducible masters, writing exercises, research topics, and more (again, directed to older students). Available from Golden Owl Publishing, P.O. Box 503, Amawalk, NY 10501; (800) 789-0022.

CC = **"Core Collection"** book (see page 8).

EARLY AND MEDIEVAL AFRICA

See also Visual Arts Grade 4: The Art of Africa.

CC *Ghana, Mali, Songhay: The Western Sudan*

by Kenny Mann
Simon & Schuster/Dillon Press, 1996
This packed and beautiful teacher/parent resource conveys much information about these three kingdoms. Illustrations include current photos, good maps, ancient artifacts, and African-inspired graphics. One chapter discusses the influence of Islam in West Africa. Sundiata and Mansa Musa are given special treatment. See also from the same author and publisher *Oyo, Benin, and Ashanti* (1996).

The Royal Kingdoms of Ghana, Mali, and Songhay: Life in Medieval Africa

by Patricia and Fredrick McKissack
Henry Holt, 1994
These award-winning authors use ancient and modern accounts, journals of African and European explorers, recent archaeological findings, and black-and-white maps and photos to bring to light the accomplishments of these three medieval African kingdoms in this informative study, written for middle school and up.

CC *Sundiata: Lion King of Mali*
written and illustrated by David Wisniewski
Clarion Books, 1992
This gorgeous picture book tells the legend of Mali's King Sundiata in the resounding voice of a tribal *griot*, illustrating it with spectacular cut-paper constructions. The story is compelling, and children (adults too!) will marvel at the pictures.

Geography of Africa

CC *Ashanti to Zulu: African Traditions*
by Margaret Musgrove
illustrated by Leo and Diane Dillon
Dial/Puffin Books, 1976
An alphabet book, yes, but an excellent way to

introduce the diversity of peoples, regions, and customs that make up Africa, "an enormous and varied continent," the author writes, "inhabited by hundreds of different peoples whose array of customs and traditions are as diverse as the land itself." The warm, rich illustrations won a Caldecott Medal.

Children's Atlas of People and Places
by Jenny Wood and David Munro
Millbrook, 1993
In readable words, maps, and many color pictures, the author discusses North Africa, West Africa, Central and East Africa, and Southern Africa.

Africa
by D. V. Georges
Childrens Press, 1986
This New True Book should be easily readable by fourth graders, with its large print and many illustrations. It provides information on various regions and peoples of Africa.

CC = "Core Collection" book (see page 8).

MEDIEVAL CHINA

CC Exploration into China
by Wang Tao
New Discovery Books, 1995
This attractive book is all about China, from prehistoric times to the present day, and it includes substantial chapters on China's "Golden Age" during the Tang dynasty, as well as on the Sung dynasty and the Mongols. There are also brief accounts of Marco Polo and Zheng He. Colorfully and informatively illustrated with current-day and period art and photos.

CC The Mongols
by Robert Nicholson
Chelsea House/Chelsea Juniors, 1994
This slender, colorfully illustrated book, readable by most fourth graders, introduces the Mongols in brief chapters on such topics as: "The Mongol World," "Horsemen and Warriors," "Genghis Khan," "Religion," "Food," "Children," and more.

WORLD HISTORY AND GEOGRAPHY

Grade 5

See also World History General Resources.

MESOAMERICAN CIVILIZATIONS

Aztec, Inca & Maya
by Elizabeth Baquedano
Alfred A. Knopf, 1993
Part of the Eyewitness series, this book is chock
full of stunning pictures, with brief paragraphs
and infobytes of explanatory text. Good for
browsing more than reading.

CC *The Aztecs* (1994)
by Robert Nicholson and Claire Watts
          The Maya (1994)
by Robert Nicholson
Chelsea House/Chelsea Juniors
Teachers might want to consider these convenient paperbacks as student texts for a class
unit on the Aztecs and the Maya. They are
clearly written, readable by fifth graders, and
generously illustrated with color drawings and
photographs. Each book addresses a number of
topics in two-page chapters. Specific topics in
The Aztecs include "The Aztec World," "The
Great Speakers," "Aztec Gods," "Aztec Temples" (including a brief discussion of human
sacrifice), "Farming," "At Home," "Crafts," and
a retelling of an Aztec legend, "Quetzalcoatl
Gives Food to the People," about the gift of
corn. *The Maya* includes brief chapters on
"Farms and Farmers," "Cities and Temples,"
"Religion and the Mayan Gods," "Writing,"
"Counting and Calendars," "Clothes and
Beauty," and a retelling of a legend, "The Hero
Twins' Revenge" (though not in especially en-
gaging prose). Each book includes a glossary

and one-page note on "How We Know" about
the ancient civilization. Granted, the writing
could be more lively, and it would help to have
a guide to pronouncing words like *uinic* and
Xbalanque, but given the books' other virtues—
concise, readable, attractive—these add up to a
good combination for fifth graders.

The Aztecs (1990)
The Incas (1989)
The Maya (1989)
by Pamela Odjik
Silver Burdett
Detailed enough but not too difficult for a fifth-
grade researcher, and useful as teacher/parent
resources as well, these photographically illustrated introductions to ancient Mesoamerican
civilizations include sections on climate, crops,
clothes, laws, art, architecture, war, and language, as well as a time line, glossary, and list
of festivals.

The Aztecs
by Tim Wood
Viking, 1992
This highly attractive visual introduction to the
Aztecs has chapters on their rise as a civilization, their army and warfare, the emperor, trade
and tribute, food and farming, and more. The
text is divided into many subsections, along
with sidebars that add interesting details. Illustrations include artifacts, maps, diagrams, and
four large architectural drawings with clear
plastic overlays that lift to reveal the inner
workings of the Great Temple at Tenochtitlán,
an Aztec house, a palace, and cliffside temples
at Malinalco. Part of the *See Through History* se-

ries, described under World History General Resources: Series.

City of the Gods: Mexico's Ancient City of Teotihuacán
by Caroline Arnold
photography by Richard Hewett
Clarion Books, 1994
A convenient way to "travel," this book concentrates on the Aztec city as it appears today, with fascinating photographs of the ruins as well as text that interprets ancient Aztec culture from the artifacts found by modern archaeologists.

CC *Pyramid of the Sun, Pyramid of the Moon*
by Leonard Everett Fisher
Macmillan, 1988
In plain yet powerful prose and elegant black-and-white illustrations, Leonard Fisher tells the history of two ancient pyramids. As Fisher frames it, these structures, built about 150 B.C. and later used by the Toltecs and the Aztecs, become silent, abiding witnesses to the sometimes violent and bloody procession of history. The book does not shy from an accurate (but not sensationalized) description of the Aztec practice of ritual sacrifice. Marginal symbols link passages in the text with a helpful time-line at the beginning of the book.

EUROPEAN HISTORY FROM THE AGE OF EXPLORATION TO THE ENGLISH BILL OF RIGHTS

The Age of Exploration

CC *Around the World in a Hundred Years: From Henry the Navigator to Magellan*
by Jean Fritz
illustrated by Anthony Bacon Venti
G. P. Putnam's Sons, 1994
We need more people like Jean Fritz, who can write good narrative history for young readers.

From the title on, this book uses a direct voice and wry humor (both in the words and in the occasional pictures) to tell the story of major European explorers in the fifteenth century. Fritz begins by examining why, for many centuries, Europeans were *not* interested in exploring, while, in contrast, the Chinese navigator Zheng He "was leading expeditions of 317 ships and 37,000 men to nearly every land bordering the China Sea and the Indian Ocean." She proceeds to organize her story by explorer, including chapters on Prince Henry the Navigator, Dias, Columbus, da Gama, Cabral, Cabot, Vespucci, de León, Balboa, and Magellan. If textbooks were written in such lucid, lively prose, maybe kids would like reading them.

Children's Atlas of Exploration
by Antony Mason
Millbrook, 1993
See description under World History General Resources: Atlases.

The Great Atlas of Discovery
by Neil Grant
illustrated by Peter Morter
Alfred A. Knopf, 1992
See description under World History General Resources: Atlases.

CC *If You Were There in 1492*
by Barbara Brenner
Bradbury Press, 1991
In lively prose that directly addresses "you," her young readers, Barbara Brenner uses the year 1492 as a lens through which to explore ideas, beliefs, and practices in fifteenth-century Europe, especially Spain. She provides fascinating details about everything from kings and queens to the fabric of clothing, and even takes you on an imaginary trip by mule through Spain. She reports on the Inquisition and the expulsion of Jews and "Moors." Read this along with Jean Fritz's *Around the World in a Hundred Years* (see above) and you'll get a good feel for the age of exploration and some of the people

who most dramatically embodied its ambitious, inquisitive, sometimes cruel spirit.

The Renaissance

See also Visual Arts Grade 5: The Art of the Renaissance.
See also Language Arts Grade 5: Shakespeare's *A Midsummer Night's Dream* and Cervantes's *Don Quixote.*

Gutenberg
by Leonard Everett Fisher
Macmillan, 1993
Bold black-and-white illustrations distinguish this readable, informative, and intriguing picture-book biography of the inventor of movable type and a mechanical printing process that made books available to ordinary people.

CC "Introduction to the Renaissance"
This May/June 1994 issue of *Calliope* (see address, page 110), the magazine of world history for young people, explores the Renaissance in several articles. An introductory article introduces the Renaissance as "A Time of Discovery and Rediscovery." A clever article cast as a short play introduces Machiavelli and the question "What Makes a Great Ruler?" Another article discusses da Vinci, Michelangelo, and Raphael (you'll want to supplement this with some of the resources in Visual Arts Grade 5). More articles and activities make this a good choice for a class text in a unit on the Renaissance.

Michelangelo
by Richard McLanathan
Harry N. Abrams, 1993
This beautifully produced volume is part of the publisher's "First Impressions" series for readers in high school and above, and so best as a teacher/parent resource. It is valuable for background on the Renaissance because it places the life story of Michelangelo into historical context, and includes chapters on "Lorenzo the Magnificent," "The Fall of the Medici," and "Julius, the Warrior Pope." The author provides helpful commentary on Michelangelo's works, many of which are superbly reproduced in the book, in color and black-and-white. Also in the "First Impressions" series is a book by the same author, *Leonardo da Vinci.*

The Renaissance
by Tim Wood
Viking, 1993
This attractive book presents in one quick overview, mainly through pictures, the achievements in art, architecture, medicine, exploration, and technology that characterize the Renaissance. The book includes four plastic overlays that lift up to show the interiors of St. Peter's Cathedral, Columbus's *Santa Maria*, a Florentine palace, and a water-wheel-powered print shop. Part of the *See Through History* series, listed under World History General Resources: Series. A good book for browsing, but we would gladly give up half its pictures for some more detailed explanatory prose.

Renaissance People
Renaissance Places
by Sarah Howarth
illustrations by Philip McNeill
Millbrook, 1992
Renaissance People follows an interesting strategy: by describing the lives of thirteen representative types of Renaissance people (banker, mercenary, artist, witch, explorer), it provides an intriguing picture of the times. It offers brief discussions of Galileo; of Machiavelli and the new ideal of the "prince" as pragmatic politician; and, of Castiglione and the ideal courtier. The companion volume, *Renaissance Places*, offers thirteen chapters, each explaining a place representative of the Renaissance: palace, chapel, monastery, theater, parliament, and even the New World. It briefly discusses Galileo, the Reformation, and Henry VIII. While informative, the prose is rather dry and "textbookish." Both books are illustrated with art of the period, including some familiar classics.

The Second Mrs. Giaconda
by E. L. Konigsburg
Aladdin Books, 1975
This wonderful work of historical fiction is set in Milan, Italy, in the sixteenth century, during the flowering of the Renaissance, and presents Leonardo da Vinci as one of its main characters. It tells the story of the relationship between Leonardo and a young rascal, Salai, who becomes an assistant to Leonardo, and eventually leads the great artist to meet the subject of perhaps the most famous portrait of all time, the *Mona Lisa*. Wonderful descriptions, witty dialogue, and challenging vocabulary—suitable for strong fifth-grade readers or for reading aloud.

The Reformation

Beliefs and Believers
by Michael Pollard
Garrett Educational Corporation, 1992
This is a concise reference book on many of the world's major religions, written for upper-elementary and middle-school students, with a brief discussion of Martin Luther and the Reformation.

Martin Luther
written and compiled by E. R. Chamberlin
Jackdaw Publications, 1972
This "Jackdaw" is a packet of posters, readings, art prints, and reproduced primary sources (including a reproduction of Luther's ninety-five theses). Though intended for older students, the materials in this package can also be useful for the teacher who is willing to select from them and adapt them for younger students. Teachers may also want to examine the optional Study Guide, which provides reproducible masters, writing exercises, research topics, and more (again, directed to older students). Available from Golden Owl Publishing, P.O. Box 503, Amawalk, NY 10501; (800) 789-0022.

CC = "Core Collection" book (see page 8).

Threads of Time: A Global History 400–1750
by Sheena Coupe and Barbara Scanlan
Longman, 1993
This textbook for the middle grades covers an awful lot in a short space, and thus does not go into much detail. Relevant here is a chapter on the Reformation, which discusses Martin Luther, the Counter-Reformation, the Inquisition, and Henry VIII and the Reformation in England.

"The World of Martin Luther"
by Merle Severy
photographs by James L. Amos
Check your library for this article in the October 1983 issue of *National Geographic* magazine, or call (800) 638-4077 to purchase a back issue. Excellent for teacher/parent background, the article offers a detailed and lively look at Martin Luther's life and times, along with vivid photographs and illustrations for which *National Geographic* is famous.

England from Elizabeth to William and Mary

CC *Good Queen Bess: The Story of Elizabeth I of England*
by Diane Stanley and Peter Vennema
Four Winds Press, 1990
This visually and verbally compelling account of the life of Elizabeth I looks at first like a picture book, but is actually a detailed and informative account of Elizabethan times focused through the life of the queen.

"Major Naval Battles"
This March/April 1991 issue of *Calliope* (see address, page 110), the magazine of world history for young people, has an article on the English defeat of the mighty Spanish Armada, as well as an interesting look at "Searching for the Armada," about the attempts of archaeologists to find remnants of ships that sank on the return voyage.

The Tower of London
by Leonard Everett Fisher
Macmillan, 1987
Stark and evocative black-and-white illustrations accompany this brief, intriguing, and selective look at English history from 1066 to 1666, as seen through the focus of what happened at the Tower of London. We learn, for example, that a wedding feast was held there to celebrate the marriage of Henry VIII to Anne Boleyn; but three years later, at the same site, she was beheaded. Other brief but interesting vignettes tell about Queen Elizabeth, Sir Walter Raleigh, James I, Guy Fawkes, and Charles II.

Threads of Time: A Global History 400–1750
by Sheena Coupe and Barbara Scanlan
Longman, 1993
This textbook for the middle grades covers an awful lot in a short space, and thus does not go into much detail. Relevant here are the chapters on "Two Ruling Families" (Tudors and Stuarts) and "Problems for the Stuarts." The latter chapter tells the story of the English Civil War, the rise of Cromwell, the execution of Charles I, and the restoration of Charles II. It only very briefly treats William and Mary and the English Bill of Rights.

FEUDAL JAPAN

The Japanese
by Pamela Odjik
Silver Burdett, 1989
A good teacher/parent resource, and readable as well by the fifth-grade researcher, this book presents a brief, informative, illustrated overview of premodern Japan's history, geography, culture, daily life, religion, art and architecture, and more. Includes a photograph of the stunning Himeji Castle, as well as pictures of the Kamakura Buddha and a landscape garden.

"Shoguns and Samurai of Japan"
This January/February 1993 issue of *Calliope* (see address, page 110), the magazine of world history for young people, focuses on the Samurai tradition, including articles, stories, and instructions on how to make a Samurai breastplate.

The Samurai's Daughter
retold by Robert D. San Souci
Dial Books, 1992
A Japanese legend set in feudal times; see description under Language Arts Grade 5: Stories.

The Samurai's Tale
by Erik Haugaard
Houghton Mifflin, 1984
Historical fiction: In this 225-page novel about turbulent sixteenth-century Japan, orphaned Taro is taken in by a general serving the great warlord Takeda Shingen. Later Taro becomes a samurai, only to discover that he is fighting for the enemies of his dead family. Written in Taro's voice, the novel is exciting and historically revealing. If you like this, you might want to see, by the same author, *The Boy and the Samurai*.

Of Nightingales That Weep
by Katherine Paterson
HarperCollins, 1974
Historical fiction: Fifth graders may enjoy this exciting and well-written novel about Takiko, daughter of a samurai, who is caught up in the civil wars in twelfth-century Japan. Katherine Paterson, an acclaimed children's author, was born in China and has studied and taught in Japan, so she draws upon personal experience as well as research. If you like this, you might also try Paterson's *The Sign of the Chrysanthemum* and *The Master Puppeteer*.

RUSSIA: EARLY GROWTH AND EXPANSION

CC *Peter the Great*
written and illustrated by Diane Stanley
Four Winds Press/Macmillan, 1986 / Aladdin, 1992
Diane Stanley mixes anecdote and history to

produce a lively and accessible biography of Peter who, as a very spoiled boy of thirteen, "believed that whatever he wanted, he should have, and the sooner the better. . . . All his life he would want fantastic things, and want them right away." As Stanley tells the story, it was this temperament, combined with boundless energy and curiosity, that would transform a Russia that "simply wished to be left alone." With detailed and brightly colored illustrations.

Russian Portraits
by Dorothy and Thomas Hoobler
illustrated by John Edens
Raintree/Steck-Vaughn, 1994
This collection of brief and engaging biographical essays, directed to middle school and above, includes chapters on Peter the Great and Catherine the Great, as well as a brief account of Ivan the Terrible in a chapter on one of Ivan's enemies, the pirate Yermak.

"Two Russian Greats: Peter and Catherine"
Scheduled for publication as the May-June 1997 issue of *Calliope* (see address, page 110), the magazine of world history for young people, this issue is to feature articles on Peter and Catherine, as well as the magazine's usual related activities and word games.

CC = "**Core Collection**" book (see page 8).

WORLD HISTORY AND GEOGRAPHY

Grade 6

See also World History General Resources.

LASTING IDEAS FROM ANCIENT CIVILIZATIONS

Judaism and Christianity

CC *The Ancient World of the Bible*
by Malcolm Day
Viking, 1994
This attractive book contains concise, skillful re-tellings of more than two dozen famous stories from the Bible, and places them in a larger context of history and geography. The book is organized in sections as follows: "The First People," "Abraham's Family," "The Israelites in Egypt," "The Promised Land," "David's Kingdom," "The Time of the Prophets," "The Exile." The text is supported by colorful illustrations, diagrams, maps, and photos of artifacts and landscapes that convey the environment of the Middle East and the daily life of ancient Israelites.

Beliefs and Believers
by Michael Pollard
Garrett Educational Corporation, 1992
This is a concise reference book on many of the world's major religions, written for upper-elementary and middle-school students, with brief chapters on "Moses and the Israelites," "The Search for a Homeland," "The First Christians," and "The Conversion of the Romans."

How Do You Spell God? Answers to the Big Questions from Around the World
by Rabbi Marc Gellman and Monsignor Thomas Hartman
Morrow Junior Books, 1995
This lively and readable book takes the approach of looking at major world religions not one at a time but through the organizing lens of a series of questions, such as: "How Are Religions Different? What Question Does Each Religion Want to Answer the Most? What Are the Holy Books? Where Are the Holy Places? Why Do Religions Split Up? How Do You Build a House for God?" This book, written by a Rabbi and a Catholic priest, was endorsed by everyone from the Dalai Lama to the National Council of Islamic Affairs.

The Israelites
by Pamela Odjik
Silver Burdett, 1989
Part of the "Ancient World" series, this book provides a concise, illustrated overview of the ancient Israelites. A number of chapters deal with geographical matters (land, climate, crops, and more), while others focus on history, beliefs, and concepts of law and justice. With many helpful photographs and drawings, in black-and-white and color.

The Rise of Major Religions
by Georgia Makhlouf
illustrated by Michael Welply
Silver Burdett, 1988
This encyclopedia of ancient religions contains sections on both Judaism and Christianity.

Ancient Greece and Rome

American Classical League Catalog of Teaching Materials for Teachers of Latin, Greek, and Classical Humanities

This catalog lists a number of helpful resources relevant to teaching ancient Greece, Rome, and classical mythology. You can order it by writing to the American Classical League, Teaching Materials and Resource Center, Miami University, Oxford Ohio 45056; or, call (513) 529-7741.

Ancient Greece
by Daniel Cohen
illustrated by James Seward
Doubleday, 1990

This big and dramatically illustrated volume looks like a picture book, and its text should be easy for most sixth-grade readers. The book presents clear but brief sections on Achilles, Homer, the Minotaur, Atlantis, Greek geography, the Olympics, the Delphic Oracle, military life, rule by the people, the Persian Wars, Greek gods, drama, philosophers, the "Golden Age," the war between Athens and Sparta, Socrates, and Alexander the Great. This book is so brief that you will want to supplement it. For a considerably more comprehensive and detailed narrative history of the ancient Greeks, see below, *The Greeks* by Roy Burrell.

Ancient Rome: A Cultural Atlas for Young People
by Michael Corbishley
Facts on File, 1989

The first half of this volume traces the growth of the Roman Empire with informative historical maps. What sets the book apart, though, are its close-up views of the varied regions of the empire, supported by excellent maps and large photographs. A good reference book for the young researcher, though the text may challenge some sixth graders.

The Assassination of Julius Caesar
by George Ochoa
Silver Burdett, 1991

This illustrated volume in the *Turning Points in*

World History series examines what led up to the assassination of Caesar, the event itself, and the consequences of it. Within this narrative frame, the book offers background information on the structure of ancient Roman society, and a glimpse at the struggles that led to the rise of the Roman empire. Good for strong readers or as a teacher/parent resource.

CC "Athens vs. Sparta"

This November/December 1994 issue of *Calliope* (see address, page 110), the magazine of world history for young people, could serve as a convenient classroom text for a unit on ideas from ancient Greece. It features brief, readable articles on "The Beginnings of Democracy," "Life in Ancient Sparta," "The Golden Age of Greece," "The Peloponnesian War," and more. With black-and-white illustrations.

The Greeks
The Romans
by Pamela Odjik
Silver Burdett, 1989

These volumes in the "Ancient World" series provide concise (forty-five-page), straightforward, readable overviews of ancient Greek and Roman civilizations, particularly the social features: how families lived, food, clothing, transportation, recreation, and the like. They devote brief two-page spreads to key figures and ideas of government and philosophy. You will probably want to supplement these with other resources that examine lasting ideas. Illustrated with many color photographs.

CC The Greeks (1989)
The Romans (1991)
by Roy Burrell
illustrated by Peter Connolly
Oxford University Press

These two books are part of Oxford's "Rebuilding the Past" series, designed, says the publisher, "to bring to life the people and places of bygone ages." Though the print is on the small side, the writing is clear and lively, occasionally directly addressing the young reader or turning the narration into a dialogue, for example, "Let's ask one of Sir Arthur Evans's men what it was like to dig up the palace at Knossos." The books examine both social life and important ideas. Chapters in *The Greeks* include: "The Minoans," "The Mycenaeans," "Greek Civilization," "The Persian Wars," "Pericles and the Golden Age," "The Peloponnesian Wars," "Alexander the Great." Chapters in *The Romans* include: "The City of Rome," "Republic and Empire," "Daily Life," "The State and Religion," "The Arena," "Barbarians at the Gate." Both books end with a brief summary of the legacy of each civilization. Both are generously illustrated with color photographs and drawings that, while historically accurate, seem melodramatic and overdone. For some strange reason, each book begins with a comic-book story (on Theseus and the Minotaur, and on Romulus and Remus). Perhaps the publishers thought, "Ahhah, here's a way to show that history can be really cool." *Wrong*—skip the bizarre comics and get to the good narrative text. Both of these books, by the way, are incorporated verbatim into the *Oxford First Ancient History* (1994), which adds to the account of Greece and Rome an account of earlier history from the Stone Age to ancient Egypt, with very brief glimpses at "other early civilizations."

"Heroes and Heroines of Early Rome"
This September/October 1995 issue of *Calliope* (see address, page 110), the magazine of world history for young people, features articles on several Roman figures of importance, including Romulus and Remus and Rome's Three *C*'s: Coriolanus, Cincinnatus, and Cornelia.

The Origins of Greek Civilization: From the Bronze Age to the Polis ca. 2500–600 B.C.
by Rhoda Himmell, Amanda H. Podnay, David Millstone, and Peter Cheoros

CC = "Core Collection" book (see page 8).

CC ***The Golden Age of Greece: Imperial Democracy 500–400 B.C.***
by Peter Cheoros, Jan Coleman-Knight, Rhoda Himmell, and Linda Symcox
University of California, National Center for History in the Schools, 1991
Teachers especially should take note of these two booklets of unit and lesson plans for teaching about ancient Greece. The lessons are written for a range of grades, so you may have to adapt some ideas for sixth grade, but most are targeted at the middle-school level. The first booklet includes ideas for teaching the Trojan War, Homer's *Odyssey*, and the nature of the Greek *polis*. The second booklet "explores Greece's most glorious century, the high point of Athenian culture." Both booklets contain teacher background materials and lesson plans with student resources (primary source documents, reproducible handouts, student background readings). Available from the National Center for History in the Schools, UCLA, 1100 Glendon Avenue, Suite 927, Box No. 951588, Los Angeles, CA 90095-1588; telephone (310) 825-4702. Write or call for price and ordering information, and if you're interested ask for a current list of available teaching units, most of which are for secondary schools.

TOWARD THE MODERN WORLD: FROM THE ENLIGHTENMENT TO THE INDUSTRIAL REVOLUTION

The Enlightenment

Creative Activities for Teaching World History: Renaissance to Revolution
Stevens & Shea Publishers, Inc.
This packet of materials for teachers includes reproducible black-line masters of "activities and puzzles . . . [that] emphasize decision making through the study of historical events." Useful here are the sections on the Age of Reason, including brief sketches (for student reading) of the thought of Rousseau, Locke, Voltaire, Spi-

noza, and Bacon, and an activity that asks students to "philosophize" about an ideal society. The packet also includes good handouts on the French Revolution (but we cannot recommend the fluffy materials on the Renaissance or the Age of Exploration). Write or call the publisher at P.O. Box 794, Stockton, CA 95201; (209) 465-1880.

The Enlightenment
by Carole Collier Frick
University of California, National Center for
   History in the Schools, 1991
A resource especially helpful for teachers, this is a teaching unit that features selections from important primary source documents by Montesquieu and Jefferson. There are many good ideas here, though you will have to adapt them for use with sixth graders. The booklet contains teacher background materials and lesson plans with student resources (primary source documents, reproducible handouts, student background readings). Available from the National Center for History in the Schools, UCLA, 1100 Glendon Avenue, Suite 927, Box 951588, Los Angeles, CA 90095-1588; telephone (310) 825-4702. Write or call for price and ordering information, and if you're interested ask for a current list of available teaching units, most of which are for secondary schools.

The French Revolution

Creative Activities for Teaching World History: Renaissance to Revolution
Stevens & Shea Publishers, Inc.
This packet of materials for teachers includes reproducible black-line masters of "activities and puzzles . . . [that] emphasize decision making through the study of historical events." Useful here are the sections on "The Trial of Louis XVI," "The French Revolution," and "The Committee of Safety." The packet also includes good handouts on the Age of Reason (but we cannot recommend the fluffy materials on the Renaissance or the Age of Exploration). Write or call

the publisher at P.O. Box 794, Stockton, CA 95201; (209) 465-1880.

Fall of the Bastille
by Kitty C. Benedict
Silver Burdett, 1991
This slender book on the French Revolution begins with an account of the storming of the hated French prison called the Bastille, then proceeds to examine what led up to that dramatic event and what followed from it. Part of the *Turning Points in World History* series, developed for middle to high school, this book is clearly written and illustrated on many pages. The text may be challenging for some sixth graders; examine it to see if you think the reading level is appropriate for your students. If so, then it can be an especially convenient single-volume resource.

The French Revolution
by Adrian Gilbert
Thomson Learning, 1995
This brief (forty-five-page) colorfully illustrated book offers a good introduction to the causes and events of the French Revolution, readable by sixth graders. It begins with an account of the execution of King Louis XVI, then moves back in time to examine what led up to that momentous event. The chronological narrative is accompanied by many sidebars that focus on key figures or topics (for example, the Three Estates, Danton, Robespierre, the guillotine). Includes helpful maps and time lines. We might wish for more lively writing, but this is one of the few decent nonfiction books for young readers on the French Revolution. Try complementing it with reading (or reading aloud) Charles Dickens's *Tale of Two Cities*—now, there's lively writing!

The King's Day: Louis XIV of France
written and illustrated by Aliki
HarperCollins, 1989
Did you know that King Louis the XIV of France took two hours to get dressed in the morning, ate with his fingers, and loved flow-

ers? Famed children's author/illustrator Aliki brings you a day in the life of Louis XIV, the Sun King, in this colorful picture book. It will be easy and enjoyable reading for sixth graders, who will enjoy its detail and marginalia.

The Industrial Revolution

Hard Times
by Charles Dickens

Published in 1854, and available in many libraries as well as many paperback editions, this is an uncharacteristically short novel for Dickens, but will still challenge many sixth-grade readers, and so may be best as a read-aloud. Dickens sets the novel in mid-nineteenth century industrial England in a place called Coketown, "a town of red brick, or of brick that would have been red if the smoke and ashes had allowed it. . . . It was a town of machinery and tall chimneys, out of which interminable serpents of smoke trailed themselves for ever and ever, and never got uncoiled." Here we meet the good-hearted laborer Stephen Blackpool; the severe schoolmaster Thomas Gradgrind who wants "nothing but Facts"; a greedy manufacturer, Josiah Bounderby; the kind and fanciful daughter of a circus clown, Sissy Jupe; and other immortal Dickens creations.

The Industrial Revolution
by Andrew Langley
Viking, 1994

Informative illustrations, some from the period but most recently drafted, constitute this mainly visual presentation of the transformation of western Europe through the introduction of labor-saving machines, and steam and coal power. Short blocks of text outline the key technological features and the social consequences of rapid industrialization and new transportation links. Four transparencies lift to reveal cutaway interiors of buildings and steam vessels. Part of the See Through History series, listed under General Resources.

CC The Industrial Revolution
edited by John D. Clare
Harcourt Brace/Gulliver Books, 1994

This handsome book aims to bring history to life through many photographs of reenacted scenes with costumed actors showing, for example, a cotton mill, a coal mine, a shipping wharf, a classroom. Unlike the busy Eyewitness Books or the See Through History series, this book does readers a favor by putting the words into nice big readable blocks of prose (instead of wrapping the words all around the pictures). The words themselves are clearly written and spiced with anecdote. Example: a skeptical member of the British Parliament asked a railroad builder, "Suppose . . . that a cow were to get in the way of the engine—would that not be an awkward circumstance?" "Very awkward," the railroad man replied, "for the cow." With brief chapters on many topics including: "The Old Order," "The First Factories," "Coal," "The First Railways," "Factory Work," "Life in the Cities," "Iron and Steel," "The Money Men," "The Scramble for Empire," "Unions, Politics, and Laws," "Women at Work," "Big Business."

LATIN AMERICAN INDEPENDENCE MOVEMENTS

José de San Martín: Latin America's Quiet Hero
by José B. Fernandez
Millbrook, 1993

This brief biography of José de San Martín begins with his childhood and ends with his elevation after death to the status of a national hero in Argentina. Along the way, the reader learns about the Latin American struggle for independence from Spain.

Miguel Hidalgo y Costilla: Father of Mexican Independence
by Frank de Varona
Millbrook, 1993

Opening with the scene of Hidalgo's execution and his brave and tender gestures to the firing squad that killed him, this clearly written narrative tells Hidalgo's life story in thirty pages. The text is accompanied by small color images and one map of Mexico. See also, from the same author and publisher, *Benito Juárez: President of Mexico*.

Simón Bolívar: Latin American Liberator
by Frank de Varona
Millbrook, 1993
This concise, well-written biography of Bolívar explains the ideas that drove him and the difficulties that came with liberation from Spain and the beginnings of self-rule.

"Spanish South America: Independence Movements"
This May/June 1993 issue of *Calliope* (see address, page 110), the magazine of world history for young people, features brief, readable articles on José de San Martín and Simón Bolívar, as well as a brief but interesting sidebar on Bernardo O'Higgins.

Toussaint L'Ouverture: Lover of Liberty
by Laurence Santrey
illustrated by Gershom Griffith
Troll Associates, 1994
This book introduces Haiti's revolutionary leader by concentrating on L'Ouverture's youth and the setting in which his ideas and fervor developed. With a few paragraphs of text and pencil drawings on every one of its fifty pages, the book should be simple but interesting for sixth graders.

AMERICAN HISTORY AND GEOGRAPHY

General Resources

The Core Knowledge Series: *What Your Kindergartner–Sixth Grader Needs to Know*, E. D. Hirsch, Jr., editor. Published by Doubleday in hardcover and Dell in paperback.

The seven current books in the Core Knowledge Series, one each for kindergarten through sixth grade, are the companion books to this resource guide. These illustrated books provide a convenient introduction to topics in the *Core Knowledge Sequence*, including the American History and Geography topics summarized on pages 94–101. Full of stories, poems, and discussions of topics in science, math, the visual arts and music, the books can be read to children or, in the upper grades, read by children. All author's proceeds from the sale of *What Your Kindergartner–Sixth Grader Needs to Know* go to the nonprofit Core Knowledge Foundation to support its mission of helping parents and teachers help children develop strong early foundations of knowledge.

CC = a "**Core Collection**" book (see p. 8).

See also World History and Geography General Resources: Geography Resources and References, and Atlases.

The American Family Album **series**
by Dorothy and Thomas Hoobler
Oxford University Press
These are powerful and moving books that combine words and pictures to present a brief chronological account of the history and "roots" of Americans from many lands. The authors provide historical background information and primary sources, which make these books an excellent resource for teachers and parents of children in about fourth grade and up. You will want to preview the books first, for a few of the pictures, which do not flinch from depicting some of the cruel and shameful episodes in our history, may disturb young children. But the books do not dwell on tragedy; they also in-

clude many words and pictures of triumph and affirmation. Titles include *The Chinese American Family Album; The Italian . . . ; The Mexican . . . ; The Irish . . . ; The African . . . ; The Japanese . . . ; The Jewish . . . ; The German . . . ; The Scandinavian . . . ;* and, *The Cuban American Family Album.*

CC *The American Reader*
edited by Diane Ravitch
HarperCollins, 1990
This is an indispensable resource for the upper elementary grades and beyond. Here are many of the words that have shaped our nation, arranged chronologically from the colonial period to the near-present. Ravitch has collected works

by political leaders, writers, poets, and social reformers. She includes not only the expected and essential essays and speeches—such as Lincoln's Gettysburg Address and John F. Kennedy's inaugural address—but also less well-known but very compelling works, such as Lucy Stone's "A Disappointed Woman" and Frederick Douglass's speech to the American Anti-Slavery Society.

The Buck Stops Here: Presidents of the U.S.
by Alice Provensen
HarperCollins, 1990
In fun rhyming couplets, Provensen relates details about the presidents from Washington to Bush, and along the way offers a minihistory of the United States. For example, for James Madison: "Now Madison is number Four,/We're fighting Englishmen once more." Illustrated with drawings of each president, surrounded by informative drawings of scenes from the times of each president, with captions noting important events and dates.

Buns Travels Across America
By "Cottonpaw"
photography by David Love
Cotton Tale Press, 1992
Cottonpaw, also known as Buns, gets a "hare brained notion to go traveling" across America. In amusing and informative photographs, we see Buns at the Statue of Liberty, the USS *Constitution* in Boston, Niagara Falls, the White House, the Lincoln Memorial, by the Mississippi River, at the Grand Canyon, and in other famous places. The book is a pleasant read-aloud for kindergartners and first graders, and older children will probably enjoy it too. (If you can't find this at your library of bookstore, write to Cotton Tale Press at P.O. Box 470275, Fort Worth, TX 76147.)

Cobblestone
Cobblestone Publishing
7 School St., Peterborough, NH 03458
Cobblestone is a magazine about American history that, says the publisher, is directed to children in grades 4–9. Each issue focuses upon a specific topic, and presents the information in lively illustrated articles, often accompanied by a game, suggested activity, and suggestions for further reading. Subscriptions and back issues are available by writing to the publisher, or by calling (800) 821-0115. Some issues on related topics have been collected as "theme packs" and are available with teacher's guides. Theme packs include: "Black History," "Civil War," "Colonial Life," "Industrialization and Beyond," "Multicultural America," "Native Americans," "Notable Women in American History," "Revolutionary Era," "The 1920s and 1930s," "U.S. Presidents and First Ladies," and "Westward Expansion." Note: The publisher also produces other good magazines for children: *Calliope* (on world history), *Odyssey* (on science), and *Faces* (on world cultures).

The Encyclopedia of Native America
by Trudy Griffin-Pierce
Viking, 1995
"The purpose of this book," says the author, a cultural anthropologist, "is to show Indians not through the eyes of whites, but through the eyes of Native Americans themselves." The book introduces many different peoples, organized by region ("The Northeast," "The Great Plains," "The Southwest," and more), and provides an epilogue on "Indians Today." The book is generously illustrated, which makes it an attractive reference, good for children to browse, but most useful as a teacher/parent resource.

CC A First Americans Book series
by Virginia Driving Hawk Sneve
illustrated by Ronald Himler
Holiday House
The language in these books is simple and clear enough to be read aloud to children in the primary grades, and read independently by children in about the third grade and up. Each book offers a brief glimpse at the history, customs, and beliefs of a specific people. The illustrations are paintings in a style that blurs fine details and depicts only vague facial features.

The series includes: *The Hopi, The Sioux, The Navajos, The Nez Perce,* and *The Seminoles.*

CC *From Sea to Shining Sea: A Treasury of American Folklore and Folk Songs*
compiled by Amy L. Cohn
Scholastic, 1993
This large, diverse, and delightful collection of stories, poems, and songs makes a wonderful complement to nonfiction texts on history. It is divided into fifteen sections with names like "In the Beginning" (on Native Americans), "The Shot Heard 'Round the World" (on Revolutionary times), and "I've Been Working on the Railroad." You'll find familiar favorites like "Yankee Doodle," "Simple Gifts," "Ol' Dan Tucker," "Take Me Out to the Ball Game," and tales of Paul Bunyan and Br'er Rabbit, as well as a wealth of less familiar but no less engaging stories and songs from diverse traditions. The book includes a very useful subject index and suggestions for further reading. Illustrated by eleven Caldecott-winning artists.

CC *Hand in Hand: An American History Through Poetry*
collected by Lee Bennett Hopkins
illustrated by Peter M. Fiore
Simon & Schuster, 1994
See entry under Language Arts, Poetry Collections: General collections.

CC *A History of US* (ten volumes)
by Joy Hakim
Oxford University Press
This series of ten slim but packed books is one of the most engaging accounts of American history, from the Ice Age to the end of the Cold War, that we've come across for reading in the home or classroom. In contrast to many textbooks, a *voice* comes through the pages here, the voice of a writer who likes history, likes children, and wants them to like history too. For Joy Hakim, history is a *story* full of characters and conflicts. It is rooted in detailed settings, and comes alive in primary sources. It veers into delightful anecdotes, and occasionally grapples with troubling contradictions. If you think history books should have a clinical objectivity about them, then you may find these books unsettling, because the author speaks her mind: she directly addresses her readers, occasionally refers to herself as a writer grappling with how to interpret a difficult issue, makes perhaps a few too many weak puns, and says what she thinks is right and wrong. The books are written for children in about grades 5 and up, and would make excellent teacher/parent resources for the earlier grades. Each volume has many maps and black-and-white illustrations. Contact the publisher for more information about a "Teaching Guide" for each volume. The series includes the following titles: (1) *The First Americans;* (2) *Making Thirteen Colonies;* (3) *From Colonies to Country;* (4) *The New Nation;* (5) *Liberty for All?;* (6) *War, Terrible War;* (7) *Reconstruction and Reform;* (8) *An Age of Extremes;* (9) *War, Peace, and All That Jazz;* (10) *All the People.*

Knowledge Unlimited, Inc.
This is a mail-order company that offers many classroom teaching aids, especially on history (which they insist on calling "Social Studies"). You'll find colorful posters, videos, CD-ROMs, and other curricular aids for teaching Early American History, the American West, the Civil War, Civil Rights, Women's Studies, and much more. Write or call for a catalog: Knowledge Unlimited, P.O. Box 52, Madison, WI 53701-0052. (800) 356-2303.

My Fellow Americans: A Family Album
written and illustrated by Alice Provensen
Harcourt Brace, 1995
American history as a portrait gallery—and what a fascinating tour it is. With colorful paintings accompanied by brief and intriguing captions, Alice Provensen takes us on a tour of American history organized according to her personally chosen themes. The people she has chosen—mostly immediately recognizable, some less familiar—are sometimes portrayed individually, sometimes grouped. For example, Henry David Thoreau gets a full page, as does Cesar

Chavez, while on another page you can find, grouped under "Guiding Lights," Horace Mann, Sequoyah, W.E.B. Du Bois, Anne Sullivan, and others. The book presents "Pilgrims and Puritans," "Woman Suffragists," "Warriors and Patriots," "Radical Reformers," "Mega-Millionaires," "The Wobblies and the Miners," "Pastoral Protectors," "Expatriates," "Writers," "Poets," "American Architects," "Visionaries," and more. For older children, this will be a fascinating browsing book. They may not always recognize the people, but it's the kind of book that will make them want to find out more.

My First Book of Biographies: Great Men and Women Every Child Should Know
by Jean Marzollo
illustrated by Irene Trivas
Scholastic, 1994
See description under World History General Resources: History Resources and References.

Native Dwellings series
by Bonnie Shemie
Tundra Books
The author combines love of architecture, art, and Native American peoples to create these unique and interesting books. Each examines "the genius of Native peoples solving problems of shelter." Each volume offers clear, attractively rendered drawings and paintings of the dwellings built by different people. These drawings are accompanied by simple text, suitable for reading aloud to young children. Other pages present more detailed information for older students, and also helpful as teacher/parent background information. The following titles are currently available: *Houses of Snow, Skin, and Bones: Native Dwellings of the Far North; Houses of Bark: Tipi, Wigwam, and Longhouse; Houses of Hide and Earth: Native Dwellings of the Plains Indians; Houses of Wood: Native Dwellings of the Northwest Coast; Mounds of Earth and Shell: Native Dwellings of the Southeast; Houses of Adobe: Native Dwellings of the Southwest.*

New True Book series
Childrens Press
New True Books are straightforward, competent little books with big print for children in about second through fifth grades: they can be read aloud in earlier grades, and read independently from about second grade on. They offer encyclopedialike factual accounts of their subjects, and provide plenty of illustrations, as well as pronunciation guides and helpful definitions of hard words. There are more than thirty New True Books on specific Native American tribes and nations, each offering a brief overview of the history, customs, and beliefs of a particular people. There are books on politics, government, leaders, geography, and more. For a listing of titles in the New True Books series, call or write Grolier Publishing Company, Customer Service, Sherman Turnpike, Danbury, CT 06816; (800) 621-1115.

Social Studies School Service
This is a mail-order company that offers many books (including some recommended in this resource guide) and classroom teaching aids, including activity books, posters, software, videos, and more. The materials vary in quality, but there's enough good stuff here to make it worth your while to write or call for their K–6 catalog: 10020 Jefferson Boulevard, Room P31, P.O. Box 802, Culver City, CA 90232-0802; (800) 421-4246.

Time Machine
Subtitled "the American history magazine for kids," *Time Machine* is published in partnership with the National Museum of American History of the Smithsonian Institution, and is devoted to the idea that "history is stories. Great stories. Stories where you really want to know what happens." The first issue, which came out in May 1996, featured stories on the Olympics, Jim Thorpe, Jesse Owens, Sonja Henie, drugs and sports, and more, written like feature articles in a newspaper rather than like dry textbooks. The magazine uses color and black-and-white illustrations, and features a more busy and "hip"-

looking layout than *Cobblestone* (see above). Suitable for readers in about fifth grade and up. For subsciption information, call (800) 742-5401.

The Young Reader's Companion to American History
edited by John A. Garraty
Houghton Mifflin, 1994
Here's a hefty encyclopedia of American history for children in about fifth grade and up, with brief articles on topics arranged alphabetically from the Abolitionist movement to the Ziegfeld Follies. Includes articles on family life, science and technology, American Indian cultures, major ethnic groups, and topical issues such as gun control and homelessness. Also includes many biographical sketches, and articles pitched to young readers, such as histories of comic books and movies. With a few black-and-white illustrations.

AMERICAN HISTORY AND GEOGRAPHY

Kindergarten

NATIVE AMERICAN PEOPLES, PAST AND PRESENT

See also Language Arts General Resources: Stories.
See also American History General Resources.

Cherokee Summer **(1993)**
Pueblo Storyteller **(1991)**
by Diane Hoyt-Goldsmith
photographs by Lawrence Migdale
Holiday House
Good to read aloud, these two attractive books are each written as though spoken by a present-day American Indian child. Crisp color photographs help us see how past and present merge in the life of the child and her people.

Cut and Make North American Indian Masks in Full Color
by A. G. Smith and Josie Hazen
Dover, 1989
Although adults will probably end up doing most of the cutting and making, kindergartners will enjoy and learn from the masks in this book, made of high-quality paper and ink, and representing several different Native American peoples. Includes Hopi Corn Man, bird mask and Aztec Fire God. (See address, page 106.)

Itse Selu: Cherokee Harvest Festival
by Daniel Pennington
illustrated by Don Stewart
Charlesbridge, 1994
This is the brightly illustrated story of Little Wolf, who lives in a Cherokee village in the days before the arrival of Columbus. It's an ex-
citing day for Little Wolf—the day of *Itse Selu,* the Green Corn Harvest Festival. The book introduces a few words from the Cherokee language, and has a helpful preface for teachers and parents.

More Than Moccasins: A Kid's Activity Guide to Traditional North American Indian Life
by Laurie Carlson
Chicago Review Press, 1994
See description under Visual Arts General Resources.

New True Book **Native Americans series**
Childrens Press
The New True Books on American Indians, with drawings, maps or photographs on every page, are a good choice for selectively reading aloud to kindergartners. The books offer a brief overview of the history, customs, and beliefs of many different peoples, and often provide glimpses of their present-day life. More than thirty volumes are available, including such titles as *The Cherokee, The Shoshoni,* and *The Sioux.*

EARLY EXPLORATION AND SETTLEMENT

Columbus

CC *Follow the Dream: The Story of Christopher Columbus*
written and illustrated by Peter Sis
Alfred A. Knopf, 1991
A simple and upbeat narrative, good for read-

ing aloud, about the life of Columbus from his childhood to the day he landed on a Caribbean island and fulfilled his dream to go beyond the edge of the known world. The award-winning illustrations are done in an unusual style: while the pictures are big, the figures in them are sometimes small, and will be most effective if children have an opportunity to pore over them up close.

CC *In 1492*
by Jean Marzollo
illustrated by Steve Björkman
Scholastic, 1991
Energetic watercolor illustrations provide a backdrop for this poem that takes off from the old couplet "In fourteen hundred ninety-two/ Columbus sailed the ocean blue." A good read-aloud.

Pilgrims

The Pilgrim's First Thanksgiving
by Ann McGovern
illustrated by Elroy Freem
Scholastic, 1973 (illustrations 1993)
The clear and simple text, along with colorful illustrations, make this a good read-aloud book It describes the hard voyage on the *Mayflower*, then moves through the seasons—winter, spring, summer, and then, in fall, to the first Thanksgiving.

CC *Samuel Eaton's Day: A Day in the Life of a Pilgrim Boy* **(1993)**
Sarah Morton's Day: A Day in the Life of a Pilgrim Girl **(1989)**
by Kate Waters
photography by Russ Kendall
Scholastic
These companion books are good for reading aloud and great for helping young children "see" what life was like for the Pilgrims. Each book tells, in first-person narration, the story of a day in the life of a Pilgrim boy and girl, including getting dressed, doing chores, eating

meals, learning lessons, and more. The words are brought to life by the illustrations, which are color photographs of historical reenactors at Plimoth Plantation. The publisher has also produced an "Innovations Teaching Guide" to accompany *Sarah Morton's Day*.

Three Young Pilgrims
written and illustrated by Cheryl Harness
Bradbury Press, 1992
This charming work of historical fiction would make a good read-aloud. It begins, "Mary, Remember, and Bartholomew stood on the deck of a little boat in the very middle of the dark blue ocean all around. They watched for mermaids and whales, pirates, and, most of all, land." The story acknowledges but does not dwell on the hardships and suffering ("Mama and the new baby" die in the hard first winter). The words are accompanied by appealing watercolor illustrations, some of which include interesting nuggets of information, perhaps of special interest to older readers.

PRESIDENTS PAST AND PRESENT

Abe Lincoln's Hat
by Martha Brenner
illustrated by Donald Cook
Random House, 1994
Here's an enjoyable story in simple words about Abe Lincoln, who buys a tall hat as a young attorney and uses it through the years to store his important papers. A good read-aloud for kindergartners, this "Step into Reading" book is written to be read independently by children in about grades 1–3.

Don't You Dare Shoot That Bear! A Story of Theodore Roosevelt
written and illustrated by Robert Quackenbush
Prentice Hall, 1984
This is too complex a book to read aloud to kindergartners, but it's a delightful and informative resource that teachers and parents could

borrow from to share with children some lively anecdotes about the president after whom "teddy bears" are named.

Honest Abe
by Edith Kunhardt
illustrated by Malcah Zeldis
Greenwillow Books, 1993
This picture book tells the story of hardworking, honest Abraham Lincoln as a boy, family man, and president. The simple words are just right for reading aloud, and the bold, vividly colored illustrations will engage the attention of your young listeners.

CC *Just Like Abraham Lincoln*
written and illustrated by Bernard Waber
Scholastic, 1964
A delightful picture book about a young boy's friendship with his neighbor who looks uncannily like Abraham Lincoln. The amusing narrative reveals a lot about the real Lincoln. A delightful read-aloud.

CC *My First Presidents' Day Book*
by Aileen Fisher
illustrated by Lydia Halverson
Childrens Press, 1987
A pleasant way to introduce George Washington and Abraham Lincoln, this slender book of charming, old-fashioned poems is just the thing to read and reread to kindergartners. The illustrations are colorful, but not quite up to the poems.

A Picture Book of George Washington (1989)
A Picture Book of Thomas Jefferson (1990)
by David A. Adler
illustrated by John and Alexandra Wallner
Holiday House
The colorful illustrations in these books should appeal to kindergartners. The books are suitable for reading aloud, though you may want to be selective since, despite the picture-book format, the author uses a few too many abstract and unfamiliar terms (for example, "talk about politics" or "legislature").

AMERICAN HISTORY AND GEOGRAPHY

Grade 1

THE EARLIEST PEOPLE: HUNTERS AND NOMADS

First Dog
written and illustrated by Jan Brett
Harcourt Brace Jovanovich, 1988
In this lovely picture-book adventure story set in prehistoric times, Paleowolf befriends Kip, a caveboy, and becomes "the first dog." Illustrations on the page borders were inspired by artifacts and cave paintings from the period.

CC *The Ice Age*
by Darlene R. Stille
Childrens Press, 1990
Part of the New True Books series, this well-illustrated overview of the Ice Age from a scientific and historical perspective is a good read-aloud introduction to why we have Ice Ages in general, and what the last one was like in particular. Plenty of drawings and photographs will help children imagine these far-off times.

Mik's Mammoth
by Mike Gerrard
Farrar, Straus & Giroux, 1990
The world of Ice Age mammals comes to life in this rhyming, picture-book adventure story about Mik and his faithful woolly mammoth.

CC *Wild and Woolly Mammoths*
written and illustrated by Aliki
HarperCollins, 1977, revised 1996
An excellent read-aloud, this book focuses on the woolly mammoth, and offers a fascinating look back to the time when these giant shaggy beasts roamed the earth. It offers a good deal of information about life in the Ice Age (how humans lived, what they wore, and how they hunted mammoths), all accompanied by bold pictures.

INTRODUCTION TO MAYA, INCA, AND AZTEC CIVILIZATIONS

CC *The Aztec*
by Patricia McKissack
Childrens Press, 1985, revised 1992
This New True Book is written to be read by children in about second to fourth grade, and would make a good read-aloud at this level. The chapter on religion very briefly mentions human sacrifice, which was central to the Aztec culture. Should you discuss this practice with first graders? Here's what we think: wait to discuss this issue until fifth grade, when—as recommended by the *Core Knowledge Sequence*—students study these civilizations in more detail. But by all means decide for yourself.

A Coloring Book of Incas, Aztecs, Mayas, and Other Precolumbian Peoples
Bellerophon Books, 1994
All the ready-to-color drawings of gods and goddesses, warriors, chiefs, and ordinary citizens in this book are taken from original pottery, statues, and documents. Captions identify most of the subjects. Many of the drawings are intricate and detailed, so don't expect children to "stay in the lines." Also available from this company, a set of five posters of Precolumbian artifacts. (See address, page 106.)

The Flame of Peace

written and illustrated by Deborah Nourse
    Lattimore
HarperCollins, 1987
Stunning Aztec-inspired art accompanies this
story of an Aztec boy who outwits seven evil
gods to bring peace to his people. The portrayal
of the Aztec gods and the vivid artwork make
this book worthwhile as a read-aloud, but the
book's emphasis on peace, however much it
may appeal to our modern sensibilities, diverts
attention from the fact that the Aztecs were
among the most warlike of Mesoamerican peoples.

How Music Came to the World: An Ancient Mexican Myth

by Hal Ober
illustrated by Carol Ober
Houghton Mifflin, 1994
Striking oil pastel illustrations distinguish this
book, which offers a retelling of an ancient Mexican legend in which the sky god and the wind
god set aside their differences and bring music
from the Sun's house to the Earth.

CC The Inca

by Patricia McKissack
Childrens Press, 1985, revised 1992
This New True Book, with many color photographs, is written to be read by children in
about second to fourth grade, and parts would
make a good read-aloud in first grade. It focuses on the Inca of the past but also discusses
their present day descendants. (Ritual sacrifice
is very briefly mentioned. For a discussion of
this issue, see the entry above for *The Aztec* by
Patricia McKissack.)

The Llama's Secret

by Argentina Palacios
illustrated by Charles Reasoner
Troll Associates, 1993
The Inca considered the llama a sacred animal.
This illustrated story tells the legendary origin

of that belief as the llama leads the others animals to safety from a great flood.

CC The Maya

by Patricia McKissack
Childrens Press, 1985, revised 1993
This New True Book is written to be read by
children in about second to fourth grade, and
would make a good read-aloud at this level. It
looks at history, customs, growing up, art, music, religion, and the Maya today. Lots of good
color photos.

The Sad Night: The Story of an Aztec Victory and a Spanish Loss

written and illustrated by Sally Schoffer
    Mathews
Clarion Books, 1994
There is much for children to think about in this
book, which tells in simple and effective terms
the complex and sometimes cruel story of the
Aztecs and the coming of Cortés. Read it yourself before you read it aloud and decide if you
are comfortable with some of the details; it tells
the truth, but the truth here includes greed, deception, cruelty, and death. The book does not
dwell on these aspects, however, and it ends by
quietly describing a recent friendly meeting between the president of Mexico and the ambassador from Spain, and notes that on the flag of
Mexico, whose people mainly speak Spanish, is
an image from Aztec lore, the eagle on the cactus. The richly colored illustrations are done in
the style of Aztec codex art.

Why There Is No Arguing In Heaven: A Mayan Myth

retold and illustrated by Deborah Nourse
    Lattimore
HarperCollins, 1989
Hunab Kw, the first Creator God of the Mayas,
challenges three lesser gods and goddesses to
create a being to worship him. This dramatically
illustrated picture book explains how Maize
God creates humankind and succeeds where
others fail. Suitable as a read-aloud for this
grade.

EARLY EXPLORATION AND SETTLEMENT

Columbus

Note: The *Core Knowledge Sequence* recommends an introduction to the story of Columbus in Kindergarten, and a review of this story in first grade in order to provide children a familiar starting point for learning about early European exploration and settlement of this country.

Christopher Columbus
by Stephen Krensky
Illustrated by Norman Greene
Random House, 1991
Readable by some first graders, this Step 2 "Step into Reading" book (written for grades 1–3) tells a simple story of Columbus's first voyage to America. Illustrated with color drawings.

Columbus Discovers America Coloring Book
by Peter F. Copeland
Dover, 1988
From Dover's series of historical coloring books, this one includes pictures of Columbus at the Spanish court, scenes of shipboard life, and, of course, landing in the New World. (See address, page 106.)

I Sailed with Christopher Columbus
by Miriam Schlein
illustrated by Tom Newsom
HarperCollins, 1991
This excellent read-aloud chapter book tells the story of a cabin boy sailing with Columbus. The child experiences the excitement of the journey and the enterprise of Columbus, but also reflects with a sense of justice on the mistreatment of the Native Americans.

 **CC** = "Core Collection" book (see page 8).

The English Colonies: An Introduction

CC *Across the Wide Dark Sea: The* **Mayflower** *Journey*
by Jean Van Leeuwen
illustrated by Thomas B. Allen
Dial Books, 1995
A beautiful portrayal of a young boy and his family, who experience the wretched nine-week journey to America and the first deadly winter at Plymouth. The author captures details that bring the experience to life—cramped living quarters on ship, storm at sea, man overboard, and the ordeal of survival at Plymouth. All rendered and expressed in a spirit of determination, faith, and courage. Excellent for reading aloud.

The First Thanksgiving
by Linda Hayward
illustrated by James Watling
Random House, 1990
Some first graders will be able to read this Step 2 Step into Reading book for beginning readers. Appealing watercolor illustrations accompany the story, which tells about the Pilgrims' reasons for leaving England, their hard voyage on the *Mayflower*, the terrible first winter, the welcome help from Samoset, Squanto, and Massasoit, and the harvest feast that has since become known as Thanksgiving.

Pocahontas: Daughter of a Chief
by Carol Greene
illustrated by Steven Dobson
Childrens Press, 1988
This Rookie Biography is written in simple language and big print. Some first graders may be able to read it with a little help; otherwise, it can be read aloud. The author begins by seeing events from Pocahontas's point of view, and puts her thoughts into imagined words. The rescue of John Smith is presented as fact, with no mention that the story might be made up or exaggerated. The book goes on to tell how Pocahontas was kidnapped by the English, married

John Rolfe, traveled to England, and died far from home. The art mixes old prints and new drawings; the old prints are better.

CC *Samuel Eaton's Day: A Day in the Life of a Pilgrim Boy* **(1993)**
  Sarah Morton's Day: A Day in the Life of a Pilgrim Girl **(1989)**
by Kate Waters
photography by Russ Kendall
Scholastic
See description under American History Kindergarten: Early Exploration and Settlement: Pilgrims. If you missed these books in kindergarten, read them now!

The Thirteen Colonies
by Dennis Fradin
Childrens Press, 1988
This is a New True Book, written in simple language and big print, with illustrations on almost every page, useful as a read-aloud in first grade. The author begins by noting that American Indians lived here long before Europeans came, and that the Spanish came before the English. The majority of the book focuses on the English. There is a brief account of the Lost Colony, followed by short chapters on "Who Were the Colonists?" (slavery is briefly noted), "How Did the Colonists Live?," "What Happened to the Indians?," and "The Colonies Break Away from England."

FROM COLONIES TO INDEPENDENCE: THE AMERICAN REVOLUTION

Betsy Ross
written and illustrated by Alexandra Wallner
Holiday House, 1994
This entertaining picture book presents Betsy Ross as an active, enterprising person. Illustrated with vivid folk art paintings.

The Boston Coffee Party
by Doreen Rappaport
illustrated by Emily Arnold McCully
HarperCollins, 1988
An I Can Read book, with large print suitable for first graders. Based on a true incident, this is a story of two young sisters during the Revolutionary War who help a group of Boston women get coffee from a greedy merchant. With color drawings and writing that is accessible to the youngest readers, this book will help students understand the struggles that took place off the battlefield.

Buttons for General Washington
by Peter and Connie Roop
illustrated by Peter E. Hanson
Carolrhoda Books, 1986
Based on a true incident during the Revolutionary War, this book tells the story of a fourteen-year-old boy who carries secret messages to George Washington in his coat buttons. With color and black-and-white illustrations, and large print, this is a good read-aloud that some strong first-grade readers, with a little help, will be able to read on their own.

Deborah Sampson Goes to War
by Bryna Stevens
illustrated by Florence Hill
Dell/Young Yearling, 1984
Women were not allowed to fight in the Revolution, but that didn't stop Deborah Sampson. This story, with black-and-white pictures, is written in big print for about a second- or third-grade reading level, and would make a good read-aloud for first grade. Ignore the cover illustration, which depicts Deborah Sampson as a sort of Michelle Pfeiffer.

The Fourth of July Story
by Alice Dalgliesh
illustrated by Marie Nonnast
Simon & Schuster/Aladdin, 1956, 1995
The author wrote this book, she says, because children "have a right to know that Independence Day is something more than fireworks

and picnics." In clear prose, good for reading aloud, she tells a concise story of the thirteen colonies, the movement for independence, the fiery speech of Patrick Henry, the writing of the Declaration of Independence, John Hancock's bold signature, the ringing of the Liberty Bell, and the carrying of the news throughout the thirteen states.

George the Drummer Boy
by Nathaniel Benchley
illustrated by Don Bolognese
HarperCollins, 1977
A Level 3 I Can Read book, directed to grades 2–4, but readable by some first graders with a little help; otherwise a good read-aloud. The author tells the story of a British drummer boy at the battles of Lexington and Concord. Read this along with a book by the same author, *Sam the Minuteman.*

George Washington: First President of the United States
by Carol Greene
illustrated by Steven Dobson
Childrens Press, 1991
Some strong first graders readers may, with help, be able to read this Rookie Biography, written in short sentences and big print; otherwise, it can be read aloud. The author looks briefly at Washington's childhood, and his work as a surveyor and a soldier. The book touches lightly upon his leadership during the Revolution, then goes on to tell some interesting details about his life as president and after. The book ends with the famous words "First in war, first in peace, and first in the hearts of his countrymen." With illustrations on nearly every page.

Heroines of the American Revolution: A Bellerophon Coloring Book
by Jill Canon
drawings by Alan Archambault
Bellerophon Books, 1994
Molly Pitcher wasn't the only one! This historical coloring book includes one-page biographies (written for adults) and ready to color drawings of over twenty women who took part in the Revolution. (See address, page 106.)

CC *The Many Lives of Benjamin Franklin*
written and illustrated by Aliki
Simon & Schuster Books for Young Readers, 1988
This is an informative and entertaining introduction to Franklin's life and many achievements. Excellent for reading aloud, but make sure the children can get a close look at the pictures, many of which feature Aliki's characteristically charming drawings with dialogue in very small print that you won't want to miss.

Phillis Wheatley: First African-American Poet
by Carol Greene
Childrens Press, 1995
This Rookie Biography, written in big print with simple language and many pictures, is a fine read-aloud introduction to an important figure on whom there are few good books for young children. It begins in the hold of a slave ship, and describes the terrible conditions the young girl was forced to suffer. It goes on to tell how the girl, now named Phillis, learned to read and write, and quickly showed her talent for poetry. It includes passages from some letters from the period, as well as a few lines from Phillis Wheatley's poetry (written in the elaborate, ornate style of her time).

CC *Sam the Minuteman*
by Nathaniel Benchley
illustrated by Arnold Lobel
HarperCollins, 1969
A Level 3 I Can Read book, directed to grades 2–4, but readable by some first graders with a little help; otherwise a good read-aloud. This is the story of Sam Brown, a boy whose quiet life on a Massachusetts farm is changed forever by the battles of Lexington and Concord. The illustrations are simple and effective. You might want to read this book along with another by the same author, *George the Drummer Boy* (described above).

Story of the American Revolution Coloring Book
by Peter F. Copeland
Dover, 1988
Fairly intricate drawings present famous scenes from the Revolutionary war—Paul Revere's ride, the signing of the Declaration of Independence, the execution of Nathan Hale, and more. (See address, page 106.)

Thomas Jefferson: Author, Inventor, President
by Carol Greene
Childrens Press, 1991
Some strong first-grade readers may, with help, be able to read parts of this Rookie Biography, written in short sentences and big print; otherwise, it can be read aloud. The story begins with a young Tom Jefferson looking at a bug— "He just wanted to learn all he could about that bug"—and goes on to emphasize his lifelong curiosity and love of learning. The author gives brief but informative accounts of Jefferson as author of the Declaration of Independence, and as president (including his disagreements with Hamilton, and the Louisiana Purchase). Illustrated with black-and-white and color photographs and paintings, including helpful photos of colonial Williamsburg and Monticello.

CC *Yankee Doodle: A Revolutionary Tail*
illustrated by Gary Chalk
Dorling Kindersley, 1993
That's right, "Tail" not "Tale." In this delightful history of the American Revolution, some of the words are written to the tune of "Yankee Doodle," and the principal players are energetic animals, garbed as Yanks and Tories. The animal characters toss the tea into Boston Harbor, cross the Delaware, sew the first American flag, and a lot more. Both entertaining and educational—a winner!

EARLY EXPLORATION OF THE AMERICAN WEST

Daniel Boone: Man of the Forests
by Carol Greene
Childrens Press, 1990
This Rookie Biography, written in simple language and large print, can be read aloud at this grade. It tells the story of Daniel Boone and the Wilderness Road, of the Shawnee resistance to the settlers moving onto their hunting grounds, and of the eventual settlement of Kentucky. The story is generally well told, though the author makes the common error of referring to the Shawnee men as "braves," and the illustrations—of which there are many, including some helpful old prints and drawings—are sometimes garish, especially the new color drawings.

CC *Lewis and Clark: Explorers of the American West*
by Steven Kroll
illustrated by Richard Williams
Holiday House, 1994
This beautifully illustrated book provides fascinating details about the Lewis and Clark expedition. The picture-book format makes it a good choice for reading aloud.

Sacagawea
by Jan Gleiter and Kathleen Thompson
illustrated Yoshi Miyake
Raintree/Steck-Vaughn, 1995
This pleasantly illustrated book in the publisher's First Biographies series provides a good deal of information about the Lewis and Clark expedition framed within a life story of Sacagawea. A good read-aloud for this grade.

CC = "Core Collection" book (see page 8).

AMERICAN HISTORY AND GEOGRAPHY

Grade 2

AMERICAN GOVERNMENT: THE CONSTITUTION

The Constitution
by Warren Colman
Childrens Press, 1987
This is a New True Book, written in simple language and big print, with illustrations on almost every page. While some second graders may be able to handle the words, it is still best read aloud with an adult to help discuss ideas and questions. The book begins, "Think what a baseball game would be like without rules," and goes on to convey, in clear and direct language, how the Constitution was conceived, drafted, and ratified. It brings up topics, such as the Articles of Confederation, that we would suggest are best left till the fourth grade. Still, you can read aloud and discuss parts of the book to introduce some basic ideas about law and government.

THE WAR OF 1812

An American Army of Two
by Janet Greeson
illustrated by Patricia Rose Mulvihill
Carolrhoda Books, 1992
Young Rebecca Bates and her sister figure out how to trick the British into believing that American troops are coming to their towns' rescue. This easy-to-read story with large print is based on a true incident in the War of 1812.

CC *By the Dawn's Early Light: The Story of the Star-Spangled Banner*
by Steven Kroll
illustrated by Dan Andreason
Scholastic, 1993
This warmly illustrated book brings drama and suspense to the story of how Francis Scott Key wrote "The Star-Spangled Banner." It includes a photograph of Key's manuscript of the poem. An afterword tells how the poem gradually became more popular and finally, in 1931, by congressional decree, our national anthem.

Cornstalks and Cannonballs
by Barbara Mitchell
illustrated by Karen Ritz
Carolrhoda Books, 1980
Children will enjoy this story of how the small town of Lewes, Delaware, resisted the British Navy during the War of 1812. It's based in fact, it's fun, and it's easy to read.

CC *The Star-Spangled Banner*
illustrated by Peter Spier
Doubleday, 1973
This large format picture book introduces our national anthem by illustrating each of its lines with a full-page, detailed watercolor. The book includes an excellent two-page spread of illustrations of our flag throughout history, a copy of Key's manuscript of the poem, and an informative historical appendix that is useful as a teacher/parent resource.

CC = "Core Collection" book (see page 8).

WESTWARD EXPANSION

Pioneers

CC *The Amazing Impossible Erie Canal*
written and illustrated by Cheryl Harness
Macmillan, 1995
Excellent pictures and an engaging story of the
canal that ran from Albany to Buffalo and facili-
tated westward movement by making transportation to the Great Lakes affordable. A great
read-aloud.

Buffalo Bill and the Pony Express
by Eleanor Coerr
illustrated by Don Bolognese
HarperCollins, 1995
Here's a lively bit of historical fiction that second graders can read independently. Part of the
I Can Read series, this is the story of young Bill
(later, Buffalo Bill), who can't resist the lure of a
sign that says WANTED: RIDERS FOR PONY EXPRESS.
YOUNG, SKINNY FELLOWS UNDER 18. ORPHANS WEL-
COME. The illustrations are competent but not
the book's real strength, which lies in the story
that manages to engage a young reader's interest while conveying information about the history of the Pony Express.

Cassie's Journey: Going West in the 1860's
by Brett Harvey
illustrated by Deborah Kogan Ray
Holiday House, 1988
This picture book with black-and-white drawings is a good read-aloud. A young girl narrates
the story of her family's westward journey from
Illinois to California in the 1860s. Based on true
accounts.

The Floating House
by Scott Russell Sanders
illustrated by Helen Cogancherry
Macmillan, 1995
Set in 1815, this is the story of the McClure family as they float down the Ohio River in a flat-
boat to find a new home farther west in Jeffer-

sonville, Indiana. This is a rich picture book and
fine piece of fiction depicting the early days and
ways of westward movement. The McClures
"were eager to reach the wild country down-
stream, where you could buy farms for a dollar
an acre and the dirt was so rich people said you
could plant a stick and it would break out in
leaves."

CC *Going West*
by Jean Van Leeuwen
illustrated by Thomas B. Allen
Dial Books, 1992
This descriptive and informative picture book of
a family's journey west is told from seven-year-
old Hannah's point of view. Warm-colored charcoal, pastel, and pencil illustrations complement
the text. A good read-aloud that can also be
read independently by some second graders.

The Golly Sisters Go West (1985)
Hooray for the Golly Sisters! (1990)
by Betsy Byars
illustrated by Sue Truesdell
HarperCollins
Back in the days before TV and movies, what
did people do for entertainment? Well, out
West, they went to see traveling shows put on
by the likes of the Golly Sisters, Rose and May-
May. A little bit of history—traveling by covered wagon, for example, and fording rivers—
comes through in these books, but let's face it,
they're mainly for fun. Children will enjoy the
antics of the Golly Sisters, and second graders
should have no trouble reading these I Can
Read books, with their simple language, big
print, and energetic illustrations.

The Josefina Story Quilt
by Eleanor Coerr
illustrated by Bruce Degen
HarperCollins, 1986
It's 1847 and young Faith doesn't want to move
west. She has to argue long and hard to get her
parents to let her bring her pet hen, Josefina. As
she travels, she pieces together a quilt which
she names the Josefina Story Quilt. This engag-

ing story is a Level 3 I Can Read book, recommended by the publisher for grades 2–4.

CC *Wagon Wheels*
by Barbara Brenner
illustrated by Don Bolognese
HarperCollins, 1978
This is a Level 3 I Can Read book, recommended by the publisher for grades 2–4. It tells the story of an African-American family who move to Kansas in the 1870s. They face a bitter winter, a prairie fire, and other hardships and adventures. Based on a true story.

Warm as Wool
by Scott Russell Sanders
illustrated by Helen Cogancherry
Bradbury Press, 1992
What would you do if you lived in cabin on the Ohio frontier in 1803 and you and your family were freezing to death? Betsy Ward raised sheep for their wool. This picture book based on a true story explains how pioneers lived and why raising sheep for wool was such a hard job. Also from this author and on a similar subject, *Aurora Means Dawn.* Both are excellent beginning historical fiction.

Native Americans

Note: The suggested focus in this grade is on the Cherokee and the Plains Indians. See also Language Arts Grade 2: Stories of Iktomi (Plains Indian trickster figure).

Buffalo Woman
written and illustrated by Paul Goble
Bradbury Press/Aladdin, 1984
A good read-aloud for this grade, this is the story of a young man who marries a female buffalo who has been transformed into a beautiful girl. When his family rejects her, he goes to join the Buffalo Nation. Told by many Plains Indian tribes, this story was meant to strengthen the bond between the people and the buffalo on whom they depended. With Goble's strikingly distinctive illustrations.

The Cherokee
by Emilie Uttag Lepthien
Childrens Press, 1985
The author describes the customs, ways of life, and history of the Cherokee nation, from its earliest days to the present, and discusses the Trail of Tears and Sequoyah. A New True Book, with many pictures and large print, readable by many second graders with some help. (There are also New True Books on various Plains Indian peoples, including these titles: *The Crow; The Shoshoni; The Pawnee;* and *The Sioux.*)

The First Strawberries: A Cherokee Story
retold by Joseph Bruchac
illustrated by Anna Vojtech
Dial Books, 1993
This gentle story tells how the sun heals a marital discord and in the process introduces strawberries to the world. Vibrant color illustrations complement the text. A good choice for a read-aloud.

CC *The Girl Who Loved Wild Horses*
written and illustrated by Paul Goble
Bradbury Press/Aladdin, 1978
In this beautifully illustrated story (a Caldecott Medal winner), a young girl prefers to live among the horses instead of with her own people. Like Goble's *Buffalo Woman* (see above), this story conveys a sense of the deep relation between the people and the animals upon which they depended. A fine read-aloud for this grade.

Sequoyah: Father of the Cherokee Alphabet
by David Petersen
Childrens Press, 1991
This illustrated book is a good read-aloud biography of the man who is most remembered "for giving his people the gift of reading and writing."

THE CIVIL WAR: AN INTRODUCTION

Abraham Lincoln: A Man for All the People
by Myra Cohn Livingston
illustrated by Samuel Byrd
Holiday House, 1993
Bold paintings and rhyming text combine in this overview of the life of Lincoln. A wonderful introduction to the sixteenth president, and a delightful read-aloud, though at times you will need to explain some of the text (such as "rode the circuit" or "called slavery a blight").

Cecil's Story
by George Ella Lyon
illustrated by Peter Catalanotto
Orchard Books, 1991
In very few words, easily readable by second graders, this moving picture book tells the story of young Cecil, whose father is away fighting in the Civil War, and of Cecil's resolution to be strong, come what may.

Civil War Paper Soldiers
by A. G. Smith
Dover Publications
Foot soldiers, commanders on horseback, cannons, tents, and flags: one hundred free-standing paper figures in gray and blue (from which the children can make a great classroom bulletin board). The diversity of uniforms gives children a sense of how we were a conglomeration of states more than a unified nation. (See address, page 106.)

The Drinking Gourd: A Story of the Underground Railroad
by F. N. Monjo
Illustrated by Fred Brenner
HarperCollins, 1993
This book tells a fictional story to dramatize historical facts about the Underground Railroad. The title refers to the Big Dipper, which runaway slaves used to guide them northward in their dangerous journey to freedom. In this story, a boy learns about the underground railroad when he finds out, to his surprise, that his father is hiding slaves in his barn and helping them get to Canada. Accessible writing and frequent illustrations make this a good book as a read-aloud or for many second graders to read on their own. A "Level 3" book in the I Can Read series.

Follow the Drinking Gourd
written and illustrated by Jeanette Winter
Alfred A. Knopf, 1988
With large, colorful illustrations and prose accessible to younger readers, this book narrates the story of the underground railroad, along which slaves were able to reach freedom by following the Big Dipper, otherwise known as the "Drinking Gourd." Includes words and music to the song named in the book's title.

The Gettysburg Address
illustrated by Michael McCurdy
foreword by Garry Wills
Houghton Mifflin, 1995
In this big picture book, McCurdy's bold, stark black-and-white prints evoke images to accompany the words of Lincoln's immortal speech. Garry Wills provides a brief foreword to describe the occasion of the speech and its larger significance.

Harriet and the Promised Land
written and illustrated by Jacob Lawrence
Simon & Schuster, 1993 (reissue of a 1968 publication)
This oversized books presents a brief biography in verse about Harriet Tubman, with magnificent illustrations by African-American artist Jacob Lawrence.

Journey to Freedom
by Courtni Wright
illustrated by Gershom Griffith
Holiday House, 1994
The inspiring story of an escaped slave family traveling to freedom on the underground railroad. Beautiful illustrations, and not without its

moments of humor, such as when these Southern-born and -bred children see snow for the first time.

CC *Just a Few Words, Mr. Lincoln: The Story of the Gettysburg Address*
by Jean Fritz
illustrated by Charles Robinson
Grosset & Dunlap, 1993
An All Aboard Reading book, Level 3 (for grades 2–3), this illustrated book does a fine job of giving a glimpse at the private life of Lincoln and dramatizing the events surrounding his brief and immortal speech. "It took longer to boil an egg" than to give this speech, the author notes. Includes the text of the Gettysburg Address.

CC *Meet Abraham Lincoln*
by Barbara Cary
Random House, 1965, 1989
A Step-Up reader, this excellent brief biography of Lincoln, written at a second-grade reading level, tells the story of Lincoln's life from the log cabin to Ford's Theater. The author is one of the few to address the issue of Lincoln's personal abhorrence of slavery.

Nettie's Trip South
by Ann Turner
illustrated by Ronald Himler
Macmillan, 1987/Scholastic, 1993
Young Nettie takes a trip from Albany to Richmond. She sees many things she will not forget—including her first glimpse of slavery. The book is written in the form of a letter from Nettie to a friend, and is based on the diary of the author's great-grandmother. A Teaching Guide is available from Scholastic.

Now Let Me Fly: The Story of a Slave Family
written and illustrated by Dolores Johnson
Macmillan, 1993
A well-illustrated and compelling read-aloud book for this grade level, this book, says the

author, "is a fictional account of one family's life in the constrictive grip of slavery. It is not a pleasant story, nor does it have a happy ending, yet it is a story that must be told." The story is told in the first-person voice of Minna, who thinks back to her childhood in Africa, then remembers all that has happened since.

A Picture Book of Harriet Tubman
by David A. Adler
illustrated by Samuel Byrd
Holiday House, 1992
In telling the life story of Harriet Tubman, Adler incorporates some of her own words, and he gives some helpful historical background to the Civil War. Along the way in this book you meet Nat Turner, John Brown (very briefly), and Abraham Lincoln. But most of all, you come to admire Harriet Tubman as, in Adler's words, "a brave, courageous woman." A fine read-aloud.

Sweet Clara and the Freedom Quilt
by Deborah Hopkinson
illustrated by James Ransome
Alfred A. Knopf, 1993
A good read-aloud, this lovely picture book tells the story of Clara, a young slave who, with determination and ingenuity, creates a patchwork quilt that depicts the route of the underground railroad, and so helps many find the way to freedom. A Reading Rainbow book.

Thunder at Gettysburg
by Patricia Lee Gauch
illustrated by Stephen Gammell
Dell Yearling, 1975
Fiction based on an autobiographical account, this brief chapter book, written at a level readable by most second graders, offers a dramatic story of one young girl's experiences as she is swept into the Battle of Gettysburg. The story powerfully, but not overwhelmingly, conveys the confusion, terror, and loss that are part of the experience of war. With evocative black-and-white drawings.

IMMIGRATION AND CITIZENSHIP

CC *Coming to America: The Story of Immigration*
by Betsy Maestro
illustrated by Susannah Ryan
Scholastic, 1996
This big, colorfully illustrated book provides a great read-aloud introduction to immigration for second graders. Betsy Maestro starts out by taking a broad historical view of immigration, from the first "immigrants" to cross the land bridge during the Ice Age, to the forced immigration of African-Americans, to the waves of immigrants from Eastern Europe in the early 1900s, as well as the arrival of refugees from Southeast Asia, Cuba, and Haiti today. She does not ignore the hardships experienced by many immigrants, but her overall view is a positive picture of *e pluribus unum*. We have only one quibble about this book: in the final two pages the language takes a sudden turn and seems to be directed more to adults than to children. That aside, this is a fine book from the author of *The Story of the Statue of Liberty* (described below).

Ellis Island: Doorway to Freedom
by Steven Kroll
illustrated by Karen Ritz
Holiday House, 1995
Haunting illustrations combine with informative text to tell the story of Ellis Island between 1800 and the present. This is a good read-aloud introduction to Ellis Island for second graders. The text is not as lively as it could be, but the illustrations carry the book and make it worth seeking out.

CC *The Story of the Statue of Liberty*
by Betsy Maestro
illustrated by Giulio Maestro
Lothrop, Lee & Shepard/Mulberry Books, 1986
This outstanding picture book tells the fascinating story of how the Statue of Liberty was designed, built in Paris, taken apart, and shipped to America to become one of our most important national symbols. Colorful, dramatic, and detailed illustrations complement the clearly written text, suitable for reading aloud. Supplemental pages provide interesting information and the text of Emma Lazarus's poem.

Statue of Liberty and Ellis Island Coloring Book
by A. G. Smith
Dover, 1985
Contains forty-five line drawings that follow the history of the statue and of immigration to Ellis Island. (See address, page 106.)

A Very Important Day
by Maggie Rugg Herold
illustrated by Catherine Stock
Morrow Junior Books, 1995
In this delightful picture book, the characters are fictional but the experience is based on important facts about what it means to become a citizen of the United States. It's a very important day in New York City for the many people from different countries who are hurrying to the courthouse to become U.S. citizens. An appendix offers a clear and helpful discussion of "Becoming a Citizen."

Historical Fiction on Immigration

Angel Child, Dragon Child
by Michele Maria Surat
illustrated by Vo-Dinh Mai
Scholastic, 1983
Ut comes to the United States from Vietnam. The children in her new American school tease her for the way she talks and dresses. But out of this conflict there grows a greater understanding. A good read-aloud.

The Butterfly Seeds
written and illustrated by Mary Watson
William Morrow/Tambourine Books, 1995
Young Jake is excited about moving to a new country but he knows he'll miss his grandfather. When Grandpa comes to say good-bye, he gives Jake some "butterfly seeds," and tells him

to plant them in America. Set in the 1910s, this is the touching story of an Eastern European immigrant family that sails to America to start a new life. Jake struggles with loneliness and homesickness but the "butterfly seeds" connect him with his past and bring hope to his American present too. The superb illustrations convey the contrast between the rural life Jake leaves behind and the bustling city in America.

How Many Days to America? A Thanksgiving Story
by Eve Bunting
illustrated by Beth Peck
Clarion Books, 1988
This is a moving story, beautifully told. Its focus is contemporary Caribbean immigration. A poor family attempts a dangerous journey in order to escape a military dictatorship and come to the United States. In the end they have much to be thankful for.

In America
written and illustrated by Marissa Moss
Dutton Children's Books, 1994
A Lithuanian grandfather shares with his American grandson the story of why he left the Old World (escaping religious persecution) and why his brother Herschel didn't (not wanting to leave the land of his youth). The tone is upbeat and the focus is on the sort of person it takes to leave the known and venture into a new culture.

CC Klara's New World
written and illustrated by Jeanette Winter
Alfred A. Knopf, 1992
This superbly illustrated book tells the story of a Swedish family that leaves the stony fields of their homeland to find a new life in fertile Minnesota. Set in the 1870s, the story traces the journey from their homeland across the Atlantic and, once in America, by steamboat and train to the Midwest, then through the stages of building their log cabin and making a home in the Minnesota wilderness. A wonderful read-aloud.

The Long Way to a New Land
written and illustrated by Joan Sandin
HarperCollins, 1981
This illustrated I Can Read book is suitable for independent reading by second graders. It tells the story of Carl Erik and his family as they leave drought-stricken Sweden to find a new life in America.

CC The Lotus Seed
by Sherry Garland
illustrated by Tatsuro Kiuchi
Harcourt Brace, 1992
A moving, stunningly illustrated story about a Vietnamese grandmother who leaves behind everything but a lotus seed in order to come to the United States. The book captures the sadness of leaving and the enormous strength needed to start anew.

CC Molly's Pilgrim
by Barbara Cohen
illustrated by Michael J. Deraney
Bantam Skylark, 1983
Molly and her family have come to America from Russia. The children in Molly's third-grade class make fun of her accent. In the end, the children learn an important lesson about religious freedom, and they learn that "pilgrims" did not come to America only in 1620. Strong second-grade readers can enjoy this book on their own (it is printed in large type); otherwise, a fine read-aloud.

Peppe, the Lamplighter
by Elisa Bartone
illustrated by Ted Lewin
Lothrop, Lee & Shepard Books, 1993
Set in a New York City tenement in the early 1900s, this is the story of Peppe, the youngest son in an Italian immigrant family, who must work to help support the family when his father falls ill. A moving and uplifting story, strengthened by evocative illustrations.

CC = "Core Collection" book (see page 8).

Silver at Night
by Susan Bartoletti
illustrated by David Ray
Crown Publishers, 1994
Set in the early twentieth century, this is the dramatically illustrated story of a diligent Italian immigrant who works in the Pennsylvania mines in order to earn enough money to bring his sweetheart to America, buy a farm, and start a family. He does, and they do!

Watch the Stars Come Out
by Riki Levinson
illustrated by Diane Goode
E. P. Dutton, 1985
A grandmother tells her grandaughter a story that begins, "When I was a little girl, my brother and I went on a big boat to America." And so we hear about the hard trip that finally brings a family together in America. Color illustrations bring the text to life. Many second graders can read this book independently.

CIVIL RIGHTS

Bloomers!
by Rhoda Blumberg
illustrated by Mary Morgan
Bradbury Press, 1993
This lively and colorful picture book humorously relates how a scandalous outfit helped Amelia Bloomer, Elizabeth Cady Stanton, and Susan B. Anthony spread the word about women's rights. A fun read-aloud (also recommended in fourth grade as independent reading).

Happy Birthday, Martin Luther King
by Jean Marzollo
illustrated by J. Brian Pinkney
Scholastic, 1993
This is a simple but sensitive and beautifully illustrated picture book that most second graders will be able to read independently.

Martin Luther King, Jr.: A Man Who Changed Things
by Carol Greene
Childrens Press, 1989
This Rookie Biography, written in large print, is a good choice for independent reading by second graders. The text is simple and interesting and there are many powerful photographs from the civil rights movement.

My First Book of Biographies: Great Men and Women Every Child Should Know
by Jean Marzollo
illustrated by Irene Trivas
Scholastic, 1994
See the description of this book under World History General Resources. Among its forty-five biographical sketches you will find Cesar Chavez, Jesse Owens, Eleanor and Franklin Roosevelt, and a "group sketch" of Elizabeth Cady Stanton, Lucretia Mott, and Susan B. Anthony.

A Picture Book of Eleanor Roosevelt
by David A. Adler
illustrated by Robert Casilla
Holiday House, 1991
About the first half of this picture book is devoted to Eleanor Roosevelt's early life. After that, a picture of her emerges as a champion of the poor and an advocate for human rights. The author works into his story some of Eleanor's strong and wise advice, such as "You must do the thing you think you cannot do." A good read-aloud that some second graders will be able to read independently.

A Picture Book of Rosa Parks
by David Adler
illustrated by Robert Casilla
Holiday House, 1993
This illustrated book gives background information on the civil rights movement and paints a portrait of Rosa Parks as a strong and committed woman. Recommended as a read-aloud for this grade level.

Rosa Parks: Hero of Our Time
written by Garnet Nelson Jackson
illustrated by Tony Wade
Modern Curriculum Press, 1993
This little paperback book, suitable for independent reading by second graders, is part of the publisher's Beginning Biographies: African-Americans series. In clear and upbeat language, it offers a look at Rosa Parks's childhood in the segregated South, and follows her up to and beyond her refusal to give up her seat on a bus. It ends with a lively poem about how Rosa Parks "changed the law." A Teaching Companion with ideas for classroom discussion and activities is available from the publisher.

CC *The Story of Ruby Bridges*
by Robert Coles
illustrated by George Ford
Scholastic, 1993
This outstanding picture books tells the true story of the first African-American child to integrate a white school in New Orleans in 1960. It is a story of prejudice and hostility met with strength and forgiveness. A beautiful and moving book.

Young Martin's Promise
by Walter Dean Myers
illustrated by Barbara Higgins Bond
Steck-Vaughn, 1993
Unlike the other recommended books on Martin Luther King, this one does not cover the achievements of his adult life. Instead it focuses on King as a boy. Why can't he play ball with the white children? Why, when his father takes him to buy a pair of shoes, does the insolent clerk demand that they go to the back of the store? Good as a read-aloud, and readable by some strong second-grade readers.

CC = "**Core Collection**" book (see page 8).

AMERICAN HISTORY AND GEOGRAPHY

Grade 3

THE EARLIEST AMERICANS

See also the listings under American History Grade 1: The Earliest People: Hunters and Nomads.

CC *The First Americans*
by Joy Hakim
Oxford University Press, 1993
This is Volume 1 in the *A History of US* series (described under American History General Resources). In engaging prose, with lots of black-and-white illustrations, the book goes way back to prehistoric times to tell the story of the first people to cross the land bridge to North America, and of the different ways of life that developed among various peoples, including the Inuit, the Anasazi ("cliff dwellers"), mound builders, Native Americans of the Southwest, Eastern Woodland Indians, and many more. It goes on to tell the story of Columbus and other early explorers. This book is an invaluable resource for teachers and parents, and is written in such a clear and lively voice that students could learn much by hearing it read aloud.

A First Americans Book **series**
by Virginia Driving Hawk Sneve
illustrated by Ronald Himler
Holiday House
The language in these books is simple and clear enough to be read aloud, and may be read independently by strong readers in the third grade. Each book offers a brief glimpse at the history, customs, and beliefs of a specific people. The illustrations are paintings in a style that blurs fine details and depicts only vague facial features. The series includes: *The Hopi, The Navajos, The Sioux,* and *The Seminoles.*

Iroquois Stories
retold by Joseph Bruchac
illustrated by Daniel Burgevin
The Crossing Press, 1985
Bruchac retells twenty-nine stories from the Iroquois. An excellent resource. (Includes the Core Knowledge selection in Language Arts Grade 3, "The Hunting of the Great Bear.")

Native Dwellings **series**
by Bonnie Shemie
Tundra Books
A very interesting and informative series, described under American History General Resources. Relevant volumes for this grade include *Houses of Bark* and *Houses of Adobe: Native Dwellings of the Southwest.*

New True Book **series**
Childrens Press
See American History General Resources for a description of the many books in this series, all of which are informative and readable in third grade, written in simple words and big print with many pictures. Relevant volumes for this grade include *The Anasazi; The Apache; The Eskimo: Inuit and Yupik; The Hopi; The Iroquois; The Navajo; The Seminole,* and others.

CC *People of the Breaking Day*
written and illustrated by Marcia Sewall
Atheneum, 1990
"We are Wampanoags, People of the Breaking Day." So begins this lovely and thoughtful book, narrated as though in the communal voice of the Wampanoag tribe that lived before the Pilgrims arrived in what we now call Massachusetts. This book is a companion volume to

the same author's award-winning *The Pilgrims of Plimoth* (see below). A fine read-aloud.

The Rough-Face Girl
    by Rafe Martin
    illustrated by David Shannon
    G. P. Putnam's Sons, 1992
Sootface: An Ojibwa Cinderella
    by Robert D. San Souci
    illustrated by Daniel San Souci
    Doubleday/Delacorte, 1994
These two picture books retell what might be called "Cinderella" stories from Algonquin folklore. Martin's book has striking illustrations.

Southwest Indians Coloring Book (1994)
Woodlands Indians Coloring Book (1995)
by Peter F. Copeland
Dover
Ready-to-color line drawings depict representative scenes from the lives of these American Indians in different regions, with different customs and ways of life. The pictures are accompanied by informative captions (for older readers). (See address, page 106.)

EARLY EXPLORATION OF NORTH AMERICA

See also World History Grade 3: The Vikings.
See also World History General Resources: Atlases.

Christopher Columbus: From Vision to Voyage
by Joan Anderson
photographs by George Ancona
Dial Books, 1991
This is a more challenging book than those about Columbus recommended for earlier grades. It traces his career from Genoa merchant to the point of departure for his first voyage to the New World. It offers interesting insights into his life and motivations, and is accompanied by color photographs of historically costumed actors recreating scenes from Columbus's life.

The Discovery of the Americas
The Discovery of the Americas Activity Book
by Betsy and Giulio Maestro
illustrated by Giulio Maestro
Lothrop, Lee & Shepard, 1992
Together, these two books, illustrated with watercolors, place Columbus's explorations in historical context by introducing a range of topics, including North and South American people and ways of life before the coming of the Europeans, other European explorers, and some less discussed issues such as "Where were the women?" The *Activity Book* suggests many interesting and fun projects, but needs to be used with discretion, as it also suggests some activities that are historically irrelevant or needlessly elaborate.

Encounter
by Jane Yolen
illustrated by David Shannon
Harcourt Brace, 1992
The author imagines the arrival of Columbus from the point of view of a Taino boy. It is not a pleasant story. It is a story of foreboding, fear, deception, and loss. The art emphasizes how, to the Taino people, the Europeans must have seemed utterly alien. One picture depicts the flesh on a European hand as a yellow, plasticlike film. Another shows a European face, almost demonic, leering at a gold ornament. The book is undeniably powerful and a bit disturbing—probably just what the author intended. Read this book yourself first to decide if it's what you want to share with your children. It will provoke questions and require thoughtful discussion.

CC *Exploration and Conquest: The Americas after Columbus: 1500–1620*
by Betsy and Giulio Maestro
illustrated by Giulio Maestro
Lothrop, Lee & Shepard, 1994
A follow-up to the same authors' *The Discovery of the Americas* (see above), this beautifully illustrated book goes on to tell the story of many explorers to the Americas after Columbus, in-

cluding Cortez, Pizarro, De Soto, Cabot, Drake, Verrazano, Champlain, and Henry Hudson. Also includes a time line and information about Native Americans. The writing is clear, though the vocabulary will challenge many third graders.

Exploration of North America Coloring Book
by Peter F. Copeland
Dover, 1992
Detailed line drawings and brief informative text (for teachers and parents) on many explorers, including the Vikings, Ponce de León, De Soto, Verrazano, Cabot, Coronado, and Champlain. (See address, page 106.)

Who Discovered America? Mysteries and Puzzles of the New World
by Patricia Lauber
illustrated by Mike Eagle
HarperCollins, 1992
The author explores clues about who reached the New World before the arrival of Columbus. Her discussion includes the Ice Age Siberians, early traders from Asia, the "first Americans," the Vikings, and fishermen sailing out of Bristol, England. As a read-aloud book, this offers clear explanations of how questions about history are explored. It is also a good teacher/parent resource for this grade level. With occasional color illustrations.

THE THIRTEEN COLONIES: LIFE AND TIMES BEFORE THE REVOLUTION

The Courage of Sarah Noble
by Alice Dalgliesh
illustrations by Leonard Weisgard
Macmillan/Aladdin Books, 1954, 1991
Third graders will be able to read for themselves this historical fiction based on a true story, which provides an engaging introduction to the difficulties faced by settlers in the American colonies. In the year 1707, when Sarah Noble is eight years old, her father heads into the

Connecticut wilderness to build a cabin, and Sarah goes along to help. "Keep up your courage, Sarah Noble," becomes Sarah's refrain as she faces hard work and many dangers. A Newbery Honor Book.

Everyday Dress of the American Colonial Period Coloring Book
by Peter Copeland
Dover, 1976
This is one in the series of the Dover coloring books (see address, page 106), with detailed line drawings and brief informative text (but not written for children). Forty-six illustrations of colonial people from various walks of life: broom seller, glass blower, wigmaker, fine lady, and more.

CC *The First Thanksgiving*
by Jean Craighead George
illustrated by Thomas Locker
Philomel Books, 1993
Substantial, well-written text, evocative illustrations, and sensitive presentation of the interaction between Pilgrims, Squanto, and Massasoit make this a superb presentation of the Pilgrim story.

If You Lived in Colonial Times
by Ann McGovern
illustrated by June Otani
Scholastic, 1964
Written in a conversational style and an accessible question-and-answer format, this illustrated book will be readable by most third graders, and will engage their interest as it answers questions about daily life in the colonies, such as "What happened if you didn't obey in school?" "How did people get the news?" "Did children have to worry about table manners?"

If You Sailed on the **Mayflower** *in 1620*
by Ann McGovern
illustrated by Anna DiVito
Scholastic, 1969 (illustrations 1991)
Written in a conversational style and an accessible question-and-answer format, this illustrated

book will be readable by most third graders and answers questions such as "What would you eat and drink on the *Mayflower*? Did they land on Plymouth Rock? Did the children go to school? Did people break the rules?"

A Lion to Guard Us
by Robert Clyde Bulla
illustrated by Michele Chessare
HarperCollins, 1981
Set in seventeenth century England and America, this is the story of three courageous English children who, after their mother dies, set out across the Atlantic to find their father in Jamestown. A wonderful read-aloud, this novel of a little more than a hundred pages can also be read independently by many third graders.

CC *Making Thirteen Colonies*
by Joy Hakim
Oxford University Press, 1993
This is Volume 2 in the *A History of US* series (described under American History General Resources). In engaging prose, with lots of black-and-white illustrations, the author begins with a look at the Woodlands Indians in Virginia, then goes on to discuss Jamestown, the Pilgrims, the Puritans, Roger Williams, King Philip's War, slavery, and a great deal more, including a discussion of the distinctive development of each and all of the original thirteen colonies. This book is an invaluable resource for teachers and parents, and is written in such a clear and lively voice that students could learn much by hearing it read aloud.

N. C. Wyeth's Pilgrims
by Robert San Souci
illustrations from paintings by N. C. Wyeth
Chronicle Books, 1991
In this lovely book, award-winning children's author Robert D. San Souci is careful to distinguish fact from legend as he gives a clear and detailed account of the Pilgrims, from their troubles in England to their hard transatlantic voyage to the first Thanksgiving. Strong readers may read this book on their own; otherwise, it

would be a good read-aloud. Illustrated with beautiful paintings by American artist N. C. Wyeth.

CC *The Pilgrims of Plimoth*
written and illustrated by Marcia Sewall
Atheneum, 1986
A companion book to the same author's *People of the Breaking Day* (see above), this book begins, "Aye, Governor Bradford calls us Pilgrims." It is written as though the words were being spoken by the communal voice of the Pilgrims, which lends immediacy to the history conveyed in the telling. Quotations from William Bradford's writings are seamlessly woven into the narration. Bright, captivating paintings by the author illuminate every two-page spread. A lovely book to read aloud.

The Plymouth Thanksgiving
written and illustrated by Leonard Weisgard
Doubleday, 1990
The story of the Pilgrims, from their exile in Holland to the friendship they forged with the Native Americans who taught them to survive in the harsh New England environment. Based on William Bradford's diary, Weisgard's prose and illustrations lend a reverent tone. Readable by many third graders, and also a good read-aloud.

The Sign of the Beaver
by Elizabeth George Speare
Houghton Mifflin, 1983
Historical fiction, good for reading aloud, this is the story of Matt, who lives in the woods of Maine, and whose life is changed as he gets to know Attean, an Iroquois boy.

Squanto and the First Thanksgiving
by Joyce K. Kessel
illustrated by Lisa Donze
Carolrhoda Books, 1983
"How did Thanksgiving start? Most of us think right away of the Pilgrims, but the story really begins with a Patuxet Indian named Squanto." This book presents Squanto as more than "the

Indian who helped the Pilgrims.'' We learn about the often sad story of his life: he was captured into slavery, taken to England, freed, captured again, taken to Spain, freed again, only to return home to find his people wiped out by smallpox. The book does not neglect the tragic aspects, but neither does it dwell on them as it goes on to tell about the many ways in which Squanto generously helped the Pilgrims. It has clear prose and big print, and is readable by third graders.

CC *The Story of William Penn*
written and illustrated by Aliki
Simon & Schuster Books for Young Readers, 1964
This is an interesting, direct, and readable picture book about Quaker leader William Penn and the founding of Pennsylvania. Aliki notes Penn's respect for the Native American people, as he learned their customs and their language.

The Thirteen Colonies
by Dennis Fradin
Childrens Press, 1988
A New True Book, easy reading for third grade, which can provide a simple general overview of the thirteen colonies. See the description under American History Grade 1: The English Colonies.

Whaling Days
by Carol Carrick
illustrated by David Frampton
Clarion Books, 1993
Dramatic woodblock prints and strong text transport the reader to a time when whaling was the main enterprise of many a colonial New England town and family. An interesting read-aloud that gives a welcome glimpse of colonial life beyond Plymouth and Jamestown.

Witch Hunt: It Happened in Salem Village
by Stephen Krensky
illustrated by James Watling
Random House, 1989
This book dramatizes, but does not sensationalize, a very difficult subject. The author conclusively asserts, ''The Salem witch hunt was a time when fear and hate ruled over common sense.'' A Step into Reading book recommended by the publisher for grades 2–4, with large print, clear prose, and occasionally challenging vocabulary.

CC = "Core Collection" book (see page 8).

AMERICAN HISTORY AND GEOGRAPHY

Grade 4

GENERAL RESOURCES

CC *From Colonies to Country* (1993)
   The New Nation (1993)
   Liberty for All (1994)
by Joy Hakim
Oxford University Press
These are Books 2–4 in the ten-volume *A History of US* series (described under American History General Resources: Series). Taken together, they offer an engaging treatment of just about every topic recommended for study in the fourth-grade American History guidelines of the *Core Knowledge Sequence* (summarized above, pages 94–101). The lively prose is written for about fifth grade and above, but will be accessible to strong readers in the fourth grade. Schools looking for classroom texts should seriously consider these. If only one volume can be afforded, then *From Colonies to Country* is the best choice. Parents: check your local library or bookstore. This is not dry "textbook" history, but history written to be read and enjoyed.

THE AMERICAN REVOLUTION

Note: The *Core Knowledge Sequence* recommends a brief introduction to the French and Indian War as background for study of the American Revolution. A number of the books listed below provide good background information (see also above Hakim, *From Colonies to Country*).

Books on the American Revolution— General Studies

The Battle of Lexington and Concord
by Neil Johnson
Four Winds Press, 1992
An excellent photographic recreation of the Battle of Lexington and Concord, with informative text providing general background on the Revolution as well as the first battle.

The Declaration of Independence
by Dennis Fradin
Childrens Press, 1988
This New True Book, written in large print for beginning readers, will be easy reading for fourth graders. With plenty of illustrations, it gives some historical background on the thirteen colonies, and goes on to describe how the Declaration of Independence was written and adopted. Along the way it introduces many figures including King George III, Tom Paine, Ben Franklin, and Thomas Jefferson.

Our Declaration of Independence
by Jay Schleifer
Millbrook, 1992
This slender but informative volume is more challenging and detailed than *The Declaration of Independence* by Fradin (see above); try to examine both books and decide which is right for your children or students. It places the Declaration in historical context and introduces the Founding Fathers. It relates a lively exchange between Jefferson and Adams about who should do the writing ("You do it!" "No, you do it!"). It offers a clear analysis of key pas-

sages. And it discusses interesting side issues such as the fate of the original document and where it is now displayed. With some color illustrations.

Paper Soldiers of the American Revolution **(1992)**
Paper Soldiers of the American Revolution: Book Two **(1994)**
Bellerophon Books
Two coloring books from Bellerophon (see address, page 106), with detailed and intricate line drawings. Here's General George Washington, there's Major General the Marquis de Lafayette. And there's an ordinary seaman, a horse and rider, a cannon, and many many more figures to cut out and color. The result could be an impressive classroom display.

Paul Revere's Ride
by Henry Wadsworth Longfellow
E. P. Dutton, 1990
See description under Language Arts Grade 4.

Stories of the American Revolution
selected by Jeanne S. Chall
Andrews & McMeel, 1994
If this convenient little paperback has an old-fashioned feel about it, that's intentional: the editor has selected chapters from standard school texts in use around 1900. There's a mixture of history and anecdote in sections on George Washington, Benjamin Franklin, Thomas Jefferson, and the War for Independence. Most selections are accompanied by a vocabulary list and a suggested activity to "improve your reading."

Story of the American Revolution Coloring Book
Uniforms of the American Revolution Coloring Book
by Peter Copeland
Dover, 1988
Part of the excellent series of the Dover coloring books (see address, page 106), with detailed line drawings and brief explanatory notes.

Biographies

CC *And Then What Happened, Paul Revere?* **(1973)**
    Can't You Make Them Behave, King George? **(1977)**
    What's the Big Idea, Ben Franklin? **(1976)**
    Where Was Patrick Henry on the 29th of May? **(1975)**
    Why Don't You Get a Horse, Sam Adams? **(1974)**
    Will You Sign Here, John Hancock? **(1976)**
by Jean Fritz
various illustrators
G. P. Putnam's Sons
After you've discovered one book by Jean Fritz, you hope there are more. And fortunately there are many. These witty, informative, fast-paced biographies are highly recommended. They bring people and history to life. History as "a lot of dull facts and dates"? Not Jean Fritz! (Note: some of the titles above are also available in editions from Scholastic.)

CC *George Washington: A Picture Book Biography*
by James C. Giblin
illustrated by Michael Dooling
Scholastic, 1992
A beautifully illustrated biography of Washington from childhood to his final days, emphasizing his quiet readiness to do the duties demanded by his country.

I Did It With My Hatchet: A Story of George Washington
written and illustrated by Robert M. Quackenbush
Pippin Press, 1989
In his characteristically lively and humorous style, Quackenbush offers a brief, readable biography of George Washington that includes both famous and little-known anecdotes about Wash-

ington's public and private life. With witty drawings by the author.

The Secret Soldier: The Story of Deborah Sampson
by Ann McGovern
illustrated by Ann Grifalconi
Scholastic, 1990
This is an engaging biography of the woman who disguised herself as a man to fight in the American Revolution. Suitable for independent reading by fourth graders. A Teaching Guide is available from Scholastic.

CC Thomas Jefferson: A Picture Book Biography
by James Cross Giblin
illustrated by Michael Dooling
Scholastic, 1994
Beautiful illustrations accompany this excellent overview of Jefferson's life, from small boy to retired president.

CC Young John Quincy
written and illustrated by Cheryl Harness
Bradbury Press, 1994
As the American colonies move to revolution, John Quincy Adams (age eight) observes events and the activities of his patriot father (John Adams). The Battle of Bunker Hill, the Continental Congress, and finally the Declaration of Independence come to life through the eyes of a child in an advantageous position to watch history in the making. Fourth graders can read this on their own, and they'll enjoy the warm, colorful illustrations.

Young Abigail Adams
by Francene Sabin
illustrated by Yoshi Miyake
Troll Associates, 1992
This slender biography depicts the young Abigail Adams as energetic, curious, and sparked by a love of learning. It also incidentally relates interesting facts about what it was like to grow up in colonial times. With black-and-white illustrations.

Historical Fiction

Ben and Me
written and illustrated by Robert Lawson
Little, Brown, 1939
Subtitled "A New and Astonishing Life of Benjamin Franklin as Written by His Good Mouse Amos." Apparently the historians have been mistaken in giving credit to Ben Franklin for all those ideas and inventions, which, as the narrator of this book, Amos the Mouse, patiently explains, were as much *his* idea as Ben's! A delightful way to get to know about an amazing man, this modern classic takes us up to the brink of the Revolution (and shows that it was Amos, after all, who made Ben such a success at the French court). Wonderful to read aloud or for students to read on their own. With humorous drawings by the author.

Early Thunder
by Jean Fritz
Puffin Books, 1967
Another gem by Jean Fritz. Fourteen-year-old Daniel begins to question his loyalty to the king in this novel set in prerevolutionary Salem. Challenging for fourth grade, perhaps best as a read-aloud.

Johnny Tremain
by Esther Forbes
illustrated by Lynd Ward
Dell, 1969; Scholastic
Winner of the Newbery Medal in 1943, this is the story of a young Bostonian who finds himself involved in the Boston Tea Party and the Battle of Lexington, and in the company of such figures as John Hancock and John and Samuel Adams. Detailed, powerful, and sometimes painful, this modern classic is challenging for younger readers, and best for this grade as a read-aloud.

CC = "Core Collection" book (see page 8).

Jump Ship to Freedom (1981)
War Comes to Willy Freeman (1983)
Who Is Carrie? (1984)
by James Lincoln Collier and Christopher
   Collier
Dell
The authors of the celebrated *My Brother Sam Is
Dead* (see below) here dramatize the lives of the
Arabus family, a family of slaves in New En-
gland, during and after the turmoil of the Revo-
lutionary War. Good for strong fourth-grade
readers and for reading aloud.

My Brother Sam Is Dead
by James Lincoln Collier and Christopher
   Collier
Four Winds Press, 1974
This Newberry Honor Book tells the exciting
and sometimes sad story of a family divided by
the Revolution. The story is told from the point
of view of young Tim, who admires his fiery
older brother, Sam. Sam is eager to fight the
British, but their father is a Loyalist. The book
does not shy away from the cruelty and suffering of war. While a challenging text for independent reading in fourth grade, it would make
a powerful read-aloud.

Phoebe the Spy
by Judith Berry Griffin
Scholastic, 1977, 1991
Originally published in hardcover as *Phoebe and
the General*, this is a story based on fact about a
free black girl, Phoebe Fraunces, who has the
dangerous job of trying to keep watch on
George Washington and protect him from an
unknown assassin. Phoebe's father owned the
famous New York City Fraunces Tavern, from
whose balcony George Washington bade fare-
well to his troops. Good for independent reading or reading aloud.

The Sign Painter's Secret
by Dorothy and Thomas Hoobler
illustrated by Donna Ayers
Silver Burdett, 1991
It's 1777 and British officers move into Annie

MacDougal's house and expect Annie's mother
to wait on them. When Annie realizes her
mother is listening to the officers' conversation
for a special reason, she finds a way to help too.
An exciting and easy-to-read tale.

MAKING A CONSTITUTIONAL GOVERNMENT

CC *The Bill of Rights* (1987)
      The Constitution (1987)
by Warren Colman
Childrens Press, 1987
These New True Books, written in simple language and big print, with illustrations on almost
every page, should be easy to read for most
fourth graders. *The Constitution* begins, "Think
what a baseball game would be like without
rules" and goes on to convey how the Constitution was conceived, drafted, and ratified. It
briefly considers a number of topics, such as the
Articles of Confederation, the three branches of
government, and amendments. A good companion to this book is *The Bill of Rights*, which includes a brief discussion of the Magna Carta,
and discusses the ideas behind the Bill of Rights
(for example, the importance of the individual,
all individuals, not just the rulers). It offers a
helpful discussion of First Amendment freedoms (you have the right to free speech but you
don't have the right to yell "fire" in a theater
when there's no fire). It goes on to discuss the
other amendments in simple terms, giving concrete examples.

CC *If You Were There When They Signed
   the Constitution*
by Elizabeth Levy
illustrated by Joan Holub
Scholastic, 1987
This illustrated book presents a behind-the-
scenes look at what went on during the writing
of the Constitution. Presented in question-and-
answer format, it asks interesting questions such
as: "What was Ben Franklin like? What were
the two sides at the convention? What was the

first big argument about? Is the word *slave* in the Constitution? Why is the Constitution called a miracle?" The conversational, untextbookish style makes this good for reading aloud or for independent reading by most fourth graders.

A More Perfect Union: The Story of Our Constitution
by Betsy and Giulio Maestro
illustrated by Giulio Maestro
Lothrop, Lee, & Shepard/Mulberry Books, 1987
This picture book describes the convention, the delegates, the ideas, and some of the arguments, and goes into more detail than the picture-book format might lead one to expect.

Our Constitution
by Linda Carlson Johnson
Millbrook, 1992
This slender but informative volume is more challenging and detailed than the Childrens Press book by Colman on the Constitution (above), but still readable by fourth graders. Illustrations and sidebars help convey both the history of the Constitution and its lasting significance.

CC *Shh! We're Writing the Constitution*
by Jean Fritz
illustrated by Tomie de Paola
G. P. Putnam's Sons, 1987
Written in Jean Fritz's characteristically lively style, this book tells an engaging story of the writing of the Constitution, describing the arguments between the Federalists and those in favor of states' sovereignty. Good for reading aloud or independent reading.

CC *Voting and Elections*
by Dennis B. Fradin
Childrens Press, 1985
This New True Book, written in simple language and big print, with illustrations on almost every page, should be easy to read for most fourth graders. It discusses the history of voting (going back to the Greeks and Romans), the gradual spread of the right to vote in the

United States, free elections (with secret ballots) versus "fixed" elections, the voting process, and the importance of voting. A solid introduction to an important topic.

EARLY PRESIDENTS AND POLITICS

Dear Benjamin Banneker
by Andrea Davis Pinkney
illustrated by Brian Pinkney
Harcourt Brace/Gulliver Books, 1994
This book about the multitalented Benjamin Banneker includes a discussion of the eloquent letter he wrote to Thomas Jefferson challenging the President for owning slaves. Jefferson responded, hence the title of this book. Good for independent reading or reading aloud. (For more books on Banneker, see Science Grade 4: Science Biographies.)

CC *George Washington: A Picture Book Biography* (1992)
    Thomas Jefferson: A Picture Book Biography (1994)
by James C. Giblin
illustrated by Michael Dooling
Scholastic
Both books are described above under American Revolution: Biographies.

The Great Little Madison
by Jean Fritz
G. P. Putnam's Sons, 1989/Scholastic
In prose that reads like a good story, Jean Fritz traces the life and contributions of the sickly child with the small voice who grew up to become the fourth president of the United States.

CC *James Madison and Dolley Madison and Their Times*
written and illustrated by Robert Quackenbush
Pippin Press, 1992
Quackenbush writes with humor and energy. This is a brief, well-told life story of James Madison and Dolley Payne (later Todd, then later Madison). It includes an account of Madison's

role in the Revolution, the writing of the Constitution, and the War of 1812. Readable by most fourth graders, who will also enjoy the author's cartoonlike illustrations.

Meet Thomas Jefferson
by Marvin Barrett
Random House, 1967, 1989
This Step-Up biography should be easy and enjoyable reading for fourth graders. In just over seventy pages, it tells Jefferson's life story, which is in many ways the story of the young nation.

The Story of the White House
by Kate Waters
Scholastic, 1991
This attractive book of photographs and old drawings, easy to read in fourth grade, offers an introduction to many aspects of the White House as a public and private home. The author gives historical background on the design of Washington, D.C., including the roles of Benjamin Banneker and Pierre L'Enfant. Pictures and brief text trace the evolution of the White House after it was burned in 1812. Behind-the-scenes photographs include the old switchboard, the office of presidential correspondence, and the presidents' private swimming pool and beauty salon!

CC Who Let Muddy Boots into the White House? A Story of Andrew Jackson
written and illustrated by Robert Quackenbush
Prentice Hall, 1986
Here's a brief, humorous portrayal of the "president of the common man," the first American president to be born in a log cabin and come to the White House without the social and educational credentials of his predecessors. An excellent book for reading independently or aloud, with the author's signature cartoonlike drawings to brighten the way.

CC = "Core Collection" book (see page 8).

REFORMERS

Bloomers!
by Rhoda Blumberg
illustrated by Mary Morgan
Bradbury Press, 1993
This lively and colorful picture book, easy to read for fourth graders, humorously relates how a scandalous new outfit helped Amelia Bloomer, Elizabeth Cady Stanton, and Susan B. Anthony spread the word about women's rights. As the author concludes, "Bloomers went out of fashion, but not the idea the costume represented."

Frederick Douglass and the War Against Slavery
by Evelyn Bennett
Millbrook, 1993
This slender but informative volume written for middle-school students is a good teacher/parent resource. It offers a good sketch of Douglass and the antislavery movement, including background on William Lloyd Garrison, the Liberator, the African slave trade, and the Underground Railroad. Occasional illustrations.

Frederick Douglass: Portrait of a Freedom Fighter
by Sheila Kenan
Scholastic, 1995
Though brief and simple, this very easy-to-read biography conveys the harshness of young Frederick's life as a slave, and then goes on to illustrate his perseverance and success. You will probably want to supplement this little book with more information about the abolitionist movement, but it can nevertheless provide good background information as preparation for reading from Douglass's Narrative (as recommended for fifth grade in the Core Knowledge Sequence). Black-and-white illustrations.

Sojourner Truth: Ain't I a Woman?
by Patricia McKissack and Frederick McKissack
illustrated by Barbara Kiwak
Scholastic, 1992
A teacher/parent resource, this is an interesting biography complemented by an appendix with

brief biographies of people Sojourner Truth knew, including Susan B. Anthony, John Brown, Frederick Douglass, Harriet Beecher Stowe, and Harriet Tubman.

CC *You Want Women to Vote, Lizzie Stanton?*
by Jean Fritz
G. P. Putnam's Sons, 1995
"Yes, Elizabeth Cady Stanton did want women to vote. It was an outlandish idea, but that's what she wanted. Not at first. As a child, she knew that girls didn't count for much, but she didn't expect to change that." So begins this book, in characteristic Jean Fritz style: direct, lively, witty. Suitable for strong fourth-grade readers and for reading aloud, this very untextbookish book offers a great way to learn about the women's rights movement. Along the way it introduces Amelia Bloomer, Lucretia Mott, Susan B. Anthony, the Seneca Falls Convention, and a great deal more.

AMERICAN HISTORY AND GEOGRAPHY

Grade 5

THE CIVIL WAR: CAUSES, CONFLICTS, CONSEQUENCES

"Abraham Lincoln"
The ten articles in this May 1994 issue of *Cobblestone* magazine (see address, page 148) focus on topics related to Lincoln. They include: his youth, his wife and family, his years as president, the Civil War, his assassination, and the Lincoln memorial.

Anthony Burns: The Defeat and Triumph of a Fugitive Slave
by Virginia Hamilton
Alfred A. Knopf, 1988/Scholastic
This award-winning book, which tells the story of Anthony Burns and the controversy surrounding the Fugitive Slave Act, provides a compelling, dramatic account of the historical issues. A Teaching Guide is available from Scholastic.

CC *The Boys' War: Confederate and Union Soldiers Talk About the Civil War*
by Jim Murphy
Clarion Books, 1990
Based on firsthand accounts of boys under the age of eighteen, this book presents a vivid picture of the life of Civil War soldiers, from the thrill of enlistment, through the rigors of camp life, to the chaos of the battlefield. With many compelling photographs.

CC *Escape from Slavery: The Boyhood of Frederick Douglass in His Own Words*
edited and illustrated by Michael McCurdy
Alfred A. Knopf, 1994
See description under Language Arts Grade 5.

CC *Lincoln: A Photobiography*
by Russell Freedman
Clarion Books, 1987
A Newbery Award winner, this outstanding biography tells Lincoln's life story with eloquent words and compelling photographs. For students (or teachers and parents) who want to know about the man, and the president, this is a fine choice.

The Long Road to Gettysburg
by Jim Murphy
Clarion Books, 1992
This book begins with Lincoln's address after the battle and then backs up to examine motives and actions of both North and South. Includes firsthand accounts from a Confederate lieutenant and a Union soldier. Their words, combined with a vivid collection of drawings and photographs, will help bring this crucial battle to life for young readers.

To Be a Slave
by Julius Lester
illustrated by Tom Feelings
Dial Books/Scholastic (paper), 1968
In this award-winning volume, the noted author has collected dramatic, often hard-hitting, sometimes painful accounts from men and women who were once slaves.

Undying Glory: The Story of the Massachusetts 54th Regiment
by Clinton Cox
Scholastic, 1991
A detailed and readable account of the valor and sacrifice exemplified by Colonel Robert Gould Shaw and his African-American troops.

Cox is a fine reporter and the black-and-white archival photographs add to the drama here.

Voices from the Civil War: A Documentary History of the Great American Conflict
edited by Milton Meltzer
HarperCollins/Crowell, 1989
A useful teacher/parent resource, this book of primary source materials can enrich classroom study of the Civil War. Weaving together excerpts from diaries, letters, interviews, newspaper articles, songs, memoirs, speeches and ballads, Meltzer creates a vivid portrait of the Civil War.

CC *War, Terrible War*
by Joy Hakim
Oxford University Press, 1994
This is Book 6 in the ten-volume *A History of US* (described under American History General Resources). It tells the story of our nation's history from Fort Sumter to the assassination of Lincoln in Ford's Theater. Schools looking for a classroom text on which to base the study of the Civil War should give this book strong consideration. Parents should examine it as well: it's written in a clear and engaging style that most fifth-graders will be able to read with pleasure.

Historical Fiction

Across Five Aprils
by Irene Hunt
Follett, 1964; Berkley, 1986
Across the five Aprils of the Civil War, nine-year-old Jethro Creighton and his family experience hardship and loss. One Creighton brother joins the Union Army, another becomes a soldier of the Confederacy. A powerful and moving novel.

Brady
by Jean Fritz
illustrated by Lynd Ward
Coward-McCann, 1960; Puffin Books, 1987
This perceptive novel is told from the point of view of a young boy, Brady Minton, whose mother grew up in the south, but whose father is an Abolitionist preacher. Between their conflicting views of slavery stands Brady. When Brady finds out that his father is an agent of the Underground Railroad, he has to decide what to do.

Bull Run
by Paul Fleischman
woodcuts by David Frampton
HarperCollins, 1993
A novel made of monologues, this is a powerful piece of historical fiction. Sixteen characters, male and female, black and white, Northern and Southern, tell the story of the Battle of Bull Run.

Freedom Train: The Story of Harriet Tubman
by Dorothy Sterling
Doubleday, 1954; Scholastic
Identified by the publisher as a biography of Harriet Tubman, this book is rather a work of historical fiction, as the writer takes imaginative license to recreate scenes, dialogue, and inner thoughts.

Red Cap
by G. Clifton Wisler
E. P. Dutton/Lodestar, 1991
This novel, based on real historical characters and events, tells the story of a thirteen-year-old boy who becomes a Union drummer, is captured, and manages to remain hopeful even as he suffers through imprisonment, watching most of his comrades die.

Which Way Freedom?
by Joyce Hansen
Walker, 1986; Avon Books, 1992
This award-winning novel based on real events tells the story of Obi, a runaway slave who ends up fighting for the Union. The goal of this novel, says the author, is to convey "a deeper understanding of African-American participation" in the Civil War.

RECONSTRUCTION

Be Ever Hopeful, Hannalee
by Patricia Beatty
Morrow Junior Books, 1988; Troll
   Associates, 1991
This dramatic novel tells the story of Hannalee and her family as they struggle to make a life in postwar Atlanta. The book gives a good sense of the hardships faced by the North and particularly the ravaged South after the Civil War.

Out from This Place
by Joyce Hansen
Walker, 1988; Avon Books, 1992
In this historical novel set during Reconstruction, we learn about one former slave in search of her family after the Civil War. A sequel to *Which Way Freedom?* (see above).

"Reconstruction"
This May 1987 issue of *Cobblestone* magazine (see address, page 148) focuses on the struggles faced by this nation in the aftermath of the Civil War.

CC *Reconstruction and Reform*
by Joy Hakim
Oxford University Press, 1994
This is Book 7 in the ten-volume *A History of US* (described under American History General Resources). It gives an engaging and detailed account of the troubled years of Reconstruction. Schools looking for a classroom text on which to base the study of this period should give this book strong consideration. Parents should examine it as well: it's written in a clear and engaging style that most fifth graders will be able to read with pleasure.

CC = "Core Collection" book (see page 8).

WESTWARD EXPANSION
See also Language Arts Grade 5: Laura Ingalls Wilder, the *Little House* books.

Across America on an Emigrant Train
by Jim Murphy
Clarion Books, 1993
Illustrated primarily with fascinating period photos, this book relates the transcontinental journey of British author Robert Louis Stevenson from New York to California by train in 1879. On the way, the reader learns about the operation of the railroads in the nineteenth century.

CC *Along the Santa Fe Trail*
by Marion Russell
adapted by Ginger Wadsworth
illustrated by James Watling
Albert Whitman, 1993
A fascinating book based on the first-person account of Marion Russell, who traveled back and forth five times on the Santa Fe Trail. She takes care of her kids, gives birth, finds shelter from hostile Indians and elements, and it's all in a day's work.

"Annie Oakley and the Wild West"
This January 1991 issue of *Cobblestone,* the magazine of American history for young readers (see address, page 148), features a lively collection of articles, readable by fifth graders, on Annie Oakley, Buffalo Bill, and the traveling "Wild West" shows.

"Buffalo Soldiers"
This February 1995 issue of *Cobblestone,* the magazine of American history for young readers (see address, page 148), is devoted to the "Buffalo Soldiers," African-Americans who, after the Civil War, joined the army and were assigned to the western mountains and southwestern deserts, where they were "expected to maintain order between the Indians and settlers, help build forts and roads, patrol borders, and

protect mail coaches and railroad construction crews"—whew!

Caddie Woodlawn
by Carol Ryrie Brink
illustrated by Trina Schart Hyman
Macmillan, 1973
Originally published in 1935, and adapted from actual childhood stories told by the author's grandmother, this Newbery Medal–winning novel tells of the many adventures of a girl who refuses to behave like a lady on the Wisconsin frontier of the 1860s.

Children of the Wild West
by Russell Freedman
Clarion Books, 1983
This extraordinary collection of photographs, accompanied by the author's informative and substantial text, helps us get to know pioneer families—especially their children—as they traveled west, as well as the Native American children who were already living out west when the pioneers arrived.

Cowboys of the Wild West
by Russell Freedman
Clarion Books, 1985
This study of "cow herders on horseback" has chapters on clothing, equipment, life on the trail, life at the ranch, and the last of the old-time cowboys. Like Freedman's other books, this one is distinguished by the many excellent photographs.

Daily Life in a Covered Wagon
by Paul Erickson
The Preservation Press, 1994
This book, exquisitely designed and beautifully illustrated (mostly with sharp color photographs), follows one family across the country on the hard journey by covered wagon from Indiana to Oregon. The text is well written and fascinating, covering all sorts of topics including wagon construction, medical procedures, food,

and entertainment. Includes a helpful time line and glossary.

If You Traveled West in a Covered Wagon
by Ellen Levine
illustrated by Mark Teague
Scholastic, 1992
Written in an easy-to-follow question-and-answer format, this book offers interesting information on many aspects of pioneer life, focusing on the people who headed to Oregon in the 1840s and 1850s. Some of the questions posed include "What kind of people traveled west? Could you send a letter or receive one? How far would you travel in a day? Where would you sleep? Without road signs, how would you know where you were?"

Lewis and Clark: Explorers of the American West
by Steven Kroll
illustrated by Richard Williams
Holiday House, 1994
This beautiful picture book, which recounts fascinating details of the Lewis and Clark expedition, was recommended as a read-aloud for first grade, and is still of value for independent reading in fifth grade. Includes a helpful map and list of important dates.

CC Reconstruction and Reform
by Joy Hakim
Oxford University Press, 1994
This is Book 7 in the ten-volume *A History of US* (described under American History General Resources: Series). It gives an engaging and detailed account of the nation's relentless push westward, of cowboys and cattle drives, of homesteaders, of the Transcontinental Railroad, and of the effects of all this on Native Americans. Schools looking for a classroom text on which to base the study of this period should give this book strong consideration. Parents should examine it as well: it's written in a clear and engaging style that most fifth graders will be able to read with pleasure.

Tecumseh
by Zachary Kent
Childrens Press, 1992
Part of the Cornerstones of Freedom series, this slender book recounts events in the life of the Shawnee leader who united a confederacy of Indians with the hopes of stopping the westward movement of settlers.

The Ten Mile Day and the Building of the Transcontinental Railroad
by Mary Ann Fraser
Henry Holt, 1993
This well-illustrated book stresses the contributions of Chinese and Irish workers, and captures the drama of the race to Promontory Point between the Central and Union Pacific companies.

CC *The Way West: Journal of a Pioneer Woman*
by Amelia S. Knight
illustrated by Michael McCurdy
Simon & Schuster, 1993
"Thursday, April 21, 1853. Rained all night; is still raining." "Saturday, April 23, 1853. Still in camp. It rained hard all night, and blew a hurricane almost. All the tents were blown down, and some wagons capsized. . . ." Steady-voiced, matter-of-fact journal entries form the text of this picture-book adaptation of a journal kept by Amelia Stewart while her family journeyed from Iowa to the Oregon Territory in 1853. The simply recorded facts are fascinating especially as, one after another, they convey the hardship of the journey, and imply the fortitude and resilience required. Michael McCurdy's highly stylized art makes a vivid impression.

NATIVE AMERICANS: CULTURE AND LIFE

Buffalo Hunt
by Russell Freedman
Holiday House, 1988
Freedman examines the importance of the buffalo in the lore and day-to-day life of the Indian tribes of the Great Plains and describes hunting methods and the uses for each part of the animal that could not be eaten. This beautiful, evocative book is illustrated with nineteenth-century paintings of buffalo, buffalo hunting, and the Plains way of life.

Death of the Iron Horse
written and illustrated by Paul Goble
Macmillan/Aladdin, 1987
With his usual spare but beautiful illustrations, author-illustrator Paul Goble tells a story based on an 1867 incident in which Cheyenne Indians derailed and raided a freight train in an act of defiance against the white man.

CC *A First Americans Book* series
by Virginia Driving Hawk Sneve
illustrated by Ronald Himler
Holiday House
This excellent series is described under American History General Resources. Recommended titles for this grade include *The Sioux* and *The Nez Perce*.

Houses of Hide and Earth
by Bonnie Shemie
Tundra Books, 1991
Part of the Native Dwellings series (described under American History General Resources), this fascinating little book examines the tepee and other dwellings, explaining in words and soft-textured illustrations how these homes were built, decorated, and inhabited.

Indian Chiefs
by Russell Freedman
Holiday House, 1987
Engaging and clearly written brief biographies, combined with carefully chosen black-and-white photographs and illustrations, make this an interesting and informative book. It includes portraits, in words and pictures, of Red Cloud, Satanta, Quanah Parker, Washakie, Joseph, and Sitting Bull.

"Joseph, A Chief of the Nez Perce"
This September 1990 issue of *Cobblestone,* a magazine of American history for young people (see address, page 148), focuses on the life and times of Chief Joseph. The brief, readable articles and photographs help provide a background to his moving "I will fight no more forever" speech. Many libraries subscribe to *Cobblestone.*

CC *The Ledgerbook of Thomas Blue Eagle*
by Jewel H. Grutman and Gay Matthaei
illustrations by Adam Cvijanovic
Thomasson-Grant, 1994
This fascinating, beautiful book speaks about the experience of young Native Americans who, in the late nineteenth century, were forcibly assimilated at institutions like the Carlisle School. The book is a fictional account by a made-up character, Thomas Blue Eagle, intended to show, as the authors note, "events that might well have occurred in the life of a Sioux boy who attended school in the East to learn about the world of the white man." Physically, it simulates ledger-book drawings, created in the late nineteenth century by young Plains Indians who had been taught in "white man's schools."

People of the Buffalo: How the Plains Indians Lived
by Maria Campbell
illustrated by Douglas Tait and Shannon Twofeathers
Firefly Books, 1976, 1983
This interesting book, the authors say, seeks to remove the layers of romantic mythology heaped on the Plains Indians and explain, in a careful and caring way, the facts about how they lived, where they slept, what they ate, and how they hunted, as well as their beliefs and rituals. Illustrated with black-and-white line drawings, suitable for independent reading or research by fifth graders.

CC = "Core Collection" book (see page 8).

CC *Red Hawk's Account of Custer's Last Battle: The Battle of the Little Bighorn, 25 June 1876*
by Paul and Dorothy Goble
Pantheon Books, 1969; University of Nebraska Press/Bison Books, 1992
With distinctive illustrations by Paul Goble, this book describes Custer's last stand at the Little Bighorn as it might have been witnessed by one of the Indians participating in the battle.

Sea and Cedar: How the Northwest Coast Indians Lived
by Lois McConkey
illustrated by Douglas Tait
Firefly Books, 1991
A brief, clear description, accompanied by helpful drawings, of the homes, tools, clothing, and beliefs of Northwest Coast Indian tribes who, as the author is quick to point out, "did not ride horses, chase buffalo, or live in tepees."

Thunder Rolling in the Mountains
by Scott O'Dell and Elizabeth Hall
Houghton Mifflin, 1992
Historical fiction. Through the eyes of Chief Joseph's daughter, this moving novel retells the events of 1877 when the Nez Perce resisted being forced onto a reservation. The book concludes with a passage from Chief Joseph's famed speech "I will fight no more forever."

Wounded Knee: The Death of a Dream
by Laurie A. O'Neill
Millbrook, 1993
This book begins with a brief account of the massacre at Wounded Knee, then moves backward to examine what led up to it. Chapters discuss the ways of life of the Sioux, the westward movement of white settlers, battles (including Little Bighorn), treaties made and broken, the Ghost Dance, and more. Written for middle school and above, the book has a few helpful illustrations.

AMERICAN HISTORY AND GEOGRAPHY

Grade 6

GENERAL RESOURCES

CC *Reconstruction and Reform* (1994)
An Age of Extremes (1994)
by Joy Hakim
Oxford University Press
These are Books 7 and 8 in the ten-volume *A History of US* (described under American History General Resources: Series). Together the two books offer engaging accounts of just about every topic recommended for study in the sixth-grade American History guidelines of the *Core Knowledge Sequence* (summarized above, pages 94–101). About the second half of *Reconstruction and Reform* deals with immigration (including the "nativist" resistance to it) and reformers (including Booker T. Washington, W.E.B. Du Bois, and Ida B. Wells). *An Age of Extremes* offers interesting, readable accounts of the rise of monopoly capitalism (including such figures as Carnegie, Rockefeller, and Morgan), William Jennings Bryan and the Populist movement, the growth of organized labor (including the Homestead and Haymarket Square strikes), immigration, reform (including the "muckrakers," Ida Tarbell, Jacob Riis, and Upton Sinclair), and the Spanish-American War. Schools looking for a classroom text should give these books strong consideration. Parents should examine them as well: they are written in a clear and direct style that sixth graders can read with pleasure.

Turn of the Century: Our Nation One Hundred Years Ago
by Nancy Smiler Levinson
E. P. Dutton/Lodestar, 1994
This engagingly written book discusses many topics recommended for study in the sixth-

grade American History guidelines of the *Core Knowledge Sequence*. Chapters include: "Inventions," "Workers Unite!," "Nation of Nations," "Rise of the City," "Souls of Black Folks," and more. A very fine volume, with many excellent photographs.

IMMIGRATION

The American Family Album series
by Dorothy and Thomas Hoobler
Oxford University Press
See description under American History General Resources.

Ellis Island: Gateway to the New World
by Leonard Everett Fisher
Holiday House, 1986
Combining many evocative photographs with clear text, this book tells the history of Ellis Island, and draws upon firsthand accounts to convey the apprehensions of the immigrants who were questioned and "processed" before being allowed to stay in America. The photographs especially help convey the personal experiences behind the historical topics.

If Your Name Was Changed at Ellis Island
by Ellen Levine
illustrated by Wayne Parmenter
Scholastic, 1993
Easy reading for this grade, this informative and interesting book proceeds in a question-and-answer format, asking such questions as "Why did people leave their homelands? Did every immigrant come voluntarily? Would everyone in your family come together? What

kind of mental tests were you given? Did you have to be able to read English? What was the Staircase of Separation? What did Americans think about the new immigrants? What contributions have immigrants made?"

CC *Immigrant Kids*
by Russell Freedman
E. P. Dutton, 1980; Puffin Books, 1995
Weaving together first-person accounts and extraordinary photographs, many of them by Jacob Riis and Lewis Hine, this book powerfully conveys what it was like to be an immigrant child in urban America about a hundred years ago. Highly recommended.

CC *Immigration: 1870–1930*
written and compiled by Christine Scriabine
Jackdaw Publications, 1995
This "Jackdaw" is a packet of posters, readings, and reproduced primary sources, including an American citizenship certificate from 1896, a little pamphlet on "What Every Emigrant Should Know," a government questionnaire, a 1920 census form, and more. Teachers may also want to examine the optional Study Guide, which provides reproducible masters, writing exercises, research topics, and more. Available from Golden Owl Publishing, P.O. Box 503, Amawalk, NY 10501; (800) 789-0022.

Multicultural America
This "Theme Pack" includes nine pertinent issues of *Cobblestone*, the magazine of American history for young readers (see address, page 148), along with a sixteen-page teacher's guide. Titles included in this package include *Immigrants I* and *Immigrants II; Chinese-Americans; Hispanic-Americans; American Jews; Italian-Americans; The Amish; Genealogy*. Individual titles, as well as the teacher's guide, may be ordered separately.

CC = "Core Collection" book (see page 8).

INDUSTRIAL AND URBAN AMERICA

"The History of Labor"
This October 1992 issue of *Cobblestone*, the magazine of American history for young readers (see address, page 148), features brief, engaging articles on the rise of labor unions; Samuel Gompers and the AFL; Labor Day; the Homestead strike and the brutal retaliation; the photography of Lewis Hine; and later developments and key figures (including A. Philip Randolph and John L. Lewis).

CC *Immigrant Kids*
by Russell Freedman
E. P. Dutton, 1980; Puffin Books, 1995
See description above under Immigration.

CC *Kids at Work: Lewis Hine and the Crusade Against Child Labor*
by Russell Freedman
Clarion Books, 1994
Students today may find it hard to believe that in the early twentieth century many children their age were working twelve-hour-a-day jobs in factories, mills, mines, and farms, often in the most unhealthy and dangerous conditions. The powerful photographs of Lewis Hine, many of which are sharply reproduced in this book, document this shameful chapter in our history. This book tells the story of Hine as a crusader for child labor laws. It is partly a biography of Hine, and partly an account of the injustices he sought to correct.

The Story of the Haymarket Riot
by Charnan Simon
Childrens Press, 1988
Suitable for sixth-grade readers, this book offers a brief, well-written account of the Haymarket Riot of 1886. It begins on the fateful day, then looks backward to causes and the condition of labor in America, then proceeds to examine the trial and the heated public debates over the whole affair. Illustrated with drawings and photographs from the period.

REFORMERS AND REFORM MOVEMENTS

CC *Bully for You, Teddy Roosevelt*
by Jean Fritz
illustrated by Mike Wimmer
G. P. Putnam, 1991
"What did Theodore Roosevelt want to do? Everything. And all at once if possible." Thus begins this lively and informative biography of our twenty-sixth president by award-winning author Jean Fritz.

Don't You Dare Shoot That Bear!: A Story of Theodore Roosevelt
written and illustrated by Robert Quackenbush
Prentice Hall, 1984
Quackenbush spins a humorous biographic tale of the twenty-sixth president, emphasizing his love of animals and wildlife, and his activities as a conservationist.

Ida B. Wells-Barnett and the Antilynching Crusade
by Suzanne Freedman
Millbrook, 1994
This brief, readable biography capably introduces the brave journalist and crusader. With black-and-white illustrations, mostly photographs.

CC *Immigrant Kids*
by Russell Freedman
E. P. Dutton, 1980; Puffin Books, 1995
See description above under Immigration. This book contains information about, and many photographs by, Jacob Riis, author of *How the Other Half Lives*.

CC *Kids at Work: Lewis Hine and the Crusade Against Child Labor*
by Russell Freedman
Clarion Books, 1994
See description above under Industrial and Urban America.

Peace and Bread: The Story of Jane Addams
by Stephanie Sammartino McPherson
Carolrhoda Books, 1993
This readable biography of Jane Addams offers a detailed discussion of her years at Hull House. With black-and-white photographs.

CC *Reconstruction and Reform An Age of Extremes*
by Joy Hakim
Oxford University Press, 1994
See description above under General Resources for this grade (page 188).

CC *The Story of Booker T. Washington*
by Patricia and Frederick McKissack
Childrens Press, 1991
Part of the Cornerstones of Freedom series, this brief, interesting, and readable biography begins with an excellent account of Washington's important speech at the 1895 Atlanta Exposition, then moves back to discuss "the times, place, and conditions that shaped his life." Illustrated with black-and-white photographs and old prints.

Votes for Women
written and compiled by Christine Scriabine
Jackdaw Publications, 1992
This "Jackdaw" is a packet of posters, readings, and reproduced primary sources, including political cartoons, handbills, pamphlets, postcards, an issue of the newsletter called *The Revolution* edited by Elizabeth Cady Stanton, and more. Teachers may also want to examine the optional Study Guide, which provides reproducible masters, writing exercises, research topics, and more. Available from Golden Owl Publishing, P.O. Box 503, Amawalk, NY 10501; (800) 789-0022.

W. E. B. Du Bois and Racial Relations
by Seamus Cavan
Millbrook, 1993
A brief, informative, and readable introduction to the life and work of W. E. B. Du Bois, with

helpful illustrations, and good discussions of the Niagara Movement and the NAACP.

Women Win the Vote
by Betsy Covington Smith
Silver Burdett, 1989
Part of the Turning Points in American History series, this book gives an overview of the history of women's rights in America from 1620 to the present, and focuses in detail on the struggle to gain the right to vote. Early chapters examine pioneers in the women's movement (as recommended for study in the fourth-grade American History guidelines of the *Core Knowledge Sequence)*, such as Lucretia Mott and Elizabeth Cady Stanton. The remainder of the book discusses Susan B. Anthony, Carrie Catt, and others. Illustrated mostly in black and white, including a photographic "Gallery of American Women Firsts."

THE SPANISH-AMERICAN WAR

CC *An Age of Extremes*
by Joy Hakim
Oxford University Press, 1994
See description above under General Resources for this grade (page 188).

The Spanish-American War
by Alden R. Carter
Franklin Watts, 1992
Suitable for sixth-grade readers and researchers, this book offers a brief (sixty-page), informative discussion of the Spanish-American War from the sinking of the Maine to America's uneasy status as a world power with imperialist ambitions. Includes many maps, drawings, and photographs.

VISUAL ARTS

Introduction

Much of the study of art in the early grades should take the form of *doing:* of drawing, painting, cutting and pasting, working with clay, and so on, sometimes for the pleasure of making things and developing artistic appreciation, and sometimes to support other studies. Accordingly, the resources suggested below include many "how-to" and activity books. (These are general books for parents and classroom teachers, not specialized resources for art teachers, who may nevertheless find some of the titles of interest.)

In addition, we suggest many books *about* works of art, artists, art history, and artistic techniques. Children should understand art not only as doing but also as seeing, in particular, *informed and active* seeing, so that the artistic concepts and works the children learn about may develop their understanding and enhance their own creative endeavors. By looking closely at art, and talking with your child about it, you can help your child develop a love of art and a habit of thoughtful, active enjoyment.

To achieve that end, however, looking and talking are not enough. Children also need materials and opportunities to be practicing artists. In school art should not be a frill or occasional distraction: it is an essential part of the core of a good education.

Visual Arts in the *Core Knowledge Sequence:* A Summary

> For information on the specific content guidelines known as the *Core Knowledge Sequence* and on the ideas behind the Core Knowledge initiative, please see in this book "Core Knowledge: Building Knowledge Year by Year" (pages 9–23, especially pages 15–17 on the *Sequence).*

The Visual Arts guidelines of the *Core Knowledge Sequence* include accepted technical concepts of visual art, such as color, line, shape, light, texture, space. Specific works are recommended to illustrate the concepts and terms introduced at each grade level. Some works are recommended because they are connected with topics in the History section of the *Sequence.* These recommended works are, of course, far from comprehensive, and are intended only to offer a coherent introduction to many kinds of arts in many media, from different cultures.

Here is **a brief summary** of the main topics in the Visual Arts section of the *Core Knowledge Sequence:*

• **Kindergarten:** Children are introduced to a variety of art activities and materials, and to a variety of artists and works of art in many media, including drawing, painting, sculpture, printmaking, and collage.

Children learn about color, and talk about the ways different colors can produce different effects and feelings, both in their own creations and in such paintings as Gauguin's "Tahitian Landscape" and Picasso's "Le Gourmet."

Children learn to identify and use different kinds of lines: straight, zigzag, curved, wavy. They look at how different artists use lines, such as Joan Miró in "People and Dog in the Sun" and Matisse in "The Purple Robe."

Children begin to look closely at pictures through being asked what the pictures make them think and feel, what details they notice, what questions the pictures make them ask, and why they think the artist chose to depict things in a certain way. Suggested works feature children and include Pieter Bruegel's "Children's Games," Mary Cassatt's "After the Bath," Winslow Homer's "Snap the Whip," Diego Rivera's "Mother's Helper," and Henry O. Tanner's "The Banjo Lesson."

Besides making their own sculptures, children learn about such sculptures as the Statue of Liberty, Northwest American Indian totem poles, and mobiles.

• **Grade 1:** Children learn more about the elements of art, including color, line, shape, and texture.

They look at the use of color in many works, such as Monet's "Tulips in Holland" and Whistler's "Arrangement in Black and Gray" (also known as "Whistler's Mother").

They continue to identify and use different kinds of lines (straight, zigzag, curved, wavy, spiral), and to note the use of line in such works as Jacob Lawrence's "The Street" and Georgia O'Keeffe's "Shell."

Children identify and use basic geometric shapes (square, rectangle, triangle, circle, oval), and note how these shapes are used by artists in such works as Grant Wood's "Stone City, Iowa."

They learn to describe qualities of texture (for example, rough, bumpy, scratchy) in natural objects and works of art, including American Indian masks and the bronze sculptures of Edgar Degas (such as "Little Fourteen-Year-Old Dancer").

Children discuss examples of different kinds of paintings—portrait, self-portrait, and still life—and create their own. Suggested portraits and self-portraits include da Vinci's "Mona Lisa," Goya's "Manuel Osorio Manrique de Zunega," and Norman Rockwell's "Triple Self-Portrait." Suggested examples of still life include Van Gogh's paintings of sunflowers and irises, and Cézanne's studies with fruit.

They learn about murals—paintings on walls—and discuss examples such as Diego Rivera's "The History of Medicine in Mexico" (which can be connected to their study of Mexico as recommended in World History and Geography Grade 1).

In connection with their learning about ancient civilizations (see World History and Geography Grade 1), children learn about the art of those civilizations. From ancient Egypt, for example, they learn about mummy cases, the Great Sphinx, and the bust of Queen Nefertiti.

• **Grade 2:** Children continue to build on their earlier learning about elements of art: color, texture, line, and shape. They learn how lines and shapes can indicate movement, as in Hokusai's "The Great Wave at Kanagawa Nami-Ura" and Blackbear Bosin's "Prairie Fire." They are introduced to examples of sculpture such as "The Discus Thrower," "Venus de Milo," and Rodin's "The Thinker."

Building on their first-grade knowledge of kinds of pictures—portraits, self-portraits, and still life—they come to understand the term *landscape*. They try their own hand at landscape painting, and look at examples such as El Greco's "View of Toledo" (also known as "Toledo in a Storm") and van Gogh's "The Starry Night."

Children are engaged in looking at, talking about, and comparing art that "looks like real things," "doesn't look exactly like real things but reminds you of things you've seen," and "doesn't try to look like something, but instead shows what the artist is thinking, feeling, or imagining." They can, for example, compare representations of animals, both lifelike (such as Albrecht Dürer's "Young Hare" and birds by John James Audubon) and abstract (such as Paul Klee's "Cat and Bird" and Picasso's "Bull's Head" made from a bicycle seat and handle bars).

In connection with what they are learning about in World History, children are introduced to architecture, including, for example, the Parthenon in Greece, the Great Stupa (a Buddhist temple in Sanchi, India), and the Himeji Castle (also known as "White Heron Castle," in Japan).

• **Grade 3:** Children build on their earlier learning about elements of art by paying attention to two new elements: light and space. They note how artists use light and shadow in various works, such as James Chapin's "Ruby Green Singing" and Johannes Vermeer's "Milkmaid." They are introduced to various ways that artists can make two dimensions look three dimensional by creating an illusion of depth in works such as Bruegel's "Peasant Wedding" and others.

The children reinforce their earlier learning about color, line, shape, and texture, as well as their new learning about light and space, by beginning to think about how all these elements work together to form a design. They look for patterns, balance, and symmetry in a variety of works, including: Matisse cutouts; early American quilts; Navajo weavings and sand paintings; and paintings by Rosa Bonheur ("The Horse Fair"), Horace Pippin ("Victorian Interior"), Mary Cassatt ("The Bath"), and others. They discuss how design can convey an idea or tell a story, in works like Edward Hicks's "The Peaceable Kingdom," Faith Ringgold's "Tar Beach," and Salvador Dalí's "The Persistence of Memory."

In connection with what they are learning about in World History, children are introduced to examples of the art of ancient Rome, such as Trajan's Column and the Pantheon, as well as some Byzantine art, such as mosaics.

• **Grade 4:** In creating their own art and learning about works of art, children continue to develop and apply what they have already learned about color, line, shape, texture, light, and space. In this grade, the suggested works and artists are more consistently connected to topics the children are learning about in history.

Children are introduced to the art of the Middle Ages in Europe, including examples of medieval Madonnas, illuminated manuscripts, the "unicorn tapestries," and Gothic cathedrals (such as Notre Dame and Chartres).

Children are introduced to Islamic art, such as the illumination of the Qur'an (Koran), and characteristic features of Islamic architecture (for example, domes and minarets), as exemplified in the Dome of the Rock (Mosque of Omar) in Jerusalem and the Taj Mahal in India.

They are introduced to the art of Africa, including masks used in religious ceremonies, sculptures by Yoruba artists, and ivory carvings and bronze sculptures of Benin.

They learn about some examples of the art of China, including silk scrolls, calligraphy (the art of brush writing and painting), and porcelain.

Children become familiar with works of art representative of the "new" nation they are learning about in their study of history, the United States after the mid-eighteenth century, including, for example, John Singleton Copley's portrait of Paul Revere, Gilbert Stuart's portrait of George Washington, and a work that has since come to symbolize the American Revolution, "Washington Crossing the Delaware." They also learn about the architecture of Thomas Jefferson's home, Monticello.

• **Grade 5:** In creating their own art and learning about works of art, children continue to develop and apply what they have already learned about color, line, shape, texture, light, and space. In this grade, the suggested works and artists are more consistently connected to topics the children are learning about in history.

Children learn the term *perspective*. They compare paintings that do not attempt to create an illusion of depth (for example, some Persian paintings) with paintings that do. They learn about the development of perspective during the Italian Renaissance, and look closely at such works as Raphael's "The Marriage of the Virgin" and Leonardo da Vinci's "The Last Supper."

Children learn about a variety of Renaissance artists and works. They observe the new emphasis on humanity and the natural world, as well as the influence of Greek and Roman art on Renaissance artists, in such works as: da Vinci's "The Proportions of Man," Botticelli's "The Birth of Venus," Michelangelo's ceiling of the Sistine Chapel, Raphael's Madonnas, Michelangelo's "David," the Florence Cathedral and St. Peter's in Rome, and (as part of the "Northern Renaissance"), works by Jan van Eyck, Albrecht Dürer, and Pieter Bruegel.

In connection with learning about nineteenth-century American history, children learn about American art and artists of the time, including: landscape painters of the Hudson River School; genre paintings such as William Sidney Mount's "Eel Spearing at Setauket"; popular prints, such as those by Currier and Ives; the Civil War photography of Matthew Brady and his colleagues; and, Augustus Saint-Gaudens's "Shaw Memorial" on Boston Common.

In connection with learning about feudal Japan, children are introduced to such works of art as the Great Buddha at Kamakura and landscape gardens.

• **Grade 6:** In creating their own art and learning about works of art, children continue to develop and apply what they have already learned about color, line, shape, texture, light, and space. In sixth grade, art history provides the context within which students can undertake creative activities as well as appreciation and analysis. For students who have studied in programs based on earlier grades in the *Core Knowledge Sequence*, the sixth-grade topics provide an opportunity for review and summation, as well as an introduction to some new works and concepts.

Students are introduced to the idea of "art history," of classifying Western art by periods and schools, with major characteristics of each period and school, as well as illustrative works. Of course the periods and characteristics are not absolute distinctions but generally helpful categories (to which there are always exceptions) often used in discussions of art. These categories, and examples of each, include Classical (the art of ancient Greece and Rome); Gothic art and architecture; Renaissance; Baroque (El Greco; Rubens); Rococo (Fragonard); Neoclassical (Jacques Louis David); Romantic (Goya; Delacroix); Realism (Millet; Courbet; Winslow Homer); and, Impressionism (Monet; Renoir; Degas; Mary Cassatt; Henry O. Tanner).

Students are introduced to the development of photography as an art form, and, in connection with their study of American history, learn about the use of photography as social criticism in the work of Jacob Riis and Lewis Hine.

(Note: twentieth-century art movements and works will be introduced in the later grades of the *Core Knowledge Sequence*.)

VISUAL ARTS

General Resources

The Core Knowledge Series: *What Your Kindergartner–Sixth Grader Needs to Know*, E. D. Hirsch, Jr., editor. Published by Doubleday in hardcover and Dell in paperback.

The seven current books in the Core Knowledge Series, one each for Kindergarten through sixth grade, are the companion books to this resource guide. These illustrated books provide a convenient introduction to topics in the *Core Knowledge Sequence*, including the Visual Arts topics summarized on pages 189–193. Full of stories, poems, history, and discussions of topics in geography, science, math, and music, the books can be read to children or, in the upper grades, read by children. All author's proceeds from the sale of *What Your Kindergartner–Sixth Grader Needs to Know* go to the nonprofit Core Knowledge Foundation to support its mission of helping parents and teachers help children develop strong early foundations of knowledge.

CC = a "Core Collection" book (see p. 8).

ART PRINTS AND REPRODUCTIONS

Many resource houses sell art prints and posters; school discounts are generally available. Here we have space to list only a few of the many resource houses, and only two major museums, though museums large and small often sell prints, slides, and postcards of their holdings.

Print Finders
15 Roosevelt Place
Scarsdale, NY 10583
914-725-2332
Fax 914-723-0218
Print Finders will send you upon request a

free listing of prints they sell that are relevant to the Visual Arts guidelines in the *Core Knowledge Sequence*.

Shorewood Fine Art Reproductions
33 River Road
Cos Cob, CT 06807
800-494-3824
Fax 203-661-2480

New York Graphic Society
P.O. Box 1469
Greenwich, CT 06836-1469
203-661-2400
Fax 203-661-2480

Knowledge Unlimited
P.O. Box 52
Madison, WI 53701-0052
800-356-2303
Knowledge Unlimited has a free catalog that lists not only art prints but many curricular materials for other disciplines as well (History, Language Arts, Science).

Metropolitan Museum of Art
Attention: Poster Shop
1000 Fifth Avenue
New York, NY 10028-0198
212-650-2924
Fax 718-628-5845

National Gallery of Art
Publications Mail Order Department
2000 B South Club Drive
Landover, MD 20785
301-322-5900
Fax 301-322-1578

Sandak
180 Harvard Avenue
Stamford, CT 06902
800-343-2806
Fax 203-967-2745
Sandak supplies *slides* (not prints). They package many of their slides in thematic sets, including a collection of "Multicultural Art" sets (African-American, African, Native American, Oriental, Middle Eastern, Latin American), and many others, such as "Art of Ancient Rome," "Art of Greece," "Dumbarton Oaks: Byzantine Art Collection," "Italian Renaissance," "Japan: A History in Art," "Egypt: An Historic Tour," "Cloisters," "Monastery and Cathedral in France," "The Royal Abbey of Saint-Denis in the Time of Abbot Suger," "Stained Glass of the Middle Ages and Renaissance," "Italian Renaissance," and dozens more. Prices vary greatly depending on the number of slides in the set,

so write or call for a catalog with pricing information.

HOW-TO AND ACTIVITY BOOKS

Block Printing
by Susie O'Reilly
Thomson Learning, 1993
With step-by-step instructions and color pictures of children engaged in projects, this book explains the materials and techniques necessary for printing activities you can do easily with children. Also nice because it opens with six pages of prints from many times and places.

CC *Brown Bag Ideas from Many Cultures*
by Irene Tejada
Davis Publications, 1993
This unusual book gives examples of traditional arts from Africa, Asia, the Middle East, Europe, Mexico, the U.S. (including American Indians), and Polynesia, and then describes how to create your own similar works of art using brown bags. You'll be surprised at what can be made out of a paper bag: moccasins, serapes, dashikis, shields, breastplates, and lots more.

First Arts and Crafts **series**
Thomson Learning
The eight books in this series were written with the youngest artists in mind. The simple, doable projects are illustrated with color photographs of children, their works in progress, and their completed masterpieces. Titles include: *Collage, Drawing, Masks, Models, Painting, Printing, Puppets,* and *Toys and Games.*

CC *Kids Create! Art and Craft Experiences for 3 to 9 Year Olds*
by Laurie Carlson
Williamson, 1990
Make dinosaurs out of your fingerprints, a cactus out of clay and bits of uncooked spaghetti, and many more fun projects. This art activity book describes over one hundred projects that

introduce the basics of working with paper and paste, clay and dough, printmaking and sculpture. Also contains seasonal activities and crafts projects.

The Kids' Multicultural Art Book: Art and Craft Experiences from Around the World
by Alexandra M. Terzian
Williamson, 1993
From the *Kids Create* publisher comes this companion volume of art and crafts projects that explore designs and traditions from around the globe. Includes projects inspired by Aztec, Japanese, Korean, African, Indian, and Native American art.

The Metropolitan Museum of Art Activity Book
by Osa Brown
Metropolitan Museum of Art/Harry N. Abrams, 1983
Make a Japanese fan or a Chinese carp kite. Build a replica of the temple of Dendur from ancient Nubia. Play a game called the "mansion of happiness." In a workbook format, this book provides color reproductions from the Met with informative discussions, games, and activities.

More Than Moccasins: A Kid's Activity Guide to Traditional North American Indian Life
by Laurie Carlson
Chicago Review Press, 1994
Instructions and diagrams for dozens of activities and projects, such as leggings, a shell necklace, masks, rattles, sand painting, as well as many recipes. We can't vouch for the authenticity of each project, but we do respect the author's responsible effort to provide information on the specific tribe or nation that inspired each activity (as opposed to lumping them together as generically "Native American"). See *Kids Create*, by the same author.

Mudworks: Creative Clay, Dough, and Modeling Experiences
by MaryAnn F. Kohl
Bright Ring, 1989
You'll never be at a loss for a dough recipe

again. Here are 117 recipes for doughs, clays, goops, and pastes that kids can use for fun and projects. About one third are edible. The book ends with a helpful list of where materials are available.

My First Activity Book
by Angela Wilkes
Alfred A. Knopf, 1989
The large format and clear, colorful explanations make this art activity book very easy to use. With twenty-one simple projects such as envelope puppets, simple papier-mâché pots, masks, and home made wrapping paper.

National Gallery of Art Activity Book: 25 Adventures with Art
by Maura A. Clarkin
Harry N. Abrams, 1994
In this delightful book, children can go on twenty-five "adventures" in which they look closely at colors, textures, point of view, light, shape, motion, balance, composition, and more, all in ways that they can understand and recreate. Many color reproductions and many interesting tidbits along the way.

Scribble Cookies and Other Independent Creative Art Experiences for Children
by MaryAnn F. Kohl
Bright Ring, 1985
Scribble cookies are the answer to the perplexing question, "What do you do with those old crayon bits?" You melt them in muffin tins to form "cookies" that draw! From elementary teacher MaryAnn Krohl comes this useful book of art projects, divided into sections by materials needed: paper, paint, printing, and more. The book concludes with recipes for the most common doughs and paints.

Start Exploring Masterpieces
by Mary Martin and Steven Zorn
Running Press, 1981
This fact-filled coloring book presents black-and-white line drawings of sixty famous paintings from the Western tradition, each accompa-

nied by informative text. Includes works by Bruegel, Cassatt, David, van Gogh, Goya, El Greco, da Vinci, Monet, Raphael, Rembrandt, and more.

ELEMENTS OF ART

CC *Learning to Look: A Complete Art History and Appreciation Program for Grades K–8*
by Sue J. Massey and Diane W. Darst
Prentice Hall, 1992
This big book is a ready-made set of units and lessons that can be adapted for various grade levels. The book is designed for all teachers, not just those with special training in the arts. It provides brief background essays for teachers, and gives detailed suggestions for activities and discussion questions. Its rather hefty price is justified by the inclusion of thirty color slides and eighteen color reproductions of European and American art masterpieces. Also included are examples of art done by children following the *Learning to Look* program. The program is designed to help children appreciate and explore the basic elements of artistic design— color, line, shape, texture, light, and space—and to complement this exploration with a range of hands-on activities.

CC *Picture This: A First Introduction to Paintings*
by Felicity Woolf
Doubleday/Delacorte Press, 1989
Picture This, an introduction to Western painting from 1400 to 1950, aims directly at kids. Here's how a paragraph in the introduction starts: "You can find out a great deal about painting by learning *how* to look at it and what questions to ask of it. It is rather like being a detective." Ten of the twenty-five paintings discussed are by artists on the *Core Knowledge Sequence*. Includes color reproductions, glossary and gallery list.

Scholastic Art
Scholastic
This magazine is available through Scholastic, Inc. It features full-color reproductions and articles about great artists, plus workshops, interviews, notes on traveling expositions and current artists. Art posters are included in the Teacher's Edition of the magazine. For ordering information, write *Scholastic Art*, P.O. Box 3710, Jefferson City, MO 65102 or call (800) 631-1586.

A Short Walk Around the Pyramids and Through the World of Art
by Phillip M. Isaacson
Alfred A. Knopf, 1993
This eclectic book discusses form, color, sculpture, and photography by looking at a fascinating collection of art from many times and places, including many artists and works from the *Core Knowledge Sequence*. A nice book for children to look at with an adult, and the text may prove helpful for teacher/parent background.

SERIES ABOUT ART AND ARTISTS

CC *Art for Children* series
by Ernest Raboff
HarperCollins
With color reproductions and clear prose printed with a handwritten look, the sixteen books in this series introduce children to the works of great artists of Western civilization. They make convenient picture books to look at with younger children, and can be read independently by children in about third or fourth grade and above. Artists examined in this series include: Renoir, van Gogh, Gauguin, Matisse, da Vinci, Michelangelo, Velázquez, Remington, Rembrandt, Raphael, Klee, Dürer, Picasso, Chagall, Rousseau, and Toulouse-Lautrec.

The Art of . . . series
by Shirley Glubok
Macmillan
Unfortunately this excellent and extensive series

for children is out of print, but it is still available in many libraries. These books are worth looking for. In them Glubok combines discussions of art with just enough historical background, all in informative, clear descriptions readable by about third or fourth graders and up. The reproductions are all in black and white, but well chosen and numerous. One great strength of the series is that it explores the art of many times and places. Titles include: *The Art of Africa, The Art of America from Jackson to Lincoln, The Art of Colonial America, The Art of Ancient Egypt, The Art of Ancient Peru, The Art of the Etruscans, The Art of the Gilded Age, The Art of Ancient Greece, The Art of China, The Art of Japan, The Art of Lands in the Bible, The Art of the New American Nation, The Art of the North American Indian, The Art of the Old West, The Art of the Southeastern Indians, The Art of the Spanish in the United States and Puerto Rico,* and *The Art of the Southwest Indians.*

CC Come Look with Me series
by Gladys S. Blizzard
Thomasson-Grant
Each of the four books in this acclaimed series pairs quality art reproductions with encouraging, thought-provoking questions for children to discuss with adults. The original volume, *Come Look with Me: Enjoying Art with Children,* is still the best place to start, but try to see the other books too: *Come Look with Me: Animals in Art; Come Look with Me: Exploring Landscape Art with Children;* and, *Come Look with Me: World of Play.*

Eyewitness Art series
Dorling Kindersley
These lavishly illustrated volumes are a delight for both adults and children. They can be used on many levels for everything from research to "just looking." Specific titles in the series include: *Watercolor, Impressionism, Perspective, Manet, Monet, Gauguin, Van Gogh.*

CC = "Core Collection" book (see page 8).

CC Getting to Know the World's Greatest Artists series
written and illustrated by Mike Venezia
Childrens Press
These books combine color reproductions, cartoons, large print, easy-to-read prose, and sometimes silly humor to introduce children to the lives and works of the great artists. The artists included in the series are: Botticelli, Bruegel, Cassatt, Dalí, da Vinci, Gauguin, Goya, Hopper, Klee, Michelangelo, Monet, O'Keeffe, Picasso, Pollock, Rembrandt, Rivera, Toulouse-Lautrec, and van Gogh.

The Key to Art series
Lerner
Each volume in this series on Western art history is devoted to the art of a specific period, and features many color reproductions. Written for children in middle school and up, so perhaps best used as a teacher/parent resource, though the color prints would be interesting to all students. Titles include: *The Key to Painting; The Key to Gothic Art; The Key to Renaissance Art; The Key to Baroque Art; The Key to Art from Romanticism to Impressionism;* and *The Key to Modern Art of the Early Twentieth Century.*

Weekend with . . . series
Rizzoli International Publications
Each of the four books in this clever series takes you on a trip into the artist's world, a trip led by the artist himself, who speaks in the first person. Artists included in the series are Degas, Picasso, Rembrandt, and Renoir. Each book includes many color reproductions, sketches, and a list important dates.

CC What Makes a . . . series
by Richard Mühlberger
Metropolitan Museum of Art and Viking
To date there are ten titles in this fine series for children of upper-elementary and middle-school age, with titles all in the form of *What Makes a Rembrandt a Rembrandt?* The books explain how to recognize the work of an artist by looking at the way color, line, shape, composition,

brushwork, and subject matter combine to form an unmistakable signature. Artists included in the series are: Bruegel, Cassatt, Degas, Goya, Leonardo, Monet, Picasso, Raphael, Rembrandt, and van Gogh.

ART HISTORIES

History of Art for Young People
by H. W. Janson and Anthony F. Janson
Harry N. Abrams, 1992 (4th edition)
Adapted from Janson's *History of Art,* the most popular textbook in introductory college courses, this children's version is still best used as a teacher/parent resource in the elementary grades. It provides an encyclopedic survey of the history of art including paintings, sculpture, architecture, and photography from prehistoric to modern times, and includes many color reproductions.

CC *The Story of Painting: The Essential Guide to the History of Western Art*
by Sister Wendy Beckett
Dorling Kindersley, 1994
In about four hundred vivid pages, this beautifully designed volume from the creators of the Eyewitness books tells the story of art from the Stone Age cave paintings to the works of the 1970s. Parents and teachers will find helpful discussions of "Gothic Painting," "The Italian Renaissance," "The Northern Renaissance," "Baroque and Rococo," "Neoclassicism and Romanticism," "The Age of Impressionism," and more.

BIOGRAPHY COLLECTIONS

Great Lives: Painting
by Shirley Glubok
Charles Scribner's Sons, 1994
A good teacher/parent resource, also readable by children in the upper elementary grades, this book provides twenty-three brief, interesting biographies of European and American artists, including David, Dürer, El Greco, Homer, van Gogh, Vermeer, and many others. With black-and-white photos and a section of color reproductions.

Lives of the Artists: Masterpieces, Messes, (and What the Neighbors Thought)
by Kathleen Krull
illustrated by Kathryn Hewitt
Harcourt Brace, 1995
Brief, gossipy biographies of da Vinci, Michelangelo, Bruegel, Sofonisba Anguissola, Rembrandt, Hokusai, Cassatt, Van Gogh, Käthe Kollwitz, Matisse, Picasso, Chagall, Duchamp, O'Keeffe, William H. Johnson, Dalí, Noguchi, Rivera, Kahlo, and Warhol. Many children may like the "daily life" details and anecdotes, but we wouldn't suggest this book be a child's *only* source of biographical information—it makes what da Vinci ate for a snack as he painted the Mona Lisa seem almost as important as the painting.

ARCHITECTURE

Architects Make Zigzags: Looking at Architecture from A to Z
by Diane Maddex
illustrated by Roxie Munro
Preservation Press, 1986
From dormers to facades and newel post, this alphabet book introduces children to the basics of architecture with wonderful drawings.

Great Moments in Architecture
by David Macaulay
Houghton Mifflin, 1978
Actually, this is a book of visual jokes that you can get only if you know the *real* great works, such as the pyramids, Eiffel Tower, and Leaning Tower of Pisa. With the assumed background knowledge, you can enjoy Macaulay's witty drawings that fondly poke fun at these and other well-recognized architectural masterpieces.

The Random House Book of How Things Were Built
by David J. Brown
Random House, 1992
Once you open this book, you won't put it down readily. This illustrated history of more than sixty of the world's greatest structures includes the Egyptian pyramids, the Lighthouse at Alexandria, Hagia Sophia, Machu Picchu, the mosque at Djenne, the leaning tower of Pisa, the Eiffel Tower, Hoover Dam, Golden Gate Bridge, Pompidou Center, and more. With a glossary of architectural terms.

CC *Round Buildings, Square Buildings, and Buildings That Wiggle Like Fish*
written and photographed by Philip Isaacson
Alfred A. Knopf, 1988
It's not adequate to call this book "an introduction to architecture" though it does introduce children to famous buildings from all over the world as well as important elements of architecture. With one hundred incredible photographs and deceptively simple prose, this book makes buildings so fascinating that it could change the way you and your children think about buildings and look at your surroundings. Includes Stonehenge, the Alhambra, the Taj Mahal, the Brooklyn Bridge, and Brunelleschi's dome for the Cathedral at Florence.

The X-Ray Picture Book of Big Buildings of the Ancient World
by Joanne Jessop
designed by David Salariya
Franklin Watts, 1993
If you're familiar with "See Through History" and Eyewitness Books, then you know what this book is like: the emphasis is on the visuals, with very detailed drawings—some of them cutaway drawings to reveal a structure's "insides"—of the Great Pyramid at Giza, the Parthenon, the Colosseum in Rome, Notre Dame cathedral, Mont St.-Michel, the Taj Mahal, the Forbidden City, Bodiam Castle, and the Basilica of St. Peter. A brief informative paragraph or two accompanies each display, as well as captions in tiny print. An attractive book, more to browse than to read.

BOOKS ABOUT ART MUSEUMS

Inside the Museum: A Children's Guide to the Metropolitan Museum of Art
by Joy Richardson
Harry N. Abrams, 1993
You don't have to be in New York to enjoy this paperback guide, which, with its gorgeous color photography, puzzles, and other activities, introduces children to the Metropolitan Museum of Art. With chapters on the art of many times and places (Egyptian, Greek, Islamic, Asian, American to name a few), and behind-the-scenes information about how the museum operates, this book can be used in many ways. It can introduce children to what art museums do, provide examples from a particular period, or let them browse as they might on a real visit.

Katie's Picture Show
by James Mayhew
Bantam, 1989
For Katie, the paintings on the museum wall are not still and distant; instead, they provide the imaginative landscapes that she actively enters. This book suggests how looking at art can be a fun, participatory experience.

The Metropolitan Museum of Art
by Howard Hibbard
Harrison House, 1988
An informative resource for parents and teachers full of beautifully photographed works of art from the Met. Covers Ancient Egyptian, Ancient Near Eastern, Greek, Roman, Early Christian, Byzantine, Islamic, Medieval, Italian Renaissance, fifteenth through nineteenth century European, American, twentieth century, Far Eastern, and Primitive Art.

CC = "Core Collection" book (see page 8).

Norman the Doorman
by Don Freeman
Viking, 1959
Fun to read when your kindergartner or first grader is learning about sculpture, this book tells the story of a small gray mouse who guards the mouse entrance to a famous museum. Then one day, he enters a contest and creates a stir with his witty sculpture of a mousetrap turned into a trapeze.

Visiting the Art Museum
by Laurene Krasny Brown and Marc Brown
E. P. Dutton, 1986
Children will probably enjoy this book because it allows them to witness the small trials and hear the funny asides as a family of five visits an art museum. In picture book format with some reproductions of well-known masterpieces.

ART AND LITERATURE

Children of Promise: African-American Literature and Art for Young People
edited by Charles Sullivan
Harry N. Abrams, 1991
Organized in a clear historical framework, this fine collection brings together words and works of art and about African-Americans, and includes works by Langston Hughes, Gwendolyn Brooks, Frederick Douglass, W.E.B. Du Bois, Jacob Lawrence, Henry Tanner, and many others. A book that's lovely to look at and think about.

CC *A Child's Book of Art: Great Pictures, First Words*
by Lucy Micklethwait
Dorling Kindersley, 1993
This beautifully designed oversized book is not only a stunning "first words" book but a magnificent collection of great art. The book gathers excellent reproductions of paintings from many times and places and organizes them in subject areas like "Pets," "Wild Animals," "Colors," "Opposites,' "Things to Do," and more. An introduction to parents and teachers gives tips for talking about the works.

Here Is My Kingdom: Hispanic-American Literature and Art for Young People
edited by Charles Sullivan
Harry N. Abrams, 1994
Following up on the success of *Children of Promise: African-American Literature and Art for Young People*, Charles Sullivan has once again collected works of literature and paired them with great art. This book features mostly writers and artists of Hispanic-American heritage. Core Knowledge teachers may want to note that the book includes works by or about Columbus, Diego Rivera, Georgia O'Keeffe, Cesar Chavez, Walt Whitman, Robert Frost, and Pablo Picasso.

Imaginary Gardens: American Poetry and Art for Young People
edited by Charles Sullivan
Harry N. Abrams, 1989
In his introduction to this beautiful collection of American poetry and art, the editor says, "This book has no rules." He means that it's a book for browsing or reading at length, and that you don't have to start at the beginning. What he doesn't say is that once you pick it up, you'll have a hard time putting it down because the collection of images is so arresting and the selection of poems so varied and so representative of our complex country.

VISUAL ARTS

Kindergarten

HOW-TO AND ACTIVITY BOOKS

See Visual Arts General Resources: How-To and Activity Books.

ELEMENTS OF ART

CC *Colors*
  Lines
  Shapes
  Stories
by Philip Yenawine
Delacorte Press, all 1991
These four books produced by the Museum of Modern Art in New York introduce basics of visual art perception in a way designed to make sense to very young children. This, for example, is from *Colors:* "The world is full of colors. That is a good thing, because colors are pretty and cheerful. But then again, colors can be serious and quiet." Through a combination of simple statements and bold color reproductions, children learn a basic vocabulary for thinking about art.

Colors Everywhere
by Tana Hoban
Greenwillow Books, 1995
This large wordless picture book by award-winning photographer Tana Hoban collects vibrant pictures for learning about colors. It also has a neat feature: to the side of each large color photo is a bar made up of the colors in the photo.

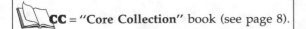
CC = "Core Collection" book (see page 8).

CC *Come Look with Me: Enjoying Art with Children* (1991)
  Come Look with Me: World of Play (1993)
by Gladys S. Blizzard
Thomasson-Grant
"This boy is holding a string in his hands. Where does it go?" "If you could feel this child's dress, how would it feel?" Gladys Blizzard asks inviting questions about twelve varied works and provides brief biographical sketches of the artists that give kids confidence in talking about art and make them curious to know more. *Enjoying Art with Children* presents twelve paintings of children by such artists as Goya, Holbein, Manet, Picasso, and others. *World of Play* includes works by Winslow Homer, Horace Pippin, Diego Rivera, Pieter Bruegel, and more. With excellent color reproductions, these books are part of the Come Look with Me series, described under Visual Arts General Resources: Series.

CC *I Spy a Lion* (1994)
  I Spy Two Eyes (1993)
by Lucy Micklethwait
Greenwillow Books
Lucy Micklethwait has found a wonderful way to make great paintings from all over the world familiar to even the smallest children. In *I Spy a Lion*, she collects twenty paintings and asks children to "spy" the animals in each. Try it! In *I Spy Two Eyes*, children practice counting as they look for a certain number of birds, apples, circles and other objects in a variety of paintings ranging from the fifteenth century to the present day. See also *I Spy: An Alphabet in Art*, listed in Visual Arts Grade 1.

Mouse Paint
written and illustrated by Ellen Stoll Walsh
Harcourt Brace, 1989
In this lighthearted introduction to colors, three white mice find pots of red, blue, and yellow paint and, you guessed it, explore the mixing of colors. Very simple prose and winning illustrations.

Pictures Tell Stories: A Collections for Young Scholars Book
by John Grandits
Open Court, 1995
With simple but appealing text and thirty-seven wonderfully chosen color illustrations from many times and places, this small book invites children to get involved in the rich possibilities of fine art. It points to things children will want to examine and it asks questions they'll want to answer. Includes many artists and a few specific works suggested in the *Core Knowledge Sequence,* such as Rivera's "Piñata" and Bruegel's "Children's Games" (with six detailed close-ups).

The Shapes Game
by Paul Rogers
illustrated by Sian Tucker
Henry Holt, 1989
"Shapes are all around us. Shall we play a game? I'll spy a shape—you say it's name!" So starts Paul Rogers's inviting poem about nine familiar shapes. Each two-page spread illustrates a shape with colorful illustrations reminiscent of Matisse cutouts. And the book ends like this: "Shapes on the ceiling,/No two the same—/Quick—before they disappear—/Give them all a name!"

ARTISTS AND WORKS

Note: The following books are recommended here to correspond with topics of study outlined for this grade in the *Core Knowledge Sequence.* **See also** Visual Arts General Resources: Art Prints and Reproductions.

Calder Creatures: Great and Small
by Jean Lipman
E. P. Dutton, 1995
This is a delightful picture book of Alexander Calder's playful animal artworks, including captions and a short biography.

Diego
by Jonah Winter
illustrated by Jeanette Winter
Alfred A. Knopf, 1991
With color-filled illustrations inspired by Rivera's murals, this bilingual picture book tells the story of the artist's life for children four and up.

 CC *Henri Matisse* **(1988)**
　　　　Pablo Picasso **(1987)**
by Ernest Raboff
HarperCollins
For this grade, these books from Raboff's fine *Art for Children* series are suggested not as a text to read to children (since their discussions are fairly technical and sophisticated), but as picture books that conveniently collect a number of works by the same artist. The book on Picasso includes *"Le Gourmet"* and "Mother and Child."

 CC *Pieter Bruegel* **(1992)**
　　　　Mary Cassatt **(1993)**
　　　　Paul Gauguin **(1992)**
　　　　Picasso **(1988)**
written and illustrated by Mike Venezia
Childrens Press
You can read aloud all or parts of these books to young children, who will delight in Venezia's own funny drawings and wacky humor as well as the many color reproductions of works by the artists. In the book on Bruegel, most of the paintings reproduced are in his realistic style depicting peasant life, but there are four Bosch-like works with strange creatures that may puzzle some children and require a little explana-

 **CC** = **"Core Collection"** book (see page 8).

tion. The book on Mary Cassatt includes color reproductions of "The Bath" and "The Boating Party." Venezia characterizes Gauguin as an artist who "led an adventurous life, traveling all over the world to find just the right place to paint." From the *Getting to Know the World's Greatest Artists* series, described under Visual Arts General Resources: Series.

CC *Pablo Picasso*
written by Tony Hart
illustrated by Susan Hellard
Barron's, 1994
This amusingly illustrated picture book about Picasso's childhood is a great read-aloud, full of interesting anecdotes and, what's more, reproductions of drawings and paintings by the young Pablo, from ages eight to twelve.

VISUAL ARTS

Grade 1

HOW-TO AND ACTIVITY BOOKS
See Visual Arts General Resources: How-To and Activity Books.

ELEMENTS OF ART
See also listings under Visual Arts Kindergarten: Elements of Art.

CC *Come Look with Me: Animals in Art*
by Gladys S. Blizzard
Thomasson-Grant, 1992
Starting with a photograph of the Lascaux cave paintings and ending with a collage made in 1987, this engaging book couples twelve varied paintings of animals with questions that engage children in looking at and talking about art. Also includes paintings by Klee, Hicks, and Matisse ("The Snail"). Part of the Come Look with Me series (described under Visual Arts General Resources: Series). Two other Come Look with Me books are described under Visual Arts: Kindergarten.

CC *I Spy: An Alphabet in Art*
by Lucy Micklethwait
Greenwillow Books, 1992
The game in this book gets children and their adult companions involved in looking closely at great paintings, and it's a lot of fun. "I spy with my little eye something beginning with *A*." An object that starts with each letter of the alphabet is hiding somewhere in each of twenty-six full-page reproductions of paintings by twenty-six different artists. There's a key for answers (some of the letters aren't easy to find) and museum locations at the end of the book.

Pictures Tell Stories: A Collections for Young Scholars Book
by John Grandits
Open Court, 1995
See description under Visual Arts Kindergarten: Looking at Pictures. Includes a reproduction of Diego Rivera's "Piñata" (as suggested in the *Core Knowledge Sequence*).

ANCIENT ART
See also World History Grade 1: Ancient Civilizations, for books with many illustrations of the art and architecture of ancient Mesopotamia and Egypt, as well as coloring and activity books.

Fun with Hieroglyphs
by Catharine Roehrig
Metropolitan Museum of Art, 1990
Lots of fun! This kit includes a book that explains hieroglyphics, an ink pad, and rubber stamps with a glyph for each letter of the alphabet. With a little help, children can "write" in hieroglyphics.

Native American Rock Art: Messages from the Past
by Yvette La Pierre
illustrated by Lois Sloan
Thomasson-Grant, 1994
Written for upper elementary students, this attractive book can be a useful teacher/parent resource at this grade level, and has many illustrations and color photos for children to look at and enjoy. The book explains what we know

about ancient rock artists—who they were, and how and why they carved in stone.

ARTISTS AND WORKS

Note: The following books are recommended here to correspond with topics of study outlined for this grade in the *Core Knowledge Sequence.* **See also** Visual Arts General Resources: Art Prints and Reproductions.

A Blue Butterfly: A Story About Claude Monet
written and illustrated by Bijou Le Tord
Doubleday/Delacorte Press, 1995
This is a welcome little book, appropriate for first graders. Using very simple words and lovely pastel illustrations modeled on Monet's water lily paintings, it introduces young children to Monet, his subjects, and his style.

CC *Camille and the Sunflowers: A Story About Vincent van Gogh*
by Laurence Anholt
Barron's, 1994
You can show children van Gogh's paintings, but what can you tell them about his sad life? This picture book offers an excellent answer. Based on an actual encounter, it tells the story of Camille Roulin, a little boy who befriends a poor painter and ends up the subject of one of his paintings. Beautifully illustrated with delicate watercolors and reproductions of seven van Gogh paintings, including "Vase with Fourteen Sunflowers."

Cézanne (1994)
Monet (1994)
by Antony Mason
Barron's
These two books from the Famous Artists series are written for older children, but first graders will enjoy the illustrations. The book on Monet reproduces paintings that span his lifetime—from schoolboy sketches to the water lilies of

his celebrated, final years. You can adapt some of the book's suggested activities for this grade level.

CC *Da Vinci* (1989)
Francisco Goya (1991)
Monet (1993)
Georgia O'Keeffe (1993)
Diego Rivera (1994)
Vincent van Gogh (1988)
written and illustrated by Mike Venezia
Childrens Press
You can read aloud all or parts of these books to young children, who will delight in Venezia's own funny drawings and wacky humor, as well as the many color reproductions of works by the artists. From the *Getting to Know the World's Greatest Artists* series, described under Visual Arts General Resources: Series.

Diego
by Jonah Winter
illustrated by Jeanette Winter
Alfred A. Knopf, 1991
See description under Visual Arts Kindergarten: Selected Artists.

CC *Henri Matisse* (1988)
Leonardo da Vinci (1987)
by Ernest Raboff
HarperCollins
For this grade, these books from Raboff's fine *Art for Children* series are suggested not as texts to read to children (since their discussions are fairly technical and sophisticated), but as picture books that conveniently collect a number of works by the same artist.

Jacob Lawrence: Thirty Years of Prints (1963–1993)
by Patricia Hills and Peter Nesbett
University of Washington Press, 1994
This teacher/parent resource collects over forty-five full-colored reproductions of Lawrence's work with valuable discussions of each.

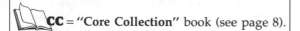

CC *Leonardo da Vinci*
by Tony Hart
illustrated by Susan Hellard
Barron's, 1993
This amusingly illustrated picture book makes da Vinci accessible by introducing the great artist as a child. Fun to read aloud. Part of a series called *Famous Children*, which also includes books on Michelangelo and Toulouse-Lautrec.

CC = "**Core Collection**" book (see page 8).

What Makes a Degas a Degas?
by Richard Mühlberger
Metropolitan Museum of Art and Viking, 1993
This interesting book is best as a teacher/parent resource at this grade level, but children will enjoy looking at the good color reproductions, and Mühlberger's discussions may give you some good ideas for talking about the artworks with your children. Looking at more than twenty paintings and sketches by Degas, the author shows us how to see Degas's characteristic use of color, line, light, composition, and subject matter. Part of the *What Makes a . . . ?* series described under Visual Arts General Resources: Series.

VISUAL ARTS

Grade 2

HOW-TO AND ACTIVITY BOOKS

See also Visual Arts General Resources: How-To and Activity Books.

ELEMENTS OF ART

See listings under Visual Arts Kindergarten: Elements of Art.

CC *Come Look with Me: Animals in Art* **(1992)**
Come Look with Me: Exploring Landscape Art with Children **(1992)**
by Gladys S. Blizzard
Thomasson-Grant
Animals in Art presents twelve varied paintings of animals with questions that engage children in looking at and talking about art; includes Matisse's "The Snail." *Exploring Landscape Art* presents twelve landscapes with thought-provoking questions and brief biographies of each artist. Includes Bruegel's "Hunters in the Snow" and works by van Gogh, Escher, Bierstadt, O'Keeffe, and Frankenthaler.

ARTISTS AND WORKS

Note: The following books are recommended here to correspond with topics of study outlined for this grade in the *Core Knowledge Sequence.* **See also** Visual Arts General Resources: Art Prints and Reproductions; and, see World History Grade 2: Ancient Greece, for books that discuss and reproduce pictures of ancient Greek art and architecture, as well as coloring and activity books.

The Art of Japan
by Shirley Glubok
Macmillan
This volume from Shirley Glubok's fine *The Art of . . .* series (described under Visual Arts General Resources: Series) is regrettably out of print, but worth looking for in libraries. In the meantime, see below, *Oriental Art;* and you can look in your library for books about Japanese civilization and culture, which often reproduce pictures of art and architecture, such as Pamela Odjik's *The Japanese* (Silver Burdett, 1989), which includes a photograph of the stunning Himeji Castle, as well as pictures of the Kamakura Buddha and a landscape garden.

CC *Camille and the Sunflowers: A Story About Vincent van Gogh*
by Laurence Anholt
Barron's, 1994
See description under Visual Arts Grade 1: Selected Artists.

CC *Henri Matisse* **(1988)**
Henri Rousseau **(1988)**
Picasso **(1987)**
Vincent van Gogh **(1988)**
by Ernest Raboff
HarperCollins
For this grade, these books from Raboff's fine *Art for Children* series are suggested not as a text to read to children (since their discussions are fairly technical and sophisticated), but as picture books that conveniently collect and clearly reproduce a number of works by the same artist.

Though many second graders may have some difficulty with the words if read aloud directly from the page, you may want to share your own versions of some of the techniques and concepts that Raboff discusses.

Oriental Art
Sandak
A set of fifteen color slides (set number 839) of masterpieces of painting and sculpture from Japan, China, and India, including a Chinese Buddha and a remarkable sculpture of a horse; a Japanese screen and Hokusai's "Great Wave off Kanagawa"; and an Indian Shiva, as well as the Taj Mahal. Part of a series of "Multicultural Art" slide collections that may be purchased from Sandak, 180 Harvard Avenue, Stamford, CT 06902; (800) 343-2806.

CC *Paul Klee* (1991)
    Picasso (1988)
    Vincent van Gogh (1988)
written and illustrated by Mike Venezia
Childrens Press
From the *Getting to Know the World's Greatest Artists* series: You can read these books aloud to second graders, or "share read" them (you read parts, they read parts). The children will enjoy Venezia's own funny drawings and wacky humor, as well as the many color reproductions of works by the artists.

What Makes a Picasso a Picasso? (1994)
What Makes a Van Gogh a Van Gogh? (1993)
by Richard Mühlberger
Metropolitan Museum of Art and Viking
These two books in the *What Makes a . . . ?* series (described under Visual Arts General Resources: Series) show each artist's characteristic use of color, line, light, composition, and subject matter. Their discussions are fairly technical, and so we suggest these books as teacher/parent resources at this grade level. Still, children will enjoy looking at the good color reproductions, and Mühlberger's discussions may give you some good ideas for talking about the artworks with your children.

CC = "Core Collection" book (see page 8).

VISUAL ARTS

Grade 3

HOW-TO AND ACTIVITY BOOKS

See Visual Arts General Resources: How-To and Activity Books.

AMERICAN INDIAN ART

Note: For other books that discuss Native American art and architecture, see American History, especially Grade 2, Grade 3, and Grade 5.

The Encyclopedia of Native America
by Trudy Griffin-Pierce
Viking, 1995
This lavishly illustrated parent/teacher resource explores the vast and diverse cultural landscape of Native America. By dividing her huge subject into seven cultural and geographic areas, the author is able to provide both a useful overview and some significant detail about rich and varied Native American cultures. Includes many informative inserts on arts and crafts of various tribes and nations.

Native American Art
Sandak
A set of fourteen color slides (set number 838) of works by past and present Native American artists and craftsmen, including adobe pueblos, a Haida shaman's rattle, a Sioux Ghost Dance shirt, and Blackbear Bosin's "Prairie Fire." Part of a series of "Multicultural Art" slide collections that may be purchased from Sandak, 180 Harvard Avenue, Stamford, CT 06902; (800) 343-2806.

North American Indian
by David Murdoch
Alfred A. Knopf, 1995
This Eyewitness book includes a great variety of art by Native Americans from many tribes and nations. Like all *Eyewitness* books, it's visually stunning, so the pictures can be shared with children (though the text is well beyond most third-grade readers).

ARTISTS AND WORKS

Note: The following books are recommended here to correspond with topics of study outlined for this grade in the *Core Knowledge Sequence*. **See also** Visual Arts General Resources: Art Prints and Reproductions; and, see World History Grade 3: Ancient Rome, for books that discuss and reproduce pictures of Roman and Byzantine art and architecture.

Faith Ringgold
by Robyn Montana Turner
Little, Brown, 1993
Lovely to look at and fascinating to read, this book tells the story of African-American artist Faith Ringgold and explains the background of her celebrated story quilts, including "Tar Beach" (suggested in the *Core Knowledge Sequence*). From the *Portraits of Women Artists for Children* series, listed in Visual Arts General Resources: Series.

 **CC** = "Core Collection" book (see page 8).

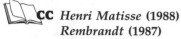 **CC** *Henri Matisse* **(1988)**
         Rembrandt **(1987)**
by Ernest Raboff
HarperCollins
You can read aloud to third graders from Raboff's fine *Art for Children* series, but since the language sometimes gets sophisticated, you will want to stop often to engage the children in talk about the ideas and pictures. Here are some representative sentences from the book on Rembrandt: "Rembrandt saw the beautiful in everything from a lion to a child, a landscape to a helmet, an old woman's face to a wrinkled root of a tree. . . . Every stroke of his brush was a caress on the surface of the painting." These books conveniently collect a number of works by the same artist, and suggest ways of enjoying the works by looking at them with careful eyes.

CC *Pieter Bruegel* **(1992)**
     Mary Cassatt **(1990)**
     Salvador Dalí **(1993)**
     Rembrandt **(1988)**
written and illustrated by Mike Venezia
Childrens Press
Many third graders will be able to read these books from the *Getting to Know the World's Greatest Artists* series, but they're so much fun that you may insist on reading them aloud! With Venezia's offbeat humor and funny drawings, each book includes many color reproductions of the artist's works.

Rosa Bonheur
by Robin Montana Turner
Little, Brown, 1991
This thirty-two-page book, appropriate for reading to third graders, tells the fascinating story of Rosa Bonheur's life. Born in 1822 to an artist father and musician mother, this French artist of realistic drawings and paintings became the first woman to receive the medal of the French Legion of Honor. Includes many color reproductions of Bonheur's works.

Tar Beach
by Faith Ringgold
Crown Publishers, 1991
This Caldecott Award–winning book brings one of Faith Ringgold's story quilts to life. With borders from the quilt and new paintings by the artist, it tells the story of a little girl whose hopes soar as she spends a hot night on a Harlem rooftop with her family. The entire quilt is pictured on the last page.

What Makes a Bruegel a Bruegel? **(1993)**
What Makes a Cassatt a Cassatt? **(1994)**
What Makes a Rembrandt a Rembrandt? **(1993)**
by Richard Mühlberger
Metropolitan Museum of Art and Viking
These books in the *What Makes a . . . ?* series (described under Visual Arts General Resources: Series) show each artist's characteristic use of color, line, light, composition, and subject matter. Their discussions are fairly technical, and so we suggest these books as teacher/parent resources at this grade level. Still, children will enjoy looking at the good color reproductions, and Mühlberger's discussions may give you some good ideas for talking about the artworks with your children. The book on Cassatt includes "The Boating Party" and "The Bath," both works suggested in the *Core Knowledge Sequence.*

VISUAL ARTS

Grade 4

See also Visual Arts General Resources: Art Prints and Reproductions.

HOW-TO AND ACTIVITY BOOKS
See Visual Arts General Resources: How-To and Activity Books.

ART AND ARCHITECTURE OF THE MIDDLE AGES IN EUROPE
See also World History Grade 4: Europe in the Middle Ages for more titles that include sections or chapters on the art of the Middle Ages.

CC *Castle* **(1977)**
Cathedral: The Story of its Construction **(1973)**
by David Macaulay
Houghton Mifflin
See description under World History Grade 4: Europe in the Middle Ages.

Cathedral Stained Glass Coloring Book
by Ed Sibbett
Dover, 1980
One of many excellent Dover coloring books, in this one children can color "see-through" pages based on windows in famous European cathedrals, and so achieve a pleasing stained-glass effect. See also World History Grade 4 for other suggested activity books from Dover (see address, page 106).

CC = "Core Collection" book (see page 8).

History of Art for Young People
by H. W. Janson
Harry N. Abrams, 1992 (fourth edition)
A teacher/parent resource; see description under Visual Arts General Resources: Art Histories.

The Key to Gothic Art
by José Bracons
Lerner, 1990
Part of the *Key to Art* Series (see Visual Arts General Resources: Series), this very helpful teacher/parent resource opens with an explanation of Gothic Art, and then takes a detailed look at cathedrals, paintings, stained-glass windows, and more.

Picture This: A First Introduction to Paintings
by Felicity Woolf
Doubleday, 1989
This is an excellent introduction to Western art from the 1400s through the 1950s, written in a clear and engaging fashion, with plenty of excellent color reproductions. Woolf also provides some helpful sample questions to get the discussion started. For children learning about the Middle Ages, see in particular the discussion of illuminated manuscripts in the chapter called "Pictures and Writing: Paintings in Books."

ISLAMIC ART AND ARCHITECTURE
See also World History Grade 4: The Rise of Islam.

Islam
This is a collection of art prints ($5^1/2'' \times 8''$) that have been prepared as part of the state of Cali-

fornia's "Visual Textbook for the California History–Social Science Framework." Prints in both black-and-white and color show mosques, illuminated manuscripts, prayer rugs, paintings, and more. Different sets of prints are available. For more information or to order, write or call The University Prints, 21 East Street, Winchester, MA 01890; (617) 729-8006.

Middle Eastern Art
Sandak
A set of ten color slides of Middle Eastern art (set number 840), with works from Iran, Syria, Israel, Egypt, and Iraq, including elaborately beautiful manuscript pages and the Dome of the Rock. Part of a series of "Multicultural Art" slide collections that may be purchased from Sandak, 180 Harvard Avenue, Stamford, CT 06902; (800) 343-2806.

THE ART OF AFRICA
See also World History Grade 4: Early and Medieval Africa.

African Art
Sandak
A set of ten color slides (set number 837) that presents art from some of the many cultures of Africa, including bronzes from Benin and masks from different regions. Part of a series of "Multicultural Art" slide collections that may be purchased from Sandak, 180 Harvard Avenue, Stamford, CT 06902; (800) 343-2806.

A Coloring Book of Ancient Africa
Ancient Africa Volume 2: The Art of Life
Bellerophon Books, 1994
These two coloring books present carefully rendered line drawings inspired by ancient African art. The first volume reproduces wall reliefs and sculptures from the ancient royal palace at Benin. Volume 2 reproduces beautiful bronze and terra-cotta works from the kingdom of Ife.

A bit of text in each volume explains the art and its origins. (See address, page 106.)

The Art of Africa
by Shirley Glubok
Macmillan
This informative book is out of print but still available in many libraries. It provides a good overview of the many styles and media of African art at a perfect level for fourth graders. Part of *The Art of . . .* series described under Visual Arts General Resources: Series.

CC *Ghana, Mali, Songhay: The Western Sudan*
Oyo, Benin, and Ashanti
by Kenny Mann
Simon & Schuster/Dillon Press, 1996
These packed and beautiful books convey much historical information, and also provide superb color photographs of the art and architecture of ancient African civilizations.

CC = "Core Collection" book (see page 8).

THE ART OF A NEW NATION: THE UNITED STATES

CC *Learning to Look: A Complete Art History and Appreciation Program for Grades K–8*
by Sue J. Massey and Diane W. Darst
Prentice Hall, 1992
This excellent resource is described under Visual Arts General Resources: Elements of Art. It includes discussions of, and activities related to, Gilbert Stuart's portrait of George Washington, and Leutze's "Washington Crossing the Delaware" (both works recommended in the *Core Knowledge Sequence* in connection with the study of American history).

Monticello Architecture
Monticello Education Department
This resource packet developed for grades 3–6 includes three lessons on the principles of architecture exemplified by Thomas Jefferson's Monticello. Students get a look at the geometry of architecture, and can examine simplified architectural drawings of Monticello. For current ordering and pricing information write Monticello Education Department, P.O. Box 316, Charlottesville, VA 22902, or call (804) 984-9853.

VISUAL ARTS

Grade 5

See also Visual Arts General Resources: Art Prints and Reproductions.

How-To and Activity Books

See Visual Arts General Resources: How-To and Activity Books.

Elements of Art

Looking at Paintings
by Frances Kennet and Terry Measham
illustrated by Malcolm Livingston
Marshall Cavendish, 1990
This book gives children ways to look at paintings by taking up different questions with paintings from different periods and cultures. For example, a discussion of light includes Rembrandt's "The Man with the Golden Helmet," a discussion of color concludes with Matisse's "The Snail," and a lesson on perspective looks at a Renaissance painting of the annunciation and five "tricks" children can use to create perspective in their own works.

Perspective
by Alison Cole
Dorling Kindersley, 1992
Using numerous color reproductions and helpful diagrams, this informative book defines linear perspective and explores its use by Renaissance artists (as well as some modern artists). The text is occasionally quite technical and complex, so this book will be most helpful as a teacher/parent resource, though children will probably find the illustrations engaging, and

will be fascinated by some of the "tricks" and devices used by painters to achieve the illusion of depth. Part of the Eyewitness Art series described in Visual Arts General Resources: Series.

Picture This: A First Introduction to Paintings
by Felicity Woolf
Doubleday, 1989
This is an excellent introduction to Western art from the 1400s through the 1950s, written in a clear and engaging fashion, with plenty of excellent color reproductions. Woolf also provides some helpful sample questions to get the discussion started.

Renaissance Art and Artists

Note: Learning about Renaissance art connects with studying the history of the Renaissance: see World History Grade 5. Many of the books recommended there discuss and reproduce pictures of Renaissance works of art.

General Books on Renaissance Art

The Key to Renaissance Art
by José Fernández Arenas
Lerner, 1988
Part of the *Key to Art* Series (see Visual Arts General Resources: Series), this book, written for middle school students, discusses Renaissance art and architecture, including works by da Vinci, Michelangelo, Brunelleschi, Dürer, and others. It has color reproductions, but since the

book itself is only six by nine inches, the pictures tend to be small.

The Renaissance: A Bellerophon Coloring Book
Bellerophon Books, 1993
From woodcuts, frescos, illuminated manuscripts, and paintings of the Renaissance come ready-to-color drawings with informative captions. (See address, page 106.)

Renaissance Art
by Nathaniel Harris
Thomson Learning, 1994
Written for middle-school students, this book can be used as a teacher/parent resource or for strong readers in fifth grade. It introduces the Renaissance in nine brief chapters with color reproductions of paintings and photographs of statues by many Renaissance artists. Includes a glossary and time line.

Books on Specific Artists

Da Vinci (1989)
Michelangelo (1991)
Pieter Bruegel (1992)
written and illustrated by Mike Venezia
Childrens Press
These books will be easy reading for fifth graders. They are not as sophisticated as some of the other series recommended in this grade, but they have a broad appeal for children of many ages, in part because of their goofy humor. Part of the Getting to Know the World's Greatest Artists series described in Visual Arts General Resources: Series.

Leonardo Da Vinci
by Antony Mason
Barron's, 1994
This brief introduction to da Vinci's life and work from apprenticeship onward includes about ten activities related to da Vinci's subjects and techniques (like mirror writing and drawing from nature). Part of the Famous Artist Se-

ries listed under Visual Arts General Resources: Series.

 CC ### Leonardo da Vinci (1987)
Michelangelo Buonarroti (1988)
Raphael (1988)
by Ernest Raboff
HarperCollins
These excellent books in the Art for Children series are readable by fifth graders. They give brief biographical background on the artist and then draw your attention to specific features and techniques in a variety of works by each artist. The book on Raphael discusses twelve of his major paintings, including The Marriage of the Virgin.

Waiting for Filippo: The Life of Renaissance Architect Filippo Brunelleschi
by Michael Bender
Chronicle Books, 1995
This is a book that makes you say "Wow!" But wait—a pop-up book for fifth graders? Sure, even for adults. The clearly written text, which most fifth graders can read, introduces Brunelleschi and Renaissance Florence. Along the way, we learn about the apprentice system, perspective, Renaissance humanist philosophy, and more. What's really fun, however, and informative, are the pop-up buildings and scenes, and the many pages with little flaps that open to reveal other structures or information. This is not gimmicky: there's a lot to learn here, and a lot to enjoy. (Chronicle Books, 275 Fifth Street, San Francisco, CA 94103)

What Makes a Bruegel a Bruegel? (1993)
What Makes a Leonardo a Leonardo? (1994)
What Makes a Raphael a Raphael? (1993)
by Richard Mühlberger
Metropolitan Museum of Art and Viking
This excellent series is more sophisticated than the books by Mike Venezia, and more technical than the books by Ernest Raboff (see above). In each book the author looks at many works by a specific artist and examines how such features as color, line, shape, composition, brushwork,

and subject matter combine to form the artist's unmistakable signature. Part of the *What Makes a . . . ?* series described under Visual Arts General Resources: Series. Good teacher/parent resources, readable by students whose interest in the subject matter makes them willing to take on the sometimes challenging text.

AMERICAN ART OF THE NINETEENTH CENTURY

American Highlights: United States History in Notable Works of Art
by Edith Pavese
Harry N. Abrams, 1993
This teacher resource book in English and Spanish, with many works of art in color and black-and-white, treats the span of American history from Colonial to modern times.

The Art of America from Jackson to Lincoln
by Shirley Glubok
Macmillan, 1973
Large black-and-white photographs depict mid–nineteenth century American painting, sculpture, architecture, furniture, and other artifacts. (Out of print but worth seeking in libraries.)

The Art of the New American Nation
by Shirley Glubok
Macmillan, 1972
Illustrated with black-and-white photographs and reproductions, this book presents the painting, inventions, architecture, and other artifacts produced by Americans during their first fifty years of independence. (Out of print but worth seeking in libraries.)

 **CC** *Learning to Look: A Complete Art History and Appreciation Program for Grades K–8*
by Sue J. Massey and Diane W. Darst
Prentice Hall, 1992
This excellent resource is described under Visual Arts General Resources: Elements of Art. A large portion of the book is devoted to "American Art: From Colonial Times to the 1890s," and examines some works recommended for fifth grade in the *Core Knowledge Sequence,* including Cole's "The Oxbow," Bierstadt's "Rocky Mountains, Lander's Peak," and Bingham's "Fur Traders Descending the Missouri." The authors also describe how to do a variety of related hands-on activities.

CC = **"Core Collection"** book (see page 8).

VISUAL ARTS

Grade 6

See also Visual Arts General Resources: Art Prints and Reproductions.

ART HISTORIES (INCLUDING BOOKS ABOUT PERIODS AND SCHOOLS)
See also the resources listed above under Visual Arts General Resources: Art Histories.

History of Art for Young People
by H. W. Janson and Anthony F. Janson
Harry N. Abrams, 1992
Adapted from Janson's *History of Art*, the most popular textbook in introductory college courses, this children's version is a good teacher/parent resource in the elementary grades, and still challenging though readable at this grade. It provides an encyclopedic survey of the history of art including paintings, sculpture, architecture, and photography from prehistoric to modern times, and includes many color reproductions.

Impressionism
by Jude Welton
Dorling Kindersley, 1993
In addition to examining works by many Impressionist painters (Manet, Monet, Renoir, Morisot, Degas, Pissarro, Sisley, and others), this book discusses their favorite subjects, defining colors, and what inspired these artists to depict the world in a new way. Part of the *Eyewitness Art* series described under Visual Arts General Resources: Series.

The Impressionists
by Yolanda Baillet
illustrations by Christian Maucler
Chelsea House, 1995
This book presents students with a young, knowledgeable, chatty, and art-loving tour guide named Tom, who describes Impressionist art and artists. Includes many color reproductions, photographs, and a glossary.

The Key to Art from Romanticism to Impressionism (1990)
    by Carlos Reyero
The Key to Modern Art of the Early Twentieth Century (1990)
    by Lourdes Cirlot
    Lerner
Both of these helpful teacher/parent resources are part of the *Key to Art* Series described under Visual Arts General Resources: Series.

CC *The Story of Painting: The Essential Guide to the History of Western Art*
by Sister Wendy Beckett
Dorling Kindersley, 1994
In about four hundred vivid pages, this beautifully designed volume from the creators of the Eyewitness books tells the story of art from the Stone Age cave paintings to the works of the 1970s. Parents and teachers will find helpful discussions of Gothic Painting, the Italian Renaissance, the Northern Renaissance, Baroque and Rococo, Neoclassicism and Romanticism, the Age of Impressionism, and more.

ELEMENTS OF ART

Investigating Art: A Practical Guide for Young People
by Moy Keightley
Facts on File, 1976, 1984
This book is divided into two sections: the first explains six important concepts in understanding art: line, shape, color, pattern, texture, and form. The second section provides eighty pages of guided projects that help students apply the concepts learned from the first part of the book. (Out of print but worth seeking in libraries.)

Looking at Paintings
by Frances Kennet and Terry Measham
illustrated by Malcolm Livingston
Marshall Cavendish, 1989
This book gives children ways to look at paintings by taking up different questions with over fourteen paintings from different periods and cultures. For example, a discussion of light includes Rembrandt's "The Man with the Golden Helmet," a discussion of color concludes with a look at Matisse's "The Snail," and a lesson on perspective looks at a Renaissance painting of the annunciation and five "tricks" children can use to create perspective for themselves. This book can work well with the sixth-grade *Core Knowledge Sequence* for art, aiding in a review of the elements of art before studying major periods and schools of art. Part of a series called *Exploring the Arts*, which also includes books on ballet, music, and theater.

Picture This: A First Introduction to Paintings
by Felicity Woolf
Doubleday, 1989
See description under Visual Arts Grade 5.

CC = "Core Collection" book (see page 8).

ARTISTS AND WORKS

Note: The following books are recommended here to correspond with topics of study outlined for this grade in the *Core Knowledge Sequence*.

Goya
by Patricia Wright
Dorling Kindersley, 1993
This visually rich book weaves biography and artistic analysis around numerous reproductions of paintings and sketches. Part of the *Eyewitness Art* series described under Visual Arts General Resources: Series

CC *Linnea in Monet's Garden*
by Christina Bjork
illustrated by Lena Anderson
Farrar, Straus & Giroux, 1987
Little wonder this book has been so popular: it makes art history into a good story. A little girl named Linnea tells us about her trip to France, where she has a great time learning about Claude Monet. As she makes her way to his country home, we see photographs of the artist and his family and many of Monet's most famous works. If you like this book, you might also like *Linnea's Windowsill Garden*, in which Linnea tells children all about growing potted plants, and *Linnea's Almanac*.

Monet
by Antony Mason
Barron's, 1994
A good introduction to Monet's life and works, which includes about a dozen related art activities on color, light, depth, and Impressionism. Part of the *Famous Artist* Series described under Visual Arts General Resources: Series.

Raphael **(1988)**
Pierre-Auguste Renoir **(1987)**
Rembrandt **(1987)**
by Ernest Raboff
HarperCollins
These excellent books in the *Art for Children* se-

ries give brief biographical background on the artist and then draw your attention to specific features and techniques in a variety of works by each artist.

Visions
by Leslie Sills
Albert Whitman, 1993
This book provides brief accounts of the lives and work of four women artists—Mary Cassatt, Betye Saar, Lenora Carrington, and Mary Frank—with photographs and color reproductions.

A Weekend with Degas (1992)
    by Rosabianca Skira-Venturi
A Weekend with Rembrandt (1991)
    by Pascal Bonafoux
A Weekend with Renoir (1992)
    by Rosabianca Skira-Venturi
    Rizzoli International Publications
What a neat idea! Each book is written as if spoken by the artist himself, who "talks" about his life and work. With photos, sketches and many color reproductions. Part of the *Weekend*

With series described in Visual Arts General Resources: Series.

CC *What Makes a Cassatt a Cassatt?* **(1994)**
    What Makes a Degas a Degas? **(1993)**
    What Makes a Goya a Goya? **(1994)**
    What Makes a Monet a Monet? **(1993)**
    What Makes a Raphael a Raphael? **(1993)**
by Richard Mühlberger
Metropolitan Museum of Art and Viking
In each book in this excellent series, the author looks at many works by a specific artist and examines how such features as color, line, shape, composition, brushwork, and subject matter combine to form the artist's unmistakable signature. Good teacher/parent resources, and readable by students whose interest in the subject matter makes them willing to take on the sometimes challenging text. Less difficult and technical discussions may be found in the excellent *Art for Children* series by Ernest Raboff (see above).

MUSIC

Introduction

Clearly the best way to appreciate music is not just to read about it but to hear it, sing it, and play it. That is why in this section we recommend not only books, but also recordings, videos, and some software.

While music teachers in schools will often use materials specifically intended for music teachers, the resources we recommend here are primarily for parents and classroom teachers with little or no formal musical training. Our goal is to direct you to resources that will help you help children enjoy music, express themselves musically, and gain a basic understanding of musical form.

Music in the *Core Knowledge Sequence:* A Summary

For information on the specific content guidelines known as the *Core Knowledge Sequence* and on the ideas behind the Core Knowledge initiative, please see in this book "Core Knowledge: Building Knowledge Year by Year" (pages 9–23, especially pages 15–17 on the *Sequence).*

The Music section of the *Core Knowledge Sequence* is made up of guidelines for:
a) Elements of music: rhythm, melody, harmony, form, notation, etc.
b) Appreciation: musical concepts, instruments, genres, and works that illustrate them
c) Suggested works (songs and instrumental).

The suggested works are of course far from comprehensive; they are provided as a starting point. Teachers and parents are encouraged to supplement them with many other works.

Here is **a brief summary** of the main topics in the Music section of the *Core Knowledge Sequence.*

• **Kindergarten:** Students learn to recognize and move to a steady beat; recognize long and short sounds; discriminate between loud and quiet, fast and slow, short and long sounds; and sing unaccompanied and in unison. They learn to recognize, by sight and sound, instruments such as the guitar, piano, trumpet, flute, violin, and drums. Suggested works include Camille Saint-Saëns's *Carnival of the Animals,* as well as songs such as "The Bear Went over the Mountain," "Bingo," "The Farmer in the Dell," "Go In and Out the Window," "Go Tell Aunt Rhody," "If You're Happy and You Know It," "Kookaburra," "Kumbaya," "London Bridge," "This Old Man," "The Wheels on the Bus," and others.

• **Grade 1:** Children reinforce musical skills learned in kindergarten and also learn to echo short rhythms and melodic patterns; play simple rhythms and melodies; and recognize like and unlike phrases. They are introduced to the concept of musical notation. They learn about the families of instruments of the orchestra, and the role of the conductor. They are introduced to classical music and composers, and to music that tells a story (such as Dukas's *The Sorcerer's Apprentice* and Prokofiev's *Peter and the Wolf*). They are introduced to ballet *(The Nutcracker)* and other types of dance, as well as to opera and jazz.

Suggested songs include "America," "Billy Boy," "Down by the Riverside," "Frère Jacques," "Michael, Row the Boat Ashore," "Oh, Susanna," "She'll Be Comin' Round the Mountain," "Take Me Out to the Ball Game," "When the Saints Go Marching In," "Yankee Doodle," and others.

• **Grade 2:** Children reinforce musical skills learned in kindergarten and first grade, and also learn to gradually slow down and get faster, and gradually increase and decrease volume; to recognize verse and refrain; to recognize a scale as a series of notes; to sing the C major scale using "do re mi" et cetera; and to recognize more musical notation.

Children build on their introduction to instruments and the orchestra in first grade by becoming more familiar with the string and percussion families, and with keyboard instruments (especially piano and organ). Suggested works for listening include African drumming; Bach's Minuet in G major, Mendelssohn's "Spring Song" and Chopin's "Minute" Waltz; Beethoven's Symphony No. 6 ("Pastoral"); Aaron Copland's "Hoe Down" from *Rodeo*; John Philip Sousa's *Stars and Stripes Forever*; and Vivaldi's *The Four Seasons*.

Suggested songs include "Auld Lang Syne," "Clementine," "Comin' Through the Rye," "Follow the Drinking Gourd," "Home on the Range," "I've Been Working on the Railroad," "Loch Lomond," "Old Dan Tucker," "Shenandoah," "Sometimes I Feel Like a Motherless Child," "The Star Spangled Banner," "Swing Low, Sweet Chariot," "This Land Is Your Land," "We Shall Overcome," "When Johnny Comes Marching Home," and others.

• **Grade 3:** Children reinforce musical skills learned in previous grades and also learn to recognize harmony and sing rounds; recognize a theme and variations; and become familiar with more musical notation.

Children build on their introduction to instruments and the orchestra in first and second grades by becoming more familiar with the brass and woodwind families. Suggested works for listening include Rossini's *William Tell Overture*; the final movement of Beethoven's Symphony No. 9; Aaron Copland's *Appalachian Spring* suite; selections from Gilbert and Sullivan's *The Pirates of Penzance*; Gustav Holst's *The Planets*; Rimsky-Korsakov's *Scheherazade*; and "The Ride of the Valkyries" from Wagner's *Ring*.

• **Grade 4:** Children reinforce musical skills learned in previous grades and also learn to name the ledger lines and spaces of the treble clef; sing or play simple melodies while reading a score; understand meter signatures (4/4, 2/4, 3/4); and understand terms such as *legato* and *staccato*. They become familiar with vocal ranges, female (soprano, mezzo-soprano, and alto) and male (tenor, baritone, and bass).

Suggested works for listening include Haydn symphonies; Mozart's *A Little Night Music*; "O Fortuna" from Carl Orff's *Carmina Burana*; and Johann Strauss, Jr.'s *On the Beautiful Blue Danube*.

• **Grade 5:** Students reinforce musical skills learned in previous grades and also participate in two- and three-part singing. They learn the term *octave* and learn to recognize chords—I (tonic), IV (subdominant), V (dominant)—and intervals. They learn more musical notation as well.

Students explore jazz: its history, the importance of improvisation, syncopation, and composers and performers such as Scott Joplin, "Jelly Roll" Morton, Louis Armstrong, and Duke Ellington. They are introduced to the influence of jazz on other music, such as Gershwin's *Rhapsody in Blue.*

Suggested works for listening include music from the Renaissance (lute songs, madrigals, choral works, dances); Mozart's Symphony No. 40; the Wedding March from Mendelssohn's music to *A Midsummer Night's Dream;* and Mussorgsky's *Pictures at an Exhibition* (as orchestrated by Ravel).

• **Grade 6:** Students reinforce musical skills learned in previous grades and also learn Italian terms used to describe tempo *(grave, largo, adagio, andante, moderato, allegro, presto)* and dynamics, from *pp (pianissimo)* to *ff (fortissimo).* They learn to recognize the introduction and coda in musical selections. They learn more about chords and musical notation.

Students explore nonwestern music and instruments. They also synthesize much of their previous exposure to musical works into a chronological overview of Western musical history from the Baroque to the Romantic. Suggested works for listening include Bach's *Brandenburg Concerto No. 2;* selections from Handel's *Messiah;* Haydn's Symphony No. 100; Mozart's Symphony No. 41 and "Hunt" String Quartet; Beethoven's Symphony No. 3 ("Eroica"), "Moonlight" Sonata, and Symphony No. 9; Berlioz's *Symphonie Fantastique;* and Chopin's "Heroic" Polonaise.

MUSIC

General Resources

**CC** = a "Core Collection" book (see p. 8).

Note: Because so many of the resources below may be effectively used in different grades, we have organized them by topic rather than grade level. In the annotations we note when a particular resource is especially suited to children in the primary grades or to older children.

MAIL-ORDER MUSIC SOURCES

Note: Your local library or vendors may carry some of the resources suggested here. If not, many are available by mail-order. There are many good music resource houses but space permits us to list only a few here.

Music for Little People
P.O. Box 1720
Lawndale, CA 90620
You can write or call (800) 727-2233 for a catalog from this mail-order service. Although recent editions of the catalog have become cluttered with nonmusical videos and toys, you'll still find a very good selection of tapes, compact discs, books, and musical instruments for children.

Music in Motion
This Texas-based vendor of musical supplies offers a well-stocked mail-order catalog, of interest to both teachers and parents, with many instruments, songbooks, recordings, videos, posters, resource books, and more. For a catalog call (800) 445-0649.

West Music
This Iowa-based vendor of musical supplies offers a well-stocked mail-order catalog, of inter-

est to both teachers and parents, with many instruments, songbooks, recordings, videos, posters, resource books, and more. For a catalog call (800) 397-9378. Other available West Music catalogs include the "Music Software Catalog" and "World Music at West: Multicultural Music and Arts Catalog."

GENERAL RESOURCES

I Wonder Why Flutes Have Holes and Other Questions About Music
by Josephine Paker
Kingfisher Books, 1995
With glossy pictures and unusually large print this book feeds a child's interest in music by offering answers to a wide-ranging collection of questions, for example: "What's double about a double bass?" "Which is the biggest instrument?" "Where can you find a gamelan?" "Are rattles just for babies?" The question-and-answer format invites dipping into the book rather than reading straight through. A good browsing book for early readers or for reading aloud.

The Kids' World Almanac of Music from Rock to Bach
by Elyse Sommer
illustrated by John Lane
World Almanac/Pharos Books, 1991
A fun book for browsers from about age eight and up. Amid abundant musical trivia on everything from who won the "Grammy" to who goofed while singing "The Star-Spangled Banner" at a baseball game, the author has cleverly included a lot of solid information about how to write and read music, what musical terms mean, and when, where, and what famous composers wrote.

Marsalis on Music
Sony Classical Film and Video, 1995
Produced for PBS, these four videos are hosted by the acclaimed jazz trumpeter Wynton Marsalis. Volume I, "Why Do Toes Tap?" explores rhythm by comparing Tchaikovsky's *Nutcracker*

with jazz arrangements of Tchaikovsky's music by Duke Ellington. Volume II, "Listening Clues," explores musical forms and introduces music by Prokofiev, Gershwin, Ellington, and Ives. Volume III, "Sousa to Satchmo," looks at the evolution of jazz. Volume IV, "Tackling the Monster," is about the "monster" of practicing to play an instrument. Marsalis, his jazz band, and a youth orchestra (led by the Boston Symphony's Seiji Ozawa) present much of the music. Also available: a companion book (also titled *Marsalis on Music*) packaged with an interactive CD, published by W. W. Norton & Company (1995).

Music!
by Geneviève Laurencin, translated by Vicki Bogard
illustrated by Claude and Denise Millet
Young Discovery Library, 1988
This brightly illustrated little book does a good job of introducing a lot of information in a small space. It would make a pleasant read-aloud in grades K–2, and can be read independently by older children. It introduces families of instruments, the orchestra, and (briefly) jazz. This and other informative volumes may be ordered directly from Young Discovery Library by calling (800) 343-7854.

SONGBOOKS

From Sea to Shining Sea: A Treasury of American Folklore and Folk Songs
compiled by Amy L. Cohn
various illustrators
Scholastic, 1993
Songs form only part of this large, diverse, and delightful collection, which also includes American stories and poems. The book is divided into fifteen sections with names like "In the Beginning" (on Native Americans), "The Shot Heard 'Round the World" (on Revolutionary times), and "I've Been Working on the Railroad." You'll find familiar songs like "Yankee Doodle," "Simple Gifts," "Ol' Dan Tucker," "Take Me Out to

the Ball Game," as well as a wealth of less familiar but no less engaging songs and stories
from diverse traditions. The book includes a
very useful subject index and suggestions for
further reading. Illustrated by eleven Caldecott-
winning artists.

Gonna Sing My Head Off! American Folk Songs for Children
collected and arranged by Kathleen Krull
illustrated by Allen Garns
Alfred A. Knopf, 1992
This attractively illustrated collection of sixty-
two American folk songs comes with simple arrangements for guitar and piano. The book includes old favorites such as "Casey Jones,"
"Clementine," "Down in the Valley," "Follow
the Drinking Gourd," "Go Tell Aunt Rhody,"
"I've Been Working on the Railroad," "Michael,
Row the Boat Ashore," "Shenandoah," "This
Land Is Your Land," "Yankee Doodle," and
many more.

Songs of the Wild West
commentary by Alan Axelrod
arrangements by Dan Fox
Simon & Schuster Books for Young Readers,
    1991
Both a visual and musical delight, this extensive
collection includes "Home on the Range," "Cielito Lindo," and "Buffalo Gals." Each musical
score is paired with western works from the
Metropolitan Museum of Art, complemented by
interesting historical commentary.

Songs from Mother Goose
compiled by Nancy Larrick
illustrated by Robin Spowart
HarperCollins, 1989
The first poems most children learn are the
handful of singable nursery rhymes with familiar tunes, such as "Twinkle, Twinkle Little Star."
This handy book presents traditional melodies
for dozens more as well, with endearing illustrations. Words appear in large-typed text both
at the side and over the notes.

SONGS—RECORDINGS

American History Through Song series
by Keith and Rusty McNeil
WEM Records
- *Colonial and Revolutionary Songs*
- *Moving West Songs*
- *Civil War Songs*
- *Cowboy Songs*
- *Working and Union Songs*

Through narration and song, this series takes
you on a musical journey through American
history. Each set includes two cassettes and historical notes on the songs, which are sung accompanied by instruments such as the banjo,
fiddle, and dulcimer. The *Moving West* collection
contains some songs that you may want to preview, because the lyrics, while historically accurate, reflect some of the prejudices of the time.

A Child's Celebration of Song
by various artists
Music for Little People
Sure to have you singing along, this award-winning and eclectic collection, available on cassette
tape or compact disc, comes with a book of suggested activities. The disc includes old favorites
by familiar performers (such as Burl Ives singing "Polly Wolly Doodle"), and delightful original songs (such as "The House at Pooh Corner"
by Loggins and Messina). Other performers include Taj Mahal, James Taylor, Sweet Honey in
the Rock, Judy Garland, and more. For ordering
information, call (800) 727-2233. Also available
from Music for Little People: *A Child's Celebration of Showtunes* and *A Child's Celebration of
Broadway.*

Disney's Children's Favorites volumes 1–4
Disney Songtapes
These four cassettes tapes, available at many toy
stores, provide pleasant renditions of many favorite children's songs, such as "Bingo," "Down
in the Valley," "Kookaburra," The A-B-C Song,"
"The Bear Went over the Mountain," "Loch
Lomond," "Waltzing Matilda," and dozens of
others. Fortunately, most of the songs are sung

in a straightforward way by Larry Croce (who also adds a few original compositions) with only rare interventions of voices of Disney cartoon characters. Another collection called *Silly Songs* is also available, though this has a bit more of Mickey, Donald, and Goofy.

Horse Sense for Kids and Other People: Authentic Sing-Along Cowboy Songs
by Horse Sense/Justin Bishop
Warner Bros./Music for Little People, 1990, 1994
Howdy, pardner! This here is a right fine collection of cowboy songs, just right for singin' round the campfire. Available on cassette tape or compact disc, with such favorites as "Git Along, Little Dogies," "Red River Valley," "Turkey in the Straw," "Cielito Lindo," and more. For ordering information, call (800) 727-2233.

CC *Shake Sugaree*
by Taj Mahal
Music for Little People, 1990
Taj Mahal is a great blues singer and superb guitarist. His gravelly voice brings a rough-edged warmth to songs such as "Brown Girl in the Ring," "Talkin' John Henry," and "Fishin' Blues." A children's chorus occasionally backs him up on this award-winning collection, available on cassette tape and compact disc. For ordering information, call (800) 727-2233.

Shake It to the One that You Love the Best: Play Songs and Lullabies from Black Musical Traditions
produced by Cheryl Warren Mattox
Warren-Mattox Productions, 1989
This songbook, with accompanying cassette tape, contains lyrics and piano score, plus color illustrations by notable black artists. Songs include: "Little Sally Walker," "Miss Lucy," "Hambone," "All the Pretty Little Horses," and twenty-two more.

Wee Sing series
Price Stern Sloan
This popular series of sixty-minute cassettes and accompanying songbooks offers a convenient

way to hear and sing along with a wide range of mostly familiar and favorite children's songs, most of which are performed on the tapes by a children's chorus. Individual titles include *Wee Sing . . . America* [see next entry]; *Around the World*; *Christmas*; *Dinosaurs*; *Fun and Folk*; *Sing-Alongs*; *Sing and Play*; and *Songs and Fingerplay*.

CC *Wee Sing America*
by Pam Beall and Susan Nipp
Price Stern Sloan, 1987
On the first side of this cassette (which comes with a small songbook), patriotic songs sung by a children's chorus are woven in with readings from important documents and speeches, such as the Preamble to the Constitution and lines from John F. Kennedy's inaugural address. Songs include "The Star Spangled Banner," "You're a Grand Old Flag," "America the Beautiful," "Anchors Aweigh," and many more. It's all very rousing without being corny. The second side has plenty of American folk songs, such as "Sweet Betsy from Pike," "John Henry," "Good-Bye, Old Paint," "Blow the Man Down," and lots more. Play the tape, march around, and sing along, good and loud!

CC *Where in the World Is Carmen Sandiego?*
performed by Rockapella and other artists
BMG Music/Zoom Express, 1992
The popular computer game that gave rise to a hit public television game show led to this rollicking collection of catchy, clever songs performed in a variety of styles—rock, doo-wop, Latin, Irish, and more. There's one old standard here, "Let's Get Away from It All." The rest are original songs, all with geographical themes (in keeping with the whole point of the *Carmen Sandiego* game and show), including "Capital," a great way to help kids remember the state capitals.

CC = "Core Collection" book (see page 8).

MUSICAL ACTIVITIES

Bingo series
by Cheryl Lavender
Jenson Publications/Hal Leonard Publishing
A very good classroom resource, and fun at
home as well (especially the games that come
with a cassette tape), these Bingo-style games
provide a lighthearted way to reinforce the
learning of musical skills and knowledge. Individual titles include: *Music Listening Bingo* (includes cassette); *Instrument Bingo* (includes cassette); *Melody Bingo; Rhythm Bingo (Level One and
Level Two); Music Symbol Bingo*; and, *Composer
Bingo*.

Kids Make Music!
by Avery Hart and Paul Mantell
Williams Publishing, 1993
A collection of all kinds of musical activities for
kids, from elements of music to styles of music
to making instruments and much more. Helpful
for parents and teachers in about grades K–4.

*Let's Make Music: An Interactive Musical Trip
Around the World*
by Jessica Baron Turner and Ronny Susan Schiff
Hal Leonard Publishing, 1995
This book comes packaged with a cassette or
compact disc. It contains songs from around the
world, and directions for making a variety of
homemade instruments from different countries,
such as a rain-stick (Chile), clappers (Australia),
castanets (Spain), *shekere* (Nigeria), and more.
Includes many helpful suggestions for related
reading.

Mini-Musicals
Milliken Publishing Company
Directed to classroom teachers, and appropriate
for home play groups as well, these resource
books, each accompanied by a cassette tape,
make it easy to produce small-scale music dra-
mas with children from about ages 4 to 7. The
books suggest activities, costume ideas, set designs, and more. The tapes provide words and
music on one side, and just music on the other.

Individual titles include "The Little Red Hen,"
"Three Piggy Opera," "Stone Soup," "Three
Nanny Goats Gruff," "Tikki Tikki Tembo," and
"Holiday Plays."

*Music Crafts for Kids: The How-To Book of
Music Discovery*
by Noel Fiarotta and Phyllis Fiarotta
Sterling, 1993
Here's a generous collection of hands-on musical projects, including ideas for making musical
instruments, activities to go along with stories
and poems, dance activities, and even some
cute ways to help learn musical notes.

*Music Through Children's Literature: Theme and
Variations*
by Donna B. Levene
illustrated by Susan Kochenberger Stroeher
Libraries Unlimited/Teacher Ideas Press, 1993
P.O. Box 6633
Englewood, CO 80155-6633
A well-organized selection of lesson plans for
elementary school teachers and librarians who
seek ideas for combining music with literature
and social studies. Each lesson begins with an
appealing children's book that contains a musical element, either in its subject matter or the
rhythms of its poetry. The lesson that follows
might include singing, dancing, or beating out
rhythms, discussing word meanings and deriva-
tions, comparing cultures, recording bird songs,
or making instruments. Geared for teachers with
a wide range of musical abilities, with clear directions and references for materials. To order
call (800) 237-6124.

CC *My First Music Book: A Life-Size
Guide to Making and Playing Simple Musical
Instruments*
by Helen Drew
Dorling Kindersley, 1993
This book provides easy-to-follow directions
with large, step-by-step photographic illustrations for making homemade instruments such
as soda-can shakers and rubber-band harps. The
projects require intermediate reading skills,

some adult assistance for younger children, and, with the exception of a few items like colored plastic tape and wallpaper paste, only ordinary household materials. Although the finished products are sometimes more eye than ear pleasing, they provide amusing and memorable lessons in the physics of sound production, especially the garden-hose horn!

MUSICAL INSTRUMENTS AND THE ORCHESTRA

CC *Carnival of the Animals*
by Camille Saint-Saëns
A wonderful way to introduce children, especially preschoolers and kindergartners, to classical music and the sounds of different instruments is through Camille Saint-Saëns's *Carnival of the Animals*. Many recordings of it are available on cassette and compact disc. If you can, play one of these recordings for your child, and join along in moving to the music and acting out the animals depicted by the different instruments. A video version of *Carnival of the Animals*, with lively puppetry, is also available (Jim Gamble Puppet Productions, Bogner Entertainment Co., 1992), but definitely go first for the music itself.

CC *Fantasia*
Walt Disney Home Video
An animated classic, now restored and available on video, which introduces children (of all ages) to the orchestra, and presents visual interpretations of such works as Dukas's *The Sorcerer's Apprentice* (starring Mickey Mouse), Beethoven's Pastoral Symphony (as the soundtrack for a mythological fantasy), selections from *The Nutcracker*, Mussorgsky's *Night on Bald Mountain*, and more. Purists may take exception to some of the musical performances, which sometimes alter the score for the sake of the visuals.

CC = **"Core Collection"** book (see page 8).

CC *Meet the Orchestra*
by Ann Hayes
illustrated by Karmen Thompson
Harcourt Brace/Gulliver Books, 1991
An orchestra of endearing animals prepares for a concert as their animal audience filters into the hall. There's a seal with a violin, an alligator on the timpani drums, and a chimp at the piano—all wearing their best concert finery. For young children, this book provides a playful introduction to the orchestra.

Microsoft Musical Instruments (CD-ROM)
Microsoft Home
Part of the *Exploration Series*, recommended for grades 4 and up, this CD-ROM is a winner of the Parent's Choice Award. It explores musical instruments in detail: their origins, inner workings, and sounds (with some fifteen hundred sound samples from two hundred instruments). Includes *Families of Instruments*, *Musical Ensembles*, *Instruments of the World*, and *A to Z of Instruments*.

Music from Strings
    by Josephine Paker
Beating the Drum
    by Josephine Paker
Rattles, Bells, and Chiming Bars
    by Karen Foster
Flutes, Reeds, and Trumpets
    by Danny Staples and Carole Mahoney
    Millbrook, all 1992
This detailed series uses plenty of photographs and illustrations to trace the development of stringed instruments, drums, percussion instruments, and wind instruments in various cultures (*da-daiko* drums, Indian sitars, and more). A few interesting projects are suggested, and each book includes a useful glossary.

Music
by Neil Ardley
Alfred A. Knopf, 1989
From a bagpipe with carved goat's head to a Stradivari violin to a Gibson Flying V electric guitar, this Eyewitness book uses detailed pho-

tographs of all kinds of beautiful and sometimes bizarre-looking instruments to teach the science and mechanics of making music. The text provides historical tidbits, and while the information is geared for middle-school age and older, even preschool children will be fascinated by looking at the pictures and learning the instruments' names.

The Orchestra
by Mark Rubin
illustrated by Alan Daniel
Firefly Books, 1992
An informative, picture-book introduction to the elements of music and the families of instruments in the orchestra. Also available as a cassette tape or video (Facets Multimedia, Inc., 1990), narrated by Peter Ustinov.

CC Peter and the Wolf
by Serge Prokofiev
We know of no more engaging way to introduce children in kindergarten and the primary grades to the orchestra than through this now-classic work. With wit and humor, Prokofiev tells the story of *Peter and the Wolf* by representing each character through an instrument in the orchestra: for example, the bird by a flute, the grandfather by a bassoon, Peter by the strings, and so on. Many recordings of this work are available on cassette and compact disc, and most feature a narrator who tells the story along with the music. Video versions are also available, including an animated version by Walt Disney; and *Peter and the Wolf: A Prokofiev Fantasy*, which mixes puppets and real actors in an energetic production (Deutsche Grammophon video). But we suggest starting with the music itself. Your child might also enjoy *Peter and the Wolf*, retold and illustrated by Michèle Lemieux (Morrow Junior Books, 1991), a lovely book that tells the story behind the music. For more fun, try *Peter and the Wolf: A Bellerophon Coloring Book* by David Brownell, with illustrations by Nancy Conkle (Bellerophon Books, 1992; see address, page 106), which tells the story of "Peter and the Wolf" with several types of ready-to-color

drawings of individual characters and whole scenes, and witty drawings that combine instruments with characters.

The Philharmonic Gets Dressed
by Karla Kuskin
illustrated by Marc Simont
HarperCollins, 1982
"Outside it's getting darker and . . . one hundred and five people are getting dressed to go to work. First they get washed. . . ." Without telling you what these people do, you follow their amusing preparations for work until they arrive onstage to become an orchestra. Along the way, there are clues to what these folks do, which the children can enjoy searching out.

Shake, Rattle, and Strum
by Sara Corbett
Childrens Press, 1995
Designed to enhance awareness of cultural diversity, this paperback book contains photos of dozens of instruments from around the world, many of which are not familiar to most Westerners. The text, which can be read aloud in the primary grades or read independently from about fourth grade and up, explains how these instruments are used in work, worship, war, and celebration.

CC What Instrument Is This?
by Rosmarie Hausherr
Scholastic, 1992
An engaging book to read aloud with children in kindergarten and the primary grades, this slim volume provides photographs of a variety of instruments, many of them being played by children, accompanied by text that poses questions like, "What instrument is played sideways and can sing like a bird? What instrument has bars that are not chocolate?" (The answers: a flute and a xylophone.) Brief discussions offer interesting details about the instruments, which include both members of the orchestra (clarinet, trumpet, violin, cello), and others (bagpipes, electric guitar).

CC *Young Person's Guide to the Orchestra*
by Benjamin Britten
Many recordings of this work by the twentieth-century British composer, Benjamin Britten, are available. Britten begins with a simple theme from a work by Henry Purcell, then explores various instruments and families in the orchestra by varying the simple theme. It's a rousing good way to learn about the orchestra, and probably most enjoyable for children in about second grade and up. (For younger children, see *Peter and the Wolf*, above.)

MULTICULTURAL MUSIC

All for Freedom
by Sweet Honey in the Rock
Music for Little People, 1989
Sing and clap along! Powerful and gorgeous harmonies are the trademark of this a capella ensemble of African-American women. On this recording, available on cassette tape and compact disc, they are sometimes joined by a children's chorus for renditions of songs both familiar and new, including spirituals ("Amen") and traditional chants. To order call (800) 727-2233.

De Colores and other Latin American Folk Songs for Children
selected, arranged, and translated by José-Luis
   Orozco
illustrated by Elisa Kleven
Dutton Children's Books, 1994
A collection of twenty-seven songs from all over Latin America with musical arrangements and exuberant illustrations.

Family Folk Festival: A Multi-Cultural Sing-Along
by various artists
Music for Little People
On this award-winning collection, available on tape or compact disc, an eclectic mix of performers (including Pete Seeger, Sweet Honey in the Rock, Taj Mahal, and the Smothers Brothers) perform such favorites as "I've Been Working

on the Railroad," "Skip to My Lou," and many more. For ordering information, call (800) 727-2233.

Favorite Songs of Japanese Children
collected and translated by Hanako Fukuda
Alfred Publishing, 1990
A simple songbook accompanies a cassette tape of Japanese folk songs, sung with some Japanese words but mostly in English, and with accompaniment by traditional Japanese instruments. A nice complement to learning about Japan (see World History Grade 2).

Fiesta! Mexico and Central America: A Global Awareness Program for Children in Grades 2–5
by Barbara Linse and Dick Judd
Fearon Teacher Aids, 1993
This book with audiocassette presents seventeen singable children's songs (with simple piano accompaniments) in Spanish with English translations, as well as instructions for activities designed to teach children about Mexican and Central American culture by emphasizing seasonal observances, feast days, and national holidays. On the tape, all songs are performed twice, once with words and once without, so that the children have a ready-made accompaniment once they know the words. The songs are linked to appropriate holidays and suggested cooking, craft, and research projects.

Let Your Voice Be Heard: Songs from Ghana and Zimbabwe
by Abraham Kobena Adzinya, Dumisani
   Maraire, and Judith Cook Tucker
World Music Press, 1986
This book-and-tape package is straightforward enough for the parent or general classroom teacher and detailed enough (with suggested multipart arrangements) for the music specialist. The one-hour tape lets you hear and sing along with a collection of call-and-response songs, game songs, story songs, and more. The book provides geographical and historical background information as well.

Let's Get the Rhythm of the Band: A Child's Introduction to Music from African-American Culture with History and Song
by Cheryl Warren Mattox
illustrated by Varnette P. Honeywood
JTG of Nashville, 1993
A lively, informative book-and-tape package. The book offers interesting essays, readable by older children, on African sources of African-American music, spirituals and gospel, ragtime and blues, jazz, rhythm-and-blues, and rap. It includes vibrant color illustrations, many helpful photographs of African-American musicians and composers, and words and music to the songs on the tape. Some of these songs are traditional, others are original; they are performed by professional musicians and singers, sometimes with a children's chorus.

Let's Make Music: An Interactive Musical Trip Around the World
by Jessica Baron Turner and Ronny Susan Schiff
Hal Leonard Publishing, 1995
See description under General Resources: Musical Activities.

Moving Within the Circle: Contemporary Native American Music and Dance
by Bryan Burton
World Music Press, 1993
This package is available as a book-and-tape or book-and-CD, with an optional set of slides. It presents songs, flute songs, and more music in performances by American Indians young and old. The book is a helpful teacher/parent resource, with plentiful information on musical styles, instruments, and six "guided listening experiences."

Shake, Rattle, and Strum
by Sara Corbett
Childrens Press, 1995
See description under Musical Instruments.

Wee Sing Around the World
Price Stern Sloan, 1994
Here's a cute tape-and-songbook package,

with singers from around the world introducing themselves and then singing a song from their homeland, and inviting you to sing along. Includes songs from Mexico, Puerto Rico, Jamaica, Guyana, Brazil, Sweden, Ireland, France (the familiar "Frère Jacques"), Germany, Spain, Greece, Ghana, Kenya, Iran, India, China, Japan, Korea, Australia ("Kookaburra"), and more.

World Music at West: Multicultural Music and Arts Catalog
A resource catalog available from West Music, an Iowa-based mail-order vendor of musical supplies, of interest to both teachers and parents. Call (800) 397-9378.

COMPOSERS (BOOKS AND RECORDINGS)

America, I Hear You: A Story about George Gershwin
by Barbara Mitchell
illustrated by Jan Hosking Smith
Carolrhoda Books, 1987
For readers in the upper elementary grades, here is an upbeat biography of the composer who brought jazz into the realm of classical music, producing the masterpieces "Rhapsody in Blue," "An American in Paris," and "Porgy and Bess."

Baby Dance
    performed by various artists
    Erato/Electra International, 1994
Classics for Kids
    performed by various artists
    RCA Victor / BMG Classics, 1993
These two compact discs collect some wonderfully catchy bits and pieces of classical music that should especially appeal to children from preschool through the primary grades. *Baby Dance* starts off with a bang with the rousing "Sabre Dance," and includes familiar works by Mozart (from *A Little Night Music*), Tchaikovsky (march from *The Nutcracker*), Chopin ("Minute Waltz"), and some less familiar but no less en-

gaging selections by Rameau, Stravinsky, and others. *Classics for Kids* presents fine performances of selections from *The Nutcracker* and *Carnival of the Animals*; "The March of the Siamese Children" from *The King and I*; "March of the Toys" from *Babes in Toyland*; *The Sorcerer's Apprentice*; Brahms's "Lullaby," and more. The discs only rarely repeat each other, and both are worth seeking out.

Bach, Beethoven and the Boys: Music History as It Ought to Be Taught
by David W. Barber
Sound and Vision, 1986
An irreverent and informative resource for teachers and parents, this book introduces the "big" composers of classical music, mixing trivia about the composers and their works with musical history and many puns along the way.

Beethoven Lives Upstairs
by Barbara Nichol
illustrated by Scott Cameron
Orchard Books, 1993
This book was developed from the very successful *Classical Kids* recording of the same name (see below). And like the recording, it weaves real incidents from Beethoven's life into the fictional letters from a young boy who had the fortune—or, as he thinks at first, misfortune—to live downstairs from Beethoven, a composer of great genius but terrible manners and temper! It's nice to have the period illustrations the book provides, but of course the recording can do what the book cannot—allow you to hear Beethoven's music. So, look first for the tape or compact disc, which is in many ways the best of the *Classical Kids* series. A well-made live-action video version of *Beethoven Lives Upstairs* is also available (BMG, 1992; approximately 50 minutes).

CC = "Core Collection" book (see page 8).

CC *Classical Kids* series
produced by Susan Hammond
BMG Music
- *Mr. Bach Comes to Call*
- *Beethoven Lives Upstairs*
- *Mozart's Magic Fantasy*
- *Tchaikovsky Discovers America*
- *Vivaldi's Ring of Mystery*

What a wonderful way to introduce children to classical music! This award-winning series, on cassette tape and compact disc, mixes fact and fiction to introduce children to the works of five great composers. Each weaves familiar musical selections into the telling of a lively and engaging story. Teacher's Guides are available for all tapes, and a special boxed "Classroom Collection" includes tapes, Teacher's Guides, poster, composer stickers, and bonus tapes (available from Music in Motion: [800] 445-0649).

CC *Famous Children* series
by Ann Rachlin
illustrated by Susan Hellard
Barron's, 1992–94
These illustrated books provide a great way to spark a child's curiosity about classical music. Ann Rachlin tells lively and engaging stories of famous composers as children. As a complement to listening to the music, the stories can be read aloud to very young children, or read independently by children from about second grade on. The stories show that these now famous musicians were once real children, who didn't like some of the things their parents wanted them to do, played practical jokes, and had secret dreams. But they also show that these real children had very special talents. Titles include: *Bach; Beethoven; Brahms; Chopin; Handel; Haydn; Mozart; Schumann; Tchaikovsky*.

The *Greatest Hits* series
Sony Classical
This series of midpriced cassette tapes or compact discs offers a convenient way to get to know some of the most famous works of a variety of composers, performed by the superb artists who recorded for the Columbia (now Sony

Classical) label. Each disc bears the name of the composer, and the composers represented include: Bach; Beethoven; Brahms; Chopin; Copland; Debussy; Gershwin; Grieg; Handel; Mozart; Ravel; Schubert; J. Strauss; Stravinsky; Tchaikovsky; Verdi; Vivaldi; and, Wagner. This is just one of many series from various recording labels—DG, Philips, EMI, RCA, London, not to mention budget labels like Naxos and Laser-Light—that conveniently package favorite classical music on middle- to budget-priced compact discs or tapes.

John Philip Sousa: The March King
by Carol Greene
Childrens Press, 1992
This readable, illustrated large-print chapter book begins with engaging anecdotes and pictures about the childhood and training of this great band leader and composer. Young readers will note that John as a child pouted in the rain because of some doughnuts, and that many years later he received seventy-two cakes on his seventy-second birthday. But to understand why Sousa was so popular, children really need to hear "The Stars and Stripes Forever" and other rousing marches.

Letters to Horseface
by F. N. Monjo
illustrated by Don Bolognese and Elaine
  Raphael
Viking, 1975
This wonderful novel for children in the upper elementary grades is based on letters written by the young Mozart as he and his father traveled through Italy for a year. It bubbles with Mozart's mischievous wit and reveals his delight in what he saw. For example, he writes to his sister, "Someday, Nannerl, I swear it, I shall squeeze all of the happy laughter, all of the colors, all of the music, and all of the perfumes of Naples into one single glorious comic opera."

CC = "Core Collection" book (see page 8).

The Lives of the Musicians: Good Times and Bad Times (And What the Neighbors Thought)
by Kathleen Krull
illustrated by Kathryn Hewitt
Harcourt Brace, 1993
These short biographies of famous composers give the high points of each composer's life along with funny tidbits and sometimes gossipy anecdotes. Older children will probably enjoy these little life stories, though the stories sometimes focus on the eccentricities of the musician and say little about the music. Some parents and teachers may want to note that the author does treat what may be considered by some people to be sensitive issues, such as Tchaikovsky's homosexuality. Includes Vivaldi, Bach, Mozart, Beethoven, Chopin, Verdi, Clara Schumann, Stephen Foster, Brahms, Tchaikovsky, Gilbert and Sullivan, Scott Joplin, Stravinsky, Gershwin, and more.

Ludwig van Beethoven: Musical Pioneer
by Carol Greene
Childrens Press, 1989
The first thing to do, of course, is give children opportunities to hear Beethoven's music. To help them get to know the man, they can read this simply written biography, which tells of the great composer's sad childhood and the later tragedy of his deafness. Illustrated with many drawings, photos of landmarks, and a mask of Beethoven. Good for reading aloud in the primary grades.

Ludwig van Beethoven: Young Composer
by Louis Sabin
illustrated by Ellen Beier
Troll Associates, 1992
This brief and clearly written biography traces the life and musical career of the great composer. It begins at the first performance of the Ninth Symphony, which Beethoven conducted, though deaf, then moves back in time to his unhappy childhood. Readable by children in about third grade and up.

Mozart: Scenes from the Childhood of the Great Composer
written and illustrated by Catherine Brighton
Doubleday, 1990
Good for reading aloud to younger students or independent reading in about third grade or above, this beautifully illustrated storybook about Mozart's childhood is told as if narrated by his musical sister, Nannerl.

Peter Tchaikovsky
written and illustrated by Mike Venezia
Childrens Press, 1994
This brief, cartoonlike biography of Tchaikovsky will appeal to children from about first grade on because of Mike Venezias's goofy humor and funny drawings.

Raggin': A Story About Scott Joplin
by Barbara Mitchell
illustrated by Hetty Mitchell
Carolrhoda Books, 1987
In this short biography, readable by children in the upper elementary grades, Scott Joplin, "King of Ragtime," is depicted as a gifted man driven to overcome all obstacles to play his music. The book clearly details the personal cost of the life Joplin chooses: separation from his family, the breakup of his marriage, the loss of money from unsuccessful ventures, and the eventual demise of his health. It does not downplay the obstacles created by racial prejudice. But with the final emphasis on the enduring nature of Joplin's compositions, the book has an uplifting message concerning the value of perseverance and originality.

Seasons Greetings from Vivaldi
written and narrated by Ann Rachlin
EMI Records/Angel Special Markets, 1992
On this cassette tape, Ann Rachlin, an educator from London, tells a fictional story that introduces children to Antonio Vivaldi and his most famous work, *The Four Seasons*. The story—about four girls, all students of Father Vivaldi—is told with zest, and the musical per-

formance is excellent. The tape says that it is recommended for listening by children from 6 to 11 years old.

Tchaikovsky Discovers America
by Esther Kalman
illustrated by Laura Fernandez and Rick Jacobson
Orchard Books, 1994
This book is based on the compact disc and cassette of the same name produced by Susan Hammond (see *Classics for Kids,* above). In this story, a thoughtful eleven-year-old girl named Jenny records in her diary the remarkable experience of meeting the great Russian composer during his trip to America in 1891 to conduct at the new Carnegie Hall. The book shows the human side of the child's larger-than-life hero as he thinks and talks about the stories that inspire his music. The dreamlike quality of the illustrations well suits the aging composer's wistful thoughts of Russia and Jenny's fantasy of dancing in his famous ballet, *Swan Lake.* (Note: the book and tape might be connected to the study of immigration; see American History Grade 2.)

Vox Music Masters **series**
Vox Music Group
This series consists of eighteen separate cassettes or compact discs, in each of which a narrator introduces children to a composer and his works, with many musical examples. The narration has the feel of an old-fashioned documentary, and the vocabulary may be daunting for the youngest listeners, but the tapes do provide a number of engaging anecdotes, and of course many selections of great music. Individual titles all begin with "The Story of . . ." and are available in three boxed sets. Set One includes Bach, Mozart, Chopin, Mendelssohn, Schubert, Schumann, and Grieg. Set Two includes Handel, Beethoven, Haydn, Wagner, Dvořák and Vivaldi and Corelli. Set Three includes Berlioz, Brahms, Johann Strauss, Tchaikovsky, Verdi and Foster and Sousa.

DANCE

All-Time Favorite Dances
Kimbo Video, 1993
Limber up! This thirty-four-minute video shows
many dances in action, including the Hokey
Pokey, the Virginia Reel, the Hora, Mexican Hat
Dance, the Limbo Rock, and more—yes, even
the Twist! Each dance is followed by brief instructions so you and your children can join in.
Also available is a guidebook with a tape or
compact disc of the music. (Available from Pop-
plers Music, [800] 437-1755.)

Barn Dance!
by Bill Martin, Jr., and John Archambault
illustrated by Ted Rand
Henry Holt, 1986

> "Right Hand! Left hand! Around you go!
> Now back-to-back your partner in a do-si-do!
> Mules to the center for a curtsey and a bow!
> An' hey there, skinny kid! Show the old cow
> how!"

Martin and Archambault perfectly capture the
rhythms of the square-dance caller in this exuberant book about a little boy who discovers all
the farm animals having a square dance in the
barn. Wonderful illustrations by Ted Rand. Fun
for reading aloud to children in preschool and
the primary grades.

Dance Me a Story: Twelve Tales from the Classic Ballets
by Jane Rosenberg
Thames & Hudson, 1985
This book is a good introduction to the world of
classical dance for children in the upper elementary grades. It describes many classic ballets, dividing them into acts and scenes, and explaining each from an onstage perspective. The text
is accompanied by black-and-white figure drawings, as well as a few color illustrations. Includes *Cinderella, Coppélia, Don Quixote, Firebird,
Giselle, The Nutcracker, Petrouchka, Romeo and Juliet,* and *Sleeping Beauty.*

Dance, Tanya
by Patricia Lee Gauch
illustrated by Satomi Ichikawa
Philomel Books, 1989
Tanya's older sister, Elsie, takes ballet lessons,
and little Tanya loves to do whatever Elsie does
at home. This engaging story for younger children conveys the imaginative excitement of ballet, and the gentle illustrations help explain
terms like *jeté* and *pas des deux* along the way. If
you like this story, there are more books about
Tanya, including *Bravo, Tanya* and *Tanya and Emily in a Dance for Two.*

Going to My Ballet Class
by Susan Kuklin
Bradbury Press, 1989
Jami and her friends invite us to join them in
the excitement of a beginning ballet class at the
Joffrey Ballet School. The story is told from
Jami's point of view in simple prose with color
photographs. One nice feature is that this ballet
class has a boy in it.

CC *The Nutcracker* (video)
by Peter Ilych Tchaikovsky
Jodav Productions, 1977
Tchaikovsky's music, American Ballet Theater's
production, and Mikhail Baryshnikov's choreography add up to a beautiful, enchanting production.

The Nutcracker Ballet
by Vladimir Vagin
Scholastic, 1995
A simple narrative of *The Nutcracker*'s plot accompanies brightly colored illustrations of the
little girl Clara with strange Herr Drosselmeier
and his life-size dolls, Clara's Nutcracker-
turned-Prince, a seven-headed Mouse King, the
Sugar Plum Fairy, and all the delightful dancing
treats in the enchanting Land of Sweets. A good
book to share with a young child before listening to a recording of the ballet.

CC *The Random House Book of Stories from the Ballet*
retold by Geraldine McCaughrean
illustrated by Angela Barret
Random House, 1994
Charmingly illustrated, lively retellings of the fantastic and romantic stories from ten well-known ballets, including *The Nutcracker, Swan Lake, Giselle, Petrouchka,* and *Romeo and Juliet.* A wonderful book to read aloud, especially as a prelude to attending a performance or watching a videotape of any of the ballets included.

Song and Dance Man
by Karen Ackerman
Alfred A. Knopf, 1988
When his grandchildren visit, Grandpa relives his days on the vaudeville stage. In the dusty attic, he digs out hat and cane and then sings, tells jokes, and tap-dances for his captivated audience. A nice read-aloud for children in the primary grades.

CC *Swan Lake: The Story of the Ballet*
written and narrated by Ann Rachlin
EMI Records/Angel Special Markets, 1992
Here is the story of *Swan Lake,* dramatically narrated by Ann Rachlin, an educator from London, and all in the service of introducing Tchaikovsky's even more dramatic music, in a first-rate performance by the London Symphony. If you can't see this ballet, this is a great way to imagine it. The tape says that it is recommended for listening by children from 5 to 11 years old.

OPERA

Aida
by Giuseppe Verdi
retold by Leontyne Price
illustrated by Leo and Diane Dillon
Harcourt Brace/Gulliver Books, 1990
In this beautiful volume, opera star Leontyne Price, who has sung *Aida* many times, retells the story of Verdi's great opera. Winner of countless awards for glorious illustrations by Caldecott Medalists Leo and Diane Dillon. Challenging text, but still a good read-aloud (especially if the children have been introduced to ancient Egypt; see World History, Grade 1).

CC *Mozart's Magic Fantasy*
produced by Susan Hammond
BMG Music
Part of the award-winning *Classical Kids* series on cassette or compact disc, this is the story of a little girl who is magically transported into the world of Mozart's opera *The Magic Flute.* A fun story and Mozart's music make for a winning combination and a great way to introduce opera to children in about first grade and up.

Music! Words! Opera!: Level 1 Teacher's Manual
by various authors
MMB Music, 1990
10370 Page Industrial Boulevard
Saint Louis, Missouri 63132
This resource book in a big three-ring binder proposes an exciting but ambitious goal: to enable elementary school teachers, including those without musical training, to help their students understand and appreciate opera, and even produce an opera of their own. Detailed lesson plans and a carefully cued cassette tape of excerpts are provided for teaching each of three fairy-tale operas: Humperdinck's *Hansel and Gretel,* Mozart's *The Magic Flute,* and Ravel's *The Child and the Enchantments* (excerpts are in the original languages, but clear English translations are provided). The lessons focus on character, plot, setting, and motivation, as well as ideas and emotions, musical motifs, and styles of singing. Another set of lessons guides the class step by step through the complex process of conceiving, rehearsing, and finally performing an original opera.

My Favorite Opera for Children
presented by Luciano Pavarotti
London Records
The world-famous tenor lends his name to this

nicely chosen collection of eighteen selections that can introduce children to the wonderful world of opera. Includes selections from Mozart's *Magic Flute,* Humperdinck's *Hansel and Gretel,* Bizet's *Carmen,* and of course, from Wagner's *Ring* cycle, "The Ride of the Valkyries."

Opera: What's All the Screaming About? The Beginner's Guide to Opera
by Roger Englander
Walker, 1983
A book for teachers and parents who are curious about opera but have wondered, as the author puts it, what all the "screaming" is about. With affection and humor, the author boils down the plots of fifty popular operas into funny tabloid headlines, introduces opera's great composers, and traces the history of opera. One version of the book comes packaged with a compact disc that includes selections from a classic recording of Bizet's *Carmen,* with the "divine" Maria Callas in the title role.

Pet of the Met
written and illustrated by Lydia and Don Freeman
Viking, 1953/Puffin Books, 1988
Maestro Petrini is a mouse who lives in the attic of the Metropolitan Opera House. Mister Mefisto is a cat who lives in the basement. They meet onstage during a production of Mozart's *Magic Flute.* A fun story to read aloud to young children, with some behind-the-scenes glimpses of an opera production as a bonus.

The Pirates of Penzance
performed by the D'Oyly Carte Opera Company
London Records
Available as a set of two compact discs, this is an authoritative and rollicking performance of the Gilbert and Sullivan musical comedy with the famous song "I am the very model of a modern major general." You may also enjoy a video of *The Pirates of Penzance,* produced by Joseph Papp (MCA Universal Home Video, 1982). This fast-paced production stars Kevin Kline, Angela Lansbury, and Linda Ronstadt. It's a de-

light from beginning to end, and a great way to get to know Gilbert and Sullivan. Lots of slapstick action, wonderful choreography, and some inside jokes for the adults (one love song turns into an Elvis Presley–style performance!).

JAZZ

Ben's Trumpet
written and illustrated by Rachel Isadora
Greenwillow Books, 1979
This book won the prestigious Caldecott Medal for its striking black-and-white illustrations that show how a young boy feels about jazz. Ben lives across the street from the Zig Zag Club and he pretends to play jazz trumpet every day. Then one day he meets the club's trumpeter and he doesn't have to pretend anymore. A fine read-aloud for first grade and up.

Charlie Parker Played Be Bop
written and illustrated by Chris Raschka
Orchard Books, 1992
"I hope children will learn that Charlie Parker and bebop had something to do with rhythm, surprise, and humor," says author and musician Chris Raschka. Read this short, delightful book aloud a few times and you'll start to see what "bebop" is all about. With its surprising rhymes and changing rhythms, Raschka's poem captures the syncopation and spirit of jazz as played by the great saxophonist Charlie Parker, whose "Night in Tunisia" inspired the book. Humorous drawings of the musician and his cat add to the fun. A fine read-aloud for first grade and up.

"Duke Ellington: A Musical Genius"
"The Jazz Sensation"
"Louis Armstrong and the Art of Jazz"
Here are three issues of *Cobblestone,* a magazine of American history for readers in the upper elementary grades. They feature many brief, readable, interesting articles that will give students a good introduction to jazz from historical and biographical perspectives. *The Jazz Sensation* (Oc-

tober 1993) includes articles on "The African Roots of Jazz," "New Orleans: The Cradle of Jazz," and "Ragtime and Scott Joplin." *Louis Armstrong* (October 1994) includes articles on "Ambassador of Goodwill," "Jazz and Art," and "Growing Up with Jazz." *Duke Ellington* (May 1993) includes articles on "Great and Glorious: Duke Ellington's Early Years," "Stepping Out in Harlem," and "The Eternal Ellington." Many libraries subscribe to *Cobblestone*. To order back issues, call (800) 821-0115.

Jazz: History, Instruments, Musicians, and Recordings
by John Fordham
Dorling Kindersley, 1993
An Eyewitness book that invites browsing, though the text is often too small and dispersed for comfortable reading, this is an engaging guide to the four aspects of jazz named in the title, with wonderful up-close photos of instruments and personalities. Includes a list of the author's choices for top 250 jazz recordings. Best as a teacher/parent resource.

Let's Get the Rhythm of the Band: A Child's Introduction to Music from African-American Culture with History and Song
by Cheryl Warren Mattox
illustrated by Varnette P. Honeywood
JTG of Nashville, 1993
A lively, informative book-and-tape package, fully described above under General Resources: Multicultural Music. One section of the book discusses jazz, in terms that you can adapt for first graders and up. Sidebars offer photographs and brief biographical sketches of Louis Armstrong, Duke Ellington, and Billie Holiday. The accompanying tape has a selection called "Play Song Jazz," an original song that improvises on the traditional song "Little Sally Walker."

CC *Marsalis on Music: Sousa to Satchmo*
Sony Classical Film and Video, 1995
In this video, the contemporary jazz trumpeter Wynton Marsalis traces the history of jazz, with musical selections from John Philip Sousa, Scott Joplin, and Louis Armstrong. Excellent for children in the upper elementary grades.

Ragtime Tumpie
by Alan Schroeder
illustrated by Bernie Fuchs
Little, Brown, 1989
Warm-toned, atmospheric paintings illustrate this fictionalized account of the childhood of Josephine Baker. Tumpie, who dreams of being a famous honky-tonk dancer, is a young girl who loves to dance, especially when she hears "a fast rag, . . . real jug band jazz."

What a Wonderful World
by Bob Thiele and George David Weiss
illustrated by Ashley Bryan
Sundance Publishing, 1995
The words of the popular Louis Armstrong song form the text of this colorfully illustrated book that conveys a message of love and tolerance. The publisher (whom you can call at [800] 343-8204) also makes this book available in "big book" form, and as part of a unit with a teacher's guide (for the primary grades). Also available from Sundance is a companion cassette tape, *What a Wonderful World* (on the MCA label), with eleven songs performed by Louis Armstrong late in his career.

STORYBOOKS ABOUT MUSIC AND SONGS

Abiyoyo
by Pete Seeger
illustrated by Michael Hays
Macmillan, 1986
With the help of artist Michael Hays, folk singer Pete Seeger has turned a song he wrote for his children into a captivating storybook. Based on a South African folktale, *Abiyoyo* tells the story of a giant who terrorized a village until a boy and his father tricked the giant with a very special song. Great for reading aloud to (and singing along with) young children.

All God's Critters Got a Place in the Choir
by Bill Staines
illustrated by Margot Zemach
E. P. Dutton, words and music, 1978; illustrations, 1989
"All God's critters got a place in the choir,/ Some sing low, some sing higher/Some sing out loud on the telephone wire." Amusing lyrics by folksinger Bill Staines accompany delightful illustrations of animal characters to introduce aspects of choral singing.

America the Beautiful
by Katharine Lee Bates
illustrations by Neil Waldman
Macmillan, 1993
Monument Valley. Niagara Falls. The Smokey Mountains. The Great Plains. This lovely picture book provides fourteen full-page paintings to illustrate the first verse of "America the Beautiful." At the end each painting is repeated in miniature in a sort of "picture glossary" with a brief description. Score included too.

Berlioz the Bear
written and illustrated by Jan Brett
G. P. Putnam's Sons, 1991
Berlioz hears a strange buzzing in his string bass, but before he can solve that problem, he must figure out how to get to town in time for the performance. A fun read-aloud for younger children.

Follow the Drinking Gourd
story and pictures by Jeanette Winter
Alfred A. Knopf, 1988
This book depicts the story behind the pre–Civil War song "Follow the Drinking Gourd." Peg Leg Joe teaches the song to slaves who want to escape to freedom, for hidden in its lyrics are directions for following the Underground Railroad (see American History Grade 2). The storybook follows the escape of one group of brave runaways as they go from danger to danger and finally reach freedom.

The Fox Went Out on a Chilly Night: An Old Song
illustrated by Peter Spier
Doubleday, 1961
This well-loved folk song with its catchy refrain takes us on an evening on the "town-o" with a daddy fox, who unapologetically raids a goose pen, then flees home to feed his family. Peter Spier's detailed drawings capture the beauty of the autumn night, the picturesque farm, the grim kidnap of the birds, the alarmed farmer's futile efforts, and the fox's happy homecoming to the little ones who feast right down to the "bones-o." At the end of the book the song is reprinted with a simple piano accompaniment and guitar chords.

Go Tell Aunt Rhody
illustrated by Aliki
Macmillan, 1974
The much-loved children's artist Aliki provides colorful paintings to accompany each line of this traditional American folk song.

CC *London Bridge Is Falling Down!*
illustrated by Peter Spier
Doubleday, 1967
Peter Spier provides wonderfully detailed, historically accurate illustrations to accompany the verses of this favorite song. An interesting essay at the end of the book also provides adults with a brief history of the real London Bridge.

The Maestro Plays
by Bill Martin, Jr.
illustrated by Vladimir Radunsky
Henry Holt, 1994
A whimsical, offbeat book with playful and bright cut-paper illustrations, appropriate as a read-aloud for preschoolers and kindergartners. The simple text introduces some probably new words, such as *maestro,* and words that describe sounds. Like most books by Bill Martin, this is catchy and fun.

CC = "Core Collection" book (see page 8).

Max Found Two Sticks
written and illustrated by Brian Pinkney
Simon & Schuster, 1994
In this fictional story, young Max imitates the sounds of his city neighborhood using sticks, buckets, and garbage cans. This picture book can interest children in looking for, listening to, and creating rhythm patterns in everyday life.

Musical Max
by Robert Kraus
illustrated by Ariane Dewey and José Aruego
Simon & Schuster, 1990
This colorful book tells a funny story that introduces younger children to many instruments. Max, a small green hippo, is mad for music. Max plays so many instruments so often that his neighbors get tired of music. Then one day Max doesn't feel like playing, and the neighbors, well, the neighbors . . . you'll have to read the book to find out what the neighbors think. If you aren't familiar with the whimsical creatures of illustrators Ariane Dewey and José Aruego (*Leo the Late Bloomer, Milton the Early Riser*), this book is a fine way to get to know them.

CC *The Star-Spangled Banner*
illustrated by Peter Spier
Doubleday, 1986
This "Reading Rainbow" selection beautifully illustrates the song and gives fascinating glimpses of history. It shows many early versions of our flag, and even a reproduction of the original manuscript of the national anthem.

Take Me Out to the Ball Game
original lyrics by Jack Norworth
illustrated by Alec Gillman
Four Winds Press/Macmillan, 1993
Illustrator Alec Gillman, a baseball fan, combines the familiar song "Take Me Out to the Ball Game" with evocative pictures based on the 1947 World Series. He also provides a brief but interesting history of the song (with music and lyrics), and a brief history of the 1947 World Series.

The Wheels on the Bus
by Maryann Kovalski
Little, Brown, 1987
Grandma, Joanna, and Jenny go shopping for coats, then wait for a bus to take them home. To pass the time, they sing the traditional song. Funny illustrations and a surprise ending breathe new life into this version of an old favorite. A good book to read aloud and sing along with.

SCIENCE

Introduction

To understand the world of plants and animals, or of seasons and weather, or of physical forces like magnetism, a child needs firsthand experience with many opportunities to observe, experiment, and get her hands dirty. Children gain knowledge about the world around them from observation and experience. But while experience counts for much, *book-learning* is also important, for it helps bring coherence and order to a child's scientific knowledge.

Only when topics are presented systematically and clearly can children make steady and secure progress in their scientific learning. The child's development of scientific knowledge and understanding is in some ways a very disorderly and complex process, different for each child. But a systematic approach to the exploration of science, one that combines experience with book-learning, can help provide essential building blocks for deeper understanding at a later time. It can also provide the kind of knowledge that one is not likely to gain from observation: consider, for example, how people long believed that the earth stands still while the sun orbits around it, a misconception that "direct experience" presented as fact.

Science in the *Core Knowledge Sequence:* A Summary

> For information on the specific content guidelines known as the *Core Knowledge Sequence* and on the ideas behind the Core Knowledge initiative, please see in this book "Core Knowledge: Building Knowledge Year by Year" (pages 9–23, especially pages 15–17 on the *Sequence*).

The *Core Knowledge Sequence* presents a grade-by-grade outline of topics in science consistent with the study of science in other countries that have had outstanding results in teaching science at the elementary level, and consistent with the aims defined by the National Academy of Sciences. Here is **a brief summary** of main topics in the Science section of the *Core Knowledge Sequence:*

• **Kindergarten:** Children learn about plants and plant growth, including what plants need to live, the basic parts of a plant, and how people use plants for food and other purposes.

Children learn about animals and their needs, including the special needs of young animals, and the special care required by pets.

Children study the human body, in particular the five senses, and taking care of their bodies.

Children learn about the four seasons, and they learn about weather (temperature, clouds, rainfall, snow, storms, and more).

Children learn about why we need to take care of the earth. They learn the terms *pollution* and *conservation,* and explore ways to recycle.

Children are introduced to magnetism, and classify materials according to whether they are or are not attracted by a magnet.

Children are introduced to the lives and achievements of scientists, including George Washington Carver, Jane Goodall, and Wilbur and Orville Wright.

• **Grade 1:** Children explore the interdependence of living things and their environments. They learn about different kinds of habitats (forest, desert, water, and others), and about the consequences of habitat destruction. They take a detailed look at oceans and undersea life. They learn about the food chain, and about different classifications used for different kinds of animals depending on what they eat (herbivores, carnivores, and omnivores). They learn the term *extinct,* both as it applies to animals long vanished (such as dinosaurs) and as it threatens to apply to animals now endangered.

Children get an overview of the major systems of the human body, including the skeletal system, the muscular system, the digestive system, the circulatory system, and the nervous system. They learn about specific organs such as the heart and brain. They learn about germs, diseases, and vaccinations, and about taking care of themselves and staying healthy.

Children are introduced to the idea that everything is made of matter, and that all matter is made up of parts too small to see. They are introduced to common examples of the three states of matter—solid, liquid, and gas—and examine water as an example of how a single substance can change states.

Children are introduced to different measuring tools and measurements, including length and temperature.

Children observe and experiment (carefully!) with electricity. They take apart and reassemble a flashlight and familiarize themselves with the functions of the parts; become familiar with a very simple circuit; sort and classify materials as conductive or nonconductive; and, learn rules for electrical safety.

Children explore the solar system. They learn about the nine planets, the sun, and the Earth in relation to the sun. They go on to learn more about our planet as they review some geographical features (continents, poles, major oceans), look at what's inside the earth, and learn about different kinds of rocks and minerals.

Children are introduced to the lives and achievements of scientists, including Rachel Carson, Thomas Edison, Edward Jenner, and Louis Pasteur.

• **Grade 2:** Children are introduced to the idea of the life cycle, and learn about the life cycles of plants and various animals (for example, butterflies and frogs). They associate life functions with seasonal cycles (for example, sprouting in spring, dormancy in winter). They undertake a more detailed exploration of the world of insects, as they learn about the parts of insects, metamorphosis, social insects (such as ants and bees), and how insects can be both helpful and harmful.

Children build on their earlier study of weather by learning about the water cycle. They learn about evaporation and condensation, about a few kinds of clouds, and about precipitation and groundwater.

The study of the human body continues with a more detailed look at how the digestive and excretory systems work. Children also learn that all living things are made up of cells, which they can only see with the aid of a microscope. They learn more about taking care of themselves, with an emphasis on a healthy diet as defined by the "food pyramid."

Building upon their introduction to magnetism in kindergarten, children in second grade learn more about magnetism, and are introduced to new ideas and terms, including magnetic poles, the law of magnetic attraction (unlike poles attract, like poles repel), and the behavior of the earth as a huge magnet. They are also introduced to orienteering using a compass.

Children begin to explore how tools and simple machines work, including the lever, pulley, wheel-and-axle (and gears), inclined plane, wedge, and screw. They observe friction and examine ways to reduce it.

Children are introduced to the lives and achievements of scientists, including Elijah McCoy, Florence Nightingale, Daniel Hale Williams, and Anton van Leeuwenhoek.

• **Grade 3:** Children are introduced to the ways in which scientists classify animals according to characteristics they share. They learn about cold-blooded and warm-blooded animals, and about vertebrates and invertebrates. They learn major characteristics and examples of fish, amphibians, reptiles, birds, and mammals.

The study of the human body continues with a more detailed look at the muscular system, the skeletal system, and the nervous system. As part of their study of the nervous system, children also learn about how they eye works and how the ear works.

Children observe and experiment with light and simple optics. They use a prism to learn about the spectrum. They learn about different kinds of mirrors and lenses and their uses (in a magnifying glass, telescope, camera, and so on). They learn the terms *transparent* and *opaque*.

Through experiments and observation, children learn about sound. They learn how sound is caused by vibration (and how the rate of vibration is related to pitch), and how sound travels through different substances. They learn about the physiology of the human voice. They learn why it is important to protect your hearing.

Children build on their earlier studies of habitats as they are introduced to ideas and terms related to ecology and ecosystems. They learn about "the food chain" and about how man-made changes can affect an ecosystem.

Children build upon their first-grade introduction to the solar system by exploring astronomy in more detail. They learn about galaxies, planetary motions (and how those motions determine the seasons, as well as day and night, on the earth), gravity, stars, eclipses, and space exploration.

Children are introduced to the lives and achievements of scientists, including Copernicus, Alexander Graham Bell, John Muir, and Mae Jemison.

• **Grade 4:** Children build upon their earlier studies of the human body by examining in more detail how the circulatory and respiratory systems work. They learn about different blood cells and blood types, about the structure of the heart, and about heart attacks. They learn about the process of taking in oxygen and getting rid of carbon dioxide, about the lungs and other organs, and about how smoking damages lung tissue.

Children are introduced to terms and concepts of chemistry in a basic way, as preparation for further study in later grades. They are introduced to a simple model of the atom, and learn about electrical charge. They are introduced to the idea of elements, and learn about familiar elements such as gold, copper, oxygen, and iron. They do simple experiments with solutions and learn about crystallization.

Building on their first-grade introduction to electricity, children study electricity in more detail. They examine the flow of electricity as they experiment with electric circuits. They learn about closed and open circuits, and about short circuits. They learn about conductors and insulators, and review rules for electrical safety.

Children are introduced to the field of geology and the study of the history of the Earth. They learn about continental drift. They examine how mountains were formed, and study earthquakes and volcanoes. They examine different kinds of rock: igneous, metamorphic, and sedimentary. They learn about forces of weathering and erosion. They study fossils as a record of the Earth's history. They are introduced to how scientists have organized the Earth's history into major eras (Precambrian, Paleozoic, Mesozoic, Cenozoic), and they learn about some life-forms and changes in each era.

Building on what they know about weather, children study topics in meteorology, including a review of the water cycle; the structure of the Earth's atmosphere; air pressure and air movement; cold and warm fronts; thunderstorms, tornadoes, and hurricanes; and tools used to forecast the weather.

Children are introduced to the lives and achievements of scientists, including Benjamin Banneker, Michael Faraday, Elizabeth Blackwell, and Charles Drew.

• **Grade 5:** Building upon their third-grade introduction to how scientists classify the natural world, children learn more about the classification of plants and animals. They learn about different kingdoms, and about how kingdoms are divided into smaller groupings. They learn why human beings are called "Homo sapiens."

Building upon their second-grade introduction to cells, children learn more about cell structures and processes. They examine different parts of plant and animal cells. They learn about single-celled organisms. They learn about the process of photosynthesis in plants. They are introduced to the process of cell division and reproduction. They build on their earlier study of life cycles to learn more about processes of plant and animal reproduction, both asexual and sexual. They also continue their study of the human body by taking a more detailed look at the endocrine and reproductive systems.

Their fourth-grade introduction to basic chemical terms and processes continues with further learning about matter and change. They learn about common compounds and how they are represented in formulas (for example, water as H_2O, salt as $NaCl$). They are introduced to the Periodic Table, and some common elements and their symbols. They learn about chemical change and physical change, and about the transfer of energy that takes place in physical change.

Children are introduced to basic concepts of physics and some simple formulas. Through observation and experiment, the concepts are connected to concrete actions, such as running, lifting a weight, and so on. Children learn about the concept of speed (formula: Speed = Distance/Time). They are introduced to the concept of work (formula: Work = Force × Distance), and to the concept of power (formula: Power = Work/Time).

Children extend their earlier studies of astronomy by taking a historical perspective: they learn about earlier models of the universe, which placed the earth at the center, and about the revolutionary ideas of Copernicus and Galileo (which can be connected to their study of the Renaissance in history).

Children are introduced to the lives and achievements of scientists, including Galileo, Percy Lavon Julian, Ernest Just, and Charles Babbage and Ada Lovelace.

• **Grade 6:** Students learn about energy. They explore different forms of energy, and the relation between potential and kinetic energy. Through observation and experiment, they learn about the conservation of energy in a system. They learn about different sources of energy, such as fossil fuels, mechanical motion, and nuclear energy.

Students build on topics introduced in earlier grades to learn in more depth and detail about light and the electromagnetic spectrum, and about sound.

Students build on earlier studies in astronomy by learning in more depth and detail about stars and galaxies.

Students are introduced to topics in genetics. They learn about Gregor Mendel's experiments. They learn about DNA, the inheritance of traits, and researchers in genetics such as Crick and Watson, Severo Ochoa, and Barbara McClintock.

Students continue their study of the human body, with a focus on the circulatory and lymphatic systems, and on the immune system and disease, including AIDS.

Students are introduced to the lives and achievements of scientists, such as Marie Curie, Charles Darwin, Albert Einstein, Lewis Howard Latimer, and Isaac Newton.

SCIENCE

General Resources

The Core Knowledge Series: *What Your Kindergartner–Sixth Grader Needs to Know,* E. D. Hirsch, Jr., editor. Published by Doubleday in hardback and Dell in paperback.

The seven current books in the Core Knowledge Series, one each for kindergarten through sixth grade, are the companion books to this resource guide. These illustrated books provide a convenient introduction to topics in the *Core Knowledge Sequence,* including the Science topics summarized on pages 247–251. Full of stories, poems, history, and discussions of topics in geography, math, the visual arts, and music, the books can be read to children or, in the upper grades, read by children. All author's proceeds from the sale of *What Your Kindergartner–Sixth Grader Needs to Know* go to the nonprofit Core Knowledge Foundation to support its mission of helping parents and teachers help children develop strong early foundations of knowledge.

CC = a "**Core Collection**" book (see p. 8).

SCIENCE CURRICULUM MODULES FOR SCHOOLS

Note: The following is a partial list of major distributors of science curriculum modules for elementary-school science programs. The modules correspond to many topics in the *Core Knowledge Sequence* Science guidelines (summarized above, pages 247–251). Most modules are specified by their developers for a certain grade level, and can generally be adapted to the sometimes different grade-level recommendations in the *Core Knowledge Sequence.* The modules usually consist of prepackaged lab materials for students, teacher's guides, reproducible masters, assessment materials, and sometimes videos or software. The modules, which are not inexpensive, typically come packaged with equipment for about thirty students. Some programs sell replacement kits of consumable materials for each module. In-service training is generally available for schools that purchase a program. For detailed information about materials and costs, please write or call the distributors of the programs and request a catalog.

FOSS: Full Option Science System
Encyclopedia Britannica Educational
  Corporation
310 South Michigan Avenue
Chicago, IL 60604-9839
Customer Service: (800) 554-9862

Insights
Optical Data Corporation
512 Means Street, Suite 100
Atlanta, GA 30318
Customer Service: (800) 524-2481

Scholastic Science Place
Scholastic Inc.
2931 East McCarty Street
Jefferson City, MO 65101
Orders: (800) 724-6527

STC: Science and Technology for Children
Carolina Biological Supply Company
2700 York Road
Burlington, NC 27215
Customer Service: (800) 334-5551

SERIES (ON VARIOUS TOPICS)

Eyewitness books
Alfred A. Knopf
All Eyewitness books are intensely visual.
They're great to browse through and pore over,
but the presentation has its pros and cons. On
one hand, these books are lovely to look at. On
the other hand, if you're looking for a coherent,
logical presentation of a topic, you'll need to
complement these books with others. In Eyewitness books, the words are secondary to the pictures. In this series, science is chopped into little
pieces rather than conveyed as a logical contin-
uum of thought. But, oh, those pictures! You'll
find yourself saying, "Oh, come look, you've
just gotta see *this!*" Science titles include: *Am-
phibian, Bird, Desert, Fish, Fossil, Insect, Mammal,
Plant, Reptile, Rocks and Minerals, Skeleton, Tree,
Volcanoes and Earthquakes, Weather,* and more.

Eyewitness Juniors
Alfred A. Knopf
Banking on the success of the Eyewitness books
(see above), this series uses a smaller page size,
fewer photos, larger type, and simpler text to
introduce primary-grade children to the basic
sciences. The wonderful pictures provide many

opportunities for looking and talking together.
Titles include: *Amazing Birds, Amazing Fish,
Amazing Frogs and Toads, Amazing Insects, Amaz-
ing Lizards, Amazing Mammals, Amazing Snakes,
Amazing Spiders,* and more.

Eyewitness Science books
Dorling Kindersley
Following the same formula as the Eyewitness
books, discussed above, this series aims for an
older audience and sets out to convey the his-
tory of each science that it portrays. Many of
the photos, therefore, are of artifacts of sci-
ence—Alexander Graham Bell's telephone,
Priestley's glass jar, for example. Titles include:
*Astronomy, Chemistry, Earth, Ecology, Electricity,
Energy, Evolution, Light, Force and Motion, Human
Body, Medicine, Technology, Time & Space.*

How Did We Find Out About . . . ? series
by Isaac Asimov
Walker
The prolific Isaac Asimov, renowned for his
ability to explain science in a clear and simple
way, took on dozens of topics in these little
books. The approach to each subject is through
the history of the science, often going back to
classical or Renaissance roots and up to the
twentieth century. The books introduce key figures (including pronunciation of the name and
dates of life) and the thought processes that car-
ried them from one idea to the next. Each book
is about fifty pages, illustrated with black-and-
white drawings, and written in language man
ageable to most fifth graders or above. Titles include *How Did We Find Out About Electricity?
Numbers? Germs? Vitamins? Energy? Atoms? Our
Human Roots? Solar Power? Life in the Deep Sea?
Genes?* and *Computers?*

How Things Work series
Thomson Learning
These attractive, intelligent books bring the
physical and engineering sciences into reach for
about second through sixth graders (can be
used as read-alouds or teacher/parent resources
for the lower grades). The series includes *It's*

Electric, Heat, Lifting by Levers, The Power of Pressure, Simple Slopes, and *Wheels at Work.* Richly illustrated with photos and attractive, well-labeled drawings, each book is clearly organized and puts relatively little text on each page. Contents proceed from simple to complex, with many cutaway drawings and clear connecting links between basic engineering science and the machines and tools we use every day.

CC *Let's-Read-and-Find-Out* **series**
HarperCollins
This classic collection of over one hundred brightly illustrated, well-written picture books sets the standard for all others. Originated by (and, in the case of quite a few titles, written by) Franklyn M. Branley, these books can be trusted to interest children and convey solid scientific information. Most can be read by second graders and above, and all work well as read-aloud books too. More recent additions to the series have been designated as "Stage 1" or "Stage 2" according to level of difficulty: "Stage 1" books explain simple and easily observable concepts, and are described by the publisher as written at an advanced first-grade reading level; "Stage 2" books explore more challenging concepts and include hands-on activities, and are described by the publisher as written at a third-grade reading level.

New True Books **series**
Childrens Press
This is a series of tried-and-true early-reader texts about many scientific subjects. The type is large and readable. The sentences are short and simple. Every book concludes with a list of "Words You Should Know" and an index. The books are all illustrated with stock color photos. The strength of these books is their good, solid coverage of so many basic scientific concepts in a simple form that makes science approachable for young readers.

CC = "Core Collection" book (see page 8).

Rookie Read-About Science **series**
Childrens Press
These informative little books introduce different science topics, written so that some first graders will be able to start reading about science for themselves. The books are organized in a clear, logical fashion, and illustrated with color photos, often including children in them. Among the more than fifty titles in this series to date are: *Flies Are Fascinating; Frogs, and Toads, and Tadpoles, Too; Gentle Gorillas and Other Apes; Hot and Cold; It Could Still Be a Leaf; It Could Still Be a Mammal; It's a Good Thing There Are Insects;* and *So That's How the Moon Changes Shape!*

GENERAL SCIENCE AND REFERENCE

The Kingfisher Science Encyclopedia
edited by Catherine Headlam
Kingfisher Books, 1991
This is a rich, colorful, and informative reference book, written in language accessible to about fourth graders and above. Organized alphabetically with almost a thousand entries, it gives basic background information in many fields and on many scientists. Very good illustrations, especially the labeled diagrams that explain processes and technologies. Entries are short, but dense and factual, with links to other entries and occasional suggestions for hands-on experiments.

My First Science Book
by Angela Wilkes
Alfred A. Knopf, 1990
This large-format book, illustrated with photos in bright, primary colors, suggests a dozen projects to get young children interested in the process of scientific experimentation. Ideas include a rain gauge and barometer, a water-bottle xylophone, and a simple electrical circuit. Big on pictures and light on text, this is more a project book than an explanation book.

The Random House Book of 1001 Wonders of Science
by Brian and Brenda Williams
Random House, 1989
This handy reference is written for about third to sixth graders. It contains information on atoms, elements, electricity, light and sound, energy and motion, space and time, the earth, inventions, and transportation, presented in a question/answer format. Color photos.

Science Matters: Achieving Scientific Literacy
by Robert M. Hazen and James Trefil
Doubleday, 1991
Having this book on hand could help any teacher or parent who is helping children learn science. "The basic ideas underlying all science are simple," says this book. Its outline reads like a primer to all science, with chapter headings like "Energy," "Electricity and Magnetism," "The Atom," "Chemical Bonding," "Relativity," and "The Code of Life."

The Way Things Work
written and illustrated by David Macaulay
Houghton Mifflin, 1988
This fascinating encyclopedia, good as a teacher/parent resource or for browsing with a child, begins with almost one hundred pages exploring simple tools and machines and the principles by which they work. The illustrations and examples are sometimes silly, harking back to Neanderthal days, and sometimes technical, but always clear and well explained in captions. The book includes helpful language and ideas about simple tools and machines, as well as about friction.

Wonders of Science
by Melvin Berger
Scholastic, 1991
The author has written many science books for children, and his broad-ranging knowledge comes in handy here. This book describes basic scientific principles and offers simple experiments for seeing them in action.

EXPERIMENTS AND ACTIVITIES

Note: Many books on science suggest some experiments and activities. This section lists books that focus almost exclusively on experiments and activities rather than explanation.

175 Amazing Nature Experiments
by Rosie Harlow and Gareth Morgan
illustrated by Kuo Keng Chen *et al.*
Random House, 1992
This book, full of ideas, illustrations, and information, embeds instructions for experiments, games, and things to make within brief discussions of background science. The experiments fall into four big categories: "How Things Grow," "Minibeasts" (meaning worms and insects), "Trees and Leaves," and "The Seasons."

175 More Science Experiments to Amuse and Amaze Your Friends: Experiments! Tricks! Things to Make!
by Terry Cash, Steve Parker, and Barbara Taylor
illustrated by Kuo Keng Chen *et al.*
Random House, 1990
Like the book above, this title gives lots of activity ideas within the context of some solid scientific discussions. Categories here are sound, electricity, chemistry, and weather.

Famous Experiments and How to Repeat Them
by Brent Filson
illustrated by Brigita Fuhrmann
Julian Messner, 1986
This unusual and interesting book provides brief biographies of great scientists and suggests ways to recreate some of their great experimental discoveries. Chapters are devoted to Archimedes, Galileo, Isaac Newton, Michael Faraday, Marie Curie (no experiment is suggested, thank goodness!), Alexander Fleming, and others.

Janice VanCleave's Science Books series
John Wiley & Sons
This series of books is designed to instruct children from about ages 8 to 12 in the scientific

method. Each book proposes twenty or more experiments, talks children through the thought processes underlying each experiment, then gives pointers on analyzing results and reporting on the experiment, as well as posing questions for further study. The format guides and encourages hands-on experience, but it offers only a bit of explanation of the scientific principles at work. Each book represents a different science, including astronomy, chemistry, earth science, geography, geometry, the human body, math, and physics. Titles (which all begin with *Janice VanCleave's . . .*) include *Janice VanCleave's Biology for Every Kid; Chemistry for Every Kid; Earth Science for Every Kid; Earthquakes; Electricity; The Human Body for Every Kid; Machines; Magnets; Volcanoes;* and *Weather.*

Science Experiments and Amusements for Children
by Charles Vivian
photographs by S.A.R. Watts
Dover, 1963
This inexpensive book describes seventy-three experiments that use everyday materials to illustrate basic concepts of the physical sciences. Instructions are brief and easy to follow, illustrated by diagrams and photos. Instructions include brief explanations of the science underlying the projects, but the book's strength is in its wealth of practical ideas. Also available from Dover Publications (31 East Second Street, Mineola, NY 11501) are a number of other inexpensive science activity and project books including *Science Projects for Children* by George Barr; *Science Research Experiments for Young People* by George Barr; *47 Easy-to-Do Classic Science Experiments* by Eugene Provenzo, Jr., and Asterie Baker Provenzo; *Safe and Simple Electrical Experiments* by Rudolf Graf; *Entertaining Science Experiments with Everyday Objects* by Martin Gardner; *Physics Experiments for Children* by Muriel Mandell, and many more.

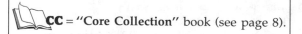

CC = "Core Collection" book (see page 8).

THE HUMAN BODY

CC *Blood and Guts: A Working Guide to Your Own Insides*
written and illustrated by Linda Allison
Little, Brown, 1976
This good-natured, well-organized book is suitably written for older elementary-level readers. Fifteen chapters discusses fifteen different systems, and each is divided into short sections, simple experiments, and interesting lists of facts. The author uses familiar language and analogies to explain physiology, like "You are a furnace, filters, and a fancy computer." Funny cartoons spice up the pages.

The Body Atlas
by Steve Parker
illustrated by Giuliano Fornari
Dorling Kindersley, 1993
This big book "maps" the human body from head to toe, exploring one major region at a time, with labeled color drawings that reveal organs and structures, complemented by occasional microphotographs and sidebars that look at systems or functions in more detail. The informative text is readable by students in about grades five and up.

Body Detectives: A Book About the Five Senses
by Rita Golden Gelman
Illustrated by Elroy Freem
Scholastic, 1994
In this fun book, the five senses are turned into paunchy guys in trench coats who "detect" the outer world and report to the brain. The amusing illustrations manage to convey some important facts. Written for about third graders and above, this book also contains a poem about the senses.

How the Body Works
by Steve Parker
Reader's Digest Association, 1994
This encyclopedic volume offers information, observations, activities, and facts to help children learn more about how the body works. It

has a number of diagrams as well as micrographs to get a clear sense of what goes on inside, plus many hands-on projects to help you understand your own physiology. The book is profusely illustrated, not only with diagrams and drawings but also with color photos of children engaged in the activities that the book describes.

How Our Bodies Work series
Silver Burdett
This series of brief (about fifty pages), informative, well-illustrated books for grades 5 through 8 explains the various functions of the human body. Titles include: *The Brain and the Nervous System; Food and Digestion; The Heart and the Bood; The Lungs and Breathing; The Skeleton and Movement; Skin, Hair, and Teeth.*

Outside and Inside You
by Sandra Markle
Bradbury Press, 1991
Using remarkable high-tech glimpses into different body systems, this book offers a realistic sense of how cells and tissues make up the body. The book includes micrographs, for example, of a cross-section of skin, rods and cones in the eye, a taste bud, and the walls of the intestine. Descriptions of each of these pictures show how cell structures determine system function.

BIOGRAPHY COLLECTIONS

Note: Biographies of individual scientists are listed in the grade levels in which they are specified in the *Core Knowledge Sequence.*

Black Pioneers of Science and Invention
by Louis Haber
Harcourt Brace Jovanovich, 1970
This book tells the life and professional stories of seven black inventors and seven black scientists, including several figures included in the

Core Knowledge Sequence: Benjamin Banneker, Elijah McCoy, Lewis Latimer, George Washington Carver, Percy Lavon Julian, Daniel Hale Williams, and Charles Drew. Each biography, ten to twenty pages long, excels in setting the figure into a social context and in explaining the technical details of his work.

Great Lives: Invention and Technology
by Milton Lomask
Charles Scribner's Sons, 1991
The *Great Lives* series (which includes volumes on Medicine, Painting, and Exploration) is a helpful parent/teacher resource for all grades, and readable by students in upper elementary grades and beyond. This volume offers twenty-seven concise, interesting biographical sketches about people whose inventions or discoveries changed our world. Includes chapters on Charles Babbage, Alexander Graham Bell, George Washington Carver, Thomas Edison, Michael Faraday, Robert Goddard, Johannes Gutenberg, Leonardo da Vinci, James Watt, Eli Whitney, Wilbur and Orville Wright, and others. With black-and-white illustrations and a bibliography of related readings.

Great Lives: Medicine
by Robert H. Curtis, M.D.
Charles Scribner's Sons, 1993
This encyclopedic book provides brief life stories of thirty-eight greats in the history of medicine, from Hippocrates and Galen to Freud and Salk. Each biography runs about ten pages long and includes significant detail, both biographical and historical. Occasional period photos or illustrations supplement the text. The book is organized according to the type of medical contribution each individual made: medical devices, infectious diseases, mental health, modern cures. Several individuals specified in the *Core Knowledge Sequence* are featured here: Edward Jenner, Louis Pasteur, Elizabeth Blackwell, Charles Drew, Marie Curie.

MAGAZINES

CC *Kids Discover*
170 Fifth Avenue
New York, NY 10010
Each issue of this magazine focuses on a specific topic, sometimes in a scientific field. The editors and writers turn each topic into a colorful eighteen-page magazine for kids. Pages are full of photography and diagrams, and lots of text. These magazines work on many levels and can be used in different ways with children from about third grade through middle school. Issues come out ten times a year, once a month except in summer. Scientific topics have included "Pyramids," "North & South Poles," "The 5 Senses," "Flight," "Trees," "Oceans," "Earthquakes," "Weather," "Space," "Deserts," "Rain Forests," "Volcanoes," "Light," "Oil," "Flowers," "Energy," "Endangered Species," and "The Solar System." Subscriptions, bulk rates, and back issues are available: call (212) 242-5133.

Ranger Rick
National Wildlife Federation
8925 Leesburg Pike
Vienna, VA 22184-0001
After they've outgrown *Your Big Backyard*, children are ready for this monthly magazine, a sort of *National Geographic* for elementary schoolchildren. The pages are full of gorgeous color photography of various plants and animals, with informative articles that can be read aloud to primary-grade children or read independently by older children. Most issues suggest a project or offer an educational game on one of the pages. Stories about "Ranger Rick" and his animal friends consistently emphasize the importance of conservation and caring for the environment; they communicate an important message, but sometimes in a heavy-handed and preachy way. Never mind—there's a great deal to enjoy and learn from in every issue.

Your Big Backyard
National Wildlife Federation
8925 Leesburg Pike
Vienna, VA 22184-0001
A magazine for preschoolers up to about first graders, *Your Big Backyard* uses vivid color photography to take children around the world and close up to coyotes, meerkats, goldfinches, squirrels, and many other animals and their habitats. The magazine gently encourages appreciation of the natural world and care for it. Most issues include a game, suggestions for easy projects, and clear, basic explanations of scientific concepts, such as the food chain. A furry, plump little character called B. B. Yardlee shows up on many pages. Children who like this magazine will, when they get a little older, probably like *Ranger Rick* too.

SCIENCE

Kindergarten

PLANTS AND PLANT GROWTH

CC *Bean and Plant*
by Christine Back
photography by Barrie Watts
Silver Burdett, 1986
With big color photographs and minimal text,
this book follows a lima bean from planting the
seed to harvesting and eating the bean. The
photos clearly demonstrate the important parts
and stages of a seed sprouting, and can help
children observe those parts and stages when
they grow their own plants from seeds.

Flowers
by Henry Pluckrose
Childrens Press, 1994
Flowers are often the most recognizable and
easily appreciated part of a plant for young children. This picture book, with pages full of color
photos displaying a variety of flower shapes
and habits, explains the function of flowers in a
plant's growth. Written with sparse yet descriptive language, this is a good kindergarten read-
aloud.

From Seed to Plant
by Gail Gibbons
Holiday House, 1991
Vividly colorful illustrations complement the
simple text about how seeds grow and the role
they play in propagating all kinds of plants.
This is a pleasant, easy-to-understand picture
book, a good introduction to seeds for kindergartners.

Growing Vegetable Soup
by Lois Ehlert
Harcourt Brace, 1987
With big, bright, geometric cutout illustrations
and simple text, this book goes step by step
from planting seeds to harvesting vegetables
and cooking soup.

CC *How a Seed Grows*
by Helene J. Jordan
illustrated by Loretta Krupinski
HarperCollins, 1960 (illustrations 1992)
This is a gentle, straightforward book about
seeds and how they grow that could be read
aloud effectively to kindergartners. It directs the
child to follow the experiment at the heart of
the book, which involves planting a handful of
bean seeds and digging them up, one a day, to
see the sequence of their sprouting. A "Stage 1"
Let's-Read-and-Find-Out book, listed under Science General Resources: Series.

The Science Book of Things That Grow
by Neil Ardley
Harcourt Brace, 1991
This colorful book has some clever experiments
designed for young children to explore the
world of growing things. See how marigold
roots can crack an eggshell; see how mold
grows on a square of bread; see how yeast gen-
erates enough gas to blow up a balloon. The
book does not offer a lot of background explanation, but it does have a lot of good ideas that
can be easily followed at home or school.

CC = "Core Collection" book (see page 8).

A Seed Is a Promise
by Claire Merrill
illustrated by Susan Swan
Scholastic, 1990
Starting with seeds that children know and moving to interesting stories of more unusual seeds, this book helps explain that seeds carry the potential of new plants within.

CC *What's Inside? Plants*
by Angela Royston
illustrated by Richard Manning
photography by Matthew Ward
Dorling Kindersley, 1992
In this book of basic botany, each spread of facing pages shows a bigger-than-life color photograph and a cutaway illustration, to explain plant physiology. Simple, straightforward language introduces each spread and labels each illustration, so the book can be read aloud effectively.

ANIMALS AND THEIR NEEDS

Animals Born Alive and Well
written and illustrated by Ruth Heller
Grosset & Dunlap, 1982; Scholastic, 1989
This pretty picture book portrays both the diversity of mammals and the characteristics they all have in common. The book's rhyming text conveys basic ideas and its appealing pictures offer much to discuss beyond its few words.

Baby Animals
by Angela Royston
photography by Steve Shott *et al.*
Dorling Kindersley, 1992
A little book for little hands. The photographs in this book still look big and give a real-life sense of each of eight animals, amplified with large-print text and accompanying illustrations. One note: since the book was originally published in England, the fawn pictured is England's fallow deer, not North America's white-tailed.

A Chick Hatches
by Joanna Cole
photography by Jerome Wexler
William Morrow, 1976
Clearly written text and remarkably revealing photographs, some black-and-white and some color, portray the incubation cycle going on inside the shell. While the text and photos may offer more detail than a kindergartner needs, this book will help children appreciate the wonderful processes that go on inside an eggshell before it gets pecked open by the hatching chick.

CC *Chickens Aren't the Only Ones*
written and illustrated by Ruth Heller
Grosset & Dunlap, 1981
Not only chickens come out of eggs. What about sea horses? Sharks? Snails? Spiny anteaters? With information likely to capture a child's interest, rhymes likely to delight a child's ear, and color illustrations that burst out from every page, this book helps children understand what eggs are all about.

CC *What's Alive*
by Kathleen Weidner Zoehfeld
illustrated by Nadine Bernard Westcott
HarperCollins, 1995
In sweet, simple prose this book puts forth the basic scientific definitions and principles that define life and distinguish plant life from animal life. Wistful illustrations follow a little girl through her neighborhood, observing nature and following simple experiments along with the text. A ''Stage 1'' Let's-Read-and-Find-Out book, listed under Science General Resources: Series.

PETS AND THEIR CARE

My New Kitten
by Joanna Cole
photography by Margaret Miller
William Morrow, 1995
With adorable (of course—they're kittens!) pho-

tographs and a readable text written in the voice of a little girl, this book goes from the pregnant mother cat to the newborn kittens to the little girl taking a kitten home for her very own.

My Puppy Is Born
by Joanna Cole
photography by Margaret Miller
William Morrow, 1991
With big color photographs of a little girl and her Norfolk terrier, and text written in the voice of the little girl, this book watches puppies being born and growing to cute little dogs. The photos do not shy away from the birth process, and the story emphasizes how both the mother dog and human caretakers must contribute to the health of the puppies.

THE HUMAN BODY: HEALTH AND THE FIVE SENSES

Dinosaurs Alive and Well! A Guide to Good Health
by Laurene Krasny Brown
illustrated by Marc Brown
Little, Brown, 1990
Dinosaur characters either follow health and safety rules or else break the rules, with dire consequences. Comical illustrations by Marc Brown (the author-illustrator of the popular "Arthur" books) make this an amusing way to teach good lessons.

Experiment with Senses
by Monica Byles
Lerner, 1994
Illustrated with color photos and block-print art, this book organizes learning about the senses into short, factual paragraphs. Some could be read aloud to kindergartners; others provide good ideas for simple experiments.

 **CC** = "Core Collection" book (see page 8).

CC I Can Tell by Touching
by Carolyn Otto
illustrated by Nadine Bernard Westcott
HarperCollins, 1994
Nice full-page color drawings and engaging text, written in the voice of a child, encourage children to tune in to their sense of touch. The main character sits at his kitchen table, then walks with his sister to the park, touching everything he can lay his hands on. The two of them roll down the hill, showing how touch can be a "whole-body experience"! A simple experiment ends the book. A "Stage 1" book in the Let's-Read-and-Find-Out series, listed under Science General Resources: Series.

Me and My Body
by David Evans and Claudette Williams
Dorling Kindersley, 1992
Bright color photos show young children doing exactly what the text suggests they do—bending, stretching, touching, sensing, all to explore the possibilities of the human body. The book is organized by the senses and offers notes to parents and teachers about these and other simple body experiments.

CC My Five Senses
written and illustrated by Aliki
HarperCollins, 1989
A classic text about the five senses and what they do for us, with Aliki's distinctive childlike illustrations. Part of the Let's-Read-and-Find-Out series, listed under Science General Resources: Series.

You Can't Smell a Flower with Your Ear! All About Your 5 Senses
by Joanna Cole
illustrated by Mavis Smith
Grosset & Dunlap, 1994
This easy-reader, targeted for grades 1 to 3, explains the basic physiology behind each of the five senses. It offers some simple experiments and basic schematics of the organs involved, and helps children understand how the senses play a part in their everyday lives. Cartoonish

drawings and funny examples keep the tone
nice and light.

MAGNETISM

See also Science Grade 2: Magnetism, for
books that may be adapted for use with kindergartners.

CC *Experiment with Magnets and
Electricity*
by Margaret Whalley
Lerner, 1994
Simple language and boldly colored photos and
illustrations make this a good introduction to
magnets. The book begins by showing where
magnets can be found in the world, then suggests a number of simple projects using magnets. Only the first half of the book involves
magnets; the second involves electricity (introduced in the first grade in schools following the
Core Knowledge Sequence).

Experiments with Magnets
by Helen J. Challand
Childrens Press, 1986
This book both defines magnets and offers a
number of simple experiments for young children to learn about them firsthand. It is written
in simple language, set in large type. Small
color photos, many of children performing the
experiments, illustrate the book. A New True
Book, listed under Science General Resources:
Series.

CC *What Magnets Can Do*
by Allan Fowler
Childrens Press, 1995
The text flows carefully and logically in this little book, accurately introducing very basic ideas
about magnets, compasses, and their uses in everyday life. Each page has no more than two or
three sentences of text and a color photograph.
A Rookie Read-About Science book, listed under Science General Resources: Series.

SEASONS AND WEATHER

Flash, Crash, Rumble, and Roll
by Franklyn M. Branley
illustrated by Barbara and Ed Emberley
HarperCollins, 1985
This book combines science, observation, and
commonsense advice about thunder and lightning storms. The illustrations are fun, and the
author does a good job explaining meteorological concepts and familiarizing children with
lightning. He includes some rules for safety
during lightning storms. Part of the Let's-Read-
and-Find-Out series, listed under Science General Resources: Series, and good as a read-aloud
for kindergartners.

CC *Seasons & Weather*
by David Evans and Claudette Williams
photography by Daniel Pangbourne
Dorling Kindersley, 1993
With large print and photos of children dressed
in primary colors, this book walks through a series of "what if?" questions and simple projects
that help young children become more aware of
weather and seasonal phenomena: "What season is it where you live?" "When can you see
the moon? "What do snowflakes look like close
up? Does crushed ice look the same?" On two
pages at the end of the book, the authors offer a
little more guidance to parents or teachers in
using the questions and activities to teach. Part
of the Let's Explore Science series.

CC *Spring* **(1994)**
Summer **(1994)**
Autumn **(1994)**
Winter **(1994)**
by Ruth Thomson and Sally Hewitt
Childrens Press
After a short introduction about the reason for
the season, each of these four volumes offers an
imaginative collection of craft and science projects, all to delve more deeply into the phenomena specific to that time of year. These books
are colorful, cheerful, and informative, and they

suggest many activities kindergartners will enjoy.

Weather: Poems for All Seasons
selected by Lee Bennett Hopkins
illustrated by Melanie Hall
HarperCollins, 1994
This easy reader, targeted for grades 2 to 4, has about thirty wonderful short poems about weather, including a few favorites like Carl Sandburg's "Fog" and Christina Rossetti's "Clouds." Pastel illustrations warm the pages.

What Will the Weather Be Like Today?
by Paul Rogers
illustrated by Kazuko
Greenwillow Books, 1990
A simple rhyme asks all the basic questions about the weather. This book gently suggests that different animals live in different habitats and that different places on earth experience different weather patterns. The cut-paper illustrations are an interesting study in themselves.

TAKING CARE OF THE EARTH

Caring for Our Air (1991)
Caring for Our Water (1991)
by Carol Greene
Enslow
In simple language and large print these books discuss air and water pollution, ending with practical lists of things children can do to keep the air and water clean.

My First Green Book
by Angela Wilkes
Alfred A. Knopf, 1991
This large-format book, illustrated with big colorful photos, suggests experiments designed both to reveal pollution problems and to practice caring for the earth. For example, one experiment helps a child replicate the effects of acid rain on plants by watering three plants with different vinegar-water solutions.

Recycle! A Handbook for Kids
written and illustrated by Gail Gibbons
Little, Brown, 1992
This lively and informative handbook on recycling focuses on five different types of garbage and describes what happens to each when recycled. Includes fun facts about garbage and recycling.

CC Recycle That!
by Fay Robinson
Childrens Press, 1995
With a little bit of text and color photos on every page, this book explains why recycling is a valuable activity. "Can you see why it's smart to recycle?" it asks. "Things that would have been wasted can be made into something useful instead." A Rookie Read-About Science book, listed under Science General Resources: Series.

Window
conceived and illustrated by Jeannie Baker
Greenwillow Books, 1991
Created out of textured collages, this book tells a wordless story about population growth and neighborhood development. We look through a window from a baby's birth, out to a forest nearby. Then, as the baby grows to manhood, the forest is cut down to make room for a city. The author's illustration technique invites children to notice and compare.

BIOGRAPHIES

George Washington Carver

George Washington Carver, Scientist and Teacher
by Carol Greene
Childrens Press, 1992
This "Rookie Biography" tells the life story of George Washington Carver. It is written for beginning readers and illustrated with many period photos and artifacts. A good read-aloud for kindergartners.

CC *A Weed Is a Flower: The Life of George Washington Carver*
written and illustrated by Aliki
Simon & Schuster, 1988
A short, touching retelling of the story of George Washington Carver, this is an early book written and illustrated by the well-known Aliki. It speaks plainly about his beginnings in a slave family, but emphasizes the work Carver did at Tuskegee, explaining it in the context of Southern agriculture.

Jane Goodall

Chimps
by Jane Goodall
Simon & Schuster/Aladdin Books, 1989
Written for children by Jane Goodall herself, this book portrays the social habits, communication abilities, mental patterns, and life cycle of the chimpanzee, all made more colorful with anecdotes about actual chimps that Goodall has known and studied. Photographs of chimps, primarily in the wild, illustrate this small paperback.

Jane Goodall, Naturalist
by J. A. Senn
Blackbirch Press, 1993
A chapter book written for children who read, this book contains anecdotes about Goodall's life that you can choose from to read aloud, and has photographs of chimpanzees that will interest kindergartners.

Wilbur and Orville Wright

The Wright Brothers: How They Invented the Airplane
by Russell Freedman
with photographs by Wilbur and Orville Wright
Holiday House, 1991
With large-format pages, extensive text, and over a hundred contemporary photos, this Newbery Honor Book will delight adults and older children who can read it, but also young children who can learn a great deal from the pictures. The Wright Brothers took pictures of every phase of their experiments, and this book has pictures of many of their models, of them in flight, even of crashes that they suffered. Seeing these events as photographs makes them all the more real.

Young Orville and Wilbur Wright: First to Fly
by Andrew Woods
illustrated by Ellen Beier
Troll Associates, 1992
This pleasant picture book focuses on the Wright Brothers as children, playing with a toy flying machine, flying kites, building their own printing press, and more. It devotes a few brief pages to their later experiments with gliders and their first flight at Kitty Hawk.

SCIENCE

Grade 1

LIVING THINGS AND THEIR ENVIRONMENTS

Cactus Hotel
by Brenda Z. Guiberson
illustrated by Megan Lloyd
Henry Holt, 1991
This attractive picture book tells the life story of a saguaro cactus that thrives in the Arizona desert and serves as a "hotel" for many animal inhabitants.

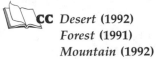 **CC** *Desert* **(1992)**
Forest **(1991)**
Mountain **(1992)**
by Ron Hirschi
illustrated by Barbara Bash
Bantam
In this series, each book has a short, friendly text that asks questions on every page, and children can use visual clues to find the answers, all adding up to an appreciation of the animals that live in these environments. The books conclude with a few more interesting facts about each animal.

The Gift of the Tree
by Alvin Tresselt
illustrated by Henri Sorensen
Lothrop, Lee & Shepard, 1972, 1992
Beautiful painterly illustrations help tell the story over decades of the life and death of a great oak tree. Over half the story occurs after the tree dies, signifying how even the rotting tree stump contributes to the cycle of life in the forest.

Habitats: Making Homes for Animals and Plants
by Pamela M. Hickman
Addison-Wesley, 1993
A teacher/parent resource, this hands-on nature book gives practical information on how to re-create ten different habitats at home, including a pond, an anthill, a worm colony, and a toad hatchery. Each chapter gives detailed instructions on how to collect the necessary materials and put the habitat together in an aquarium or jar. Each chapter concludes with a section called "The Big Picture," showing how the tabletop habitat fits into the outside world of nature. Many color illustrations help convey instructions.

How to Be a Nature Detective
by Millicent E. Selsam
illustrated by Marlene Hill Donnelly
HarperCollins, 1995
This book takes a clever approach to nature observation, enlisting children as "nature detectives." Pretty watercolors on each page invite the child to come to conclusions based upon observations within the book and then outside in nature, as children are asked to do things such as matching tracks with animals. Part of the Let's-Read-and-Find-Out series, listed under Science General Resources: Series.

Life in the Rainforests: Animal, People, Plants
by Lucy Baker
Scholastic, 1990
This is one title in a series of books that uses colorful illustrations and photographs to introduce young readers to various habitats. Written for readers in about third to fifth grade, these

books are best as read-alouds in this grade. Other titles in this series (by various authors): *Life in the Deserts; Life in the Mountains; Life in the Oceans; Life in the Islands;* and *Life in the Polar Lands.*

Under the Ground
by Henry Pluckrose
Childrens Press, 1994
With a simple read-aloud text and fascinating cutaway photos, this book makes you think about what goes on under the earth. It shows how plants grow, how animals live and burrow, and how human beings dig and build beneath the earth.

CC *A Walk in the Desert*
by Caroline Arnold
illustrated by Freya Tanz
Simon & Schuster/Silver Press, 1990
This easy-to-read book uses attractive, realistic watercolor illustrations to introduce native plants and animals of the desert. A map of the world's major deserts is included. Other books in this series include *A Walk up a Mountain, A Walk in the Woods,* and *A Walk by the Seashore.*

Welcome to the Green House
by Jane Yolen
illustrated by Laura Regan
Scholastic, 1993
Paintings full of life and words like poetry invite you to visit the "green house"—the rain forest. The author draws attention to the sounds of this environment, and both text and illustrations emphasize its remarkable diversity of plant and animal life.

CC *Who Eats What? Food Chains and Food Webs*
by Patricia Lauber
illustrated by Holly Keller
HarperCollins, 1995
This book brings children into food chains in two ways: first, by showing where humans fit in, and second, by asking them to draw food chains and webs that they know. The book

culminates in a clear description of a complex food web in the ocean. Bold color illustrations and a few drawings, as if done by a child, help clarify concepts. Part of the Let's-Read-and-Find-Out series listed under Science General Resources: Series.

OCEANS AND UNDERSEA LIFE

Amazing Fish
by Mary Ling
photographed by Jerry Young
Alfred A. Knopf, 1991
One of many colorfully illustrated volumes in the Eyewitness Juniors series, this book presents interesting facts about many creatures of the deep, and plenty of close-up pictures on every page.

A Day Underwater
by Deborah Kovacs
Scholastic, 1987
Enter an experimental submarine and, through spectacular underwater photography, take an engaging visual voyage to the ocean floor. A Reading Rainbow selection.

At Home in the Tide Pool
by Alexandra Wright
illustrated by Marshall Peck III
Charlesbridge, 1992
With colorful illustrations and informative text, this book draws children close to the details of life of a tide pool. Each page portrays a broad view, then in the margins offers detailed drawings of plants or creatures that the child looks for in the bigger drawing. The book manages to introduce a number of different species, offering interesting details on each one.

CC *The Magic School Bus on the Ocean Floor*
by Joanna Cole
illustrated by Bruce Degen
Scholastic, 1992
Using a touch of fantasy to convey the facts,

this book presents Ms. Frizzle and her class as they don scuba tanks and travel down to the ocean floor, identifying the plants and animals they find at each level. The book concludes with a classroom mural depicting the full sweep of terrains and habitats that they visited.

CC *Ocean*
by Ron Hirschi
illustrated by Barbara Bash
Bantam, 1991
This is a lovely and simple introduction to the sea and its inhabitants, with vivid, realistic watercolors and text that asks children to guess the name of each animal depicted.

Seashore Life Coloring Book
by Anthony D'Attilio
Dover, 1973
Here are forty-six pages of black-and-white line drawings, ready to color, including anemones, jellyfish, coral, barnacles, hermit crabs, and many different kinds of fish. (See address, page 106.)

HABITAT DESTRUCTION AND ENDANGERED SPECIES

All the King's Animals: The Return of Endangered Wildlife to Swaziland
written and photographed by Cristina Kessler
Boyds Mills Press, 1995
Though the text of this book is far above a first-grade level, parts of it are worth reading aloud or sharing with children, who will enjoy the vivid color photographs. As the author states, "So often, only African disasters get attention. This is a book celebrating an African success story," the story of how conservationist Ted Reilly, with the support of the country's monarchy, has struggled against, and begun to overcome, the problems of poaching, disease, and overpopulation that threaten such wildlife as impala, elephants, rhinos, and lions.

Bringing Back the Animals
by Teresa Kennedy
illustrated by Sue Williams
Amethyst, 1991
This appealing book combines a big chalk illustration with a page of interesting, factual text about a dozen endangered animals, including the giant panda, the bottle-nosed dolphin, the blue whale, and the hooded cobra. The author describes each animal's life habits and explains why they have become endangered.

CC *The Great Kapok Tree*
by Lynne Cherry
Harcourt Brace, 1990
All the animals that live in a great kapok tree in the South American rain-forest explain to a tree cutter why he should not cut down the tree. Vivid, engaging illustrations strengthen the book's message.

Oil Spill!
by Melvin Berger
illustrated by Paul Mirocha
HarperCollins, 1994
Dramatic illustrations, both close up and distant, offer children different perspectives on oil spills. The book is not just a call for sympathy for animal victims, but also an attempt to explain the technologies involved in cleaning up oil spills. Part of the Let's-Read-and-Find-Out series, listed under Science General Resources: Series.

Sam the Sea Cow
by Francine Jacobs
illustrations by Laura Kelly
Walker, 1979, 1991
This book evokes concern over the manatee, nearing extinction, by telling the story of a young manatee rescued from a sewage drain and raised at a seaquarium. The prose is poetic and simple; realistic drawings illustrate the story.

CC = "Core Collection" book (see page 8).

Will We Miss Them? Endangered Species
by Alexandra Wright
illustrated by Marshall Peck III
Charlesbridge, 1992
This book asks an interesting question. Since
you rarely see a rhinoceros, a whooping crane,
or a panda, will we really miss them if they
disappear? The lively text, describing each animal's distinctive habits, along with endearing
color illustrations, help children answer "Yes!"
and know why.

EXTINCT ANIMALS (MOSTLY DINOSAURS)

CC *Digging Up Dinosaurs*
written and illustrated by Aliki
HarperCollins, 1988
Playful paleontology from Aliki: this easy-to-
read book (though probably best as a read-
aloud for many first graders) offers fun illustrations and a simple text that proceeds from the
basic identification list of dinosaurs to a discussion of the study of bones found in the ground.

CC *Dinosaur Time*
by Peggy Parish
illustrated by Arnold Lobel
HarperCollins, 1974
Written by the creator of Amelia Bedelia, this
"Reading Rainbow" book describes eleven dinosaurs in language easy enough for many begin-
ners to manage. Arnold Lobel—creator of the
popular "Frog and Toad" books—provides illustrations that combine realism and whimsy.

Tyrannosaurus Was a Beast
by Jack Prelutsky
illustrated by Arnold Lobel
William Morrow/Greenwillow, 1988
Here's a pleasant way to add a little poetry to
the study of dinosaurs, with these humorous
verses about the ever-popular creatures.

CC = "Core Collection" book (see page 8).

CC *Wild and Woolly Mammoths*
written and illustrated by Aliki
HarperCollins, 1977, revised 1996
This book introduces the woolly mammoth: its
life habits, how prehistoric peoples hunted the
mammoth, how the species became extinct, and
how scientists learn about mammoths. The illustrations in this book look as if they were coloring book drawings filled in with crayon by children—a simple and appealing technique. Part of
the Let's-Read-and-Find-Out series, listed under
Science General Resources: Series.

THE HUMAN BODY: BASIC BODY SYSTEMS AND HEALTH

Basic Body Systems

The Magic School Bus Inside the Human Body
by Joanna Cole
illustrated by Bruce Degen
Scholastic, 1989
This book mixes fantasy with science as the
Magic School Bus takes Ms. Frizzle and the
class for a fantastic voyage. They follow food as
it enters Arnold's body, moves into the blood-
stream, and circulates to the heart, lungs, and
brain. Back in the classroom, the children draw
a diagram of the body.

The Skeleton Inside You
by Philip Balestrino
illustrated by True Kelly
HarperCollins, 1989
Halloween skeletons will never look the same to
children after they have read or heard this fact-
filled book that explains the human skeleton
and considers the functions of bones. Part of the
Let's-Read-and-Find-Out series, listed under Science General Resources: Series.

What's Inside? My Body
conceived and designed by DK Direct Limited
Dorling Kindersley, 1991
This vividly illustrated book uses imaginary

cutaways to look inside the body. On the first two-page spread, for instance, a full-color photo shows a little boy spreading arms and legs wide. Opposite him, as if his outer layers have been peeled off, we see a drawing of his skeleton in the same position. Similar illustrations show us the brain, the eye, the ear, the heart, the digestive system, the limbs, and the hand. Brief read-aloud labels provide basic terminology and explain how internal parts work.

Why I Cough, Sneeze, Shiver, Hiccup, and Yawn
by Melvin Berger
illustrated by Holly Keller
HarperCollins, 1983
Starting with body phenomena every child knows—sneezes, hiccups, shivers—the author explains reflexes and the nervous system. Cute cartoon characters display body parts inside, and the book includes a simple experiment children can do with each other (tickle the bottom of their feet) to experience reflex actions.

CC *Your Insides*
by Joanna Cole
illustrated by Paul Meisel
Putnam & Grosset, 1992
This wonderful book explains each body system by comparing it to a familiar everyday object: your skeleton is like the frame of a house; your knee joint is like a hinge. Illustrated with appealing drawings of children using their bodies at work and play. Also includes a section of plastic overlays showing the insides of the body, which will fascinate young learners.

Health and Disease: Taking Care of Your Body

Bacteria and Viruses
by Leslie Jean LeMaster
Childrens Press, 1985
With large type and clearly defined concepts about the causes of disease, this book could be read aloud to teach children the scientific basis for health and hygiene practices. Brief chapters discuss germs, bacteria, viruses, fever, food spoiling, and medicines, among other topics. A number of magnified color photographs give realistic visual images of bacteria and viruses. A New True Book, listed under Science General Resources: Series.

CC *Germs Make Me Sick!*
by Melvin Berger
illustrated by Marylin Hafner
HarperCollins, 1985
This easy-reader explains the scientific meaning of that slippery word *germ*. It distinguishes viruses and bacteria in ways that a young child can understand. It helps children "see" microscopic components of blood, like white blood cells and antibodies. In the end, it offers a number of understandable explanations that underlie all those adult words of wisdom about staying healthy and clean. Pleasant color illustrations accompany the text. Part of the Let's-Read-and-Find-Out series, listed under Science General Resources: Series.

What Food Is This?
by Rosmarie Hausherr
Scholastic, 1994
A riddle-and-answer format and appealing photographs spark this study of nutritious foods. All the foods discussed are healthy and wholesome, and information on each has been shaped with an eye to explaining how they grow and why they are nutritious. The entire book is organized around the food pyramid, which is described in detail in an appendix for teachers and parents.

MATTER

Air Is All Around You
by Franklyn M. Branley
illustrated by Holly Keller
HarperCollins, 1986
With gentle language and illustrations, this book explains a difficult concept for children: that air is matter with weight and characteristics. It uses

a simple experiment that could be done at home or in the classroom to demonstrate the basic principle, and touches upon the presence of air in water and the absence of air in space. A Let's-Read-and-Find-Out book, listed under Science General Resources: Series.

Experiments with Air
by Ray Broekel
Childrens Press, 1988
This book explains a dozen simple experiments to demonstrate the properties of air, using handy materials like an aquarium, glass, string, and newspaper. Each chapter explains the principles involved in simple, readable prose and uses photos of children to demonstrate the experiments.

CC *It Could Still Be Water*
by Allan Fowler
Childrens Press, 1992
Attractive color photographs accompany simple descriptions of water's importance to life. This book introduces water's ability to change from liquid to solid or gas and ends with a two-page photo glossary. Part of the Rookie Read-About Science series; see listing in Science General Resources: Series.

Water
by Graham Peacock
Thomson Learning, 1994
Organized around simple-to-do experiments, this book helps young children understand some basic physical properties of water, including floating, water pressure, and solutions. It uses plenty of photos and drawings to illustrate every point it makes.

CC *What Happened?*
by Rozanne Lanczak Williams
illustrated by Gwen Connelly
Creative Teaching Press, 1994
This very simple reader presents changes in the state of matter through the eyes of a child. On the pond where I skated, what happened to the ice? It melted. In the water where I poured the sugar, what happened to the sugar? It dis-

solved. Soft watercolors and few words to a page help children learn these concepts while practicing their reading.

ELECTRICITY

CC *All About Electricity*
by Melvin Berger
illustrated by Marsha Winborn
Scholastic, 1995
Electricity isn't so hard a topic for first grade when it's presented in a clear, friendly way as this book does, with colorful illustrations and good ideas for activities such as making a battery out of coins and becoming an "Electric Detective" to monitor electrical safety at home.

Experiment with Magnets and Electricity
by Margaret Whalley
Lerner, 1994
See description under Science Kindergarten: Magnetism.

THE SOLAR SYSTEM

Discovering the Stars
by Laurence Santrey
illustrated by James Watling
Troll Associates, 1982
This book, simple enough to read aloud to first graders, begins with our view of the stars in the heavens, then offers an astronomer's view of stars and asteroids, using simple language, evocative illustrations, and helpful analogies. The author also introduces several familiar constellations by telling the myths behind them.

The Magic School Bus Lost in the Solar System
by Joanna Cole
illustrated by Bruce Degen
Scholastic, 1990
The Magic School Bus takes Ms. Frizzle and her class on a fantastic field trip to outer space, including a visit to each of the nine planets. A fun and informative read-aloud.

CC *The Moon Seems to Change*
by Franklyn M. Branley
illustrated by Barbara and Ed Emberley
HarperCollins, 1987
Clear text and friendly cartoon figures help project a child's imagination out to a global scale in order to understand the phases of the moon. The author also describes an easy experiment to help children see the phenomenon. Part of the Let's-Read-and-Find-Out series, listed under Science General Resources: Series.

CC *My Picture Book of the Planets*
by Nancy E. Krulik
Scholastic, 1991
The organization and simple language of this book make it an ideal starting point for the study of the planets. The author moves, planet by planet, from Mercury outward. Each planet gets two to four pages of its own, with a few basic facts conveyed in large-typesize text. Computer-enhanced NASA graphics give a sense of surface texture and colors.

The Planets in Our Solar System
by Franklyn M. Branley
illustrated by Don Madden
HarperCollins, 1987
With photos of planets, cute illustrations, and a clear text that starts with the earth and moves out through the planets, this book refers when possible to observations that can be done on earth. The book ends with two ideas for making a solar system mobile, one that hangs and one a wall mural that more accurately reflects distances between planets. A "Stage 2" book in the Let's-Read-and-Find-Out series, listed under Science General Resources: Series. Good as a read-aloud or very strong readers may be able to handle it on their own.

Postcards from Pluto: A Tour of the Solar System
written and illustrated by Loreen Leedy
Holiday House, 1993
Join a group of children on a lively tour with Dr. Quasar as they "visit" and learn about the sun and the planets from Mercury to Pluto.

CC *The Sun Is Always Shining Somewhere*
by Allan Fowler
Childrens Press, 1991
This introductory book introduces the concept that the sun is a star, and discusses our need for the sun, why it looks so large, and how the earth moves. Part of the Rookie Read-About Science series written at a first-grade reading level, listed in Science General Resources: Series.

What Makes Day and Night
by Franklyn M. Branley
illustrated by Arthur Dorros
HarperCollins, 1986
This book provides a simple discussion of how the rotation of the earth causes day and night. It suggests a demonstration using a flashlight in the dark, letting the child's body be the earth. Simple color illustrations, including a couple of lovely sunsets, enhance the book. Part of the Let's-Read-and-Find-Out series, listed under Science General Resources: Series.

THE EARTH (OUTSIDE AND INSIDE)

Earth
by Dennis B. Fradin
Childrens Press, 1989
This easy-reader book presents basic facts about the earth; it begins by identifying it as a planet in the solar system, then brings the focus down to earth's oceans and land masses. One chapter discusses its motions in space, another the layers going down to the core. Many small color photos and diagrams illustrate the book. A New True Book, listed under Science General Resources: Series.

CC = "Core Collection" book (see page 8).

CC *How to Dig a Hole to the Other Side of the Earth*
by Faith McNulty
illustrated by Marc Simont
HarperCollins, 1979
This easy reader, illustrated with two-color drawings, invites children to imagine that they are tunneling down through the center of the earth to the other side. The main character dons a diving suit to travel through water, an asbestos suit to brave the core, and makes it to the far side of the globe thanks to a specially designed submarine.

CC *It Could Still Be a Rock*
by Allan Fowler
Childrens Press, 1993
"A rock could be any size and still be a rock"—so opens this small, easy-to-read book about different rock types, rock formations, and fossils. Part of the Rookie Read-About Science series written at a first-grade reading level; see listing in Science General Resources: Series.

CC *The Magic School Bus Inside the Earth*
by Joanna Cole
illustrated by Bruce Degen
Scholastic, 1987
For those who enjoy the antics of Ms. Frizzle and her magic school bus, this book will fit right into the study of the earth's crust and core. The class jackhammers through the earth's outer layers, then plummets into a limestone cave, explores the various types of rock, and bursts out the other side, through a volcanic island.

Rocks and Minerals
by Illa Podendorf
Childrens Press, 1982
This New True Book, with large print and plenty of color pictures, provides clear and simple explanations of rocks and minerals. The author gently introduces the terms *igneous, metamorphic,* and *sedimentary.* A good book for shared reading (you read some, the child reads some) or reading aloud. For even more striking pictures, try the Eyewitness Book called *Rocks*

and Minerals by R. F. Symes (Knopf, 1988), which has extraordinary color photographs but is written for adults.

Volcanoes
by Franklyn M. Branley
illustrated by Marc Simont
HarperCollins, 1985
Branley's straightforward writing style and Simont's eye for geological perspectives combine to make this book a useful teacher/parent resource that, selectively read aloud and explained, will help first graders get a sense of how volcanoes work. The book balances between technical discussions and descriptions and pictures conveying the experience of being in or around a volcano eruption. Part of the Let's-Read-and-Find-Out series, listed under Science General Resources: Series.

BIOGRAPHIES

Rachel Carson

CC *Rachel Carson*
written and illustrated by William Accorsi
Holiday House, 1993
This picture book turns the high points of Rachel Carson's life into a story that first graders can follow. The color illustrations, primitive in style, manage to take many abstract events and turn them more literal. The text uses elementary language to talk about a number of environmental and political issues.

Rachel Carson, Friend of the Earth
by Francene Sabin
illustrated by Yoshi Miyake
Troll Associates, 1993
This book, written for slightly older children than first grade, tells Carson's life story in simple terms. Illustrated on almost every page with ink-wash drawings, the book is not divided into chapters, but could be read aloud in two or three sittings.

Thomas Edison

Thomas Edison, Great American Inventor
by Shelly Bedik
Scholastic, 1995
This black-and-white picture-book biography of
Edison begins with his boyhood and tells the
story of his youthful experiments and his great
inventions, including the light bulb, phono-
graph, and motion picture projector. A good,
brief read-aloud for this grade.

Thomas Alva Edison, Great Inventor
by David A. Adler
illustrated by Lyle Miller
Holiday House, 1990
Written in simple language and divided into
short chapters, this large-format biography
could be read aloud to first graders. It singles
out some amusing incidents in Edison's life, as
well as relating the expected key events. Every
spread has a pencil drawing.

Louis Pasteur

Louis Pasteur
by Rae Bains
illustrated by Dick Smolinski
Troll Associates, 1985
A short book with color illustrations on every
spread, this biography spans Pasteur's lifetime
and briefly introduces the concepts of bacteria,
fermentation, pasteurization, and vaccination.
All or part could be used for reading aloud.

Louis Pasteur: Enemy of Disease
by Carol Greene
Childrens Press, 1990
Parts of this informative, large-print biography
can be read to first graders, especially the chapter on testing the rabies vaccine.

SCIENCE

Grade 2

SEASONAL CYCLES

Animals in Winter
written and illustrated by Susanne Riha
Carolrhoda, 1989
This is a beautiful book featuring twelve animals that hibernate. Each animal is examined in a two-page spread, with four to five paragraphs on one page describing the animal's habits and, on the facing page, a large illustration framed by ten smaller illustrations showing the animal's habits at different points in the year. The one drawback of this book is that many of the animals are European, such as the hedgehog, the dormouse, and the European hamster. The publisher, aware of this potential problem for American children, includes a list of parallel North American animals in the back.

Dear Rebecca, Winter Is Here
by Jean Craighead George
illustrated by Loretta Krupinski
HarperCollins, 1993
A poetical grandmother writes a letter to her granddaughter, evoking all the feelings and experiences of winter, and in the meantime explaining what the winter solstice means. Beautiful paintings illustrate this quiet, affectionate book about winter.

Red Leaf, Yellow Leaf
written and illustrated by Lois Ehlert
Harcourt Brace, 1991
A child describes the life of a sugar maple, observing it through all the seasons. The illustrations of this book are fascinating collages that combine cut-paper art and real objects, like maple twigs, burlap, ribbon, and a nursery tag for a maple tree. The book is fun to read and fun to look at too.

Spring (1990)
Summer (1991)
Winter (1990)
Fall (1991)
by Ron Hirschi
photography by Thomas D. Mangelsen
Cobblehill Books
Quiet, lyrical language and sensitive photographs in these four large-format companion volumes explore the phenomena of the seasons.

Why Do Leaves Change Color?
by Betsy Maestro
illustrated by Loretta Krupinski
HarperCollins, 1994
This book combines nice descriptions of autumn with scientific explanations of how and why the leaves change color and fall in autumn. Friendly color illustrations help children identify the trees from which they find autumn leaves. A Level 2 book in the Let's-Read-and-Find-Out series, listed under Science General Resources: Series.

LIFE CYCLES

The Caterpillar and the Polliwog
written and illustrated by Jack Kent
Simon & Schuster/Half Moon Books, 1982
In this delightful book, a little polliwog watches his caterpillar friend change into a butterfly without realizing that he is changing too.

Egg: A Photographic Story of Hatching
by Robert Burton
photography by Jane Burton and Kim Taylor
Dorling Kindersley, 1994
This beautifully designed book begins by considering general topics having to do with the developing egg, then shows in crisp color photographs the hatching process of twenty-seven different animals, including fifteen different birds, from swan to starling, and twelve other animals, including snake, gecko, goldfish, and slug. A few facts about each animal are included on the pages, but the strength of this book comes from its wonderful pictures of a range of animals that hatch out of eggs.

From Tadpole to Frog
by Wendy Pfeffer
illustrated by Holly Keller
HarperCollins, 1994
An easy-to-read book with pleasant illustrations, chronicling the life cycle of a frog from spring awakening and egg-laying to maturity and winter hibernation. The last two pages identify five common frog species. Part of the Let's-Read-and-Find-Out series, listed under Science General Resources: Series.

CC *A Nest Full of Eggs*
by Priscilla Belz Jenkins
illustrated by Lizzy Rockwell
HarperCollins, 1995
Using observations of a robin as a frame for discussion, this book displays the diversity of nests, eggs, and feathers. Cheery color illustrations accompany the simple text. It includes a four-stage diagram of a bird developing inside an egg and suggestions on how to set out nesting materials for wild birds nearby. Part of the Let's-Read-and-Find-Out series, listed under Science General Resources: Series.

CC *The Reason for a Flower*
written and illustrated by Ruth Heller
Grosset & Dunlap, 1983
Bursting with lovely color illustrations and sparse, careful text, this book explains a plant's

cycle through flowers, pollen, and seeds to roots and trees, and introduces a few technical terms for flower parts.

Tadpole and Frog
by Christine Back
photographs by Barrie Watts
Silver Burdett, 1986
With clear language, color photos that focus precisely on important details, and accompanying sketches, this book provides a good basic rendition of the life cycle of the frog that you can read aloud to second graders.

WEATHER

The Cloud Book
written and illustrated by Tomie de Paola
Holiday House, 1975
De Paola uses his familiar storybook-style drawings to help children learn to identify many types of clouds. The text does a nice job linking myths and legends about clouds with a child's own imaginary tendency to see shapes in the sky.

Feel the Wind
written and illustrated by Arthur Dorros
HarperCollins, 1989
With pretty drawings and readable text, this book explores the mysteries of the wind, which we cannot see but which we feel and hear. Some pages discuss the wind as a function of global air masses, and others describe how wind affects weather and climate. The book includes directions on how to make a weather vane.

CC *How's the Weather?*
by Melvin and Gilda Berger
illustrated by John Emil Cymerman
Ideals, 1993
This is an easy reader designed to help get children thinking and talking about the weather. In prose that most second graders can manage, it asks and answers "why" questions about

weather phenomena, suggests basic scientific experiments, and tells about modern weather-prediction techniques. Friendly color illustrations.

It's Raining Cats and Dogs: All Kinds of Weather and Why We Have It
by Franklyn M. Branley
illustrated by True Kelley
Houghton Mifflin, 1987
This is a fun book, divided into bite-sized pieces but offering a lot of information for a second-grade study of weather. Branley mixes scientific fact with funny asides like "How many snow-flakes in a snowstorm?" He includes a number of easy experiments, weather observation tips, and weather safety practices, as well as clear explanations, helped by amusing drawings, of common and not-so-common weather phenomena.

CC Sun Up, Sun Down
written and illustrated by Gail Gibbons
Harcourt Brace, 1983
Written in the voice of a little girl, this book weaves together commonsense observations and basic scientific facts to introduce important weather concepts. "The storm clouds begin to drift away. Although it is still sprinkling, the sun appears once again and shines through the raindrops. I see a beautiful rainbow. My mom says the light of the sun shining through the raindrops makes the rainbow." This accessible language and cute, colorful geometric drawings help convey complex concepts like the earth's water cycle and how rainbows form.

Water, Water Everywhere
by Mark J. Rauzon and Cynthia Overbeck Bix
Sierra Club Books for Children, 1994
With careful, poetic language and crisp, colorful photographs, this book explains the omnipresence and the preciousness of water on our planet. It moves through the water cycle, through the regions of the world, and through a discussion of pollution.

Weather Words and What They Mean
written and illustrated by Gail Gibbons
Holiday House, 1990
Gibbons takes a straightforward approach to introducing the most basic ideas about weather, by defining and using the most common words in meteorology. She includes simple words like *hot, cold, sun,* and *rain,* but also more complex words like *air pressure, dew, front,* and *sleet.* The book's simple language and picture-book illustrations help to convey facts and lay the groundwork for understanding the phenomena of weather.

CC Where Do Puddles Go?
by Fay Robinson
Childrens Press, 1995
Most second graders will be able to read this book about the water cycle, which helps them learn about evaporation and condensation by observing things in their daily life. Most of the illustrations are color photos of children, and the book includes one excellent diagram conveying the principles of the water cycle. A Rookie Read-About Science book, listed under Science General Resources: Series.

INSECTS

Amazing Insects
by Laurence Mound
photography by Frank Greenaway
Alfred A. Knopf, 1993
Like others in this series, this book offers facts and tidbits about insects in bite-sized pieces. It combines larger-than-life photos and color illustrations, both realistic and comical. Part of the Eyewitness Junior series, listed under Science General Resources: Series.

CC = "Core Collection" book (see page 8).

Ant
by Michael Chinery
illustrated by Nichola Armstrong
photographs by Barrie Watts
Troll Associates, 1991
This book's strength lies in the intelligent inter-action of huge color photographs and delicate color drawings on every facing page. The photos show real-life ants; the illustrations are geared to reveal facts and features discussed in the simple, factual text. Also in this Life Story series: *Butterfly, Snake,* and *Spider.*

Armies of Ants
by Walter Retan
illustrated by Jean Cassels
Scholastic, 1994
Written for the second- and third-grade reader, this book dives deeply into the world of ants. Chapters focus on soldier ants in the rainforest, on ant physiology, on social cooperation, among other things. Detailed illustrations: every page is swarming with ants!

CC *The Bee, Friend of the Flowers*
written and photographed by Paul Starosta
Charlesbridge, 1992
This book's clearly written factual text tells the life cycle of the bee and the hive. Sharp color photographs, three or more on every page, make you feel as though you are right there in-side the beehive.

The Big Bug Book
by Margery Facklam
illustrated by Paul Facklam
Little, Brown, 1994
This book intrigues young readers by introduc-ing a baker's dozen of the world's largest in-sects. The illustrator conveys just how large the insects are by setting them among familiar ob-jects, like a baseball and bat or a box of crayons. Each insect gets two pages, filled with a life-sized color illustration and a few interesting paragraphs each.

CC *Bugs*
by Nancy Winslow Parker and Joan Richards Wright
illustrations by Nancy Winslow Parker
Greenwillow/Mulberry Books, 1987
The pages of this entertaining Reading Rainbow book alternate between simple rhyming ques-tions and answers ("What bug fell into Ben's broth? A moth.") on the left-hand page and brief scientific descriptions of the insect being featured on the right, with well-labeled color drawings. Several pages at the end of the book present a visual glossary, defining terms about insect life cycles and body parts.

Caterpillar Caterpillar
by Vivian French
illustrated by Charlotte Voake
Candlewick Press, 1993
A girl with a wise gardener for a grandfather learns about caterpillars by observing eggs hatch on nettles, then distinguishing many types of caterpillars, and finally watching a pupa hatch into a butterfly on her windowsill. The illustrations, done with a light touch, add fur-ther information.

It's a Good Thing There Are Insects
by Allan Fowler
Childrens Press, 1990
This book introduces language and ideas about insects in large type, making it a good book for beginning readers to use to practice research, es-pecially considering its photo-keyed glossary of insect terms and index at the back. Color photo-graphs display many familiar insects. Part of the Rookie Read-About Science series, listed under Science General Resources: Series.

Ladybug
by Barrie Watts
Silver Burdett, 1987
Each page, headed by a thematic sentence, de-scribes a different stage in the life cycle of a ladybug, from mating through eggs, larvae, pupa, to adult. The text of this Reading Rain-bow book can probably be read by many sec-

ond graders. Photos illustrate the entire process and also review the full cycle on one page at the end.

Where Butterflies Grow
by Joanne Ryder
illustrated by Lynne Cherry
Lodestar, 1989
With lyrical language and color illustrations rich in detail, this book invites children to imagine themselves as a maturing swallowtail, first as a hatching egg, then a caterpillar, then a butterfly. The book's last two pages repeat the story more technically, giving advice on how to hatch butterflies at home.

Where's That Insect?
by Barbara Brenner and Bernice Chardiet
illustrated by Carol Schwartz
Scholastic/Cartwheel, 1993
Vivid color illustrations accompany interesting text that introduces a variety of insects, including leafcutter ants, monarch butterflies, dragonflies, honeybees, crickets, aphids, and more. A good read-aloud, and fun to look at, as the text often asks the child to look for the insects in the pictures.

THE HUMAN BODY

Cells

CC *Cells and Tissues*
by Leslie Jean LeMaster
Childrens Press, 1985
This book uses simple yet technically accurate language, color photos of people, microscopic views of cells and tissues, and labeled drawings to provide a solid basic introduction to the concepts of cells, tissues, organs, and body systems. A New True Book, listed under Science General Resources: Series.

CC = "Core Collection" book (see page 8).

Greg's Microscope
by Millicent E. Selsam
illustrated by Arnold Lobel
HarperCollins, 1963
This easy reader makes a story out of a young boy's first experiences with his microscope. He views salt, sugar, onion skin, and his own hair, and makes all the common mistakes, like presuming air bubbles are huge cells. This book would be fun for children who have shared Greg's experience as well as for those who are just learning about microscopes and the world of things we can't see with the naked eye.

Digestive and Excretory Systems

CC *Nutrition: What's in the Food We Eat*
by Dorothy Hinshaw Patent
photography by William Munoz
Holiday House, 1992
Straightforward text and pictures convey the basics of nutrition, including carbohydrates, protein, fat, vitamins, and minerals, as well as principles of healthy eating by way of explaining how the body uses food. The book includes a recipe for homemade soft pretzels, charts of calories and fat contents for several foods, and the federally approved food pyramid.

CC *What Happens to a Hamburger*
by Paul Showers
illustrated by Anne Rockwell
HarperCollins, 1985
With simple language and diagrams, this informative book describes the process of digestion, from the first bite of food on down, and how the food we digest is essential for energy, bones, and muscles. The labeled pictures help children get a mental picture of what goes on inside their bodies, and the full text can be read by some second graders. A Reading Rainbow book, part of the Let's-Read-and-Find-Out series, listed under Science General Resources: Series.

Magnetism

📖 **CC** *All About Magnets*
by Stephen Krensky
illustrated by Paul Meisel
Scholastic, 1992
Cute, cartoony drawings accompany text that gets quite serious, discussing the arrangements of molecules in a magnet, magnetic poles of the earth, and Oersted's early work in electromagnetism. The clear writing makes these big ideas understandable, and offers a number of projects to learn about magnetic phenomena. A tiny bar magnet comes attached to the inside back cover of this book.

Experiment with Magnets and Electricity
by Margaret Whalley
Lerner, 1994
See description under Science Kindergarten: Magnetism.

Experiments with Magnets
by Helen J. Challand
Childrens Press, 1986
See description under Science Kindergarten: Magnetism.

The Science Book of Magnets
by Neil Ardley
Harcourt Brace/Gulliver Books, 1991
This attractive introductory book suggests fifteen hands-on experiments with magnets. The experiments are arranged by level of difficulty.

Tools and Simple Machines

Experiment with Movement
by Bryan Murphy
Scholastic, 1991
Vivid color photographs and simple hands-on activities help children understand the sometimes abstract terms and concepts introduced in this book, including *force, movement, inertia, friction*, and *gravity*. Brief chapters address gears, pulleys, and levers.

Forces
by Graham Peacock
Thomson Learning, 1994
This book contains a series of simple experiments and explores several different physical forces, including gravity, friction, centrifugal force, flotation, and magnetic force. The text is clearly addressed to the young reader and many illustrations, both drawings and photos, illuminate the directions. For each experiment, the principles involved are summarized clearly.

Lifting by Levers
by Andrew Dunn
illustrated by Ed Carr
Thomson Learning, 1993
This book defines basic concepts of physics, like *lever* and *machine*, and invites children to find examples of physics in use in the world around them. It has clear, simple language and illuminating drawings accessible to second graders. Part of the How Things Work series, listed under Science General Resources: Series. Companion books in the series are equally good: *Simple Slopes* and *Wheels at Work*, for example.

Machines
written and illustrated by Anne and Harlow
 Rockwell
Macmillan, 1972
Very simple text and watercolor paintings identify simple tools and machines, from levers and wheels to egg beaters and bicycles.

📖 **CC** *Simple Machines*
by Ann Horvatic
photographs by Stephen Bruner
E. P. Dutton, 1989
Clear text and excellent black-and-white photographs describe simple machines we use every day, from seesaws to scissors. Others include wedges, inclined planes, screws, wheels, and levers. The book will help children identify these simple machines in their daily lives and group them together according to the jobs they perform.

BIOGRAPHIES

Anton van Leeuwenhoek

CC *The Microscope*
by Maxine Kumin
illustrated by Arnold Lobel
HarperCollins, 1984
In this little volume, the text of a fanciful poem about van Leeuwenhoek is illustrated with round and jolly ink drawings by the popular children's illustrator Arnold Lobel. The poem is spread out, few words to every page, making this an enjoyable easy reader for adults and children alike.

Elijah McCoy

Elijah McCoy, Inventor
by Garnet Nelson Jackson
illustrated by Gary Thomas
Modern Curriculum Press, 1993
With some help on the big words, many second graders should be able to read this short, colorfully illustrated story of the man who invented a way to lubricate the wheels of railroad cars while they were still moving. This story ends on an upbeat note by explaining the origin of the phrase *the real McCoy*. For a more detailed life story of McCoy, best as a read-aloud at this grade level, see Wendy Towle's *The Real McCoy: The Life of an African-American Inventor*, illustrated by Wil Clay (Scholastic, 1993).

Five Notable Inventors
by Wade Hudson
illustrated by Ron Garnett
Scholastic, 1995
In this easy reader, second graders can acquaint themselves with Elijah McCoy and four other African-American inventors. The section on McCoy is seven pages long, illustrated with both period photos and attractive watercolors, and tells of the high points of McCoy's career.

Florence Nightingale

Florence Nightingale
by Anne Colver
Chelsea House, 1992
Part of the publisher's Discovery Biographies series directed to children from seven to twelve years old, this eighty-page life story of the English pioneer of nursing is a good teacher/parent resource at this grade level.

Daniel Hale Williams

Black Pioneers of Science and Invention
by Louis Haber
Harcourt Brace Jovanovich, 1970
A twenty-four page chapter in this helpful teacher/parent resource book is devoted to Williams, a pioneer in heart surgery and founder of the first interracial hospital in the United States. See also the description of this book under Science General Resources: Biography Collections.

SCIENCE

Grade 3

FISH

Do Fishes Get Thirsty?
by Les Kaufman
New England Aquarium/Franklin Watts, 1991
Books that use a question-and-answer format can be mechanical, but not this one. The questions were selected to engage children—Do fishes make good parents? Can fishes talk? Do fishes go to school? The answers are full of clear, detailed information, and are amplified with excellent color photography.

CC *What Is a Fish?*
by Barbara R. Stratton
New England Aquarium/Franklin Watts, 1991
Well coordinated text and photographs make this book almost as good as a guided tour of the aquarium. For example, the page that explains how fish breathe faces a full-page color close-up of fish gills. Advanced readers will be able to make it through the whole book, while others can dip in and find facts and explanations that interest them, or navigate the book with an adult.

AMPHIBIANS AND REPTILES

CC *Frog*
by Michael Chinery
photography by Barrie Watts
illustrated by Martin Camm
Troll Associates, 1991
Intelligent interactions between text, illustrations, and a larger-than-life photo on every page make this book a valuable guide to the life cycle and habits of frogs. The text is written at an appropriate level for most third-grade readers.

Frogs and Toads
by Bobbie Kalman and Tammy Everts
Crabtree, 1994
The photo on the front cover says it all: a horny toad, his pink slimy mouth gorging on a grimy worm. Yucky and wonderful! Big color photographs show many varieties of frogs and toads, with accompanying text that most third graders can read on their own.

CC *Snake*
by Michael Chinery
photography by Barrie Watts
illustrated by Denys Ovenden
Troll Associates, 1991
This book combines large color photos, related illustrations, and just the right amount of text to make for a satisfying source of information on snakes, readable by most third graders.

BIRDS

Amazing Birds
by Alexandra Parsons
photography by Jerry Young
Alfred A. Knopf, 1990
This generously illustrated book defines birds, then singles out nine interesting birds, from the hummingbird to the vulture and ostrich, with color photos and brief spans of text. One section explains how birds fly. An Eyewitness Junior book, listed under Science General Resources: Series.

Birds
by Peter Alden and Fiona Reid
illustrated by John Fill
Houghton Mifflin, 1987
This Peterson Field Guide Coloring Book begins
with a few pages introducing the biology and
identification of birds, then presents a book full
of carefully drawn outlines of the birds of North
America, with accompanying text just as one
would read in a field guide. It's a nice way to
encourage the observation of detail and color.

MAMMALS

Amazing Mammals
by Alexandra Parson
photography by Jerry Young
Alfred A. Knopf, 1990
Like other Eyewitness Junior books, this vividly
illustrated volume spends two pages establish-
ing the defining characteristics of a mammal,
then introduces nine different interesting mammals, from bats to monkeys to tigers, with color
photos and small bits of text.

Forest Mammals
written and illustrated by Glen Loates
Crabtree, 1993
This book about North American forest-dwell-
ing mammals is a vehicle for the author's lovely
wilderness art. For each of about fifteen mammals, he presents a full-color painting that captures the animal's spirit. Facing the paintings
are passages about that animal's habitat and
features. The book begins with a discussion of
basic ecology and ends with a personal note
from Loate, which may inspire observation, creativity, and environmental consciousness among
young readers.

Mammals
by Peter Alden and Fiona Reid
illustrated by Fiona Reid
Houghton Mifflin, 1987
This Peterson Field Guide Coloring Book combines basic information about North American
mammals and how to identify them with pages
of carefully drawn outlines, accompanied by
field-guide–like text.

Sea Mammals
by Anita Ganeri
illustrated by Dennis Ovenden and Malcolm
    McGregor
Raintree/Steck-Vaughan, 1994
By grouping polar bears and sea otters along
with whales, dolphins, and porpoises, this book
makes clear which seagoing animals are mammals. Each animal gets two pages of attention,
with color illustrations and a small number of
interesting facts keyed to illustrations.

THE HUMAN BODY
See also Science General Resources: The Human Body.

The Brain: What It Is, What It Does
by Dr. Ruth Dowling Bruun and Dr. Bertel
    Bruun
illustrated by Peter Bruun
Greenwillow Books, 1989
This easy reader, illustrated with little cartoon
drawings, makes the brain and its functions accessible to young students. The book includes
not only basic nervous system physiology, but
also discussions of intelligence, emotions, and
sleep.

A Book About Your Skeleton
by Ruth Belov Gross
illustrated by Steve Björkman
Scholastic, 1978 (illustrations 1994)
This easy-to-read book offers lively writing ("If
you didn't have bones, you would flop around
like spaghetti") and amusing illustrations to introduce children to the skeletal system. An earlier edition with different illustrations (by Deborah Robison) may be available in some libraries.

Discover Bones: Explore the Science of Skeletons
by Lesley Grant
Addison-Wesley, 1992
This book about bones suggests more than forty
activities, all designed to reveal such things as
the structure of the human spine, what happens
when bones break, the role of bones in archeol-
ogy, and more. The book contains games, fun
facts, and art activities.

Professor I.Q Explores the Brain
by Seymour Simon
illustrated by Dennis Kendrick
Boyds Mills Press, 1993
Funny, cartoonish illustrations and clear writing, good for reading aloud with third graders,
distinguish this introduction to the brain and
how it works. The lively presentation, hosted by
the rather daffy Professor I.Q., makes it easy to
deal with terms such as "cerebral cortex," "syn-
apse," and "electroencephalograph." Sprinkled
throughout the book are interesting "Try This"
activities that help children understand the
sometimes challenging concepts.

Your Brain and Nervous System
by Leslie Jean LeMaster
Childrens Press, 1984
With clear language in large type, color photos,
and well-labeled drawings, this serious book introduces the basic anatomy and functions of the
brain and the nervous system. It defines and
uses a number of technical concepts, like the au-
tonomic, central, and peripheral nervous systems. It offers basic information on the spinal
cord and nerve-cell formations, and discusses
reflex movements and sleep. A New True Book,
listed under Science General Resources: Series.

CC = **"Core Collection"** book (see page 8).

SOUND AND HEARING

All About Sound
by Melvin Berger
illustrated by Cynthia Fisher
Scholastic, 1994
This easy-to-read book clearly explains interesting facts about sound and offers ideas for some
simple experiments and activities, such as finding your vocal cords, making a simple stetho-
scope, and making a string telephone.

Ears Are for Hearing
by Paul Showers
illustrated by Holly Keller
HarperCollins, 1990
This book explains the workings of the ear in
simple words and pictures. Some pages are perhaps too simple, but the anatomical cross-sections of the ear are sophisticated enough to inform and engage most third graders. Part of the
Let's-Read-and-Find-Out series, listed under Science General Resources: Series.

Sound
by Graham Peacock
Thomson Learning, 1993
Most third graders will be able to read this
book and, with a little help, work through some
of its many suggested activities. The text discusses basics such as sound waves, echoes, and
the speed of sound. Clever drawings and cheerful photos of children performing the experiments perk up every page of the book.

CC *Sound Experiments*
by Ray Broekel
Childrens Press, 1983
Many third graders will be able to read this
New True Book on their own, but you will want
to help discuss the concepts and carry out some
of the many simple experiments suggested in
the book. The author offers clear, concise explanations of many topics including sound and vibration, pitch, sound waves, how sound travels
in different media, and more. Illustrated with
color photographs.

LIGHT AND OPTICS: AN INTRODUCTION

All About Light: A Do-It-Yourself Science Book
by Melvin Berger
illustrated by Blanche Sims
Scholastic, 1995
This friendly and colorful book offers simple explanations of light, lenses, and various terms (such as *transparent* and *opaque),* as well as ideas for easy hands-on experiments with light, for example, seeing light bend and making a color wheel.

Bending Light
by Pat Murphy
illustrated by Denise Brunkus
Little, Brown, 1992
Devoted to the spirit of "fooling around" as a way to explore the physical world, this book describes fifteen experiments with light and lenses, including full explanations of the science involved and further questions to keep you thinking. Experiments include making lenses of Jell-O and ice. The book comes with a small plastic lens.

Lenses! Take a Closer Look
by Siegfried Aust
illustrated by Helge Nyncke
Lerner, 1991
A colorful romp through the history and sciences of lenses, this book engages a child's curiosity with a different topic on every page, from glasses and optical illusions to the telescope and the microscope. The author offers suggestions and plans for several activities, including building your own periscope and kaleidoscope. Tests for vision and color blindness are included.

Light
by Graham Peacock
Thomson Learning, 1993
Funny drawings and attractive photos of children make this book an appealing way to explore the world of light and sight. It is divided into a number of sections and projects, written at a level that most third graders will understand and enjoy. Instructions for a flipbook, a pinhole camera, a periscope, and other projects are included.

ECOLOGY

Air Pollution
by Darlene R. Stille
Childrens Press, 1990
Building upon a good discussion of air and how we breathe, this easy reader gives a lot of specific information about air pollution: how it happens, why it is dangerous, and what to do about it. The book is illustrated with color photos and has large type. A New True Book, listed under Science General Resources: Series.

Earth Child: Games, Stories, Activities, Experiments & Ideas About Living Lightly on Planet Earth
by Kathryn Sheehan and Mary Waidner
Council Oaks Books, 1991
This is a generous collection of activities and ideas meant to promote ecological consciousness and respect. Each chapter includes a list of further resources. It may be ordered directly from the publisher: (800) 247-8850.

CC *50 Simple Things Kids Can Do to Save the Earth*
by The Earth Works Groups
Andrews & McMeel, 1990
Instead of preaching, this book organizes its ideas into fifty subjects on which the authors want to build children's environmental consciences—Styrofoam, water consumption, batteries, heat escape, and more. Each subject unfolds through a quiz question, a short bit of information, and then a list of project activities.

Global Change
by Theodore P. Snow
Childrens Press, 1990
In careful, readable prose accompanied by small color photographs, this book explains how the

forces of weather and human culture affect global change. Chapters include "Changes Long Ago," "The Loss of Ozone," and "Destruction of Habitats." The book concludes with a chapter on large- and small-scale efforts to protect our planet. A New True Book, listed under Science General Resources: Series.

Scavengers and Decomposers: Nature's Clean Up Crew
by Pat Hughey
illustrated by Bruce Hiscock
Atheneum, 1984
This is a lovely little book about an unappetizing but important subject: the animals that clean up the world. Seagulls, vultures, raccoons, rats, hyenas, dung beetles, earthworms, slugs are all introduced here, showing how their work fits into the cycles of nature. The language is clear and precise, the science is expressed well, and the line illustrations are delicate and informative.

CC *Tree of Life: The World of the African Baobab*
written and illustrated by Barbara Bash
Little, Brown/Sierra Club Books, 1989
Vivid, detailed watercolor illustrations and clearly written text tell a story of the interdependence of plants, animals, and people in an African ecosystem at the center of which is the extraordinary baobab tree. Good as a read-aloud or for independent reading. If you like this book, also see, by the same author, *Desert Giant: The World of the Saguaro Cactus* (Little, Brown, 1989).

Water Pollution
by Darlene R. Stille
Childrens Press, 1990
With easy-to-read text and color photos on every page, this book introduces the importance of water to the world, then explores the nature and extent of water pollution today. It uses some technical language, taking care to introduce it properly, and builds upon the concept of the balance of nature to explain problems in

the world's bodies of water. A New True Book, listed under Science General Resources: Series.

ASTRONOMY

The Beginning of the Earth
by Franklyn M. Branley
illustrated by Giulio Maestro
HarperCollins, 1988
With clear language and illustrations, some close to abstract art, this book outlines a theory of how the earth and solar system began to form out of a massive cloud of dust and gases billions of years ago. The author and illustrator take events and concepts that are hard to imagine and manage to bring them to some level of concrete reality. Part of the Let's-Read-and-Find-Out series, listed under Science General Resources: Series.

CC *Comets, Meteors, and Asteroids*
by Seymour Simon
William Morrow, 1994
With a large-page format and up-to-date information, this book includes some amazing photos, not only those taken in space but also several on land, conveying the scale and power of comets and meteors. For a book on the same topic that third graders can read independently, try the New True Book called *Comets, Asteroids, and Meteors* by Dennis Fradin (Childrens Press, 1984).

Discovery Atlas of Planets and Stars
Rand McNally, 1990
This book gives a broad-reaching combination of photographs from space, illustrations, diagrams, and maps. It discusses the Earth, the planets, stars, galaxies, and constellations.

Earth: Our Planet in Space
by Seymour Simon
Four Winds Press, 1984
This striking book, with large pages in black and white, uses recent photographs of earth taken from space to convey a sense of the globe

as a planet. It explains seasons, discusses the atmosphere and earth's magnetic field, and uses aerial shots to portray the earth's surface and how it has changed under human influence.

Eclipse: Darkness in Daytime
by Franklyn M. Branley
illustrated by Donald Crews
HarperCollins, 1988
The author begins where we all begin—amazed, even scared, by an eclipse—and carries children through systematic scientific explanation to an understanding of how an eclipse happens. Crews's pastel airbrush illustrations help explain the concepts. The book includes advice and instructions on how to view an eclipse. Part of the Let's-Read-and-Find-Out series, listed under Science General Resources: Series.

CC Find the Constellations
written and illustrated by H. A. Rey
Houghton Mifflin, 1976
A revised edition of a classic book on constellations, written and illustrated with great humor by the beloved author of the Curious George books. Rey shares his fascination with the constellations, telling the myths and stories behind them as well as offering practical advice on how to find them in the night sky. Many star maps illustrate the book. This popular book is in its twenty-sixth printing.

CC Gravity Is a Mystery
by Franklyn M. Branley
illustrated by Don Madden
HarperCollins, 1986
Why does a ball come down when you throw it? Why do astronauts bounce around so easily on the moon? This book answers such questions and links a child's experience of gravity—sitting in a chair or lifting a rock—with the gravity one would feel on the other planets. Like all the books in this series, it combines clear explanations about important scientific topics with lighthearted yet reliably factual illustrations. A Let's-Read-and-Find-Out book, listed under Science General Resources: Series.

Jupiter (1985)
Saturn (1985)
Mars (1987)
Uranus (1987)
Neptune (1991)
Mercury (1992)
Venus (1992)
by Seymour Simon
Morrow Junior Books
Each of the books in this handsome series takes a detailed look at one planet, through explanatory text and terrific color photographs. The advantage of the series is its large-page format, which allows big photos and big print. The author moves through the history of discovering and naming the planets and their moons, and gives some explanation of how contemporary images of outer space have been generated.

Moon Flights
by Dennis B. Fradin
Childrens Press, 1985
The author begins this book with a quick history of flight, then details the Apollo 11 moon launch, that culminated in "one small step for a man, one giant leap for mankind." He then outlines what we have learned from moon launches and what we may yet accomplish from more. Photos from the launches help illustrate the text. The language is serious but easy to read. A New True Book, listed under Science General Resources: Series.

CC Our Solar System
by Seymour Simon
William Morrow, 1992
Teachers and parents can share parts of the text with third graders; the remarkable photographs will enthrall all. A handsome, large-format, full-color book that starts big—with a vision of where our solar system fits into the galaxy—then zeroes in on each planet and many of their moons.

CC = "Core Collection" book (see page 8).

Shooting Stars
by Franklyn M. Branley
illustrated by Holly Keller
HarperCollins, 1989
This book quickly explains that shooting stars
are not stars but meteoroids and (when they hit
the earth) meteorites. Keller's cute cartoons and
several actual photos of craters accompany the
basic, readable text, which plays around with
the concept of "catch a falling star." Part of the
Let's-Read-and-Find-Out series, listed under Science General Resources: Series.

CC *Space*
by Ian Ridpath
Kingfisher Books, 1992
This large-format book, with many color illustrations and a sensible design, offers basic information about stars, the planets, and galaxies. A
significant portion of the book focuses on the
exploration of space, explaining how rockets are
propelled, how Skylab and the Hubble space
telescope work, and what the future of space
exploration may bring.

The Universe: Think Big
by Jeanne Bendick
illustrated by Lynne Willey and Mike Roffe
Millbrook, 1991
This attractive book, written at about fourth-
grade reading level, explains what the universe
is and where we live in it. It also explains how
we measure the great distances in space and introduces the Big Bang Theory. Other titles in
this series, also written by Bendick, are: *The
Sun, The Planets,* and *The Stars.*

Why Doesn't the Earth Fall Up?
by Vicki Cobb
illustrated by Ted Enik
E. P. Dutton, 1988
This book answers nine not-so-dumb questions
like "If the earth is spinning, why don't we feel
it move?" The text uses a combination of common sense and simple experiments to replicate
the historical findings of great scientists like Copernicus, Galileo, and Newton.

BIOGRAPHIES

Alexander Graham Bell

*Ahoy! Ahoy! Are You There? A Story of
Alexander Graham Bell*
written and illustrated by Robert Quackenbush
Prentice Hall, 1981
With its lively writing and witty illustrations,
this book would make a good read-aloud. It
tells the story of the boy with "an inventive and
inquisitive mind" who grew up to invent the
telephone. Some technical vocabulary will require explanation, but in general the book keeps
things clear and accessible.

Mae Jemison

Mae Jemison, Astronaut
by Garnet Nelson Jackson
illustrated by Fred Willingham
Modern Curriculum Press, 1994
The doctor and astronaut on the space shuttle
Endeavour emerges as a role model in this positive, upbeat little biography, easily readable at
this grade level. Available as part of a series
(Beginning Biographies: African Americans II),
with optional posters and a teaching guide.

John Muir

John Muir: Man of the Wild Places
by Carol Greene
Childrens Press, 1991
Illustrated on every page with many photographs and drawings, this Rookie Biography
can be read by third graders, who will learn
from it about the pioneering protector of the
wilderness who helped to found the Sierra
Club.

SCIENCE

Grade 4

THE HUMAN BODY

See also Science General Resources: The Human Body.

CC *A Drop of Blood*
by Paul Showers
illustrated by Don Madden
HarperCollins, 1989 (revised edition)
This Let's-Read-and-Find-Out Science Book offers a friendly, easy-to-read introduction to what makes up our blood, with amusing, cartoon-like illustrations. Also recommended is another volume by the same author, out of print but worth seeking in libraries, called *Hear Your Heart,* which offers a straightforward, readable introduction to the circulatory system.

The Heart and Blood
by Jan Burgess
Silver Burdett, 1988
This forty-five-page book introduces students to the circulatory system, including how to keep it healthy. Clear diagrams and color photographs accompany the text, suitable for strong readers or as a teacher/parent resource.

The Lungs and Breathing
by Mark Lambert
Silver Burdett, 1988
Written for fifth to eighth graders, this book, with clear diagrams and color photographs, can be used as a parent/teacher resource for introducing students to the respiratory system, including how to keep it healthy.

CC = "Core Collection" book (see page 8).

Ouch! A Book About Cuts, Scratches, and Scrapes
by Melvin Berger
illustrated by Pat Stewart
Lodestar, 1991
Any child who has asked for a Band-Aid will be interested in this little book, which explains in clear and readable words how the body stops bleeding and works to heal itself when a cut, scratch, or scrape occurs.

Your Heart and Blood
by Leslie Jean LeMaster
Childrens Press, 1984
This New True Book should be easy reading for fourth graders, but nonetheless very informative. Chapters address questions like What is blood? Why does a cut bleed? What are blood vessels? How does the heart pump blood? The book also offers a brief introduction to different blood types. Illustrated with many color drawings and photographs, including photos of the human heart.

CHEMISTRY: BASIC TERMS AND CONCEPTS

See also the listings under Science General Resources: Experiments and Activities. Schools may want to examine the prepackaged materials for experiments available in various elementary school science programs; see the list of Science Curriculum Modules in Science: General Resources.

CC *Adventures with Atoms and Molecules: Chemistry Experiments for Young People*
by Robert C. Mebane and Thomas R. Rybolt
Enslow, 1985
This is the first of five books by the same title from the same authors and publisher (Book II, 1987; Book III, 1991; Book IV, 1992; Book V, 1995). Each book presents clear, concise directions for thirty experiments, all framed as questions, for example, "Can the flavor of apples be separated from apple cider vinegar? Does air have weight? Can large crystals be made from small molecules? Are there carbon dioxide molecules in your breath?" Each experiment includes a brief "Discussion" section that explores relevant chemical terms and concepts. The authors have designed the experiments for children from fourth to sixth grade.

Janice VanCleave's Chemistry for Every Kid: 101 Easy Experiments that Really Work
by Janice VanCleave
John Wiley & Sons, 1989
This book gives clear directions for plenty of experiments and offers brief—sometimes a little *too* brief—explanations of the related chemical concepts.

ELECTRICITY

The Ben Franklin Book of Easy and Incredible Experiments
by the Franklin Institute Science Museum
illustrated by Cheryl Kirk Noll
John Wiley & Sons, 1995
This book combines glimpses at Benjamin Franklin as a historic figure and as a scientist, offering instructions for a number of experiments that parallel his own. No, it doesn't encourage tying a key to the end of a kite string, but it does explain how to make an electroscope out of cardboard, aluminum foil, and a paper clip, so you can sense the static electricity in the air. The book is divided into sections on weather, electricity, music, paper and printing, and light and sight.

CC *It's Electric*
by Andrew Dunn
illustrated by Ed Carr
Thomson Learning, 1993
Starting with a clear discussion of atoms and electrons, this book uses clear language and well-designed illustrations to introduce electricity. Breakaway drawings and logical text explain such equipment as a copying machine, a car battery, and a dry-cell battery. Part of the How Things Work series, listed under Science General Resources: Series.

CC *Switch On, Switch Off*
by Melvin Berger
illustrated by Carolyn Croll
HarperCollins, 1989
With simple language and cute, colorful drawings, this book introduces basic concepts and terminology about electricity and electrical circuits. Early in the book, children are given directions for making a copper wire coil and inducing the flow of electricity with a bar magnet. That experience becomes the foundation for understanding how a power plant works. The book includes good explanations and diagrams of a house's electrical system and the incandescent light bulb. A Let's-Read-and-Find-Out book, listed under Science General Resources: Series.

GEOLOGY: THE EARTH AND ITS CHANGES

Adventures with Rocks and Minerals Book I: Geology Experiments for Young People
by Lloyd H. Barrow
Enslow, 1991
The author offers thirty experiments, with clear directions and black-and-white line drawings, as well as follow-up discussions, designed to help students in grades 4–9 understand how geologists study the earth. A second volume by the same title is available (Book II, 1995).

Continents
by Dennis B. Fradin
Childrens Press, 1986
This short, straightforward book combines geography and geology for a detailed definition of the concept of a "continent," accessible to a fourth grader. Cutaway drawings illustrate discussions of the earth's inner core and the ocean landscape. The author discusses Pangaea and the history of continents, as well as the difference between a country and a continent. The book concludes by listing countries and capitals found on each continent, as well as with a glossary and index. A New True Book, listed under Science General Resources: Series.

CC *The Dillon Press Book of the Earth*
by Tom Mariner and Anyon Ellis
Simon & Schuster School Division, 1991
This is a remarkably comprehensive book about many topics in earth science. It includes information and diagrams about the earth's crust, types of rocks, the continents, the oceans, wind, weather, and climate. It is illustrated with large, readable drawings and diagrams that interact well with the text, giving a good visual sense of the earth's phenomena. The book concludes with an almanac of continents, listing many facts, features, and figures.

Earthquakes
by Franklyn M. Branley
illustrated by Richard Rosenblum
HarperCollins, 1990
Clear explanations and colorful pictures make this Let's-Read-and-Find-Out Science Book a friendly introduction to the how and why of earthquakes. The author also briefly discusses some major earthquakes in history and safety procedures during an earthquake.

Icebergs and Glaciers
by Seymour Simon
William Morrow, 1987
This book combines large-format color photos, many spectacular, with clear text explaining why and how glaciers and icebergs form. Com-

panion volumes by Simon include *Earthquakes* (William Morrow, 1991) and *Volcanoes* (William Morrow, 1988).

The Super Science Book of Rocks and Soils
by Robert Snedden
illustrations by Frances Lloyd
Thomson Learning, 1995
This book intelligently links rocks, soils, volcanoes, erosion, and fossils, as well as building with stone and farming the earth. It uses clearly labeled drawings, interesting photos, and a number of simple projects to amplify the text.

This Dynamic Planet
U.S. Geological Survey
This huge color map of the world, nearly three feet tall by five feet wide, shows the locations of volcanoes, earthquakes, and impact craters. A significant amount of information is conveyed in tiny type on the bottom one-fifth of the map. Order it from the Map Distribution Center, U.S. Geological Survey, Federal Center, Box 25286, Denver, CO 80225, for $4.00 each plus $3.50 shipping.

Volcano
by John Dudman
Thomson Learning, 1993
Spectacular color photos and clear diagrams and cross-sections fill this book. The book ends with instructions for building a model volcano with the classic baking-soda-and-vinegar recipe for bubbling lava (but *be careful*—too much can be dangerous). One volume among four in Thomson Learning's Violent Earth series, which also includes the titles *Earthquake, Flood,* and *Storm.*

CC *Volcanoes*
by Franklyn M. Branley
illustrated by Marc Simont
HarperCollins, 1985
Branley's straightforward writing style and Simont's eye for geological perspectives combine to give a clear picture of how volcanoes work. The book balances between technical dis-

cussions and descriptions and pictures conveying the experience of being in or around a volcano eruption. Should be easy reading for most fourth graders; part of the Let's-Read-and-Find-Out series, listed under Science General Resources: Series.

HISTORY OF THE EARTH

CC *The Beginning of the Earth*
by Franklyn M. Branley
illustrated by Giulio Maestro
HarperCollins, 1988
With clear language and illustrations, some close to abstract art, this book outlines in elementary terms the theory of how the earth and solar system began to form out of a massive cloud of dust and gases billions of years ago. The author and illustrator take events and concepts that are hard to imagine and manage to bring to them a degree of concrete reality.

Dinosaur Dig
by Kathryn Lasky
photography by Christopher G. Knight
William Morrow, 1990
Imagine actually participating in a dinosaur dig! That's what the two children in this book do, and it becomes an engaging way to explain to children just what paleontologists do and just how we learned what we know about dinosaurs. The book is illustrated throughout with color photographs from the dig.

Dinosaurs Walked Here and Other Stories Fossils Tell
by Patricia Lauber
McGraw Hill, 1987
"Like entries in a diary, fossils tell of the earth's history," says this book, which offers wonderful eye-opening photographs and illustrations, including many pictures of paleontologists at work discovering fossils, bones, and footprints. The book offers detailed explanations of how we know what we know about prehistoric ani-

mals, based upon what scientists have found in fossil form.

Evolution
by Joanna Cole
illustrated by Aliki
HarperCollins, 1987
Starting with a farmer who finds a bone as he plows, this clever book introduces the basic concepts of evolution, including the progression of species, extinction, natural selection, and human ancestors. It presents geologic eras as a natural follow-up to the discoveries of William Smith as he built a canal in England and began to notice rock strata filled with layers of plant and animal fossils. Aliki's colored-pencil drawings add a gentle touch. Part of the Let's-Read-and-Find-Out series, listed under Science General Resources: Series.

Fossils Tell of Long Ago
written and illustrated by Aliki
HarperCollins, 1990 (revised edition)
Fourth graders will enjoy this Let's-Read-and-Find-Out book that features Aliki's distinctive cartoonlike drawings and informative text, sometimes set off in little word balloons.

METEOROLOGY

CC *Hurricane Watch*
by Franklyn M. Branley
illustrated by Giulio Maestro
HarperCollins, 1985
This interesting book, readable by most fourth graders, describes the effects of hurricanes and explains the forces that cause them. The illustrations are sometimes technical and sometimes evocative. Part of the Let's-Read-and-Find-Out series, listed under Science General Resources: Series.

CC = "Core Collection" book (see page 8).

Storm
by Jenny Wood
Thomson Learning, 1993
Bringing together thunderstorms, snowstorms, dust and sandstorms, tornadoes, and hurricanes, this book describes both the atmospheric conditions and the human experience of violent storms. It includes a number of clearly drawn, well-labeled diagrams that explain the phenomena involved in various types of storm, along with some rather spectacular photos of the damage storms can cause.

CC *Tornado Alert*
by Franklyn M. Branley
illustrated by Giulio Maestro
HarperCollins, 1988
This book combines scientific descriptions of tornadoes with advice on what to do if a tornado approaches. Its chalk illustrations are powerful. The author uses plenty of numbers in his technical discussions of how tornadoes form, what effects they might have, and where they most often occur. Part of the Let's-Read-and-Find-Out series, listed under Science General Resources: Series.

Weather Forecasting
written and illustrated by Gail Gibbons
Four Winds Press, 1987
In a very friendly format, the book introduces major ideas about the changing weather and how we observe and record those changes. The book describes not only weather phenomena but also technology and communications. The text is very readable, the color illustrations clear and pleasant.

The Weather Sky
by Bruce McMillan
Farrar, Straus & Giroux, 1991
This is an ingenious and illuminating book about the weather. Many books tell youngsters what this cloud or that cloud means to the weather forecaster, but this book goes into a good deal more detail. The author keeps four things going on page after page: a representative photo of the cloud type; a graduated dia-

gram, showing at what altitude the cloud type can be found; typical weather-map symbols; and a paragraph pulling the three together, explaining the weather changes involved.

CC *Weatherwatch*
by Valerie Wyatt
illustrated by Pat Cupples
Addison-Wesley, 1990
This book is lively in text, in illustrations, and in ideas. Its enthusiasm will inspire children to enjoy noticing the weather and how it influences our lives. The author suggests a number of easy and fun projects, including preserving a snowflake, creating smog in a jar, and making a small barometer.

BIOGRAPHIES

Benjamin Banneker

What Are You Figuring Now? A Story About Benjamin Banneker
by Jeri Ferris
illustrated by Amy Johnson
Carolrhoda Books, 1988
Easily readable by most fourth graders, this chapter book capably recounts the inspiring life of Benjamin Banneker, the astronomer, surveyor, printer, and abolitionist who helped design Washington, D.C.

Elizabeth Blackwell

Elizabeth Blackwell: The First Woman Doctor
by Francene Sabin
illustrated by Ann Toulmin-Rothe
Troll Associates, 1982
This short storybook, illustrated with ink-wash drawings, concentrates on Blackwell's childhood, showing the elements that led up to her ambition and success in later life. Her actual accomplishments as a physician take only three pages of this forty-eight-page book.

Charles Drew

Black Pioneers of Science and Invention
by Louis Haber
Harcourt Brace Jovanovich, 1970
This book includes a chapter on Charles Drew, combining his struggles as an African-American with his accomplishments as a health-care professional. There is an interesting section on his determination to integrate blood banks during World War II.

Charles Drew, Doctor
by Garnet Nelson Jackson
illustrated by Gary Thomas
Modern Curriculum Press, 1994
This brief, upbeat picture-book biography focuses on Dr. Drew's medical achievements, and should be very easy reading for fourth graders.

Michael Faraday

Famous Experiments and How to Repeat Them
by Brent Filson
illustrated by Brigita Fuhrmann
Julian Messner, 1986
See description under Science General Resources: Experiments and Activities.

Great Lives: Invention and Technology
by Milton Lomask
Charles Scribner's Sons, 1991
A chapter of this teacher/parent resource book offers a brief anecdotal portrait of the humble beginnings, hard work, and important discoveries of this pioneer in electricity.

SCIENCE

Grade 5

LIFE SCIENCES: LIFE CYCLES AND CELL PROCESSES

See also Science Grade 3: Classification of Animals, for books about specific classes of animals.

Janice VanCleave's Biology for Every Kid: 101 Easy Experiments that Really Work
by Janice VanCleave
John Wiley & Sons, 1989
This book gives clear directions for many experiments with readily available materials, but only minimal explanations.

Hidden Worlds: Pictures of the Invisible
by Seymour Simon
William Morrow, 1983
Breathtaking pictures and concise, clear text make this yet another fine book from Seymour Simon, filled with photos, some color and mostly black and white. Simon explains the technology that allows us to see inside the body, as well as such marvels of the world around us as a snowflake, or even a drop falling into a platter of milk (captured using split-second high-speed flash photography). In five chapters, Simon takes us to hidden worlds "Around You," "Inside Your Body," "Of Time," "Of the Earth," and "Of Space." A book sure to elicit many oohs and ahhs, or at least a "Wow, cool!"

Inside an Egg
by Sylvia Johnson
photography by Kiyoshi Shimizu
Lerner, 1982
This clear and detailed book is written for about fourth grade and up, and has remarkable, large-

scale embryonic photographs. Note that unlike many other books about chickens and eggs, this book frankly illustrates mating and fertilization, with cutaway drawings of both the female and the male reproductive systems. One interesting digression shows how closely early chick embryos resemble early fish embryos.

Outside and Inside You
by Sandra Markle
illustrated by Susan Kuklin
Bradbury Press, 1991
Using remarkable high-tech glimpses into different body systems, this book offers a realistic sense of how cells and tissues make up the body. The book includes micrographs, for example, of a cross-section of skin, rods and cones in the eye, a taste bud, and the walls of the intestine. Descriptions of each of these pictures show how cell structures determine system function.

Plant Families
by Carol Lerner
William Morrow, 1989
This elegant book begins with the basics of botanical identification, then proceeds to give pointers on how to classify plants into their twelve major families. For each family, the author provides a page of text, with some description of the plant family's usefulness, and one page of delicate color illustration, labeled to point out the most important identifying traits.

Plants Without Seeds
by Helen J. Challand
Childrens Press, 1986
With discussions of algae, fungi, bacteria, lichens, mosses, and ferns, this factual book tells

a lot about how non–seed-bearing plants reproduce. It also shows how reproductive processes in plants serve as a classifying features. Illustrated with small color photographs, typeset with large, bold type, and composed in short, simple sentences, this book may seem too elementary for some fifth graders, but it is full of interesting information. A New True Book, listed under Science General Resources: Series.

THE HUMAN BODY

Note: Different schools and districts have different local requirements about the grade level at which to introduce the study of human sexuality, and what topics to study. The following books are listed here because they deal with topics suggested in the fifth-grade Science section of the *Core Knowledge Sequence.* Teachers and parents may want to compare these suggestions to local programs and requirements.

Adolescence

Asking About Sex and Growing Up
by Joanna Cole
illustrated by Alan Tiegreen
William Morrow, 1988
This book asks and answers many of a young person's questions about sexuality, like "At what age do girls get their first period?," "What is a wet dream?," and "At what age can a girl get pregnant?" Chapters move from adolescent development issues into adult sexuality, including pregnancy, homosexuality, sex abuse, and sexually transmitted diseases. The author treats contraception, abortion, and homosexuality without judgment. A few line drawings illustrate the book. Includes a note to parents, bibliographies for both children and parents, and a good index.

CC = "Core Collection" book (see page 8).

CC *The What's Happening to My Body?*
Book for Boys
by Lynda Madaras
illustrated by Jackie Aher
New Market Press, 1988
This friendly, informative book was written by a woman who teaches sex education to preteens and teens, and she clearly knows her audience. The book ranges through every topic of interest to boys approaching or in the midst of puberty, from body changes to issues of sexual health and relationships. The book is illustrated with line drawings and topics are often handled through a question-answer format, helping boys feel okay about wondering what's happening to them.

CC *The What's Happening to My Body?*
Book for Girls
by Lynda Madaras
illustrated by Claudia Ziroli and Jackie Aher
New Market Press, 1987
This book approaches an adolescent girl's physiology and questions about sex with the same understanding and frankness as Madaras's book for boys. Each book includes a chapter about changes going on in the other sex, as well as issues particular to the audience.

Human Reproduction

Being Born
by Sheila Kitzinger
photography by Lennart Nilsson
G. P. Putnam's Sons, 1992
Kitzinger, a British nurse midwife who has written many books for the expectant mother, now writes a book about conception, gestation, and birth for children. Her frankness is matched by the awe-inspiring intrauterine photography of Lennart Nilsson. The text is unswerving in the way it addresses the facts yet poetical in its style, addressing "you" as if the child reader were the growing fetus. The photos include sperms diving at the surface of the egg, the downy texture of a five-month-old fetus's skin,

and a head emerging from between the mother's legs.

How You Were Born
by Joanna Cole
photographs by Margaret Miller and others
William Morrow, 1994
This book combines gentle, direct language with photographs and color drawings to explain human conception, gestation, and birth. It uses a few of Lennart Nilsson's remarkable intrauterine photos, a number of happy-family photos, and drawings for those aspects of the story that might cause some embarrassment if shown through photography instead. The book does not end at birth, but describes bonding between parents and infant, nursing, and early learning. The book begins with a five-page note to parents from the author, with advice on the wisest way to handle children's questions and partial understanding.

CHEMISTRY: MATTER AND CHANGE
See also the listings under Science General Resources: Experiments and Activities. Schools may want to examine the prepackaged materials for experiments available in various elementary school science programs; see the list of Science Curriculum Modules that opens Science General Resources.

CC *Adventures with Atoms and Molecules: Chemistry Experiments for Young People*
by Robert C. Mebane and Thomas R. Rybolt
Enslow, 1985
See description under Science Grade 4: Chemistry.

Chemically Active: Experiments You Can Do at Home
by Vicki Cobb
illustrated by Theo Cobb
J. B. Lippincott, 1985
Many ideas for experiments with common materials make this a helpful book for the home or classroom. More than other books of science activities, this one goes into some useful detail about chemical terms and concepts, offering clear explanations of challenging material.

Chemistry
by Ann Newmark
Dorling Kindersley, 1993
Not so much a book for continuous reading as occasional browsing, this book's vivid illustrations might spark interest and curiosity in a budding young scientist. The text takes a historical approach in its explanation of chemistry, the elements, the periodic table, and chemical reactions. Most sections of the book include vivid color photos with lengthy captions (in small type), and incorporate historical moments in chemistry with the introduction of basic scientific ideas. Topics discussed include the periodic table, metals, gases, reactions, and organic chemistry. An Eyewitness Science book, listed under Science General Resources: Series.

CC *Our Atomic World*
by Melvin Berger
Franklin Watts, 1989
Melvin Berger has a knack for explaining difficult concepts clearly and concisely. While this book goes into a bit more detail than you might want to introduce in fifth grade (including brief discussions of superconductivity, radioactivity, and quarks), the first five chapters offer readable and interesting discussions to go along with your studies in chemistry, including: "Meet the Atom," "Inside the Atom," "The Elements," "Solids, Liquids and Gases," and "Molecules and Compounds." With color photographs and illustrations.

CC = **"Core Collection"** book (see page 8).

INTRODUCTION TO PHYSICS: SPEED, WORK, POWER

Energy
by Illa Podendorf
Childrens Press, 1982
Although the short, simple sentences and large type of this book may seem elementary to some fifth graders, there is an advantage in taking an abstract concept like "energy" and presenting it in such a simple, down-to-earth way. The book is divided into short chapters, each about a different form of energy—wind, water, electrical, magnetic, heat. It uses familiar examples like flashlight batteries and the combination of vinegar and baking soda inside a jar to convey the concept of energy that can do work. Color photos illustrate each page. A New True Book, listed under Science General Resources: Series.

CC *Exploring Uses of Energy*
by Ed Catherall
Steck-Vaughn, 1991
Using a number of everyday examples, this book introduces basic physical concepts like energy, work, weight, and energy conservation, as well as basic tools like the lever, the ramp, wheels, pulleys, and gears. The book's design promotes constant interplay between textbook-like discussion and hands-on projects. Each topic is introduced in a two-page spread: the first page explains new terms and concepts, the second page describes a project or activity designed to illustrate the new information. Color photos and drawings illustrate every page.

Wheels at Work
by Andrew Dunn
illustrated by Ed Carr
Thomson Learning, 1993
This book explains how wheels and rotating power drive much of the work done today. It explains gears and pulleys, discusses inertia, and reveals the workings of an automobile's wheels and steering system. More than is needed for an introduction, but nonetheless helpful as a teacher/parent resource, and for the illustrations. Part of the How Things Work series, listed under Science General Resources: Series.

BIOGRAPHIES

Galileo

Note: Teachers following the *Core Knowledge Sequence* will find in these books about Galileo useful information for lessons on changing concepts of the universe, which may be connected to the study of the Renaissance (see World History Grade 5).

Famous Experiments and How to Repeat Them
by Brent Filson
illustrated by Brigita Fuhrmann
Julian Messner, 1986
See description under Science General Resources: Experiments and Activities.

Five Secrets in a Box
by Catherine Brighton
E. P. Dutton, 1987
Although this is a picture book with very little text, it packs in an entire lesson about Galileo's interests and studies. Fifth graders can move far beyond the simple story line to learn the meaning of each of the five "secrets" that Galileo's daughter finds in a box on her father's table.

Galileo
written and illustrated by Leonard Everett Fisher
Macmillan, 1992
In a black-and-white picture-book format, this is an intelligent biography that describes the science and controversy in Galileo's work. The author gives enough information about several phases of the great scientist's work, so that his advances in physics, instrumentation, and astronomy can be grasped.

Percy Lavon Julian

Black Pioneers of Science and Invention
by Louis Haber
Harcourt Brace Jovanovich, 1970
The chapter on Julian in this book provides chilling accounts of the discouragement and prejudice he faced, as well as clear technical discussions of his accomplishments in organic chemistry and drug synthesis. See Science General Resources: Biography Collections for a longer description of this book.

Ernest Just

Black Pioneers of Science and Invention
by Louis Haber
Harcourt Brace Jovanovich, 1970
A chapter of this book is devoted to the life and achievements of Ernest Just, a pioneer in marine biology and research in cell structure. The discussion is sometimes quite technical, so this book is best used as a teacher/parent resource.

SCIENCE

Grade 6

HISTORY OF SCIENCE

***Eyewitness Science* series**
Dorling Kindersley
Following the same formula as the Eyewitness books—lots of informative pictures, text (sometimes complex) spread out in captions around the page—this series aims to convey the history of each science that it portrays. Many of the photos, therefore, are of artifacts of science: for example, Alexander Graham Bell's telephone, or Priestley's glass jar. Titles include *Chemistry, Evolution, Human Body,* and *Ecology.*

CC *Secrets of the Universe: Discovering the Universal Laws of Science*
by Paul Fleisher
illustrated by Patricia A. Keeler
Atheneum, 1987
This engaging book explores the history of science through the great discoveries of scientific laws. It includes the work of Archimedes, Galileo, Newton, Pascal, Ohm, Joule, Einstein, and Heisenberg. The book emphasizes the significance of mathematics in expressing universal laws, and also does a good job of asking just what is a scientific law. There are a few ideas on how to recreate some of history's great experiments. Line drawings and diagrams illustrate the book, which includes a bibliography and index.

CC = "Core Collection" book (see page 8).

ENERGY

CC *Exploring Energy Sources*
by Ed Catherall
Steck-Vaughn, 1991
This book proceeds from a basic definition of energy, through principles of energy conservation, to brief introductions to many modern energy sources: coal, oil, gas, solar, wind, hydroelectricity, and nuclear power. Each topic receives two pages of treatment: one page of background text, a second page offering some sort of activity or experiment, and a set of questions to test the reader's understanding. Photos and illustrations accompany each two-page spread. Some activities are not very scientific: for example, the section on nuclear power suggests that youngsters poll people on their opinions about nuclear power. (Which, come to think of it, is more feasible than building a home reactor!) See also by the same author, *Exploring Uses of Energy* (Steck-Vaughn, 1991), listed under Science Grade 5: Introduction to Physics.

The Greenhouse Effect: Life on a Warmer Planet
by Rebecca L. Johnson
Lerner, 1994 (revised edition)
For the enterprising sixth grader, this book of one hundred pages offers a matter-of-fact review of research on carbon dioxide levels and possible global warming, as well as projections of the potential impact of the "greenhouse effect" on humans and natural systems. With many color photographs and diagrams.

Nuclear Energy
by Nigel Hawkes
Franklin Watts, 1981
This brief but informative book offers clear and readable discussions of nuclear energy in chapters on "Nuclear Power," "Splitting the Atom," "Reactor Fuel," "Nuclear Engines," and "Nuclear Waste," including a discussion of "What Might Go Wrong." With color illustrations and diagrams on every page.

Our Atomic World
by Melvin Berger
Franklin Watts, 1989
See Science Grade 5: Chemistry for a description of this readable introduction to challenging topics. The closing chapters of the book address radiation and nuclear energy.

Putting the Sun to Work
by Jeanne Bendick
Garrard, 1979
Building from a common experience—the feeling of heat on a summer day—this slightly dated book explains how the sun creates weather phenomena, then shows how technology has been designed to capture sun, water, and wind power and transform them into electricity. The book includes a number of interesting projects that allow children to experience the power of sun for themselves, like cooking an egg within the arc of a sheet of aluminum foil set out in the sunshine. Simple cartoon drawings illustrate a number of points and provide a bit of technical information on such things as solar cells, hydroelectric dams, and a solar space station.

LIGHT AND THE ELECTROMAGNETIC SPECTRUM

How Did We Find Out About Lasers?
by Isaac Asimov
illustrated by Erika Kors
Walker, 1990
In his clear, logical style, Asimov explains the historical sequence of ideas and developments that allowed Planck to develop quantum theory, then allowed scientists after Planck to transform his ideas into actual technology. A companion title asks *How Did We Find Out About Microwaves?* (Walker, 1989). Excellent black-and-white drawings illustrate major ideas in both books, and the final chapters give overviews of the uses of these technologies in industry and medicine today. Part of the How Did We Find Out About . . . ? series, listed under Science General Resources: Series.

CC *Lights, Lenses, and Lasers*
by Melvin Berger
illustrated by Greg Wenzl
G. P. Putnam's Sons, 1987
Divided into chapters on the three topics in its title, this book combines history of science, hands-on experiments, and serious explanations of current technologies, adding up to a fine introduction to the science of optics. It explains the workings of the eye and how they relate to various lenses, including eyeglasses and telescopes. It gives a basic history of lasers, then explores some of their current applications. Line drawings and black-and-white photographs illustrate most pages. Includes a glossary and an index.

Mirrors: Finding Out About the Properties of Light
by Bernie Zubrowski
illustrated by Roy Doty
William Morrow/Morrow Junior Books, 1992
This Boston Children's Museum Activity Book offers clear instructions for about fifty experiments on light and optics, making use of a variety of plane, transparent, and curved mirrors. While the activities are clearly described, the author does not go into much detail about the scientific principles they illustrate.

CC = "Core Collection" book (see page 8).

ASTRONOMY: STARS AND GALAXIES

CC *Galaxies*
by Seymour Simon
William Morrow, 1988
This beautiful book uses color photos to convey the reality of nebulae, supernovae, and galaxies. Reading through it feels almost like a trip into outer space, the pages are so big and so many are filled with amazing photos.

How Did We Find Out About the Speed of Light?
by Isaac Asimov
illustrated by David Wool
Walker, 1986
The prolific Isaac Asimov here tells an engaging story of how we came to understand the speed of light and why this understanding is crucial to our sense of the scale of the universe. Along the way we meet a variety of scientists and astronomers, including Galileo, Albert Michelson, and Albert Einstein. Fans of *Star Trek* may be disappointed by Asimov's conclusion that "the scientists, from Galileo to Michelson, who tried to measure the speed of light, little knew they were measuring the prison bars that may keep us in the solar system forever."

Odyssey
Cobblestone Publishing
7 School Street, Peterborough, NH 03458
(800) 821-0115
In nine issues a year, this appealing magazine makes the study of stars, galaxies, planets, outer space, and the planet Earth (volcanos, tides, gravity, and more) interesting and accessible for the older elementary grade levels. Each issue includes features about researchers and their discoveries, plus departments like Mind Bogglers and Backyard Observations. The magazine also runs some contributions from readers. School and public libraries often subscribe to this magazine. Back issues are available from the publisher.

Our Universe: A Guide to What's Out There
by Russell Stannard
Kingfisher Books, 1995
Written by a British professor of physics, this book has style and a winning sense of humor. It begins its tour of the universe by discussing atoms, but soon takes off, passing by the moon, the planets, and the sun, and on to the vaster and more mystifying aspects of the universe. In two chapters, it considers the Big Bang and the creation of the universe. The book contains all illustrations, no photos—a combination of forceful chalk images of stars and nebulae and a running series of spot black-and-whites, through which we track three characters: the professor, the earthling boy, and the alien.

The Third Planet: Exploring the Earth from Space
by Sally Ride and Tam O'Shaughnessy
Crown Publishers, 1994
This fascinating book goes in several different directions, but the starting point is always the view of the earth from outer space, thanks to remarkable photographs taken during space shuttle flights. Sally Ride, first American woman astronaut, and O'Shaughnessy, a biology teacher, team up to use the shuttle's-eye view to explain about the atmosphere, storms and air masses, the oceans, and the changing surface features of the earth. This view really does give new perspectives on the planet, informing our most modern models of the earth. The book is vividly illustrated with photos and computer-enhanced maps.

CC *The Universe for the Beginner*
by Patrick Moore
Cambridge University Press, 1990
Written by the BBC's astronomy commentator, this book begins with basics but moves swiftly and logically to discussions of the Big Bang theory, supernovae, pulsars, giant and dwarf stars, and black holes, moving through our galaxy and beyond to others. It is illustrated with excellent diagrams and color photos, and is very well organized into chapters.

GENETICS, ADAPTATION, AND EVOLUTION

Amazing Schemes Within Your Genes
by Fran Balkwill
illustrations by Mic Rolph
Carolrhoda Books, 1993
This book fools around a bit—it's a playful picture book designed to make the study of genes and chromosomes fun. At a glance, it looks like an easy reader, but it doesn't read like one—pages are dense with text and information, and the basics of DNA, amino acids, chromosomes, heredity, and evolution are all here. For those students who aren't put off by the storybook look, or for those who need a storybook to make science go down more easily, this might be a good starting point.

Genetics: Nature's Blueprints
by Lynn Byczynski
Lucent Books, 1991
This book is a clearly written introduction to genetics, incorporating history, science, health, ethics, and behavior into the discussion. It presents introductory information about such matters as cell division, DNA structure, and recombinant DNA, intertwined with life stories of DNA researchers and interesting examples of the force of genetic determination in human life. Black-and-white photos and diagrams appear on every page, and the book includes a glossary, bibliography, and thorough index.

Hominids: A Look Back at Our Ancestors
by Helen Roney Sattler
illustrated by Christopher Santoro
Lothrop, Lee & Shepard, 1988
In this handsome book, the author brings together the findings of cultural and physical anthropologists into a species-by-species portrayal of our hominid forebears, from Australopithecus to Homo sapiens. Maps and text identify where fossils were found and what they might mean in the overall map and time line of human civilization. Text and charcoal illustrations on every page depict both bone and tool fragments, often

comparing actual findings with hypotheses. One set of drawings, for instance, shows how scientists flesh out an Australopithecine skull, visualizing how the being actually looked.

How Did We Find Out About Genes?
by Isaac Asimov
illustrated by David Wool
Walker, 1983
In his characteristically breezy, conversational way, Asimov chronicles the work of five major figures in the history of genetics: Mendel and pea plants, de Vries and primrose mutations, Fleming and cell division, Morgan and fruit flies, Müller and radiation-induced mutations. The book gives a quick overview of major steps in experimental work and thought, leading up to Crick and Watson. One of the How Did We Find Out About . . . ? series, listed under Science General Resources: Series.

The Human Body: How We Evolved
by Joanna Cole
illustrated by Walter Gaffney-Kessell and Juan Carlos Barberis
William Morrow, 1987
"As different as humans are from other animals," this book says, "we are part of the animal world." This look at human evolution begins 15 million years ago, when our ancestors were apelike tree dwellers in Africa. With helpful pencil drawings and explanations of evolutionary steps that can be tested with personal observation today (the thumb, the grip, stereoscopic vision, for example), this book outlines the stages of human development up to Neanderthal.

Medicine: Great Lives
by Robert H. Curtis, M.D.
Charles Scribner's Sons, 1993
This encyclopedia of great figures in the history of medicine includes a ten-page entry on Watson and Crick. It contains background material on DNA and the history of genetic discoveries, including the work of Mendel, before it goes on to chronicle the life and work of Watson and

Crick, including much of the interplay and competition among scientists at that time. The text is written at a level appropriate for sixth graders. See book listing under Science General Resources: Biography Collections.

Traces of Life: The Origins of Humankind
by Kathryn Lasky
illustrated by Whitney Powell
William Morrow, 1989
One way to learn about human evolution is to read about the work of those who have pieced together our current picture of it: that's the approach of this handsome and good-humored book. The author introduces some great anthropologists, beginning with Lyell and Darwin, and our great human ancestors, too, including Lucy and the Taung baby. Clear, well-labeled drawings accompany every page. Chapters are interspersed with passages on how hominid ancestors must have lived.

THE HUMAN BODY: IMMUNE SYSTEM AND DISEASE
See also Science General Resources: The Human Body.

CC *AIDS: How It Works in the Body*
by Lorna Greenberg
Franklin Watts, 1992
With interesting analogies and carefully chosen language, this book builds upon the basic science of bacteria and viruses into a discussion of AIDS and the search for AIDS treatments. Actual micrographic images of cells, color enhanced by computer, help depict the biology of the HIV virus.

Understanding AIDS
by Ethan A. Lerner
Lerner, 1987
This book, written by an immunologist, gets right to the point in its discussions of difficult subjects like AIDS, homosexuality, and drug use. The author has conceived seven life stories, from a youngster whose swollen glands make

him ask, "Do I have AIDS?" to a young man who comes home for Christmas to tell his family he is gay and has AIDS. After each story, told with care and directness, the book asks and answers questions, and clarifies issues of medical science that are often clouded by issues of morality. This book is blunt and nonjudgmental. The life stories may interest young readers, since they tell the tales that often stay hidden.

BIOGRAPHIES

Marie Curie

Marie Curie, Brave Scientist
by Keith Brandt
illustrated by Karen Milone
Troll Associates, 1983
Most of this brief (forty-eight-page) volume, easily readable in this grade, focuses on the childhood and youth of Manya Sklodowska, the precocious child who, when she entered the great French university, the Sorbonne, began to call herself Marie, and later married a professor of physics there, Pierre Curie. So, while there's little science here, there is a pretty good story.

Medicine: Great Lives
by Robert H. Curtis, M.D.
Charles Scribner's Sons, 1993
Marie Curie receives a ten-page biography in this encyclopedia of great figures in the history of medicine. The author tells her life story in clear, readable prose with emphasis on the personal, although he includes basic information about the science that made her great. Two full-page period photos illustrate the text. See book listing under Science General Resources: Biography Collections.

CC = "Core Collection" book (see page 8).

Charles Darwin

Charles Darwin and Evolution
by Steve Parker
Chelsea House, 1995
Attractively designed, with many contemporary
color illustrations, this brief book about Darwin's life and times is both accessible and intelligent. The story line is punctuated with explanatory sidebars. The book concludes with a
glossary, an index, and an interesting comparative time line of events in science, exploration,
politics, and art during Darwin's time.

Charles Darwin, Revolutionary Biologist
by J. Edward Evans
Lerner, 1993
This handsome little biography, written in narrative style, tells of Darwin's life, work, and significance. It is extensively illustrated with
photos, political cartoons, and engravings from
Darwin's times. It reasons through a number of
Darwin's theoretical findings and discusses the
public response to his ideas during his lifetime
and after. Includes an index and bibliography.

Albert Einstein

Albert Einstein
by Karin Ireland
Silver Burdett, 1989
This colorfully written hundred-page biography
weaves together historical information and intriguing threads from Einstein's life, including
his troubles in school, his family life, and his
contributions to science. The thought processes
that led to his innovations are clearly explained
in nontechnical language. Contemporary photographs illustrate the book.

Albert Einstein and the Theory of Relativity
by Robert Cwiklik
Barron's, 1987
This book provides not only a readable biography of Einstein but also an intelligent attempt at
explaining his most important ideas in language
that most middle schoolers will appreciate. The
book includes a glossary, list of discussion topics, bibliography, and index.

Lewis Howard Latimer

Black Pioneers of Science and Invention
by Louis Haber
Harcourt Brace Jovanovich, 1970
Not only Latimer's inventions and patents but
also his poetry are remembered in the chapter
of this book devoted to him. The author briefly
depicts the state of the city, too, in which Latimer's work on lighting made such significant
changes. One period portrait and a period en-
graving of the incandescent light illustrate the
sixteen-page section on Latimer. See Science
General Resources: Biography Collections for
more on this book.

Lewis Howard Latimer
by Glennette Tilley Turner
Silver Burdett, 1991
Written for upper-middle to high-school students, this is a well written account of the life
and times of the African-American electrical en-
gineer who found ways to develop Thomas Edison's research into practical municipal lighting
systems in New York, Philadelphia, and London. Illustrated with black-and-white photographs, diagrams, and documents.

MATHEMATICS: SUPPLEMENTARY RESOURCES

Introduction

In international evaluations of math performance by students in various countries, students in the United States have in recent years consistently performed near the bottom. One reason is that students in countries such as France and Japan begin building a secure foundation in mathematics in the earliest years of their schooling, and that they receive more consistent practice and more challenging work than American students. Students in this country deserve to have the same kind of foundation in mathematics.

Compared to other countries, American schools spend less time on mathematics and more time on language arts. But math deserves at least as much time, in part because math is itself a kind of language. Just as we expect English to become second nature to American schoolchildren, so should math.

Research in cognitive psychology has made clear that learning math is in some ways like learning to read. Both are mostly "unnatural" activities: they require the brain and mind to do things that they are not designed by nature to do.

Granted, we are born with some limited natural capacity for both language and math. Language is "natural" to the extent that children, without apparent effort, learn to speak the language they are exposed to. Similarly, we are born with a few basic, natural math abilities. For example, we have an innate geometrical sense that enables us to develop rough "mental maps" of familiar environments, so that even if the electricity goes out one evening, we can navigate from one room to another without suffering much more than a stubbed toe (these mental maps aren't perfect). Also, in the preschool years, human infants develop the ability to determine the number of items in sets of three to four objects.

But the natural ability to acquire spoken language, or to count a set of three or four objects, can only take you so far. In the Introduction to the Language Arts section of this book, we discuss the fact that reading is not a natural process, and what this means for teaching. As for math, our natural sense of quantities up to three or four does not enable us to add or multiply larger quantities, or provide a natural ability to borrow when doing a two-digit subtraction problem, or give us an automatic understanding of place value or square roots. Our natural knowledge may even run counter to the unnatural learning that math requires, as is the case, for example, in the notation of fractions, which sometimes initially puzzle young learners because as the bottom number gets bigger, the fraction gets smaller.

Because most math is unnatural, we cannot expect children to learn it through math-related games or projects or social activities. Rather, the competencies need to be taught directly, explicitly, and systematically. A project or activity may occasionally help reinforce a competency or demonstrate its "real-world" usefulness: for example, a simulated grocery store in the classroom can help children practice adding and subtracting as they figure out how much items cost and how much change to give a "customer." But, while such an activity can demonstrate the usefulness of knowing how to add and subtract money, it cannot be the primary route to developing the necessary skills. One cannot expect children to learn to add and subtract with speed, proficiency, and accuracy simply by letting them play in a classroom store or participate in other "real-world" activities designed to allow children to "discover" the math they need to know.

Because almost all math knowledge is unnatural knowledge, it is not something that children discover; rather, it is something they must be taught. Moreover, because math is a discipline with its own vocabulary, conventions, and patterns of thinking, it is critically important to attend to *math as math.* We point this out because of the current emphasis in many schools on linking math to other disciplines, and the proliferation of programs and materials with disorienting names like "Literature-Based Math." True, some lessons in literature, history, or science may offer occasional opportunities for introducing a math problem or concept: for example, first graders studying the forest habitat may be asked to solve a problem like "There were six squirrels gathering acorns. Three more squirrels joined them. How many squirrels are there in all?" But these are at best activities to reinforce math, not the primary means by which to teach it. They can supplement, but not replace, regular attention to the operations, concepts, and procedures of math as math.

Every successful program for teaching math to young children follows these three cardinal rules: 1) practice, 2) practice, and 3) practice. Not mindless, repetitive practice, but thoughtful and varied practice, in which children are given opportunities to approach problems from a variety of angles, and in which, as they proceed to learn new facts and operations, they consistently review and reinforce their earlier learning. Practice in small doses is generally more effective than extended sessions: sixty minutes of practice in a single sitting is not as beneficial for young learners as three sessions of twenty minutes each.

Regular practice is essential: beginning in kindergarten, children should study math regularly if not daily. This practice needs to be part of a coherent, long-term plan because, for most math competencies, practice needs to be distributed across many weeks, months, or even years, in order to ensure that children can effortlessly and automatically perform the basic operations upon which all "problem solving" and other sophisticated math applications depend.

Some well-meaning people fear that practice in mathematics—for example, memorizing the times tables up to twelve, or doing timed worksheets with one hundred addition and subtraction problems—leads to joyless, soul-killing drudgery. Nothing could be further from the truth. The destroyer of joy in learning mathematics is not practice but anxiety—the anxiety that comes from feeling that one is mathematically stupid or lacks any "special talent" for math. For young children, learning math requires no special talent. It requires only practice, effort, and, of course, competent instruction. Regular practice will give children the absolute familiarity they need with basic operations so that, for example, a second grader *automatically* knows the addition facts up to eighteen, and doesn't have to stop and think about them as he goes on to learn multiplication in third grade. This automatic fluency with basic operations—which is needed for insight and problem-solving skill, even when using a calculator—gives a child a sense of mastery and self-confidence, and makes learning math engaging and interesting rather than frustrating and intimidating.

Math in the *Core Knowledge Sequence:* A Summary

> For information on the specific content guidelines known as the *Core Knowledge Sequence* and on the ideas behind the Core Knowledge initiative, please see in this book "Core Knowledge: Building Knowledge Year by Year" (pages 9–23, especially pages 15–17 on the *Sequence).*

Note: In *The Learning Gap* (Summit Books, 1992), an important comparative study of elementary education in the United States, Japan, and China, Harold Stevenson and James Stigler point out that because math textbooks in the United States are often very long and repetitive, "American teachers often omit some topics. Different topics are omitted by different teachers, thereby making it impossible for the children's later teachers to know what has been covered at earlier grades—they cannot be sure what their students know and what they do not" (page 140).

This practice of individual teachers omitting topics and making isolated decisions about what to teach needs to be replaced by a more coherent approach. It is unfair that the children in Ms. Jones's third grade class work through the textbook chapter on fractions while Ms. Smith's class skips that chapter because "we ran out of time" or because Ms. Smith "thought it was more important to do the chapter on graphs."

Whatever math textbook a school adopts, it is important that the teachers in the school agree on clear and specific learning goals for math in each grade, and focus instruction on helping students to achieve these goals. The *Core Knowledge Sequence* provides a detailed outline of mathematical topics and competencies for the elementary grades. These recommendations reflect research into the math standards of nations that produce consistently excellent results in math achievement at the elementary level, especially France and Japan. The math competencies described in the *Sequence* can be developed only though regular, repeated, and long-term practice.

Here is a *summary* of the Math guidelines in the *Core Knowledge Sequence.*

• **Kindergarten:** Children work with patterns and classification, both with concrete objects and pictorial representations. They compare sets of objects and pictorial representations to practice the concepts of more than, less than, equal to, most, and least. Over time they learn to count forward from 1 to 31, first beginning with 1 and then from any given number. They learn to count backward from ten; from 1 to 10 by twos; and, to 50 by fives and tens. They learn to recognize and write the numbers from 1 to 31. Given a number, they learn to identify one more and one less. They learn what a pair is and how to identify a pair. They learn to identify $1/2$ as one of two equal parts of a region or object, and find $1/2$ of a set of concrete objects.

Children work with money and learn to identify pennies, nickels, dimes, quarters, and the one-dollar bill. They identify the dollar sign ($) and cents sign (¢), and write money amounts using the ¢ sign.

Using concrete objects, children add and subtract to ten, and learn the meaning of the + and − signs.

Children identify familiar tools of measurement and their functions, including a ruler, scale, and thermometer. They measure length in nonstandard units (for example, "How many paper clips long is this?"), and they begin to measure length in inches. They compare the weight of objects and identify which is heavier or lighter. They compare the capacity of containers. They compare temperature (hotter and colder). They learn to read a clock face to the hour, and learn the days of the week and the months of the year. They practice orienting themselves in time using such words as *today, yesterday, tomorrow, this morning* and so on.

Children gain geometrical knowledge and skills, such as identifying left and right, top and bottom, and terms of relative orientation and position such as *closed/open, over/under, above/below, to the right of/to the left of*. They identify basic plane figures: square, rectangle, triangle, and circle. They learn to recognize shapes as the same or different, and to make congruent shapes and designs.

• **Grade 1:** Children continue work with patterns and classification and reinforce concepts of likeness and difference by sorting and classifying objects according to various attributes: size, shape, color, amount, function, and so on. They define a set by the common property of its elements and, in a given set, indicate which item does not belong. They recognize patterns and predict the extension of a pattern.

In working with numbers and counting, children review and build on topics from kindergarten. Over time they learn to recognize and write numbers 0–100; to count from 0–100 by ones, twos, fives, and tens; to count by tens from a given single-digit number; to count forward and backward; to identify ordinal position, 1st to 10th; to identify a dozen, a half dozen, and a pair. They are introduced to the concept of place value, and begin to identify ones, tens, and hundreds. Given a number, they identify one more and one less, as well as ten more and ten less. They compare quantities using the signs $<$, $>$, and $=$. They recognize fractions as part of a whole: $1/2$, $1/3$, $1/4$. They use tallies and create and interpret simple pictorial graphs and bar graphs.

They continue to work with money and learn to identify and recognize the relative value of a penny, nickel, dime, quarter. They learn to use dollars and cents signs (\$ ¢). They show how different combinations of coins equal the same amounts of money.

First-grade computation skills focus on basic addition and subtraction. Over time children learn their addition facts up to 12 and *practice them until mastered*. They learn to add in any order, and they understand what happens when you add zero. They work with different ways of writing addition problems (horizontally and vertically). They learn that when adding three numbers, they get the same sum regardless of how they group the addends. They do two-digit addition without regrouping.

They practice subtraction (using concrete objects, as well as paper and pencil). Over time they learn the subtraction facts to 12 and *practice them until mastered*. They become familiar with different ways of writing subtraction problems (horizontally and vertically). They practice two-digit subtraction without regrouping, as well as subtracting ten from a two-digit number.

Children learn to solve basic one-step story and picture problems, as well as simple equations in the form of ___ $- 2 = 7$; $5 +$ ___ $= 7$.

First graders learn more about measurement. They move from measuring length using nonstandard units (for example, paper clips) to measuring length in inches and feet, as well as in centimeters. They measure and draw line segments in inches and centimeters. They compare weights of objects using a balance scale, and measure weight in nonstandard units and in pounds. They estimate and measure capacity in cups, and learn to measure capacity in quarts and gallons. They use a common thermometer to measure temperature in degrees Fahrenheit. In working with time, they practice sequencing events, and comparing the duration of events. They learn to read a clock face and tell time to the half hour, and they come to know the days of the week and the months of the year, both in order and out of sequence.

Children review and reinforce all the geometrical skills, terms, and concepts introduced in kindergarten. In addition, they learn to describe a square, rectangle, and triangle according to number of sides, and to identify basic solid figures: sphere, cube, and cone.

• **Grade 2:** Children learn to recognize and write numbers to 1,000, and to read and write words for numbers from one to one hundred. They order and compare numbers to 1,000, using the signs $<$, $>$, and $=$. They practice counting (forward and backward) by twos, threes, fives, and tens, and learn to count by tens from any given number. They practice counting by hundreds and fifties to 1,000. They practice using a number line. They learn to identify ordinal position, 1st to 20th, and to identify even and odd numbers. They continue to develop their understanding of place value (ones, tens, hundreds), and practice writing numbers in expanded form (for example $64 = 60 + 4$; $367 = 300 + 60 + 7$). Given a number, they identify one more and one less; ten more and ten less. They learn to round to the nearest ten. They create and interpret simple bar graphs. They practice with fractions: one half, one third, one fourth, one fifth, one sixth, one eighth, one tenth (and corresponding numerical symbols). They review money values, and solve problems in which different combinations of coins equal the same amounts of money.

Second graders develop their computation skills through further work with addition and subtraction, as well as an introduction to multiplication. They learn the addition facts to 18 and *practice them until mastered.* They estimate sums, and solve problems with two-digit and three-digit addends with and without regrouping. They add three two-digit numbers, and practice finding the sum (up to 999) of any two whole numbers. They use addition to check subtraction. They learn subtraction facts to 18 and *practice them until mastered.* They estimate the difference in subtraction problems. They practice two-digit and three-digit subtraction with and without regrouping, such that, given two whole numbers of 999 or less, they can find the difference.

In beginning to study multiplication, second graders learn what *factor* and *product* mean, and they practice multiplying a single-digit number by 1, 2, 3, 4, 5. They come to understand what happens when you multiply, by 1, by 0, and by 10. They solve simple word problems, and solve simple equations in the form of ___ $- 9 = 7$; $7 +$ ___ $= 16$; $4 \times$ ___ $= 8$.

Second graders build on their previous work with measurement. They make linear measurements in feet and inches, and in centimeters. They know that one foot $= 12$ inches, and they learn the abbreviations: *ft., in.* They practice measuring and drawing line segments in inches (to $^1/_2$ inch), and in centimeters. They estimate linear measurements, then measure to check their estimates. They compare weights of objects using a balance scale, estimate and measure weight in pounds, and use the abbreviation, *lb.* They estimate and measure liquid volumes in cups, pints, quarts, gallons. They compare U.S. and metric liquid volumes, the quart and liter (one liter is a little more than one quart). They measure and record temperature in degrees Fahrenheit (to the nearest 2 degrees), and use the degree sign °. They learn to read a clock face and tell time to five-minute intervals, and use the terms *A.M.* and *P.M.,* as well as noon and midnight. They solve problems on elapsed time (how much time has passed?). They write the date using words and numbers, and only numbers.

Second graders review and reinforce topics in geometry from Grade 1 as necessary (left and right, orientation and position, etc.). They learn to measure the perimeter in inches of squares and rectangles. They associate solid figures with planar shapes: sphere (circle), cube (square), pyramid (triangle). They make congruent shapes and designs, and learn to identify lines as horizontal, vertical, perpendicular, parallel. They practice naming lines and line segments (for example, line AB; segment CD). They identify a line of symmetry and create simple symmetric figures.

• **Grade 3:** Third graders learn to read and write numbers (in digits and words) up to six digits. They practice identifying place value up to hundred thousands, and they learn to order and compare numbers to 999,999, using the signs <, >, and =. They practice counting by twos, threes, fives, and tens; counting by tens from any given number; writing numbers in expanded form; and, using a number line. They practice rounding numbers to the nearest ten and to the nearest hundred. They learn to identify perfect squares (and square roots) to 100, and recognize the square root sign. They learn to read Roman numerals from 1 to 20 (I–XX). They are introduced to the concept of negative numbers, and practice locating positive and negative whole numbers on a number line. They create and interpret bar graphs and line graphs.

In working with fractions and decimals, third graders learn to identify the numerator and denominator, to write mixed numbers, to recognize equivalent fractions (for example, $1/2 = 3/6$), and to compare fractions with like denominators, using the signs <, >, and =. They practice reading and writing decimals to the hundredths. They write amounts of money using \$ and ¢ signs and the decimal point, and practice making change using as few coins as possible.

Computation for third grade involves further practice of basic addition facts to ensure mastery, mentally estimating a sum, using mental computation strategies, adding with and without regrouping, and finding the sum (up to 10,000) of any two whole numbers. Children practice basic subtraction facts to ensure mastery, as well as mentally estimating the difference, using mental computation strategies, subtracting with and without regrouping, and solving problems in which, given two whole numbers of 10,000 or less, they find the difference. Children practice until they have mastered basic multiplication facts to 10×10, and come to understand what happens when you multiply, by 10, 100, and 1,000. They practice multiplying two whole numbers, with and without regrouping, in which one factor is 9 or less and the other is a multidigit number up to three digits. They write numbers in expanded form using multiplication, for example $9,278 = (9 \times 1,000) + (2 \times 100) + (7 \times 10) + 8$. They estimate a product and solve word problems involving multiplication.

Third graders are introduced to multiplication and division as opposite operations. They learn the meaning of *dividend, divisor,* and *quotient,* and practice until they master basic division facts to $100 \div 10$. They learn that you cannot divide by 0, and that any number divided by 1 = that number. They divide two- and three-digit dividends by one-digit divisors, and solve division problems with remainders. They practice solving two-step word problems; equations in the form of ____ $\times 9 = 63$ or $81 \div$ ____ $= 9$; and, problems with more than one operation, as in $(43 - 32) \times (5 + 3) =$ ____ .

Third graders practice making linear measurements in yards, in feet and inches, and in centimeters and meters. They know that 1 foot = 12 inches; 1 yard = 36 inches; 3 feet = 1 yard; 1 meter = 100 centimeters; 1 meter is a little more than 1 yard. They measure and draw line segments in inches (to $1/4$ inch), and in centimeters. They estimate linear measurements, then measure to check estimates. They estimate and measure weight in pounds and ounces, and in grams and kilograms. They use the abbreviations *lb, oz., g, kg.* They estimate and measure liquid capacity in cups, pints, quarts, gallons, and liters, and they learn that 1 quart = 2 pints; 1 gallon = 4 quarts. They compare U.S. and metric liquid volumes: quart and liter (one liter is a little more than one quart). They measure and record temperature in degrees Fahrenheit and Celsius, and identify the freezing point of water as $32\,°F = 0\,°C$. They learn to tell time to the minute, and solve problems on elapsed time.

Children review and reinforce topics in geometry from earlier grades. They go on to learn about polygons, and identify sides as line segments (for example, side CD). They can recognize and define a pentagon, hexagon, and octagon. They learn to identify angles, and learn about right angles, as well as the fact that there are four right angles in a square or rectangle. They compute area in square inches (in^2) and square centimeters (cm^2).

• **Grade 4:** Fourth graders read and write numbers (in digits and words) up to nine digits, and recognize place value up to hundred millions. They order and compare numbers to 999,999,999 using the signs $<$, $>$, and $=$. They write numbers in expanded form, and locate positive and negative whole numbers on a number line. They round to the nearest ten; to the nearest hundred; to the nearest thousand. They identify perfect squares (and square roots) to 144, and recognize the square root sign. They learn to identify Roman numerals from 1 to 1,000 (I–M), and identify years as written in Roman numerals. They create and interpret bar graphs and line graphs, and plot points on a coordinate plane (grid), using ordered pairs of positive whole numbers.

In fourth grade children review and extend earlier work with fractions and decimals. They write mixed numbers; change improper fractions to mixed numbers, put fractions in lowest terms, rename fractions with unlike denominators to fractions with common denominators, and compare fractions with like and unlike denominators, using the signs $<$, $>$, and $=$. They solve problems in the form of $2/3 = {}^?/12$. They practice reading and writing decimals to the nearest thousandth. They read and write decimals as fractions (for example, $0.39 = {}^{39}/100$), write decimals in expanded form, round decimals to the nearest tenth and hundredth, and compare decimals using the signs $<$, $>$, and $=$.

By fourth grade, *children should have mastered all basic whole number operations.* They review and reinforce basic multiplication facts to 10×10, identify multiples of a given number as well as common multiples of two given numbers. They multiply by two-digit and three-digit numbers, estimate a product, and use mental computation strategies for multiplication such as breaking a problem into partial products, for example: $3 \times 27 = (3 \times 20) + (3 \times 7) = 60 + 21 = 81$. They solve word problems involving multiplication. They review and reinforce basic division facts to $100 \div 10$, and practice different ways of writing division problems:

$$28 \div 7 \qquad 7\,\overline{)28} \qquad 28/7$$

They learn to identify factors of a given number, as well as the common factor of two given numbers. They practice estimating the quotient, and dividing dividends up to four digits by one-digit and two-digit divisors.

Fourth graders practice solving two-step word problems, and equations in the form of ____ $\times 9 = 63$; $81 \div$ ____ $= 9$. They solve problems with more than one operation, as in $(72 \div 9) \times (144 \div 12) =$ ____ .

Fourth graders build upon and extend earlier work with measurement. They learn the following equivalences among U.S. customary units of measurement, and solve problems involving changing units of measurement:

1 ft = 12 in	1 lb = 16 oz	1 cup = 8 fl oz (fluid ounces)
1 yd = 3 ft = 36 in	1 ton = 2,000 lb	1 pt = 2 c
1 mi = 5,280 ft		1 qt = 2 pt
1 mi = 1,760 yd		1 gal = 4 qt

They learn the following equivalences among metric units of measurement, and solve problems involving changing units of measurement:

1 cm = 10 mm (millimeters)	1 cg (centigram) = 10 mg (milligrams)	
1 m = 100 cm = 1,000 mm	1 g = 100 cg = 1,000 mg	1 liter = 1,000 ml = 100 cl
1 km = 1,000 m	1 kg = 1,000 g	1 cl (centiliter) = 10 ml (milliliters)

Fourth graders build upon previous work in geometry by identifying and drawing points, segments, rays, and lines (horizontal, vertical, perpendicular, parallel, and intersecting). They identify angles as right, acute, or obtuse. They learn to identify various polygons, and to identify and draw diagonals of quadrilaterals. In studying circles, they learn to identify the radius and diameter, and learn that radius = $^1/_2$ diameter. They practice finding the area of a rectangle using the formula Area = Length × Width, and they solve problems involving finding area in a variety of square units (such as mi^2; yd^2; ft^2; in^2; km^2; m^2; cm^2; mm^2). They compute the volume of rectangular prisms in cubic units (cm^3, in^3).

• **Grade 5:** Fifth graders read and write numbers (in digits and words) up to the hundred billions, and identify place value up to billions. They write numbers in expanded form, locate positive and negative whole numbers on a number line, and round to the nearest ten, hundred, thousand, and hundred thousand. They review perfect squares (and square roots) to 144. They identify a set and the members of a set, as indicated by { }. They learn to identify prime numbers less than 50, to determine the greatest common factor (GCF) of given numbers, as well as the least common multiple (LCM) of given numbers.

Fifth graders are introduced to ratio and percent. They determine and express simple ratios, use ratio to create a simple scale drawing, and solve problems on speed as a ratio, using the formula S = d/t. They learn to recognize the percent sign (%) and understand percent as "per hundred." They practice expressing equivalences between fractions, decimals, and percent, and learn common equivalences: $^1/_{10}$ = 10%; $^1/_4$ = 25%; $^1/_2$ = 50%; $^3/_4$ = 75%. They practice finding the given percent of a number.

In building on their earlier work with fractions and decimals, fifth graders determine the least common denominator (LCD) of fractions with unlike denominators, put fractions in lowest terms, compare fractions with like and unlike denominators (using the signs <, >, and =), identify the reciprocal of a given fraction, and learn that the product of a given number and its reciprocal = 1. They practice adding and subtracting fractions with like and unlike denominators, as well as mixed numbers and fractions. They multiply mixed numbers and fractions, round fractions to the nearest whole number, and write fractions as decimals (e.g., $^1/_4$ = 0.25; $^{17}/_{25}$ = 0.68; $^1/_3$ = 0.3333 . . . or 0.33, rounded to the nearest hundredth). They write decimals in expanded form, read and write decimals on a number line, and round decimals to the nearest tenth, hundredth, and thousandth. They estimate decimal sums, difference, and products by rounding.

They add and subtract decimals through ten thousandths, and practice multiplying decimals (by 10, 100, and 1,000; by another decimal).

Fifth graders learn to name and understand the commutative and associative properties of addition, as well as the commutative, associative, and distributive properties of multiplication. They practice multiplying two factors of up to four digits each, writing numbers in expanded form using multiplication, estimating a product, and using mental computation strategies for multiplication. They solve word problems using multiplication and division. They practice estimating the quotient, and moving the decimal point when dividing by 10, 100, or 1,000. They practice dividing dividends up to four digits by one-digit, two-digit, and three-digit divisors. They solve word problems with multiple steps, and problems with more than one operation.

Fifth graders review and practice measurement, and solve problems involving addition and subtraction of different units requiring conversion to common units.

Further work with geometry includes measuring the degrees in angles, learning that a right angle is 90°; an acute angle is less than 90°; an obtuse angle is greater than 90°; and a straight angle is 180°. They learn to identify and construct different kinds of triangles: equilateral, right, and isosceles. They identify and draw various polygons. They identify an arc, chord, radius, and diameter of a circle, and use a compass to draw circles with a given diameter or radius. They practice finding the circumference of a circle using the formulas $C = \pi \times d$, and $C = 2 \pi \times r$, using 3.14 as the value of *pi*. They review the formula for the area of a rectangle (Area = length × width) and solve problems involving finding area in a variety of square units (such as mi^2; yd^2; ft^2; in^2; km^2; m^2; cm^2; mm^2). They practice finding the area of triangles using the formula $A = 1/2(b \times h)$. They compute the area of a parallelogram using the formula $A = b \times h$. They learn how to find the area of an irregular figure (such as a trapezoid) by dividing it into regular figures for which they know how to find the area. They compute volume of rectangular prisms in cubic units (cm^3, in^3), using the formula $V = l \times w \times h$.

Fifth graders are introduced to the concept of probability as a measure of the likelihood that an event will happen. Using simple models, they express the probability of a given event as a fraction. They collect and organize data in graphic form (bar, line, and circle graphs). They solve problems requiring interpretation and application of graphically displayed data. They learn to find the average (mean) of a given set of numbers. They practice plotting points on a coordinate plane, using ordered pairs of positive and negative whole numbers, as well as graphing simple functions.

Fifth graders learn to recognize variables and solve simple equations with one variable. They practice writing and solving equations for word problems.

• **Grade 6:** Sixth graders review and reinforce all skills with numbers and number sense specified above for fifth grade (place value, ordering, understanding integers, rounding, squaring and square roots, identifying prime numbers, greatest common factor, and least common muiltiple). They learn to use exponents, and the terms *squared, cubed,* and *to the nth power*. They read and evaluate numerical expressions with exponents, identify value of powers of ten up to 10^6, and write numbers in expanded notation using exponents.

Sixth graders continue work with ratio and percent. They solve problems, including word problems, involving proportions with one unknown. They use ratios and proportions to interpret map scales and scale drawings. They express equivalences between fractions, decimals, and percents; find the given percent of a number; find what percent a given number is of another number; solve problems involving percent increase and decrease; find an unknown number when a percent of the number is known; and, use expressions with percents greater than 100%.

Further work with fractions and decimals for sixth graders includes adding and subtracting mixed numbers and fractions with like and unlike denominators; multiplying and dividing mixed numbers and whole numbers and fractions; dividing by a fraction (i.e., multiplying by reciprocal); and, writing fractions as decimals and as percents. Sixth graders review earlier work with decimals and solving problems with decimals.

Sixth graders review and apply computation skills in problem solving. They multiply multidigit factors, with and without a calculator. They divide multidigit dividends by up to three-digit divisors, with and without a calculator. They solve word problems with multiple steps, and problems with more than one operation according to order of operations (with and without a calculator).

Sixth graders solve problems requiring conversion of units within the U.S. Customary System, and within the metric system. They learn to associate prefixes used in metric system with quantities: kilo = thousand; hecto = hundred; deka = ten; deci = tenth; centi = hundredth; milli = thousandth.

In geometry, sixth graders identify and use signs that mean "is congruent to," "is similar to," "is parallel to," and "is perpendicular to." They construct parallel lines and a parallelogram, as well as a perpendicular bisector. They learn that if two lines are parallel, any line perpendicular to one is also perpendicular to the other; and, that two lines perpendicular to the same line are parallel. They identify and measure the degrees in angles (review terms: right, acute, obtuse, straight); practice bisecting angles; construct an angle congruent to a given angle; and construct a figure congruent to a given figure, using reflection over a line of symmetry, and identify corresponding parts. They learn how congruent plane figures can be made to correspond through reflection, rotation, and translation. They solve problems based on the fact that the sum of the measures of the angles of a triangle is 180°. They construct different kinds of triangles, and learn the terms by which we classify kinds of triangles: by length of sides (equilateral, isosceles, scalene) and by angles (right, acute, obtuse). They identify congruent angles and sides, and axes of symmetry, in parallelograms, rhombuses, rectangles, and squares. They practice finding the area (A) and perimeter (P) of plane figures, or given the area or perimeter find the missing dimension, using the following formulas:

rectangle: $A = lw$ $P = 2(l + w)$
square: $A = s^2$ $P = 4s$
triangle: $A = \frac{1}{2}bh$ $P = s1 + s2 + s3$
parallelogram: $A = bh$ $P = 2(b + s)$

Sixth graders solve problems involving application of the formulas for finding the circumference of a circle: $C = \pi d$, and $C = 2\pi r$, using 3.14 as the value of *pi*. They find the area of a circle using the formula $A = \pi r^2$. They find volume of rectangular solids, or given the volume find a missing dimension, using the formulas $V = lwh$, or $V = bh$ [in which b = area of base].

Building upon their prior study of probability and statistics, sixth graders express probability of a given event as a fraction or ratio, and solve problems requiring interpretation and application of graphically displayed text. Given a set of data, students find the mean, median, range, and mode. They construct a histogram and a tree diagram. They plot points on a coordinate plane, using ordered pairs of positive and negative whole numbers, and learn the terms "origin" (0,0); "x-axis"; and, "y-axis." They graph simple functions and solve problems involving use of a coordinate plane.

Sixth graders recognize variables and solve equations with one variable, and practice writing and solving equations for word problems.

MATHEMATICS

Supplementary Resources

The Core Knowledge Series: *What Your Kindergartner–Sixth Grader Needs to Know*, E. D. Hirsch, Jr., editor. Published by Doubleday in hardcover and Dell in paperback.

The seven current books in the Core Knowledge Series, one each for kindergarten through sixth grade, are the companion books to this resource guide. These illustrated books provide a convenient introduction to topics in the *Core Knowledge Sequence*, including the Math topics summarized on pages 307–314. Full of stories, poems, history, and discussions of topics in language arts, history, geography, science, the visual arts and music, the books can be read to children or, in the upper grades, read by children. All author's proceeds from the sale of *What Your Kindergartner–Sixth Grader Needs to Know* go to the nonprofit Core Knowledge Foundation to support its mission of helping parents and teachers help children develop strong early foundations of knowledge.

CC = a "**Core Collection**" book (see p. 8).

Note: Here we recommend resources that can *supplement but not replace* the math textbooks and workbooks used in schools. Our recommendations are directed primarily to parents who want to reinforce and supplement what their children learn in school, but not teach math in a home-schooling program, for which more extensive materials are needed, such as the primary grade materials of the Saxon Math program, which offers a systematic, easy-to-follow set of daily lessons with regular review and reinforcement. This program, while not ideal, is, according to our consultants, one of the more effective currently available. (For information on Saxon Math, call [800] 284-7019.)

GENERAL RESOURCES

Anno's Math Games
written and illustrated by Mitsumasa Anno
Philomel Books, 1987
Two little gnomelike characters, Kriss and Kross, take us on a tour of a variety of mathematical topics. Through clever illustrations, the author encourages children to engage in mathematical thinking about relationships of quantity and size, sameness and difference, proportion, shapes, direction, and much more. Some of these are real mind-teasers! Suitable for children in about kindergarten through third grade. If you like this book, there are two more: *Anno's Math Games II* (1989) and *Anno's Math Games III* (1991).

CC *Family Math*
by Jean Kerr Stenmark, Virginia Thompson, and
  Ruth Cossey
Regents of the University of California, 1986
This generous, helpful book provides clear directions for math activities that parents can do
with children from 5 to 12 years old. It includes
word problems, measurement, geometry, estimation, arithmetic, and lots of ideas for things
to make. The book is easy to follow, and the
activities are both fun and substantial, providing
a great way to supplement (not replace) math
instruction in school. For more information on
ordering the book, write or call Lawrence Hall
of Science, Attention: Family Math, University
of California, Berkeley, CA 94720; (510) 642-
1910.

The I Hate Mathematics! Book
by Marilyn Burns
illustrated by Martha Hairston
Little, Brown, 1975
The title, while unfortunate, is probably all too
accurate for many people. The author provides
puzzles, mind-teasers, riddles, sidewalk games
and other problems and activities, suitable for
children in about grades 4–8. With amusing,
cartoonlike illustrations. If you like this book,
then try, by the same author, *Math for Smarty
Pants* (Little, Brown, 1982).

*Janice VanCleave's Math for Every Kid: Easy
Activities that Make Learning Math Fun*
by Janice VanCleave
illustrated by Barbara Clark
John Wiley & Sons, 1991
For children in about second through sixth
grade, here are lively explanations of a variety
of math topics, with suggested activities and
problems.

Math Made Meaningful
Cuisinaire Company of America
There's a big emphasis in schools on teaching
math through the use of "manipulatives,"
hands-on concrete objects, especially in the primary grades. Children use the most readily

available manipulatives—their fingers—when
first learning to count and compute (this practice, by the way, should *not* be discouraged in
young children, as reliable researchers have
found that finger counting helps children make
a faster transition to more symbolic math operations). Manipulatives, then, make sense in the
early learning of math, but the idea is to use
them in order to get beyond them, so that by
the upper elementary grades children are doing
more "mental math." All this is by way of introducing the Cuisinaire Company and its
"Math Made Meaningful" kit, which can be
used at home or school for children in preschool
and up. It consists of more than 150 rods (in
plastic or wood) and a manual that explains
how to use them. The kit can be purchased directly from the Cuisinaire Company of America,
P. O. Box 5026, White Plains, NY 10602-5026.
For current price and ordering information, call
(914) 997-2600.

Tangram
by Joost Elffers
Penguin, 1977
Many children from kindergarten on enjoy playing with a tangram, a puzzle, thought to have
been created in China long ago, which consists
of a square that has been marked off into seven
geometric shapes. Try also *Fun with Tangrams
Kit* and *Tangrams ABC Kit* by Susan Johnston
(Dover Publications, 31 East Second Street, Mineola, NY 11501).

Young Explorers in Mathematics series
by JoAnne Nelson
various illustrators
Modern Curriculum Press
This series of six books is appropriate for children in kindergarten through second grade.
Each colorful book tells a little story that introduces a math concept and associated skills.
The publisher markets to schools, so the books
are only available in packages of six or more.
Each book is also available in "big book" format, along with optional Activity Mats and a
Teaching Companion. For more information, call

the publisher at (800) 321-3106. Individual titles include: *How Tall Are You?*; *Neighborhood Soup*; *One and One Make Two*; *Count by Twos*; *Half and Half*; *The Magic Money Machine*.

COMPUTER SOFTWARE

Note: For those who have access to computers capable of running these software programs, they can provide fun ways to practice mathematical skills and thinking through a variety of different games and activities. Like all the math resources, these are supplementary materials, not the primary media for learning math. The children's software field is growing rapidly; while these were some of the best programs available when this book was complied, there are no doubt more available now.

Early Math Software (prekindergarten through grade 2)

Early Math
Sierra On-Line
Children from about 3 to 6 will enjoy the basic math activities that take place inside an asteroid with a funny alien named Loid.

James Discovers Math
Broderbund
When the screen comes up you see James in his kitchen. By clicking different objects, you start different activities, including measurement (using an illustration of a pencil as the unit of measurement, and measuring such objects as an alligator!), counting, simple adding and subtracting, and more, with occasional songs and puzzles adding to the fun.

Math Rabbit
The Learning Company
Basic skills—including counting, matching numbers to sets of objects, recognizing patterns, and adding and subtracting—are reinforced through

a variety of activities that take place in a fun circus setting. Designed for children from about 4 to 7 years old.

Millie's Math House
Edmark
For preschoolers to kindergartners, this program, which has received many awards, uses children's voices, sound effects, music, and funny characters, including Millie the Cow, in activities designed to help children recognize and name shapes, recognize sizes, count, match numbers with sets of objects, and other basic skills.

Intermediate Math Software (grades 3–6)

Adi's 2nd and 3rd Grade Mathematics
Adi's 4th and 5th Grade Mathematics
Sierra On-Line
These ambitious packages aim to provide a solid math curriculum that educates as it entertains. There's a lot packed into these CD-ROMs, hosted by an extraterrestrial being named Adi. Besides many activities designed to help children practice math computation and concepts (such as ordering and estimation), there are full-motion animated video clips that explain math concepts, and a collection of games that can be accessed by answering questions. Lessons are organized by "chapters," and completed lessons are logged on a Student Progress screen. The math gets pretty challenging on the discs for grades 4 and 5, so be prepared to offer some occasional advice and encouragement. (Sierra On-Line also offers "Adi" programs for English and Science.)

Math Blaster 1: In Search of Spot
Davidson
With plenty of problems and a variety of skill levels, this program provides fun ways to practice mental math skills in addition, subtraction, multiplication, division, fractions, decimals, percents, estimation, and number patterns. The

video-arcade-style games are part of a story in which the child solves problems as part of a battle against the "Trash Alien" who has littered the universe and captured Spot. To the rescue! For more advanced students try *Math Blaster 2* and *Math Blaster Mystery.*

Math Workshop
Broderbund

This popular program, designed for children ages 6 to 10, helps children develop computation and problem-solving skills through a variety of games, including "Bowling for Numbers," "Puzzle Patterns," "Rhythm Generator," and more, all with funny animated characters, music, and sound effects.

Super Solvers OutNumbered!
The Learning Company

Morty Maxwell, Master of Mischief, threatens to destroy the Shady Glen TV station. Well, go ahead—but no, that's not the point! The point is for children from about 7 to 10 years old to use their computation skills and solve word problems in order to collect clues and, before time runs out, foil the dastardly Morty and his evil scheme. Besides the game, the program also offers a "Drill for Skill" option, which allows focused practice of basic math facts.

NUMBERS AND COUNTING

Note: Many counting books are appropriate for preschoolers, but they can be enjoyed by kindergartners and first graders as well, for whom the illustrations and the rhymes or stories provide a delightful way to reinforce and review.

Animal Numbers
written and illustrated by Bert Kitchen
Dial Books, 1987

The numbers from 1 to 10 are represented in this attractive oversized book by a mother animal with the corresponding number of off-

spring. Children can trace the large number and count the number of offspring. Also depicts the numbers 15, 25, 50, 75, and 100.

CC Anno's Counting Book
written and illustrated by Mitsumasa Anno
HarperCollins, 1977

This wordless picture book depicts the numbers 0–12. Beautiful illustrations show activities of people and animals through the twelve months of the year. Each double-page spread provides many sets of objects for children to count. As the illustrations change to show increasing numbers, a tower of cubes also grows in the left margin. There are notes about numbers at the end of the book. (A paperback edition is also available from Scholastic.)

Feast for 10
written and illustrated by Cathryn Falwell
Clarion Books, 1993

Colorful collages of cut paper and other materials illustrate a pleasant rhyming story about buying groceries and then preparing a big dinner—which lets you count to ten twice. A nice read-aloud for preschoolers and kindergartners.

How Many Bugs in a Box?
written and illustrated by David A. Carter
Simon & Schuster, 1987

This is a sturdy pop-up book that introduces the numbers 1–10. The reader is asked, "How many bugs are in the (blue, yellow, small, thin, etc.) box?" on each double page. Each pop-up is a new surprise, such as "4/four/fast/fleas," which run off the page as the pop-up appears! If you like this book, you may also want to see its sequel, *More Bugs in Boxes* (Simon and Schuster, 1990).

How Much Is a Million?
by David M. Schwartz
illustrated by Steven Kellogg
Lothrop, Lee & Shepard, 1985

Aided by the vivid, imaginative interpretations of illustrator Steven Kellogg, the wizard Marvelosissimo introduces four children to the magnitude of large numbers. How long does it take to count to one million? How high would the column reach if one million children stand on one another's shoulders?

I Spy Two Eyes
by Lucy Micklethwait
Greenwillow Books, 1993
This book reproduces paintings from around the world and asks children to practice counting as they look for a certain number of birds, apples, circles, and other objects in paintings ranging from the fifteenth century to the present day.

Monster Math
by Grace Maccarone
illustrated by Marge Hartelius
Scholastic, 1995
To help children count backward and understand the concept of "one less than," here's a cute rhyming poem, something like the old song about "Five little monkeys jumping on the bed, one fell off," etc. The brightly colored illustrations depict playful, friendly-looking monsters. This book is part of the publisher's Hello Math Reader series, and while we can recommend this volume, we cannot say the same for all books in the series.

One Bear at Bedtime
by Mick Inkpen
Little, Brown/Dell (paper), 1987
As a little boy is getting ready for bed, numerals and word names for the numbers 1–10 help describe his activities. There are many opportunities for children to count, for example, the four giraffes who sit in the bath and nine caterpillars who wander through the pages of the book. On the last page the little boy faces a challenge: how can he sleep surrounded by all of the animals who helped him get ready?

Numbears: A Counting Book
by Kathleen Hague
illustrated by Michael Hague
Henry Holt, 1986
"Kathleen's seen a nest out her window,/Up

high on the second floor;/ Snug inside the basket of twigs/ Are blue eggs—she counted four." Each Teddy bear in this charming picture book has a rhyme, and each rhyme gives the child an opportunity to practice counting up to twelve. A paperback is available from Scholastic.

One Was Johnny
written and illustrated by Maurice Sendak
HarperCollins, 1962
Count from one to ten and then back again in this funny, sometimes silly rhyming story that young children will enjoy hearing over and over again. Available as a separate title or as part of the "Nutshell Library" package (with *Chicken Soup with Rice*—described below under Time—*Alligators All Around*, and *Pierre*.)

Rooster's Off to See the World
written and illustrated by Eric Carle
Picture Book Studio, 1987/Scholastic
Through striking illustrations and a pleasant story about a rooster who, on his way to see the world, is joined by fourteen animals, this book offers a fun way to reinforce the meaning of numbers and sets for children in kindergarten and first grade.

Too Many Balloons
by Catherine Matthias
illustrated by Gene Sharp
Childrens Press, 1982
A little girl buys balloons at the zoo and shows them to the animals. On each page she buys a different number—first one red, then two yellow, and so on. The number of animals she shows them to on each page is equivalent to the number of balloons.

The Very Hungry Caterpillar
written and illustrated by Eric Carle
G. P. Putnam's Sons, 1981
A modern classic for preschoolers and kindergartners, this clever and brightly illustrated book reinforces counting and the days of the week as it tells the story of how much a little caterpillar eats on his way to becoming a butterfly.

What Comes In 2's, 3's & 4's?
by Suzanne Aker and Bernie Karlin
illustrated by Bernie Karlin
Simon & Schuster, 1990
How many sides to a piece of pizza? How
many wheels on a wagon? This boldly illustrated counting book depicts various things that
can be found in 2's, 3's, and 4's in daily life.

COMPUTATION

Bunches and Bunches of Bunnies
by Louise Mathews
illustrated by Jeni Bassett
Dodd, Mead/Scholastic, 1978
The title sums up the pictures in this counting
book with a twist: the rhyming story presents
bunnies in groups (of two, three, four, up to
twelve), and so introduces the idea that multiplication is a quick form of addition: for example, "Count the bunnies at the ball, / Rabbit
partners, short and tall. / Now the music comes
alive, / And 5×5 is 25."

The Doorbell Rang
written and illustrated by Pat Hutchins
Greenwillow Books, 1986
A book about sharing, and about how to divide
a dozen. The story begins in Ma's kitchen with
a dozen cookies and two children. But then the
doorbell rings and neighbors drop by. Then the
doorbell rings again, and again. . . .

A Grain of Rice
written and illustrated by Helena Clare Pittman
Bantam Skylark, 1992
A classic Chinese tale in which, for a reward, a
farmer asks for one grain of rice doubled every
day for a hundred days—which doesn't sound
like much until you figure it out. For another
version of this story, set in India, try *The King's
Chessboard* by David Birch (Dial Books for
Young Readers, 1988).

CC = "Core Collection" book (see page 8).

Mental Math in the Primary Grades (1988)
Mental Math in the Middle Grades (1987)
by Jack Hope, Larry Leutzinger, Barbara J. Reys,
    and Robert E. Reys
Dale Seymour
These books developed for classroom teachers
can also be used at home (if you're prepared to
offer some explanation and assistance). They
provide activities designed to help children "do
math in their heads." The *Primary Grades* book,
for grades 1–3, focuses on mental math abilities
with addition and subtraction. The *Middle
Grades* book, for grades 4–6, provides activities
for addition, subtraction, multiplication, and division. May be ordered directly from the publisher, a supplier of a variety of math materials
(of varying quality), by calling (800) 872-1100.

One Hundred Hungry Ants
by Elinor J. Pineczes
illustrated by Bonnie Mackain
Houghton Mifflin, 1993
Here's a whimsical story in verse of ants trying
out different formations to get to a picnic faster:
shall they go in two lines of 50? four lines of
25? five of 20? The story is a fun way to introduce factors of 100. The same author and illustrator have also produced a charming story to
illustrate the concept of remainders in division,
called *A Remainder of One* (Houghton Mifflin,
1995).

FRACTIONS

Eating Fractions
written and photo-illustrated by Bruce McMillan
Scholastic, 1991
Colorful photographs and very simple text (just
single words on the pages) introduce children to
wholes, halves, thirds, and fourths of pizza,
strawberry pie, and other foods. Be prepared for
a snack after reading!

Fraction Action
written and illustrated by Loreen Leedy
Holiday House, 1994
The dust jacket claims this book "is HALF for

fun and HALF for learning," and it's right. Children love the zany illustrations and silly asides as Miss Prime, a slender hippopotamus, teaches her students about fractions. Her lessons cover halves, thirds, fourths, dividing whole sets into fractions, and more.

TIME (INCLUDING TELLING TIME, DAYS OF THE WEEK, MONTHS OF THE YEAR):

Chicken Soup with Rice: A Book of Months
written and illustrated by Maurice Sendak
HarperCollins, 1962
A wonderful rhyming story, with Sendak's humorous drawings, takes us through the months of the year, with a serving of chicken soup with rice in every month. A fun book to read aloud and enjoy over and over again. Available as a separate title or as part of the "Nutshell Library" package (with *One Was Johnny*—described above under Counting Books—*Alligators All Around*, and *Pierre.*)

Clock-O-Dial
Educational Insights
Young children enjoy this "hands-on" kit for learning to tell time with a funny crocodile clock. Available at many teacher supply stores and some toy stores, or direct from the manufacturer in California by calling (213) 979-1955 (if you call the manufacturer, ask first about their minimum order policy).

My First Book of Time
by Claire Llewellyn
Dorling Kindersley, 1992
This big book, with lots of brightly colored photographs, introduces children to the four seasons, the days of the week, and telling time. It includes a foldout clock with movable hands, as well as suggestions for a few timely (sorry, we couldn't resist!) projects.

Time to . . .
written and illustrated by Bruce McMillan
Lothrop, Lee & Shepard, 1989
An hour-by-hour introduction to telling time that follows a kindergartner through his day from waking up to bedtime.

Today Is Monday
illustrated by Eric Carle
Philomel Books, 1993
Eric Carle adapts the traditional song, which repeats the names of the days of the week, and adds his distinctive bold, colorful illustrations. A delight to look at and read aloud to young children.

MONEY

Alexander, Who Used to Be Rich Last Sunday
by Judith Viorst
Simon & Schuster Children's/Aladdin, 1978
Alexander receives a dollar from his grandparents and spends it a little at a time. The reader can discover if Alexander has any money left.

If You Made a Million
by David M. Schwartz
illustrated by Steven Kellogg
Lothrop, Lee & Shepard, 1989
From the team that brought us *How Much Is a Million?* comes another exuberantly illustrated book. The pages combine Kellogg's illustrations with photographs of money that clearly depict how many pennies make up a nickel, how many nickels make up a dime, how many one- and five-dollar bills make up a ten-dollar bill, etc. The story proceeds to the sum of a million dollars. Along the way it introduces the idea of putting money in a bank and earning interest, which may be a difficult concept for very young listeners. A Teaching Guide is available from Scholastic.

INDEX

A

Abe Lincoln's Hat (Brenner), 153

Abiyoyo (Seeger), 243

Abraham Lincoln: A Man for All the People (Livingston), 164

Accorsi, William, 272

Ackerman, Karen, 241

Across America on an Emigrant Train (Murphy), 184

Across Five Aprils (Hunt), 183

Across the Wide Dark Sea: The Mayflower Journey (Van Leeuwen), 157

Adam of the Road (Gray), 132

Adler, David A., 154, 165, 168, 273

Adolescence, 295

Adventures of Pinocchio, The (adap. Kassirer), 57

Adventures of Sherlock Holmes, The (Sadler), 85–86

Adventures of Tom Sawyer, The (Twain), 84

Adventures of Ulysses, The (Evslin), 90

Adventures with Atoms and Molecules: Chemistry Experiments for Young People (Mebane and Rybolt), 289, 296

Adventures with Rocks and Minerals Book I: Geology Experiments for Young People (Barrow), 289

Adzinya, Abraham Kobena, 235

Aeneid (Virgil), 91

Aesop for Children, The, 54

Aesop's Fables, 54–55

Aesop's Fables (illus. Hague), 54

Aesop's Fables (illus. Holder), 54

Africa

    art of, 216

    early and medieval, 133–134

Africa (Georges), 134

African Art (Sandak), 216

Age of Exploration, 136–137

Age of Extremes, An (Hakim), 188, 190, 191

Ageorges, Véronique, 132

Aher, Jackie, 295

Ahoy! Ahoy! Are You There? A Story of Alexander Graham Bell (Quackenbush), 287

Aida (Verdi), 241

AIDS: How It Works in the Body (Greenberg), 303

Aiken, Riley, 74

Air Is All Around You (Branley), 269–270

Air Pollution (Stille), 284

A Is for Africa (Onyefulu), 111

Aladdin and the Magic Lamp (Hautzig), 73

Aladdin and the Wonderful Lamp (Carrick), 73

Albers, Dave, 61, 67

Albert Einstein (Ireland), 304

Albert Einstein and the Theory of Relativity (Cwiklik), 304

Alcott, Louisa May, 84–85

Alden, Peter, 282

Alderson, Brian, 73

Aldred, Cyril, 113

Alexander, Who Used to Be Rich Last Sunday (Viorst), 323

Ali Baba and the Forty Thieves (McVitty), 73

Alice in Wonderland (Carroll), 73

Aliki, 52, 69, 71, 74, 114, 130, 144–145, 155, 159, 174, 244, 261, 264, 268, 291

Alison's Zinnia (Lobel), 47

All About Electricity (Berger), 270

All About Light: A Do-It-Yourself Science Book (Berger), 284

All About Magnets (Krensky), 279

All About Sound (Berger), 283

Allen, Thomas B., 157, 162

All for Freedom (Sweet Honey in the Rock), 235

All God's Critters Got a Place in the Choir (Staines), 244

Allison, Linda, 256

All the King's Animals: The Return of Endangered Wildlife to Swaziland (Kessler), 267

All-Time Favorite Dances, 240

Along the Santa Fe Trail (Russell), 184

Alphabears: An ABC Book (Hague), 47

Alphabet books, 47

Amazing Birds (Parsons), 281

Amazing Fish (Ling), 266

Amazing Impossible Erie Canal, The (Harness), 162

Amazing Insects (Mound), 276

Amazing Mammals (Parsons), 282

Amazing Schemes Within Your Genes (Balkwill), 302

Ambrus, Victor G., 78

America, I Hear You: A Story about George Gershwin (Mitchell), 236

American Army of Two, An (Greeson), 161

American Classical League Catalog of Teaching Materials for Teachers of Latin, Greek, and Classical Humanities, 122, 125, 142

American Family Album series (Hoobler and Hoobler), 147, 188

American government, 161, 178–179

American Highlights: United States History in Notable Works of Art (Pavese), 220

American History Through Song series, 230

American Indian Myths and Legends (ed. Erdoes and Ortiz), 87

American Reader, The (Ravitch), 147–148

American Revolution, 158–160, 175–178

American Tall Tales, 70–71

American Tall Tales (Osborne), 70

American West, 160, 162–163, 184–186

America the Beautiful (Bates), 244

Amos, James L., 138

Amphibians and reptiles, 281

Anansi and the Moss-Covered Rock (Kimmel), 57, 61

Anansi and the Talking Melon (Kimmel), 57

Anansi Goes Fishing (Kimmel), 57

Ancient Africa Volume 2: The Art of Life (Bellerophon Books), 216

Ancient art, 208–209

Ancient China, 120–121

Ancient China (Nicholson and Watts), 120

Ancient civilizations, 112–114, 141–143

Ancient Civilizations: Mesopotamia (Pofahl), 112

Ancient Civilizations Time Traveler series (Pofahl), 105

Ancient Egypt, 113–114

Ancient Egypt (Hart), 113

Ancient Greece, 122–123, 142–143
    mythology, 68–70, 75–76, 90–91

Ancient Greece (Cohen), 122, 142

Ancient Greece (Nicholson and Watts), 122–123

Ancient Greece (Pearson), 123

Ancient India: A Bellerophon Coloring Book, 119

Ancient Near East, The: A Bellerophon Coloring Book, 112

Ancient Rome, 125–126, 142–143

Ancient Rome: A Cultural Atlas for Young People (Corbishley), 142

Ancient World of the Bible, The (Day), 103, 114, 141

Ancient World series, 105–106

Ancona, George, 171

Andersen, Hans Christian, 42, 59, 62, 66, 74

Anderson, Joan, 171

Andreason, Dan, 161

Androcles and the Lion (Stevens), 75

Angel Child, Dragon Child (Surat), 166

Angeli, Marguerite de, 132

Anholt, Laurence, 209, 211

Animal Fables from Aesop, 55

Animal Numbers (Kitchen), 320

Animals and pets, 260–261

Animals Born Alive and Well (Heller), 260

Animals in Winter (Riha), 274

Animal Tales (Weiss), 51

Anno, Mitsumasa, 129, 317, 320

Anno's Counting Book (Anno), 320

Anno's Math Games (Anno), 317

Anno's Medieval World, 129

Ant (Chinery), 277

Anthony Burns: The Defeat and Triumph of a Fugitive Slave (Hamilton), 182

Apple and the Arrow, The: The Legend of William Tell (Buff and Buff), 74–75

Applebaum, Stanley, 113

Appleby, Ellen, 53, 54

Arabian Nights, The (Alderson), 73

Arabian Nights, The (Philip), 73
Arabian Nights Entertainments, The (ed. Lang), 73
Arabs in the Golden Age, The (Moktefi), 132
Arab World and Islamic Resources and School
    Services (AWAIR), 132
Archambault, Alan, 159
Archambault, John, 47, 240
Archipowa, Anastassija, 74
*Architects Make Zigzags: Looking at Architecture
    from A to Z* (Maddex), 202
Architecture, 202–203, 215–216
Ardley, Neil, 233–234, 259, 279
Arenas, José Fernández, 218–219
Armies of Ants (Retan), 277
Armstrong, Nicholas, 277
Arnold, Caroline, 136, 266
*Around the World in a Hundred Years: From Henry
    the Navigator to Magellan* (Fritz), 136
Arrow and the Lamp, The: The Story of Psyche
    (Hodges), 75
Arrow to the Sun: A Pueblo Indian Tale
    (McDermott), 52
Art
    American, 216–217, 220
    ancient, 208–209
    elements of, 200, 205–206, 208, 210, 218, 222
    histories, 202, 221
    how-to and activity books, 198–200
    and literature, 204
    Renaissance, 218–220
Art for Children series (Raboff), 200, 206, 209,
    211–212, 214, 219, 222, 223
Arthur, High King of Britain (Morpurgo), 80
Arthur, Malcolm, 60
Arthurian legends, 80–82
Artists, 200–202, 206–207, 209–214, 219–220, 222–
    223
Art museums, 203–204
Art of . . . , The series (Glubok), 200–201, 210,
    216
Art of Africa, The (Glubok), 216
Art of America from Jackson to Lincoln, The
    (Glubok), 220
Art of Japan, The (Glubok), 211
Art of the New American Nation, The (Glubok),
    220
Art prints and reproductions, 197–198

Aruego, José, 145
Ashanti to Zulu: African Traditions (Musgrove),
    133–134
Ashby, Ruth, 104
Asimov, Isaac, 253, 300–302
Asking About Sex and Growing Up (Cole), 295
Assassination of Julius Caesar, The (Ochoa), 142
Astronomy, 285–287, 301
At Home in the Tide Pool (Wright), 266
Atlases, 108–111
A to Zen (Wells), 121–122
Aust, Siegfried, 284
Autumn (Thomson and Hewitt), 262
Avery, Gillian, 38, 83, 88
A Was Once an Apple Pie (Lear), 47
Axelrod, Alan, 230
Aztec, Inca & Maya (Baquedano), 135
Aztec, The (McKissack), 155
Aztec civilization, 135–136, 155–156
Aztecs, The (Nicholson and Watts), 135
Aztecs, The (Odjik), 135
Aztecs, The (Wood), 135–136

B

Baby Animals (Royston), 260
Baby Dance, 236–237
*Bach, Beethoven and the Boys: Music History as It
    Ought to Be Taught* (Barbers), 237
Back, Christine, 259, 275
Backstein, Karen, 65
Bacteria and Viruses (LeMaster), 269
Bailey, Donna, 127
Baillet, Yolanda, 221
Bains, Rae, 273
Baker, Alan, 81
Baker, Jeannie, 263
Baker, Lucy, 265–266
Baldwin, James, 75
Balestrino, Philip, 268
Balkwill, Fran, 302
Bang, Molly Garrett, 67
Baquedano, Elizabeth, 135
Barber, David W., 237

Barberis, Juan Carlos, 302
Bard of Avon: The Story of William Shakespeare (Stanley and Vennema), 85
Barn Dance! (Martin and Archambault), 240
Barret, Angela, 53, 241
Barrett, Marvin, 180
Barrie, J. M., 67
Barrow, Lloyd H., 289
Bartoletti, Susan, 168
Bartone, Elisa, 167
Bash, Barbara, 267, 285
Bassett, Jeni, 322
Bates, Katharine Lee, 244
Battle of Lexington and Concord, The (Johnson), 175
Baumann, Kurt, 116
Bayley, Rosalind, 112
Beall, Pam, 231
Bean and Plant (Back), 259
Beating the Drum (Paker), 233
Beatty, Patricia, 184
Beauty and the Beast, 65
Beckett, Sister Wendy, 202, 221
Bedik, Shelly, 273
Bee, Friend of Flowers, The (Starosta), 277
Beethoven Lives Upstairs (Nichol), 237
Be Ever Hopeful, Hannalee (Beatty), 184
Beginning of the Earth, The (Branley), 285, 291
Beginning reading materials (not phonetically controlled), 48–49
Beier, Ellen, 238, 264
Being Born (Kitzinger), 295–296
Beliefs and Believers (Pollard), 115, 138, 141
Ben and Me (Lawson), 177
Benchley, Nathaniel, 159
Bender, Michael, 219
Bendick, Jeanne, 287, 300
Bending Light (Murphy), 284
Beneath a Blue Umbrella (Prelutsky), 36
Benedict, Kitty C., 144
Ben Franklin Book of Easy and Incredible Experiments, The, 289
Bennett, Evelyn, 180
Bennett, William J., 75
Benson, Patrick, 65
Ben's Trumpet (Isadora), 242
Berenzy, Alix, 60

Berger, Gilda, 275
Berger, Melvin, 255, 267, 269, 270, 275, 283, 284, 288, 289, 296, 300
Berkin, Mark, 133
Berlioz the Bear (Brett), 244
Best-Loved Folktales of the World (ed. Cole), 38–39, 74, 78, 80, 86
Best of Aesop's Fables, The, 54
Betsy Ross (Wallner), 158
Bewick, Thomas, 38, 83, 88
Bicycle Man, The (Say), 122
Big Bug Book, The (Facklam), 277
Bill and Pete Go Down the Nile (De Paola), 113
Bill of Rights, The (Colman), 178
Bingo series (Lavender), 232
Biographies, 44, 176–177, 202, 257, 263–264, 272–273, 281, 287, 292–293, 297–298, 303–304
Birds, 281–282
Birds (Alden and Reid), 282
Birling, Paul, 120
Bix, Cynthia Overbeck, 276
Bjork, Christina, 222
Björkman, Steve, 282
Black Pioneers of Science and Invention (Haber), 257, 280, 293, 298, 304
Black Ships Before Troy: The Story of the Iliad (Sutcliff), 90
Blind Men and the Elephant, The, 65
Blizzard, Gladys S., 201, 205, 208, 211
Block Printing (O'Reilly), 198
Blood and Guts: A Working Guide to Your Own Insides (Allison), 256
Bloom, Frances, 48
Bloomers! (Blumberg), 168, 180
Blue Butterfly, A: A Story About Claude Monet (Le Tord), 209
Blumberg, Rhoda, 168, 180
Bob Books; More Bob Books; Even More Bob Books (Maslen), 48
Body Atlas, The (Parker), 256
Body Detectives: A Book About the Five Senses (Gelman), 256
Bogard, Vicki, 229
Bolin, Frances Schoonmaker, 83, 89
Bolognese, Don, 159, 163, 238
Bombarde, Odile, 126
Bonafoux, Pascal, 223

Bond, Barbara Higgins, 169
Book About Your Skeleton, A (Gross), 282
Book of Nonsense, A (Lear), 33–34
Book of Virtues, The (ed. Bennett), 75
Books that Build Character (Kilpatrick, Wolfe and Wolfe), 32–33
Boston Coffee Party, The (Rappaport), 158
Boy's War, The: Confederate and Union Soldiers Talk About the Civil War (Murphy), 182
Boy Who Held Back the Sea, The (Hort), 57–58
Bracons, José, 215
Brady (Fritz), 183
Brain, The: What It Is, What It Does (Bruun and Bruun), 282
Brandt, Keith, 303
Branley, Franklyn M., 262, 269–272, 276, 285–287, 290–292
Bremen-Town Musicians, The, 51
Brenner, Barbara, 136–137, 153, 163, 278
Brenner, Fred, 164
Brett, Jan, 51, 56, 65, 155, 244
Brighton, Catherine, 239, 297
Bringing Back the Animals (Kennedy), 267
Brink, Carol Ryrie, 185
Britten, Benjamin, 235
Brocaded Slipper, and Other Vietnamese Tales, The (Vuong), 62
Broekel, Ray, 107, 270, 283
Broutin, Christian, 114
Brown, David J., 203
Brown, Laurene Krasny, 204, 261
Brown, Marc, 204, 261
Brown, Marcia, 51
Brown, Osa, 199
Brown Bag Ideas from Many Cultures (Tejada), 198
Brownell, David, 234
Bruchac, Joseph, 41, 74, 86–87, 163, 170
Bruner, Stephen, 279
Brunkus, Denise, 66, 284
Bruun, Bertel, 282
Bruun, Ruth Dowling, 282
Bryan, Lorinda, 54
Buck Stops Here, The: Presidents of the U.S. (Provenson), 148
Buddha (Roth), 119
Buddhism, 119–120
Buff, Conrad, 74–75

Buff, Mary, 74–75
Buffalo Bill and the Pony Express (Coerr), 162
Buffalo Hunt (Freedman), 186
Buffalo Woman (Goble), 163
Bugs (Parker), 277
Bulla, Robert Clyde, 173
Bull Run (Fleischman), 183
Bully for You, Teddy Roosevelt (Fritz), 190
Bunches and Bunches of Bunnies (Mathews), 322
Buns Travels Across America (Cottonpaw), 148
Bunting, Eve, 167
Burgess, Jan, 288
Burgevin, Daniel, 74, 170
Burkert, Nancy Eckholm, 53
Burnett, Frances Hodgson, 89–90
Burns, Marilyn, 318, 323
Burrell, Roy, 142–143
Burton, Bryan, 236
Burton, Jane, 275
Burton, Robert, 275
Burton, Virginia Lee, 66
Butterfly Seeds, The (Watson), 166–167
Buttons for General Washington (Roop and Roop), 158
Byars, Betsy, 162
Byczynski, Lynn, 302
Byers, Helen, 118
Byles, Monica, 261
Byrd, Samuel, 164, 165
By the Dawn's Early Light: The Story of the Star-Spangled Banner (Kroll), 161

C

Cache of Jewels and Other Collective Nouns, A (Heller), 44
Cactus Hotel (Guiberson), 265
Caddie Woodlawn (Brink), 185
Caduto, Michael, 41
Calder Creatures: Great and Small (Lipman), 206
Calliope magazine, 110, 112, 125, 130, 132–133, 137–140, 142, 143, 145
Calmenson, Stephanie, 48, 55, 57, 66
Cameron, Scott, 234

Camille and the Sunflowers: A Story About Vincent Van Gogh (Anholt), 209, 211
Camm, Martin, 281
Campbell, Maria, 187
Canada, 127
Canada (Bailey), 127
Canada (Schemenaur), 127
Candlewick Book of Fairy Tales, The (ed. Hayes), 39
Canon, Jill, 159
Canterbury Tales (Chaucer), 129
Care for Our Air (Greene), 263
Care for Our Water (Greene), 263
Carle, Eric, 321, 323
Carlson, Laurie, 152, 198–199, 199
Carnival of the Animals (Saint-Saëns), 233
Carol for Christmas, A (Tompert), 117
Carr, Ed, 279, 289, 297
Carrick, Carol, 73, 174
Carrick, Donald, 63, 73
Carroll, Lewis, 73
Carter, Alden R., 191
Carter, David A., 320
Cary, Barbara, 165
Caselli, Giovanni, 105
Casey at the Bat (Thayer), 83
Cash, Terry, 255
Casilla, Robert, 168
Cassels, Jean, 277
Cassie's Journey: Going West in the 1860's (Harvey), 162
Castle (Gravett), 129
Castle (Macaulay), 130, 215
Castle in the Attic, The (Winthrop), 132
Castles (Steele), 129
Catalanotto, Peter, 164
Caterpillar and the Polliwog, The (Kent), 274
Caterpillar Caterpillar (French), 277
Cathedral: The Story of its Construction (Macaulay), 130, 215
Cathedrals: Stone Upon Stone (Gandiol-Coppin), 130
Cathedral Stained Glass Coloring Book (Sibbett), 215
Catherall, Ed, 297, 299
Cat Who Went to Heaven, The (Coatsworth), 119
Cavan, Seamus, 190–191

Cecil's Story (Lyon), 164
Cells, 278, 294–295
Cells and Tissues (LeMaster), 278
Cervantes, Miguel de, 84
Cézanne (Mason), 209
Chaikin, Miriam, 116
Chalk, Gary, 160
Chall, Jeanne S., 176
Challand, Helen J., 262, 279, 294–295
Chamberlin, E. R., 138
Chardiet, Bernice, 60, 278
Charles Darwin, Revolutionary Biologist (Evans), 304
Charles Darwin and Evolution (Parker), 304
Charles Drew, Doctor (Jackson), 293
Charlie Parker Played Be Bop (Raschka), 242
Charlotte's Web (White), 65
Chaucer, Geoffrey, 129
Chelepi, Chris, 123
Chemically Active: Experiments You Can Do at Home (Cobb), 296
Chemistry, 288–289, 296
Chemistry (Newmark), 296
Chen, Ju-Hong, 73
Chen, Kuo Keng, 255
Chen, Tony, 115
Cheoros, Peter, 143
Cherokee, The (Lepthien), 163
Cherokee Summer (Goldsmith), 152
Cherry, Lynne, 267, 278
Chessare, Michele, 173
Chicka Chicka Boom Boom (Martin and Archambault), 47
Chicken Little and the Little Half Chick (Hader and Hader), 51
Chickens Aren't the Only Ones (Heller), 260
Chicken Soup with Rice: A Book of Months (Sendak), 323
Chick Hatches, A (Cole), 260
Child, Lydia Maria, 56
Child Is Born, A: The Christmas Story (Winthrop), 115
Children of Promise: African-American Literature and Art for Young People (ed. Sullivan), 204
Children of the Wild West (Freedman), 185
Children's Aesop, The, 55
Children's Atlas of Civilizations (Mason), 108

Children's Atlas of Exploration (Mason), 108, 136

Children's Atlas of People and Places (Wood), 108, 134

Children's Classics: A Book List for Parents (The Horn Book), 33

Children's Homer, The: The Adventures of Odysseus and the Tale of Troy (Colum), 90

Child's Book of Art, A: Great Pictures, First Words (Micklethwait), 204

Child's Celebration of Song, A, 230

Child's First Bible, A (Stoddard), 115

Child's Garden of Verses, A (Stevenson), 36, 50, 56

Chimps (Goodall), 264

China
    ancient, 120–121
    medieval, 134

Chinaberry Book Service, 33

Chinery, Michael, 277, 281

Chocolate, Deborah M. Newton, 61, 67

Chorzempa, Rosemary, 131

Christianity, 115–117, 141

Christmas Carol, A (Dickens), 65

Christopher Columbus (Krensky), 157

Christopher Columbus: From Vision to Voyage (Anderson), 171

Chung, Chi, 83, 89

Church, Alfred J., 90

Ciardi, John, 37, 65, 72

Cinderella, 51

Circling the Globe: A Young People's Guide to Countries and Cultures of the World, 107

Cirlot, Lourdes, 221

Citizenship, 166

City of the Gods: Mexico's Ancient City of Teotihuacán (Arnold), 136

Civil rights, 168–169

Civil War
    causes, conflicts, and consequences, 182–183
    introduction to, 164–165

Civil War Paper Soldiers (Smith), 164

Clare, John D., 145

Clark, Barbara, 318

Clark, Margaret, 54

Clarkin, Maura A., 199

Classical Kids series, 237, 241

Classic Myths to Read Aloud (ed. Russell), 39, 68, 75, 90–91

Classics for Kids, 236–237, 239

Classics to Read Aloud to Your Children (ed. Russell), 39, 52, 68, 75, 79

Clements, Andrew, 114

Clever Gretchen and Other Forgotten Folktales (Lurie), 74

Climo, Shirley, 62, 113

Clock-O-Dial, 323

Cloud Book, The (De Paola), 275

Coastworth, Elizabeth, 119

Cobb, Theo, 296

Cobb, Vicki, 287, 296

Cobblestone magazine, 85, 148, 151, 182, 184, 187, 189, 242–243

Coerr, Eleanor, 162–163

Cogancherry, Helen, 162, 163

Cohen, Barbara, 117–118, 129, 167

Cohen, Daniel, 122, 142

Cohn, Amy L., 40, 149, 229–230

Cole, Alison, 218

Cole, Joanna, 38–39, 48, 57, 74, 78, 80, 86, 260–262, 266–270, 272, 291, 295, 296, 302

Coleman-Knight, Jan, 143

Coles, Robert, 169

Collier, Christopher, 178

Collier, James Lincoln, 178

Collodi, C., 57

Colman, Warren, 161, 178

Colonial America, 157–158, 172–174

Coloring Book of Ancient Africa, A (Bellerophon Books), 216

Coloring Book of Ancient China, A (Bellerophon Books), 121

Coloring Book of Ancient Egypt, A (Aldred), 113

Coloring Book of Ancient Greece, A (Bellerophon Books), 123

Coloring Book of Incas, Aztecs, Mayas, and Other Precolumbian Peoples (Bellerophon Books), 155

Coloring Book of Rome, A (Bellerophon Books), 125

Coloring Book of the Middle Ages, A (Bellerophon Books), 131

Coloring Book of the New Testament, A, 115

Coloring Book of the Old Testament, A, 115

Colors Everywhere (Hoban), 205

Colors (Yenawine), 205

Colum, Padraic, 90

Columbus, Christopher, 152–153, 157, 171

Columbus Discovers America Coloring Book (Copeland), 157

Colver, Anne, 280

Come Look with Me: Animals in Art (Blizzard), 208, 211

Come Look with Me: Enjoying Art with Children (Blizzard), 205

Come Look with Me: Exploring Landscape Art with Children (Blizzard), 211

Come Look with Me: World of Play (Blizzard), 205

Come Look with Me series (Blizzard), 201

Comets, Asteroids, and Meteors (Fradin), 285

Comets, Meteors, and Asteroids (Simon), 285

Coming to America: The Story of Immigration (Maestro), 166

Comparing Religions series, 115

Complete Nonsense Book of Edward Lear, The, 34

Composers, 236–239

Computation, 322

Computer software, mathematics, 319–320

Conkle, Nancy, 234

Connelly, Gwen, 270

Connolly, Peter, 142–143

Constitution, The (Colman), 161, 178

Continents (Fradin), 290

Cook, Donald, 153

Cook, Roy J., 88–89

Copeland, Peter F., 157, 160, 171, 172, 176

Corbett, Sara, 234, 236

Corbishley, Michael, 125, 126, 142

Cornstalks and Cannonballs (Mitchell), 161

Corrin, Sara, 74

Corrin, Stephen, 74

Cossey, Ruth, 318

Cottonpaw, 148

Count Your Way Through India (Haskins), 119

Count Your Way Through Mexico (Haskins), 118

Coupe, Sheena, 138, 139

Courage of Sarah Noble, The (Dalgliesh), 172

Courlander, Harold, 67, 78

Courtalon, Corinne, 114

Cowboys of the Wild West (Freedman), 185

Cow-Tail Switch, The, 67

Cox, Clinton, 182–183

Coyote: A Trickster Tale from the American Southwest (McDermott), 52

Crane, Lucy, 42

Crane Wife, The, 65

Creative Activities for Teaching World History: Renaissance to Revolution (Stevens & Shea), 143–144

Crews, Donald, 286

Cricket magazine, 48–49

Crisp, Peter, 126

Croll, Carolyn, 289

Cuentos: Tales from the Hispanic Southwest (Maestas and Rael), 74

Cupples, Pat, 292

Curtis, Robert H., 257, 302–303

Cut and Make Egyptian Masks (Smith and Hazen), 113

Cut and Make North American Indian Masks in Full Color (Smith and Hazen), 152

Cut from the Same Cloth: American Women of Myth, Legend, and Tall Tale (San Souci), 70

Cvijanovic, Adam, 187

Cwiklik, Robert, 304

Cyclops, 68

Cymerman, John Emil, 275

D

Dagan, Bernard, 123

Daily Life in a Covered Wagon (Erickson), 185

Dalgliesh, Alice, 158–159, 172

Dance, 240–241

Dance, Tanya (Gauch), 240

Dance Me a Story: Twelve Tales from the Classic Ballets (Rosenberg), 240

Dancing Teepees: Poems of American Indian Youth (ed. Sneve), 34, 50

Daniel Boone: Man of the Forests (Greene), 160

Danile, Alan, 234

Dark Ages, The (Gregory), 125

Darst, Diane W., 200, 216, 220

D'Attilio, Anthony, 267

D'Aulaire, Edgar Parin, 68, 76

D'Aulaire, Ingri Parin, 68, 76

D'Aulaire's Book of Greek Myths (D'Aulaire and D'Aulaire), 68, 76

D'Aulaire's Norse Gods and Giants, 76

Davidson, Diane, 43, 85, 89

Da Vinci (Venezia), 209, 219

Day, Malcolm, 103, 111, 114, 141

Day, Michael, 109, 124

Day Underwater, A (Kovacs), 266

Dear Benjamin Banneker (Pinkney), 179

Dear Rebecca, Winter Is Here (George), 274

Death of the Iron Horse (Goble), 186

Deborah Sampson Goes to War (Stevens), 158

Declaration of Independence, The (Fradin), 175

De Colores and other Latin-American Folk Songs for Children (Orozco), 235

Defoe, Daniel, 79

Degen, Bruce, 162, 266, 268, 270

Delf, Brian, 104, 109–110

Demi, 67–68, 121

Democracy Reader, The (ed. Ravitch and Thernstrom), 103

De Paola, Tomie, 35, 52, 113, 117, 179, 275

Deraney, Michael J., 117–118, 167

Desert (Hirschi), 265

Design Your Own Coat of Arms: An Introduction to Heraldry (Chorzempa), 131

Desimini, Lisa, 40, 52

Dewey, Ariane, 245

Diamond, Donna, 75

Dickens, Charles, 65, 90, 145

Dickinson, Emily, 83–84, 89

Diego (Winter), 206, 209

Diego Rivera (Venezia), 209

Digestive and excretory systems, 278

Digging Up Dinosaurs (Aliki), 268

Dillon, Diane, 41, 74, 133, 241

Dillon, Leo, 41, 74, 133, 241

Dillon Press Book of the Earth, The (Mariner and Ellis), 290

Dinosaur Dig (Lasky), 291

Dinosaurs, 268

Dinosaurs Alive and Well! A Guide to Good Health (Brown), 261

Dinosaurs Walked Here and Other Stories Fossils Tell (Lauber), 291

Dinosaur Time (Parish), 268

Discover Bones: Explore the Science of Skeletons (Grant), 283

Discovering the Stars (Santrey), 270

Discovery Atlas of Planets and Stars (Rand McNally), 285

Discovery of the Americas, The (Maestro and Maestro), 171

Discovery of the Americas Activity Book, The (Maestro and Maestro), 171

Disease, 303

Disney's Children's Favorites, 230–231

DiSomma, Elizabeth V., 80

DiVito, Ann, 172

Dobson, Steven, 157, 159

Dr. Jekyll and Mr. Hyde (Stevenson), 89

Dodson, Liz Brenner, 119

Do Fishes Get Thirsty? (Kaufman), 281

Dolch, Edward, 78, 79

Dolch, Marguerite, 78, 79

Donnelly, Judy, 114

Donnelly, Marlene Hill, 265

Don Quixote and Sancho Panza (Cervantes), 84

Don't You Dare Shoot That Bear! A Story of Theodore Roosevelt (Quackenbush), 153–154, 190

Donze, Lisa, 173

Dooling, Michael, 79, 176, 177, 179

Doorbell Rang, The (Hutchins), 321

Door in the Wall, The (Angeli), 132

Dorros, Arthur, 271, 275

Doty, Roy, 300

Doubleday Children's Atlas, The (ed. Olliver), 108

Dover Activity Books, 106

Dover Children's Books, 39

Downing, Julie, 60

Dragon's Robe, The (Lattimore), 121

Dream Keeper and Other Poems, The (Hughes), 34, 83, 88

Drew, Helen, 232–233

Drinking Gourd, The: A Story of the Underground Railroad (Monjo), 164

Drop of Blood, A (Showers), 288

Dubowski, Cathy East, 67

Dudman, John, 290

Dunn, Andrew, 279, 289, 297

Duntze, Dorothée, 59

Dyer, Jane, 37

E

Eagle, Michael, 70, 126, 172
Earliest people, 155, 170–171
Early, Margaret, 73, 74
Early Thunder (Fritz), 177
Ears Are for Hearing (Showers), 283
Earth: Our Planet in Space (Simon), 285–286
Earth, the, 271–272, 289–291
Earth (Fradin), 271
Earth Child: Games, Stories, Activities, Experiments & Ideas About Living Lightly on Planet Earth (Sheehan and Waidner), 284
Earthquakes (Branley), 290
Earthquakes (Simon), 290
Easter Story, The (Heyer), 115
Eastman, P. D., 49
Eating Fractions (McMillan), 322
Eclipse: Darkness in Daytime (Branley), 286
Ecology, 284–285
Educators Publishing Service (EPS), 48
Edward Lear's Nonsense, 34
Edwards, June, 84
Eggs: A Photographic Story of Hatching (Burton), 275
Egyptian Cinderella, The (Climo), 113
Egyptian Punch-Out Mummy Case (Smith), 113
Ehlert, Lois, 259, 275
Ehrlich, Amy, 41, 51, 60, 62, 117
Eisen, Armand, 42
Electricity, 270, 289
Electromagnetic spectrum, 300
Elephant's Child and Other Just So Stories, The (Kipling), 66
Elffers, Joost, 318
Elijah McCoy, Inventor (Jackson), 280
Elizabeth Blackwell: The First Woman Doctor (Sabin), 292
Ellis, Anyon, 290
Ellis Island: Doorway to Freedom (Kroll), 166
Ellis Island: Gateway to the New World (Fisher), 188
Emberley, Barbara, 262, 271
Emberley, Ed, 262, 271
Emperor's New Clothes, The (Andersen), 66
Empty Pot, The (Demi), 121
Encounter (Yolen), 171

Encyclopedia of Native America, The (Griffin-Pierce), 148, 213
Endangered species, 267–268
Energy, 299–300
Energy (Podendorf), 297
England, from Elizabeth to William and Mary, 138–139
Englander, Roger, 242
Enik, Ted, 287
Enlightenment, 143–144
Enlightenment, The (Frick), 144
Environment, 263, 265–267, 284–285
Erdoes, Richard, 87
Erickson, Paul, 185
Escape from Slavery: The Boyhood of Frederick Douglass in His Own Words (ed. McCurdy), 85, 182
Esther's Story (Wolkstein), 115–116
Europe
    from Age of Exploration to English Bill of Rights, 136–139
    in Middle Ages, 129–132
Evans, David, 261, 262
Evans, J. Edward, 304
Everts, Tammy, 281
Everyday Dress of the American Colonial Period Coloring Book (Copeland), 172
Everyday Life in Roman Times (Corbishley), 125
Everyman Anthology of Poetry for Children, The (ed. Avery), 38, 83, 88
Evolution, 302
Evolution (Cole), 291
Evslin, Bernard, 90
Ewing, Carolyn S., 116
Exodus (Chaikin), 116
Experiments and activities, science, 255–256
Experiments with Air (Broekel), 270
Experiments with Magnets (Challand), 262, 279
Experiment with Magnets and Electricity (Whalley), 262, 270, 279
Experiment with Movement (Murphy), 279
Experiment with Senses (Byles), 261
Exploration and Conquest: The Americas after Columbus: 1500–1620 (Maestro and Maestro), 171–172
Exploration into China (Tao), 134

Exploration of North America Coloring Book (Copeland), 171
Exploring Energy Sources (Catherall), 299
Exploring Uses of Energy (Catherall), 297, 299
Extinct animals, 268
Eyewitness Art series, 201, 222
Eyewitness Atlas of the World, The, 109
Eyewitness Juniors series, 253, 266, 276, 281
Eyewitness Science books series, 253, 299

F

Faber, Doris, 44
Faber, Harold, 44
Faces magazine, 128
Facklam, Margery, 277
Facklam, Paul, 277
Fadden, John Kahionhes, 86
Faerie Queen (Spenser), 79
Fairytale Favorites in Story and Song (Weiss), 58
Faith Ringgold (Turner), 213
Fall (Hirschi), 274
Fall of the Bastille (Benedict), 144
Falwell, Cathryn, 320
Family Folk Festival: A Multi-Cultural Sing-Along, 235
Family Math (Stenmark, Thompson, and Cossey), 318
Famous Children series (Rachlin), 237
Famous Experiments and How to Repeat Them (Filson), 255, 293, 297
Fantasia, 233
Farrell, Kate, 38
Faulkner, Matt, 59
Favorite Fairy Tales Told Around the World (ed. Haviland), 39, 59
Favorite Fairy Tales Told in India (ed. Haviland), 67
Favorite Fairy Tales Told in Spain (ed. Haviland), 59
Favorite Greek Myths (ed. Osborne), 68–69, 91
Favorite Norse Myths (ed. Osborne), 76
Favorite Poems of Childhood (ed. Smith), 36

Favorite Poems Old and New (ed. Ferris), 34, 72, 77, 83, 88
Favorite Songs of Japanese Children (Fukuda), 235
Feast for 10 (Falwell), 320
Feelings, Tom, 182
Feel the Wind (Dorros), 275
Fernández, José B., 145
Fernandez, Laura, 239
Ferris, Helen, 34, 72, 77, 83, 88
Ferris, Jeri, 292
Festival of Freedom: The Story of Passover (Silverman), 116
Festivals Together: A Guide to Multi-cultural Celebration (Fitzjohn, Weston, and Large), 103–104, 120
Feudal Japan, 139
Fiarotta, Noel, 232
Fiarotta, Phyllis, 232
Field, Eugene, 57
Fiesta! Mexico and Central America: A Global Awareness Program for Children in Grades 2–5 (Linse and Judd), 118, 235
50 Simple Things Kids Can Do to Save the Earth (Earth Works Groups), 284
Fill, John, 282
Filson, Brent, 255, 293, 297
Find the Constellations (Rey), 286
Fiore, Peter M., 34, 149
Fire on the Mountain and Other Ethiopian Stories, The (Courlander and Leslau), 78
First Americans, The (Hakim), 170
First Americans Book series (Sneve), 148–159, 170, 186
First Arts and Crafts series (Stocks), 198
First Christmas, The (illus. National Gallery), 116
First Dog (Brett), 155
First Strawberries, The: A Cherokee Story (Bruchac), 163
First Thanksgiving, The (George), 172
First Thanksgiving, The (Hayward), 157
Fish, 281
Fisher, Aileen, 154
Fisher, Cynthia, 283
Fisher, Leonard Everett, 68, 76, 121, 136, 137, 139, 188, 297
Fisherman and His Wife, The, 66
Fitzgerald, Robert, 90

Fitzjohn, Sarah, 103, 120
Fitzjohn, Sue, 103–104, 120
Five Notable Inventors (Hudson), 280
Five Secrets in a Box (Brighton), 297
Flame of Peace, The (Lattimore), 156
Flash, Crash, Rumble, and Roll (Branley), 262
Fleischman, Paul, 183
Fleisher, Paul, 299
Floating House, The (Sanders), 162
Florence Nightingale (Colver), 280
Flowers (Pluckrose), 259
Flutes, Reeds, and Trumpets (Staples and Mahoney), 233
Follow the Dream: The Story of Christopher Columbus (Sis), 152–153
Follow the Drinking Gourd (Winter), 164, 244
Forbes, Esther, 177
Forces (Peacock), 279
Ford, George, 169
Ford, Pamela Baldwin, 42
Fordham, John, 243
Foreman, Michael, 43, 66, 80
Forest (Hirschi), 265
Forest Mammals (Loates), 282
For Laughing Out Loud: Poems to Tickle Your Funnybone (ed. Prelutsky), 36
Fornari, Giuliano, 256
Fossils Tell of Long Ago (Aliki), 291
Foster, Karen, 233
Fourth of July Story, The (Dalgliesh), 158–159
Fowler, Allan, 262, 270–272, 277
Fox, Dan, 230
Fox Went Out on a Chilly Night, The: An Old Song, 244
Fraction Action (Leedy), 322–323
Fractions, 322–323
Fradin, Dennis B., 158, 174, 175, 179, 271, 285, 286, 290
Frampton, David, 174, 183
Francisco Goya (Venezia), 209
Fraser, Mary Ann, 186
Frederick Douglass: Portrait of a Freedom Fighter (Kenan), 180
Frederick Douglass: The Black Lion (McKissack and McKissack), 85
Frederick Douglass and the War Against Slavery (Bennett), 180

Freedman, Russell, 182, 185, 186, 189, 264
Freedman, Suzanne, 190
Freedom Train: The Story of Harriet Tubman (Sterling), 183
Freem, Elroy, 153
Freeman, Don, 204, 242
Freeman, Lydia, 242
French, Fiona, 62
French, Vivian, 65, 277
French Revolution, 144–145
French Revolution, The (Gilbert), 144
Frick, Carole Collier, 144
Friedman, Ina R., 122
Fritz, Jean, 136, 165, 176, 177, 179, 181, 183, 190
Frog (Chinery), 281
Frog Prince, The, 58
Frog Prince Continued, The (Scieszka), 58
Frogs and Toads (Kalman and Everts), 281
From Colonies to Country (Hakim), 175
From Sea to Shining Sea: A Treasury of American Folklore and Folk Songs (ed. Cohn), 40, 149, 229–230
From Seed to Plant (Gibbons), 259
From Tadpole to Frog (Pfeffer), 275
Frost, Robert, 38, 84, 89
Fuchs, Bernie, 243
Fuhrmann, Brigita, 255, 293, 297
Fukuda, Hanako, 235
Fuller, Margaret, 85
Fun with Hieroglyphics (Roehrig), 113, 208

G

Gaffney-Kessell, Walter, 302
Gag, Wanda, 74
Galaxies (Simon), 301
Galdone, Paul, 51, 52, 60
Galileo (Fisher), 297
Gammell, Stephen, 34, 165
Gandiol-Coppin, Brigitte, 130
Ganeri, Anita, 282
Garfield, Leon, 43–44
Garland, Sherry, 167
Garnett, Eve, 36

Garnett, Ron, 280

Garns, Allen, 230

Garraty, John A., 151

Gauch, Patricia Lee, 165, 240

Gellman, Marc, 115

Gelman, Rita Golden, 256

Genetics, 302–303

Genetics: Nature's Blueprints (Byczynski), 302

Geography From A to Z: A Picture Glossary (Knowlton), 107

Geography of the Americas, 123–124

Geology, 271–272, 289–291

George, Jean Craighead, 172, 274

Georges, D. V., 124, 134

George the Drummer Boy (Benchley), 159

George Washington: A Picture Book Biography (Giblin), 176, 179

George Washington: First President of the United States (Greene), 159

George Washington Carver, Scientist and Teacher (Greene), 263

Georgia O'Keeffe (Venezia), 209

Germs Make Me Sick! (Berger), 269

Gerrard, Mike, 155

Getting to Know the World's Greatest Artists series (Venezia), 201, 207, 212, 214, 219

Gettysburg Address, The (illus. McCurdy), 164

Ghana, Mali, Songhay: The Western Sudan (Mann), 133, 216

Gibbons, Gail, 127, 259, 263, 276, 292

Gibbs, John, 103

Giblin, James Cross, 176, 177, 179

Gift of the Tree, The (Tresselt), 265

Gilbert, Adrian, 144

Gilgamesh the King (Zeman), 112

Gillman, Alec, 245

Gillon, Edmund V., Jr., 131

Girl Who Loved Wild Horses, The (Goble), 163

Glass, Andrew, 85

Gleiter, Jan, 160

Global Change (Snow), 284–285

Glubok, Shirley, 200–202, 211, 216, 220

Goble, Paul, 66, 163, 186, 187

Gods and Goddesses of Olympus, The (Aliki), 69

Going to My Ballet Class (Kuklin), 240

Going West (Van Leeuwen), 162

Golden Age of Greece, The: Imperial Democracy 500–400 B.C. (Cheoros, Coleman-Knight, Himmell, and Symcox), 143

Golden Deer, The (Hodges), 120

Golden Slipper, The: A Vietnamese Legend, 62

Goldilocks and the Three Bears, 51

Goldstein, Peggy, 121

Golly Sisters Go West, The (Byars), 162

Gone Is Gone (Gag), 74

"Gone Is Gone" (Lurie), 74

Gonna Sing My Head Off! American Folk Songs for Children (Krull), 230

Goodall, Jane, 264

Goode, Diane, 41, 168

Good Queen Bess: The Story of Elizabeth I of England (Stanley and Vennema), 138

Gorey, Edward, 37, 65

"Gorgon's Head, The" (Hawthorne), 76

Gorsline, Douglas, 64

Go Tell Aunt Rhody, 244

Government, American, 161, 178–179

Goya (Wright), 222

Grahame, Kenneth, 75

Grain of Rice, A (Pittman), 322

Grammatical topics, 44

Grandits, John, 206, 208

Grandville, J. J., 79

Grant, Lesley, 283

Grant, Neil, 109, 136

Gravett, Christopher, 129–130

Gravity Is a Mystery (Branley), 286

Gray, Elizabeth Jane, 132

Great Alexander the Great, The (Lasker), 123

Great Atlas of Discovery, The (Grant), 109, 136

Greatest Hits series, 237–238

Great Kapok Tree, The (Cherry), 267

Great Little Madison, The (Fritz), 179

Great Lives: American Literature (Faber and Faber), 44

Great Lives: Invention and Technology (Lomask), 257, 293

Great Lives: Medicine (Curtis), 257, 302–303

Great Lives: Painting (Glubok), 202

Great Moments in Architecture (Macaulay), 202

Great St. Lawrence Seaway, The (Gibbons), 127

Great Wall of China, The (Fisher), 121

Greek Myths for Young Children (Williams), 69

Greek Myths (Weiss), 52, 69

Greeks, The (Burrell), 142–143

Greeks, The (Odjik), 142

Greeks, The (Williams), 123

Green, John, 113, 123

Greenaway, Frank, 276

Greenberg, Lorna, 303

Greene, Carol, 157–160, 168, 238, 263, 273, 287

Greene, Norman, 157

Greenhouse Effect, The: Life on a Warmer Planet
    (Johnson), 299

Greeson, Janet, 161

Gregory, Tony, 125

Greg's Microscope (Selsam), 278

Grifalconi, Ann, 177

Griffin, Judith Berry, 178

Griffin-Pierce, Trudy, 148, 213

Griffith, Gershom, 164

Grimm brothers, 42, 54, 58, 60

Grimms' Tales for Young and Old (trans.
    Mannheim), 40

Gross, Gwen, 80

Gross, Ruth Belov, 51, 66, 282

Growing Up in Ancient China (Hook), 121

Growing Up in Ancient Greece (Chelepi), 123

Growing Up in Ancient Rome (Corbishley), 125

Growing Up in Viking Times (Tweddle), 127

Growing Vegetable Soup (Ehlert), 259

Grutman, Jewel H., 187

Guiberson, Brenda Z., 265

Gulliver's Stories (Dolch, Dolch, and Jackson), 78

Gulliver's Travels (Swift), 78

Gutenberg (Fisher), 137

H

Haber, Louis, 257, 280, 293, 298, 304

Habitats: Making Homes for Animals and Plants
    (Hickman), 265

Hader, Berte, 51

Hader, Elmer, 51

Hafner, Marylin, 269

Hague, Kathleen, 47, 321

Hague, Michael, 35, 47, 55, 61, 64, 67, 321

Hakim, Joy, 149, 170, 173, 175, 183–185, 188, 190,
    191

Haley, Gail E., 61

Hall, Donald, 34

Hall, Elizabeth, 187

Halverson, Lydia, 154

Hamilton, Edith, 41

Hamilton, Virginia, 41, 74, 182

Hammond, Susan, 237, 239, 241

*Hand in Hand: An American History Through
    Poetry* (ed. Hopkins), 34, 149

Hansel and Gretel (Grimm brothers), 58

Hansen, Joyce, 183, 184

Hanson, Peter E., 158

Hanukkah: The Festival of Lights (Koralek), 116

Happy Birthday, Martin Luther King (Marzollo),
    168

Hard Times (Dickens), 145

Harlow, Rosie, 255

Harness, Cheryl, 153, 162, 177

Harriet and the Promised Land (Lawrence), 164

Harris, Nathaniel, 219

Harrison, James, 110

Hart, Avery, 232

Hart, George, 113

Hart, Tony, 207, 210

Hartelius, Marge, 321

Hartman, Thomas, 115

Harvey, Brett, 162

Haskins, Jim, 118, 119

Hastings, Selina, 81

Haugaard, Erik, 139

Hausherr, Rosmarie, 234, 269

Hautzig, Deborah, 59, 65, 73

Haverfield, Mary, 57

Haviland, Virginia, 39, 59, 67

Hawkes, Nigel, 300

Hawthorne, Nathaniel, 42–43, 52, 76

Hayes, Ann, 233

Hayes, Sarah, 39

Hays, Michael, 117, 243

Hayward, Linda, 157

Hazen, Josie, 113, 152

Hazen, Robert M., 255

Headlam, Catherine, 254

Heart and Blood, The (Burgess), 288

Hear Your Heart (Showers), 288

Heckedy Pig (Wood), 54

Heins, Paul, 53

Hellard, Susan, 207, 210, 237

Heller, Ruth, 44, 62, 113, 260, 275

Henny Penny, 51

Henri Matisse (Raboff), 206, 209, 211, 214

Henri Rousseau (Raboff), 211

Henry-Biabaud, Chantal, 123

Henterly, Jarmichael, 82

Here Is My Kingdom: Hispanic-American Literature and Art for Young People (ed. Sullivan), 204

Heroines of the American Revolution: A Bellerophon Coloring Book (Canon), 159

Herold, Maggie Rugg, 166

Herstory: Women Who Changed the World (ed. Ashby and Ohrn), 104

Herzog, George, 67

Hewett, Richard, 136

Hewitt, Kathryn, 44

Hewitt, Sally, 262

Hey Diddle Diddle and Other Mother Goose Rhymes (illus. De Paola), 35

Heyer, Carol, 115

Heyer, Marilee, 80

Hibbard, Howard, 203

Hickman, Pamela H., 265

Hidden in Sand (Hodges), 120

Hidden Worlds: Pictures of the Invisible (Simon), 293

Hill, Florence, 158

Hills, Patricia, 209

Himler, Ronald, 148, 165, 170

Himmell, Rhoda, 143

Hinduism, 119–120

Hirsch, E. D., Jr., 111

Hirschi, Ron, 265, 267, 274

Historical fiction, 132, 177–178, 183

History of Art for Young People (Janson and Janson), 202, 215, 221

History of US, A (Hakim), 149, 173, 175, 184, 185, 188

Hoban, Lillian, 49

Hoban, Tana, 205

Hodges, Margaret, 75, 79–80, 81, 84, 120

Hoff, Syd, 49

Hoggan, Pat, 71

Holder, Heidi, 55

Holdren, John, 111

Holling, Holling Clancy, 127–128

Holub, Joan, 178

Hominids: A Look Back at Our Ancestors (Sattler), 302

Honan, Linda, 131

Honest Abe (Kunhardt), 154

Honeywood, Varnette P., 236, 243

Hoobler, Dorothy, 140, 147, 178, 188

Hoobler, Thomas, 140, 147, 178, 188

Hook, Richard, 121

Hooks, William H., 53, 63

Hooray for the Golly Sisters! (Byars), 162

Hopkins, Lee Bennett, 34, 37, 64, 149, 263

Hopkinson, Deborah, 165

Horn Book, Inc., The, 33

Horse Sense for Kids and Other People: Authentic Sing-Along Cowboy Songs, 231

Hort, Lenny, 57–58

Horvatic, Ann, 279

House at Pooh Corner, The (Milne), 54, 58

Houses of Hide and Earth (Shemie), 186

Howarth, Sarah, 130–131, 137

How a Seed Grows (Jordan), 259

How Did We Find Out About . . . ? series (Asimov), 253, 300

How Did We Find Out About Lasers? (Asimov), 300

How Did We Find Out About Genes? (Asimov), 302

How Did We Find Out About the Speed of Light? (Asimov), 301

How Do You Spell God? Answers to the Big Questions from Around the World (Gellman and Hartman), 115, 141

Howe, John, 59

Howell, Troy, 68, 91

How Many Bugs in a Box? (Carter), 320

How Many Days to America? A Thanksgiving Story (Bunting), 167

How Many Spots Does a Leopard Have? and Other Tales (Lester), 52

How Much Is a Million? (Schwartz), 320–321

How Music Came to the World: An Ancient Mexican Myth (Ober), 156

How My Parents Learned to Eat (Friedman), 122

How Our Bodies Work series, 257

How's the Weather? (Berger and Berger), 275–276

How the Body Works (Parker), 256–257

"How the Camel Got His Hump" (Kipling), 66

How Things Work series, 253–254

How-to and activity books, 198–200

How to Be a Nature Detective (Selsam), 265

How to Dig a Hole to the Other Side of the Earth (McNulty), 272

How You Were Born (Cole), 296

Hoyt-Goldsmith, Diane, 152

Hu, Ying-Hwa, 34, 72, 77

Hudson, Wade, 280

Hughes, Langston, 34, 83, 88

Hughey, Pat, 285

Human body, 256–257, 261–262, 268–269, 278–279, 282–283, 288, 295–296, 303

Human Body, The: How We Evolved (Cole), 302

Human reproduction, 295–296

Hundredth Name, The (Oppenheim), 117

Hunt, April, 183

Hunt, Jonathan, 130

Hurricane Watch (Branley), 291

Hutchins, Pat, 322

Hutton, Warwick, 69–70, 76, 116

Hyman, Trina Schart, 53, 60, 79, 81, 129, 185

I

I Can Tell by Touching (Otto), 261

Ice Age, The (Stille), 155

Icebergs and Glaciers (Simon), 290

Ichikawa, Satomi, 240

Ida B. Wells and the Antilynching Crusade (Freedman), 190

I Did It With My Hatchet: A Story of George Washington (Quackenbush), 176–177

If You Lived in Colonial Times (McGovern), 172

If You Made a Million (Schwartz), 323–324

If Your Name Was Changed at Ellis Island (Levine), 188–189

If You Sailed on the Mayflower in 1620 (McGovern), 172–173

If You Traveled West in a Covered Wagon (Levine), 185

If You Were There in 1492 (Brenner), 136–137

If You Were There When They Signed the Constitution (Levy), 178–179

I Hate Mathematics! Book, The (Burns), 318

Iktomi and the Berries, 66

Iktomi and the Boulder, 66

Iktomi and the Buffalo Skull, 66

Iktomi and the Ducks, 66

Iliad, The (Homer), 90

Iliad and the Odyssey of Homer, The (Church), 90

Illuminations (Hunt), 130

Imaginary Gardens: American Poetry and Art for Young People (ed. Sullivan), 204

Immigrant Kids (Freedman), 189, 190

Immigration, 166–168, 188–189

Immigration: 1870–1930 (Scriabine), 189

Impressionism (Welton), 221

Impressionists, The (Baillet), 221

In a Circle Long Ago: A Treasury of Native Lore from North America (ed. Van Laan), 40, 52

In America (Moss), 167

In a Pickle and Other Funny Idioms (Terban), 45

Inca, The (McKissack), 156

Incas, The (Odjik), 135

Inca civilization, 135, 155–156

Inch Boy, The, 62

India, 119

India: The Culture (Kalman), 119

Indian Chiefs (Freedman), 186

Industrial and urban America, 189

Industrial Revolution, 145

Industrial Revolution, The (ed. Clare), 145

Industrial Revolution, The (Langley), 145

In 1492 (Marzollo), 153

Inkpen, Mick, 321

Insects, 276–278

Inside an Egg (Johnson), 294

Inside Story series, 106

Inside the Museum: A Children's Guide to the Metropolitan Museum of Art (Richardson), 203

In the Beginning: The Nearly Complete History of Almost Everything (Platt), 104

In the Month of Kislev: A Story for Hanukkah (Jaffe), 117

Into the Mummy's Tomb: The Real Life Discovery of Tutankhamun's Treasures (Reeves), 114

Investigating Art: A Practical Guide for Young People (Keightley), 222

Invincible Louisa (Meigs), 85

Ireland, Karin, 304

Iroquois Stories: Heroes and Heroines, Monsters and Magic (Bruchac), 74, 170

Irving, Washington, 78, 79

Isaacson, Phillip M., 200, 203

Isadora, Rachel, 74, 242

I Sailed with Christopher Columbus (Schlein), 157

I Saw Esau: The Schoolchild's Pocket Book (ed. Opie and Opie), 45

Ishii, Momoko, 67

Islam, 215–216

Islam
    art and architecture, 215–216
    rise of, 132–133

Islamic Calligraphy Coloring Book (Massasati), 116

Isles, Joanna, 36

I Spy: An Alphabet in Art (Micklethwait), 47, 205, 208

I Spy a Lion (Micklethwait), 205

I Spy Two Eyes (Micklethwait), 205, 321

Israelites, The (Odjik), 141

It Could Always Be Worse (Zemach), 58–59

It Could Still Be a Rock (Fowler), 272

It Could Still Be Water (Fowler), 270

It Figures! Fun Figures of Speech (Terban), 44

I Think I Thought and Other Tricky Verbs (Terban), 44

It's a Good Thing There Are Insects (Fowler), 277

It's Electric (Dunn), 289

Itse Selu: Cherokee Harvest Festival (Pennington), 152

It's Raining Cats and Dogs: All Kinds of Weather and Why We Have It (Branley), 276

It's Snowing! It's Snowing! (Prelutsky), 37

It's Thanksgiving (Prelutsky), 36

I Wonder Why Flutes Have Holes and Other Questions About Music (Paker), 229

I Wonder Why Pyramids Were Built and Other Questions About Ancient Egypt (Steele), 114

J

Jack and the Beanstalk, 59

Jackson, Beulah, 78, 79

Jackson, Garnet Nelson, 169, 280, 287, 293

Jacob Lawrence: Thirty Years of Prints (Hills and Nesbett), 209

Jacobs, Francine, 267

Jacobsen, Karen, 118, 122

Jacobson, Rick, 239

Jaffe, Nina, 117

Jakobsen, Kathy, 52

James, John, 126, 130

James Madison and Dolley Madison and Their Times (Quackenbush), 179–180

Jane Goodall, Naturalist (Senn), 264

Janice VanCleave's Biology for Every Kid: 101 Easy Experiments that Really Work (VanCleave), 294

Janice VanCleave's Chemistry for Every Kid: 101 Easy Experiments that Really Work (VanCleave), 289

Janice VanCleave's Geography for Every Kid: Easy Activities That Make Learning Geography Fun (VanCleave), 107

Janice VanCleave's Math for Every Kid: Easy Activities That Make Learning Math Fun (VanCleave), 318

Janice VanCleave's Science Books series (VanCleave), 255–256

Janson, Anthony F., 202, 215, 221

Janson, H. W., 202, 215, 221

Japan, 121–122
    feudal, 139

Japan (Jacobsen), 122

Japan: Land of Samurai and Robots (Ottenheimer), 122

Japanese, The (Odjik), 139, 211

Jarrell, Randall, 53, 66

Jason and the Golden Fleece (Fisher), 76

Jazz, 242–243

Jazz: History, Instruments, Musicians, and Recordings (Fordham), 243

Jeffers, Susan, 51, 57, 58, 62

Jenkins, Priscilla Belz, 275

Jessop, Joanne, 203

John Henry (Lester), 70

John Henry: An American Legend (Keats), 70

John Henry and His Mighty Hammer (Troll Associates), 71
John Muir: Man of the Wild Places (Greene), 287
Johnny Appleseed (Lindbergh), 52
Johnny Appleseed: A Tall Tale (Kellogg), 71
Johnny Appleseed Goes a'Planting (Troll Associates), 71
Johnny Tremaine (Forbes), 177
John Philip Sousa: The March King (Greene), 238
Johnson, Amy, 292
Johnson, Dolores, 165
Johnson, Linda Carlson, 179
Johnson, Rebecca L., 299
Johnson, Stephen T., 117
Johnson, Sylvia, 294
Jonah and the Great Fish (Hutton), 116
Jones, Malcolm, 40
Jordan, Helene J., 259
Jorjensen, David, 61
José de San Martín: Latin America's Quiet Hero (Fernández), 145
Josefina Story Quilt, The (Coerr), 162–163
Journey of Meng, The (Rappaport), 121
Journey to Freedom (Wright), 164–165
Judaism, 141
Judd, Dick, 118, 235
Julius Caesar (Shakespeare), 89
Julius Caesar for Young People (ed. Davidson), 89
Jump Again! More Adventures of Brer Rabbit (ed. Parks and Jones), 40
Jump Ship to Freedom (Collier and Collier), 178
Jump! The Adventures of Brer Rabbit (ed. Parks and Jones), 40
Jupiter (Simon), 286
Just a Few Words, Mr. Lincoln: The Story of the Gettysburg Address (Fritz), 165
Just Like Abraham Lincoln (Waber), 154
Just So Stories (Kipling), 66

K

Kalman, Bobbie, 118, 119, 281
Kalman, Esther, 239
Kassirer, Sue, 57

Katie's Picture Show (Mayhew), 203
Kaufman, Les, 281
Kazuko, 263
Keats, Ezra Jack, 70
Keeler, Patricia A., 299
Keepers of Life: Discovering Plants Through Native American Stories and Earth Activities for Children (Caduto and Bruchac), 41
Keepers of the Animals: Native American Stories and Wildlife Activities for Children (Caduto and Bruchac), 41
Keepers of the Earth: Native American Stories and Environmental Activities for Children (Caduto and Bruchac), 41, 86
Keepers of the Night: Native American Stories and Nocturnal Activities for Children (Caduto and Bruchac), 41
Keightley, Moy, 222
Keller, Holly, 266, 269, 275, 283, 287
Kellogg, Steven, 52, 71
Kelly, Laura, 117, 267
Kelly, True, 268
Kemp, Richard, 109–110
Kenan, Sheila, 180
Kendall, Russ, 153, 158
Kennedy, Dorothy M., 37
Kennedy, Paul E., 131
Kennedy, Teresa, 267
Kennedy, X. J., 37
Kennet, Frances, 218, 221
Kent, Jack, 51, 66, 274
Kent, Zachary, 186
Kessel, Joyce K., 173–174
Kessler, Cristina, 267
Key to Art from Romanticism to Impressionism, The (Reyero), 221
Key to Art series, 201, 215, 218, 221
Key to Gothic Art, The (Bracons), 215
Key to Modern Art of the Early Twentieth Century, The (Cirlot), 221
Key to Renaissance Art, The (Arenas), 218–219
Kids at Work: Lewis Hine and the Crusade Against Child Labor (Freedman), 189, 190
Kids Create: Art and Craft Experiences for 3 to 9 Year Olds (Carlson), 198–199
Kids Discover magazine, 110, 126, 127, 258
Kids Make Music! (Hart and Mantell), 232

Kids' Multicultural Art Book, The: Art and Craft Experiences from Around the World (Terzian), 199

Kids' World Almanac of Music from Rock to Bach, The (Sommer), 229

Kiesler, Kate, 114

Kilpatrick, William, 32–33, 78

Kimmel, Eric, 57, 73

King Arthur and His Knights (Weiss), 80–81

Kingfisher Book of the Ancient World, The: From the Ice Age to the Fall of Rome (Martell), 104

Kingfisher Illustrated History of the World, The (ed. Zevin), 104

Kingfisher Science Encyclopedia, The (ed. Headlam), 254

"King Midas and the Golden Touch" (Hawthorne), 52

King's Day, The: Louis XIV of France (Aliki), 144–145

Kipling, Rudyard, 66

Kitchen, Bert, 320

Kitchen Knight, The: A Tale of King Arthur (Hodges), 81

Kites Sail High: A Book About Verbs (Heller), 44

Kitzinger, Sheila, 295–296

Kiuchi, Tatsuro, 167

Kiwak, Barbara, 180

Klara's New World (Winter), 167

Kleven, Elisa, 235

Kliros, Thea, 36

Knee-High Man and Other Tales, The (Lester), 59

Knight, Amelia S., 186

Knight, Christopher G., 291

Knight, Hilary, 37, 56–57

Knight (Gravett), 129–130

Knights and Armour Coloring Book (Smith), 131

Knights of the Kitchen Table (Scieszka), 81

Knights of the Round Table (Gross), 80

Knowledge Unlimited, Inc., 104–105, 149

Knowlton, Jack, 107

Koch, Kenneth, 35, 38

Kohl, MaryAnn F., 199

Konigsburg, E. L., 132, 138

Koralek, Jenny, 116

Korean Cinderella, The, 62

Kosmer, Ellen, 131

Kovacs, Deborah, 266

Kovalski, Maryann, 245

Krapesh, Patricia, 90

Kraus, Robert, 245

Krensky, Stephen, 157, 174, 279

Kroll, Steven, 160, 161, 166, 185

Krulik, Nancy E., 271

Krull, Kathleen, 44, 202, 230, 238

Krupinski, Loretta, 259, 274

Kuklin, Susan, 240, 294

Kumin, Maxine, 280

Kunhardt, Edith, 126, 154

Kuskin, Karla, 234

L

Lacome, Julie, 47

Ladybug magazine, 48–49

Ladybug (Watts), 277–278

Laiken, Deidre, 80

Lambert, Mark, 288

Lane, Rose Wilder, 84

Lang, Andrew, 73

Langley, Andrew, 145

La Pierre, Yvette, 208–209

Large, Abigail, 103–104, 120

Large, Judy, 103–104, 120

Larrick, Nancy, 230

Lasker, Joe, 123, 131

Lasky, Kathryn, 291, 303

Latin American independence movements, 145–146

Lattimore, Deborah Nourse, 121, 156

Lauber, Patricia, 172, 266, 291

Laurencin, Geneviève, 229

Lavender, Cheryl, 232

Lawrence, Jacob, 164

Lawson, Robert, 132, 177

Lear, Edward, 33–34, 47

Learning to Look: A Complete Art History and Appreciation Program for Grades K–8 (Massey and Darst), 200, 216, 220

Ledgerbook of Thomas Blue Eagle, The (Grutman and Matthaei), 187

Lee, Alan, 90

Lee, Jeanne M., 120

Leedy, Loreen, 271, 322–323

Le Gallienne, Eva, 42

Legend of King Arthur, The (Lister), 81

Legend of Scarface, The: A Blackfeet Indian Tale (Bruchac), 86–87

Legend of Sleepy Hollow, The (Irving), 78

Legend of the Bluebonnet, The (De Paola), 52

Legend of the Indian Paintbrush, The (De Paola), 52

LeMaster, Leslie Jean, 269, 278, 283, 288

Lemieux, Michèle, 234

Lenses! Take a Closer Look (Aust), 284

Leonardo da Vinci (Hart), 210

Leonardo da Vinci (Mason), 219

Leonardo da Vinci (Raboff), 209, 219

Lepthien, Emilie Uttag, 163

Lerner, Carol, 294

Lerner, Ethan A., 303

Leslau, Wolf, 78

Lesser, Rika, 58

Lester, Julius, 42, 52, 59, 61, 70, 182

Le Tord, Bijou, 209

Let's Get the Rhythm of the Band: A Child's Introduction to Music from African-American Culture with History and Song (Mattox), 236, 243

Let's Make Music: An Interactive Musical Trip Around the World (Turner and Schiff), 232, 236

Let's-Read-and-Find-Out series, 254, 265–267, 269–271, 274, 275, 279, 286–288, 290, 291

Letters to Horseface (Munjo), 238

Let Your Voice Be Heard: Songs from Ghana and Zimbabwe (Adzinya, Marire, and Tucker), 235

Levene, Donna B., 232

Levine, Ellen, 185, 188–189

Levinson, Nancy Smiler, 188

Levinson, Riki, 168

Levy, Elizabeth, 178–179

Lewin, Ted, 120, 167

Lewis and Clark: Explorers of the American West (Kroll), 160, 185

Lewis Howard Latimer (Turner), 304

Liang and the Magic Paintbrush, 67–68

Liberty for All (Hakim), 175

Life cycles, 274–275, 294–295

Life in Ancient Egypt Coloring Book (Applebaum), 113

Life in Ancient Greece Coloring Book (Green), 123

Life in the Rainforests: Animals, People, Plants (Baker), 265–266

Lifting by Levers (Dunn), 279

Light and optics, 284, 300

Light (Peacock), 284

Light in the Attic, A (Silverstein), 38, 72, 78

Lights, Lenses, and Lasers (Berger), 300

Lincoln: A Photobiography (Freedman), 182

Lindbergh, Reeve, 52

Lines (Yenawine), 205

Ling, Mary, 266

Linnea in Monet's Garden (Bjork), 222

Linse, Barbara, 118, 235

Lion to Guard Us, A (Bulla), 173

Lipman, Jean, 206

Lipson, Eden Ross, 33

Lister, Robin, 81

Little, Emily, 70

Littledale, Freya, 66, 79

Little House on the Prairie (Wilder), 84

Little Inchkin, 62

Little Lama of Tibet, The (Raimondo), 120

Little Match Girl, The (Andersen), 74

Little Red Hen, The, 52

Little Red Riding Hood, 53

Little Women (Alcott), 84–85

Litzinger, Roseanne, 71

Lives of the Artists: Masterpieces, Messes (and What the Neighbors Thought) (Krull), 202

Lives of the Musicians: Good Times and Bad Times (and What the Neighbors Thought) (Krull), 238

Lives of the Writers: Comedies, Tragedies (and What the Neighbors Thought) (Krull), 44

Living in Ancient Rome (Bombarde and Moatti), 126

Living in India (Singh), 119

Living in South America (Henry-Biabaud), 123

Livingston, Myra Cohn, 164

Livingstone, Malcolm, 218, 221

Llama's Secret, The (Palacios), 156

Llewellyn, Clare, 323

Lloyd, David, 58

Lloyd, Frances, 290

Lloyd, Megan, 37, 265

Loates, Glen, 282

Lobel, Anita, 47

Lobel, Arnold, 35, 47, 49, 72, 77, 268, 278, 280

Locker, Thomas, 54, 57–58, 79, 172

Lomask, Milton, 257, 293

London Bridge Is Falling Down!, 244

Longfellow, Henry Wadsworth, 77, 176

Lóng Is a Dragon: Chinese Writing for Children (Goldstein), 121

Long Road to Gettysburg, The (Murphy), 182

Long Way to a New Land, The (Sandin), 167

Lon Po-Po: A Red Riding Hood Story from China, 62

Looking at Paintings (Kennet and Measham), 218, 221

Lotus Seed, The (Garland), 167

Louie, Ai-Ling, 63

Louis Pasteur (Bains), 273

Louis Pasteur: Enemy of Disease (Greene), 273

Love, David, 148

Low, Alice, 69, 76

Ludwig van Beethoven: Musical Pioneer (Greene), 238

Ludwig van Beethoven: Young Composer (Sabin), 238

Lum, Darrell, 62

Lungs and Breathing, The (Lambert), 288

Lurie, Alison, 74

Lynch, P. J., 39

Lyon, George Ella, 164

M

Macaulay, David, 130, 202, 215, 255

MacDonald, Fiona, 130, 133

MacGill-Callahan, Sheila, 117

Machines (Rockwell), 279

Mackain, Bonnie, 322

Macmillan Book of Greek Gods and Heroes, The (Low), 68, 69, 76

Madaras, Lynda, 295

Madden, Don, 271, 288

Maddex, Diane, 202

Mae Jemison, Astronaut (Jackson), 287

Maestas, José, 74

Maestro, Betsy, 166, 171–172, 179, 274

Maestro, Giulio, 45, 166, 171–172, 179, 285, 291, 292

Maestro Plays, The (Martin), 244

Magic Fish, The (Littledale), 66

Magic School Bus Inside the Earth, The (Cole), 272

Magic School Bus Inside the Human Body, The (Cole), 268

Magic School Bus Lost in the Solar System, The (Cole), 270

Magic School Bus on the Ocean Floor, The (Cole), 266–267

Magnetism, 262, 279

Mahan, Ben, 81

Mahoney, Carole, 233

Mahy, Margaret, 121

Mai, Vo-Dinh, 166

Maid of the North, The: Feminist Folktales from Around the World (Phelps), 41

Makar, Barbara, 48

Make a Joyful Sound: Poems for Children by African-American Poets (ed. Slier), 34, 72, 77

Makhlouf, Georgia, 141

Making Thirteen Colonies (Hakim), 173

Mammals, 282

Mammals (Alden and Reid), 282

Mangelsen, Thomas D., 274

Mann, Kenny, 133, 216

Mannheim, Ralph, 40

Manning, Richard, 260

Mantell, Paul, 232

Many Lives of Benjamin Franklin, The (Aliki), 159

Many Luscious Lollipops: A Book About Adjectives (Heller), 44

Maps and Globes (Broekel), 107

Maps and Globes (Knowlton), 107

Maraire, Dumisani, 235

Marcellino, Fred, 60

Marchesi, Stephen, 84

Marcus, Pablo, 78

Marie Curie, Brave Scientist (Brandt), 303

Mariner, Tom, 290

Markle, Sandra, 257, 294

Mark Twain — What Kind of a Name Is That? A Story of Samuel Langhorne Clemens (Quackenbush), 84

Marsalis on Music, 229
Marsalis on Music: Sousa to Satchmo, 243
Marshall, Edward, 49
Marshall, James, 49, 51, 53, 58, 64
Mars (Simon), 286
Martell, Hazel Mary, 104
Martin, Bill, Jr., 47, 240, 244
Martin, Mary, 199–200
Martin, Rafe, 63, 171
Martin Luther (Chamberlin), 138
Martin Luther King, Jr.: A Man Who Changed Things (Greene), 168
Mary Cassatt (Venezia), 206, 207, 214
Marzollo, Jean, 105, 150, 153, 168
Maslen, Bobby Lynn, 48
Maslen, John R., 48
Mason, Anthony, 108, 136, 209, 219, 222
Massasati, Ahmas, 116
Massey, Sue J., 200, 216, 220
Match Wits with Sherlock Holmes series (Shaw), 86
Mathews, Louise, 322
Mathews, Sally Schoffer, 156
Math Made Meaningful (Cuisinaire Company), 318
Matter, 269–270, 296
Matthaei, Gay, 187
Matthias, Catherine, 321
Mattox, Cheryl Warren, 37, 50, 231, 236, 243
Maucler, Christian, 221
Max and Ruby's Midas (Wells), 52
Max Found Two Sticks (Pinkney), 245
Maya, The (McKissack), 156
Maya, The (Nicholson), 135
Maya, The (Odjik), 135
Maya civilization, 135, 155–156
Mayer, Marianna, 54, 65
Mayer, Mercer, 60, 65
Mayhew, James, 203
Maynard, Christopher, 105
McBride, Angus, 127
McCaughrean, Geraldine, 241
McClintock, Barbara, 55
McConkey, Lois, 187
McCully, Emily Arnold, 158
McCurdy, Michael, 70, 85, 164, 182, 186
McDermott, Gerald, 52

McGovern, Ann, 79, 153, 172–173, 177
McGregor, Malcolm, 282
McKissack, Frederick, 85, 133, 180–181, 190
McKissack, Patricia, 85, 133, 155, 156, 180–181, 190
McLanathan, Richard, 137
McMillan, Bruce, 292, 322, 323
McNeil, Keith, 230
McNeil, Rusty, 230
McNeill, Philip, 137
McNulty, Faith, 272
McPherson, Stephanie Sammartino, 190
McTiernan, Mary Louise, 80
Me and My Body (Evans and Williams), 261
Measham, Terry, 218, 221
Mebane, Robert C., 289, 296
Medearis, Angela Shelf, 67
Medieval Alphabet to Illuminate, A (Bellerophon Books), 131–132
Medieval Cathedral, A (MacDonald and James), 130
Medieval China, 134
Medieval Feast, A (Aliki), 130
"Medio Pollito," 59
Meet Abraham Lincoln (Cary), 165
Meet the Orchestra (Hayes), 233
Meet Thomas Jefferson (Barrett), 180
Meigs, Cornelia, 85
Meisel, Paul, 269, 279
Meltzer, Milton, 183
Mercury (Simon), 286
Merrill, Clare, 260
Merry-Go-Round: A Book About Nouns (Heller), 44
Mesoamerican civilizations, 135–136
Mesopotamia (Bayley), 112
Meteorology, 291–292
Metropolitan Museum of Art, The (Hibbard), 203
Metropolitan Museum of Art Activity Book, The (Brown), 199
Mexican Folktales from the Borderland (Aiken), 74
Mexico, 118, 145–146
Mexico (Jacobsen), 118
Mexico: The Culture (Kalman), 118
Michelangelo (McLanathan), 137
Michelangelo (Venezia), 219
Michelangelo Buonarroti (Raboff), 219

Micklethwait, Lucy, 47, 204, 205, 208, 321
Microscope, The (Kumin), 280
Microsoft Musical Instruments, 233
Middle Ages, 129–134
    art and architecture, 215
Middle Ages, The (Gillon), 131
Middle Ages, The (Howarth), 130–131
Middle Eastern Art (Sandak), 216
Midsummer Night's Dream, A (ed. Stewart), 85
Midsummer Night's Dream for Young People, A
    (ed. Davidson), 85
Migdale, Lawrence, 152
*Miguel Hidalgo y Costilla: Father of Mexican
    Independence* (Varona), 145–146
Mikolaycak, Charles, 115, 116
Mik's Mammoth (Gerrard), 155
Miles, Elizabeth, 60
Miller, Lyle, 273
Miller, Margaret, 260–261, 296
Millet, Claude, 229
Millet, Denise, 229
Millstone, David, 143
Milne, A. A., 37, 50, 54, 57, 58
Milone, Karen, 303
Minarik, Else Homelund, 49
Ming-Yi, Yang, 121
Mini-Musicals, 232
Minn of the Mississippi (Clancy), 127–128
Mirocha, Paul, 267
Mirrors: Finding Out About the Properties of Light
    (Zubrowski), 300
Mitchell, Barbara, 236, 239
Mitchell, Hetty, 239
Mitchell, Kathy, 65, 73
Mitra, Annie, 65
Miyake, Yoshi, 160, 177, 272
Moatti, Claude, 126
Moktefi, Mokhtar, 132
Molly's Pilgrim (Cohen), 167
Monet (Mason), 209, 222
Monet (Venezia), 209
Money, 323–324
Mongols, The (Nicholson), 134
Monjo, F. N., 164, 238
Monster Math (Maccarone), 321
Monticello Architecture, 217

Moon Flights (Fradin), 286
Moon Seems to Change, The (Branley), 271
Moore, Clement Clark, 64
Moore, Lillian, 54
Moore, Patrick, 301
More Classics to Read Aloud to Your Children (ed.
    Russell), 39, 68
*More Perfect Union, A: The Story of Our
    Constitution* (Maestro and Maestro), 179
More Surprises (ed. Hopkins), 37, 64
*More Tales of Uncle Remus: Further Adventures of
    Brer Rabbit, His Friends, His Enemies, and
    Others* (Lester), 61
*More Than Moccasins: A Kid's Activity Guide to
    Traditional North American Indian Life*
    (Carlson), 152, 199
Morgan, Gareth, 255
Morgan, Mary, 168, 180
Morimoto, Junko, 62
Morley, Jacqueline, 126
Morpurgo, Michael, 80
Morter, Peter, 109
Moser, Barry, 40
Moses in the Bulrushes (Hutton), 116
Moss, Marissa, 167
Moss Gown (Hooks), 63
*Mother Goose: A Collection of Classic Nursery
    Rhymes* (ed. Hague), 35
"Mother Goose" poems, 35–36
Mound, Laurence, 276
Mountain (Hirschi), 265
Mouse Paint (Walsh), 206
*Moving Within the Circle: Contemporary Native
    American Music and Dance* (Burton), 236
Moxley, Sheila, 73
*Mozart: Scenes from the Childhood of the Great
    Composer* (Brighton), 239
Mozart's Magic Fantasy, 241
*Mudworks: Creative Clay, Dough, and Modeling
    Experiences* (Krohl), 199
Mufaro's Beautiful Daughters: An African Tale, 63
Mühlberger, Richard, 201–202, 210, 212, 214,
    219–220, 223
Multicultural music, 235–236
Mulvihill, Patricia Rose, 161
Mummies Made in Egypt (Aliki), 114
Mummy (Putnam), 113

Murdoch, David, 213
Murphy, Brian, 279
Murphy, Jim, 182, 184
Murphy, Pat, 284
Musgrove, Margaret, 133–134
Musical activities, 232–233
Musical instruments, 233–235
Musical Max (Kraus), 245
Music (Ardley), 233–234
Music Crafts for Kids: The How-to Book of Music Discovery (Fiarotta and Fiarotta), 232
Music for Little People, 228
Music from Strings (Paker), 233
Music in Motion, 228
Music! (Laurencin), 229
Music Through Children's Literature: Theme and Variations (Levene), 232
Music! Words! Opera!: Level 1 Teacher's Manual, 241
MvVitty, Walter, 73
My Brother Sam Is Dead (Collier and Collier), 178
Myers, Walter Dean, 169
My Favorite Opera for Children (Pavarotti), 241–242
My Fellow Americans: A Family Album (Provenson), 149–150
My First Activity Book (Wilkes), 199
My First Book of Biographies: Great Men and Women Every Child Should Know (Marzollo), 105, 150, 168
My First Book of Time (Llewellyn), 323
My First Green Book (Wilkes), 263
My First Music Book: A Life-Size Guide to Making and Playing Simple Musical Instruments (Drew), 232–233
My First President's Day Book (Fisher), 154
My First Science Book (Wilkes), 254
My Five Senses (Aliki), 261
My New Kitten (Cole), 260–261
My Parents Think I'm Sleeping! (Prelutsky), 37
My Picture Book of the Planets (Krulik), 271
My Puppy Is Born (Cole), 261
Mystery! Mystery! for Children (Weiss), 86
Mythology (Hamilton), 41
Myths and legends, 68–70, 75–76, 80–82, 86–87, 90–91

N

Nagano, Makiko, 53, 62
Naprstek, Joel, 84
Nason, Thomas W., 38, 84
National Gallery of Art Activity Book: 25 Adventures with Art (Clarkin), 199
National Geographic, 138
National Geographic World, 110
National Wildlife Federation, 258
Native American Art (Sandak), 213
Native American Rock Art: Messages from the Past (La Pierre), 208–209
Native Americans, 152, 163, 170–171
   art, 213
   culture and life, 186–187
Native Dwellings series (Shemie), 150, 170, 186
Nativity, The (illus. Sanderson), 116
N.C. Wyeth's Pilgrims (San Souci), 173
Nelson, JoAnne, 318
Neptune (Simon), 286
Nesbett, Peter, 209
Nest Full of Eggs, A (Jenkins), 275
Nettie's Trip South (Turner), 165
New Kid on the Block, The (Prelutsky), 36
Newmark, Ann, 296
New Nation, The (Hakim), 175
New Puffin Children's World Atlas: An Introductory Atlas for Young People (Tivers and Day), 109, 111, 124
New Read-Aloud Handbook, The (Trelease), 33
Newsom, Tom, 157
New True Book series, 106, 150, 170, 254, 271, 278, 288, 290, 295, 297
   on the continents, 111
   Native Americans series, 152
New York Times Parent's Guide to the Best Books for Children, The (Lipson), 33
Nichol, Barbara, 237
Nicholson, Robert, 120, 122–123, 127, 134, 135
Night Before Christmas, The (Moore), 64
Nilsson, Lennart, 295, 296
Nipp, Susan, 231
Noah's Ark (illus. Ray), 116
Nolan, Dennis, 70
Noll, Cheryl Kirk, 289
Nonnast, Marie, 158

Norman the Doorman (Freeman), 204
Norse mythology, 76
North America (Georges), 124
North American Indian (Murdoch), 213
Norworth, Jack, 245
Now Let Me Fly: The Story of a Slave Family (Johnson), 165
Now We Are Six (Milne), 37, 50, 57
Nuclear Energy (Hawkes), 300
Numbears: A Counting Book (Hague), 321
Numbers and counting, 320–322
Nutcracker, The (Tchaikovsky), 240
Nutcracker Ballet, The (Vagin), 240
Nutrition: What's in the Food We Eat (Patent), 278
Nyncke, Helge, 284

O

Ober, Carol, 156
Ober, Hal, 156
Ocean (Hirschi), 267
Oceans, 266–267
Ochoa, George, 142
O'Dell, Scott, 187
Odjik, Pamela, 135, 139, 141, 142, 211
Odyssey, The (Homer), 90
Odyssey magazine, 301
Of Nightingales that Weep (Paterson), 139
Ohrn, Deborah Gore, 104
Oil Spill! (Berger), 267
Olliver, Jane, 108
Once and Future King, The (White), 81
175 Amazing Nature Experiments (Harlow and Morgan), 255
One Bear at Bedtime (Inkpen), 321
175 More Science Experiments to Amuse and Amaze Your Friends: Experiments! Tricks! Things to Make (Cash, Parker, and Taylor), 255
One Hundred Hungry Ants (Pineczes), 322
O'Neill, Laurie A., 187
One Hundred and One Famous Poems (ed. Cook), 88–89
One Was Johnny (Sendak), 321

On Market Street (Lobel), 47
On the Banks of the Pharaoh's Nile (Courtalon), 114
On the Way Home (Wilder and Lane), 84
Onyefulu, Ifeoma, 111
Opera, 241–242
Opera: What's All the Screaming About? The Beginner's Guide to Opera (Englander), 242
Opie, Iona, 36, 45
Opie, Peter, 36, 45
Oppenheim, Shulamith Levey, 117
Orchestra, 233–235
Orchestra, The (Rubin), 234
O'Reilly, Susie, 198
Oriental Art (Sandak), 211, 212
Origins of Greek Civilization, The: From the Bronze Age to the Polis ca. 2500–600 B.C. (Himmell, Podnay, Millstone, and Cheoros), 143
Ormerod, Jan, 58
Orozco, José-Luis, 235
Ortiz, Alfonso, 87
Osborne, Mary Pope, 68–69, 70, 76, 91
O'Shaughnessy, Tam, 301
Otani, June, 53
Ottenheimer, Laurence, 122
Otto, Carolyn, 261
Ouch! A Book About Cuts, Scratches, and Scrapes (Berger), 288
Our Atomic World (Berger), 296, 300
Our Constitution (Johnson), 179
Our Declaration of Independence (Schliefer), 175–176
Our Solar System (Simon), 286
Our Universe: A Guide to What's Out There (Stannard), 301
Out from This Place (Hansen), 184
Outside and Inside You (Markle), 257, 294
Ovenden, Dennis, 282
Overlie, George, 86
Over the River and Through the Woods (Child), 56
Owl and the Pussycat, The (Lear), 56–57
Owl and the Pussycat and Other Nonsense Poems, The (Lear), 33–34, 64
Oxford Book of Children's Verse in America, The (ed. Hall), 34
Oyo, Benin, and Ashanti (Mann), 133, 216

P

Pablo Picasso (Hart), 207
Pablo Picasso (Raboff), 206
Paddle to the Sea (Holling), 128
Paker, Josephine, 229, 233
Palacios, Argentina, 156
Paper Soldiers of the American Revolution (Zlatich), 176
Paper Soldiers of the American Revolution: Book Two (Zlatich), 176
Parables of Jesus, The (De Paola), 117
Parish, Peggy, 49, 268
Parker, Nancy Winslow, 277
Parker, Steve, 255–257, 304
Parks, Van Dyke, 40
Parmenter, Wayne, 188
Parsons, Alexandra, 281, 282
Patent, Dorothy Hinshaw, 278
Paterson, Katherine, 65, 67, 139
Paul Bunyan (Kellogg), 71
Paul Bunyan and His Blue Ox (Troll Associates), 71
Paul Gauguin (Venezia), 206, 207
Paul Klee (Venezia), 212
Paul Revere's Ride (Longfellow), 77, 176
Pavarotti, Luciano, 241–242
Pavese, Edith, 220
Peace and Bread: The Story of Jane Addams (McPherson), 190
Peach Boy (Hooks), 53
Peach Boy: A Japanese Legend (Nagano), 53
Peacock, Graham, 270, 279, 283, 284
Pearson, Anne, 123
Peck, Beth, 167
Peck, Marshall, III, 266, 268
Pecos Bill: The Roughest, Toughest, Best (Troll Associates), 71
Pels, Winslow Pinney, 66
Pennington, Daniel, 152
People Could Fly, The: American Black Folktales (Hamilton), 41, 74
People of the Breaking Day (Sewall), 170–171, 173
People of the Buffalo: How the Plains Indians Lived (Campbell), 187
Peppe, the Lamplighter (Bartone), 167
Perrault, Charles, 60

Persephone (Hutton), 69
Persephone and the Pomegranate: A Myth from Greece (Waldherr), 69
Perseus (Hutton), 76
Perspective (Cole), 218
Peter and the Wolf (Lemieux), 234
Peter and the Wolf (Prokofiev), 234
Peter and the Wolf: A Bellerophon Coloring Book (Brownell), 234
Peter Pan (Barrie), 67
Petersen, David, 163
Petersham, Maud, 37, 50
Petersham, Miska, 37, 50
Peter Tchaikovsky (Venezia), 239
Peter the Great (Stanley), 139–140
Pet of the Met (Freeman and Freeman), 242
Pfeffer, Wendy, 275
Phelps, Ethel Johnston, 41, 42
Philharmonic Gets Dressed, The (Kuskin), 234
Philip, Neil, 73
Phillis Wheatley: First African-American Poet (Greene), 159
Phoebe the Spy (Griffin), 178
Phonetically controlled readers, 47–48
Physics, 297
Picard, Barbara Leonie, 90
Picasso (Raboff), 211
Picasso (Venezia), 206, 212
Picture Book of Eleanor Roosevelt, A (Adler), 168
Picture Book of George Washington, A (Adler), 154
Picture Book of Harriet Tubman, A (Adler), 165
Picture Book of Rosa Parks, A (Adler), 168
Picture Book of Thomas Jefferson, A (Adler), 154
Pictures Tell Stories: A Collection for Young Scholars Book (Grandits), 206, 208
Picture the Middle Ages: The Middle Ages Resource Book (Honan), 131
Picture This: A First Introduction to Paintings (Woolf), 200, 215, 218, 221
Pidgeon, Jean, 71
Pied Piper of Hamelin, The, 59
Pierre-Auguste Renoir (Raboff), 222
Pieter Bruegel (Venezia), 206, 214, 219
Pilgrims, 153
Pilgrim's First Thanksgiving, The (McGovern), 153
Pilgrims of Plimoth, The (Sewall), 171, 173
Pineczes, Elinor J., 322

Pinkney, Andrea Davis, 179
Pinkney, Brian, 70, 83, 88, 168, 179, 245
Pinkney, Jerry, 42, 61, 63, 70
Pinocchio (Collodi), 57
Pinto, Ralph, 59
Pioneers, 162–163, 185, 186
Pirates of Penzance, The (Gilbert and Sullivan), 242
Pittman, Helena Clare, 322
Planets in Our Solar System, The (Branley), 271
Plant and Animal Alphabet Coloring Book (Tillett), 47
Plant Families (Lerner), 294
Plants, 259–260
Plants Without Seed (Challand), 294–295
Platt, Richard, 104
Pluckrose, Henry, 259, 266
Plume, Ilse, 51
Plymouth Thanksgiving, The (Weisgard), 173
Pocahontas: Daughter of a Chief (Greene), 157–158
Podendorf, Illa, 297
Podnay, Amanda H., 143
Poe, Edgar Allan, 89
Poetry, 33–38, 50, 56–57, 64–65, 72–73, 77–78, 83–84, 88–89
Poetry for Young People (Dickinson), 83–84, 89
Pofahl, Jane, 105, 112
Polacco, Patricia, 83
Pollard, Michael, 115, 138, 141
Pollyanna (Porter), 78
Pompeii . . . Buried Alive (Kunhardt), 126
Poole, Josephine, 53
Porter, Eleanor H., 78
Postcards from Pluto: A Tour of the Solar System (Leedy), 271
Potter, Beatrix, 61
Powell, Whitney, 303
Prelutsky, Jack, 35–37, 72, 77, 268
Presidents, American, 153–154, 159, 160, 179–180
Price, Leontyne, 241
Priceman, Marjorie, 36
Primary Phonics Workbooks and Storybooks (Makar), 48
Princess and the Pea, The (Andersen), 59
Principal's New Clothes, The (Calmenson), 66
Professor I.Q. Explores the Brain (Simon), 283
Prokofiev, Serge, 234

Proud Taste for Scarlet and Miniver, A (Konigsberg), 132
Provenson, Alice, 148–150
Pueblo Storyteller (Goldsmith), 152
Puss in Boots (Perrault), 60
Putnam, James, 113
Putting the Sun to Work (Bendick), 300
Pyramid (Putnam), 113
Pyramid of the Sun, Pyramid of the Moon (Fisher), 136

Q

Quackenbush, Robert, 84, 153–154, 176–177, 179–180, 190, 287
Questions and Answers About Explorers (Maynard), 105

R

Raboff, Ernest, 200, 206, 209, 211, 214, 219, 222, 223
Rachel Carson (Accorsi), 272
Rachel Carson, Friend of the Earth (Sabin), 272
Rachlin, Ann, 237, 239, 241
Rackham, Arthur, 42–43, 76, 78, 79
Radunsky, Vladimir, 244
Rael, Juan, 74
Raggin': A Story about Scott Joplin (Mitchell), 239
Ragtime Tumpie (Schroeder), 243
Raimondo, Lois, 120
Ram, Govinder, 120
Rama and Sita: A Folk Tale from India (Ram), 120
Rand, Ted, 77
Rand McNally Children's Atlas of World History, 109
Rand McNally Children's Atlas of World Wildlife, 109
Rand McNally Picture Atlas of the World (Kemp), 109–110

Random House Book of Fairy Tales, The (ed. Ehrlich), 41

Random House Book of How Things Were Built, The (Brown), 203

Random House Book of Mother Goose (ed. Prelutsky), 35

Random House Book of 1001 Wonders of Science, The (Williams and Williams), 255

Random House Book of Poetry for Children, The (ed. Prelutsky), 35, 72, 77

Random House Book of Stories from the Ballet, The (McCaughrean), 241

Ranger Rick magazine, 258

Ransome, James, 165

Raphael, Elaine, 238

Raphael (Raboff), 219, 222

Rappaport, Doreen, 121, 158

Rapunzel, 60

Raschka, Chris, 242

Rattles, Bells, and Chiming Bars (Foster), 233

Rauzon, Mark J., 276

Raven and Other Favorite Poems, The (Poe), 89

Ravitch, Diane, 103, 147–148

Ray, David, 168

Ray, Deborah Kogan, 162

Ray, Jane, 116

Read Me a Story: A Child's Book of Favorite Tales, 41

Ready . . . Set . . . Read: The Beginning Reader's Treasury (ed. Cole and Calmenson), 48, 57

Ready . . . Set . . . Read—and Laugh! A Funny Treasury for Beginning Readers (ed. Cole and Calmenson), 48, 57

Real Mother Goose, The (illus. Wright), 35

Reasoner, Charles, 156

Reason for a Flower, The (Heller), 275

Recipe for Reading (Traub and Bloom), 48

Reconstruction, 184

Reconstruction and Reform (Hakim), 184, 185, 188, 190

Recordings, 230–231

Recycle! A Handbook for Kids (Gibbons), 263

Recycle That! (Robinson), 263

Red Cap (Wisler), 183

Red Hawk's Account of Custer's Last Battle: The Battle of the Little Bighorn, 25 June 1876 (Goble), 187

Red Leaf, Yellow Leaf (Ehlert), 274

Red Riding Hood, 53

Reed, Allison, 116

Reeves, Nicholas, 114

Reformation, 138

Reformers, 180–181, 190–191

Regan, Laura, 266

Regniers, Beatrice Schenck de, 35

Reid, Barbara, 35

Reid, Fiona, 282

Religion, 114–118, 141

Rembrandt (Raboff), 214, 222

Rembrandt (Venezia), 214

Renaissance, 137–138

Renaissance, The: A Bellerophon Coloring Book, 219

Renaissance, The (Wood), 137

Renaissance art, 218–220

Renaissance Art (Harris), 219

Renaissance People (Howarth), 137

Renaissance Places (Howarth), 137

Retan, Walter, 277

Rey, H. A., 286

Reyero, Carlos, 221

Richardson, Joy, 203

Ride, Sally, 301

Ride a Purple Pelican (Prelutsky), 36

Ridpath, Ian, 287

Riha, Susanne, 274

Ringgold, Faith, 214

Riordan, James, 78

Rip Van Winkle (Irving), 79

Rip Van Winkle/Gulliver's Travels (Weiss), 79

Rise of Major Religions, The (Makhlouf), 141

Ritz, Karen, 161, 166

Rivers, 127–128

Robin Hood of Sherwood Forest (McGovern), 79

Robin Hood/The Three Musketeers (Weiss), 79

Robinson, Fay, 263, 276

Robinson Crusoe (Defoe), 79

Robison, Deborah, 282

Rockwell, Anne, 279

Rockwell, Harlow, 279

Rockwell, Lizzy, 275

Roehrig, Catharine, 113, 208

Roffe, Mike, 287

Rogasky, Barbara, 60

Rogers, Paul, 206, 263

Rolph, Mic, 301
Romans, The (Burrell), 142–143
Romans, The (Crisp), 126
Romans, The (Odjik), 142
Roman Villa, A (Morley), 126
Roop, Connie, 158
Roop, Peter, 158
Rooster Crows, The: A Book of American Rhymes and Jingles (Petersham and Petersham), 37, 50
Rooster's Off to See the World (Carle), 321
Rosa Bonheur (Turner), 214
Rosa Parks: Hero of Our Time (Jackson), 169
Rosenberg, Jane, 240
Rosenberry, Vera, 67
Rosenblum, Richard, 290
Rosenthal, Marc, 108
Rosenthal, Paul, 108
Rose, Where Did You Get That Red? Teaching Great Poetry to Children (Koch), 35
Roth, Susan, 120
Rough-Face Girl, The (Martin), 63, 171
Round Buildings, Square Buildings, and Buildings That Wiggle Like Fish (Isaacson), 203
Rounds, Glen, 53, 54
Royal Kingdoms of Ghana, Mali, and Songhay: Life in Medieval Africa (McKissack and McKissack), 133
Royston, Angela, 260
Rubin, Mark, 234
Rumpelstiltskin (Grimm brothers), 60
Russell, Marion, 184
Russell, William F., 39, 52, 68, 75, 79, 90–91
Russia, early growth and expansion, 139–140
Russian Portraits (Hoobler and Hoobler), 140
Ryan, Susannah, 166
Rybolt, Thomas R., 289, 296
Ryder, Joanne, 278

S

Sabin, Francene, 177, 272, 292
Sabin, Louis, 238
Sacagawea (Gleiter and Thompson), 160
Sacred River (Lewin), 120

Sadler, Catherine Edwards, 85–86
Sad Night, The: The Story of an Aztec Victory and a Spanish Loss (Mathews), 156
Sage, Alison, 60
Saint George and the Dragon (Hodges), 79–80
Saint-Saëns, Camille, 233
Sakuri, Gail, 53
Salvador Dalí (Venezia), 214
Sam the Minuteman (Benchley), 159
Sam the Sea Cow (Jacobs), 267
Samuel Eaton's Day: A Day in the Life of a Pilgrim Boy (Waters), 153, 158
Samurai's Daughter, The: A Japanese Legend (San Souci), 86, 139
Samurai's Tale, The (Haugaard), 139
Sancha, Sheila, 131
Sandak, 211–213, 216
Sanders, Scott Russell, 162, 163
Sanderson, Ruth, 116
Sandin, Joan, 167
San José, Christine, 74
San Souci, Daniel, 54, 63, 70, 78, 120, 171
San Souci, Robert D., 78, 82, 86, 139, 171, 173
Santoro, Christopher, 302
Santrey, Laurence, 146, 270
Sarah Morton's Day: A Day in the Life of a Pilgrim Girl (Waters), 153, 158
Sattler, Helen Roney, 302
Saturn (Simon), 286
Saunders, Susan, 60
Say, Allen, 122
Scanlan, Barbara, 138, 139
Scavengers and Decomposers: Nature's Clean Up Crew (Hughey), 285
Schemenaur, E., 127
Schiff, Ronny Susan, 232, 236
Schindler, S. D., 59
Schlein, Miriam, 157
Schliefer, Jay, 175–176
Scholastic Art magazine, 200
Schroeder, Alan, 243
Schwartz, Carol, 278
Schwartz, David M., 320–321, 323–324
Science Book of Magnets, The (Ardley), 279
Science Book of Things that Grow, The (Ardley), 259

Science Experiments and Amusements for Children (Vivian), 256

Science Matters: Achieving Scientific Literacy (Hazen and Trefil), 255

Scieszka, Jon, 58, 81

Scriabine, Christine, 189, 190

Scribble Cookies and Other Independent Creative Art Experiences for Children (Krohl), 199

Sea and Cedar: How the Northwest Coast Indians Lived (McConkey), 187

Seabird (Holling), 128

Sea Mammals (Ganeri), 282

Seashore Life Coloring Book (D'Attilio), 267

Seasons, 262–263, 274

Seasons Greetings from Vivaldi (Rachlin), 239

Seasons & Weather (Evans and Williams), 262

Second Mrs. Giaconda, The (Konigsburg), 138

Secret Garden, The (Burnett), 89–90

Secrets of the Universe: Discovering the Universal Laws of Science (Fleisher), 299

Secret Soldier, The: The Story of Deborah Sampson (McGovern), 177

Seed Is a Promise, A (Merrill), 260

Seeger, Pete, 243

See Through History series, 106

Selsam, Millicent E., 265, 278

Sendak, Maurice, 42, 321, 323

Senn, J. A., 264

Sequoyah: Father of the Cherokee Alphabet (Petersen), 163

Seuss, Dr., 49

Seven Blind Mice (Young), 65

Seven Chinese Brothers, The (Mahy), 121

Seven Tales (Andersen), 42

Severy, Merle, 138

Sewall, Marcia, 170–171, 173

Seward, James, 122, 142

Shake, Rattle, and Strum (Corbett), 234, 236

Shake It to the One that You Love the Best: Play Songs and Lullabies from Black Musical Traditions (ed. Mattox), 37, 50, 231

Shakespeare: The Animated Tales (ed. Garfield), 43–44

Shakespeare, William, 43–44, 85, 89

Shakespeare for Children (Weiss), 43

Shakespeare for Young People series (ed. Davidson), 43

Shakespeare Stories (Garfield), 43

Shake Sugaree, 231

Shannon, David, 52, 63, 171

Shapes (Yenawine), 205

Shapes Game, The (Rogers), 206

Shaw, Charles, 89

Shaw, Martin, 86

She and He: Adventures in Mythology (Weiss), 69

Sheehan, Kathryn, 284

Shemie, Bonnie, 150, 170, 186

Shepard, Ernest H., 37, 57, 58, 75

Sherlock Holmes for Children (Weiss), 86

Sherman, Ori, 117

Shh! We're Writing the Constitution (Fritz), 179

Shimizu, Kiyoshi, 294

Shooting Stars (Branley), 287

Short Walk Around the Pyramids and Through the World of Art, A (Isaacson), 200

Shott, Steve, 260

Showers, Paul, 278, 283, 288

Sibbett, Ed, 215

Side by Side: Poems to Read Together (ed. Hopkins), 37

Sign of the Beaver, The (Speare), 173

Sign Painter's Secret, The (Hoobler and Hoobler), 178

Silent Lotus (Lee), 120

Sills, Leslie, 223

Silver at Night (Bartoletti), 168

Silverman, Maida, 116

Silverstein, Shel, 38, 72, 78

Simon, Charnan, 189

Simon, Seymour, 283, 285–286, 290, 294, 301

Simón Bolívar: Latin American Liberator (Varona), 146

Simont, Marc, 234, 272, 290

Simple Machines (Horvatic), 279

Sims, Blanche, 284

Sing a Song of Mother Goose (illus. Reid), 35

Sing a Song of Popcorn (ed. Regniers), 35

Singh, Anne, 119

Sir Gawain and the Green Knight (Hastings), 81

Sir Gawain and the Loathly Lady (Hastings), 81

Sis, Peter, 152–153

Sixteenth Century Mosque, A (MacDonald and Bergin), 133

Skeleton Inside You, The (Balestrino), 268

Skira-Venturi, Rosabianca, 223
Sleeping Beauty, 60–61
Sleeping Beauty and Other Fairy Tales (Grimm brothers), 42, 60
Sleeping Ugly (Yolen), 60–61
Slier, Deborah, 34, 72, 77
Smith, A. G., 113, 127, 131, 152, 164, 166
Smith, Betsy Covington, 191
Smith, Jan Hosking, 236
Smith, Jessie Willcox, 36
Smith, Joseph A., 115
Smith, Lane, 81
Smith, Mavis, 261
Smith, Philip, 36
Smolinski, Dick, 273
Snake (Chinery), 281
Snedden, Robert, 290
Sneve, Virginia Driving Hawk, 34, 50, 148–149, 170, 186
Snow, Theodore P., 284–285
Snow White, 53
Social Studies School Service, 105, 150
Sojourner Truth: Ain't I a Woman? (McKissack and McKissack), 180–181
Solar system, 270–271
Something BIG Has Been Here (Prelutsky), 36
Sommer, Elyse, 229
Song and Dance Man (Ackerman), 241
Songs, 230–231
Songs from Mother Goose (Larrick), 230
Songs of the Wild West (Axelrod and Fox), 230
Sootface: An Ojibwa Cinderella (San Souci), 171
Sorensen, Henri, 265
Sound and hearing, 283
Sound (Peacock), 283
Sound Experiments (Broekel), 283
South America (Georges), 124
Southwest Indians Coloring Book (Copeland), 171
Space (Ridpath and Muirden), 287
Spanish-American War, 191
Spanish-American War, The (Carter), 191
Speare, Elizabeth George, 173
Spenser, Edmund, 79
Spider and the Sky God: An Akan Legend, 61
Spider magazine, 48–49
Spier, Peter, 161, 244, 245
Spirin, Gennady, 60

Spowart, Robin, 230
Spring (Hirschi), 274
Spring (Thomson and Hewitt), 262
Squanto and the First Thanksgiving (Kessel), 173–174
Stained Glass Windows Coloring Book (Kennedy), 131
Staines, Bill, 244
Stalker, Geoffrey, 107–108
Stanley, Diane, 85, 138–140
Stannard, Russell, 301
Staples, Danny, 233
Starosta, Paul, 277
Star-Spangled Banner, The, 161, 245
Start Exploring Masterpieces (Martin and Zorn), 199–200
Statue of Liberty and Ellis Island Coloring Book (Smith), 166
Steele, Philip, 114, 129
Stenmark, Jean Kerr, 318
Steptoe, John, 63
Sterling, Dorothy, 183
Stevens, Bryna, 158
Stevens, Janet, 51, 53, 59, 66, 75
Stevenson, Robert Louis, 36, 50, 56, 80, 89
Stevenson, Suçie, 59
Stewart, Arvis, 69, 76
Stewart, Diana, 85, 89
Stewart, Don, 152
Stewart, Pat, 288
Stille, Darlene R., 155, 284, 285
Stock, Catherine, 166
Stoddard, Sandol, 115
Stories (Yenawine), 205
Stories for Seven-Year-Olds (ed. Corrin and Corrin), 74
Stories of the American Revolution (ed. Chall), 176
Story a Story, A, 61
Story of Booker T. Washington, The (McKissack and McKissack), 190
Story of Hanukkah, The (Ehrlich), 117
Story of Johnny Appleseed, The (Aliki), 52, 71
Story of Jonah, The (Baumann), 116
Story of Jumping Mouse, The, 53
Story of Painting, The: The Essential Guide to the History of Western Art (Beckett), 202, 221
Story of Ruby Bridges, The (Coles), 169

Story of the American Revolution Coloring Book (Copeland), 160, 176

Story of the Haymarket Riot, The (Simon), 189

Story of the Statue of Liberty, The (Maestro), 166

Story of the Vikings Coloring Book (Smith), 127

Story of the White House, The (Waters), 180

Story of William Penn, The (Aliki), 174

Stratton, Barbara R., 281

Strom (Wood), 292

Sugarman, Tracy, 79

Sullivan, Charles, 204

Summer (Hirschi), 274

Summer (Thomson and Hewitt), 262

Sundiata: Lion King of Mali (Wisniewski), 133

Sun Is Always Shining Somewhere, The (Fowler), 271

Sun Up, Sun Down (Gibbons), 276

Super Science Book of Rocks and Soils, The (Snedden), 290

Surat, Michele Maria, 166

Surprises (ed. Hopkins), 37, 64

Sutcliff, Rosemary, 90

Swan, Susan, 260

Swan Lake: The Story of the Ballet (Rachlin), 241

Sweet Clara and the Freedom Quilt (Hopkinson), 165

Swift, Jonathan, 78

Switch On, Switch Off (Berger), 289

Sword in the Stone, The (White), 81

Symcox, Linda, 143

T

Tadpole and Frog (Back), 275

Tail Feathers from Mother Goose (Opie and Opie), 36

Tait, Douglas, 187

Take Me Out to the Ballgame, 245

Tale of Aladdin and the Wonderful Lamp, The: A Story from the Arabian Nights (Kimmel), 73

Tale of Peter Rabbit, The (Potter), 61

Tale of Two Cities, A (Dickens), 90

Tales from the Old Testament (Weiss), 117

Tales of Uncle Remus, The: The Adventures of Brer Rabbit (Lester), 42, 61

Talk, Talk: An Ashanti Legend (Chocolate), 67

Talking Eggs, The, 63

Talking Like the Rain: A First Book of Poems (ed. Kennedy and Kennedy), 37

Talking to the Sun: An Illustrated Anthology of Poems for Young People (Koch and Farrell), 38

Tames, Richard, 133

Tangram (Elssers), 318

Tanz, Freya, 266

Tao, Wang, 134

Tar Beach (Ringgold), 214

Tarcov, Edith, 58

Tatterhood and Other Tales (ed. Phelps), 42

Taylor, Barbara, 255

Taylor, Kim, 275

Tchaikovsky, Peter Ilych, 240

Tchaikovsky Discovers America (Kalman), 239

Teague, Ken, 121

Tecumseh (Kent), 186

Tejada, Irene, 198

Temple, Frances, 67

Temple Cat (Clements), 114

Ten Mile Day and the Building of the Transcontinental Railroad, The (Fraser), 186

Tenniel, John, 73

Terban, Marvin, 44, 45

Terzian, Alexandra M., 199

Thayer, Ernest L., 83

There Was an Old Man: A Gallery of Nonsense Rhymes (Lear), 33

Thernstrom, Abigail, 103

Theseus and the Minotaur (Hutton), 69–70

Thibault, Dominique, 130

Thiele, Bob, 243

Third Planet, The: Exploring the Earth from Space (Ride and O'Shaughnessy), 301

Thirteen Colonies, The (Fradin), 158, 174

This Dynamic Planet (U.S. Geologic Survey), 290

Thomas, Gary, 280, 293

Thomas Alva Edison, Great Inventor (Adler), 273

Thomas Edison, Great American Inventor (Bedik), 273

Thomas Jefferson: A Picture Book Biography (Giblin), 177, 179

Thomas Jefferson: Author, Inventor, President
   (Greene), 160
Thompson, Karmen, 233
Thompson, Kathleen, 160
Thompson, Virginia, 318
Thomson, Ruth, 262–263
Threads of Time: A Global History 400–1750
   (Coupe and Scanlan), 138, 139
Three Billy Goats Gruff, The, 53–54
Three Gold Pieces (Aliki), 74
Three Little Pigs and Other Favorite Nursery
   Stories, The, 54
"Three Words of Wisdom," 74
Three Young Pilgrims (Harness), 153
Thumbelina (Andersen), 62
Thunder at Gettysburg (Gauch), 165
Thunder Rolling in the Mountains (O'Dell and
   Hall), 187
Tiegreen, Alan, 295
"Tiger, the Brahman, and the Jackal, The," 67
Tiger Soup: An Anansi Story from Jamaica, 67
Tillett, Leslie, 47
Time, 323
Time Machine magazine, 150–151
Time to . . . (McMillan), 323
Tivers, Jacqueline, 109, 111, 124
To Be a Slave (Lester), 182
Today is Monday (Carle), 323
Tomes, Margot, 74
Tompert, Ann, 117
Tom Sawyer (Twain), 84
Tom Thumb (Andersen), 62
Tongue-Cut Sparrow, The, 67
Tools and machines, 279
Too Many Balloons (Matthias), 321
Too Much Talk (Medearis), 67
Tornado Alert (Branley), 292
Toulmin-Rothe, Ann, 292
Tournament of Knights, A (Lasker), 131
Toussaint L'Ouverture: Lover of Liberty (Santrey),
   146
Tower of London, The (Fisher), 139
Traces of Life: The Origins of Humankind (Lasky),
   303
Traub, Nina, 48
Treasure Island (Stevenson), 80
Treasury of Children's Literature, A (ed. Eisen), 42

Tree of Life: The World of the African Baobab
   (Bash), 285
Trefil, James, 255
Trelease, Jim, 33
Tresselt, Alvin, 265
Trivas, Irene, 105, 150, 168
Trojan Horse, The: How the Greeks Won the War
   (Little), 70
Trojan Horse, The (Hutton), 70
Trojan War, The (Evslin), 90
Truesdell, Sue, 162
True Story of the Three Little Pigs, The (Scieszka),
   58
Tseng, Jean, 121
Tseng, Mou-sien, 121
Tucker, Judith Cook, 235
Tucker, Sian, 206
Tudor, Tasha, 89
Turkle, Brinton, 56
Turner, Glennette Tilley, 304
Turner, Jessica Baron, 232, 236
Turner, Robyn Montana, 213, 214
Turn of the Century: Our Nation One Hundred
   Years Ago (Levinson), 188
Tut-Ankh-Amun and His Friends (Aldred), 113
Tut's Mummy: Lost . . . and Found (Donnelly),
   114
Twain, Mark, 84
Tweddle, Dominic, 127
Twofeathers, Shannon, 187
Tye May and the Magic Brush, 67
Tyrannosaurus Was a Beast (Prelutsky), 268

U

Ugly Duckling, The, 54
Understanding AIDS (Lerner), 303
Under the Ground (Pluckrose), 266
Undying Glory: The Story of the Massachusetts 54th
   Regiment (Cox), 182–183
Uniforms of the American Revolution Coloring Book
   (Copeland), 176
Universe, The: Think Big (Bendick), 287
Universe for the Beginner, The (Moore), 301

Up Up and Away: A Book About Adverbs (Heller), 44

Uranus (Simon), 286

V

Vagin, Vladimir, 240

VanCleave, Janice, 107, 255–256, 289, 294, 318

Van Laan, Nancy, 40, 52

Van Leeuwen, Jean, 49, 157, 162

Van Rynbach, Iris, 56

Van Wright, Cornelius, 34, 72, 77

Van Zandt, Eleanor, 110

Varona, Frank de, 145–146

Velveteen Rabbit, The (Williams), 61

Venezia, Mike, 201, 206–207, 209, 212, 214, 219, 239

Vennema, Peter, 85, 138

Venti, Anthony Bacon, 136

Venus (Simon), 286

Verdi, Giuseppe, 241

Very Hungry Caterpillar, The (Carle), 321

Very Important Day, A (Herold), 166

Vikings, 126–127

Vikings, The (Nicholson and Watts), 127

Vincent van Gogh (Raboff), 211

Vincent van Gogh (Venezia), 209, 212

Viorst, Judith, 323

Virgil, 91

Visiting the Art Museum (Brown and Brown), 204

Visions (Sills), 223

Visual Dictionary of the Earth, The (ed. Stalker), 107–108

Vitale, Stefano, 67

Vivian, Charles, 256

Voake, Charlotte, 54, 277

Vogel, Malvina G., 75, 78, 79

Voices from the Civil War: A Documentary History of the Great American Conflict (ed. Meltzer), 183

Vojtech, Anna, 163

Volcano (Dudman), 290

Volcanoes (Branley), 272, 290–291

Volcanoes (Simon), 290

Votes for Women (Scriabine), 190

Voting and Elections (Fradin), 179

Vox Music Masters series, 239

Vuong, Lynette Dyer, 62

W

Waber, Bernard, 154

Wade, Tony, 169

Wadsworth, Ginger, 184

Wagon Wheels (Brenner), 163

Waidner, Mary, 284

Waiting for Filippo: The Life of Renaissance Architect Filippo Brunelleschi (Bender), 219

Waldherr, Kris, 60, 69

Waldman, Neil, 244

Walk in the Desert, A (Arnold), 266

Wallner, Alexandra, 154, 158

Wallner, John, 154

Walsh, Ellen Stohl, 206

Walter Dragun's Town: Crafts and Trade in the Middle Ages (Sancha), 131

War, Terrible War (Hakim), 183

War Comes to Willy Freeman (Collier and Collier), 178

Ward, Lynd, 177

Ward, Matthew, 260

Warm as Wool (Sanders), 163

War of 1812, 161

Warrs, S. A. R., 256

Washington Irving's Rip Van Winkle (Locker), 79

Watch the Stars Come Out (Levenson), 168

Water, Water Everywhere (Rauzon and Bix), 276

Water (Peacock), 270

Water Pollution (Stille), 285

Waters, Kate, 153, 158, 180

Watling, James, 114, 174, 184, 270

Watson, Mary, 166–167

Watson, Richard Jesse, 62

Watts, Barrie, 259, 275, 277–278, 281

Watts, Bernadette, 51

Watts, Claire, 120, 122–123, 127, 135

Way Things Work, The (Macaulay), 255

Way West, The: Journal of a Pioneer Woman (Knight), 186

Weather, 262–263, 275–276, 291–292

Weather: Poems for All Seasons (Hopkins), 263

Weather Forecasting (Gibbons), 292

Weather Sky, The (McMillan), 292

Weatherwatch (Wyatt), 292

Weather Words and What They Mean (Gibbons), 276

Weaving of a Dream, The: A Chinese Folktale (Heyer), 80

W.E.B. Du Bois and Racial Relations (Cavan), 190–191

Weed Is a Flower, A: The Life of George Washington Carver (Aliki), 264

Weekend with . . . series, 201

Weekend with Degas, A (Skira-Venturi), 223

Weekend with Rembrandt, A (Bonafoux), 223

Weekend with Renoir, A (Skira-Venturi), 223

Wee Sing America, 231

Wee Sing Around the World, 236

Wee Sing series, 231

Weisgard, Leonard, 34, 72, 77, 83, 88, 172, 173

Weiss, George David, 243

Weiss, Jim, 43, 51, 52, 58, 79, 80–81, 86, 117

Welcome to the Green House (Yolen), 266

Wells, Rosemary, 52

Wells, Ruth, 121–122

Welply, Michael, 141

Welton, Jude, 221

Wenzl, Greg, 300

Westcott, Nadine Bernard, 260

Westerman, Johanna, 57

West Music, 228–229

Weston, Minda, 103–104, 120

Westward expansion, 160, 162–163, 184–186

Wexler, Jerome, 260

Whaling Days (Carrick), 174

Whalley, Margaret, 262, 270, 279

What Are You Figuring Now? A Story About Benjamin Banneker (Ferris), 292

What a Wonderful World (Thiele and Weiss), 243

What Do We Know About the Romans? (Corbishley), 126

What Food Is This? (Hausherr), 269

What Happened? (Williams), 270

What Happens to a Hamburger (Showers), 278

What Instrument Is This? (Hausherr), 234

What Is a Fish? (Stratton), 281

What Magnets Can Do (Fowler), 262

What Makes a . . . series (Mühlberger), 201–202, 210, 212, 214, 219–220

What Makes a Bruegel a Bruegel? (Mühlberger), 214, 219

What Makes a Cassatt a Cassatt? (Mühlberger), 214, 223

What Makes a Degas a Degas? (Mühlberger), 210, 223

What Makes a Goya a Goya? (Mühlberger), 223

What Makes a Leonardo a Leonardo? (Mühlberger), 219

What Makes a Monet a Monet? (Mühlberger), 223

What Makes a Picasso a Picasso? (Mühlberger), 212

What Makes a Raphael a Raphael? (Mühlberger), 219, 223

What Makes a Rembrandt a Rembrandt? (Mühlberger), 214

What Makes a Van Gogh a Van Gogh? (Mühlberger), 212

What Makes Day and Night (Branley), 271

What's Alive (Zoehfeld), 260

What's Happening to My Body? Book for Boys (Madaras), 295

What's Happening to My Body? Book for Girls (Madaras), 295

What's Inside? My Body (DK Direct), 268–269

What's Inside? Plants (Royston), 260

What Will the Weather Be Like Today? (Rogers), 263

Wheels at Work (Dunn), 297

Wheels on the Bus, The (Kovalski), 245

When Solomon Was King (MacGill-Callahan), 117

When We Were Very Young (Milne), 37, 50, 57

Where Butterflies Grow (Ryder), 278

Where Do Puddles Go? (Robinson), 276

Where in the World Is Carmen Sandiego?, 231

Where on Earth: A Geografunny Guide to the Globe (Rosenthal), 108

Where's That Insect? (Brenner and Chardiet), 278

Where the Sidewalk Ends (Silverstein), 38, 72, 78

Which Way Freedom? (Hansen), 183, 184

White, E. B., 65

White, T. H., 81

Who Discovered America? Mysteries and Puzzles of the New World (Lauber), 172

Who Eats What? Food Chains and Food Webs (Lauber), 266
Who Is Carrie? (Collier and Collier), 178
Who Let Muddy Boots into the White House? A Story of Andrew Jackson (Quackenbush), 180
Why Doesn't the Earth Fall Up? (Cobb), 287
Why Do Leaves Change Color? (Maestro), 274
Why I Cough, Sneeze, Shiver, Hiccup, and Yawn (Berger), 269
Why Johnny Can't Tell Right from Wrong (Kilpatrick), 32–33, 78
Why There Is No Arguing in Heaven: A Mayan Myth (Lattimore), 156
Wijngaard, Juan, 81, 115–116
Wild and Wooly Mammoths (Aliki), 155, 268
Wilder, Laura Ingalls, 84
Wilkes, Angela, 199, 254, 263
Willey, Lynne, 287
Williams, A. Susan, 123
Williams, Brenda, 255
Williams, Brian, 255
Williams, Claudette, 261, 262
Williams, Garth, 36, 65
Williams, Marcia, 69
Williams, Margery, 61
Williams, Richard, 160, 185
Williams, Rozanne Lanczak, 270
Williams, Sue, 267
William Tell (Early), 74
Willingham, Fred, 287
Wills, Garry, 164
Will We Miss Them? Endangered Species (Wright), 268
Winborn, Marsha, 270
Windham, Sophie, 41
Wind in the Willows, The (Grahame), 75
Window (Baker), 263
Wings (Yolen), 70
Winnie-the-Pooh (Milne), 54
Winter, Jeanette, 164, 167, 206, 209, 244
Winter, Jonah, 206, 209
Winter, Milo, 54
Winter (Hirschi), 274
Winter (Thomson and Hewitt), 262
Winthrop, Elizabeth, 115, 132
Wishes, Lies, and Dreams: Teaching Children to Write Poetry (Koch), 35

Wisler, G. Clifton, 183
Wisniewski, David, 133
Witch Hunt: It Happened in Salem Village (Krensky), 174
Wolf and the Seven Little Kids, The (Grimm brothers), 54
Wolfe, Gregory, 32–33
Wolfe, Suzanne M., 32–33
Wolkstein, Diane, 115–116
Women Win the Vote (Smith), 191
Wonder Book for Boys and Girls, A (Hawthorne), 42–43, 52, 76
Wonders of Science (Berger), 255
Wonders of the World (Caselli), 105
Wood, Audrey, 54
Wood, Jenny, 108, 134, 292
Wood, Tim, 135–137
Woodlands Indians Coloring Book (Copeland), 171
Woods, Andrew, 264
Wool, David, 301, 302
Woolf, Felicity, 200, 215, 218, 221
World Music at West: Multicultural Music and Arts Catalog, 236
World of Islam, The (Tames), 133
"World of Martin Luther, The" (Severy), 138
Wounded Knee: The Death of a Dream (O'Neill), 187
Wright, Alexandra, 266, 268
Wright, Blanche Fisher, 35
Wright, Joan Richards, 277
Wright, Orville, 264
Wright, Patricia, 222
Wright, Wilbur, 264
Wright Brothers, The: How They Invented the Airplane (Freedman), 264
Wyatt, Valerie, 292
Wyeth, N. C., 173
Wynken, Blynken, and Nod (Field), 57

X

X-Ray Picture Book of Big Buildings of the Ancient World, The (Jessop), 203

Y

Yagawa, Sumiko, 65
Yankee Doodle: A Revolutionary Tail (illus. Chalk), 160
Yeh-Shen: A Cinderella Story from China, 63
Yenawine, Philip, 205
Yolen, Jane, 60–61, 70, 171, 266
Yoshi, 121–122
You Can't Smell a Flower with Your Ear! All About Your 5 Senses (Cole), 261–262
You Come Too: Favorite Poems for Young Readers (Frost), 38, 84, 89
Young, Ed, 62, 65
Young, Jerry, 266, 281, 282
Young Abigail Adams (Sabin), 177
Young Discovery Library, 106–107
Young Explorers in Mathematics series (Nelson), 318–319
Young Guinevere (San Souci), 82
Young John Quincy (Harness), 177
Young Martin's Promise (Myers), 169
Young Orville and Wilbur Wright: First to Fly (Woods), 264
Young People's Atlas of the United States, The (Harrison and Van Zandt), 110
Young Person's Guide to the Orchestra (Britten), 235
Young Reader's Companion to American History, The (Garraty), 151
Your Big Backyard (National Wildlife Federation), 258
Your Brain and Nervous System (LeMaster), 283
You Read to Me, I'll Read to You (Ciardi), 37, 65, 72
Your Foot's on My Feet (Terban), 44
Your Heart and Blood (LeMaster), 288
Your Insides (Cole), 269
You Want Women to Vote, Lizzie Stanton? (Fritz), 181
Yussel's Prayer (Cohen), 117–118

Z

Zallinger, Jean, 67
Zeldis, Malcah, 154
Zelinsky, Paul O., 58, 60
Zemach, Margot, 52, 58–59, 66, 244
Zeman, Ludmila, 112
Zevin, Jack, 104
Ziroli, Claudia, 295
Zoehfeld, Kathleen Weidner, 260
Zorn, Steven, 199–200
Zubrowski, Bernie, 300

"The best year of teaching I ever had. This year has
been so much fun: fun to learn, fun to teach."
Joanne Anderson, teacher,
Three Oaks Elementary School
Fort Myers, Florida

Collect the entire Core Knowledge series

ISBN	TITLE	PRICE
31026-9	What Your First Grader Needs to Know	$10.95/13.95 Can
31027-7	What Your Second Grader Needs to Know	$10.95/14.95 Can
31257-1	What Your Third Grader Needs to Know	$10.95/14.95 Can
31260-1	What Your Fourth Grader Needs to Know	$10.95/14.95 Can
31464-7	What Your Fifth Grader Needs to Know	$10.95/14.95 Can
31467-1	What Your Sixth Grader Needs to Know	$10.95/14.95 Can

READERS:

The titles listed above are available in your local bookstore. If you are interested in mail ordering any of the Core Knowledge books listed above, please send a check or money order only to the address below (no C.O.D.s or cash) and indicate the title and ISBN book number with your order. Make check payable to Dell Consumer Services (include $2.50 for postage and handling). Allow 4–6 weeks for delivery. Prices and availability subject to change without notice.

Please mail your order and check to:
Dell Consumer Services, Dept. CK
2451 South Wolf Road
Des Plaines, IL 60018

EDUCATORS AND LIBRARIANS:

For bulk sales or course adoptions, contact the Bantam Doubleday Dell Education and Library Department. Outside New York State call toll-free 1-800-223-6834 ext. 9238. In New York State call 212-492-9238.

FOR MORE INFORMATION ABOUT CORE KNOWLEDGE:

Call the Core Knowledge Foundation at 1-800-238-3233.